Adult Career Development

Concepts, Issues and Practices

Third Edition

Edited by: Spencer G. Niles

National Career Development Association

Tulsa, Oklahoma

Adult Career Development

Concepts, Issues and Practices

Third Edition

Edited by: Spencer G. Niles

National Career Development Association

Tulsa, Oklahoma

© Copyright 2002 by the National Career Development Association
10820 E. 45 Street, Suite 210
Tulsa, OK 74146
Phone: 866-367-6232
Fax: 918-663-7058

Library in Congress Cataloging-in-Publication Data

ISBN 1-885333-09-9

HF5381.7.C69 2002
153.9'4'000295—dc21

Preface

The National Career Development Association is proud to present the third edition of the Adult Career Development: Concepts, Issues and Practices. Spencer G. Niles identified authors who were able to provide the most thoughtful and current expression of theory and practice in the area of adult career development.

Knowledge of the importance of adult career development has grown over the past decades as we have seen rapid changes in the world that affects all of our lives. Changes in technology have added new occupations and reformed existing ones. The current world of work has continued to reshape the working lives of all adults, bringing economic opportunities to some and hardships to others. Better knowledge of healthful living and medical advances have increased the life span and thereby raised new questions for many about the meaning of work and income in the second half of life.

Change is continuous and we need to address how these changes will affect our clients' life career. NCDA offers this book to help qualified counselors and other career development professionals provide informed services to adults who face life's challenges and opportunities.

The association expresses its gratitude to Spencer G. Niles and all of the authors who have contributed to this important book. It is through their hard work and dedication that this resource becomes a reality. We know that you will appreciate the knowledge you will gain from this work.

Roger Lambert
NCDA President 2001-2002

Acknowledgments

Many thanks to the Board of Directors of the National Career Development Association and the Executive Director, Deneen Pennington, for their tremendous support of this project. Carri Hoffman provided excellent editorial expertise and took the lead in pulling together the final version of the book. I am very grateful for Carri's hard work on this project. I am also deeply appreciative of the time and effort the chapter authors contributed to this book. They are a group with whom it is an honor for me to be associated. They are inspiring in the quality of their work and in their commitment to the profession.

As always, I am thankful to my family (Hugh, Polly, Kathy, Jenny, Jonathan, Susan, and Sandra) for teaching me that career development occurs within the context of life development.

To the readers, I sincerely hope that you find this book to be useful to you as you strive to help others consider how they will spend the most precious commodity they have—their time on this earth.

Spencer G. Niles

Penn State University

Table of Contents

SECTION VI: TRAINING COUNSELORS, EVALUATING PROGRAMS, AND FUTURE SCENARIOS

Introduction

The second edition of this book begins by noting "just when I had the answers…the questions changed!" I think the experience of encountering changing questions and evolving career challenges is the typical experience for adults in contemporary society. Clearly, Super's notion that the self-concept evolves over time making choice and adjustment a continuous process (Super, Savickas, & Super, 1996) can also be applied to the workplace (i.e., work evolves over time making the need to choose and adjust a continuous requirement). Change is the constant and also the challenge. In this, the third edition of this book, we seek to address the changing scenarios and emerging challenges confronting adults today. We offer theoretical concepts and practical interventions for career practitioners seeking to help adults move forward in their careers.

To this end, this book represents the collective efforts of leaders within the field of career development theory and practice. Readers will quickly recognize that they are fortunate to have the opportunity to learn the latest thinking about concepts, issues, and practices for fostering adult career development. Chapter authors provide current and useful information for addressing the career concerns of diverse adult populations.

In chapter one, Spencer Niles, Edwin Herr, and Paul Hartung discuss the career concerns confronting adults in contemporary society. They also identify important trends that are influencing the emergence of these career concerns. Finally, they note the need for career practitioners to reconceptualize their theories and practices to address adult career concerns effectively.

Section II (Theories and Concepts) begins with Fred Vondracek and Erik Porfeli providing new thinking related to developmental perspectives applied to adult career development. John Krumboltz and Sheila Henderson continue our focus on theoretical concepts by offering extensions of the learning theory of career counseling. Sunny Hansen brings a holistic focus to this discussion by explaining the ways in which integrative life planning can be helpful in coping with life role concerns confronting adults as they seek to manage their work and their lives.

Bob Lent and Steve Brown also offer an important and highly useful discussion of ways in which social cognitive career theory connects to concerns adults experience in their career development. Finally, Gary Peterson and his colleagues at Florida State help us understand that their cognitive information processing model has very useful concepts for working with adult clients in career counseling.

The next section of the book (Strategies, Methods, and Resources) highlights specific practices for fostering career development in adult clients. Chapters in this section provide strategies for: (a) appraising adults' career capabilities (John Crites and Brian Taber), (b) empowering clients to become actively engaged in the career counseling process (Amundson), and (c) using technology in the career intervention process computer delivery systems in resolving career concerns (Harris-Bowlsbey). Each of these chapters provide readers with cutting edge ideas for making career counseling and assessment more comprehensive, collaborative, and efficacious.

Many readers know that the field of career development theory and practice has been criticized for being limited in its usefulness in a pluralistic society. The next section of the book (Diverse Populations) attempts to address this criticism by focusing on specific groups and discussing career interventions that may be most useful to the career concerns that members of these respective groups may encounter. Ellen Cook, Mary Heppner, and Karen O'Brien describe how an ecological perspective can be especially useful to the career concerns confronting women in contemporary society. Jerry Trusty then offers important information that career practitioners need to know as they assist persons of color. Mark Pope and Bob Barret offer very helpful information and advice as to how career interventions can be made more applicable for the concerns experienced by adults who are also gay, lesbian, or bisexual. Ed Levinson provides ideas for career counselors working with adults who have learning disabilities. Denny Engels and Hank Harris outline the importance of all career practitioners having knowledge about, and skills in, helping military personnel and their dependents cope with the unique career challenges presented by military life. Finally, Julie Miller addresses the growing population of "mature" workers.

Career interventions also occur in diverse settings. Thus, the next section of the book (Diverse Settings) addresses the special considerations relevant to the particular setting in which career services are provided. Kerr Inkson and Michael Arthur offer a new framework ("organization careers") for conceptualizing career development in business and industry. Of course, many adults seek career assistance in their communities and do not work in business and industry settings. Thus, Jane Goodman and Sandra McClurg provide a very useful description of community-based career services for adults. Deborah Marron and Jack Rayman focus on the career concerns of adult students attending research universities. Lastly, Darrell Luzzo provides useful information for the growing number of adults enrolled in community colleges.

The final section of the book (Training Counselors, Evaluating Programs, and Future Scenarios) helps those training career practitioners (Jane Swanson and Karen O'Brien) and those overseeing the administration of career services (Susan Whiston and Briana Brecheisen) consider important factors in the quality of service delivery. Finally, Edwin Herr delineates important perspectives on the future of career development theory and practice for adults.

Before concluding this introduction, it is also important to point out that this book represents the continuation of the work conducted by H. Daniel Lea and the late Zandy B. Leibowitz. Daniel and Zandy edited the first two outstanding editions of this book. Thus, I am honored to have the opportunity to receive the baton from them. My sense is that, thanks to the stellar contributors to the third edition, we are continuing in the Lea and Leibowitz tradition.

Spencer G. Niles

Penn State University

SECTION I:

CONTEMPORARY CAREER CONCERNS

CHAPTER 1
Adult Career Concerns in Contemporary Society

Spencer G. Niles
Edwin L. Herr
Pennsylvania State University

Paul J. Hartung
Northeastern Universities College of Medicine

Career concerns evolve as the nature of work changes. Harsh evidence exists to indicate that the nature of work is changing substantially. To call our attention to these changes, authors use such dramatic phrases as "the career has died" and "work has ended" (Bridges, 1994; Rifkin, 1995). Although such declarations are not to be taken literally, they are to be taken seriously. The "career is dead" authors alert us to the fact that understanding changes occurring in the nature of work is essential for responding effectively to the career concerns confronting adults in contemporary society.

Indicators revealing ways in which work is changing include statistics about high levels of global unemployment, corporate downsizing, and a jobless economic recovery. Reports of these events appear daily in various news media. Technological advances change how business is conducted as small companies compete globally via the information highway and computers perform tasks once assigned to workers, thereby creating near workerless factories. Underlying these changes is the clear message that the social contract between employers and employees is being redefined (Rifkin, 1995; Savickas, 1993). New challenges and career tasks emerge from these substantial changes in the nature of work.

Contemporary workers struggle to balance their various life role commitments as predictions concerning ways in which technology would create a leisure society long ago gave way to reality. Rather than creating more leisure time, advances in technology have made it easier (and often necessary) to work more hours. Americans now take fewer vacation days per year than workers in any other industrialized country (Reich, 2001). Unfortunately, technology can change work, but it can not change the fact that days still occur in 24-hour cycles and more of those hours are being filled by work activity.

Other evidence that the nature of work is changing is found in media reports describing increases in the number of (a) companies offering day-care and parental leave, (b) families with dual earners, and (c) people working from home. Work concerns do not occur in separation from life concerns. These reports highlight the increased intertwining of work and family roles and have important implications for the career concerns confronting workers.

Career Concerns Evolve Over Time

Savickas (1993) reminds us that such shifts are not to be unexpected because they occur with each transition to a new century. Specifically, Savickas (1993) eloquently delineates the transitory nature of work ethics and evolving career concerns throughout the course of American history. Each ethic presents particular career development tasks to workers. For example, a vocational ethic valuing independent effort, self-sufficiency, frugality, self-discipline, and humility predominated in the 19th century (Maccoby & Terzi, 1981; Savickas, 1993). Most workers during this era engaged in physical labor for their work. Farming, managing a household, or developing a craft were the primary career options available. During the 20th century, or modern era, a "career ethic" predominated (Savickas). This ethic emphasized working for corporations and climbing the corporate ladder. Workers migrated from rural to urban areas and turned their attention to finding their place within organizational structures. Workers were required to fit into, and commit to, organizational hierarchies. This ethic created a shift in attributes prized within the workplace. Rather than prizing attributes such as self-sufficiency, independence, and humility, attributes such as loyalty, commitment, and dedication to the organization were valued. In return for demonstrating these latter attributes, there was the implicit assumption that employers would demonstrate loyalty to their employees. This "assumption of reciprocity" regarding loyalty was often powerful enough to cause workers to subjugate feelings of career dissatisfaction. Job security, especially for post-depression era workers, was a precious commodity.

Clearly, the "rules of the game" are changing. Large scales layoffs have led many workers to realize that blind loyalty to corporate employers is unwise. Long-term employees are being replaced by "on demand workers" (Rifkin, 1995). These new contingent workers are hired to complete a particular project and once the project is completed, so is their employment. Adults are forced to acknowledge that although they have a job today, they may be unemployed tomorrow- regardless of how competent they are or how hard they work. Corporate downsizing results in flattened organizational structures and fewer career ladders to climb. Those workers who continue to adhere to the twentieth century career ethic are left feeling confused and bewildered as they continue to display attributes and attempt to fulfill goals that are, for the most part, no longer relevant.

As adults attempt to smooth their career turbulence they realize that old solutions for increasing job security (e.g., being competent and working harder) often have little impact on new situations. Workers who have lost their jobs via corporate downsizing are now less willing to sacrifice everything for their careers when the organizations they work for are so willing to sacrifice them. Those who have been "sacrificed" are often left feeling betrayed, anxious about competing, and insecure about the future (Savickas, 1993).

Given these shifts, it is not surprising that many adult career counseling clients express concerns related to low career self-efficacy, anxiety due to ambiguous career paths and a lack of job security, confusion over how to obtain training to update their skills, and frustration related to conflicting life role demands (Anderson & Niles, 1995). Super, Savickas, and Super (1996) also note that many adult career counseling clients present with concerns related to life structure issues rather than more isolated work concerns.

The life structure is comprised of the social elements that constitute a life, which are arranged in a pattern of core and peripheral roles. This arrangement, or life structure, forms the basic configuration of a person's life; a design that organizes and channels the person's engagement in society, including occupational choice. Usually two or three core roles hold a central place and other roles are peripheral or absent (Super, et al., 1996, p. 128).

Super and his colleagues (1996) note that life structure concerns reflect the fact that work occurs within a holistic life context. The demise of the assumption of reciprocity regarding loyalty in the workplace confronts workers with the need (and the opportunity) to be more responsive to questions concerning work and life satisfaction. It is not surprising, therefore, that adults in career counseling seek solutions for coping more effectively with their multiple life role commitments and often discuss non-work related concerns (e.g., relationship issues, ego dystonic emotional concerns, etc.) with their career counselors (Anderson & Niles, 1995). Apparently, the emerging work ethic is leading many contemporary workers to view their lives more holistically than workers in previous historical periods. This shift clearly illustrates the fact that few things are more personal than a career choice (Niles & Pate, 1989). Career concerns are personal and workers today evaluate career decisions within the context of the life roles they play.

Such statements suggest contemporary workers cope with a different set of career development tasks than did their earlier counterparts. For example, Maccoby and Terzi (1981) predicted that adults in contemporary society would focus more on achieving personal and professional growth than being solely focused on work success. Maccoby and Terzi described this emerging approach to work as a "self-fulfillment ethic." Those adhering to the "self-fulfillment ethic" seek work that is not so consuming that it denies opportunities for involvement in family, community, leisure, and other life roles. Rather than "living to work," many adults are more interested in "working to live." And, workers now must assume the primary responsibility for creating the lives they live- especially as those creative activities relate to work.

"Old" Ethics Continue as "New" Ethics Emerge

Although many workers seem to be turning away from the career ethic and turning toward the self-fulfillment ethic described by Maccoby and Terzi (1981), work continues to play a central role in the life experience of most people in the United States. Support for this statement is found in our everyday experience by considering the ways in which individuals typically introduce themselves to each other. Experience tells us that the most common question people ask when they meet for the first time is: "What do you do?" Seldom do people respond to this question by noting their community service initiatives, parenting activities, or leisure pursuits. Responses to this seemingly innocuous question typically focus on what one does to earn a living. Such interactions reinforce the contention that in a fluid industrial society occupation is the principal determinant of social status (Super, 1976). For better or worse, our choice of work tends to color the perceptual lens through which others view us. For many people, work identifies a person more clearly than any other single characteristic.

Many people also continue to take a view toward work that is steeped in values emanating from the historical context dating to the founding of the United States (in essence, this represents the perpetuation of the vocational ethic into contemporary society). For example, those operating from an individualistic perspective emphasize individual control in career development (e.g., self-sufficiency, discipline, perseverance, goal-directedness) and de-emphasize the role that contextual variables (e.g., the opportunity structure, the economy, the family, socioeconomic status, racism, sexism) play in shaping one's career. Thus, if a person has a "successful career," many people associate very positive attributes to the person who is a "success." The corresponding assumption is that the "unsuccessful" person is inferior. The application of attributes associated with the vocational ethic, the denial of contextual factors influencing the pattern of one's career development, and the dominant status of work in identity development, become problematic because they each create an inextricable link between work and self-worth. The centrality of work in identity formation also clearly diminishes the important ways in which non-work life roles contribute to self-worth and self-efficacy. As workers in contemporary society experience periods of unemployment, they are confronted directly with the problematic nature of linking work with self-worth.

Obviously, these changes in the nature of work are not benign. They have important implications for work and workers. For example, when work situations go awry, other life domains also suffer. Many jobless workers must cope with economic and family responsibilities without adequate financial resources. Increases in unemployment correlate significantly with increases in substance abuse, referrals to mental health centers, physical ailments (e.g., coronary heart disease), child abuse, and spouse abuse (Herr, 1989). Thus, the ripple effects and the costs of unemployment are substantial to the individual, the family, and society. The move away from the career ethic to the emerging ethic focused on nurturing life structure involvements suggests that adults in contemporary society will search more intentionally to identify effective strategies for managing the fluid demands of multiple life role activities.

The "self-fulfillment ethic" described by Maccoby and Terzi (1981) suggests that sociological conceptualizations of work will become more prominent and work will become more contextualized. Another implication of the self-fulfillment ethic is that people will search for life satisfaction and self-expression in multiple life roles. As more workers focus on working to live rather than living to work, the question becomes what is one working to live for? That is, what other life role commitments influence the goals that one hopes to accomplish through work activity? The importance of clarifying the values one hopes to express in the life roles comprising one's life structure also becomes a prominent career counseling concern. These questions have implications for the sort of assistance adults will require when attempting to clarify, articulate, and implement their life-role self-concepts (Super et al., 1996).

These shifts in the nature of work make it impossible to deny that career development is an evolutionary process. This evolutionary process occurs against a backdrop of constant economic, social, cultural, technological, and historical change. Careers develop within a process that is dynamic, interactive, contextual, and relational. For example, most workers today need at least basic competence in using computer technology, must engage in lifelong learning, and must be able to interact with diverse co-workers. Obviously, these requirements differ significantly from those experienced by workers just several decades ago. Thus, static descriptions of career development are not useful and static career interventions are, in the long run, inadequate. Just as the evolutionary shifts occurring in work require people to re-think work, career practitioners must re-think how they can be most useful in helping their clients cope with their career concerns in contemporary society.

In conceptualizing their interventions for the current context, career practitioners must be guided by an understanding of how technological and cultural factors influence what is required for people to move forward in their careers. Savickas (1993) predicted that in the 21st century career counselors would move from supporting the 20th century notion of careerism to fostering self-affirmation in their clients. To achieve this goal, counselors must respond creatively to help their clients manage their careers effectively. Moreover, career practitioners must understand the emerging trends that are shaping the nature of work in contemporary society.

Heterogeneity in the Workplace and Emerging Career Concerns

The "typical" American worker is no longer an employed father married to a full-time homemaker and mother. More typical is the family in which both partners are employed, or in which a single parent is employed. Media stories depicting the experiences of increasing numbers of dual-career parents and single parent households are common today, Dual-career parents, once the anomaly, are now the norm. The term, "single-parent household" describes many households today. Dual-career parents and single parents struggle to balance work and family responsibilities. Children from all ethnic and economic backgrounds lament the lack of parental attention and guidance they receive today (Reich, 2001). Often, the demands required to cope successfully with multiple life roles create stress levels that are overwhelming for adults who are parents.

To make matters worse, results of most studies indicate that although men and women share the workplace, they often do not share the household responsibilities (Niles & Goodnough, 1996). In most instances, women carry major responsibilities for household and parenting tasks—even when they are also working outside the home. The stress experienced by dual-career parents often manifests itself in increasing tension between couples, children feeling isolated from parents, and parents feeling as though they are living fragmented lives. Single parents in the workforce tend to fare no better when confronted with the task of managing work and family responsibilities—which in all likelihood the must do with fewer financial resources than dual-career parents.

Once reserved primarily for White men, the workplace is now increasingly heterogeneous. In the 21st century, people of color will continue to experience significant growth in numbers while the White population will decline significantly (Lee & Richardson, 1991). The influx of new immigrants into the United States will also continue in large numbers (Spencer, 1989). From 1980 to 1990, while the White population grew about 5 percent, the African American population increased by approximately 10 percent, Hispanics by almost 55 percent, Asian Americans by almost 110 percent, and Native Americans by about 38 percent. Hispanics are expected to surpass African Americans to become the largest minority group in the United States sometime within the next two decades (Herr and Cramer, 1996, p. 273).

Despite the fact that the workforce is increasingly heterogeneous, Niles and Harris-Bowlsbey (in press) note that there is ample evidence to suggest that women, people of color, persons with disabilities, gay men, and lesbian women encounter tremendous obstacles in their career development. For example, over 50 percent of young urban African American men were unemployed, worked part-time jobs involuntarily, or earned poverty-level wages in the 1980s (Lichter, 1988). The unemployment rate for African Americans has been above 11 percent each year since 1978 and was about 2.5 times the rate for Whites in the last decades of the 20th century (Swinton, 1992). Swinton also noted that only 36.9 percent of African American men are employed as executives, administrators, salespersons, and managers as compared to 61.8 percent of White men.

Hispanic Americans are also concentrated in lower-paid, lesser-skilled occupations. For example, "more than half of the employed Hispanic women are either clerical workers or nontransport operatives (dress-makers, assemblers, machine operators, and so on) (Herr & Cramer, 1996, p. 277). Herr and Cramer also noted that "no other minority group in the United States has experienced deeper prejudice or is in a less-advantaged posture than Native Americans" (p. 281). The poverty rate of Native Americans families is twice the rate (23.7 percent) of the general population in the United States (U.S. Bureau of Census, 1992). The 1980 U.S. Census report indicated that only 56 percent of Native Americans over the age of 25 had completed four or more years of high school (as compared to 66.5 percent of the general U.S. population). The unemployment rate for Native Americans living on reservations is 45 percent and 14 percent of those living on reservations have incomes of less than $2,500 per year (Johnson, Swartz, & Martin, 1995).

Despite legislation aimed at protecting their rights (e.g., Public Law 93-112, the Rehabilitation Act of 1973; Public Law 94-142, the Education for All Handicapped Children Act of 1975; Public Law 95-602, the Rehabilitation, Comprehensive Services, and Developmental Disabilities Amendment of 1978; Public Law 101-476, the Education of the Handicapped Amendments of 1990; Public Law 101-336, the Americans with Disabilities Act of 1990) Americans with disabilities have fared no better. "Of the 13 million people considered to have a work disability, 33.6 percent are in the labor force and 15.6 percent are unemployed; thus nearly half of those with a work disability are outside the work structure" (Isaacson & Brown, 1997, p. 313).

Gay, lesbian, and bisexual individuals also experience discriminatory treatment in the labor force. Goleman (1990) suggested that the negative bias toward this group is often more intense than that directed toward any other group. Herr and Cramer (1996, p. 292) noted that gay, lesbian, and bisexual persons are essentially barred from certain occupations and find vertical mobility blocked simply because of their sexual orientation.

These statistics reveal that many women, people of color, persons with disabilities and gay/lesbian/bisexual individuals regularly experience discriminatory practices in hiring and promoting, insufficient financial resources, and a lack of role models and mentors. Thus, traditional career interventions may not be appropriate for assisting members of diverse groups in their career development. Career development interventions in contemporary society must be reconceptualized to more adequately meet the career development needs of the members of an increasingly pluralistic society and heterogeneous workplace.

Regardless of one's demographic variables, all workers must cope effectively with emerging trends in work if they are to be successful. Thus, career practitioners must also understand, and be able to communicate to others, the emerging work trends that will influence their clients' career development.

Ten Factors Drive the Emerging Trends in Work

The rapidity of change in the nature of work, the language of work, and the content of work in the United States are proceeding more comprehensively and quickly than it is possible to comprehend fully. The underlying factors driving the emerging trends in work are profound and diverse. They include at least the following:

1. ***The pervasive effects of advanced technology in workplaces of all kinds and in virtually all occupations.*** It is difficult to overstate the degree to which advanced forms of technology have altered and are continuing to modify the content and the processes of work. The application of computer technology, telecommunications, and the Internet has allowed work to be done throughout the world without regard to space, time, or political boundaries. But, perhaps more pragmatically, advanced technology in its multiple forms has changed the nature of jobs in many occupational sectors; reduced the number of workers required to maintain and operate "high tech" factories and other workplaces; given rise to the need for "knowledge workers," persons who not only know how to do particular work, but why it is being done; elevated the general level of education required for work; made workplaces more information-rich, dependent on information to control and operate machines (robots, lathes, aircraft, etc.), for quality control, and for decision-making about such areas as inventory management, tracking the distribution of products shipped, and understanding the nature of one's consumers of products or services.

    Embedded within the meaning of the term "advanced technology" are many resources. Certainly central to this arena are computers, their software systems, and their increasing sophistication. The omnipresence of computers in homes and workplaces, in transportation and financial services, in international trade, in entertainment and in other spheres of life, rely on the rapidity and accuracy with which computers process, analyze, and transmit information. But, in these senses, computers are only tools, enablers if you will, by which other forms of advanced technology can flourish. The Internet, for example, is an international linkage of computers, telecommunications, graphics and knowledge bases from sites around the world, making comprehensive information accessible to persons in any setting or geographic location as long as they have computer access to an Internet portal. But, the ability of computers to analyze and model information, to calculate its characteristics and to transmit such analyses is the support system for the advances in the understanding and treatment of diseases that have a genetic base; in pharmaceuticals, particularly medicines; in the development of multi-fuel vehicles; in developing composite and smart materials, with built in sensors to monitor stress and fatigue in materials used for construction of bridges and buildings, for aircraft, automobiles, space stations, propulsion systems; in biotechnology, altering foods to make them more abundant and disease free, custom tailored to environmental conditions in which they need to thrive; in neurosciences; in global positioning and tracking of satellites and vehicles; in the transfer of currencies among nations electronically, and in many other applications of science and technology. In large measure, the global economy as it is emerging would be impossible to achieve without the availability of computers, sophisticated software, telecommunications and related processes.

2. *A changing social psychology of work.* In large part due to the effects of advanced technology in the workplace (as well as changing management styles that encourage workers to participate more fully in decision-making, problem-solving, and related issues of flextime and the scheduling of work) the social psychology of work is changing. The relationships between managers and employees, co-workers, workers and customers tend.to be more fluid as the use of technologies frees persons from some aspects of their work and requires more interaction among them. More work is being done by teams. Employers at more levels of the workplace have access to information and the opportunity to make work decisions that was previously reserved for mangers only. For some workers, computers have provided them more autonomy in their work. For other workers, however, the needs for continuous data entry to computers and monitoring them to interact with customer orders, etc., has imposed a new form of "assembly line" mentality and new ways to implement surveillance of worker productivity. Depending upon particular workplace cultures, the introduction of advanced technology in the workplace can reduce personal privacy and autonomy, change the flow of information among workers and managers, and enhance or demean workers' feelings and self-perceptions related to their interactions with computers or other forms of advanced technology.

3. *Participation in international economic competition*, as reflected in the growing global economy as well as in regional competitive structures such as the North American Free Trade Agreement, the European Union, the Association of South East Asian Nations. As a result, workers who are bilingual and understand the economic and political systems of nations with which trade is being conducted will have skills that are increasingly prized. More workers are likely to spend some part of their career working abroad, or in communication with persons in other nations with whom they conduct export-import, financial, industrial or business transactions.

4. *Changing employment opportunities as corporations and other organizations of work reduce in number their permanent workforces*, and increase the number of workers who are part-time or temporary employees and outsource, or subcontract, particular functions to other work organizations. In such contexts, many former full-time or new workers are now working several part-time jobs to earn adequate

income, in some cases without the likelihood of permanent institutional identity or adequate benefits (e.g., health care).

5. ***New concepts of careers are emerging.*** A new language of career is emerging, which suggests that because workplaces are changing rapidly, frequently downsizing the number and characteristics of their permanent workforces, more and more workers are becoming responsible for their own career management. During the earlier era of long-term worker employment in one firm, the career development of a worker tended to be primarily the role of the workplace and its managers. As the workplace found it necessary to do so, workers were retrained and reassigned to new jobs within the firm, and there was a frequently implicit "social contract" between employer and employee, which emphasized worker loyalty to the firm that was rewarded by retention and loyalty to the worker by the employer. Increasingly, that historical social contract is being set aside, requiring that individual workers be able to keep their occupational skills and competencies at a high level, constantly engaged in learning to sustain their marketability, and to be able to "sell" their competencies to employers. Part of the uncertainty of sustained employment for individual workers in such scenarios is reflected in the propensity of many workers to work harder and harder, having less and less time for other aspects of their life, including marriage and children. Americans, as a group, now work harder and longer than almost any other people on earth (Reich, 2001). An interesting corollary to the changes in work is that as workplaces and the occupational structures undergo dramatic change, there are both employment uncertainties for many workers and, at the same time, serious skill shortages. In instances, where such skill shortages exist, many workers that are employed in such contexts are under significant pressure to make up for the shortage of needed workers by "slaving away" and intensifying the hours they work. Thus, there are multiple patterns of uncertainty and over-commitment reflected throughout the occupational structure. And, there are analyses that strongly urge persons to prepare themselves to engage in Protean Careers (Hall, 1996), careers in which they are prepared to change with change, to be personally flexible, and able to anticipate emerging trends and to transform their skills and attitudes to accommodate such changes.

6. ***As a function of the increases in the use of advanced technology throughout the occupational structure and the transfer of selected industries to other nations, there has been an increase in the average educational requirements necessary for employment in many occupations.*** In some industries, advanced technology has eliminated the need for some unskilled and semi-skilled jobs and, in other instances, middle management jobs, which tended to be the positions which collected and analyzed data for decision-making, have been eliminated because information is now likely to be shared throughout the entire job spectrum as a function the utilization of computers to monitor and control specific tasks of fabrication, painting, assembly line operations, maintaining inventory and distribution of raw materials, financial transactions, quality control, etc. Thus, the interaction of person and machines has grown in symbiotic terms, modifying what persons do in manufacturing and other industries. For example, in the automobile industry, more and more of the work of building a car is performed by robots which are in turn controlled by

computers which are in turn the subject of programming, trouble-shooting, and operating by human beings. Such a scenario is replayed in different ways throughout the occupational structure. The results include "high tech" factories that need far fewer persons involved in manufacturing or in other industries even though the productivity of such factories continues to increase. The corollaries include the expectation that the human being operating the advanced technology in virtually any context, will be required to take on more responsibility and know more than was true when most industrial or business operations were done manually, not technologically. Few emerging occupations exist for people who cannot read, write, and do basic mathematics. Thus, people who have weak educational backgrounds are likely to be increasingly vulnerable to unemployment and to job opportunities that are uncertain.

7. **Because of the growing educational requirements of jobs**, the importance of science and technology to product development and marketing, and the need to find the competitive edge in new processes, many workplaces are essentially "learning organizations" populated by various kinds of "knowledge workers." The dictum that "knowledge is power" can be revised to focus on the fact that in today's job marker "knowledge of science and technology is power."

8. **An increased proportion of workers will not remain in a specific job in the same company for an extended period of time.** Because of the dynamic quality of work and work organizations, persons will likely engage in seven or more jobs in their work life, frequently engaging in retraining within a context of lifelong learning in order to manage their own career development. Many workers in the near future will essentially be "world workers," moving among nations in pursuit of suitable work. Currently, there is a global labor surplus that is continuing to spur widespread immigration to nations, like the U.S. where the unemployment rate is low and job creation is high. In such circumstances, persons compete for work wherever they can be found, competing for jobs with domestic workers, sometimes filling skill shortages in particular nations where they exist. But, such transnational mobility may cause "rootlessness and culture shock" for many workers. In such cases, nations will need to alter their education and support systems to accommodate the growing numbers of guest workers, immigrants, and temporary residents moving across national boundaries.

9. **Another trend has to do with the changing demographics of the workforce.** In particular, in an increasing number of nations, women are entering the paid workforce in large numbers and remaining in the workforce after marriage and childbearing. Many of these women are single parents, many are one part of a dual career couple, and most of them have children. Such circumstances change patterns of childrearing as well as the nature of the workplace. For example, many workers expect their employers to offer daycare for workers' children, flexible work schedules for parents to have more ability to attend to their children's needs as well as their work responsibility, and more opportunities, for certain categories of workers, to engage in telecommuting from home.

10. **A final trend relates to the shift away from developing career "maturity" and toward career "adaptability".** Savickas (1997)

noted that adaptability refers to "the quality of being able to change, without great difficulty, to fit new or changed circumstances" (p. 254). Given the rate of change occurring in the world-of-work and the various demands workers experience, moving to conceptualizing career development from an adaptability perspective seems reasonable. The adaptability construct represents the interplay between person and environment within the career development process. Coping effectively with the contemporary career context requires workers to develop career adaptability.

Understanding the Emerging (and Expanding) Context of the Worker

As suggested by the ten factors identified above, the changes in the workplace and the various types of pressure workers experience are reflected in the home and within families. In families in which both parents work, parents frequently come to their childrearing or other marital roles in a state of fatigue. The strain of their work carries into the home. In selected occupations, where parents are subjected to pressures to work significant amounts of overtime, because of skill shortages in their workplace, time for balancing non-work and other life roles becomes limited and problematic. In other circumstances, where one or both parents are under continuous pressure to keep their competencies sharp and new, they may find that much of their discretionary time composed of taking courses and learning new skills to be able to successfully compete for work. The pressures for persons in dual-career or dual-income families to work harder, to push themselves to remain at a high level of skill competence is also often indirectly changing the nature of childrearing in the United States. Just as corporations outsource tasks that they previously did within the corporation to organizations outside the corporation that have specific specialties in security, food services, custodial work, advertising, marketing, accounting, transportation, or many other possibilities, many families are doing the same with regard to maintaining their home and children. They are outsourcing day care and birthday parties, they are "eating out" or "ordering food to be delivered," they are ordering groceries online rather than going to the store and selecting them; they are using cleaning services, lawn and snow removal services, and other mechanisms to try to balance work and non-work roles. The term "virtual parenting" has come into the language to describe parents whose work requires them to work late or travel a lot. Their solution is to try to use e-mail, fax, audiotapes, family conference calls, and voice mail to stay in touch with their children (Schellenbarger, 1999).

But, many of these sorts of strains on families and the responses cited are really for the affluent parts of society, not persons of low economic wealth or the single parents. Single parents who work two jobs or more to maintain financial viability may also have to use day care, but, where possible, they are likely to use a relative or a friend to do so, rather than an expensive pre-school or day care. Frequently, the impoverished of the nation, whose institutional work is uncertain, who are frequently "laid off" or terminated, as unskilled jobs are replaced by outsourcing or other mechanisms, may spend much of their discretionary time seeking work and/or engaging in several part-time jobs. Many of these persons are on the edge of financial insolvency all of the time, trying to engage in multiple ways to obtain funds while taking on all of the tasks required by their children and their homes. They are persons for whom "life structure issues" triangulate around financial strain and creating some sense of hope for a better future. Such divides between the affluent and those of low economic wealth continue to fragment this nation and its people. The economically poor are not just rich people without money. Their culture, their worldviews, their expectations, and their realities about the roles they do and can play are quite at odds with other segments of the population. In a stunning statistic that affirms such disparities in how different the roles of persons are. Reich has written that "Bill Gates' [the founder/owner/CEO of Microsoft] net worth alone is equal to the total net worth of the bottom 50 percent of American families." Thus, to be useful in today's context, career development theories and career practitioners must be responsive to the myriad contextual factors driving intraindividual and extraindividual factors that foster career development. The growing socioeconomic divide can not be ignored. Theories must be applicable and career services available, to persons from all socioeconomic strata.

Career Development Expands to Human Development

Prompted by social and political action focused on diversity issues, shifting demographics in many parts of the world, fluctuating economic conditions, increasingly sophisticated technology and information systems, and the changing nature of work, scholars endeavor to reevaluate past and present understandings of the very notion of careers. Examining the future of career as a construct leads to the obvious conclusion that cultural issues figure prominently in efforts to help individuals move forward in their career development (Leong & Hartung, 2000).

Increased attention to social issues has surfaced in discussions about de-emphasizing careers and instead theorizing about and helping people to develop the role of work in their lives relative to roles in non-work domains (Herr & Niles, 1998; Richardson, 1993, 1994, 1996). This perspective calls for a shift from talking about career development, with its socioeconomic status, educational, and privilege implications, to considering human development through work and non-work roles; a perspective that may be more relevant to people of diverse social statuses and cultural backgrounds. As Richardson (1993) commented, this perspective shift emphasizes work as "a central human activity that is not tied to or solely located in the occupational structure...[and] a basic human function among populations for whom work has a multiplicity of meanings, including but not restricted to a career meaning" (p. 427). So conceived, work represents a culture-general human life role, whereas career represents a more culture-specific form of occupational life.

Adapting an epistemology that interprets *career* choice and development to mean *human* development through a constellation of work and non-work life roles holds great promise for contemporary career counseling practice and for society (Cook, 1994; Richardson, 1993; Savickas, 2000; Super & Sverko, 1995). Some career theories currently converge on this theme. For example, the sociological perspective on work and career development articulated by Hotchkiss and Borow (1996) recognizes that as members of social institutions people play a variety of social roles. Similarly, Gottfredson's (1996) theory of circumscription and compromise attends to issues of social identity, orientation to sex roles, and social valuation. The Theory of

Work Adjustment (Dawis, 1996) describes career development as "the *unfolding* of capabilities and requirements in the course of a person's interaction with environments of various kinds (home, school, play, work) across the life span" (p. 94). Perhaps the most obvious example is Super's life span, life space theory (Super et al., 1996) which emphasizes the multiple roles that form the basis of the human life space. Clearly, the theories advanced in subsequent chapters of this book address *career* development from a comprehensive perspective that conceptualizes career from a human development framework.

The movement to human development and away from more narrowly defined notions of career development is also reflected in more recent approaches to career counseling. For example, Peavy (1992) and Cochran (1997) present constructivist approaches to career intervention that highlight the client's narrative life story in constructing career plans. These career interventions approaches rely on card sorts, autobiographies, and other techniques that emphasize the individual's life-span development rather than relying upon the use of standardized tests that locate person's interests, aptitudes, and values on a normal curve. The latter approach (i.e., the use of standardized tests) emphasizes career development in a comparative sense. The former acknowledges the individual's unique life history in composing a life that includes multiple life-role development. Amundson (1998) focuses on actively engaging clients in the process of developing as humans who sort through career questions within a greater life context. These models are excellent examples of intervention strategies grounded in more expansive views of career development that incorporate the individual's subjective experience into the career counseling process.

As noted earlier, cross-cultural psychology also takes that perspective that life roles are fundamental elements of subjective culture — defined as the human-made part of people's environments (Triandis, 1994). Roles are etic constructs in that all cultures transmit expectations about social role behavior. Individual behavior in social roles differs as a function of the range of behavioral role options a culture makes available to its members. For example, the roles of father, spouse, and worker for a fifth-generation European-American man likely mean something very different than what these roles mean for a first-generation Japanese-American man. In addition, the changing nature of work, the growing diversity of society, the global economy and marketplace, and occupational and other barriers limit and influence the viability of different roles for people. Career practitioners, therefore, must remain cognizant of two facts as they help adults cope with career concerns in contemporary society. First, people differ in terms of which life roles are most viable and salient for them. Second, personal, structural, and cultural factors such as gender expectations, social class, discrimination, personal choice, and family expectations influence individuals' levels of commitment to and participation in work (Fitzgerald & Betz, 1994; Fouad & Arbona, 1994; Niles & Goodnough, 1996). These two facts influence the self-concepts, goals, and concerns adults clients present to career counselors. They also indicate that career interventions must be oriented to the client's context. A "one size fits all" "shotgun" orientation will "miss" clients concerns more than it will address them.

Career Counseling for Social Action

The need to reconceptualize career interventions for the current context led Herr and Niles (1998) to suggest that incorporating social action strategies in the career intervention process is one way career practitioners can respond more effectively to the career concerns confronting many adults in contemporary society. Lee agrees with Herr and Niles stating that career counselors must act as "career development advocates for disenfranchised clients by actively challenging long-standing traditions that stand in the way of equity in the workplace (Lee, 1989, p. 219).

Career counseling for social action requires counselors to provide multifaceted career interventions and to expand their roles beyond traditional individual career counseling practice. For example, although advocacy is also required in the career counseling process to instill hope in clients and empower them to manage their careers, career counseling for social action also requires counselors to integrate the roles of facilitator and community counselor into the career counseling process.

Career counseling for social action begins with career counselors possessing the multicultural competencies (i.e., knowledge, skills, and attitudes) necessary for understanding how the environments their clients occupy interact to influence the interpretations and meanings clients attach to work and occupational opportunities. Blustein and Noumair (1996) noted the importance of understanding how contextual factors (e.g., history, family, economics, culture) interact with clients' intrapersonal experiences to shape their life-role identities. Acquiring this understanding requires the use of career counseling interventions that are sensitive to the life structure needs of clients (Bowman, 1993; Leong, 1996; Super et al., 1996) and serves as the foundation for identifying social action strategies aimed at facilitating career development.

Career practitioners engaged in social action use interventions that address career concerns systemically. In part, this occurs when career counselors use community resources to provide clients access to information and opportunities (e.g., employment offices, "on-stop career shops," support groups). Learning about career resources available in the community facilitates appropriate referrals and increases the probability that clients will receive the services they need. Therefore, career counselors engaging in social action also play the role of facilitator and providing information, referrals, and encouragement to clients (Enright, Conyers, & Szymanski, 1996). Playing this role effectively requires career counselors to maintain files of useful resources, including names of potential mentors representing a diversity of backgrounds (e.g., African American, Asian American, individuals with disabilities, gay and lesbian men and women), information on accommodations for disabled individuals with different functional limitations, names of employers willing to provide opportunities for job shadowing and internship experiences, and names of individuals willing to participate in informational interviewing experiences (Enright et al., p. 111).

Having a thorough knowledge of career resources available in the community also allows counselors to identify areas where services are lacking. In these instances, counselors once again take on a strong advocacy role and seek to rectify service deficiencies in their communities (Lee, 1989).

Advocacy is also important when clients' career concerns are the result of external factors such as large-scale downsizing. In these instances, counselors concerned with social action address not only the career concerns of individual clients, but also the career concerns of the community at-large (Cahill & Martland, 1996). This is accomplished by integrating individual career counseling skills with community counseling skills. Integrating career counseling and community counseling strategies is especially critical in rural communities where economic restructuring can threaten the very existence of the community. Cahill and Martland argue that community career counseling builds on the strength of individual career counseling and offers assistance to people in their struggle to maintain their communities as they create opportunities for career development. Thus, in addition to individual career counseling skills, counselors need skills in facilitating group problem-solving, consensus building, and an understanding of the social and economic development process to help clients advance their careers in contemporary society.

Essentially, career counselors who instill hope in their clients and empower them to manage their careers are multiculturally competent, act as facilitators of information and referrals, advocate for their clients when employment practices and community traditions stand in the way of equity in the workplace, and integrate individual career counseling skills with community counseling skills to assist people in their struggle to maintain their communities and create opportunities for career development.

Because work concerns occur within a life context, contemporary career counselors also use family interventions strategies to help family members work together to cope with work-related concerns and to make career-related decisions that are sensitive to the family context. This combination of skills expands traditional approaches to career counseling and equips counselors for effective social action aimed at facilitating career development in clients.

Summary

Clearly, career interventions must evolve to respond effectively to the emerging career concerns of adult workers. In this respect, career practitioners are not excluded in the call for all workers to be more adaptable and flexible in their work situations. The theories and interventions presented in this book represent an effort to help career practitioners increase their range of knowledge pertaining to the variety of career concerns clients present and the numerous career interventions than can be used to help adult clients resolve their career concerns in contemporary society.

References

Amundson, N. E. (1998). *Active engagement: Enhancing the career counselling process.* Richmond, BC: Ergon Communications.

Anderson, W., & Niles, S. (1995). Career and personal concerns expressed by career counseling clients. *The Career Development Quarterly*, 43, 240-245.

Blustein, D. L., & Noumair, D. A. (1996). Self and identity in career development: Implications for theory and practice. *Journal of Counseling and Development*, 74, 433-441.

Bowman, S. L. (1993). Career intervention strategies for ethnic minorities. *The Career Development Quarterly*, 42, 14-25.

Bridges, W. (1994). *Job shift*. Reading, MA: Addison-Wesley.

Cahill, M., & Martland, S. (1996). Community career counseling for rural transition. *Canadian Journal of Counselling*, 30, 155-164.

Cochran, L. (1997). *Career counseling: A narrative approach*. London: Sage.

Cook, E. P. (1994). Role salience and multiple roles: A gender perspective. *The Career Development Quarterly*, 43, 85-95.

Dawis, R.V. (1996). The theory of work adjustment and person-environment correspondence counseling. In D. Brown & L. Brooks (Eds.) *Career choice and development: Applying contemporary theories to practice* (3rd ed., pp. 75-120). San Francisco: Jossey-Bass.

Enright, M. S., Conyers, L. M., & Szymanski, E. M. (1996). Career and career-related educational concerns of college students with disabilities. *Journal of Counseling and Development*, 75, 103-114.

Fitzgerald, L. F., & Betz, N. E. (1994). Career development in cultural context: The role of gender, race, class, and sexual orientation. In M.L. Savickas & R.W. Lent (Eds.), *Convergence in career development theories: Implications for science and practice* (pp. 103-117). Palo Alto, CA: Consulting Psychologists Press.

Fouad, N. A., & Arbona, C. (1994). Careers in a cultural context. *The Career Development Quarterly*, 43, 96-104.

Goleman, D. (1990). Homophobia: Scientists find clues to its roots. *The New York Times*, pp. C1, C11.

Gottfredson, L. S. (1996). Gottfredson's theory of circumscription and compromise. In D. Brown & L. Brooks (Eds.) *Career choice and development: Applying contemporary theories to practice* (3rd ed., pp. 179-232). San Francisco: Jossey-Bass.

Hall, D. T., & Associates (Eds.). (1996). *The career is dead—long live the career: A relational approach to careers*. San Francisco: Jossey-Bass.

Herr, E. L. (1989). Career development and mental health. *Journal of Career Development*, 16, 5-18.

Herr, E. L., & Cramer, S. H. (1996). *Career guidance and counseling through the lifespan: Systemic approaches*. New York: HarperCollins.

Herr, E. L., & Niles, S. G. (1998). Career: A source of hope and empowerment in a time of despair. In C. Lee & G. Walz (Eds.), *Social action: A mandate for counselors* (pp. 117-136). Greensboro, NC: ERIC/CASS.

Hotchkiss, L., & Borow, H. (1996). Sociological perspective on work and career development. In D. Brown & L. Brooks (Eds.) *Career choice and development: Applying contemporary theories to practice* (3rd ed., pp. 281-334). San Francisco: Jossey-Bass.

Isaacson, L. E., & Brown, D. (1997). *Career information, career counseling, and career development* (6th ed.). Boston, MA: Allyn & Bacon.

Johnson, M. J., Swartz, J. L., & Martin, W. E., Jr. (1995). Applications of psychological theories for career development with Native Americans. In F.T.L. Leong (Ed.), *Career development and vocational behavior of racial and ethnic minorities* (pp. 103-136). Mahwah, NJ: Erlbaum.

Lee, C. C. (1989). Needed: A career development advocate. *The Career Development Quarterly*, 37, 218-220.

Lee, C. C., & Richardson, B. L. (Eds.). (1991). *Multicultural issues in counseling: New approaches to diversity*. Alexandria, VA: American Counseling Association.

Leong, F. (1996). Toward an integrative model for cross-cultural counseling and psychotherapy. *Applied and Preventative Psychology*, 5, 189-209.

Leong, F. T. L., & Hartung, P. J. (2000). Adapting to the changing multicultural context of career. In A. Collin & R. Young (Eds.) *The future of career* (pp. 212-227). Cambridge, England: Cambridge University Press.

Levey, J., & Levey, M. (1998). *Living in balance: A dynamic approach for creating harmony and wholeness in a chaotic world*. New York: MJF Books.

Lichter, D. (1988). Race, employment hardship and inequality in American non-metropolitan south. *American Sociological Review*, 54, 436-446.

Maccoby, M., & Terzi, K. (1981). What happened to work ethic? In J. O'Toole, J. Scheiber, & L. Wood (Eds.), *Working, changes, and choices* (pp. 162-171). New York: Human Services Press.

Niles, S. G., & Goodnough, G. (1996). Life-role salience and values: A review of recent research. *The Career Development Quarterly*, 45, 65-86.

Niles, S. G., & Harris-Bowlsbey, J. (in press). *Career development interventions in the 21st century*. Englewood Cliffs, NJ: Prentice-Hall.

Niles, S. G., & Pate, R. H. Jr. (1989). Competency and training issues related to the integration of career counseling and mental health counseling. *Journal of Career Development*, 16, 63-71.

Peavy, R. (1992). A constructivist model of training for career counselors. *Journal of Career Development*, 18, 215-228.

Reich, R. (2001). *The future of success*. New York: Knopf.

Richardson, M. (1993). Work in people's lives: A location for counseling psychologists. *Journal of Counseling Psychology*, 40, 425-433.

Richardson, M. S. (1994). Pros and cons of a new location: Reply to Savickas (1994) and Tinsley (1994). *Journal of Counseling Psychology*, 41, 112-114.

Richardson, M. S. (1996). From career counseling to counseling/psychotherapy and work, jobs, and career. In M. L. Savickas, & W. B. Walsh (Eds.) *Handbook of career counseling theory and practice* (pp. 347-360). Palo Alto, CA: Davies-Black.

Rifkin, J. (1995). *The End of Work*. New York: Putnam.

Savickas, M. (1993). Career in the post-modern era. *Journal of Cognitive Psychotherapy: An International Quarterly*, 7, 205-215.

Savickas, M. (1997). Career adaptability: An integrative construct for life-span, life-space theory. *The Career Development Quarterly*, 45, 247-259.

Savickas, M. L. (2000). Renovating the psychology of careers for the 21st century. In A. Collin & R. Young (Eds.) *The future of career* (pp. 53-68). Cambridge, England: Cambridge University Press.

Schellenbarger, S. (1999). *Work & family*. New York: A Ballantine Book.

Spencer, G. (1989). *Projections of the population of the United States by age, sex, and race: 1998-2008*. Current Population Reports. Population estimates and projections. Series P-25, No. 1018. Washington, DC: Government Printing Office.

Super, D. E. (1976). *Career education and the meaning of work*. Monographs on career education. Washington, DC: The Office of Career Education, U.S. Office of Education.

Super, D. E., Savickas, M. L., & Super, C. M. (1996). The life-span, life-space approach to careers. In D. Brown & L. Brooks (Eds.), *Career choice and development: Applying contemporary theories to practice* (3rd ed., pp. 121-178). San Francisco: Jossey-Bass.

Super, D. E., & Sverko, B. (Eds.). (1995). *Life roles, values, and careers: International findings of the work importance study*. San Francisco: Jossey-Bass.

Swinton, D. H. (1992). The economic status of African Americans: Limited ownership and persistent in quality. In B. J. Tidwell (Ed.), *The state of black America* (pp. 61-117). New York: National Urban League.

Triandis, H. C. (1994). *Culture and social behavior*. New York: McGraw-Hill.

U.S. Bureau of Census, (1992). *Population projections of the United States, by age, sex, race, and Hispanic origin: 1992-2005*. Current Population Reports. Series P-25, No. 10920. Washington, DC: Government Printing Office.

SECTION II:

THEORIES AND CONCEPTS

CHAPTER 2
Life-Span Developmental Perspectives on Adult Career Development: Recent Advances

Fred W. Vondracek
Erik J. Porfeli
Pennsylvania State University

A career, as Donald Super was fond of reminding people, is "the sequence of positions, jobs, and occupations that a person occupies and pursues during the course of a life of preparing to work, working, and retiring from work" (Super, 1992, p.422). Having been influenced by the life-course perspective of Charlotte Bühler, Super was acutely aware of the fact that boundaries between the vocational development of children and adolescents, on the one hand, and the career development of young, middle-aged and older adults, on the other, were arbitrary and artificial. In his chapter in the previous edition of this volume (Super, 1992), he maintained that preparation for work, working and retirement are integral and interconnected parts of the individual's career over the course of life. Super lamented the fact that both clients and professional counselors and psychologists tend to focus on the individual person, as if the person were operating in a vacuum, thereby neglecting the complex environments in which people actualize their careers. At the same time, he empathized with those who despaired at the complexity of developmental-contextual, life-span models like that presented by Vondracek, Lerner, and Schulenberg (1986) and wondered whether future methodological advances would provide the means for handling the complex models that would be needed in a future that he viewed as ever more complex, more uncertain, and more rapidly changing.

The good news is that there are, indeed, more sophisticated methodologies that can cope quite well with the tremendous complexity of person-context models in the study of career development, without loosing the individual in the process (e.g., Blustein, Phillips, Jobin-Davis, Finkelberg, & et al., 1997; Heinz, Kelle, Witzel, & Zinn, 1998; Reitzle & Vondracek, 2000). The bad news is that much work remains to be done to further develop these complex models and to apply them specifically to the field of career development (Vondracek & Kawasaki, 1995). Moreover, customary ways of doing things seem to change much more slowly than the circumstances that warrant change. In the area of career counseling, well-established assessment instruments and typologies, in spite of their proven utility, may have become impediments to progress and to the integration of vocational psychology into the mainstream of psychological theory, research and practice. Clearly, the challenge today is to present novel and complex models in a way that describes the essential parameters in a clear and concise manner, without unnecessary jargon and without undue preoccupation with the technical details. A further concern deals with the applicability of theoretical models and complex research findings in the everyday practice of professionals in the field of career counseling. It is our aim to address some of these challenges and concerns in the following pages.

The Developmental-Contextual, Life-span Perspective

Super's insistence on viewing the entire "life-career" and not disconnecting the preparation to enter work from "post-entry" work or adolescent vocational development from adult career development, represents a tradition in vocational psychology that is honored and strengthened in the life-span perspective. His concern about contextualizing development is also fully represented in the developmental-contextual approach to career development, and while it is impossible to account for every context in which persons develop, several ways of determining the relative importance of specific contexts are provided (e.g., Bronfenbrenner, 1979; Gibson, 1982). The details of the developmental-contextual, life-span perspective on career development were presented by Vondracek, et al. (1986) and do not need to be repeated here. An extension and elaboration of this framework, particularly with reference to adult career development (Vondracek & Kawasaki, 1995) was published in the *Handbook of Vocational Psychology*. It relied extensively on advances in developmental theory that have come to be known as the Living Systems Framework (Ford, 1987), Developmental Systems Theory (Ford & Lerner, 1992), and Motivational Systems Theory (Ford, 1992). In the meantime, significant advances have been made in life-span developmental theory since the 1986 publication of the Vondracek, et al., book on life-span career development. We would be remiss in our aim to present an up-to-date version of the developmental-contextual, life-span approach to career development if we did not introduce some of the key features of contemporary advances in life-span developmental theory. Specifically, we would like to introduce a general model of life-span development that has evolved during the past decade under the leadership of Paul Baltes and his colleagues (e.g., Baltes, 1997; Baltes & Baltes, 1990; Baltes, Lindenberger, & Staudinger, 1998).

The Model of Selective Optimization with Compensation (SOC)

This model was developed as part of an effort to account for and enhance understanding of successful development. Although the main focus was on successful aging (Baltes & Baltes, 1990), it was formulated quite generally to make it broadly deployable and amenable to domain-specific refinements (Baltes, et al., 1998). The field of life-span career development is an excellent candidate for application and adaptation of the SOC model, in part because in career development there is less controversy with regard to what constitutes successful development than might be the case in, for example, the domains of moral or social development. The basic proposition of the model is that selection, optimization, and compensation represent lifelong processes in development that converge around the objectives of maximizing gains and minimizing losses (Baltes, et al., 1998). Moreover, it is the coordinated use of selection, optimization, and compensation strategies that is most likely to result in successful development, i.e., maximizing gains and minimizing losses.

24

As an example, when a man fractures a leg, he has a few compensatory options. He could choose to employ a cane, crutches, or a wheel chair. Although all three are viable options, most people and physicians choose crutches. Why? Each of the three choices affords mobility to an otherwise immobile person, and if the selection criteria only included mobility then any of the three would compensate adequately for the injury. If a person's only consideration is their ability to master the device (i.e., a specific selection criterion which involves optimization), then the cane may be the best option if a person has exceptional balance. This person would deem the wheelchair and the crutches unnecessary. Once we add more explicit selection criteria, however, then the choice across individuals may become more consistent. The criteria could include mobility, stability, and exercise to the uninjured leg. A wheelchair permits mobility, but limits exercise to the uninjured leg. A cane permits mobility but affords less stability than the crutches; hence, the cane option may be too risky. Crutches tend to be favored because they force the user to exercise the uninjured leg and yet afford a reasonable amount of stability while in the act of being mobile.

The key to the example is that selection criteria act as the frame, and within this context people develop gain/loss ratios to determine their plans of action. During the calculation of this ratio, people who consider issues associated with optimization and compensation will tend, so the theory suggests, to arrive at an optimal solution that best suits their current needs, resources, and barriers.

Although it is clear that selection, optimization, and compensation behaviors can be conceptualized as deliberate behavioral strategies, Baltes, et al., (1998) make the point that the implementation of these behaviors can range from relatively passive to active, and they may be motivated internally or externally. A person who is fully conscious and intentional about these behaviors may execute them, or they may be carried out in a relatively unconscious manner by a person who is on "automatic pilot" and who behaves in a functionally autonomous manner. Moreover, selection, optimization, and compensation (SOC) behaviors may change from being deliberate to being automatic, from passive to active, and so forth. Although these variable dimensions of SOC behaviors add to the complexity of the explanatory model, they also expand the possible focal points and range of interventions that may be applied to change a person's SOC behaviors, an observation that will be addressed at a later point in this chapter.

Because development represents a complex process that involves multi-causality (i.e., multiple causes may contribute to the occurrence of any particular feature of development) and multi-functionality (i.e., a given event or behavior may contribute toward the accomplishment of different developmental objectives in different ways), it is not always clear whether a given event is an instance of selection, optimization, or compensation. Moreover, the definition of what constitutes instances of selection, optimization, and compensation changes as people age and their capabilities change, and as people change their contextual circumstances. Once more, we observe that human development is a exceedingly complex process that defies oversimplification, making resistance too simple, "one size fits all" models essential. What stays constant in this explanatory model is the implication that selection, optimization, and compensation typically collaborate in achieving "successful development" (Baltes, et al., 1998, p. 1057).

Selection, Optimization, and Compensation in Life-span Career Development

The SOC model is particularly well suited for conceptualizing career development and work performance across the life-span. When one examines what it takes to develop a successful career and to maintain a high level of work performance over a period of many decades, it is readily apparent that most individuals endeavor to accomplish this in spite of various deficiencies in the resources available to them. These resource deficiencies may be age-related, as would be the case in a loss of physical stamina or strength, declines in memory, or chronic health conditions. They could also be related to macro-economic conditions, such as recessions or hyperinflation, or to other contextual circumstances, including accidents or natural disasters. In all such cases, the SOC framework would predict that those individuals who successfully employ selection, optimization, and compensation strategies are the ones most likely to have successful careers over long periods of time and to maintain a high level of work performance. It may be helpful, at this time, to define and provide some examples of selection, optimization, and compensation behaviors with special reference to their role in adult career development.

SELECTION

This is the first component of the SOC model, representing processes that are central to the structuring and choice of goals (Wiese, Freund, & Baltes, 2000). Moreover, in this model selection refers to the identification of domains of behavior and the direction of behavior toward the development of that domain. Clearly, in career development, selection plays a central role. As an individual considers the broad range of possibilities in the occupational domain, as well as the range of consequences associated with these possibilities, selections (choices) are made which, in turn, eliminate alternative selections. For example, if an individual selects as his or her goal to pursue an occupation in medicine, it means that other possible goals (e.g., being a ballet dancer) are "unselected." Moreover, it means that behaviors become directed toward obtaining the requisite training and skills to actualize this occupational goal selection.

Carstensen, Hanson and Freund (1995) have suggested that as people get older they become increasingly different from one another and that this increasing differentiation is the consequence of two forms of selection. They suggest that structural selection may occur through societal practices that limit opportunities depending on various factors including gender, race, class, and age. Clearly, these are factors that have been of primary concern to life-course sociologists who have focused on the social structuring of developmental trajectories and transitions (e.g., Elder, 1997). The second kind of selection is referred to as behavioral selection, which according to Carstensen, et al. (1995) involves actively choosing one or more life paths from among many.

In adult career development, structural selection based on race, social class, and gender, have been well documented (Fouad & Bingham, 1995; Schneider, 1994). In structural selection, individuals' occupational choices are constrained or channeled by forces that are relatively independent of the characteristics of the individual. For example, in spite of expectations that match or exceed those of white students,

African-American students end up being unemployed or in occupations that generally pay less, in part reflecting the fact that hiring decisions continue to be based on race to some extent (Kohn & Schooler, 1983). Social class-linked occupational socialization may also constrain occupational choices (Kohn & Schooler, 1983), and women continue to consider a narrower range of occupational options, possibly because they continue to be conflicted by societal expectations that they invest in having a family as well as a career (Gutek, Searle, & Klepa, 1991).

Behavioral selection, however, also plays a major role in occupational choice. This process of behavioral selection incorporates the essentials of what Lerner and Busch-Rossnagel (1981) refer to as producing one's own development, and what Elder (1997) refers to as human agency in choice making and actions. Individual characteristics, including abilities, motivation, and personality, tend to drive behavioral selection. An interesting distinction is made in the SOC model between two kinds of behavioral selection, namely, elective selection and loss-based selection (Freund, Li, & Baltes, 1999). Elective selection in the field of career or occupation refers, for example, to choosing between several desirable options or setting up a goal hierarchy to develop occupational choice priorities. Loss-based selection is likely to occur when one's ability to achieve a certain goal becomes compromised. Examples would be running out of money in pursuing the requisite education or training for a particular occupation or suffering an injury in a car accident that precludes a previously made choice of becoming a performing artist.

OPTIMIZATION

Within the SOC model, optimization revolves around the development and employment of "goal appropriate means" (e.g., skills) in the attainment of goals or preferences (Marsiske, Lang, Baltes, & Baltes, 1995, p. 58). It is readily apparent that this process of skill (or knowledge) development is applicable in the area of career development. Optimization in career development could also be focused around identifying and seeking environments that enhance one's career development and work performance. Moving to a new location that has better job prospects or moving to another company that offers better chances for advancement would be additional examples of optimization. In other words, optimization in career development might involve moving to New York City if one is an aspiring theater actor, or moving to silicon valley if one is gifted in computer technology. Other examples of optimization in career development include the investment of energy and time in the acquisition of occupational skills, modeling oneself after others who are successful in a given occupation, showing long-term persistence in the face of difficult goals (e.g., in entrepreneurship), and being able to delay gratification (Wiese, et al., 2000).

In today's challenging and rapidly changing occupational environment, optimization in the domain of cognition and intellectual development is a prerequisite for advancement. Indeed, the avoidance of technological obsolescence and the pursuit of occupational advancement require that individuals apply themselves to bring about a convergence of "cognitive, motivational, and goal-appropriate means" (Marsiske, et al., 1995). Such goal appropriate means are certainly not confined to the development of cognitive skills and capabilities. They also include motor skills, such as those required to operate a lathe or to fly an airplane. In addition, the development of social skills that are necessary to build occupational networks and to gain access to potential mentors and colleagues are also critical optimizing activities with special import in the world of work (Marsiske, et al., 1995). In summary, individuals who engage in optimizing behaviors are much more likely to successfully reach their career development and work performance goals than people are who do not effectively engage in such behaviors.

COMPENSATION

Compensation within the SOC model results from internal or external limits or losses. It is a complex construct and theoreticians and researchers are not completely in agreement regarding its definition (Dixon & Bäckman, 1995). It may thus be useful to start with a comprehensive and inclusive definition of compensation: "Compensation can be inferred when an objective or perceived mismatch between accessible skills and environmental demands is counterbalanced (either automatically or deliberately) by investment of more time or effort (drawing on normal skills), utilization of latent (but normally inactive) skills, or acquisition of new skills, so that a change in the behavioral profile occurs, either in the direction of adaptive attainment, maintenance, or surpassing of normal levels of proficiency or of maladaptive outcome behaviors or consequences" (Bäckman & Dixon, 1992, p. 272).

Although this definition was written to be applicable across a broad range of domains, it is readily apparent that compensation strategies and behaviors are critically important in career development and in the achievement and maintenance of satisfactory work performance. It is important to note (with Dixon & Bäckman, 1992) that a mismatch between a person's capabilities or skills and the demands of the situation must exist for compensation to be an appropriate and necessary behavioral strategy, because without such a mismatch or deficit there is no need or rationale for compensation. Indeed, Elder (1997) has noted that mismatches between expectations and reality are likely to give rise to attempts by individuals and families to find new ways to master their situations. Conceptualized from the perspective of the SOC framework, when the previously effective internal and external resources are no longer adequate to cope with a new situation, compensatory strategies must be employed as a means to adapt.

Compensation is an essential strategy in adult career development and in the maintenance of satisfactory work performance. This assertion can be brought into focus with reference to the mismatches between individuals and the demands of their environments in situations of rapid and sometimes dramatic change. One such circumstance occurred as a result of the fall of the iron curtain and the reunification of Germany (Vondracek, 1999; Vondracek, Reitzle, & Silbereisen, 1999). The rapid social change experienced in the former East Germany produced huge discrepancies between expectations based on many years of experience in a Communist society, where the state took care of everything, on the one hand, and the requirements of a new, competitive, capitalist society on the other. Those individuals who were able to compensate by developing entrepreneurial skills, for example, were able not only to survive but also to thrive under the new conditions.

Other circumstances that necessitate compensation as an adaptive strategy in adult career development include unemployment, divorce, or the loss of strength, endurance, or acuity of senses, and other deficits associated with the processes of aging. Successful workers compensate for such deficits in many different ways, depending on the internal and external resources they have available. For example, they may seek to expand their social contacts to cope with unemployment and divorce, and to cope with age-related deficits they may reduce the strength required to perform their tasks by sub-dividing these tasks into smaller ones and spending more time doing them. They may also seek to acquire new skills (i.e., a more efficient way of doing a task) in order to compensate for a decline in speed. Finally, individuals may compensate by seeking assistance from others or through the use of aides, such as mechanical or electronic devices.

Selective Optimization with Compensation in Adult Career Development

As previously noted, Baltes, et al. (1998) acknowledges that selection, optimization, and compensation are defined in relation to their functional and contextual location. This means that whether something represents selection, optimization, or compensation depends on the circumstances and cannot be defined in an absolute sense without reference to the developmental status and contextual circumstances of the person. Nevertheless, some examples from the real-life experiences of successful individuals will serve to illustrate the ubiquity of SOC behaviors and define them in relation to specific contexts. This is best illustrated by means of some biographical examples, as presented in Table 1 by Marsiske, et al., (1995, p. 68). What is readily apparent from the table is that work- and performance-related behaviors occupy a very central position in individuals' SOC behaviors. This is to be expected, because work- and performance-related goals are likely to be of central importance in the goal selections made by most individuals.

The examples also clearly show that the use of all three strategies, selection, optimization, and compensation, are critically important in attaining success. A legitimate question, however, is whether this holds true for ordinary people as well as for the "superstars" featured in the example. There is some recent empirical evidence that suggests that selection, optimization, and compensation represent fundamental strategies of successful life management across a number of domains. For example, Wiese, et al. (2000) demonstrated that individuals who reported more extensive use of SOC strategies were more likely to report being generally successful and particularly being more successful in the domains of work and partnership. Similarly, Abraham and Hanson (1995) reported that adults who used SOC strategies were more likely to maintain a feeling of competence and of successful goal attainment in the occupational domain.

TABLE 1: SELECTIVE OPTIMIZATION WITH COMPENSATION: BIOGRAPHICAL EXAMPLES

Source	Selection	Optimization	Compensation
Concert Pianist Rubinstein (Baltes & Baltes, 1990)	Played smaller repertoire of pieces in late life	Practiced more hours with age	Slowed performance before fast movements to heighten contrast
Athlete Michael Jordan (Greene, 1993)	Focused only on basketball in youth, excluding swimming and skating	Daily line drills and upper body training	Reliance on special footwear to deal with chronic foot injury
Scientist Marie Curie (Curie, 1937)	Excluded political and cultural activities from her life	Spent a fixed number of hours daily in isolation in her laboratory	Turned to the advice of specific colleagues when encountering scientific problems that were beyond her expertise

(Marsiske, et al., 1995, p. 68.)

If the use of selection, optimization, and compensation strategies enhances individuals' chances of experiencing successful development across a wide range of domains, it would clearly be advantageous for them to do anything that would improve their proficiency in using them. In fact, there may be both domain-general and domain-specific SOC strategies, although individuals who use SOC strategies in one domain are likely to use them in others, as well (Wise, et al., 2000). Several issues related to the use of SOC strategies would clearly be of particular interest to career counselors and career consultants:

1. What are the most commonly used SOC-related behaviors employed by adults who successfully pursue their occupational careers?
2. Are there specific SOC-related behaviors that work better for men or for women?
3. Are there specific SOC-related behaviors that are particularly effective for certain age groups or for individuals with specific educational attainment or belonging to certain socio-economic groups?
4. Are SOC-related behaviors more applicable and more helpful to members of some occupational groups than to others
5. Can career professionals teach individuals the effective use of SOC-related behaviors?

While most of these questions await thoughtful longitudinal research before they can be answered in any kind of definitive manner, it may be useful at this point to examine how the SOC model can be applied in the practice of career counseling and career consultation.

Applying the Life-Span Model of Selective Optimization with Compensation in Career Interventions

The life-span model of selective optimization with compensation has been proposed as a universal model of development (Baltes & Baltes, 1990; Marsiske, et al, 1995). Its very general nature has been cited as evidence that it is open with regard to its deployability and that domain-specific refinement (in this case to the domain of adult career development) is not only appropriate but necessary (Baltes, et al., 1998). In the general model, *antecedent conditions* can be identified that conceptualize development as a process of selective adaptation, with selection pressures arising from limitations and changes in internal and external resources or from one's desire to improve or simply alter their life course. For each domain of development, domain-specific selection pressures can be specified. The antecedent conditions result in the activation of *adaptive processes*, which consist of selection, optimization, and compensation. When used effectively, these processes result in *outcomes* that minimize losses and maximize gains.

When the general SOC model is applied to adult career development, *antecedent conditions* are represented primarily by *selection pressure*, i.e., the necessity or desire to select one set of goals or objectives rather than another, which arises from the fact that people have finite internal and external resources that they seek to optimize. Particularly relevant in adult career development are internal resources such as intelligence, motivation, personality dispositions, temperament, knowledge, skills, health and energy, and external resources such as money, opportunity, family support, facilitative economic and political conditions, and the like. Additional selection pressure derives from age-related changes, including losses in internal resources (e.g., a decline in strength and stamina, visual acuity, steadiness of hand, flexibility) and in external resources (e.g., opportunity, family support, other support networks). *Adaptive processes* in adult career development are represented by domain-specific selection, optimization, and compensation strategies and behaviors which, when effectively used, result in *outcomes* that include the successful attainment of occupational goals, maintenance of performance at the highest possible level, and successful coping with obstacles and losses that have the potential for impacting occupational performance and career success.

Career counselors are often called upon to work with clients who face complex problems of balancing conflicting demands, such as those posed by work on the one hand and family on the other. There is evidence that the use of compensation-related behaviors is most adaptive and can be used effectively when dealing with work/family conflict. In the area of work, however, optimization behaviors and strategies appear to be more relevant and effective in leading to successful development (Wiese, et al., 2000). In counseling adolescents about their initial career choices, selection-related behaviors and strategies are more important. Although this suggests that, depending on the circumstances, one or another SOC-related behavior should receive primary attention, it must be remembered that the combined application of all three is likely to produce the best outcomes.

Illustrations of the use of Selection, Optimization, and Compensation in Career Interventions

In the biographical illustrations introduced earlier (see Table 1), some career-related examples of selection, optimization, and compensation behaviors and strategies were presented. Table 2 augments these examples to show the kinds of SOC-related behaviors that are most likely the focus of career interventions, as well as the alternative, non-SOC behaviors that are often encountered in the process of career counseling. Following Table 2, we present three fictitious case summaries and analyses, which intentionally represent a diverse range of clients across a variety of demographic variables, as a means of demonstrating the model's range of applicability.

TABLE 2: EXAMPLES OF SALIENT SOC-RELATED BEHAVIORS (AND ALTERNATIVES) THAT COULD BE THE FOCUS OF CAREER INTERVENTIONS

	Target Behavior	Alternative
Selection	Single-mindedly focusing on specific career goals	Dividing attention among many goals
	Choosing occupation that is congruent with intellectual capability	Choosing occupation significantly above or below intellectual ability
	Finding and selecting the best available job after unexpected unemployment	Refusing to consider jobs outside of one's area of specialization
Optimization	Persistent pursuit of goal-relevant means, e.g., acquiring relevant training, skills, education	Giving up when success does not come as easily as expected
	Working overtime in order to acqire important experience	Insisting on strictly limiting intrusion of work into personal time
	Attending motivational workshops to enhance and maintain peak performance and enthusiasm for work	Accepting reduced performance as inevitable signs of aging
Compensation	Persistently searching for alternative behaviors when new deficits, conflicts, or barriers prevent obtaining accustomed or desired outcomes/performance	Accepting reduced performance, income, demotion, that occur as a result of new deficits, conflicts, or bariers
	Compromising with regard to the division of household labor with a partner or spouse	Insisting on traditional, gender-based division of household labor
	Investing time and effort in learning new technological skills in order to avoid obsolescence/job loss	Believing that excellence will be recognized and rewarded, even if it is situated in "yesterday's" skills

Adapted from Baltes & Dickson (2000) and Wiese, et al., (2000)

The case of Lee: Lee is a 25 year-old glazier in a ceramics factory. He is married and has two pre-school-aged children. His and his wife's families have lived in this town for generations. Having worked in the same factory from the time he graduated from high school, Lee was slated for promotion into a supervisory position, but the factory was sold and was subsequently shut down before Lee obtained the expected promotion. The factory was situated in Lee's small town and is approximately two hours from any related industry. There are few occupational choices in his town. Lee faces either significant retraining and a possible pay reduction or relocation to a new community. Lee is seeking career guidance as a means of finding work, preferably in his hometown, which will continue to support his family of five at an economic level close to his former salary.

Lee represents the majority of young adults who have received little or no post-secondary education, yet are clearly motivated to succeed in their occupational lives. Unfortunately, Lee, in spite of his competence and motivation, has lost his job. Such a loss can be quite difficult to resolve, particularly given his family and community circumstance. In SOC terms, Lee has experienced detrimental structural selection (the plant closing) that has prompted Lee to explore a loss-based selection strategy (retraining or relocation). Applying the SOC framework to Lee's current problem offers a structure and starting point to a clearly complex problem.

SELECTION

Lee's ability to advance toward a supervisory position and obtain commensurate recognition from his former supervisor demonstrates that he has the ability to select and meet obtainable goals that yield favorable outcomes. Based on this history, Lee probably has effective SOC occupational strategies that could be used to facilitate the shift to another job or occupation. Lee has made firm commitments to goals in the occupational (glazier and potential supervisor) and interpersonal (husband and father) domain, which could imply a decrease in plasticity, but, given his age and occupational status, he is likely to have the flexibility needed to undergo occupational re-exploration and re-training. Lee may profit from some career guidance and education during the re-exploration phase but given his apparent goal selection strengths, such guidance should be offered on an as-needed basis and the counselor should foster a healthy measure of self-direction as a means of empowering Lee to employ his selection strengths

OPTIMIZATION

Having selected a new occupation, Lee will have to add to and hone his current occupational skills. Lee's past performance suggests that he is quite willing and capable of acquiring and applying new occupational skills; therefore, he seems to be a good candidate for a structured school or apprenticeship experience.

COMPENSATION

Given the relative lack of well-paying available work in Lee's community and his financial obligations to his family, Lee may have to take temporary work during the retraining phase. This compensatory action may and probably will prolong the training period, yet may also be the only way for Lee to satisfy his long-term interpersonal and occupational goals.

The shift away from manufacturing and heavy industry in the US has forced many men and women like Lee to radically alter their career pathway or to relocate to those communities where related industry continues to offer work in skilled and semi-skilled trades. Lee could choose to relocate. This choice would involve a different set of selective optimization with compensation goals and behaviors but the counselor could just as easily frame such a pathway in SOC terms.

In either the retraining or the relocation option, Lee appears to be predominantly addressing occupational issues and employing behavioral strategies associated with the selection phase of the SOC model, but recall that this behavioral episode was precipitated by a loss, hence Lee, at a relatively young age, is also compensating. The selective optimization with compensation meta-model presents an integrative, developmentally sensitive model. A behavior can be interpreted as being selective, optimizing, or compensatory in nature depending on the individual's situation and the developmental status of the individual. Imagine how the scenario would be different for Lee and the career counselor if Lee were 60 years old. Lee would likely invoke a compensatory orientation by seeking out part-time work and limiting frivolous spending; yet selection strategies would exist and could center on the search for available and appropriate jobs within his community. Relocation could be cast as a compensatory strategy to mitigate further financial loss if no available work existed. Although retraining is a possibility, it seems unlikely that Lee would select this option at the twilight of his working life. Altering Lee's age demonstrates how occupational developmental status can cast a very different light on a person's circumstances and how this can lead to an alternative set of strategies. In other words, SOC is a developmental model that is applicable across the lifespan; hence, it can act as a tool to appropriately and effectively frame the client's circumstance and the subsequent plan of action in a developmentally sensitive fashion.

The case of David: David is a 35 year-old district sales manager for an international manufacturer and distributor of automobile parts, situated in a major metropolitan city. In this position, David is required to do an extensive amount of domestic and international travel. David has been married for 10 years and has a 7 year-old daughter. Since accepting the promotion to district manager, David's travel requirements have increased and he is now concerned that the travel is affecting his marriage and that he is "missing-out" on significant events in his daughter's life. David is considering a job change to reduce the time he is away from home, but he is concerned that such a change will require relocation or a step-down in his salary. David is seeking career counseling to attempt to find a job that will utilize his skills and abilities, but that will require less travel and, preferably, will be situated within commuting distance from his current home.

Although David clearly aspired to attain his current position and probably engaged SOC strategies and behaviors effectively, he now finds the adage, "be careful what you wish for..." apropos. In short, he is experiencing the common conflict between occupational demands and interpersonal goals. Returning to the language of SOC and lifespan theory, David's resources are limited to the point that he is unable to meet life goals, which demand similar resources (in this case time spent engaging in work and family activities is the resource). By the time he arrives at the counselor's office, he has already engaged the SOC system by selecting career counseling and exploration as a goal to resolve his current crisis. This strategy implies that David feels unable to restructure his current work demands or to transfer to an alternative position within the organization. Although such a conclusion may be premature and a reevaluation of this position could be a goal of counseling, we will operate under the assumption that no options exist with his current employer.

SELECTION

David has marketable skills that can be easily transferred to a wide range of occupational settings; hence, selection issues may revolve around David's relocation and income concerns. Depending on David's skills, he may or may not need to be concerned about a salary change or relocation. If either is likely, exchanges between David and his wife and David and the career counselor concerning these issues could be classified as a part of the goal selection process.

OPTIMIZATION

Having selected the goal of seeking a similar job with a different employer in the same city, optimizing strategies could include improving his marketability. In order to achieve this goal David could engage in a variety of optimizing behaviors including creating or revising his resume, networking with friends and associates in related businesses in order to generate leads, and/or rehearsing for potential job interviews. One essential feature of optimizing involves identifying, honing, and effectively using one's strengths and minimizing weaknesses. Therefore, David and the counselor will need to determine which job acquisition strategies to further develop and employ and which to ignore.

COMPENSATION

Simultaneously maintaining a demanding job and engaging in job search can lead to additional time pressures; therefore, David may need to engage in a time management compensatory strategy. Related compensatory behaviors could include abstaining from extracurricular activities or devoting even less time to family obligations. In either event, such compensatory strategies may be more palatable to David and his family since they are, in all likelihood, short-term and offer the promise of more time for both if he carefully engages in his job search and effectively engages in the optimizing behaviors discussed above.

Upon David's arrival at the counseling setting, he has engaged in a significant amount of selection. Although he still needs to make some goal choices, his strategic emphasis appears to be grounded in the optimizing domain. Therefore, career counseling could center on assisting David to further define his goals, but the bulk of the work would focus on optimizing strategies, such as the improvement of his resume and interviewing skills and tapping into his ability to use computer and recruiter resources to generate job prospects. In summary, David is a successful salesman and behaviors associated with sales can be optimized. Instead of selling automobile parts, metaphorically and literally, David will have to devise and employ strategies and behaviors to sell himself.

The case of Tom: Tom is a 55 year-old, furniture-grade, master carpenter living in a mid-sized town that acts as a hub for several smaller satellite communities in a rather rural portion of the state. Approximately three months ago, Tom sustained serious injuries during an automobile accident. He lost his right hand and he has limited use of the left arm and hand. The strong consensus amongst the medical and rehabilitation team is that he will be unable to return to his former job. Tom currently resides with his sister and her family as he is unmarried and in need of personal care assistance at this time. Tom wants to seek work in a woodworking trade but he is unsure of his options given his medical realities. Tom is willing to undergo occupational therapy and some re-training, yet he is quite adamant about remaining in the field of woodworking. His former employer has expressed an interest in keeping Tom as an employee but, like Tom, is uncertain about what role Tom could fill. Tom hopes that career counseling will offer him a setting where he can further define his career options given his physical limitations.

Tom has suffered a serious loss that will affect many different aspects of his life. Although Tom may not have been active in acquiring rehabilitation and counseling services, his continued participation demonstrates his desire to return to work and his ability and motivation to access compensatory strategies and employ related behaviors. Given his firm stance on the type of work he is willing to perform and his current employer's expressed interest, the goal of career counseling could be to aid Tom in the exploration of work options and to assist him in potential negotiations with his employer.

SELECTION

Tom will have to work quite hard and set a range of sub-goals in order to accomplish his major goal of returning to the woodworking trade. Therefore, with the aid of the career counselor and the rehabilitation team, he will need to: (a) identify and organize those necessary activities associated with occupational and physical therapy, (b) identify skills and abilities that are independent of his physical limitations, (c) gather information associated with the needs of his current employer, (d) identify and choose educational opportunities and finally, (e) fit his existing and newly acquired abilities to the needs of his employer. Although there may be a natural sequencing to these goals, Tom will need to make choices and these choices will ultimately determine the pace and effectiveness of the rehabilitation and counseling process.

OPTIMIZATION

Tom is a master carpenter and, by definition, has demonstrated the ability to optimize occupational skills. A significant goal in counseling will be to identify and further develop Tom's other but perhaps less refined occupational skills. For example, if Tom's employer needs someone to fill a supervisor or mentor role, then Tom could further refine his ability to be an effective manager or educator by taking coursework. Given his former position within the wood shop, he has probably engaged in similar behaviors as a peripheral aspect of his previous job, but may now have to enhance these skills should they become central aspects of a new position. This point needs to be underscored, because in most cases optimization involves the enhancement of existing skills while compensation typically involves the application and perhaps the acquisition of alternative or related skills in order to maintain or enhance a certain aspect of life. As Tom probably already has some mentorship skills, he would focus on "optimizing" those skills.

COMPENSATION

Limiting the impact of Tom's disability through the use of counseling, education, and assistive technology could be a primary goal of counseling. The career counselor, for example, could empower Tom to seek and acquire additional or specialized training in the field of automated CAD-based woodworking or in the use of assistive technology. Returning to school and learning to use assistive devices would require Tom to employ previously ignored or infrequently used internal and external resources to accomplish occupational goals that were essentially created or redefined by the injuries he sustained.

As an individual facing the last 10 to 15 years of his working life, Tom is clearly engaging the compensation system. Although he may be capable of more plasticity than he realizes, he is currently unwilling to entertain re-training in an alternative occupation, and as a counselor it may be wise to support this position until reasonable efforts have been made to return Tom to his current employer. Given the report from the rehabilitation team, it is highly unlikely that Tom will be capable of attaining the level of skill he once had. However, given his expertise and understanding of woodworking, he may be able to successfully take on a supervisory or mentorship role that would allow him to continue working within his current work setting. Given the information we have, any conclusion concerning the exact nature of Tom's future job may be premature but the point to be made here is that the SOC model affords the ability to cast a presenting problem into a cohesive and developmentally sensitive framework that aides the counselor in generating a series of action steps and strategies that, in turn, lead to a host of predictable outcomes.

Conclusions

The model of selective optimization with compensation was presented as being particularly applicable to the pursuit and achievement of career-related goals. The model attends to selection, which revolves around the construction of goal systems or goal hierarchies—unquestionably central issues or tasks in career development across the life-span. It also focuses on the strategies of optimization and compensation, which describe how individuals use goal-relevant means, i.e., behaviors that are relevant and important for the accomplishment of the goals that are being pursued. Career counseling that is specifically designed to enhance individuals' ability to effectively use selection, optimization and compensation behaviors in pursuing their career development objectives was presented as a novel approach, especially in the area of adult career development.

With the introduction of any new approach it is reasonable to question what evidence exists to warrant the investment of time and energy required for its adoption into practice. Moreover, it is also to be expected that questions would be raised regarding the uniqueness of any approach presented as an advancement or innovation. The first question is undoubtedly one that can be addressed by empirical research. Some initial studies are encouraging. For example, one study has demonstrated that individuals who report more SOC-related behaviors tend to score significantly higher on work-related well-being than individuals who show fewer SOC-related behaviors, leading the authors to state that "findings support the hypotheses that SOC-related strategies are efficient means for planning and managing the occupational and partnership challenges of adult life" (Wiese, et al., 2000, p. 295). Other authors have proposed that the SOC framework can serve as an organizing framework for the work of industrial/organizational psychologists as they address a wide range of organizational (occupational) behaviors (B. Baltes & Dickson, 2000). Moreover, it should be clear that SOC-related interventions do not need to be focused exclusively on helping individuals to effectively use SOC strategies; selection, optimization, and compensation can also be used as coordinated strategies for changing the work environment for individuals, especially as they become older and have to cope with various losses and deficits (Charness & Bosman, 1995).

The uniqueness of the SOC framework derives in large part from the fact that it is well integrated into current and emergent theoretical perspectives in the broad field of life-span developmental psychology (e.g., Baltes, et al., 1998). It differs from other career development and career counseling models in that it offers a cohesive and developmentally sensitive guide or template to frame an individual's past and present circumstance. The SOC framework assumes that an individual has finite resources to achieve a wide range of goals, and that SOC behaviors and strategies serve to maximize gains and minimize losses on the way to accomplishing these goals. The model prompts practitioners to consider more than their particular domain of practice or research by suggesting that interrelationships between domains and their respective goals are of critical importance when examining or guiding the allocation of resources in a focal domain. In a sense, the SOC model sees resources as fluid, where the individual acts as an agent constantly redirecting the flow from one goal to another. Problems arise, extending the analogy, when goals simultaneously compete for similar resources or when disaster strikes and resources dry up. Moreover, the model and the foundational research associated with the lifespan approach lend predictive power to the researcher and the counselor when they attempt to identify the potential consequences of current client behaviors and strategies. Returning to target behaviors and the respective alternatives in Table 2, we can see how different compensatory behaviors and strategies may increase the chances of maintenance or even growth in the occupational domain and how others may increase the chance of further decline. Paraphrasing Baltes, et al., (1998, p. 1045), career development can be conceptualized as a "gain-loss dynamic," and in principle, career counseling would then focus on employing SOC strategies in maximizing occupational or work-related gains and minimizing losses throughout the occupational life-span of the person.

Career counselors are not novices in developing strategies to assist individuals in choosing their goals wisely, in making the most of their resources (optimizing), or in overcoming setbacks (compensating). They could undoubtedly benefit, however, from placing their interventions within a broader, more comprehensive developmental framework as is represented by the SOC metatheory of successful development. It not only offers guidance with regard to the allocation of resources in the face of competing goals (e.g., work versus family; Wiese, et al., 2000), but it also offers an explicit developmental framework that stresses the continuity of development from infancy through old age. The latter observation often gets lost in the work of career counselors who work with adults. Yet, understanding development in adulthood must be an integral feature of any career intervention focused on adults. Presentation of the SOC framework is intended to be a first step toward a re-integration of the field of adult career counseling with the broader field of and adult development.

References

Abraham, J. D., & Hansson, R. O. (1995). Successful aging at work: An applied study of selection, organization, optimization, and compensation through impression management. *Journals of Gerontology Series B-Psychological Sciences & Social Sciences*, 50B(2), 94-103.

Bäckman, L., & Dixon, R. A. (1992). Psychological compensation: A theoretical framework. *Psychological Bulletin*, 112, 259-283.

Baltes, B. B., & Dickson, M. W. (2000, Aug. 4-8). *Using life-span models in Industrial/organizational psychology: The theory of selective optimization with compensation.* Paper presented at the 108th Annual Convention of the American Psychological Association, Washington DC.

Baltes, P. B. (1997). On the incomplete architecture of human ontogeny: Selection, optimization, and compensation as foundation of developmental theory. *American Psychologist*, 52(4), 366-380.

Baltes, P. B., & Baltes, M. M. (1990). Psychological perspectives on successful aging: The model of selective optimization with compensation. In P. B. Baltes & M. M. Baltes (Eds.), *Successful aging: Perspectives from the behavioral sciences.* (pp. 1-34). Cambridge, MA: Cambridge University Press.

Baltes, P. B., Lindenberger, U., & Staudinger, U. M. (1998). Life-span theory in developmental psychology. In W. Damon (Series Ed.) & R.M. Lerner (Vol. Ed.), *Handbook of child psychology: Vol. 1. Theoretical Models of Human Development* (5th ed., pp. 1029-1143). New York: Wiley.

Blustein, D. L., Phillips, S. D., Jobin-Davis, K., Finkelberg, S. L., & et al. (1997). A theory-building investigation of the school-to-work transition. *Counseling Psychologist*, 25(3), 364-402.

Bronfenbrenner, U. (1979). *The ecology of human development.* Cambridge, MA: Harvard University Press.

Carstensen, L. L., Hanson, K. A., & Freund, A. M. (1995). Selection and compensation in adulthood. In R.A. Dixon & L. Bäckman (Eds.), *Compensating for psychological deficits and declines: Managing losses and promoting gains.* (pp. 107-126). Mahwah, NJ: Erlbaum.

Charness, N., & Bosman, E. A. (1995). Compensation through environmental modification. In R. A. Dixon & L. Bäckman (Eds.), *Compensating for psychological deficits and declines: Managing losses and promoting gains* (pp. 147-168). Mahwah, NJ: Erlbaum.

Dixon, R. A., & Bäckman, L. (1995). Concepts of compensation: Integrated, differentiated, and Janus-faced. In R. A. Dixon & L. Bäckman (Eds.), *Compensating for psychological deficits and declines: Managing losses and promoting gains.* (pp. 3-19). Mahwah, NJ: Erlbaum.

Elder, G. H., Jr. (1997). The life course and human development. In R.M. Lerner (Ed.), *Theoretical Models of Human Development*, (Vol. 1). New York: Wiley.

Ford, D. H. (1987). *Humans as self-constructing living systems: A developmental perspective on behavior and personality.* Hillsdale, NJ: Erlbaum.

Ford, D. H., & Lerner, R. M. (1992). *Developmental systems theory: An integrative approach.* Newbury Park, CA: Sage.

Ford, M. E. (1992). *Motivating humans: Goals, emotions, and personal agency beliefs.* Newbury Park, CA: Sage.

Fouad, N. A., & Bingham, R. P. (1995). Career counseling with racial and ethnic minorities. In W.B. Walsh & S.H. Osipow (Eds.), *Handbook of vocational* psychology: Theory, research, and practice. Contemporary topics in vocational psychology. (2nd ed., pp. 331-365). Mahwah, NJ: Erlbaum.

Freund, A. M., Li, K. Z. H., & Baltes, P. B. (1999). The role of selection, optimization, and compensation. In J. Brandtstaedter & R. M. Lerner (Eds.), Action & self-development: Theory and research through the life span (pp. 401-434, 540). Thousand Oaks, CA: Sage.

Gibson, E. J. (1982). The concept of affordances in development: The renascence of functionalism. In W.A. Collins (Ed.), The concept of development. The Minnesota symposia on child psychology (Vol. 15, pp. 55-81). Hillsdale, NJ: Erlbaum.

Gutek, B. A., Searle, S., & Klepa, L. (1991). Rational versus gender role explanations for work and family conflict. Journal of Applied Psychology, 76(4), 560-568.

Heinz, W. R., Kelle, U., Witzel, A., & Zinn, J. (1998). Vocational training and career development in Germany: Results from a longitudinal study. International Journal of Behavioral Development, 22(1), 77-101.

Kohn, M. L., & Schooler, C. (1983). Work and Personality: An inquiry into the impact of social stratification. Norwood, NJ: Ablex.

Lerner, R. M., & Busch-Rossnagel, N. (Eds.). (1981). Individuals as producers of their development: A life-span perspective. New York: Academic Press.

Marsiske, M., Lang, F. B., Baltes, P. B., & Baltes, M. M. (1995). Selective optimization with compensation: Life-span perspectives on successful human development. In R.A. Dixon & L. Bäckman (Eds.), Compensating for psychological deficits and declines: Managing losses and promoting gains. (pp. 35-79). Mahwah, NJ: Erlbaum.

Reitzle, M., & Vondracek, F. W. (2000). Methodological avenues for the study of career pathways. Journal of Vocational Behavior, 57, 445-467.

Schneider, B. (1994). Thinking about an education: A new developmental and contextual perspective. Research in Sociology of Education and Socialization, 10, 239-259.

Super, D. E. (1992). Toward a comprehensive theory of career development. In D. H. Montross & C. J. Shinkman (Eds.), Career development: Theory and practice. (pp. 35-64). Springfield, IL: Charles C Thomas, Publisher.

Vondracek, F. W. (1999). Meeting challenges in the new Germany and in England: New directions for theory and data collection. In R. K. Silbereisen & J. Bynner (Eds.), Meeting challenges in the new Germany and in England (pp. 291-302). London: Macmillan.

Vondracek, F. W., & Kawasaki, T. (1995). Toward a comprehensive framework for adult career development theory and intervention. In W. B. Walsh & S. H. Osipow (Eds.), Handbook of vocational psychology: Theory, research, and practice. Contemporary topics in vocational psychology. (2nd ed., pp. 111-141). Mahwah, NJ: Erlbaum.

Vondracek, F. W., Lerner, R. M., & Schulenberg, J. E. (1986). Career development: A life-span developmental approach. Hillsdale: Erlbaum.

Vondracek, F. W., Reitzle, M., & Silbereisen, R. (1999). The influence of changing contexts and historical time on the timing of initial vocational choices. In R. K. Silbereisen & A.V. Eye (Eds.), Growing up in times of social change. (pp. 151-169). New York: DeGruyter.

Wiese, B. S., Freund, A. M., & Baltes, P. B. (2000). Selection, optimization, and compensation: An action-related approach to work and partnership. Journal of Vocational Behavior, 57, 273-300.

CHAPTER 3
A Learning Theory for Career Counselors

John D. Krumboltz
Sheila Henderson
Stanford University

Whenever work begins with a new client, the career counselor faces a decision on what theory will be the most effective framework to guide the counseling work. A good theory is like a road map. It offers a big picture of the territory and its most important features without confusing the reader with unnecessary details. Just as a map oversimplifies the real land (omitting swimming pools, buildings and flower beds), so a theory for career counselors may oversimplify the career development process (omitting descriptions of love affairs, eating habits and a good night's sleep.) Krumboltz (1994) has suggested that a good theory should be accurate, responsible, comprehensive, integrative, and adaptive. In the contemporary world of career counseling, this is no small task.

Change will be the one constant people can count on. The world of work in the 21st century was forecasted to be dynamic and fluid by a recent symposium on the "new career" (Arnold & Jackson, 1997). In summarizing the major forecasts from the symposium, Krumboltz (1998a) identified some interesting ways the world of work will be different in the future. If these forecasts are accurate, the traditional career ladder will be replaced by more frequent occupational shifts due to industry and workplace transitions as well as changes in personal interests. Nontraditional careers will be more commonplace as work and family responsibilities become more and more interwoven. The dominance and security of large company employers is obsolete. More people will be self-employed or will work in small and medium-sized companies. An attitude of career self-reliance has already begun to replace traditional loyalties between employer and employee (Waterman, Waterman & Collard, 1994). Commitment to lifelong learning and occupation resiliency in the face of constantly changing workplace demands will be essential coping strategies. The ante for career counselors is higher than ever. A career counselor must be able to teach flexible and adaptive skills for career entry and change that are relevant and appropriate to this changing market.

There are two critical questions that must be addressed by contemporary career development theory:

1. How do we explain how people find their way into such a diverse array of occupational endeavors?
2. How can career counselors help clients achieve a more satisfying life?

The central theses of the learning theory discussed in this chapter are that: from infancy onward everyone is exposed to a multitude of diverse learning experiences that shape the career path, and 2) career counselors can build on their clients' past learning experiences by working with them to create new learning experiences in the future. The present formulation of this theory is based on an integration of three prior contributions: A social learning theory of career decision making (Krumboltz, 1979); A learning theory of career counseling (Krumboltz, 1996); and Planned happenstance: Constructing unexpected career opportunities (Mitchell, Levin & Krumboltz, 1999).

Trait-and-factor theory has dominated career counseling for nearly a century. Under this model, first articulated by Frank Parsons (1909), career counselors were taught to match individuals with available occupations. Career counseling was conducted under a three-step model:

1. Know the individual's characteristics,
2. Know the occupational requirements, and
3. Exercise "true reasoning" to match the individual to the occupation.

This simple mechanical process of counseling is part of the reason that career counseling has drawn less social esteem than other branches of psychology and is often dismissed as less demanding and less interesting than other types of counseling work.

While career counseling has changed with time, the vestiges of the old model still pervade the field and still influence client expectations. Many clients want to be told the name of the one occupation that would be right for them for their lifetime. Counselors struggling conscientiously to satisfy their clients' unrealistic wishes give them tests, provide occupational information, and try to locate the name of an occupation that will be perfect for the client. If the client is unable or unwilling to name an occupational goal, then the counselor's work has been unsuccessful. Someone must bear the responsibility. In most cases it is the client who is labeled as "undecided" or even "chronically indecisive."

In the 1970's job satisfaction—defined as the positive evaluative attitude toward one's job experiences (Nichols, 1990)—was the focus of many studies which attempted to correlate external work factors (e.g., compensation, benefits, work environment) with global measures of satisfaction (Locke, 1976). As the relevance of this perspective waned, popular literature began drawing on mythology and philosophy to suggest a deeper meaning in work (for example, Clark, 2000; Frankl, 1984; Moore, 1992; Potter, 1995). The concept of job satisfaction has been replaced with broader meanings of happiness in both career and in life (Henderson, 2000a), where the internal factors within a person (e.g., values, experiences, goals, desires) direct the search for meaningful professional endeavor. The traditional focus on helping clients to make a "career decision" is far too narrow now. A more holistic view of career counseling now places the search for a satisfying career within the context of a broader search for a satisfying life. Career counselors are finding that the process of helping clients create satisfying lives for themselves involves much more than "deciding" on a suitable occupation. It involves an understanding of how personal relationships, hobbies, aesthetic appreciations and spiritual values will be intertwined with the pursuit of a fulfilling career.

What used to be a process of mechanical assessment of interests, aptitudes, job skills and the associated job market has changed into a fluid process of supporting clients as they improvise their own personal career paths. Instead of influencing clients to choose and stick, career counselors need to teach their clients to watch for, recognize and capitalize on opportunity on a daily basis. The question is no longer

"What do you want to do with the rest of your life?" but rather "What would be fun and satisfying to try next?" This new conceptualization of career is that of an adventure and a journey (Henderson, 2000b). Career decision-making skills are no longer focused on merely naming one lifetime occupation. In these days where career is likely to follow one of an almost infinite number of possible trajectories, effective career decision-making is a daily process. Career decision-making has become so much more constant and complex, career counselors are now teaching lifetime rather than one-time skills in effective decision-making.

Explaining Occupational Diversity

Since there are an almost infinite number of ways to make a living, how is it that people end up doing the work that they do? The Social Learning Theory of Career Decision-Making (Krumboltz, 1979) explains how an innumerable number of learning experiences combine to shape a career path and thus provide a coherent model for adult career development. This theory provides a framework for addressing why people have pursued particular career activities, why they change careers, and why they express preferences for certain career experiences over others.

DIVERSE LEARNING EXPERIENCES EXPLAIN DIVERSE OCCUPATIONAL CHOICES

An occupational choice is the result of a lifelong sequence of *learning experiences* unique to each individual. Therefore, it is the role of learning experiences from infancy to adulthood that are central to this theory. Both *instrumental* and *associative* learning experiences systematically shape our attitudes, standards, preferences and behavior. This process occurs within the context of an individual's unique internal innate predispositions and psychological context as well as the prevailing external economic, social and cultural conditions at the time.

When discussing the issue of what we're born with versus what we experience through our lives, it is paramount that we avoid thinking about thoughts, feelings and behaviors in deterministic terms. For example, Sapolsky (1997) argued, "Again and again, behavioral biologists have long been insisting that one cannot talk meaningfully about nature or nurture, only about their interaction" (p. 42). This point of view applies directly to career development. The interaction between innate predispositions and learning experiences within the intra-individual, family, social, educational and cultural context will have a profound effect on career opportunity and an individual's ability to capitalize on it. Particularly in adulthood, people make minute-to-minute choices about what they will experience and how they will interpret those experiences. Every e-mail, every phone conversation, every conversation with a friend, every occupational association, and every new risk taken will influence learning and future opportunity. As Csikszentmihalyi (1990) so deftly explained, "We create ourselves by how we invest energy" (p. 33), and "each person must use whatever tools are available to carve out a meaningful, enjoyable life" (p. 16).

LEARNING OCCURS FROM CONSEQUENCES AND FROM OBSERVATIONS

Let's take a look at learning experiences in more detail. *Instrumental* learning occurs from the direct consequences of a behavior. For example, a child who takes tennis lessons and receives attention and encouragement for hitting the ball well will generate a more positive self-observation generalization about tennis than will a child who is not reinforced in this way. The child learns from the consequences of his or her own performance.

Associative learning experiences occur from observing others. Watching tennis matches on TV, listening to tennis players describe their technique, and reading about the careers of famous tennis players illustrate how interest, or disinterest, in the game of tennis can be generated. Both instrumental and associative learning experiences will influence an individual's *worldview generalizations*. Depending on the context of these learning experiences, an individual might develop a worldview that the field of professional tennis is either a welcoming occupation offering encouragement, excitement and opportunity or a gritty occupation threatening discouragement and probable failure.

Both *instrumental* and *associative* learning experiences will have a profound effect on a child's development of *task approach skills*. Positive experiences will result in work habits, mental sets (including emotional responses), perceptual and thought processes, and problem orientations that are critical to the ability to craft and maintain satisfying careers. However, learning experiences are not always positive. Sometimes after a series of occupational defeats, discouragement from others and unsuccessful attempts to get new employment, a client will come to counseling confused, beleaguered and doubtful of their future career potential. As counselor and client work together to make sense of past experiences in this way, particular sensitivity must be paid to how social, cultural, economic, geographic and political circumstances can both create and obliterate opportunity for different individuals.

For example, the case of the child being taken to dance lessons presupposes that there is a dance teacher, a building where dance lessons can be held, parents who want their children to learn about dancing, automobiles and roadways to transport the children, a police force and fire department to protect them from harm, and an economic structure that permits time and money to be devoted to dance beyond that needed for mere survival. Learning experiences of various types are made possible by the institutions that exist, or do not exist, in the society where the children grow up. Libraries, churches, water departments, factories, schools, governments, labor unions, community organizations, tennis courts and cricket fields are a few of the institutions and facilities than enable such a wide variety of learning experiences for each individual.

Ward and Bingham (1993) posited that one important element in multicultural competency for career counselors is the close attention paid to how race, ethnicity and gender discrimination may be bearing on an individual's difficulty in career progression. With an nonjudgmental and empathic attitude, counselors can view lost opportunity, confusion about interests, blocking beliefs, contradictory values, problematic work habits, skill gaps, and inhibited personality patterns not as permanent career limiting factors but as the basis for designing new learning experiences.

The Goal of Career Counseling

Now that we understand that clients come to us from a rich cultural learning history about which we initially know virtually nothing, let's consider what actions a career counselor can take to be of help to a confused client. The profoundly challenging work of contemporary career counseling begins the moment that clients dare to explore their future. *"The goal of career counseling is to facilitate the learning of skills, interests, beliefs, values, work habits, and personal qualities that enable each client to create a satisfying life within a constantly changing work environment"* (Krumboltz, 1996, p. 61). This goal is a radical departure from traditional goal statements that focus on the making of a single career decision. Now career counselors can be seen as coaches, educators, advocates and mentors to clients endeavoring to achieve the components of a more satisfying life. This is a challenging mix of roles that requires a flexible yet systematic approach.

When approaching work with a client, the career counselor is encouraged to take a broad view of the meaning of a career concern. The search for meaningful work happens in the context of a quest for a meaningful and satisfying life. Career endeavor occurs in a broader life setting, so it is incumbent on career counselors to make room for a discussion of broader life challenges integrated with career issues. The integration of personal and vocational counseling is becoming paramount in state-of-the-art career counseling work (Krumboltz, 1993; Richardson, 1993). There are many personal, work/life balance, lifespan, cultural and adjustment issues that act as powerful shaping forces on career needs and interests (Blustein & Spengler, 1995; Helms, 1994; Krumboltz, 1993; Seligman, 1994; Super, 1980). Several key influences deserve mention:

1. ***Locus of control and personal self-efficacy*** will influence a client's enthusiasm for embarking on a career exploration effort (Bandura, 1997). To what degree are clients taking responsibility for their job searches? Or, are they hoping a job will come to them? Do clients believe in their personal competence? Or, have they lost a sense of their ability to make a meaningful contribution in the world of work?

2. ***Interpersonal approach and communication skills*** will have a profound influence on a client's past, present and future career (Covey, 1990). Interpersonal skills in meeting, relating to and working with others will also influence both, a client's approach to a job search and, that client's ability to acquire and maintain employment. Written and verbal skills will not only determine the success of phone, postal and e-mail contact but also are critical to success on the job. Clients will vary in their sophistication in this regard. Immigrants, for example, are particularly vulnerable due to their difficulty with the language and lack of familiarity with the unwritten rules, traditions and customs for interpersonal communication in their new culture (Lee & Westwood, 1996) and may seek career counseling support to acquire cultural knowledge and assistance with successful communication (McCarthy & Mejía, 2000).

3. ***Values about work/life balance*** will determine how much time the client has to invest in career and what kind of career alternatives will be of interest. More and more individuals and couples are finding ways to craft creative employment alternatives in order to accommodate family and relationship priorities (Jackson & Wilde, 2000; Perrone, 2000).

4. *Developmental stages across the lifespan* are critical to shaping career interests. A college graduate, early in the process of developing effective technical skills and a work ethic, will require a different counseling approach than a retiring professional looking for a way to make a meaningful contribution during retirement (Harris, 2000; Seligman, 1994; Super, 1980). Career counseling need not stop when retirement begins. Oman and Thoresen (2000) have shown that non-paid work for seniors is an important occupational outlet that contributes to happiness and longevity.

5. *Culture* will bear significantly on a client's career goals, interests and struggles and the manner in which a client will pursue career exploration (Helms, 1994; Sue & Sue, 1999). To what extent is career exploration an individual effort or one done in concert with immediate or extended family relationships and commitments? How are issues of race and ethnicity affording or limiting a client's ability to pursue a career of interest? Ward and Bingham (1993) encourage counselors to be especially sensitive to the pressures women and people of color are facing due to issues of discrimination. Immigrants may be particularly vulnerable to occupational stress due to financial pressures, adjustment issues, and lack of experience with dominant cultural norms (Lee & Westwood, 1996; McCarthy & Mejía, 2000).

Guidelines for the Practice of Career Counseling

In trying to grapple with the complexity of contemporary career counseling amidst a rapidly changing workforce while taking into consideration broader life concerns, there can be no rigid step-by-step sequence of actions. However, the following ten guidelines can be used judiciously by career counselors in mutual collaboration with their clients to help them create more satisfying lives:

1. Establish accurate case conceptualizations;
2. Set action goals for the counseling process;
3. Identify past significant career events and pleasures;
4. Teach the advantages of open-mindedness;
5. Normalize and reframe unplanned events as opportunities;
6. Use assessment instruments to stimulate new learning and gauge progress;
7. Transform fascinations into opportunities for learning;
8. Encourage clients to create beneficial unplanned events;
9. Overcome blocks to action; and
10. Use life-long education for prevention.

ESTABLISH ACCURATE CASE CONCEPTUALIZATIONS

Effective counseling work begins with an accurate case conceptualization. The first step in the case conceptualization process is the initial interview. Here the counselor will get a sense of clients' educational and work histories. As clients tell their stories, an effective career counselor will pay close attention for key learning events that have shaped the clients' self-observation generalizations and worldview generalizations. Here it is important to understand how clients' unique family and social histories as well as the broader culture have shaped their career aspirations and beliefs in their personal career potential. The present context of their lives is critical to understanding how family life, hobbies, personal interests, and career hopes may interweave. Structured guides to gathering case histories (e.g., Morrison, 1995) can assist this process. It is important to understand whether serious health habits and concerns as well as emotional difficulties bear on the counseling work. For example, maladaptive health habits (e.g., alcohol and substance abuse) or serious psychological conditions (e.g., depression, anxiety or personality disorders) may require concurrent interventions. Effective career counselors will have a good referral list of community resources at their fingertips.

Initial sessions are critical to forming a good relationship with the client. Career counselors must develop multicultural competence in their work. Sue, Arredondo and McDavis (1992) suggested that multicultural competence has the following characteristics: 1) Counselor awareness of assumptions, values, stereotypes and biases that may bear on client work; 2) Interest in and awareness of the life experiences, historical background and cultural heritage of the client; and 3) Use of strategies, techniques and interventions that are appropriate and compatible with the client's needs and culture. The Multicultural Career Counseling Checklist (Ward & Bingham, 1993) can be especially helpful in orienting the counselor to the client's expectations for the counseling process.

Clients vary in their initial willingness to be open with a professional. Comfort with self-disclosure is an attribute that will vary across cultures (Ishiyama, 1989; Sue & Sue, 1999). Some clients will come to career counseling wanting only career testing and may resent questioning that extends beyond simple assessment. Other clients may be wary and disinterested in the testing process, preferring to pursue a more action-oriented approach. An awareness of verbal and nonverbal clues will help counselors gauge clients' comfort level with the counseling process (Fouad, 1994). Clients will be more likely to respond positively if a career counselor has the ability to mirror their pace for self-disclosure, formality, eye contact, interpersonal distance and pace for the counseling process (Fouad, 1994; Martin, 1983; Sue & Sue, 1999). In these circumstances, it is not at all unusual for clients to disclose more once a good therapeutic alliance is formed.

SET ACTION GOALS FOR THE COUNSELING PROCESS

The task of finding a suitable niche in the world of work can be arduous, especially when the workplace is changing so rapidly. Some clients will come to counseling feeling beleaguered, fearful and without hope. Zeteophobia, the fear of searching for a future direction, is a common emotional reaction (Krumboltz, 1993). Some of the fear is based on the false belief that they must make one decision now that will determine their fate forever. Some of it is based on the false assumption that they must investigate the pros and cons of 12,000 occupations, a task of overwhelming magnitude. Counselors can play an active role in reducing zeteophobia by countering faulty assumptions and orienting clients in advance to the career counseling process.

The counselor is responsible for the counseling process, but the client is in charge of the goals. Clients will come to career counseling with career direction goals (e.g., find a new job), interpersonal goals (e.g., get along better with my boss), emotional goals (e.g., manage my anger about getting passed over for promotion), dual career goals (e.g., find employment that accommodates my child care schedule), and/or retirement goals (e.g., finding worthwhile retirement activities).

The counselor has an important role in providing empathy, support, encouragement, enthusiasm and openness to the client's goal setting process. Some clients will start slowly with the smallest of goals (e.g., dust off that old resume and bring it in to the next session); other clients will come to counseling already motivated to pursue ambitious goals (e.g., arrange three informational interviews before the next session). When the client's pace is very different from that of the counselor, more energy has to be invested in keeping in step with the client.

IDENTIFY PAST SIGNIFICANT CAREER EVENTS AND PLEASURES

Some clients come to counseling depressed, discouraged and doubtful that any work could be satisfying to them. When clients are feeling particularly unclear about what vocational activities might be of interest, it is helpful for them to remember times in the past when they have felt deeply engaged in an activity. Narrative therapy has been shown to be effective as a guided exercise to assist clients in discovering significant past occasions (Henderson & Oliver, 2000; Savickas, 1995). Sometimes memories of more meaningful times in the past can spur some hope and enthusiasm about the career exploration process. The technique is simple, fun, and can be used with individuals or in groups. More structured workbook exercises are also available (see Nichols, 1991). For example, a counselor might ask: *Tell me about a time, in a job or in a hobby, that you remember really enjoying or feeling exceptionally engaged or involved in an activity... a special moment of enjoyment.*

The client might tell a story about a moment in school or an experience on a trip or a particular compelling hobby endeavor. After listening to the story, the counselor can then ask: *Now, tell me the story again ... but this time emphasize what you did that made the story happen and might make such an event possible again.*

Narrative restorying exercises can generate more positive feelings and perspectives about the past and instill hope in the counseling process. That hope is often the beginning of an action-oriented process to creating happiness in the future.

TEACH THE ADVANTAGES OF OPEN-MINDEDNESS

Indecisiveness is often disparaged in our culture. It is true that an inability to make good and timely decisions can lead to lost opportunities in business, finance and social circumstances. However, in traditional career counseling, indecision has become the label counselors hang on clients who are their failures. If the whole purpose of career counseling is to make a career decision, then the clients' inability or unwillingness to state an occupational goal means that the counseling has failed. A rich vocabulary on degrees of indecision has accumulated (Gordon, 1998).

If, on the other hand, the goal of counseling is to help people create satisfying lives for themselves, then the speed with which clients declare an occupational goal is irrelevant. In fact, some would go so far as to say that people should never make a career decision if that means one lifetime choice. Instead of struggling to arrive at this permanent lifetime commitment (a futile task), a career counselor should focus on encouraging interesting activities that clients might want to try next. Experimentation is the key. Clients cannot know whether they will really like something until they try it. Explorations can give them hints as to whether they want to move forward in the same direction or change directions. It is never necessary to make a permanent career decision. Consequently indecision is not a sign of failure—it can be a sign of success! However, since the word "indecision" still has a negative connotation, let's call it "open-mindedness."

Career counselors have an important role of not only normalizing the state of indecision but also advocating the benefits of open-mindedness (Krumboltz, 1992). If counselors can see the wisdom in indecision, they can teach clients to remain open to and create new and unexpected opportunities. Blustein (1997) supported this view by suggesting that counselors have a role in helping clients to tolerate the ambiguity associated with career exploration.

In the early 1900's when making a career choice began a one-dimensional career trajectory, Frank Parsons (1909) advocated the career decision as pivotal to the career counseling process. Now nearly a century later, emphasis on the pivotal career decision is outdated and in most cases inappropriate. The workplace is changing too quickly; jobs come and go as fast as new opportunities appear. It is understandable that people come to career counseling in an undecided state, given the immense number of choices and the unforeseeable future. Contrary to popular view, fast decision-making in the world of career could easily preclude many valuable experiences (Baumgardner, 1982). Along these lines, Blustein (1997) advocated an "open and nonrigid approach to the world" as a way of encouraging growth and opportunity.

NORMALIZE AND REFRAME UNPLANNED EVENTS AS OPPORTUNITIES

At times during counseling interviews, clients will refer to significant events in their lives but diminish their personal role by saying, "It was an accident," "I just got lucky," or "The opportunity just fell in my lap."

Everyone's career is affected by events that could not have been predicted (Krumboltz, 1998b). Mitchell et al. (1999) posited that, "Unplanned events are not only inevitable, but they are desirable" (p. 118). Some of the leaders in career counseling have begun to recognize, to some degree, that chance events are present in the career exploration process (Bandura, 1982; Betsworth & Hansen, 1996; Cabral & Salomone, 1990; Hart, Rayner & Christensen, 1971; Miller, 1983, 1995; Scott & Hatalla, 1990). For example, Betsworth and Hansen (1996) found that two thirds of the participants in their study (237 people) spoke of the role of chance events in their careers. Up until recently, researchers were uncertain as to how to incorporate consciously the role of serendipity into the career counseling process and called for a model that might incorporate happenstance into career counseling (Cabral & Salomone, 1990; Miller, 1983; Scott & Hatalla, 1990).

Since the days of the Parsonian model, planning has underscored the career counseling process. It still remains important, but a radical new view is that counselors must learn to teach clients to plan for serendipitous events. Luck can be generated. Hence, we have the intentional oxymoron advocated by Mitchell et al. (1999): Planned *happenstance*. The goal of the planned happenstance model is to provide ways that counselors can teach clients to generate, recognize, and incorporate chance events into the process of their career development. Clients need to learn to generate and take advantage of pivotal opportunities in their careers. Counselors have the opportunity to make this new philosophy the mainstream in career counseling. Mitchell et al. (1999) offer the following questions as prompts for counselors to encourage discussion of past happenstance events:

1. How have unplanned events influenced your career?
2. How did you enable each event to influence you?
3. How do you feel about unplanned events in your future?

The goal at this stage is to help clients see from their own histories that unplanned events are normal, that they have benefited from them, that they had a hand in enabling the unplanned event to happen to them, and that they took some action to capitalize on the unplanned event. The desired generalization then is, "If I did it before, I can do it again."

USE ASSESSMENT INSTRUMENTS TO STIMULATE NEW LEARNING AND GAUGE PROGRESS

Aptitude and achievement tests summarize skills and knowledge that has been learned in the past. Interest inventories summarize past likes and dislikes. Personality assessments give a picture of interpersonal styles acquired so far. Belief inventories identify career assumptions that have been interfering with career progress in the past.

This summary of past learning can be a valuable starting point for career explorations. It provides a benchmark against which future progress can be measured. However, the important goal is helping clients learn how to create satisfying lives for themselves in the future. Assessment instruments can be used to stimulate new learning, not merely to tabulate prior learning (Krumboltz & Jackson, 1993). This is an important distinction. For example, the Strong Interest Inventory can be used to identify interests that a client has not yet developed but would like to develop. Interests are not fixed for life. They change as clients acquire new experiences. For example, millions of people are now interested in computers. Before computers were invented, such an interest was obviously impossible. Exposure to computers stimulated the interest. New interests can be learned.

A comprehensive assessment profile can be a good exploration tool to discover what clients would like to learn in the future. When cast in an enthusiastic light, the review of assessment scores can be affirming and encouraging to a client. Action goals can be set to revive old interests and explore new ones. A snapshot of job skills can set the direction for exciting new learning. A personality profile can open discussion about interpersonal skills that the client may have always wanted to develop. Discussions of this nature can be prompted with the following kinds of questions:

1. Which skill would you most like to build next?
2. What curiosities do you have that you would like to explore further?
3. What dimensions of your personality would you like to develop in the future?
4. Which of these career beliefs are interfering with your career exploration? Which of them would you like to change?

One useful exercise is to ask clients to guess assessment scores before the results are reported back. Unexpected scores can be the source of rich conversation and stimulate the desire to learn more.

Administration of assessment instruments involves not only an understanding of the technical aspects of scoring and reporting but also an understanding of an assessment's relevance across cultures. Career assessment instruments that are developed on normative samples of limited ethnic and racial diversity may have limited generalizability to other populations (Fouad, 1994; Sue, Arredondo & McDavis, 1992). Assessments that evaluate aptitude, vocational skill and general knowledge are particularly liable to discriminate against people of color and immigrants who may not have had extensive exposure to many aspects of the dominant culture. Difficulty with language makes the accuracy of assessment results even more dubious. In the spirit of multicultural competence in career counseling, Fouad (1994) advised counselors to:

1. evaluate the relevance of certain assessment tools before using them with any client,
2. report results cautiously and in a way that does not perpetuate cultural stereotypes, and
3. remember that assessments that encourage self-exploration may not be appropriate for some clients who place a higher priority on familial or ethnic group career decision-making.

TRANSFORM FASCINATIONS INTO OPPORTUNITIES FOR LEARNING

Clients will reveal different ideas, intriguing activities and hobbies directly or indirectly as counseling progresses. Career counselors can capitalize on initial fascinations to begin the career exploration process. For example, a client fascinated by the sport of Ultimate Frisbee might find an opportunity to coach the sport to inner city kids. Or, a client who has a keen interest in growing tropical plants might join an organization devoted to preserving the Amazon rain forest. By getting involved in activities like this, clients are likely to meet people who share their interests, some of whom may actually earn a living in a related occupation. Whether they themselves become employed in these fields is not as important as learning new skills and making new contacts from which future opportunities may arise. In the meantime they are engaged in a new activity that adds to their enjoyment of life.

Researchers have suggested that an exploratory and experimental approach to one's environment is a fundamental human motivation (Cassidy, 1999; Piaget, 1954; White, 1959). Humans by their very nature seem to seek out contact and stimulation from the environment. Novelty and variety in the environment are inherently pleasing to most people. However, exploration of any environment often involves unexpected circumstances and problems to be solved. When unexpected events occur, clients must be taught to see these occurrences as opportunities. At times, even disappointments are merely veiled opportunities. Missing a scheduled train, while initially disappointing, might afford an interesting and valuable chance meeting while waiting for the next train. As an unknown Internet contributor expressed it, "A pessimist sees the difficulties in opportunities; an optimist sees the opportunities in difficulties."

A counselor who is knowledgeable about written, electronic and Internet resources for job exploration and who is skillful in teaching job search skills (e.g., resume and letter writing, informational and job interviewing) will be all that much more effective in helping clients get started with their exploration process. Other counseling techniques, such as role-play, may be effective with assisting clients in effecting change on a more personal level. Research in social psychology demonstrates rather convincingly that improvisational role-playing of behavior inconsistent with one's previous behavior is an effective mechanism for change (McGuire, 1985, cited in Zimbardo & Leippe, 1991).

ENCOURAGE CLIENTS TO CREATE BENEFICIAL UNPLANNED EVENTS

The opportunity to benefit from chance, according to Mitchell et al. (1999), depends on two principles: 1) exploration generates opportunities to experience unplanned events which may potentially increase the quality of one's life, and 2) timely and skilled action empowers people to capitalize on the opportunities presented by the unplanned events. The job of the career counselor is to motivate and instruct clients both to engage in the exploratory behavior and to recognize and act on the opportunities. Theorists have postulated that curiosity, preparedness, receptivity, and a solid set of career entry skills are critical to creating pivotal serendipity in career (Austin, 1978; Bandura, 1982; Salomone & Slaney, 1981). What is absolutely critical in realizing serendipitous events, according to Salomone and Slaney (1981), is the willingness to take timely and effective action. Mitchell et al. (1999) have offered five skills that can assist clients in making the most out of the opportunity in their lives:

1. *Curiosity:* Exploring new learning opportunities.
2. *Persistence:* Exerting effort despite setbacks.
3. *Flexibility:* Changing thinking about alternative methods and goals.
4. *Optimism:* Viewing new opportunities as possible and attainable.
5. *Risk-Taking:* Taking action in the face of uncertain outcomes.

OVERCOME BLOCKS TO ACTION

Many classic tales, such as the Wizard of Oz, teach us that any meaningful journey will involve many obstacles to be overcome. The career journey is an endeavor that involves confronting obstacles. While some people face more obstacles than others, no one has a perfectly smooth path through life. Everyone experiences career disappointments and thwarted opportunities along with some joys and successes. It is in this realm that counselors have the opportunity to help clients the most. Some clients, discouraged by repeated disappointments, may begin to inhibit productive action with self-defeating beliefs.

1. "It's impossible to find a job in that field."
2. "I don't have the experience required for that position."
3. "She wouldn't be interested in talking with me."
4. "I don't interview well."

These are all examples of self-defeating generalizations and worldviews. The process of cognitive restructuring involves teaching clients to see a problem from another viewpoint. Counselors can often effectively counter self-defeating beliefs by offering positive observations about the client (Nevo, 1987). When the client avoids arranging an informational interview with the fear that, "She wouldn't be interested in talking with me," the counselor can respond with a statement such as, "I find that I'm very interested in talking with you. It's not at all hard for me to imagine that she would be too." Such positive affirmations can help to counter faulty presumptions about the self and the world.

Some troublesome beliefs are merely misunderstandings or based on incorrect facts. For example, when a client believes that there are no opportunities available in a particular field of interest, sometimes just a little bit of research can reveal that there are indeed jobs available in a competitive field. Every field is competitive to some extent. Not trying for something you want because a field is reputed to be competitive is self-defeating.

The Career Beliefs Inventory (Krumboltz, 1991) is one tool that can be useful in assessing blocking beliefs and initiating conversations about ways to examine them. For example, Scale 15 (Career Path Flexibility) explores clients' beliefs about the sequence of steps needed to enter an occupation. Someone scoring low on this scale tends to believe that an occupation must be pursued by following a prescribed sequence of steps. A higher score indicates a belief that there could be multiple routes to a particular occupation. The evidence suggests that modern careers take many innovative trajectories (Bateson, 1989; Henderson, 2000b). For example, graduate school might be pursued right after college or very late in life, depending on the individual's career interests and resources at the time.

Reframing, which involves seeing an obstacle from another perspective, is also an effective counseling technique. An obstacle can be seen as an insurmountable roadblock or a challenge to be mastered. The evidence is now clear that cognitive structure— the way clients view themselves and the world of work—will influence their career exploration behaviors, decision-making processes and career planning (Neimeyer, Nevill, Probert & Fukuyama, 1985; Sampson, Peterson, Lenz & Reardon, 1992). In one experimental study, Mitchell and Krumboltz (1987) compared a cognitive restructuring intervention with the teaching of decision skills. A no-treatment control group was also included. The cognitive restructuring treatment proved most effective in reducing anxiety and promoting career exploration among college students.

USE LIFE-LONG EDUCATION FOR PREVENTION

The life-long pursuit of education is a necessity in the modern world. People should never complete their education. Education does not necessarily involve going to school, however. Education takes place everyday in multiple settings. Learning occurs in formal organizations and in informal conversations. Museums, libraries, television, newspapers, religious institutions, community organizations, business and industry supplement the work of schools and colleges. By enrolling in courses of interest, clients are very likely to meet other people who may be instrumental to new career directions (Bandura, 1982). The career counselor can take an active role in this process. By inquiring about a client's reaction to the course material and experiences with classmates, the counselor can encourage a watchful eye for potential opportunities.

Job clubs, in which members support each other in their search for work, have been amazingly successful (Azrin & Besalel, 1980). Self-help books on career issues have been popular and helpful for millions of people (e.g., Bolles, 2000). Virtual Job Experiences are on the horizon as ways of giving young people a realistic experience at performing in various occupations (Krumboltz, 1997). The Internet is filled with websites offering advice and information about careers (e.g., http://stats.bls.gov/k12/html/ edu_over.htm). Career counseling need not necessarily be one-counselor-with-one-client. People can educate themselves in a variety of ways, and career counselors can multiply the effectiveness of their efforts by reaching people in groups, workshops or through the Internet.

Conclusion

When the world changes, so do our theoretical models. What we are witnessing now is a huge paradigm shift in what it means to be a career counselor. The goal has changed from making a career decision to creating a satisfying life. The methods have changed from matching individuals with occupations to encouraging continual learning and experimentation. Do we throw out the old? No, we build on career assessment tests by using them in new ways—to stimulate new learning in a culturally sensitive manner. Is counseling over when a career decision has been made? No. Career counselors are now needed more than ever to offer lifelong educational, emotional and motivational support for their clients' personal career journey.

The litmus test to any theory of career development is whether it can effectively guide the actual career counseling work. In the past, outcome measures for career counseling focused on whether or not a career decision was made. In this new learning model, more appropriate outcome measures would include whether clients are learning new skills, experimenting with new interests, challenging blocking beliefs and expanding their network of social and career contacts. Ultimately, the outcome measure of interest is whether clients rate themselves as making progress toward creating personally satisfying lives for themselves. The result of such a model will be clients who learn to be career adventurers, seeking opportunity, exploring alternatives, and trying things out—all with the goal of increasing happiness in their lives. The pursuit of happiness is more than a cliché in the Declaration of Independence—it is the ultimate goal of career counseling.

References

Arnold, J., & Jackson, C. (1997). The new career: issues and challenges. *British Journal of Guidance and Counselling*, 25, 427-433.

Austin, J. H. (1978). *Chance, chase, and creativity: The lucky art of novelty*. New York: Columbia University Press.

Azrin, N. H., & Besalel, V. A. (1980). *Job club counselor's manual*. Baltimore: University Park Press.

Bandura, A. (1982). The psychology of chance encounters and life paths. *American Psychologist*, 37, 747-755.

Bandura, A. (1997). *Selfl-efficacy: The Exercise of Control*. New York: W. H. Freeman & Company.

Bateson, M. C. (1989). *Composing a Life*. New York: Penguin Books.

Baumgardner, S. R. (1982). Coping with disillusionment, abstract images, and uncertainty in career decision making. *Personnel and Guidance Journal*, 61, 213-217.

Betsworth, D. G., & Hansen, J. I. C. (1996). The categorization of serendipitous career development events. *Journal of Career Assessment*, 4, 91-98.

Blustein, D. L. (1997). A context-rich perspective of career exploration across the life role. *The Career Development Quarterly*, 45, 260-274.

Blustein, D. L., & Spengler, P. M. (1995). Personal adjustment: Career counseling and psychotherapy. In W. B. Walsh & S. H. Osipow (Eds.), *Handbook of vocational psychology: Theory, research, and practice* (2nd ed., pp. 295-329). Mahwah, NJ: Erlbaum.

Bolles, R. N. (2000). *What color is your parachute?* Berkeley, CA: Ten Speed Press.

Cassidy, J. (1999). The nature of a child's ties. In J. Cassidy and P.R. Shaver (Eds.), *Handbook of attachment theory, research and clinical applications (pp. 3-20). New York: Guilford Press.*

Cabral, A. C., & Salomone, P. R. (1990). Chance and careers: normative versus contextual development. *The Career Development Quarterly*, 39, 5-17.

Clark, John. (2000). *The money or your life: Reuniting work and joy!* London: Random House UK.

Covey, S. (1990). *The 7 habits of highly effective people: Restoring character ethic.* (1st Fireside Ed.) New York: Simon & Schuster.

Csikszentmihalyi, M. (1990). *Flow: The psychology of optimal experience.* New York, NY: HarperCollins.

Frankl, V. E. (1984). *Man's search for meaning.* New York: Washington Square Press.

Fouad, N. A. (1994). Career assessment with Latinos/Hispanics. *Journal of Career Assessment*, 2, 226-239.

Gordon, V. N. (1998). Career decidedness types: A literature review. *The Career Development Quarterly*, 46, 386-403.

Harris, A. H. S. (1999-2000). Using adult development theory to facilitate career happiness. *Career Planning and Adult Development Journal*, 15(4), 27-36.

Hart, D. H., Rayner, K., & Christensen, E. R. (1971). Planning, preparation, and chance in occupational entry. *Journal of Vocational Behavior*, 1; 279-285.

Helms, J. E. (1994). Racial identity and career development. *Journal of Career Assessment*, 2, 199-209.

Henderson, S. J. (1999-2000a). Career happiness: More fundamental than job satisfaction. *Career Planning and Adult Development Journal*, 15(4), 5-10.

Henderson, S. J. (2000b). "Follow your bliss": A process for career happiness. *Journal of Counseling and Development*, 78(3), 305-315.

Henderson, S. J., & Oliver, L. (1999-2000). Enjoyment and happenstance—Central themes in career happiness. *Career Planning and Adult Development Journal*, 15(4), 105-118.

Ishiyama, F. I. (1989). Understanding individuals in transition: A self-validation model. *Canadian Journal of School Psychology*, 4, 41-56.

Jackson, A. P., & Wilde, S. V. (1999-2000). Constructing family-friendly work: Three real dreams. *Career Planning and Adult Development Journal*, 15(4), 37-48.

Krumboltz, J. D. (1979). A social learning theory of career decision making. In A. M. Mitchell, G. B. Jones, & J. D. Krumboltz (Eds.), *Social Learning and Career Decision Making* (pp. 19-49). Cranston, RI: Carroll Press.

Krumboltz, J. D. (1991). *Manual for the career beliefs inventory.* Palo Alto, CA: Consulting Psychologist Press.

Krumboltz, J. D. (1992). The wisdom of indecision. *Journal of Vocational Behavior*, 41, 239-244.

Krumboltz, J. D. (1993). Integrating career and personal counseling. *The Career Development Quarterly*, 42, 143-148.

Krumboltz, J. D. (1994). Improving career development theory from a social learning perspective. In M. L. Savickas & R. W. Lent (Eds.), *Convergence in career development theories: Implications for science and practice* (pp. 9-31). Palo Alto, CA: Davies-Black.

Krumboltz, J. D. (1996). A learning theory of career counseling. In Mark L. Savickas & W. Bruce Walsh (Eds.), *Handbook of career counseling theory and practice* (pp. 55-80). Palo Alto, CA: Davies-Black.

Krumboltz, J. D. (1997, August 19). *Virtual job experience.* Symposium presented at the Annual Meeting of the American Psychological Association, Chicago, IL.

Krumboltz, J. D. (1998a). Counsellor actions needed for the new career perspective. *British Journal of Guidance and Counseling*, 26(4), 559-564.

Krumboltz, J. D. (1998b). Serendipity is not serendipitous. *Journal of Counseling Psychology*, 45, 390-392.

Krumboltz, J. D., & Jackson, M. A. (1993). Career assessment as a learning tool. *Journal of Career Assessment*, 1, 393-409.

Lee, G., & Westwood, M. J. (1996). Cross-cultural adjustment issues faced by immigrant professionals. *Journal of Employment Counseling*, 33, 29-42.

Locke, E. A. (1976). The nature and cause of job satisfaction. In M. D. Dunette (Ed.), *Handbook of industrial organizational psychology* (pp. 1297-1350). Chicago, IL: Rand McNally.

Martin, D. G. (1983). *Counseling and therapy skills.* Prospect Heights, IL: Waveland Press.

McCarthy, C., & Mejía, O. L. (1999-2000). Promoting immigrants' career happiness through developing coping resources. *Career Planning and Adult Development Journal*, 15(4), 11-26.

McGuire, W. (1985). Attitudes and attitude change. In G. Lindzey & E. Aronson (Eds.). *Handbook of social psychology: Volume II* (3rd ed., pp. 233-346). New York: Random House.

Miller, M. J. (1983). The role of happenstance in career choice. *The Vocational Guidance Quarterly*, 32, 16-20.

Miller, M. J. (1995). A case for uncertainty in career counseling. *Counseling and Values*, 39, 162-168.

Mitchell, K. E., Levin, A. S., & Krumboltz, J. D. (1999). Planned happenstance: Constructing unexpected career opportunities. *Journal of Counseling and Development*, 77, 115-124.

Mitchell, L. K., & Krumboltz, J. D. (1987). The effects of cognitive restructuring and decision-making training on career indecision. *Journal of Counseling and Development*, 66, 171-174.

Moore, T. (1992). *Care of the soul.* New York, NY: Harper Perrenial.

Morrison, J. (1995). *The first interview: Revised for DSM IV.* New York: Guilford Press.

Neimeyer, G. J., Nevill, D. D., Probert, B., & Fukuyama, M. (1985). Cognitive structure in vocational development. *Journal of Vocational Behavior*, 27, 191-201.

Nevo, O. (1987). Irrational expectations in career counseling and their confronting arguments. *The Career Development Quarterly*, 35, 239-250.

Nichols, C. W., Jr. (1990). An Analysis of the sources of dissatisfaction at work, (Doctoral dissertation, Stanford University, 1990). *Dissertation Abstracts International*, 51-11B, p. 5623.

Nichols, C. W., Jr. (1991). *Assessment of core goals: A sampler set, manual and workbook.* Redwood City, CA: Mind Garden.

Oman, D., & Thoresen, C. E. (1999-2000). Role of volunteering in health and happiness. *Career Planning and Adult Development Journal*, 15(4), 59-70.

Parsons, F. (1909). *Choosing a vocation*. Boston, MA: Houghton Mifflin.

Perrone, K. M. (1999-2000). Balancing life roles to achieve career happiness and life satisfaction. *Career Planning and Adult Development Journal*, 15(4), 49-58.

Piaget, J. (1954). *The construction of reality in the child*. New York, NY: Basic Books.

Potter, B. (1995). *Finding a path with a heart: How to go from burnout to bliss*. Berkeley, CA: Ronin.

Richardson, M. S. (1993). Work in people's lives: A location for counseling psychologists. *Journal of Counseling Psychology*, 40, 425-433.

Salomone, P. R., & Slaney, R. B. (1981). The influence of chance and contingency factors on the vocational choice process of nonprofessional workers. *Journal of Vocational Behavior*, 19, 25-35.

Sapolsky, R. (1997, October). A gene for nothing. *Discover* (pp. 40-46).

Sampson, J. P, Jr., Peterson, G. W., Lenz, J. G., & Reardon, R. C. (1992). A cognitive approach to career services: Translating concepts into practice. *The Career Development Quarterly*, 41, 67-74.

Savickas, M. L. (1995). Constructivist counseling for career indecision. *The Career Development Quarterly*, 43, 363-373.

Scott, J., & Hatalla, J. (1990). The influence of chance and contingency factors on career patterns of college-educated women. *The Career Development Quarterly*, 39, 18-30.

Seligman, L. (1994). *Developmental career counseling and assessment*. (2nd ed.). Thousand Oaks, CA: Sage.

Sue, D. W., Arredondo, P., & McDavis, R. J. (1992). Multicultural counseling competencies and standards: A call to the profession. *Journal of Multicultural Counseling and Development*, 20, 64-88.

Sue, D. W., & Sue, D. (1999). *Counseling the culturally different: Theory and practice*. (3rd ed.). New York: Wiley.

Super, D. E. (1980). A life-span, life-space approach to career development. *Journal of Vocational Behavior*, 16, 282-298.

Ward, C. M., & Bingham, R. P. (1993). Career assessment of ethnic minority women. *Journal of Career Assessment*, 1, 246-257.

Waterman, R. H., Waterman, J. A., & Collard, B. A. (1994, July-August), Toward a career-resilient workplace. *Harvard Business Review* (pp. 87-95).

White, R. W. (1959). Motivation reconsidered: The concept of competence, *Psychological Review*, 66(5), 297-333.

Zimbardo, P. G., & Leippe, M. R. (1991). *The psychology of attitude change and social influence*. New York: McGraw-Hill.

CHAPTER 4
Integrative Life Planning (ILP): A Holistic Theory For Career Counseling with Adults

L. Sunny Hansen
University of Minnesota

This chapter presents a new way of thinking about life planning for career professionals who work with adults, not only in career counseling but also in training, workshops, and systems interventions. It describes a conceptual framework for Integrative Life Planning (ILP), discusses the relevance and applications of ILP for adults, and provides examples of present and potential applications to diverse adult populations.

In describing a theory of ILP, the chapter departs from some of the traditional characteristics of theory prescribed by empirical approaches. ILP is comprehensive rather than parsimonious or reductionist; it does not easily lend itself to measurement; it centrally addresses ethnic, racial, gender, socioeconomic status, and other diversity issues; and it is interdisciplinary, drawing not only from the psychology of individual development but from sociology, economics, adult development, multiculturalism, feminism, and constructivism. It is focused not only on choosing an occupation but also on developing and connecting the various parts of one's life.

The phrase "Integrative Life Planning" was deliberately chosen instead of career planning. *Integrative* means to renew, to make whole by bringing different parts of mind, body, and spirit together. *Life planning* includes work but also multiple aspects of life and their interrelatedness. In spite of controversy about whether planning is possible in these uncertain times, the word *planning* is retained because it still connotes a sense of agency or control on the part of the person.

Counselors are quite accustomed to using metaphors and visualizing images, and quilts (and quilters) are a primary metaphor for Integrative Life Planning. Quilting is an important tradition in many cultures, usually performed by women but increasingly by men. The quilt is created from pieces that fit together to make a whole and create a product, often a work of art that provides warmth and symbolizes the care and nurturing expected of the counseling profession. The second metaphor is of Mother Earth, an image that evokes wholeness and connectedness.

Rather than an individual counseling model, ILP is probably best described as a new worldview, an expanded holistic framework for addressing the career

Portions of this chapter have been adapted from *Integrative Life Planning: Critical Tasks for Career Development and Changing Life Patterns* by L. Sunny Hansen, San Francisco: Jossey-Bass, 1997.

development of adults at different life stages. While our knowledge of adult development is still limited, there has been an abundance of literature on it in the last three decades. One aspect on which there is almost universal agreement is that adults become more heterogeneous with age. Another is that many adults, especially at midlife, make career changes that require a variety of interventions. New conceptualizations and considerable research have emerged on sub-populations of adults such as early, middle, and older adults. Within this part of the life span, researchers have addressed unique needs of specific groups, including women, ethnically diverse groups, people with disabilities, and gays and lesbians, as well as addressing different settings, as in this chapter.

In the last quarter century career counselors and psychologists have become much more focused on the context of people's lives. Especially in response to the women's movement and multiculturalism, career counselors and psychologists have added "contextualism" to traditional concerns about intrapsychic or interpersonal influences on career development and choice. Contextualism is also a major part of ILP.

Overview of Integrative Life Planning (ILP)

Integrative Life Planning is part of a new paradigm for helping young, middle, and older adults reflect and act on their life career choices and decisions in some different ways. It is a distinctly new way of thinking about old problems in that it pulls together several aspects of life not always included in career planning—aspects which foster thinking about connectedness and wholeness in contrast to separation and fragmentation. Briefly, it is a model which:

- Relates *societal contexts* to the individual, to families, to education, and to work.
- Is a lifelong process of identifying primary needs, roles, and goals and integrating them within self, work, family, and community.
- Is interactive and relationship oriented and designed to help individuals achieve greater satisfaction, meaning, wholeness, and a sense of community.
- Is a means to help shape the direction of one's life, empower others, manage change, and contribute to the larger society and common good,

RATIONALE

Dramatic global societal changes point to the need for counselors and other career professionals to re-examine their profession and ways in which members are being prepared to function effectively in the new millennium. Integrative Life Planning offers a holistic lens through which to examine the contexts of people's lives and determine ways to assist them with emerging career and life planning issues.

ILP is an interdisciplinary concept that focuses on systems and connectedness; a life planning process that helps counselors and clients develop a "big picture" perspective, to see "work within a life," but also work and life roles beyond national boundaries. It advocates developing worldviews and life plans that not only provide satisfaction to individuals but benefit to society or community.

VALUES ASSUMPTIONS

As with any theory, innovation, program, or curriculum, certain value assumptions undergird Integrative Life Planning. They are:

1. Societal changes in demographics, workplaces, families, and communities require counseling professionals to broaden their concepts of career development and career guidance in the 21st century.
2. Changes in the nature of knowledge support the addition of new ways of knowing to career development theory, research, and practice.
3. Career professionals need to help students, clients, and employees develop skills of *integrative thinking*—seeing connections in their lives and in their local and global communities.
4. Broader kinds of self-knowledge (beyond interests, abilities, and values) and societal knowledge (beyond occupational and educational information) are critical to an expanded view of career, including multiple roles, identities, and critical life tasks in diverse cultures.
5. Career counseling needs to focus on career professionals as change agents, helping clients to achieve more holistic lives and become advocates and agents for positive societal change through the choices and decisions they make.

Critical Life Tasks of ILP

ILP theory is developed around six critical themes or life tasks facing adults in the new millennium. The tasks are identified through recurring trends in the career development literature, investigated by researchers in several disciplines, and voiced in reports of people's lived experience. Though focused originally on U.S. culture, the tasks appear to have some relevance across cultures, with variations in priorities depending on the culture. Each of the life tasks will be briefly described:

1. Finding work that needs doing in changing global contexts
2. Weaving our lives into a meaningful whole
3. Connecting family and work (Negotiating roles and relationships)
4. Valuing pluralism and inclusivity
5. Managing personal transitions and organizational change
6. Exploring spirituality and life purpose

1) FINDING WORK THAT NEEDS DOING IN CHANGING GLOBAL CONTEXTS

The first task emphasizes work yet to be done to make society a better place. It contrasts with typical ways of job search where individuals gather information about themselves (often through tests and inventories), scan the environment, and find the piece of the occupational pie they think will be most satisfying to them. ILP reflects on the kinds of universal societal problems that need to be addressed and seem especially important, in the new millennium, i.e. work that needs doing on both global and local levels. The ten challenges below, most of them self-explanatory, were identified by the author:

- Preserving the environment
- Constructive use of technology

- Understanding work and family changes
- Accepting changing gender roles
- Understanding and celebrating diversity
- Reducing violence
- Promoting economic opportunity (reducing poverty)
- Advocating for human rights
- Discovering and applying new ways of knowing
- Exploring spirituality, meaning, and purpose

Many of these have a social justice, social equity, and social change theme not present in most current vocational theories. Some writers differentiate between "good work" and "bad work." Good work that needs doing is the work that will help achieve sustainable development on the planet as well as enhance the human condition. "Bad work," which should be eliminated, includes crime, drugs, sexual slavery, violence, and pornography (Fox, 1994). Career professionals (and their adult clients, students, or employees) are urged to identify their own human challenges and priorities and to reflect on how they can "think globally and act locally" in addressing these superordinate needs. It is perhaps apparent that one's own socioeconomic status, values, barriers, and opportunities may affect the selection of these challenges.

2) WEAVING OUR LIVES INTO A MEANINGFUL WHOLE

There are many kinds of wholeness, including finding balance, connecting career and personal lives, linking spirituality and work, and striving for wholeness through telling one's story. An important aspect of wholeness is the recognition by many people that the work role or family role cannot meet all needs and a desire to find more balance in life. Workers who have been laid off or "downsized" may turn crisis into opportunity and begin to attend to what may have been the missing parts of their lives, that is, besides the vocational or career dimension, the social, intellectual, physical, spiritual, and emotional dimensions.

From a systems perspective, it is well-known that what happens in one part of life affects other parts, and often there is a connection between the career and the personal. Herr (1989) made a strong case for the linkage between personal issues and career development. In a special issue of *The Career Development Quarterly* the question was asked, "How personal is career counseling?" Several well-known leaders in career psychology, including Super, Betz, Krumboltz, and others, answered "very personal" and attested to the important connection between personal mental health and career and work issues (Subich, 1993).

"Career as Story" offers one vehicle for adults to find wholeness. Students and clients may move toward wholeness by telling their story as they see it, then reconstructing it (and planning it) as they would like it to be (Jepsen, 1995; Cochran, 1997; Savickas, 1997). For more than 30 years traditional age and adult students in my regular career development classes and in my independent distance learning class have completed an assignment to write their "life career story." Through reading these stories, one finds impressive learning and insight that occurs in the telling of the story and even greater satisfaction as students incorporate it into their career and life planning.

Maria Valdez (name disguised), an immigrant from Mexico, was especially successful in turning her story into reality. In taking a distance learning class on Integrative Life Planning, she shared several "chapters" of her life: she reflected on her life roles, examined her values, clarified her mission, developed a sense of agency, defined her own spirituality, made several voluntary and involuntary transitions, stayed off welfare, utilized community resources, found a meaningful job, and set some priorities for her next steps, including to work more on her family and personal relationships, and continuing to learn through distance education. Maria was truly doing holistic life planning, and she appreciated the opportunity to learn how to do so.

It should be pointed out that for many in society wholeness may be an elusive goal, especially for those struggling with basic needs of food, clothing, and shelter. Yet striving for wholeness should not be available only to the economically and educationally privileged.

3) CONNECTING FAMILY AND WORK (NEGOTIATING ROLES AND RELATIONSHIPS)

With the U.S. population increasingly reflecting multiple family types, especially single parent, two earner and dual career families, considerable attention has been given to issues of family and work. As more women enter the workforce in greater numbers and men begin to assume more roles in the family, researchers have begun to investigate how work affects family and how family affects work. One noted sociologist some years ago asked the important question, in essence, "Why does family always have to fit around work? Why can't work sometimes fit around family?" (Kanter, 1977). Changing family patterns create career dilemmas, such as family requirements for a desired lifestyle (How much is enough?), livelihood for single parents, the need for reliable and affordable childcare, maternal and paternal leave, flexible schedules, adequate transportation, work and marital satisfaction, decision-making conflicts, and stress and coping strategies. In the 70s and 80s, much emphasis in the work and family literature was put on role conflict and stress, based on an assumption that time and energy are fixed and that individuals in multiple roles inevitably experience conflict that affects their well-being. A new approach being advanced is that of work and family integration, that there is opportunity for enhancement of well being through participation in multiple roles. In the new century, there is need to assess the impact of work experiences on family life and of family experiences on work life (Greenhaus & Parasuraman, 1999).

Gender-role expectations derived from socialization and stereotyping also create work-family problems, and each culture may be at a different place on a continuum of change with regard to this issue. Stereotypes create barriers for both women and men, and stereotypes of what men and women are like or should be like are still pervasive. For example, the pattern that still prevails in many Western wedding ceremonies of a father "giving 'his' daughter away" and the bride giving up her birth name reinforces the traditional attitudes toward women as property as subordinate to men. Although women obtain more of the bachelor's degrees in U.S. colleges and universities today, institutional structures and policies, such as a "glass ceilings" or "concrete walls" which limit occupational opportunity or mobility may still block their career options. Men are limited also, by societal stereotypes and expectations and barriers which keep them from participating more widely in stereotypically female occupations or activities, such as nursing, child-rearing, household tasks, and freedom for emotional expressiveness. Counselors of adults need to be aware of the facilitators and barriers in the life planning of each. The impact of gender on career is a continuing issue across cultures, though it may be phrased differently depending on the status of women and men and the political and cultural context.

Another context for thinking about work and family is Super's (1980) life-span model (of the roles and theaters of a person's life (student, homemaker, worker, citizen, and leisurite) (Super & Sverko, 1995). A related way of looking at the differential socialization of women and men and roles in work and family is through self-sufficiency and connectedness. Many years ago Bakan (1966) used the terms "agency" and "communion" to define what he called male and female ways of ordering reality. He linked *agency* with males (using descriptors like rational, logical objective, analytic, competitive, and instrumental); and *communal* with females (using descriptors such as subjective, nurturing, cooperative intuitive, expressive, and integrative). He suggested that a developmental task for both women and men is to integrate both the agentic and the communal into their lives. ILP has incorporated this concept, but the terms used are "self-sufficiency," usually identified with men, and "connectedness," usually identified with women, as characteristics needed by both.

ILP presents a vision of women and men as partners at home and in the workplace, being empowered to meet their needs for both self-sufficiency and connectedness. Partnerships occur when each partner (a) treats the other with dignity and respect; (b) demonstrates flexibility in negotiating roles and goals; and (c) enables the other to choose and enact roles and responsibilities congruent with his or her talents and potentials and the partners' mutual goals for work, the relationship, the family, and the community (Hansen, 1997). For many adults at different life stages today, negotiating changing roles and relationships in families and in the workplace offer sometimes difficult challenges.

4) VALUING PLURALISM AND INCLUSIVITY

In ILP a strong emphasis exists on the critical life task of learning to deal with differences—understanding how to approach "the Other" who may be different in some way from oneself. This task is important because interpersonal skills and intercultural sensitivity in the new millennium will continue to be important on and off the job. Effective relationships in the workplace may require a new set of counseling skills, such as to: (a) gain an understanding of the meaning and implications of valuing diversity; (b) better understand one's own culture as well as biases and attitudes toward others; (c) assist clients to develop a worldview that helps them to function in a multicultural environment; and (d) utilize that knowledge to help diverse clients, students, and workers to be free from bias and have opportunities to make choices that further their own self-actualization and societal betterment.

Pluralism reinforces the importance of difference, recognizes many parts, groups, experiences, and truths, and establishes a context for valuing diversity. An awareness of all kinds of difference, e.g. racial, ethnic, religious, disability, sexual orientation, age, gender, socioeconomic class, and geographical origins—the multiple identities each person brings to a work or family relationship—is essential to understanding the people with whom career professionals and their clients will interact in the future. Of course, along with accepting differences is the need to recognize similarities or commonalities. While this task is also important for children and youth, the present generation of adults will need help in addressing it if this society is going to move closer to achieving its democratic goals.

5) MANAGING PERSONAL TRANSITIONS AND ORGANIZATIONAL CHANGE

Wholeness in life also involves the capacity to manage personal transitions and organizational change. With changes occurring in all stages of life—especially with early, middle, and older adults—transition counseling (along with gerontological counseling) may be one of the most needed skills in the career counseling profession of the future. One important need is for clients to understand the transition process, as Schlossberg (1994) points out. Understanding the four S's (Situation, Self, Supports, and Strategies (for coping) involved in the process is a key to better negotiating a transition (Goodman & Pappas (2000).

Another important aspect of transitions is decision-making. Although the most common models for decision-making in the past have been logical, linear models that lead to prediction and a certainty of choice, new thinking about decision-making is helping adults become more conscious of complexity and of risks and risk-taking. Two new models of decision-making that focus on paradox and uncertainty are "Positive Uncertainty" (Gelatt, 1989) and "Planned Happenstance" (Mitchell, Levin, & Krumboltz, 1999). Positive uncertainty combines both reason and intuition and is designed to help prepare individuals for the change, instability, and complexity they may face in the future. It urges people to learn to live with paradox, to recognize the positive characteristics of uncertainty, and to not be afraid to change one's mind. Many traditional age and adult college students in my classes seem to resonate with this philosophy. One young woman exposed to this ILP task in a senior seminar in psychology expressed the point well when she said:

> There is nothing wrong with feeling that there is an element of ambiguity to my goals and that I expect them to change. What I am experiencing is "positive uncertainty." It surprised me that what I saw as a flaw in me, never being able to stick with one plan, is actually the strength of flexibility. Since I am extremely rational, it sometimes bothers me that it takes me so long to determine and decide what I am going to do. Now I realize there is nothing wrong with me, and it is perfectly OK to have a plan yet not be certain that it will become reality.

Taking into account the global context and the changing nature of work structures across cultures, Herr (1997) also expressed this need for personal flexibility as one of the competencies needed for adults in the 21st century. Planned Happenstance, another paradoxical model, was developed more recently; it provides a systematic way of using curiosity to take advantage of the unexpected and unanticipated. It involves preparing clients to capitalize on surprising life events by learning to carve a positive response to them so that what may be an unexpected or unplanned event can be used to further opportunity.

A third equally important aspect of transitions is to help adults become change agents, in their personal and family lives and in their organizations, facilitating their sense of agency. Organizational change can be facilitated by any of several systematic models of change process. Career professionals can help clients engage in systems change by assessing their institution as it is now and determining how they would like it to be. Clients also need to be taught strategies for implementing change. A rich body of literature on systems change and organizational development can be helpful in this process. By becoming a change agent, adults also can directly or indirectly work toward the betterment of the larger society.

6) EXPLORING SPIRITUALITY AND LIFE PURPOSE

One distinct trend with adult populations is the search for spirituality, purpose, and meaning. Including spirituality as part of career development and holistic career planning has been triggered in part by the women's movement and multiculturalism. It has become central in career counseling in the last approximately ten years and has become a main theme in professional counseling and career counseling conferences.

Although there are many definitions of spirituality, the following are the most relevant to ILP: (a) The core of the self that gives meaning to life; (b) A higher power outside of oneself; (c) The center of the person from which meaning, self, and life understanding are generated; and (d) The deep integration, wholeness, a sense of the interrelatedness of all of life.

Spirituality is linked with meaning and purpose, a desire to contribute to community, and achieve a sense of wholeness and connection with others. It may or may not be defined as religion, but it will be part of the task of career counselors to help adult clients, students, or workers define what spirituality means in their own lives. Along with a search for meaning, a number of young adults are seeking more balance in life and refuse to give their whole lives to their jobs. Some are moving away from materialism by downshifting and redefining success for themselves. Meijers (1998), in discussing a "career identity," suggests that individuals need to be able to answer what seem to be two very important questions: "What does work mean in and for my life?" and "What do I want to mean to others through my work?"

A theologian encourages re-examination of the material values driving society and suggests that a primary value in life is "living life fully" (Fox, 1994, p. 1). Work should be more spiritual, he observes, based on a larger meaning and purpose—not just to fit into a job but to benefit the community through giving back one's talents. He sees the work role as the place where "mind, heart, and health come together in a harmony of life experiences that celebrate the whole person" (p. 2).

Although spirituality is a topic often ignored in the rational, logical career decision-making of the past, many career counselors have begun to recognize that spirituality is central to life. Women and ethnic groups who have tended to view life more holistically have reinforced that centrality. The growing connection between spirituality and work has become a prominent topic in career development in the U.S. Today there seems to be a new openness to including spirituality as part of career and life planning, expressed in a number of professional books, including *Connections between Spirit and Work in Career Development* (1997) and *SoulWork* (1998), both by Bloch and Richmond. "Career as Story," mentioned earlier, is also linked to meaning and purpose by some authors (e.g. Amundson, 1998; Peavy, 1990; and Savickas, 1997).

Relevance of the ILP Model to Adults

It is the task of career counselors and HRD professionals to help adult clients understand these tasks, to help them see the interrelatedness of the various tasks, and to help them prioritize the tasks according to their needs and the needs of society. Another young adult, also a senior in a college seminar in psychology, states it well:

> Integrative Life Planning is not just a new approach to job seeking and talent finding; it is a working example of how to put together all the parts of life one encounters in a successful and meaningful way. Some of these tasks will occur at different times for different people as they live and plan their lives. I think that three of these tasks are particularly relevant to my life right now, and these are probably the parts of ILP I will carry with me.

CLARIFYING THE TASKS

Although all six life tasks are a blend of the internal and external, some relate more to individual development (weaving our lives into a meaningful whole, inclusivity and relating to difference, and spirituality and purpose). The contextual tasks relate more to societal development and change (finding work that needs doing, exploring the positive connection between work and family, and managing personal transitions and organizational change).

These tasks grow out of the author's concern that counseling and career development—and what preservice and inservice counselors and other career professionals are taught—are still based heavily on a linear approach to career planning and a focus on matching, currently called person/environment fit. While trait and factor approaches always will be needed—especially in times of job search—there are signs that people's visions of their life journey include much more than fitting into the job market. For those at Maslow's survival level of existence, however, basic survival needs likely have to be met before one can do holistic life planning. Many adults recognize that the dramatic changes in work, family, and the larger society require more expansive thinking about their lives and life choices. ILP was begun more than ten years ago in response to both the external societal changes and the internal changes in people's lives.

Another aspect that career counselors and their adult clients need to understand is the changing nature of knowledge and increasing acceptance of different ways of knowing—recognition that the logical positivist and empirical tradition presents only one way of knowing, and that qualitative ways of knowing provide another valid way of seeking answers to some types of clinical and career psychology research questions. The work of scholars such as Gama (1992) and Hill and Associates (1997) has helped counseling psychology broaden its scope of knowledge. Theory-building also has undergone some changes. The old ways in which theory defined practice are being complemented with new ways of practice stimulating theory.

PAST AND PRESENT APPLICATIONS TO ADULTS

The critical life tasks of ILP are at a cognitive level that the average adult at different stages of the life span can understand. While much of career counseling has emphasized self-concept and self-actualization, there is growing awareness of the need for societal contribution which ILP has emphasized. One student in a career development class had this to say: "I am fascinated with the idea of what might happen if career counselors...begin to encourage others to take on this global view in the preparation of future goals and plans. Wouldn't it be inspiring to know individuals were being counseled to better society with their lives instead of just bettering themselves?"

Career development theory, which has emerged since the 1950s, focused on such concepts as career readiness, career maturity, planfulness, and developmental tasks. Recognition of the difficulty of defining developmental tasks of adulthood has led to great variety in addressing adult needs and concerns. Campbell and Cellini (1981) developed a "Taxonomy of Adult Problems" based on four components: 1) adult decision-making, 2) implementing career plans, 3) organizational-institutional performance, and 4) organizational-institutional adaptation (work adjustment). Much of the emphasis was still on choice of an occupation as a final outcome with little indication that today's emerging themes, changing social values, or new work and work patterns were part of the career and life planning process.

Attempts to make career development a science have been replaced with the recognition that, with adults especially, it is more of an art. And even as an art it has been, until recently, bereft of concepts of wholeness, integration, and spirituality and other neglected areas related to career development. Much adult career counseling has dealt with keeping up with occupational changes, maintaining oneself in an occupation, and preparing for a next stage (such as retirement). One of the foremost theorists advancing the notion of life roles and life stages, Super in 1996 renamed his later life stages from "decline" to "disengagement," a word that seems more appropriate in the new century. In more recent literature, Amundson (1998) approaches adult career counseling in a more integrated way, including eight competencies especially needed for preparing counselors: purpose, problem-solving, communication skills, theoretical knowledge, applied knowledge, organizational adaptability, human relations, and self confidence.

While one cannot ignore the importance of economics in career planning, especially with segments of the population that are unemployed, underemployed, "burned out," dislocated, downsized, and restructured, one needs to add dimensions that have been left out in career planning and emphasize that career development is connected to all aspects of life—the intellectual, physical, social, emotional, and spiritual—not only occupational.

It is also true that most adults desire a sense of agency, some sense of control over their lives. They do not want career counselors to tell them what to do; yet guidance toward both self-development (self-actualization) and societal development (leaving this world a better place) is important. Controlling one's destiny is not just egotistical self-enhancement but altruistic societal betterment. This emphasis on both is a major characteristic of ILP.

GENERAL ADULT DEVELOPMENT APPLICATIONS

Recognizing that "one size does not fit all," career counseling using Integrative Life Planning provides a large umbrella to help adults at different life stages address their unique issues and stretch their thinking about themselves in society.

Briefly, ILP can be used with young adults, mid-life adults, and older adults in some of the following ways.

Traditional-age college students who have been exposed to Integrative Life Planning (such as graduate students in counseling classes, undergraduates in distance learning, and seniors about to graduate) seem to understand and relate to ILP very easily. The concept has been demonstrated to be understandable and helpful to college seniors, as several have attested. It makes sense that after four years in college programs that are disparate and fragmented, they welcome a theory that pulls their ideas together and gives them a sense of wholeness. Several quotes cited in this paper indicate that the cognitive level is appropriate for college students, but also that they have affective reactions to these concepts that stimulate their feelings of connectedness, wholeness, and spirituality.

Mid-life clients may also relate to ILP, especially if they are in crisis when feelings of loss and a search for meaning and purpose may become paramount. Divorce situations often create economic problems, but many going through divorce also need to deal with affective issues. This is especially true with women who are dislocated or men who are downsized. A substantial body of literature on midlife women and midlife men indicates there are gender differences that require different kinds of interventions. Current attempts in some states to eliminate programs for dislocated workers (most of whom are women) and replace them with "All-in-One" Workforce Centers are misguided and ignore the diversity of adults. While economic issues are very important to women on welfare, for example, many, in addition to information, need support, counseling, and spirituality to help them through crises.

Older adults who have worked many years during their lives but have exited the workforce may be most receptive to ILP philosophy. They may be in a state of renewal, seeking answers to aspects of life that have been neglected. This is a stage of life in which spirituality often becomes more important, gender roles change, work and family issues take on a different character, and connectedness becomes more central because of loss of spouses, partners, friends, and other loved ones. Stereotypes of aging make the themes of ILP very relevant, as issues of inclusion and exclusion, and meaning and purpose, as well as economic security, take center stage. Specific examples as to how Integrative Life Planning has been used with diverse adult populations may be instructive.

SPECIFIC APPLICATIONS OF ILP TO DIVERSE ADULT POPULATIONS

Although still an evolving concept, Integrative Life Planning has major applications to individuals of diverse backgrounds. Anecdotal feedback and evaluations from numerous training workshops has indicated that women and ethnic minorities find the ILP concept extremely relevant

As pointed out early in this chapter, Integrative Life Planning is a comprehensive concept difficult to measure in traditional ways. While no formal studies have been conducted, research has begun on an experimental self-assessment instrument designed to help clients or workshop participants assess where they are in relation to integrative thinking and planning. The *Integrative Life Planning Inventory* (Hansen, Hage, & Kachgal, 1999), a 20-item Likert-type questionnaire, has been used in a number of ILP workshops and with graduate students in counseling classes. The instrument helps users assess where they are on the critical tasks of ILP on a scale from traditional to holistic. The primary evidence of the viability of the ILP concept has been from participants (mostly counselors and other career professionals) in ILP workshops, feedback from counselor educators teaching ILP in counseling or psychology classes, and various applications reported to the author from different settings and cultures. These are described briefly below.

SENIOR SEMINAR IN PSYCHOLOGY AT AMERICAN COLLEGES

An assistant professor in psychology at a liberal arts college used ILP as a basis for her Senior Seminar in Psychology class. She excitedly reported that students were very enthusiastic, and she shared a number of quotations from students in the class. A few of them, with their permission, are reported in this paper. Students seemed to appreciate the holistic approach and found three or four of the critical life tasks to which they related. For example, one young woman described what the tasks of work-family balance and self-sufficiency and connectedness meant to her, as she and her fiancé had just begun talking about how they would live their lives, carry out their work, and their hopes and dreams for family. Several students saw implications in their own lives for some of the other life tasks as well.

Other colleges, some with high proportions of ethnic minorities, reported that ILP has been adapted as a philosophical framework for college career centers. One liberal arts college is exploring the use of Integrative Life Planning as a conceptual framework for a "Senior Year" program fashioned after John Gardner's "Freshman Year." In another adaptation, one community college instructor used ILP as the basis for a course in "Philosophy of Work."

FEMALE PRISON INMATES IN SOUTH AFRICAN UNIVERSITY PROJECT

The following application was described and implemented by an assistant professor at a South African university. Exposed to ILP through an international counseling institute, he involved his counseling students in an intervention to help female inmates think about career and life planning prior to their release. The inmates' responses to the program in 1999 and 2000, led by a Master's student, were reported as extremely positive. The researchers pointed out that since most of the inmates had never been exposed to career planning, this was an important new idea to them and their future. The honors student who conducted the second intervention stated:

> I have learnt much from applying the ILP framework and find that it is well suited to the South African context. Our country is going through radical changes that leave citizens apprehensive about the future and has caused our crime rate to soar. ILP appears to have the ability to make the social processes of change open to observation. It is then my wish, in employing the ILP paradigm, to enable each to make his/her personal change a process of deliberation and choice" (e-mail, 2000, August 23).

This project is being expanded to include male inmates as well. The ILP concept, as well as other models of life-span development, is being taught by the original instructor at a South African university. Other kinds of implementation need to be explored across cultures for their appropriateness and cross-cultural utility. Already

ILP has been piloted in the Philippines, Japan, Italy, Sweden, Australia, and New Zealand.

PROGRAM FOR LOW-INCOME WOMEN ON WELFARE

Another ILP intervention was undertaken by a project director of a program for low-income women on welfare in the Minneapolis-St. Paul area. She reported a high level of satisfaction among the female participants and shared copies of a special lifeline, the "Circle of Life" (a common Native American symbol), drawn by the participants. On a very basic level they were able to express their need for spirituality and their own interpretation of purpose in their lives through the circle lifeline.

TEACHING ILP TO TEACHERS AND COUNSELORS

Inservice teachers and counselors in a two-week summer ILP workshop taught by the author created their own ILP Program plans to incorporate into their classes in secondary and postsecondary settings. The programs were implemented during the following school year in a variety of interventions/innovations, and feedback from the teachers and counselors was quite positive.

TEACHING ILP IN COUNSELOR EDUCATION

After more than 10 years of teaching Integrative Life Planning to adult students in career development and counseling classes, the author found a high level of interest in the expanded concept of career. Several students in the counselor education career development classes framed their own career stories around the ILP themes and tasks. Many of the female and minority students especially resonated with the holistic concept. Students had some good questions, however, including such queries as:

- Can you integrate too much or where do you draw the line?
- How do you communicate the importance of incorporating all parts of life into a whole with younger people?
- How do you bring incorporation of all parts of life into counseling with older persons?
- How do you address spirituality with clients who are not in touch with this part of their lives?
- How do you help students become more conscious of their own socialization to gender roles, cultural norms, and the mechanized society?
- Does Integrative Life Planning apply across cultures?
- What are the arguments for and against using more holistic approaches to career and life development?

For some brief answers to these questions, see Hansen in *The Career Development Quarterly* Special Millennium Issue, Spring 2001.

INDEPENDENT DISTANCE LEARNING AND CONFERENCE WORKSHOPS

For several years the author has taught the independent study distance learning course called Integrative Career Planning, a course that has attracted enrollees from around the world. (Maria, mentioned earlier, was one of them). Some have taken the course because their international schools are being downsized, and they need more credits or courses in order to be certified in new schools. Some were from military bases that had been closed down and were making an involuntary transition. Some take the course for their own self development and enlightenment. And still others, many of them present or prospective counselors, take it because they want to update their knowledge and skills in career development. Enrollees report that the course is a helpful vehicle for them to better understand themselves and societal changes and to develop or revise at least a tentative life plan. Another strategy being considered for reaching distance learning students is to offer holistic life planning through the Internet in a format that goes beyond simple matching models or person-environment assessment. Currently the course is being revised and will be offered through the University of Minnesota Continuing Education in Fall, 2001, as Integrative Life Planning.

A number of local, national, and international workshops have been offered at conferences in the years that ILP has been in existence. ILP has been the topic of conference keynotes in several cultures, including the Philippines, Japan, Sweden, Canada, and the U.S.

POTENTIAL APPLICATIONS TO HRD

Because of its comprehensiveness, Integrative Life Planning has potential for use with human resource development programs in government, business, and education. In business, Wellness Programs and Family-Work Balance are growing concerns, which well might be addressed through holistic life planning. Aspects of ILP can help HRD personnel to attend to such dilemmas as child care, work and family salience, task sharing, marital satisfaction, work satisfaction, money, stress and coping strategies, social supports, power, spirituality, decision-making, etc. Specific applications to HRD are described in another volume (see Hanson in Kummerow, 2000). ILP also can act as a facilitator of team-building including development of relational skills among members of organizations. It is likely that ILP could be used in Outplacement or Career Coaching programs where workers have been downsized or laid off. Employees can be taught to use Schlossberg's Transition model and strategies for dealing with change and uncertainty.

By linking career counseling to "Self-in-Relation Theory," as Hall and Associates (1996) have done, HRD personnel and career counselors can help systems teach workers a new set of skills including (a) lifelong learning, teamwork, adaptability, valuing diversity, communication, and decision making; and (b) 'relational competencies' of self-reflection, active listening, empathy, self-disclosure, and collaboration to better understand themselves and others in a dynamic and diverse workplace. These are just a few examples of the application of ILP to diverse adult populations and settings.

ILLUSTRATIVE STRATEGIES FOR IMPLEMENTATION

A number of strategies have been included in the ILP model, many of which can be useful in implementing ILP into counselor education, workshops, or private practice. The following are illustrative, with many others available in the original book in which ILP is described (Hansen, 1997). Space precludes further description of the strategies here.

ILLUSTRATIVE STRATEGIES

Critical Life Events	Mutuality Planning
Risk-taking and Decision-making	Life Planning Influences
Storytelling – Career as Story	Career Rainbow
Life Role Identification	Partnerships
Visualization and Metaphor	Rethinking Work
Patches of the Quilt	A Sense of Time

SYNTHESIS AND CONCLUSION

The Circle of Life (see Figure 1), is an activity which is central to ILP, demonstrates how all the pieces of Integrative Life Planning fit together. An important symbol of Native cultures, it offers opportunity for reflection on one's own wholeness, connectedness, and integrative thinking.

Figure 1
CIRCLE OF LIFE — SYNTHESIS OF INTEGRATIVE LIFE PLANNING

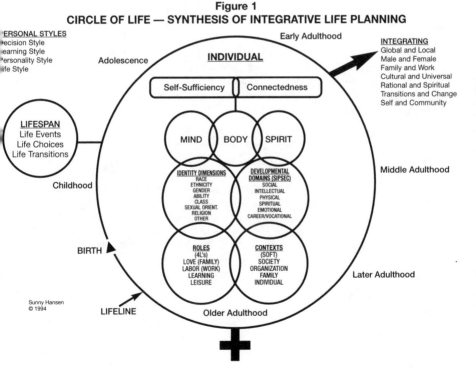

Some users of ILP may find it overwhelming since it is so comprehensive and inclusive. Because of this, it is important to parse out the tasks that are most relevant for a given population or setting. It should also be remembered that ILP is intended to be primarily complementary to traditional matching, job search, or work adjustment approaches. Using Integrative Life Planning with adults will result in some shifts in worldviews.

INTEGRATIVE LIFE PLANNING MEANS MOVING FROM . . .		
Thinking locally	to	Sharing globally
Planning for work	to	Planning for life roles and how they relate to one another
Focus on self-sufficiency only	to	Focus on self-sufficiency and connectedness for both women and men
Expecting stability	to	Expecting and managing change and transitions in both family and work
Monoculturalism	to	Multiculturalism and inclusivity
Fragmentation	to	Wholeness and community

As pointed out, the critical life tasks of ILP are interactive. Some deal with individual development (spirituality, holistic planning, and interpersonal effectiveness), and others are more contextual (finding work in global contexts, negotiating roles and relationships in work and family, and managing change and transitions). All nonetheless are linked to one another. For example, understanding the interrelationship of family, work, and other life roles and dealing with difference are central tasks of living, learning, and working in a global society. Helping individuals, partners, and families explore how the various parts of their lives fit together is an important goal for counselors of adults, as is creating awareness of the changing contexts that affect our life choices and decisions.

Career counselors in each culture will have to decide what in ILP is relevant and applicable, depending on their own contexts, priorities, and worldviews. No counselor or career professional could expect to absorb or implement the entire ILP concept at once. Each will have to select those life tasks that are more important or meaningful at a given time with a given population or setting and work with them. How well holistic life planning approaches to human development will be able to compete with the technological approaches focused on information and economic development may well depend on both personal and contextual changes and how well the diverse needs of both individuals and society are articulated.

COMPLETING THE QUILT METAPHOR

To return to the quilt metaphor, the quilt pulls the pieces of ILP together so that it makes sense and is meaningful to counselors and career professionals who help clients make their own choices and decisions through integrative thinking and life planning. Counselors of adults can help students, clients, and employees design the roles and goals of their lives and see how the pieces fit together in meaningful ways. They can especially help clients understand that life planning is not just planning for self-satisfaction but also for the betterment of society. And, finally, they can help adults at early, midlife, and later life stages address their needs to not only fit into jobs or deal with crises but to learn to view themselves and society through a lens of wholeness and community.

REFERENCES

Amundson, N. E. (1998). *Active engagement – Enhancing the career counseling process*. Richmond, BC: Ergon Communications.

Bakan, D. (1966). *The duality of human existence: An essay on psychology and religion*. Skokie, IL: Rand McNally.

Bloch, D. P., & Richmond, L. J. (Eds). (1997). *Connections between spirit and work in career development*. Palo Alto, CA: Davies-Black.

Bloch, D. P., & Richmond, L. J. (1998). *SoulWork – Finding the work you love, loving the work you have*. Palo Alto, CA: Davies-Black.

Campbell, R. E., & Cellini, J. V. (1981). A diagnostic category of adult career problems. *Journal of Vocational Behavior*, 19, 175-190.

Cochran, L. (1997). *Career counseling: A narrative approach*. Thousand Oaks, CA: Sage.

Fox, M. (1994). *The reinvention of work: A new vision of livelihood for our time*. San Francisco: Harper.

Gama, E. P. (1992). Toward science-practice integration: Qualitative research in counseling psychology. *Counseling and Human Development*, 25(2), 1-12.

Gelatt, H. B. (1989). Positive uncertainty: A new decision-making framework for counseling. *Journal of Counseling Psychology*, 36(2), 252-256.

Goodman, J., & Pappas, J. G. (2000, Spring). Applying the Schlossberg 4S transition model to retired university faculty: Does it fit? *Adultspan Journal*, 2(1), 15-28.

Greenhaus, J. H., & Parasuraman, S. (1999). Research on work, family, and gender: Current status and future directions. In G. N. Powell (Ed). *Handbook of gender in organizations* (pp. 391-412). Newbury Park, CA: Sage.

Hall, D. T., & Associates. (1996). *Career is dead—Long live career: A relational approach to careers*. San Francisco: Jossey-Bass.

Hansen, L. S. (1997). *Integrative life planning – Critical tasks for career development and changing life patterns*. San Francisco: Jossey-Bass.

Hansen, L. S. (2000). Integrative life planning: A new world view for career professionals. In J. Kummerow, (Ed.), *New directions in career planning and the workplace* (2nd ed., pp.123-159). Palo Alto, CA: Davies-Black.

Hansen, L. S. (2001, March). Integrating career and life development in the new millennium. *The Career Development Quarterly*, 49(3).

Hansen, L. S., Hage, S., & Kachgal, M. (1999). *Integrative Life Planning Inventory*. Integrative Life Planning, Counseling and Student Personnel Psychology, University of Minnesota, Minneapolis.

Herr, E. L. (1989). Career development and mental health. *Journal of Career Development*, 16, 5-18.

Herr, E. L. (1997). Perspectives on career guidance and counseling in the 21st century. *Educational and Vocational Guidance Bulletin*, 60, 1-15.

Jepsen, D. (1995, June). *Career as story: A narrative approach to career counseling*. Paper presented at National Career Development Association Conference, San Francisco, CA.

Hill, C. E., Thompson, B. J., & Williams, E. N. (1997, October). A guide to conducting consensual qualitative research. *The Counseling Psychologist*, 25 (4), 571-572.

Kanter, R. M. (1977). *Work and family in the United States: A critical review and agenda for research and policy*. New York: Russell Sage Foundation.

Meijers, F. (1998). The development of a career identity. *International Journal for the Advancement of Counselling*, 20, 191-207.

Mitchell, K., Levin, A. S., & Krumboltz, J. D. (1999). Planned happenstance: Constructing unexpected career opportunities. *Journal of Counseling and Development*, 77, 115-124.

Peavy, R. V. (1990). *SocioDynamic counseling – A constructivist perspective.* Vancouver, BC: Trafford.

Savickas, M. L. (1997). The spirit in career counseling: Fostering self-completion through work. In D. Bloch & L. Richmond (Eds.), *Connections between spirit and work in career development.* (pp. 3-25), Palo Alto, CA: Black-Davies.

Schlossberg, N. K. (1994). *Overwhelmed: Coping with life's ups and downs.* New Lexington Press. (Original work published 1989).

Subich, L. M. (1993). How personal is career counseling? *The Career Development Quarterly*, 42(2), 129-131.

Super, D. E. (1980). A life-span, life-space approach to career development. *Journal of Vocational Behavior*, 16(3), 282-298.

Super, D. E., & Sverko, B. (Eds.). (1995). *Life roles, values and careers.* San Francisco: Jossey-Bass.

CHAPTER 5
Social Cognitive Career Theory and Adult Career Development

Robert W. Lent
University of Maryland

Steven D. Brown
Loyola University Chicago

Social cognitive career theory (SCCT) is intended to provide a unifying framework for understanding the processes through which people develop vocational interests, make (and remake) occupational choices, and achieve varying levels of career success and stability (Lent, Brown, & Hackett, 1994). The foundation for this approach lies in Albert Bandura's (1986) general social cognitive theory, which emphasizes the complex, reciprocal interplay between people, their behavior, and environments. Taking its cue from Bandura's theory, SCCT highlights people's capacity to direct their own vocational behavior (i.e., human agency), yet it also acknowledges the many personal and environmental influences (e.g., socio-structural barriers and supports, culture, disability status) that serve to strengthen, weaken or, in some cases, even override human agency in career development.

In this chapter, we first overview the basic theory and its implications for adult career development. After briefly considering SCCT's research base, we illustrate how the theory can be used in counseling aimed at career choice and change issues. Finally, we discuss the theory's applications with a variety of adult populations, such as persons of color, women, persons with disabilities, and gay and lesbian workers. Readers wishing a more thorough treatment of SCCT, its research base, conceptual underpinnings, or relation to earlier career theories are referred to other recent sources (e.g., Lent et al., 1994, 2000; Lent & Hackett, 1994).

Basic Elements of SCCT

SCCT considers the interplay among a number of constructs (e.g., interests, abilities, and goals) that are dealt with to varying degrees by earlier career theories. It also posits cognitive and experiential processes that may complement or extend important aspects of other career theories (e.g., the means by which people come to develop primary vocational interests in Holland's, 1985, theory). While incorporating a variety of person, contextual, and behavior variables, SCCT proposes a

Portions of this chapter were adapted from Lent and Brown (1996) and Brown and Lent (1996). Reprinted material was used with the permission of the National Career Development Association. Correspondence concerning this chapter should be addressed to Robert W. Lent, Department of Counseling and Personnel Services, University of Maryland, College Park, MD 20742. Electronic mail may be sent via Internet to RL95@umail.umd.edu.

few central mechanisms and paths through which these variables influence career developmental outcomes.

The theory highlights three intricately-linked variables through which individuals help to regulate their own career behavior: *self-efficacy beliefs, outcome expectations,* and *personal goals.* Self-efficacy beliefs refer to "people's judgments of their capabilities to organize and execute courses of action required to attain designated types of performances" (Bandura, 1986, p. 391). These beliefs represent the most central and pervasive mechanism of personal agency in Bandura's (1986, 1997) framework. In the social cognitive view, self-efficacy is not a singular static, passive, or global trait, but rather involves dynamic self-beliefs that are linked to particular performance domains and activities, such as different academic and work tasks. An individual might, for instance, hold high self-efficacy beliefs regarding his or her ability to perform artistic tasks but feel much less competent at entrepreneurial or mechanical tasks.

Self-efficacy beliefs are assumed to be acquired and modified via four primary informational sources:

1. Personal performance accomplishments
2. Vicarious learning
3. Social persuasion, and
4. Physiological and affective states and reactions.

Although the specific effects of these informational sources on self-efficacy depends on how they are patterned within a particular learning context and how they are processed cognitively, personal accomplishments are generally seen as exerting the greatest influence on self-efficacy. Success experiences tend to raise (and failures tend to lower) self-efficacy beliefs within a given performance domain. Efforts to enhance career-related self-efficacy have typically employed a combination of methods based on these four sources (e.g., Betz, 1992).

Outcome expectations refer to beliefs about the consequences or outcomes of performing particular behaviors. Bandura contends that people's behavior is affected both by their sense of their personal capabilities (self-efficacy) and by their beliefs about the likely effects of various actions (outcome expectations). However, he views self-efficacy as generally being the more influential determinant of behavior, noting that there are many instances in which people hold positive outcome expectations about a given course of action (e.g., the common belief in the U.S. that pursuing a medical career will yield a high income), but avoid such action if they doubt they possess the requisite capabilities. Outcome expectations regarding potential career paths are derived from a variety of direct and vicarious learning experiences, such as perceptions of the outcomes one has received in relevant past endeavors and the information one acquires through second-hand sources about the working conditions and rewards of different fields.

Personal goals, which play a central, if often implicit, role in career choice and decision-making theories, may be defined as one's intention to engage in a certain activity or to produce a particular outcome (Bandura, 1986). Goals provide an important vehicle for self-empowerment. By setting personal goals, people help to organize, guide, and sustain their own efforts, even over long intervals without external reinforcement. Social cognitive theory posits that the goals people set for themselves are influenced by their self-efficacy and outcome expectations. For example, strong positive beliefs about one's artistic capabilities and about the outcomes of artistic pursuits are likely to nurture corresponding personal goals, such as the intention to pursue training or a career in the arts.

SCCT's Models of Vocational Interests, Choice, and Performance

The social cognitive framework organizes career-related interest, choice, and performance processes into three interlocking models (Lent et al., 1994). We will overview these models, focusing on the interplay among the social cognitive variables (e.g., self-efficacy, goals) along with other important aspects of persons (e.g., gender, race/ethnicity), their contexts, and learning experiences.

VOCATIONAL INTERESTS

Childrens' and adolescents' environments expose them, directly and vicariously, to a variety of activities, such as crafts, sports, music, and mechanical tasks, that have potential career relevance. In addition to their exposure to such activities, young people are selectively reinforced by parents, peers, teachers, and other important persons (including, eventually, themselves) for pursuing, and performing well at, certain activities from among those that are possible. Through continued activity practice and feedback, children and adolescents refine their skills, develop personal performance standards, form a sense of their efficacy in particular tasks, and acquire certain expectations about the outcomes of their performance.

Our interest model (see Figure 1) holds that self-efficacy and outcome expectations regarding particular activities exert important effects on the formation of career interests (i.e., one's particular pattern of likes, dislikes, and indifferences regarding various occupations and career-relevant tasks). In particular, SCCT asserts that people form enduring interest in an activity when they view themselves as competent at it and when they anticipate that performing it will produce valued outcomes (Bandura, 1986; Lent et al., 1994). Conversely, people are likely to develop disinterest or even aversion toward activities in which they doubt their efficacy and expect to receive negative outcomes.

Emergent interest, self-efficacy, and positive outcome expectations are hypothesized to promote goals for further activity exposure. That is, as people develop an affinity for an activity at which they feel efficacious and expect positive outcomes, they are likely to form goals for sustaining or increasing their involvement in the activity. These goals, in turn, increase the likelihood of subsequent activity practice. Practice efforts give rise to a particular pattern of attainments (e.g., successes, failures), which then serve to revise self-efficacy and outcome expectations within an ongoing feedback loop.

FIGURE 1

MODEL OF HOW BASIC CAREER INTERESTS DEVELOP OVER TIME

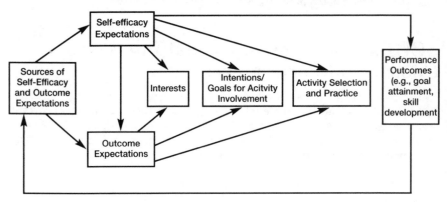

This model highlights cognitive and behavioral influences during childhood and adolescence. Copyright 1993 by R. W. Lent, S. D. Brown, and G. Hackett. Reprinted by permission.

We believe this process repeats itself continuously over the lifespan, though it is perhaps most fluid up until late adolescence or early adulthood, at which point interests tend to stabilize. Although broad occupational interests are often quite stable in adulthood (Hansen, 1984), SCCT is sanguine about the prospect of interests (both vocational and avocational) changing and shifting over time. Change versus stability in basic interests is determined by such factors as whether initially preferred activities become restricted and whether people are exposed (or expose themselves) to compelling learning experiences that enable them to expand their sense of efficacy and positive outcome expectations into new activity spheres.

Fatherhood, for example, provides an occasion for many men to revisit their interests in social pursuits, such as helping and teaching. Similarly, changing work assignments (e.g., taking on managerial responsibilities), advances in technology (e.g., the proliferation of personal computers in the workplace), and organizational and economic changes (e.g., corporate down-sizing) provide the context for adults to cultivate wholly new or dormant interests. As suggested above, whether such events promote a new path for interest development will likely depend on the extent to which people come to: (a) view themselves as efficacious at a new activity, and (b) see the activity as leading to valued outcomes. Unfortunately, many adults may experience narrowed vocational interests either because their environments have exposed them to a restricted range of efficacy-building experiences, or because of the manner in which they have cognitively processed the efficacy-building experiences that they have had (e.g., by attributing successes to external factors, such as task ease or luck). We will later describe two strategies that counselors can use to help clients identify and revisit career paths that may have been prematurely foreclosed on the basis of biased self-efficacy percepts or outcome expectations.

Aptitudes and Values

SCCT posits that aptitudes/abilities and values are also important to interest formation, but that their effects are largely funneled through self-efficacy and outcome expectations. That is, rather than determining interests directly, objective ability is seen as affecting self-efficacy beliefs which, in turn, influence interests (Lent et al., 1994). Work values, meanwhile, are incorporated within SCCT's concept of outcome expectations. Such expectations may be conceptualized as a combination of people's preferences for particular work conditions and reinforcers (e.g., status, money), which is how work values are often defined, together with personal beliefs about the extent to which these reinforcers are present in particular occupations.

Other Person and Contextual Variables

The social cognitive variables do not operate alone in shaping vocational interest, choice, and performance. Indeed, these variables are accompanied and affected by other important qualities of persons and their contexts, such as gender, race/ethnicity, genetic endowment, and socioeconomic status. Let us single out race and sex for special consideration. While they are often thought of as physical aspects of persons, SCCT is particularly concerned with the psychological and social effects of these factors. Their primary relevance to career development is seen as linked to the sort of reactions they evoke from the social/cultural environment — as well as from their relation to the opportunity structure that pervades career development. Thus, race and sex may be viewed as statuses that are socially conferred and constructed, transcending their mere biological properties. It has been argued that researchers distinguish between sex (a biological variable) and gender (a sociocultural construction involving the psychological ramifications of sex) (Unger, 1979). Similar distinctions may be made between race and ethnicity (see Casas, 1984).

Framing gender and ethnicity as socially constructed aspects of experience leads naturally to a consideration of socio-structural conditions that mold the learning opportunities to which particular individuals are exposed, the characteristic reactions (e.g., support, discouragement) they receive for performing different activities, and the future outcomes they anticipate. It is particularly important to consider how gender and ethnicity influence the contexts in which percepts about personal efficacy are acquired. Hackett and Betz (1981) have discussed the biasing effects of gender role socialization on boys' and girls' access to sources of information necessary for developing strong efficacy percepts in male-typed (e.g., science) versus female-typed (e.g., artwork) activities. As a result of this socialization, boys and girls are more likely to develop abilities and self-efficacy at tasks that are culturally defined as gender-appropriate.

In sum, the effects of gender and ethnicity on career interest, choice, and performance are seen as operating largely through self-efficacy and outcome expectations — or, more precisely, through the differential learning experiences that give rise to these beliefs. Gender and cultural factors are additionally linked to the opportunity structure within which career goals are framed and pursued; we will highlight this linkage within the context of SCCT's model of occupational choice behavior, below.

OCCUPATIONAL CHOICE

As in Holland's (1985) theory, SCCT assumes that, under supportive environmental conditions, people's vocational interests tend to orient them toward particular fields in which they might perform preferred activities and interact with others who are like themselves in important ways. Persons with social interests, for instance, are likely to gravitate toward socially-oriented occupations, allowing them to work with others in a helping or teaching capacity. However, it is apparent that people's career choices do not always reflect their interests (Williamson, 1939), and that their environments are not always supportive (Betz, 1989; Holland, 1985). There are many instances where choice may be constrained, for example, by economic need, family dictate, discrimination, or educational considerations. In such instances, career choice may be less an expression of personal interests than of other factors. SCCT, therefore, highlights the function of additional variables that influence the choice process, either apart from or in concert with interests.

As presented in our interest model, self-efficacy and outcome beliefs are seen as jointly promoting career-related interests. Interests foster corresponding career choice **goals** (e.g., intentions to pursue a given career path) which, in turn, motivate **actions** designed to implement one's goals (e.g., enrolling in a particular course of training). These actions are followed by a particular pattern of performance successes and failures. For instance, after deciding to enroll in a computer training program, a trainee may have difficulty mastering the requisite skills. This experience may prompt the trainee to revise his or her self-efficacy beliefs, leading to a change in goals (e.g., selection of a new training program or occupational option).

In addition to interests, choice behavior may be influenced directly by self-efficacy and outcome expectations (see Figure 2). That is, people are likely to adopt and implement particular career goals for which they view themselves to be efficacious and that they perceive as leading to desirable outcomes, such as adequate pay and working conditions. These additional paths help to explain occupational choice in instances where people must compromise their primary interests (Bandura, personal communication, March 1, 1993). In such cases, choice may be guided by such considerations as what work is available, whether the individual feels competent to perform it (self-efficacy), and whether the expected outcomes (e.g., pay) are worth the effort.

FIGURE 2
MODEL OF PERSON, CONTEXTUAL, AND EXPERIENTIAL FACTORS
AFFECTING CAREER-RELATED CHOICE BEHAVIOR

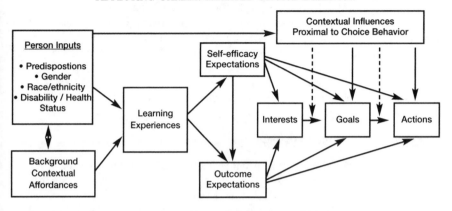

Copyright 1993 by R. W. Lent, S. D. Brown, and G. Hackett. Adapted by permission. Dashed lines indicate that contextual influences can moderate interest-goal and goal-action relations.

Contextual Influences on Choice Behavior

We believe that an adequate account of the choice process requires consideration of the ways in which people are able to exercise personal agency in their career development. Thus, SCCT highlights the role of personal goals in choice-making. By the same token, a satisfactory account of how choices are made must also reckon with those conditions that either support or hobble personal agency. In conceptualizing how environments affect the choice process, our model draws upon the constructs of "contextual affordance" (Vondracek et al., 1986) or "opportunity structure" (Astin, 1984), which emphasize the resources (or hardships) that environments provide with respect to individuals' career development. Our model divides contextual affordance/opportunity structure variables into two types, based on their relative proximity to career choice points: (a) more distal, background influences that precede and help shape interests and self-cognitions, and (b) proximal influences that come into play during the active phases of choice-making.

We had earlier discussed the more distal role of contextual variables in shaping the acquisition of self-efficacy and outcome expectations. Here we highlight the impact of contextual factors during the process of devising and implementing career choice goals. SCCT posits that certain features of the opportunity structure influence people's ability to translate their interests into career goals and their goals into actions. In particular, we hypothesize that people's career interests will be more likely to blossom into goals (and they will be more likely to act on their goals) when they experience beneficial environmental conditions (e.g., presence of ample support, few barriers) as opposed to non-supportive or hostile conditions. SCCT also recognizes the potent, direct influences that certain conditions exert on choice formation or implementation (e.g., discrimination in hiring, cultural practices wherein career choices are deferred to one's elders).

These aspects of SCCT's choice model suggest the importance of assisting adult clients both to negotiate career choice barriers, such as racism and sexism, and to marshal support for their career choices. Recent evidence suggests that the support that adolescents (McWhirter, Torres, & Rasheed, 1998) and adults (Richie et al., 1997) experience for their career plans can have a potent influence on their career aspirations and successes, in some cases helping to offset the effects of barriers. Proactive barrier-coping and social support-building interventions may be particularly helpful for those persons— such as women of color (Hackett & Byars, 1996) or individuals of lower socioeconomic status (Chartrand & Rose, 1996) — who are likely to encounter oppressive conditions in school, training, or work environments.

VOCATIONAL PERFORMANCE

SCCT is concerned with two primary aspects of performance: the level of attainment individuals achieve in their work tasks (e.g., measures of success or proficiency) and the degree to which they persist at a particular work activity or career path (e.g., perseverance at problem-solving, job stability), despite obstacles. Performance is seen as influenced by ability, self-efficacy, outcome expectations, and performance goals (see Figure 3). (The latter refer to the level of attainment toward which one aspires in a given work domain, such as striving for a particular level of sales performance.) Ability, as assessed by achievement, aptitude, or past performance indicators, is assumed to affect performance both directly and indirectly, through its effects on self-efficacy and outcome expectations. Self-efficacy and outcome expectations, in turn, affect the level of performance goals that people set for themselves. Higher self-efficacy and positive outcome beliefs promote higher goals, which help to mobilize and sustain performance efforts.

Consistent with Bandura's (1986) theory, SCCT posits a feedback loop between performance attainments and subsequent behavior. Mastery experiences promote development of abilities and, in turn, self-efficacy and outcome expectations in a dynamic cycle. As noted earlier, people also develop their abilities, self-efficacy, outcome expectations, and goals within a sociocultural context that is substantially affected by such factors as the structure of opportunity (e.g., economic status, educational access, social supports), gender role socialization, and community and family norms.

We should emphasize that self-efficacy is seen as providing an important complement to (but not a substitute for) ability. Complex performances require adequate capabilities as well as self-efficacy, which help people to organize and orchestrate their talents. Self-efficacy that is optimistic yet reasonably congruent with assessed competencies promotes effective performance behavior. Problems are likely to result, however, when individuals either do not possess sufficient ability to succeed at a given course of action or where they greatly misconstrue their efficacy. Underestimates of efficacy relative to documented ability diminish achievement behavior; where people doubt their competence they may give up more easily, set lower goals, suffer from debilitating performance anxiety, and avoid challenges of which they are capable. Serious overestimates of self-efficacy, on the other hand, may embolden people to attempt tasks for which they are ill-prepared, increasing the likelihood of failure and discouragement.

SCCT's analysis of performance behavior holds a number of implications for career and academic interventions. For example, efficacy-enhancing procedures, which will be discussed in a subsequent section, may be helpful for clients exhibiting vocational performance (or choice) problems who possess adequate skills but weak efficacy beliefs in a given performance domain. More extensive efforts, such as remedial skill-building, may be necessary in instances where performance problems are linked to both skill deficits and weak self-efficacy.

FIGURE 3
MODEL OF TASK PERFORMANCE, HIGHLIGHTING THE ROLES OF
ABILITY, SELF-EFFICACY, OUTCOME EXPECTATIONS, AND
PERFORMANCE GOALS

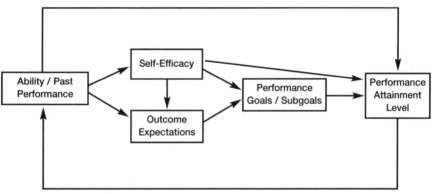

Copyright 1993 by R.W. Lent, S. D. Brown, and G. Hackett.
Reprinted by permission.

Selected Research Applications

Research relevant to, or stemming directly from, SCCT's hypotheses has grown at a rapid rate in recent years. While a comprehensive review of this literature is beyond the scope of the present chapter, we will summarize some of the major findings, paying particular attention to their implications for adult career development. A number of qualitative (e.g., Bandura, 1997; Hackett, 1995; Swanson & Gore, 2000) and quantitative (e.g., Lent et al., 1994; Sadri & Robertson, 1993; Stajkovic & Luthans, 1998) reviews may be consulted for a more in-depth analysis of research linking social cognitive theory to career development processes and outcomes.

There is now ample evidence indicating that social cognitive variables aid understanding of career behavior during the preparatory, transition (e.g., school-to-work, work change), and post-entry (work adjustment) phases of career development. For example, meta-analyses of research, primarily involving late adolescents and young adults, indicate that: (a) self-efficacy and outcome expectations are each good predictors of occupational interests and choices; (b) interests are strong predictors of career-related choices; and (c) self-efficacy and outcome expectations may impact career choice both directly and through their linkage to interests (refer to Figure 2) (Lent et al., 1994). Findings also provide support for the hypothesized experiential sources of self-efficacy. Of the four source variables (prior personal performance, vicarious learning, social persuasion, physiological and affective states and reactions), personal performance experiences typically show the strongest relation to self-efficacy, which is, in turn, a good predictor of outcome expectations. Such findings provide useful implications for the design of interventions designed to promote self-efficacy and outcome expectations.

The linkage of self-efficacy to future performance outcomes has been of particular concern to researchers wishing to understand the factors that promote optimal work performance. Meta-analyses have shown that self-efficacy is a useful predictor of performance in both academic (Multon, Brown, & Lent, 1991) and vocational (Stajkovic & Luthans, 1998) settings, and that certain factors affect the strength of self-efficacy's predictive utility. For instance, self-efficacy tends to be more strongly related to performance in older vs. younger students, and in low-achieving vs. adequately-achieving students (Multon et al., 1991), suggesting that self-efficacy-based interventions intended to promote performance may be particularly useful for late adolescents and young adults and for those who evidence achievement difficulties.

To this point, we have been discussing social cognitive research findings at the aggregate, or meta-analytic, level. However, it may also be useful to convey a flavor of the range of topics and populations that have been examined at the level of individual studies. We will, therefore, cite several noteworthy examples of social cognitive career research, primarily involving the career self-efficacy percepts of adult workers (see Bandura, 1997, for a more complete analysis of this literature).

One socially significant application of social cognitive theory has involved study of those who are either looking for initial employment or who have lost their jobs and must locate new work options. A number of researchers have examined the role of self-efficacy in the job search process. Saks and Ashforth (1999) found that self-efficacy regarding job search behaviors was associated with more active search efforts and successful employment outcomes in students making the transition from college to career. Other researchers have found that self-efficacy predicts successful reemployment following job loss (Kanfer & Hulin, 1985). Vinokur and his colleagues developed a preventive intervention for unemployed adults. They found that the program, which was effective at promoting reemployment (Caplan, Vinokur, Price, & van Ryn, 1989), worked, in part, by raising job search self-efficacy which, in turn, enhanced motivation and job search behavior (van Ryn & Vinokur, 1992).

Another large set of studies have focused on factors that promote adaptation to, and success in, different work settings and job roles. Examples of research in this category include studies linking self-efficacy to organizational socialization outcomes. Newcomers possessing strong self-efficacy beliefs regarding their work skills at organizational entry were found to cope better with situational demands and to perform their jobs more successfully than did those with lower self-efficacy. Training that offered mastery experiences, coworker modeling, and feedback — elements that reflect the sources of self-efficacy — was effective at promoting self-efficacy which, in turn, predicted later occupational success and satisfaction (Saks, 1994, 1995; Saks & Ashforth, 1997). The benefits of self-efficacy are not, however, limited to new employees. Among job incumbents, certain facets of self-efficacy have also been shown to be predictive of such career adjustment and well-being outcomes as job stress-coping (Chwalisz, Altmaier, & Russell, 1992), work attendance (Frayne & Latham, 1987), enrollment in training activities (Hill, Smith, & Mann, 1987), job satisfaction (Jex & Bliese, 1999), work productivity (Taylor, Locke, Lee, & Gist, 1984), and managerial decision-making (Wood & Bandura, 1989). Some of these (and other) studies have also confirmed the hypothesized roles of ability, goals, and other social cognitive variables as they operate in unison with self-efficacy to promote school/work adjustment or success outcomes.

In sum, the research literature offers support for a number of theoretical assumptions (from SCCT as well as from the larger social cognitive theory) regarding how self-efficacy and outcome expectations function in relation to career interests, choice, performance, and other career development outcomes. However, there is need for a great deal more research on such understudied topics as the role of contextual supports and barriers in the career choice process (Lent, Brown, & Hackett, 2000), and the effects of SCCT-based interventions on various aspects of school and work functioning. Despite the need for additional study, we believe the existing literature justifies efforts to translate SCCT into career interventions with adults. In the next section, we consider one such intervention aimed at counseling for career choice and change.

Using SCCT in Career Choice/Change Counseling

SCCT contains many useful implications for preventive, developmental, and remedial career development interventions. In this section we will show how basic hypotheses of the theory can be applied to one common class of problems experienced by adult clients, namely, difficulty in choosing and changing (or re-choosing) occupational options. We first highlight three basic tenets of SCCT that we consider to have important implications for practice. We then describe several counseling strategies (with case examples) that have the potential to help clients (a) generate a broad array of occupational possibilities that are as uncontaminated as possible by perceptual and cognitive distortions, (b) identify and overcome barriers to implementing preferred occupational choices, and (c) modify inaccurate self-efficacy beliefs so that optimum choices can be developed and implemented.

The basic hypotheses of our interest and choice models suggest three fundamental tenets that have important implications for the treatment of vocational choice difficulties. First, because SCCT suggests that occupational interests develop primarily from self-efficacy beliefs and outcome expectations — which may or may not match more objective indicators of abilities or reinforcers — some (perhaps many) clients enter counseling having already eliminated potentially rewarding occupational possibilities due to faulty self-efficacy beliefs or outcome expectations. Second, because SCCT posits that barriers moderate the relations between interests and occupational choices, clients may be less likely to translate their interests into choices if they perceive insurmountable barriers to implementing those choices. Third, because self-efficacy beliefs and outcome expectations are assumed to develop primarily from performance accomplishments, faulty self-efficacy percepts and outcome expectations may be modified by helping clients to acquire new success experiences, to review prior performance accomplishments, and to benefit cognitively from such experiences.

It may be useful to illustrate the psychological and economic implications of these self-efficacy, outcome expectation, and choice-barrier processes with an example. Some mathematically talented women show low interest in math and science-related occupations because their socialization experiences led them to acquire inaccurately low self-efficacy beliefs (e.g., Campbell & Hackett, 1986; Eccles, 1987; Hackett, Betz, O'Halloran, & Romac, 1990) or unfavorable outcome expectations (e.g., Eccles, 1987). And even mathematically-capable women, as we shall suggest in our case examples, may not express interest in occupations requiring a moderate level of mathematics sophistication if they inaccurately discount their capabilities. Moreover, even those who accurately gauge their efficacy at math tasks, and who perceive positive outcomes associated with careers involving math tasks, may not elect to pursue such careers if they perceive significant barriers to entry, success, or advancement.

According to the first tenet, then, some persons may prematurely eliminate potentially rewarding occupational pursuits because of inaccurate self-efficacy and/or outcome expectations. In such instances, we advocate helping clients to identify foreclosed possibilities and to develop more accurate perceptions of their occupational competencies and of potential outcomes. According to the second tenet, even persons with well developed and differentiated interests in a particular career path will be unlikely to pursue that path if they perceive (accurately or inaccurately) substantial barriers to entering or advancing in that career. In such cases, career choice counseling would profitably include helping clients to (a) identify barriers to choice implementation, (b) evaluate both the realism and surmountability of identified barriers, and (c) develop supportive networks that can facilitate their career plans or help them to overcome identified barriers. According to the third tenet, assistance in identifying foreclosed occupational paths and overcoming choice barriers should involve helping clients to acquire new experiences and to reprocess old experiences in such a way that faulty efficacy and outcome percepts may be counteracted. Although these tenets are not without precedent in the career literature, the theoretical context offered by SCCT may suggest new or redesigned counseling possibilities. We now describe several theory-derived strategies for assisting career clients to maximize their occupational options and to manage anticipated barriers to choice implementation.

IDENTIFYING FORECLOSED OCCUPATIONAL OPTIONS

Like most other approaches to career choice counseling, the social cognitive perspective is aimed at helping clients choose from an array of occupations that correspond with important aspects of their work personalities. We further believe that it is generally valuable to help clients construct the broadest possible array of occupational possibilities by enabling them to identify and consider further those career paths that they might have already eliminated on the basis of faulty self-efficacy percepts and/or outcome expectations. Thus, rather than simply generating occupational possibilities from expressed or measured interests (or other sources of information), we suggest that counselors also explore with clients those occupations that are of lower interest and analyze more fully the experiences and beliefs upon which these interests are based. Any options that seem to be based on inaccurately low self-efficacy beliefs or faulty occupational information could then be explored more fully with the client and, on the basis of this exploration, added to the other options that the client is considering.

The basic processes for facilitating interest exploration are, therefore, fairly straightforward and include assessing discrepancies between self-efficacy and demonstrated skill, and between outcome expectations and occupational information. Substantial discrepancies then become the target for further exploration. Up to this point, these straightforward processes have been limited by the dearth of available measures for assessing self-efficacy and outcome expectations in relation to a broad spectrum of occupations or work activities. However, this limitation has begun to abate with the recent introduction of innovative measures, like the Self-Confidence Inventory (Betz, Borgen, & Harmon, 1996), which are tied to established occupational classification systems.

Although more such measurement advances would aid application of SCCT to choice counseling, we have begun to pilot in our practices some strategies that do not require formal measurement devices but seem, at least anecdotally, to work well. The first strategy involves comparing discrepancies among scores obtained from standardized measures of aptitude, vocational need, and occupational interest. The second involves a modified vocational card sort procedure.

Analyzing discrepancies

It is widely recognized in career counseling that discrepancies among scores on different measures of a client's work personality provide important information for discussion and clarification (Dawis & Lofquist, 1984; Holland, 1985). We agree, and further hypothesize that discrepancies in scores on aptitudes/skills and interest measures suggest the operation of inaccurate self-efficacy beliefs, while score discrepancies on work-related needs/values and interest measures suggest the presence of faulty outcome expectations. For example, clients who obtain high scores on measures of occupationally-relevant aptitudes but express low interests in occupations requiring those aptitudes *may* be underestimating their self-efficacy and, therefore, foreclosing on potentially rewarding occupational options. Similarly, clients who express low interests in occupations that would seem to reinforce their major work-related needs and values *may* be basing their interest judgments on faulty outcome expectations — and thereby also prematurely narrowing their occupational options.

One approach that we have used to identify foreclosed occupational options begins by administering standardized measures of vocational interests, needs, and aptitudes. Using an occupational classification framework, we then compare the occupations generated by need and aptitude data to those generated from interest data. Occupations generated from need and aptitude indexes but not from interest assessments are considered to represent potentially foreclosed possibilities and are targeted for further discussion. As an example, consider the case of a 35-year old woman who entered counseling because of significant dissatisfaction with her job as a picture editor for a major publisher. The client, who had previously obtained a masters degree in art history, reported that her job was unchallenging and that it did not make adequate use of her abilities. Her testing results were quite dramatic from a social cognitive perspective. Her aptitudes and vocational needs were quite correspondent with, among other options, post-secondary teaching in a variety of socially-oriented fields, such as sociology, social sciences, psychology, and counseling. She had, however, responded to the interest measure with a large number of indifferent responses and, therefore, had a very flat and undifferentiated interest profile.

When these discrepancies were discussed with her, she indicated that she had earlier in her life considered these occupational possibilities but had failed to take them seriously because she did not believe she had the writing and quantitative skills necessary for success in such occupations. Her counselor pointed out that her aptitude data indicated that she did, indeed, seem to have the basic verbal and quantitative aptitudes required in these occupations, and that her general learning ability seemed correspondent with that required in college teaching. Further exploration of her past school performance identified rather well-developed writing skills that she seemed to discount because of her excessive performance standards. Her counselor helped her to reconsider these intimidating standards, and to gather additional data on her quantitative skills, for instance, by taking a college-level statistics course. She eventually chose to enter a doctoral program in urban sociology at a major university, where she performed well academically. She required several follow-up sessions with her counselor during her first year of doctoral study to work on her intimidating performance standards and to maintain her expectations of efficacy in her chosen career.

Modified card sort

Our second strategy for identifying foreclosed occupational possibilities is based on a modified vocational card sort procedure. Similar to standard card sort methods (Slaney & Mackinnon-Slaney, 1990), we first ask the client to sort occupations into three categories: (a) might choose, (b) would not choose, and (c) in question. The remainder of the procedure, however, focuses exclusively on those occupations that were sorted initially into the "would not choose" and "in question" categories. The client is encouraged to sort these occupations into more specific categories reflecting self-efficacy beliefs (i.e., "might choose if I thought I had the skills"), outcome expectations (i.e., "might choose if I thought it offered me things I value"), definite lack of interest (i.e., "wouldn't choose under any circumstance"), or other. Occupations sorted into the self-efficacy and outcome expectation subcategories are then explored for accuracy of skill and outcome perceptions; further testing or information-gathering may be employed for these purposes.

The use of this strategy to identify foreclosed occupational possibilities can be illustrated with another client, a 24-year old woman who expressed dissatisfaction in her occupation as a free-lance production assistant in the film industry, citing lack of security and advancement opportunities. She also indicated that her work lacked "social importance." The client completed our modified card sort procedure, initially sorting a variety of teaching options into the "Might Choose" category, though she sorted several teaching-related options involving supervision and leadership responsibilities (e.g., school principal, dean of students) into the "Would Not Choose" category. In subsequent sorting she placed all of the latter occupations into the subcategory reflecting low self-efficacy beliefs (i.e., "might choose if I thought I had the skills") because, as the ensuing discussion revealed, she did not believe she had (or could acquire) the leadership and influencing skills required in these occupations.

In order to gather additional data on her influencing and leadership skills, she was asked to complete the Skills section of the *Campbell Interests and Skills Survey* (CISS; Campbell, 1989), and to give the same inventory to three friends to complete it "as she should have completed it." Average raw scores on the CISS's seven primary orientations were calculated for both the client's responses and her friends' responses. A plot comparing her scores to a composite average of her friends' scores was shared with her. It revealed a substantial discrepancy between self- and other-ratings of her influencing skills. She was encouraged to discuss this finding with her friends. These discussions prompted the client to reevaluate her efficacy beliefs in her leadership and influencing skills, as well as her interest in leadership positions in education. She later decided to pursue a graduate degree in a department of educational leadership along with a teaching certificate, and she reported being satisfied with her choice.

ANALYZING BARRIER PERCEPTIONS

Our theoretical position holds that perceived barriers to choice attainment will moderate the relation of interests to choice goals, and goals to actions. Because barriers may, thus, compromise the ability of some clients to translate their primary occupational interests into choices (and to implement their choices), it may be important for counselors to help clients to identify, analyze, and prepare for possible career choice barriers. We have found it useful to adapt Janis and Mann's (1977) decisional balance sheet procedure to help our clients identify possible consequences, for themselves and their significant others, related to their preferred option(s). We then focus on those anticipated negative consequences that might serve as choice implementation barriers. The client is helped both to (a) consider the likelihood that each barrier will be encountered and (b) develop strategies to prevent or manage the most likely barriers.

To illustrate, consider again our 35-year old client. Using the balance sheet procedure, she generated one significant barrier to the pursuit of an academic career in urban sociology. Specifically, in considering the negative consequences that might follow from pursuing this career, she indicated that she was in a long-standing intimate relationship with a man who was self-employed in the local area. Because the area contained only one relevant graduate program, she feared that she might have to move elsewhere, thereby jeopardizing this relationship. She considered this to be a highly likely barrier to her moving forward with the sociology option. The counselor encouraged her to discuss this issue with her significant other in order to gather more data on its actual status as a barrier and to develop strategies for managing it. Together, the client and her partner concluded that it, indeed, represented a significant concern for both of them. They decided mutually that she would apply to graduate programs nationwide, but reserve the local program as her first choice. In the event that she was not accepted locally, her partner agreed to move with her. Although she was ultimately accepted at the local university, the prior discussions helped her to anticipate and prepare for an important potential barrier to implementing her preferred career choice.

MODIFYING SELF-EFFICACY BELIEFS

There are times when it may be valuable to attempt to modify clients' self-efficacy beliefs. Such a goal may be useful in career choice counseling, for example, to maximize clients' chances of succeeding at desired career options. As suggested earlier, it may also be a helpful part of counseling directed at enhancing or remediating clients' performance skills. SCCT and general social cognitive theory (Bandura, 1986) both point to perceived performance accomplishments as generally being the most potent source of information for altering self-efficacy beliefs. Thus, it may be valuable to assist clients in structuring new performance experiences (such as course work) in areas where *aptitude seems to be sufficient* but self-efficacy is low.

As we attempted to show in our case examples, there are also other methods at the counselor's disposal that can be used creatively to challenge faulty self-efficacy percepts. For example, clients can be asked to seek out information (e.g., how one's GRE scores correspond to those of graduate students in a foreclosed field) or gather data (e.g., friends' ratings of one's influencing abilities on a standardized inventory) that might counteract detrimental self-efficacy percepts. Additional testing could also be employed to challenge unrealistically low self-perceptions. In sum, provision of new performance experiences, reanalysis of past experiences, or gathering and presenting effective counter-attitudinal data can all be used to help the client counteract faulty self-efficacy percepts.

In addition, it is important that clients process efficacy-relevant data in ways that will have maximum impact on their self-efficacy beliefs. Success experiences (whether new or based on reviewing past performances) must be perceived as success experiences by the client if they are to boost his or her sense of efficacy. Persons, like our first client, who hold intimidating standards for performance are unlikely to credit themselves for accomplishments that are objectively excellent, but seem substandard when viewed through a distorting lens. Thus, counselors may need to help such clients construct developmentally appropriate performance standards and learn to reinforce themselves for developmental progress rather than ultimate performance. Many clients may also need to learn to attribute successful performance accomplishments to internal stable (i.e., ability) rather than to internal unstable (effort) or external (luck or task ease) causes.

To illustrate these methods, as our first client (the 35 year-old woman) began to take quantitative coursework, she tended to attribute her success to the effort she put into the course. Her counselor challenged these effort attributions by inviting her on several occasions to consider the possibility that she was more quantitatively skilled than she thought (an ability attribution). Follow-up sessions were devoted primarily to maintaining and further developing self-efficacy beliefs in areas critical to success in her chosen field, in fostering adaptive performance standards, and in setting realistic performance goals.

SCCT and Client Diversity

SCCT was explicitly designed to aid understanding of the career development of a wide range of students and workers, including persons who are diverse with respect to race/ethnicity, culture, gender, socioeconomic status, age, and disability status. It is, therefore, fitting that many of the research and practical applications of the theory have thus far reflected this focus on diversity and individual difference. In this section, we will overview some of these applications.

In the earliest work extending social cognitive theory to the career domain, Hackett and Betz (1981) demonstrated how the construct of self-efficacy might be used to explain certain aspects of women's career development. For instance, many women underutilize their career talents, gravitate toward traditionally-female fields, and avoid options that are male-dominated. Hackett and Betz posited that such occupational stereotyping may result from gender role socialization experiences in which both girls and boys tend to be encouraged by socialization agents (e.g., parents, teachers, peers) to pursue activities that are culturally defined as gender-appropriate, and to refrain from activities viewed as more appropriate for the opposite sex. Through differential access to the four sources of efficacy information (e.g., exposure to gender-traditional role models, lack of exposure to nontraditional ones), girls tend to develop self-efficacy beliefs, over time, that mirror these socialization biases.

Subsequent studies have tended to provide support for Hackett and Betz's theoretical analysis. For instance, women tend to report more self-efficacy for performing occupations that are traditionally held by women than for those that are male-dominated, though men report equally high self-efficacy for both traditionally male and female fields (Betz & Hackett, 1981). These differences in self-efficacy stand in contrast to the lack of differences between the male and female research participants in measured verbal and quantitative ability. This pattern of findings suggests that women's career pursuits can be constricted by the self-limiting effects of low self-efficacy. That is, environment-imposed barriers may become internalized in the form of biased self-efficacy beliefs, which may then supersede considerations of actual ability in the career choice process.

Related research has shown that self-efficacy beliefs mediate gender differences in scientific/technical field interests (e.g., Lapan, Boggs, & Morrill, 1989). Also, general samples of men and women tend to report self-efficacy differences relative to gender-typed tasks and fields (e.g., mathematics), though such self-efficacy differences are less likely to be manifest in samples of women and men who have had comparable efficacy-building experiences. Moreover, some evidence suggests that patterns of occupational sex stereotyping with respect to self-efficacy are less pronounced in younger cohorts (see Bandura, 1997; Hackett & Lent, 1992).

Collectively, the work discussed here highlights several social and cognitive mechanisms through which potential career paths can be stymied in women. The hopeful message is that such work also points to several developmental routes for redressing or preventing socially-imposed limitations on women's career development. However, as Bandura (1997) observed, apart from the role of self-efficacy beliefs in promoting gender differences in occupational pursuits, "cultural constraints, inequitable incentive systems, and truncated opportunity structures are also influential in shaping women's career development" (pp. 436). This caveat serves as a reminder that larger systemic issues, and not only self processes, require attention in the effort to foster women's career options.

Paralleling Hackett and Betz's (1981) earlier discussion of social cognitive factors affecting the career development of women in general, Hackett and Byars (1996) provided a theoretical analysis of the career development of persons of color, in particular, African American women. Hackett and Byars pointed to cultural learning experiences, mediated by the four sources of efficacy information (e.g., social encouragement to pursue certain options; exposure to racism; role modeling), that may differentially influence African American women's sense of career self-efficacy, outcome expectations, goals, and subsequent career progress. These authors offer a host of insightful, theory-based recommendations, including developmental interventions, social advocacy, and collective action, for promoting the career growth of African American women.

Other applications of SCCT to diverse client populations should be noted. Chartrand and Rose (1996) adapted the theory to a career intervention program for adult female prison inmates. Szymanski and Hershenson (1998) discussed how SCCT could be applied to persons with disabilities, noting that self-efficacy and outcome expectations are particularly useful constructs to consider in a vocational rehabilitation context. Likewise, Fabian (2000) considered how SCCT could be used to inform career interventions specifically for adults with mental illness. Morrow, Gore, and Campbell (1996) considered SCCT's potential in understanding the career development of lesbian women and gay men, noting how social-contextual influences can help shape self-efficacy and outcome expectations as well as the process through which interests are translated into choice. SCCT has also been extended to a number of cross-cultural or cross-national applications (e.g., de Bruin, 1999; Kantas, 1997; Nota & Soresi, 2000; Van Vianen, 1999).

We believe the applications mentioned in this section convey SCCT's potential utility in studying and facilitating the career development of a diverse range of adults. While such applications are exciting in their promise, they need to be accompanied by far more research that clarifies how various social cognitive variables (e.g., contextual supports and barriers, self-efficacy at managing the multiple demands of career and family roles), interface with culture, ethnicity, socioeconomic status, sexual orientation, and disability/health status to shape the career development trajectories of particular groups of adults.

Summary

We have provided a brief introduction to social cognitive career theory, an evolving framework that furthers earlier efforts to extend Bandura's (1986) general theory to career development phenomena. This framework highlights social cognitive variables that enable the exercise of personal agency, and incorporates the effects of other person and environmental factors (e.g., gender, ethnicity) on career development outcomes. Our theory-building effort is intended to help explain individual variability in career interest, choice, and performance. We believe that it also has useful implications for the design of developmental, preventive, and remedial career interventions. Accordingly, we illustrated how SCCT might be used in counseling aimed at career choice or change. We also overviewed the theory's research base and its applications to diverse groups of adult career clients.

References

Astin, H. S. (1984). The meaning of work in women's lives: A sociopsychological model of career choice and work behavior. *The Counseling Psychologist*, 12, 117-126.

Bandura, A. (1986). *Social foundations of thought and action: A social cognitive theory*. Englewood Cliffs, NJ: Prentice-Hall.

Bandura, A. (1997). *Self-efficacy: The exercise of control*. New York: Freeman.

Betz, N. E. (1989). Implications of the null environment hypothesis for women's career development and for counseling psychology. *The Counseling Psychologist*, 17, 136-144.

Betz, N. E. (1992). Counseling uses of career self-efficacy theory. *The Career Development Quarterly*, 41, 22-26.

Betz, N. E., Borgen, F. H., & Harmon, L. W. (1996). *Skills Confidence Inventory: Applications and technical guide.* Palo Alto, CA: Consulting Psychologists Press.

Betz, N. E., & Hackett, G. (1981). The relationship of career-related self-efficacy expectations to perceived career options in college women and men. *Journal of Counseling Psychology*, 28, 399-410.

Brown, S. D., & Lent, R. W. (1996). A social cognitive framework for career choice counseling. *The Career Development Quarterly*, 44, 354-366.

Campbell, D. (1989). *Manual for the Campbell Interest and Skill Survey.* Minneapolis, MN: National Computer Systems.

Campbell, N. K., & Hackett, G. (1986). The effects of mathematics task performance on math self-efficacy and task interest. *Journal of Vocational Behavior*, 28, 149-162.

Caplan, R. D., Vinokur, A. D., Price, R. H., & van Ryn, M. (1989). Job seeking, reemployment, and mental health: A randomized field experiment in coping with job loss. *Journal of Applied Psychology*, 74, 759-769.

Casas, J. M. (1984). Policy, training, and research in counseling psychology: The racial/ethnic minority perspective. In S. D. Brown & R. W. Lent (Eds.). *Handbook of counseling psychology* (pp. 785-831). New York: Wiley.

Chartrand, J. M., & Rose, M. L. (1996). Career interventions for at-risk populations: Incorporating social cognitive influences. *The Career Development Quarterly*, 44, 341-353.

Chwalisz, K. D., Altmaier, E. M., & Russell, D. W. (1992). Causal attributions, self-efficacy cognitions, and coping with stress. *Journal of Social and Clinical Psychology*, 11, 377-400.

Dawis, R. V., & Lofquist, L. H. (1984). *A psychological theory of work adjustment.* Minneapolis, MN: University of Minnesota Press.

de Bruin, G. P. (1999). Social cognitive career theory as an explanatory model for career counselling in South Africa. In G. B. Stead & M. B. Watson (Eds.), *Career psychology in the South African context.* Pretoria, South Africa: J. L. van Schaik.

Eccles, J. S. (1987). Gender roles and women's achievement. *Psychology of Women Quarterly*, 9, 15-19.

Fabian, E. S. (2000). Social cognitive theory of careers and individuals with serious mental health disorders: Implications for psychiatric rehabilitation programs. *Psychiatric Rehabilitation Journal*, 23, 262-269.

Frayne, C. A., & Latham, G. P. (1987). Application of social learning theory to employee self-management of attendance. *Journal of Applied Psychology*, 72, 387-392.

Hackett, G. (1995). Self-efficacy in career choice and development. In A. Bandura (Ed.), *Self-efficacy in changing societies.* Cambridge, UK: Cambridge University Press.

Hackett, G., & Betz, N. E. (1981). A self-efficacy approach to the career development of women. *Journal of Vocational Behavior*, 18, 326-336.

Hackett, G., Betz, N. E., O'Halloran, M. S., & Romac, D. S. (1990). Effects of verbal and mathematics task performance on task and career self-efficacy and interest. *Journal of Counseling Psychology*, 37, 169-177.

Hackett, G., & Byars, N. E. (1996). Social cognitive theory and the career development of African American women. *The Career Development Quarterly*, 44, 322-340.

Hackett, G., & Lent, R. W. (1992). Theoretical advances and current inquiry in career psychology. In S. D. Brown & R. W. Lent (Eds.), *Handbook of counseling psychology* (2nd ed., pp. 419-451). New York: Wiley.

Hansen, J. C. (1984). The measurement of vocational interests: Issues and future directions. In S. D. Brown & R. W. Lent (Eds.), *Handbook of counseling psychology* (pp. 99-136). New York: Wiley.

Hill, T., Smith, N. D., & Mann, M. F. (1987). Role of efficacy expectations in predicting the decision to use advanced technologies: The case of computers. *Journal of Applied Psychology, 72*, 307-313.

Holland, J. L. (1985). *Making vocational choices: A theory of vocational personalities and work environments* (2nd ed.). Englewood Cliffs, NJ: Prentice-Hall.

Janis, I. L., & Mann, L. (1977). *Decision making.* New York: Free Press.

Jex, S. M., & Bliese, P. D. (1999). Efficacy beliefs as a moderator of the impact of work-related stressors: A multilevel study. *Journal of Applied Psychology, 84*, 349-361.

Kanfer, R., & Hulin, C. L. (1985). Individual differences in successful job searches following lay-off. *Journal of Vocational Behavior, 38*, 835-847.

Kantas, A. (1997). Self-efficacy perceptions and outcome expectations in the prediction of occupational preferences. *Perceptual and Motor Skills, 84*, 259-266.

Lapan, R. T., Boggs, K. R., & Morrill, W. H. (1989). Self-efficacy as a mediator of Investigative and Realistic General Occupational Themes on the Strong-Campbell Interest Inventory. *Journal of Counseling Psychology, 36*, 176-182.

Lent, R. W., & Brown, S. D. (1996). Social cognitive approach to career development: An overview. *The Career Development Quarterly, 44*, 310-321.

Lent, R. W., Brown, S. D., & Hackett, G. (1994). Toward a unifying social cognitive theory of career and academic interest, choice, and performance [Monograph]. *Journal of Vocational Behavior, 45*, 79-122.

Lent, R. W., Brown, S. D., & Hackett, G. (2000). Contextual supports and barriers to career choice: A social cognitive analysis. *Journal of Counseling Psychology, 47*, 36-49.

Lent, R. W., & Hackett, G. (1994). Sociocognitive mechanisms of personal agency in career development: Pantheoretical prospects. In M. L. Savickas & R. W. Lent (Eds.), *Convergence in theories of career development: Implications for science and practice* (pp. 77-95). Palo Alto, CA: Consulting Psychologists Press.

McWhirter, E. H., Torres, D., & Rasheed, S. (1998). Assessing barriers to women's career adjustment. *Journal of Career Assessment, 6*, 449-479.

Morrow, S. L., Gore, P. A., & Campbell, B. W. (1996). The application of a sociocognitive framework to the career development of lesbian women and gay men. *Journal of Vocational Behavior, 48*, 136-148.

Multon, K. D., Brown, S. D., & Lent, R. W. (1991). *Journal of Counseling Psychology, 38*, 33-38.

Nota, L., & Soresi, S. (2000). *Autoefficacia nelle scelte: La visione sociocognitiva dell'orientamento.* Firenze, Italy: Institute for Training, Education, and Research.

Richie, B. S., Fassinger, R. E., Linn, S. G., Johnson, J., Prosser, J., & Robinson, S. (1997). Persistence, connection, and passion: A qualitative study of the career development of highly achieving African American-Black and White women. *Journal of Counseling Psychology, 44*, 133-148.

Sadri, G., & Robertson, I. T. (1993). Self-efficacy and work-related behaviour: A review and meta-analysis. *Applied Psychology: An International Review*, 42, 139-152.

Saks, A. M. (1994). Moderating effects of self-efficacy for the relationship between training method and anxiety and stress reactions of newcomers. *Journal of Organizational Behavior*, 15, 639-654.

Saks, A. M. (1995). Longitudinal field investigation of the moderating and mediating effects of self-efficacy on the relationship between training and newcomer adjustment. *Journal of Applied Psychology*, 80, 211-225.

Saks, A. M., & Ashforth, B. E. (1997). Organizational socialization: Making sense of the past and present as a prologue for the future. *Journal of Vocational Behavior*, 51, 234-279.

Saks, A. M., & Ashforth, B. E. (1999). Effects of individual differences and job search behaviors on the employment status of recent university graduates. *Journal of Vocational Behavior*, 54, 335-349.

Slaney, R. B., & Mackinnon-Slaney, F. (1990). The use of vocational card sorts in career counseling. In C. E. Watkins, Jr. & V. L. Campbell (Eds.), *Testing in counseling practice* (pp. 317-371). Hillsdale, NJ: Erlbaum.

Stajkovic, A. D., & Luthans, F. (1998). Self-efficacy and work-related performance: A meta-analysis. *Psychological Bulletin*, 124, 240-261.

Swanson, J. L., & Gore, P.A. (2000). Advances in vocational psychology theory and research. In S. D. Brown & R. W. Lent (Eds.), *Handbook of counseling psychology* (3rd ed., pp. 233-269). New York: Wiley.

Szymanski, E. M., & Hershenson, D. B. (1998). Career development of people with disabilities: An ecological model. In R. M. Parker & E. M. Szymanski (Eds.), *Rehabilitation counseling: Basics and beyond* (3rd ed., pp. 327-378). Austin, TX: Pro-Ed.

Taylor, M. S., Locke, E. A., Lee, C., & Gist, M. E. (1984). Type A behavior and faculty research productivity: What are the mechanisms? *Organizational Behavior and Human Performance*, 34, 402-418.

Unger, R. K. (1979). Toward a redefinition of sex and gender. *American Psychologist*, 34, 1085-1094.

van Ryn, M., & Vinokur, A. D. (1992). How did it work? An examination of the mechanisms through which an intervention for the unemployed promoted job-search behavior. *American Journal of Community Psychology*, 20, 577-597.

Van Vianen, A. E. M. (1999). Managerial self-efficacy, outcome expectations, and work-role salience as determinants of ambition for a managerial position. *Journal of Applied Social Psychology*, 29, 639-665.

Vondracek, F. W., Lerner, R. M., & Schulenberg, J. E. (1986). *Career development: A life-span developmental approach*. Hillsdale, NJ: Erlbaum.

Williamson, E. G. (1939). *How to counsel students*. New York: McGraw-Hill.

Wood, R. E., & Bandura, A. (1989). Social cognitive theory of organizational management. *Academy of Management Review*, 14, 361-384.

CHAPTER 6
Using A Cognitive Information Processing Approach in Career Counseling with Adults

Gary W. Peterson
Jill A. Lumsden
James P. Sampson Jr.
Robert C. Reardon
Janet G. Lenz
Florida State University

There is an old adage, "Give people a fish and they eat for a day, but teach them how to fish and they eat for a lifetime." This wise shibboleth succinctly captures the ultimate aim in using the cognitive information processing (CIP) approach to career counseling; that is, to enable individuals to become skillful career problem solvers and decision makers. We believe that by taking a career problem of the moment through the CIP approach, individuals not only learn how to solve the problem at hand, but to generalize this experience to future career problems when such incidents inevitably arise. Although this theoretical frame of reference has been described in earlier writings (Peterson, Sampson, Reardon, 1991; Peterson, Sampson, Reardon, & Lenz, 1996; Reardon, Lenz, Sampson, & Peterson, 2000; Sampson, Peterson, Lenz, & Reardon, 1992; Sampson, Peterson, Reardon, & Lenz, 2000), a discussion of how it specifically applies to counseling with adults has not yet been undertaken. For the purposes of this chapter, we refer to an adult as anyone who is beyond the post-adolescent years and who possesses sufficient autonomy so as to no longer rely on parental support for the basic necessities of life. Adults are typically in committed relationships and often involved in family responsibilities and property ownership.

We begin this chapter with a brief review of the basic tenants of CIP theory. We then discuss ways to apply CIP theory to help career counselors understand the problems and learning needs of adult clients, choose career assessments, and provide learning experiences to facilitate the development of a client's career problem-solving and decision-making skills. We conclude with describing the case of Evelyn to demonstrate how CIP theory can be used to assist adults in making satisfying career decisions.

Background of Cognitive Information Processing Theory

The historical antecedents of cognitive information processing (CIP) theory may extend back to the early 20th century when Parsons (1909) declared there were three key factors involved in making career choices:

1. A clear self understanding,
2. Knowledge of occupations, and
3. The ability to draw relationships between them.

He speculated that if individuals possessed these three capabilities, they would not only be more likely to make appropriate career choices, but that society would be served as well through better person-job matches, thereby resulting in greater productivity.

Parson's three factors have led to three distinct paths of inquiry:

1. The pursuit of measuring personality traits and factors,
2. The development of taxonomies of occupations, and
3. The advancement of theories of career problem solving and decision making.

For example, modern interest appraisals such as the *Self-Directed Search* (SDS; Holland, 1994), the *Strong Interest Inventory* (SII; Consulting Psychologists Press, 1994), human abilities tests such as the *Inventory of Work-Related Abilities* (American College Testing, 1998), and values inventories such as the *Values Scale* (Super & Nevill, 1986) may be traced to the initial formulations of the Minnesota Group in the late 1930s (Patterson & Darley, 1936; Williamson, 1939). The development of occupational classification systems such as the *Dictionary of Occupational Titles* (U.S. Department of Labor, Employment Service, 1977), *Dictionary of Holland Occupational Codes* (Gottfredson & Holland, 1996), and the *O*NET* (U.S. Department of Labor and the National O*NET Consortium, 1999) have enabled individuals to systematically acquire knowledge about the world of work. The development of career problem-solving and decision-making theories may be traced to decision models advanced by Gelatt (1962), Katz (1963, 1969), Miller-Tiedeman and Tiedeman (1990), and Janis and Mann (1977). These models can be subsumed under an over-arching five-step sequence:

1. Define the problem.
2. Understand its causes.
3. Formulate plausible solutions.
4. Prioritize the alternatives and arrive at a first choice.
5. Implement the solution and evaluate the outcomes.

All three of these forces became integral components in the CIP model.

The Cognitive Information Processing Theory in Career Choice

In the early 1970s, a line of inquiry emerged from the field of cognitive science that offered a new way of thinking about career choice and decision making. This paradigm, referred to as *cognitive information processing* (CIP), was initially formulated in the works of Hunt (1971), Newell and Simon (1972), and Lackman, Lackman, and Butterfield (1979). This paradigm provides a way to describe the fundamental memory structures and thought processes involved in solving career problems and making career decisions. With this knowledge, we can now ask, "What can we do as career counselors to enable adults to enhance their skills as career problem solvers and decision makers?" Theorizing about career choice and career development requires a theory about the nature of theories themselves. Here, we refer to both the structure and content of any psychological theory (Slife & Williams, 1997).

Psychological theories may be thought of as being comprised of four fundamental attributes: 1) definitions, 2) assumptions and propositions, 3) operations, and 4) implications for practice, (Hall & Lindzey, 1978). The definitions, assumptions and operations on which the CIP model is based follow while implications for practice are presented through the use of a case study later in the chapter.

DEFINITIONS

The following definitions may be visualized in terms of a series of concentric rings from the smallest inner circle, a career problem, to the problem space, to career problem solving, to career decision making, to ultimately career development with each succeeding concept encompassing the previous concept.

Career problem. A *gap* between an existing state of career indecision and a more desired state. The gap creates cognitive dissonance (Festinger, 1964) that becomes the primary motivational source driving the problem solving process. The gap results in a tension or discomfort that individuals seek to eliminate.

Problem space. All cognitive and affective components contained in working memory as individuals approach a career problem-solving task (Peterson, 1998; Sinott, 1989). In adults, the problem space entails the career problem at hand in addition to all the issues associated with it, such as marital and family relationships, financial considerations, and prior life experiences, as well as the emotional states embedded in them.

Career problem solving. A complex set of thought processes involved in the acknowledgement of a gap, an analysis of its causes, the formulation and clarification of alternative courses of actions, and the selecting of one of these alternatives to reduce the gap. A career problem is solved when a career choice is made from among the alternatives.

Career decision making. A process that not only encompasses career choice, but also entails a commitment to and the carrying out of the actions necessary to implement the choice.

Career development. The implementation of a series of career decisions that comprise an integrated career path throughout the life span.

ASSUMPTIONS

The following are key assumptions on which the application of CIP to adult populations is based.

- Career problem solving in adulthood is a complex, ambiguous cognitive activity. Unlike solving ordinary classroom mathematics, physics, or chemistry problems, the stimulus is ambiguous, the solution requires an optimization of alternatives, and the correctness of a choice can be uncertain.
- One's capability as a career problem solver depends on the ability to access knowledge components and cognitive skill components stored in long-term memory (LTM). Successful career problem solving depends on the extent of one's self-knowledge and one's knowledge of occupations, as well as a

storehouse of cognitive operations one can use to derive relationships between the two knowledge domains.

- Career development involves the continual growth and change in knowledge structures. Self-knowledge and occupational knowledge structures consist of networks of inter-connected knowledge domains called *schemata* that evolve over the life span. Because both the occupational world and individuals are ever changing, the need to develop and integrate these domains never ceases.

- The goal of career counseling is to facilitate the development of information processing skills. From a CIP perspective, career counseling involves providing the conditions of learning that enhance the acquisition of self-knowledge and occupational knowledge and the development of cognitive problem-solving and decision-making skills that are necessary to transform information into satisfying and meaningful career decisions.

OPERATIONS

Two fundamental learning processes form the cornerstones of CIP: 1) the development of self-knowledge and occupational knowledge structures that form the contents that undergird career problem solving and decision making, and 2) the development information transformation processes that take one from the recognition of a career problem to the implementation of a decision to rectify it.

Structural Components of CIP: The Pyramid of Information Processing

In order for individuals to become independent and responsible career problem solvers and decision makers, certain information processing capabilities must undergo continual development throughout the life span. From an adaptation of the works of Robert Sternberg (1980,1985), these capabilities may be envisioned as forming a pyramid of information processing domains with three hierarchically arranged domains (See Figure 1). The knowledge domain lies at the base, the decision-making skills domain comprises the mid level, while the executive processing domain is at the apex.

FIGURE 1
PYRAMID OF INFORMATION PROCESSING DOMAINS
IN CAREER DECISION MAKING

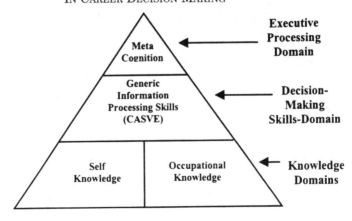

The knowledge bases. Two knowledge domains, self-knowledge and occupational knowledge, lie at the base of the pyramid. *Self-knowledge* includes knowledge about one's interests, abilities, skills and values based on an on-going construction of one's life's experiences. *Occupational knowledge* consists of one's own unique structural representation of the world of work, as well as an understanding of individual occupations in terms of their duties and responsibilities as well as their education and training requirements to attain them (Peterson, 1998).

The mid-level processing components. The decision-making skills domain involves generic information processing skills that combine occupational knowledge and self knowledge to solve a career problem and to make a decision. A 5-step recursive information transformation process (See Figure 2), the CASVE Cycle (pronounced "ca- Sah-veh), is used as a heuristic to frame the career counseling process as follows.

1. *Communication* (**C**). Information is received and encoded which signals that a problem exists. One then queries oneself and the environment to formulate the gap (or discontinuity) that is the problem. It also entails getting "in touch" with all components of the problem space including thoughts, feelings, and related life circumstances.

2. *Analysis* (**A**). The causes of the problem are identified and the relationships among problem components are placed in a conceptual framework or mental model.

3. *Synthesis* (**S**). Possible courses of action are formulated through the creation of possibilities (synthesis elaboration) and then narrowed (synthesis crystallization) to a manageable set of viable alternatives.

4. *Valuing* (**V**). Each course of action or alternative is evaluated and prioritized according to its likelihood of success in removing the gap and its probable impact on self, significant others, cultural group, and society. Through this process a first choice emerges and the career problem is solved.

5. *Execution* (**E**). An action plan is formulated to implement the choice, which becomes a goal for the client. A series of milestones are laid out in the form of means-ends relationship that will lead step by step to the attainment of the goal. Thus, a career decision is made when individuals move deliberately toward a goal, such as enrolling in a training program or taking a job in a chosen occupational field.

6. Upon executing the plan, there is a return to the Communication phase of the cycle to evaluate whether the decision successfully removed the gap. If so, the individual moves on to solve succeeding problems that arise from the implementation of the solution. If not, one recycles through the CASVE cycle with new information about the problem, one's self and occupations acquired from the initial pass through the CASVE cycle.

FIGURE 2

THE FIVE STAGES OF THE CASVE

(COMMUNICATION, ANALYSIS, SYNTHESIS, VALUING, EXECUTION)

CYCLE OF INFORMATION PROCESSING SKILLS USED IN CAREER DECISION MAKING

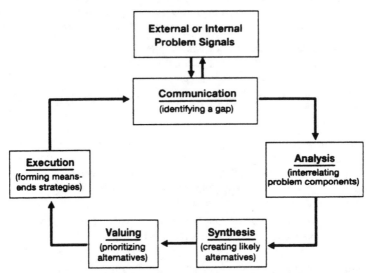

The Apex. The apex of the pyramid, the executive processing domain, contains metacognitive components that guide and regulate the lower order functions. We describe this domain as "thinking about thinking," which entails the ability to view one's self as a career problem solver from a detached perspective. The domain involves metacognitive components (Flavel, 1979) that (a) control the selection and sequencing of cognitive strategies to achieve a goal, and (b) monitor the execution of a given problem-solving strategy to determine if a goal has been reached. The domain also consists of one's own beliefs, assumptions, and thoughts about the activity of career problem solving itself. Positive beliefs or thoughts facilitate the career problem solving process while dysfunctional career thoughts pertaining to any facet of the respective domains will inhibit or arrest the career problem-solving and decision-making process (Sampson, Peterson, Lenz, Reardon, & Saunders, 1996a).

We turn now to applying the CIP theory of career choice to the adult experience. Specifically, we ask the question, "How can we, as career counselors, help adults enhance their career problem-solving and decision-making skills through career counseling?"

The Nature of Adult Career Problems

An initial consideration in the application of the CIP model in career counseling with adults is acquiring an understanding of important factors in the life context associated with the career problem (Cochran, 1994; Peterson, Sampson, Lenz, & Reardon, 1999; Spokane, 1991). Such factors must be taken into account in administering assessments or undertaking learning experiences to enhance career problem solving and decision-making skills. The following three factors are not exhaustive of factors that may bear on career counseling with adults, but they do represent ones that occur over and over again.

Urgency. Adults often differ from adolescents with respect to the limited amount of time, in which to learn career problem-solving skills and to make a career decision. For adolescents, the process of learning career problem solving skills can take years. A high school junior can take several years to choose a career field in the form of a college major. A college sophomore can take a full semester to explore the choice of major prior to declaring a major in the junior year. However, adults who are in a transition from one job to the next may have only days in which to make a decision and secure employment, otherwise they may encumber financial debts. In CIP terms, adult career clients may feel pressured to traverse the stages of the CASVE cycle as quickly as possible.

Complexity. The career problems of adults often emanate out of highly complex lives (Sampson et al., 2000). The career problem space often includes personal issues related to committed intimate relationships (or the desire to have one), children and family responsibilities, the ownership of property, insurance and financial investments, community and spiritual involvement, leisure pursuits, and an existing job. In addition, the problem space may include issues related to getting along in the workplace, economic conditions, and cultural influences. All of these aspects of adult life, inter-related with the specific career issue, directly influence how a client engages the respective stages of the CASVE cycle in arriving at a solution to a career problem in the Valuing phase and implementing it in the Execution phase.

Capability. Third, there is a term in chaos theory (Gleick, 1988), *sensitivity to initial conditions,* commonly referred to as the butterfly effect, which connotes that small differences in the beginning diverge and become greater and greater as time progresses. In applying chaos theory to career counseling (Peterson & Krumboltz, 1997), we as career counselors often observe the inexorable and powerful effects of prior learning, family background, and personality factors acquired early in life, on both the career counseling process as well as its outcomes. Thus, there are broad individual differences in terms of the extent to which adult clients bring prior learning experiences and general problem-solving abilities to the career decision-making process. Moreover, clients vary in terms of aptitudes for further education and training, attitudes toward risk taking, self-esteem or self-efficacy, family support and values, and thoughts, beliefs and assumptions about the world of work. All of these factors contribute to an adult client's capability for career problem solving and decision making.

Upon gaining an understanding of the life context through an appraisal of a client's states of urgency, complexity, and capability, a career counselor is now ready to identify a client's learning needs through assessment procedures grounded in CIP theory.

The Assessment of Adult Learning Needs

The important assessment question from a CIP perspective is, "What do adults need to learn through career counseling to enhance their career problem-solving and decision-making skills so as to become independent problem solvers and decision makers?" The Pyramid and the CASVE Cycle serve as heuristics for the identification of adult learning needs.

ASSESSING READINESS FOR CAREER COUNSELING

Readiness, in CIP theory, alludes to the ability of a client to acquire self-knowledge and occupational knowledge and to use this information to solve a career problem and to make a career decision (Sampson et al., 2000). Some clients come to career counseling centers in high states of readiness with well-formulated career questions and have few related stress factors in the problem space. Others are in low states of readiness with severe states of anxiety, depression, and confusion and require considerable professional assistance to help them manage the complexities of their career problem and related issues in the career problem space (Saunders, Peterson, Sampson, & Reardon, 2000). Yet others may be limited in their ability to consider plausible career options and opportunities because of dysfunctional career thoughts (Hill & Peterson, 2001). Thus, not all clients are prepared to immediately engage the career problem solving process—they may require intensive personal assistance from a career counselor to manage factors in the problem space that impede learning before they are able to begin.

The assessment of readiness may be accomplished through the integration of information gathered from a self-report measure followed by a client interview. A useful readiness measure for adults, based on CIP theory, is the *Career Thoughts Inventory* (CTI; Sampson et al., 1996a). The CTI assesses the level of client's dysfunctional thinking through three principal construct scales, Decision Making Confusion (DMC), Commitment Anxiety (CA), and External Conflict (EC). Scale scores along with responses to individual items enable a career counselor to identify and locate blocks in the Pyramid or in the CASVE cycle that impede career problem solving and decision making. A follow-up interview then identifies historical and present life circumstances that underlie the blocks. The extent of debilitating emotional states such as anxiety and depression can also be ascertained.

On the basis of the readiness assessment, clients may be assigned to one of three levels of career service, self-help, brief staff-assisted, and individual case-managed (Sampson et al., 2000). Clients determined to be in a high state of readiness (i.e., low complexity, and high capability) progress directly to the formulation of counseling objectives and learning activities to attain them. They will typically engage in self-help or brief staff-assisted modes of utilization of career services. Clients who are assessed to be in a moderate state of readiness (e.g., moderate complexity, and moderate capability) often require brief-staff assisted and sometimes individual case-managed career services to clarify career and personal issues and to use appropriate career services. On the other hand, clients in a low state of readiness (e.g., high urgency, high complexity, and moderate capability) will most likely be assigned directly to individual case-managed career services including a series of private individual counseling sessions and the removing the blocks through the use of the *Career Thoughts Inventory Workbook* (Sampson, Peterson, Lenz, Reardon, & Saunders, 1996b). In severe cases in which there are strong emotional states that impair higher order cognitive functioning or complex personal issues related to the career problem, clients are often advised to seek psychiatric evaluation or conjoint mental health counseling.

Assessing Career Problem-Solving Skills

At this stage in the assessment process we ask, "Which domains of the Pyramid require further development in order to be able to solve the career problem at hand?" Domain assessments may be as follows:

Self-knowledge. The assessment of self-knowledge is often a confirmatory process in which interest inventories, such as the *Self-Directed Search* (Holland, 1994), allow clients to clarify and reaffirm their interests. Computer-assisted career guidance (CACG) systems, card sorts (values, interests, skills), and autobiographical sketches may also be useful.

Occupational knowledge. Occupational knowledge may be assessed through traditional vocational card sorts (Tyler, 1961; Slaney, Moran, & Wade, 1994) or through using a card sort as a cognitive mapping task (Peterson, 1998). Through the use of a think-aloud procedure, clients reveal their knowledge about occupations as they sort the cards into "Like", "Dislike", or "Maybe" piles. In a cognitive mapping task, clients reveal a schema of the world of work by sorting cards into piles of related occupations and then identifying the pile "Most like me."

Decision making skills. The *Career Thoughts Inventory* (CTI; Sampson et al., 1996a) may be used to identify specific phases in the CASVE Cycle in which a client is experiencing blocks in the career problem solving process brought about by dysfunctional career thoughts. The Decision Making Confusion (DMC) scale reveals dysfunction in the Communication, Analysis, and Synthesis phases which entail the derivation of career alternatives; the Commitment Anxiety (CA) scale alludes to the transition from arriving at a solution to the career problem in the Valuing phase to a commitment to action in the Execution phase; and the External Conflict (EC) scale addresses the Valuing phase in which clients weigh the importance of their views in relation to the views of significant others.

Additionally, through the interview process, a career counselor may inquire about how a client has successfully solved career problems in the past and has made ensuing decisions. Themes and patterns may emerge that provide an indication of the level of skill employed in the career decision process as well as the extent to which there may be reoccurring constraints or barriers in the process. Further, a counselor may gain a sense of a client's approach to career problem solving by asking the client to recall several episodes of how they went about solving a career problem in which they were pleased with the outcome, and then recall episodes in which the client was not pleased. The client then explores the potential causes of the different outcomes. This assessment method is referred to as the critical incident method (Flanagan, 1954).

Executive processing. Dysfunctional thoughts in this domain may also be assessed through responses to individual items on the Executive Processing content scale of the CTI. In addition, during interviews with a client, a career counselor may listen carefully for instances of negative self-talk, ineffective cognitive strategies, and lack of control in staying focused on the task at hand. A counselor may also listen for the capacity for self-detachment and for being aware of one's self as a career problem solver.

The outcome of the assessment process is having prepared a client for initiating the career problem solving process (if needed) and having determined the domains of the Pyramid in which new knowledge or skills must be learned to solve the career problem at hand. The gaps between the existing state and required state of mastery in the respective domains are reformulated to become the objectives of counseling. The objectives of counseling and the learning activities to attain them comprise the individualized learning plan (ILP; Peterson et al, 1996).

Helping Adults Acquire Career Problem Solving and Decision Making Skills

Here, we ask the question, "What are interventions and special considerations that must be made with adults to facilitate the acquisition of self-knowledge, occupational knowledge, and career problem solving and decision-making skills?" To address this question, we again return to the Pyramid and the CASVE cycle.

Acquiring self-knowledge. Adults bring with them a wealth of personal experiences not only about the world of work, but about relationships, leisure pursuits and spiritual commitments. These experiences are stored in the form of episodes or stories (Tulving, 1984). From the on-going reconstruction of life experiences (Neisser, 1981), individuals acquire perceptions of their interests, abilities, skills, values, attitudes, beliefs, and a philosophy of life. In career counseling, when discussing career options, adults are able to tell stories about both direct experiences with a potential alternative as well as indirect experiences in the form of "I know someone who...." Thus the writing of a 5-page autobiography often provides a way to help clients organize their life experiences and to observe emergent patterns of how they respond to changes in work and family.

Additionally, the use of interest inventories, values inventories, and ability and skills assessments typically affirm and clarify the elements of the self-knowledge domain. When counseling adults, because of time demands (i.e., urgency), clients may prefer to use inventories that require little time to complete, ones that they can take home between sessions, or measures they can complete on-line via the internet (Sampson, 1999).

Acquiring occupational knowledge. Adults are likely to bring with them to career counseling a mature representation of the world of work (Peterson, 1998). In a vocational card sort mapping task, they are typically able to sort cards into coherent cognitive structures we refer to as schemata. Often, adults are also able to demonstrate considerable knowledge about individual occupations as well as capabilities for clearly differentiating between and among them. Thus, in career counseling, adults are apt to continue the processes of *schema specialization* (Rummelhart & Ortony, 1976) in which they are able to make finer discriminations (Neimeyer, 1988) among occupations because of prior learning. They also engage in *schema generalization* in which they form more extensive networks of connections among extant occupational knowledge structures. In other words, in career counseling, adults with broad backgrounds of life experiences and work histories continue to perfect the occupational knowledge structures they already possess.

When career counseling takes place within comprehensive career centers, the acquisition of occupational knowledge may be facilitated through the use of a variety of media. Print materials in the form of occupational briefs, vocational biographies, reference books, and special topics books are an efficient means to acquire factual knowledge about occupations. Interactive media can be used to enable clients to project themselves into an occupational environment and experience indirectly.

Internet web sites enable clients to access occupational information in the career center or at home. Reality testing through job shadowing or interviews with incumbents allows clients to experience occupations even more directly. Again, when counseling adults, brevity and convenience are important characteristics to keep in mind when formulating learning experiences to facilitate the acquisition of occupational knowledge.

Acquiring career problem solving and decision making skills. It is quite likely that adults have already made very important career decisions in their lifetimes. They may even have acquired their own method for approaching the career problem-solving task. Some may approach the career problem solving in a methodical, linear fashion while others may go about it in more circuitous ways. To be successful, a career counselor must be able to assess an adult's preferred approach and to integrate the approach into the CASVE Cycle framework. We have found the CIP model to be sufficiently flexible and adaptable so as to serve as a useful learning heuristic for the vast majority of adult clients.

In mastering career problem-solving and decision-making skills, the content or substance of learning involves both declarative knowledge (i.e., what) and procedural knowledge (i.e., how). The concept of the Pyramid of Information Processing Domains is presented directly to clients in the form of a handout, "What's Involved in Career Choice" (See Figure 3). The concepts of Communication, Analysis, Synthesis, Valuing, and Execution, as well as the cyclical relationship among these concepts, are learned through presenting a visual representation in the form of a handout with a figure depicting the CASVE Cycle with easy-to-grasp statements describing each stage (See Figure 4). Then, through subsequent considerations of activities included in the ILP, clients begin to accommodate (Piaget, 1977) their own decision-making style to the CIP model. The counselor provides encouragement and operant reinforcement as clients allude to the model in their own thought processes. At the termination of counseling, the counselor reviews the decision-making process undertaken and demonstrates how the CIP model can be used in future career problem situations. This process we refer to as *generalization of learning.*

FIGURE 3
PYRAMID OF INFORMATION PROCESSING
DOMAINS: CLIENT VERSION
WHAT'S INVOLVED IN CAREER CHOICE

FIGURE 4
CLIENT CASVE CYCLE
A GUIDE TO GOOD DECISION MAKING

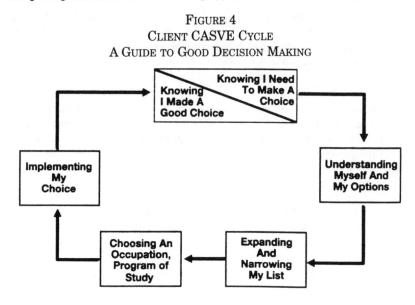

Acquiring metacognitive skills in the Executive Processing Domain. Adult clients approach the career problem-solving task with a wide range of attitudes about their capabilities for engaging in career problem solving. Some may approach the task with a great deal of confidence and have high expectations, while others may be cautious, lacking confidence, or even cynical. Some may want to engage in self-examination by taking interest inventories and engaging in a counseling process, while others merely want to be shown a list of available job openings to which they may apply. Some may believe the world of work holds boundless opportunities for wealth and self-fulfillment while others view it as threatening and hostile. To engage in successful career problem solving and decision making, a career counselor should become aware of such attitudes and how they may facilitate or interfere with the process, since dysfunctional career thoughts (Sampson et al., 1996a) or irrational beliefs (Krumboltz, 1991) are likely to set the process up for failure from the outset. The use of the *Career Thoughts Inventory* (CTI) is especially important in identifying impediments to career problem solving residing in this domain.

When dysfunctional or negative thoughts have been identified in the assessment process, clients learn how to change their dysfunctional, or negative career thoughts using the ICAA algorithm (Identify, Challenge, Alter, and Act). *The CTI Workbook* (Sampson et al., 1996b) takes clients step-by-step through a cognitive restructuring process (Meichebaum, 1977; Beck, 1976). Clients are then directed to transfer their learning from the workbook to everyday life through homework assignments in which they regularly rehearse and practice engaging new thoughts in the presence of old negative thought-inducing stimuli (Sampson et al). Clients also learn how to self-monitor their progress through the CASVE Cycle. The importance of attending to the Executive Processing Domain cannot be over emphasized. In applying the CIP model to counseling adults, we have often found that it is the primary source of the blockage to solving the career problem, and once it is cleared up, the solution and decision immediately follow with little additional assistance from a career counselor.

We now turn to the case of Evelyn (pseudonym) to demonstrate how the CIP model, with the Pyramid and CASVE Cycle, was used in career counseling to help her to make a satisfying career decision through the development of her career problem-solving and decision-making skills. A 7-step career service delivery sequence (Peterson et al., 1991; 1996) is used to frame the presentation.

THE CASE OF EVELYN

Evelyn is a 49-year old divorced white female who came to a comprehensive career center to find a more satisfying occupation. She is presently an Account Executive in an insurance firm of 35 employees in a medium-sized community of 250,000 people. This career center has a front desk in a large open area where a career advisor greets the client and conducts a brief initial interview typically lasting no more than 5-10 minutes. Behind the reception desk, there are large working tables for clients to read, to complete inventories, or to talk with career advisors. There are also individual counseling offices and a computer room equipped with computer-assisted career guidance (CACG) systems.

1. **Initial Interview.** Upon greeting the career advisor at the reception desk, Evelyn, speaking about her present job as an Account Executive, revealed that, like all previous positions she has held, she was able to master her duties in a short span of time, no more than a couple of years. She stated that her present job offers job security, good benefits, and a salary sufficient to meet her needs, she has grown tired and bored of the job and no longer finds it meaningful or satisfying. Although she is unable to state explicitly what she is searching for, she believes she can find more fulfilling work.

2. **Preliminary Assessment.** Because Evelyn was not looking for specific information and was in a state of indecision, the career advisor at the front desk suggested that she schedule an individual counseling session to more fully examine factors related to her career problem. Although her verbal expressions were clear and coherent, her voice sounded bland and unemotional, thus suggesting a depressed mood state. Evelyn made an appointment to see a career counselor. She was also assigned to take the *Career Thoughts Inventory* (CTI) prior to attending the scheduled counseling session.

3. **Define the Problem and Explore the Problem Space.** Evelyn is presently experiencing a gap between where she is (i.e., a job that she finds boring, routine, and unfulfilling), and where she wants to be (i.e., in a job that is more satisfying). Thus, she is in a state of indecision and wishes to attain a state of decidedness. This cognitive dissonance between the existing state and desired state provides the motivation to engage in the career problem-solving and decision-making processes.

Early in the scheduled counseling session, Evelyn revealed that she has held steady employment for 27 years. She began her career path earning a Masters Degree in Education and worked for over a decade as a High School English Teacher. Growing bored with the routines of teaching, she became a successful Real Estate Broker in the local area for several years. Then, seeking to combine her business knowledge with her interest in schooling, she became an Educational Technology Consultant. This job provided an opportunity to travel, which she found exciting for a while. Evelyn then said she became tired of the fast-paced life style associated with this position and sought a more stable life in the community. She has no children.

Evelyn also revealed additional important elements in the problem space. Three years ago, Evelyn obtained a divorce from her husband after 25 years of marriage, which she explained was an emotionally traumatic experience. During the first year after the divorce, she totally immersed herself in the job she presently holds, forgoing any social life. During the past year, she has made a concerted effort to expand her social life. She stated she has always had close friends, but now is seeking more involvement with them. Evelyn, while owning a home, is able to pay her monthly bills and she possesses a limited amount of debt. Thus, elements in the problem space revealed thus far in the counseling session included career indecision, limited social life, and no evidence of fulfilling leisure activities.

Midway into the session, the career counselor and Evelyn reviewed the results of the CTI. Evelyn's percentile scores for adult norms on the CTI were Total = 42, Decision Making Confusion (DMC) = 90, Commitment Anxiety (CA) = 84, and External Conflict (EC) = 69. She endorsed the following CTI statements as AGREE: I'm afraid I'm overlooking an occupation; There are several fields of study or occupations that fit me, but I can't decide on the best one; I can narrow down my occupations to a few, but I don't seem to be able to pick just one; I worry a great deal about choosing the right field of study or occupation; The hardest thing is settling on just one field of study or occupation; and I get so depressed about choosing a field of study or occupation that I can't get started.

The career counselor said to Evelyn, "The results of the CTI indicate that, while total dysfunctional thinking was typical for adults, there were specific issues related to committing to a career goal (i.e., Commitment Anxiety) and to feelings of depression (i.e., Decision Making Confusion) that definitely should be addressed." Evelyn agreed with the counselor's interpretation.

Approaching the close of the counseling session, Evelyn was handed a printed sheet depicting the Client Versions of the Pyramid and CASVE Cycle (See Figures 3 and 4) to show her how the career counseling process is conducted in this career center. The counselor recommended that, to arrive at a satisfying career decision, she and the counselor schedule three counseling sessions to work together to explore all domains of the Pyramid and to progress step by step through the CASVE Cycle. Evelyn concurred with the recommendation and scheduled a second counseling session. Before the second counseling session, Evelyn agreed to take the Self-Directed Search (SDS) to enable her to clarify her interests and to provide useful information to formulate goals for of career counseling.

4. **Formulate Counseling Objectives.** At the opening of the second counseling session Evelyn and the career counselor again reviewed the individual items of the CTI as well as the results of the SDS. Evelyn's raw scores and (percentile scores) for adult female norms of the SDS were R = 25 (84), I = 14 (50), A = 32 (81), S = 37 (61), E = 40 (91), and C = 12 (14). The Summary Code was **ESA**. She listed only two occupations, Florist (ARE) and Emergency Medical Technician (RSI) as possible career aspirations.

Based on a review of Evelyn's CTI and SDS scores, and a review of her work history, she and the career counselor together formulated the following objectives to enable her to advance her career problem solving and decision making skills:

    a) Identify and explore occupations that are consistent with interests;
    b) Apply the CASVE Cycle to solving Evelyn's career problem and making a decision;

    c) Reframe negative career thoughts related to the difficulty in committing to a career choice; and

    d) Review related issues e.g., relationships, leisure pursuits, and mood.

5. **Develop Individualized Learning Plan (ILP).** At this comprehensive career center, the ILP is a one-page handout that contains lines for the counseling goals at the top, with columns below containing Learning Activity, Purpose/Outcome, Estimated time, Objective number, and Objective Priority in terms of sequence (Peterson et al., 1996). The ILP serves as a concrete step-by-step plan to achieve the objectives of counseling, and ultimately the goal of improving Evelyn's career problem- solving and decision-making skills. It also serves to foster a working alliance and to affirm the career counseling relationship.

The following learning activities were developed by Evelyn and the counselor and recorded on the ILP:

    a) Use the *CTI Workbook* to learn how to reframe the negative career thoughts endorsed on the CTI. (Objective 3, Priority 1)

    b) Review ESA and SEA occupations in the *Occupations Finder;* select potentially interesting occupations for further exploration. (Objective 1, Priority 2)

    c) Follow up with the counselor to review results of activities 1 and 2 and to explore related issues in the problem space. (Objective 1,3,4, Priority 3)

    d) For high priority occupations identified in activity #2, read about them in the *Occupational Outlook Handbook* (OOH) and in occupations folders in the Career Center library. (Objective 1, Priority 4)

    e) Identify and contact local firms for information interviews. (Objective 1, Priority 5)

    f) Explore leisure pursuits. (Objective 4, Priority 6)

    g) Monitor progress through the CASVE Cycle. (Objective 2; Priority on-going)

After having developed the ILP, Evelyn scheduled two follow-up sessions to meet with the career counselor. A copy of the ILP was made for Evelyn and one for her folder. The *CTI Workbook* was given to her for homework prior to the next session to reframe items she endorsed as Agree on the CTI.

6. **Execute ILP.** In the first counseling session following the development of the ILP, Evelyn discussed progress she had made using the *CTI Workbook*. In this session, she began to see how negative career thoughts related to Commitment Anxiety were preventing her from considering any potentially satisfying occupation. She found using the Identify-Challenge-Alter-Act (ICAA) sequence on the items daily as homework to be very helpful. She also began to realize the importance of leading a balanced life in terms of work, relationships and leisure pursuits. She expressed the hope that she would be able to remarry sometime in the future after she first began to feel more comfortable with herself as a single woman. She also recognized she had been exploring the Communication and Analysis phases of the CASVE Cycle in the first and second interview as well as making improvement in the Executive Processing Domain.

Upon review of ESA and SEA occupations in the Holland *Occupations Finder*, Evelyn selected the following occupations for further exploration: Lobbyist, Chamber of Commerce Administrator, Convention Manager, and Community

Organization Director. She then read about the occupations in the OOH and other resources in the library. She found Lobbyist and Convention Manager particularly interesting and decided to conduct a site visit to Hotels and Lobbying firms in the local community. Here, Evelyn engaged in the Synthesis Elaboration, expanding possible alternatives, and Synthesis Crystallization, narrowing options to a manageable few. She also advanced her self-knowledge as she related her interests to occupations.

Also, in the third interview she also examined her social life and leisure activities. She said she always had an interest in growing flowers and in gardening, but never took the time to participate in these activities. She thought she might like to join an Orchid club. In such a club, she might find people with whom she may have interests in common besides work. Evelyn decided to schedule the fourth counseling session after she had completed the site visits to two Lobbying firms and two convention hotels. This activity would advance her mastery of occupational knowledge.

Three weeks later, in the fourth counseling session, Evelyn compared her present employment as an Account Executive in an insurance firm to that of a Convention Manager. She ruled out the option of Lobbyist. She feared it would require even more time away from friends and leisure activities than her present job. Evelyn weighed the respective advantages and disadvantages of Account Executive and Convention Manager. After thoughtful consideration, she decided she would remain in her present job for the time being while she continued to pursue her leisure interests and to become more active socially. Upon reflection, she began to realize that she was asking her job to meet too many of her needs and interests and that was an unreasonable expectation for any job. With this insight, she began to view her job more positively. In fact, her general level of happiness and well being began to increase. Here, Evelyn identified that she had engaged the Valuing Phase and was moving on to the Execution Phase. All of the learning activities scheduled in the ILP had been completed.

Evelyn said she would like to schedule a follow up counseling session in about six weeks to review the progress she had made in becoming more comfortable and satisfied with her career choice to remain in her present job and in leading a more balanced life style. This step would return her to the Communication Phase to examine whether the gap between the existing state of indecision and desired state at entry to career counseling had closed.

7. **Summative Review and Generalization.** Before leaving the session (not the follow-up session), Evelyn and the counselor traced the steps Evelyn had taken through the Pyramid and the CASVE Cycle. Evelyn was pleased with her feeling of accomplishment and what she had learned about potential occupations and herself in the process. She had strengthened each domain of the Pyramid thereby improving her capabilities as a career problem solver and decision maker. Evelyn and her counselor then discussed how she could continue to use the CIP model not only with career problems, but also work problems and personal problems as well. Evelyn and her counselor together had a truly rewarding CIP career counseling experience.

Summary

A career problem-solving and decision-making paradigm has been presented with implications for working with adult populations. The intent of the CIP approach is to serve as a heuristic to enable individuals to systematically think through career problems that will open opportunities for career and lifestyle enhancement. The model includes assessing readiness for career problem solving by identifying dysfunctional thoughts that may interfere with the acquisition of self-knowledge and occupational knowledge or impede progress through the CASVE Cycle. Dysfunctional thoughts relate to self-imposed constraints or stereotypic thoughts that limit options or lead to immobility. Ultimately, through the application of the model, adult clients, as in the Case of Evelyn, are helped to enhance their career problem-solving and decision making capabilities that will lead to satisfying, meaningful, and productive lives.

References

American College Testing. (1998). *Inventory of Work-Related Abilities: Career planning survey technical manual*. Iowa City, IA: Author.

Beck, A. (1976). *Cognitive therapy and the rational disorders*. New York: International University Press.

Cochran, L. (1994). What is a career problem? *Career Development Quarterly*, 42, 204-215.

Consulting Psychologists Press. (1994). *Strong Interest Inventory*. Palo Alto, CA: Author.

Festinger, L. (1964). Motivations leading to social behavior. In R. C. Teevan & R. C. Burney (Eds.), *Theories of motivation in personality and social psychology* (pp. 138-161). New York: Van Nostrand.

Flanagan, J. D. (1954). The critical incident technique. *Psychological Bulletin*, 51(4), 327-358.

Flavell, J. H. (1979). Metacognition and cognitive monitoring: A new idea of cognitive-developmental inquiry. *American Psychologist*, 34, 906-911.

Gelatt, H. B. (1962). Decision-making: A conceptual frame of reference for counseling. *Journal of Counseling Psychology*, 9(3), 240-245.

Gleick, J. (1988). *Chaos: Making of a new science*. New York: Penguin Books.

Gottfredson, G. D., & Holland, J L. (1996). *Dictionary of Holland occupational codes*. Odessa, FL: Psychological Assessment Resources.

Hall, C. S., & Lindzey, G. (1978). *Theories of personality* (3rd ed.). New York: Wiley.

Hill, S., & Peterson, G. W. (2001, April). *The impact of decision-making confusion on the processing of occupational information*. Paper presented at the annual convention of the American Educational Research Association, Seattle, WA.

Holland, J. L. (1994). *Self-Directed Search*. Odessa, FL: Psychological Assessment Resources.

Hunt, E. B. (1971). What kind of computer is man? *Cognitive Psychology*, 2, 57-98.

Janis, I. L., & Mann, L. (1977). *Decision making: A psychological analysis of conflict, choice, and commitment*. New York: Free Press.

Katz, M. R. (1963). *Decisions and values: A rationale for secondary school guidance*. New York: College Entrance Examination.

Katz, M. R. (1969, Summer). Can computers make guidance decisions for students? *College Board Review*, 72, 13-17.

Krumboltz, J. D. (1991). *Manual for the Career Beliefs Inventory.* Palo Alto, CA: Consulting Psychologists Press.

Lackman, R., Lackman, J. L., & Butterfield, E. C. (1979). *Cognitive psychology and information processing.* Hillsdale, NJ: Erlbaum.

Meichebaum, D. (1977). *Cognitive-behavior modification.* New York: Plenum.

Miller-Tiedeman, A., & Tiedeman, D. (1990). Career decision making: An individualistic perspective. In D. Brown & L. Brooks (Eds.), Career choice and development (2nd ed., pp. 308-337). San Francisco, CA: Jossey-Bass.

Neimeyer, G. J. (1988). Cognitive integration and differentiation in vocational behavior. *The Counseling Psychologist*, 16, 440-475.

Neisser, U. (1981). John Dean's memory: A case study. *Cognition*, 9, 1-22.

Newell, A., & Simon, H. (1972). *Human problem solving.* Englewood Cliffs, NJ: Prentice-Hall.

Parsons, F. (1909). *Choosing a vocation.* Boston: Houghton Mifflin.

Patterson, D. G., & Darley, J. G. (1936). *Men, women, and jobs.* Minneapolis: Minnesota Press.

Peterson, G. W. (1998). Using a vocational card sort as an assessment of occupational knowledge. *Journal of Career Assessment*, 6, 49-76.

Peterson, G. W., & Krumboltz, J. D. (1997, March). *Career development and career counseling in an uncertain world of work.* Paper presented at the annual convention of the American Educational Research Association, Chicago, IL.

Peterson, G. W., Sampson, J. P. Jr., Lenz, J. G., & Reardon, R. C. (1999, May). *Three contexts of career problem solving and decision making: A cognitive information processing perspective.* Fourth Biennial Vocational Society Conference. Milwaukee, WI.

Peterson, G. W., Sampson, J. P., Jr., & Reardon, R. C. (1991). *Career development and services: A cognitive approach.* Pacific Grove, CA: Brooks/Cole.

Peterson, G. W., Sampson, J. P., Jr., Reardon, R. C., & Lenz, J. G. (1996). Becoming career problem solvers and decision makers: A cognitive information processing approach. In D. Brown & L. Brooks (Eds.), *Career choice and development* (3rd ed., pp. 423-475). San Francisco, CA: Jossey-Bass.

Piaget, J. (1977). The development of thought: Equilibrium of cognitive structures. New York: Viking Press.

Reardon, R. C., Lenz, J. G., Sampson, J. P., Jr., & Peterson, G. W. (2000). *Career development and planning: A comprehensive approach.* Belmont, CA: Wadsworth/Thompson Learning.

Rummelhart, D. E., & Ortony, A. (1976). Representation of knowledge in memory. In R. C. Anderson, R. J. Spiro, & W. E. Montague (Eds.), *Schooling and the acquisition of knowledge* (pp. 99-135). Hillsdale, NJ: Erlbaum.

Sampson, J. P., Jr. (1999). Integrating Internet-based guidance with services provided in career centers. *The Career Development Quarterly*, 47, 243-254.

Sampson, J. P., Jr., Peterson, G. W., Lenz, J. G., & Reardon, R. C. (1992). A cognitive approach to career services: Translating concepts into practice. *The Career Development Quarterly*, 41, 67-74.

Sampson, J. P., Jr., Peterson, G. W., Lenz, J. G., Reardon, R. C., & Saunders, D. E. (1996a). *The Career Thoughts Inventory (CTI).* Odessa, FL: Psychological Assessment Resources.

Sampson, J. P., Jr., Peterson, G. W., Lenz, J. G., Reardon, R. C., & Saunders, D. E. (1996b). *Improving your career thoughts: A workbook for the Career Thoughts Inventory.* Odessa, FL: Psychological Assessment Resources.

Sampson, J. P., Jr., Peterson, G. W., Reardon, R. C., & Lenz, J. G. (2000). Using readiness assessment to improve career services: A cognitive information processing approach. *The Career Development Quarterly*, 49, 146-174.

Saunders, D. E., Peterson, G. W., Sampson, J. P., Jr., & Reardon, R. C. (2000). Relation of depression and dysfunctional career thinking to career indecision. *Vocational Behavior*, 56, 288-298.

Sinnott, J. D. (1989). A model for the solution of ill-structured problems: Implications for everyday and abstract problem solving. In J. D. Sinnott (Ed.), *Everyday problem solving* (pp. 72-99). New York: Praeger.

Slaney, R. B., Moran, W. J., & Wade, J. C. (1994). Vocational card sorts. In J.T. Kapes, M. M. Mastie, & E. A. Whitfield (Eds.), *A counselor's guide to career assessment instruments* (pp. 347-360). Alexandria, VA: National Career Development Association.

Slife, B. D., & Williams, R. N. (1997). Toward a theoretical psychology. *American Psychologist*, 52, 177-129.

Spokane, A. (1991). *Career intervention*. Englewood Cliffs, NJ: Prentice-Hall.

Sternberg, R. J. (1980). Sketch of a componential subtheory of human intelligence. *Behavioral and Brain Sciences*, 3, 573-584.

Sternberg, R. J. (1985). Instrumental and componential approaches to the nature of training on intelligence. In S. Chapman, J. Segal, & R. Glaser (Eds.), *Thinking and learning skills: Research and open questions*. Hillsdale, NJ: Erlbaum.

Super, D. E., & Nevill, D. (1986). *Values Scale*. Palo Alto, CA: Consulting Psychologists Press.

Tulving, E. (1984). Precison elements of episodic memory. *Behavioral and Brain Sciences*, 7, 223-268.

Tyler, L. E. (1961). Research explorations in the realm of choice. *Journal of Counseling Psychology*, 8, 195-201.

U.S. Department of Labor, Employment Service. (1977). *Dictionary of Occupational Titles* (4th ed.). Washington DC: U.S. Printing Office.

U.S. Department of Labor and The National O*NET Consortium. (1999, July). *Abilities Questionnaire*. O*NET Data Collection Program. Author.

Williamson, E. G. (1939). *How to counsel students*. New York: McGraw-Hill.

SECTION III:

STRATEGIES, METHODS, AND RESOURCES

CHAPTER 7
Appraising Adults' Career Capabilities: Ability, Interest, and Personality

John O. Crites
Crites Career Consultants
Boulder, Colorado

Brian J. Taber
Kent State University

In his Model of Career Maturity, Crites (1978, p. 4) made the distinction between career choice content and career choice process in decision making:

> The former encompasses the Consistency of Career Choices and Realism of Career Choices factors in the model (Figure 1 *[see next page]*). To operationally define these dimensions it is necessary to elicit a career choice from an individual. A question like, "Which occupation do you intend to enter when you have completed your schooling or training" (Crites, 1969, p. 139) is asked, and, if the individual has made a choice, an occupational title, e.g. machinist, copywriter, or dancer, is given in response. This is career choice content. In contrast, career choice process refers to the variables involved in arriving at a decision of career choice content. These variables include the group factors of Career Choice Competencies and Career Choice Attitudes in the model of career maturity.

A chapter on "Instruments for Assessing Career Development" (Crites, 1984), in the third National Vocational Guidance Association commemorative volume Designing Careers (Gysbers, 1984), reviewed contemporary measures of career choice process such as Crites' (1978) Career Maturity Inventory and the Career Pattern Study's (Thompson, Lindeman, Super, Jordaan, & Myers, 1981, 1982) Career Development Inventory. More recent reviews of career choice process measures including the Adult Career Concerns Inventory (Super, Thompson, & Lindeman, 1988) have been conducted by Savickas (1992, 2000). This chapter describes and discusses some of the tests and inventories available to appraise adults' capabilities (both intellective and nonintellective) for career choice content.

With the increased focus on adult career development well exemplified by this book devoted entirely to the topic, more and more career counselors and career development specialists, particularly in business and community organizations, find themselves confronted with the task of assisting adults in appraising their career capabilities – abilities, interests, and personality characteristics. Yet many of these professionals are either unaware of existing standardized measures for adult career appraisal and use none, or they construct homemade surveys and questionnaires that have unknown or uncertain reliability and validity. The need for a review of appropriate tests and inventories for career counseling and group work with adults seems apparent. To identify these assessment instruments, a search was first made

Figure 1
A Model of Career Maturity in Adolescence and Adulthood

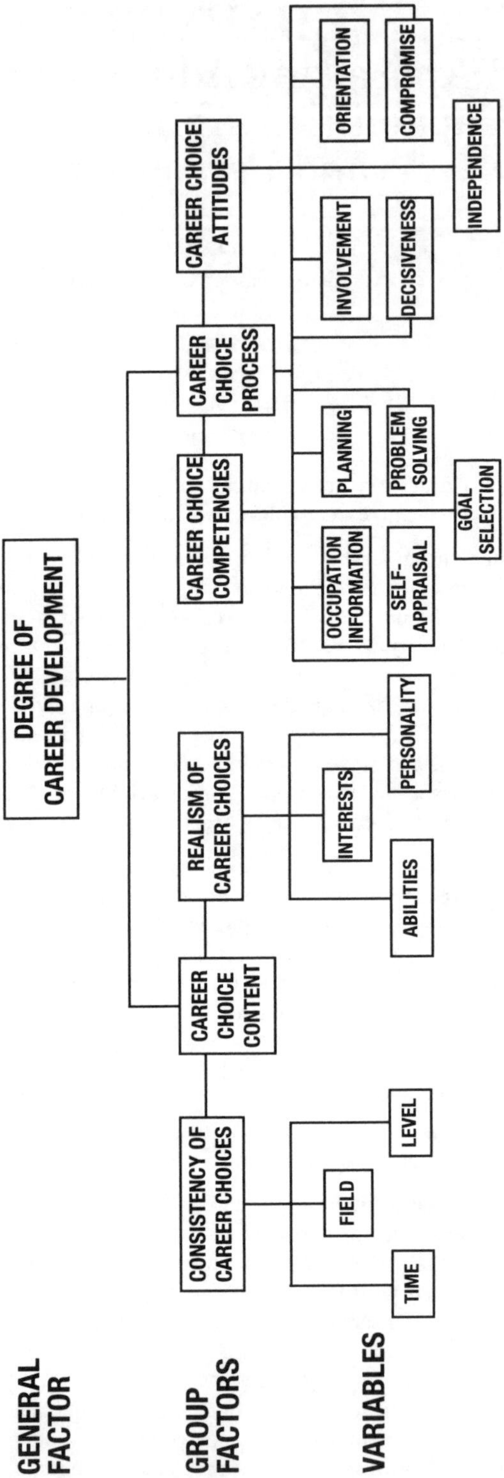

GENERAL FACTOR

GROUP FACTORS

VARIABLES

for all measures listed in the fourth edition of TESTS (Maddox, 1997) that were applicable to adults. Then, for each instrument, the number of references cited in the Thirteenth Mental Measurements Yearbook (MMY; Impara & Plake, 1998) was calculated. The most extensively researched instruments were selected for review, the assumption being that they would have sufficiently documented psychometric characteristics to be useful in career counseling and career development programs.

In addition to these well-established tests and inventories, other less studied but promising instruments, are mentioned so that users can assess their usefulness for particular situations (see Sweetland & Keyser, 1983). Certain judgmental constraints have been imposed on the selection of the adult appraisal instruments included in this review, in terms of career counseling pragmatics (Crites, 1981). Experience indicates that some are better than others. This review and critical analysis is, therefore, a synthesis of scientific findings on appraisal instruments for adult career capabilities (career choice content) and informed experience with them. Ability tests, including measures of general intelligence, achievement, aptitudes (multifactor) are presented first and are followed by a discussion of vocational interest inventories, with a final section on personality measures.

Ability Tests

There are certain desiderata that ability tests, including general intelligence, achievement, and aptitude, should have for the appraisal of adult career capabilities. Foremost among these is that the test be a power measure, that is, untimed, because adults beyond the ages 25 – 30 have a decrement in performance under hurried conditions (Super & Crites, 1962). In addition, all tests, but particularly those for intelligence and aptitude, should have evidenced vocational validity – that is, be predictive of occupational level or occupational aptitude patterns (OAPs). Two other, different parameters are whether both (a) verbal and nonverbal and (b) group and individual tests are available. Given these specifications, only a few ability tests can be recommended for the appraisal of adult capabilities.

INTELLIGENCE TESTS

The assessment of general intelligence or "g" does not receive a great deal of attention in career counseling even though "g" has been found to covary with academic achievement, work performance, income, and occupational level (Lubinski, 2000; Lindemann & Matarazzo, 1990). No one test of general intelligence has all the characteristics desired in such measures for appraising the intellectual functioning of adults. If there is sufficient administration time and a qualified examiner, then the Wechsler Adult Intelligence Scales III (WAIS III; Wechsler, 1997) has much to recommend it, particularly its extensive age norms, which allow the comparison of an adult's score with those of peers (Matarazzo, 1972). It has only modest vocational validity (Super & Crites, 1962), but can yield a good estimate of an adult's probable level of occupational attainment, which corresponds generally to the levels axis in Roe's occupational classification system (Roe, 1956), as well as to the DOT ratings of general ability given in Holland's Dictionary (Gottfredson & Holland, 1996). Another possible test of "g" that was specifically designed for business and industry is the Wonderlic Personnel Test (Wonderlic, 1989), which is a group administered paper and pencil instrument that can be given either timed (12 minutes) or untimed conditions. The Wonderlic Personnel Test is also available in a computer version through The Psychological Corporation. It has had extensive use in employee selection situations, as has the Wesman Personnel Classification Test (Wesman, 1965), a timed (28 minutes) paper-and-pencil measure of the verbal and numerical components in general intelligence. The Kaufman Brief Intelligence Test (KBIT; Kaufman & Kaufman, 1990) measures both verbal and nonverbal domains of intelligence and provides percentile ranks by age. Finally, for a brief, nonverbal assessment of intelligence, the Beta-III (Kellog & Morton, 1999) is an excellent option.

ACHIEVEMENT TESTS

Although achievement tests are usually associated with school assessment programs, their use with adults has increased over the years with the introduction of career development workshops in business/industrial organizations and the establishment of Private Industry Council programs for the unemployed. There is often the need to assess level of educational development, particularly with the latter group, to determine whether remedial basic education is indicated before proceeding with job search. There are three widely used measures of adult achievement: Adult Basic Learning Examination (ABLE; Karlsen & Gardner, 1986), Tests of Adult Basic Education, Forms 7 & 8 (TABE; CTB/McGraw Hill, 1996), and the Wide Range Achievement Test 3 (WRAT 3; Wilkinson, 1993). Of these ABLE (Second edition) has the best-established psychometric properties. It appraises vocabulary, reading comprehension, spelling, arithmetic computation, and problem-solving skills, at three different levels: grades 1 to 4, grades 5 to 8, and grades 9 to 12. A short screening test called SelectABLE (sic), is used to determine which level of testing is appropriate. Tests at levels I and II take approximately 2 hours, whereas level III takes 3 hours and 25 minutes to administer. Percentile rank norms and stanines are reported for all levels. The purpose of the TABE is to measure achievement of skills commonly associated with basic adult education curricula. The TABE includes tests of reading, mathematics, and language/spelling with five different levels: L (Literacy), E (Easy), M (Medium), D (Difficult), and A (Advanced). As with the ABLE, there is a brief Locator Test used to select the appropriate level for the examinee. While the TABE, Forms 7 & 8 and its predecessors have been widely used, criticisms of its psychometric properties, norming procedures and criterion-referenced data have led to calls for caution when using these measures (Beck, 1998; Osterlind, 1994). Recent additions to the TABE series are the TABE Work-Related Foundation Skills (TABE WF; CTB/McGraw Hill, 1996) and the TABE Work-Related Problem Solving (TABE PS; CTB/McGraw Hill, 1996). The TABE WF has four subtests: Reading, Mathematics Computation, Applied Mathematics, and Language. The TABE PS tests the examinees ability to use reading and math skills to identify a problem, asking the right questions, decision making ability, evaluating outcomes, and demonstrate learning. While these measures are potentially useful, unfortunately they are susceptible to the same criticisms as other tests in the TABE series. The WRAT 3 subtests include Reading, Spelling, and Arithmetic. Unlike the TABE Forms 7 & 8, norms are referenced to age rather than grade, which is obviously much more appropriate for adults (cf., WAIS III). The WRAT series of tests have been in use for more than 60 years with seven revisions. The revisions in the WRAT 3 have attempted to correct some of the shortcomings of previous editions of the measure. However, questions about the psychometric properties persist, and results of the WRAT 3 should used in conjunction with other types of data (Ward, 1995).

APTITUDE TESTS

Clearly, the best documented and most widely applicable aptitude tests for adults are in the USES General Aptitude Test Battery (GATB; United States Employment Services, 1982). Not only were they developed on and for adults (Super & Crites, 1962), but also they have an extensive "Occupational Aptitude Pattern" (OAP) database, which Hunter (1983) extended to 12,000 occupations, using the new techniques of validity generalization. There are now 66 OAPs that encompass most of the distinct occupations in the world of work (Droege & Padgett, 1979). A major drawback with the GATB, however, is that it is tightly controlled by local employment services, and can be administered only by them or certified examiners. As a result, this highly developed instrument is also highly restricted in its availability. Fortunately, there is an equally useful alternative, Although it does not include the performance tests as the GATB does. The Employee Aptitude Survey (EAS; Grimsley, Ruch, Warren, & Ford, 1980) is a battery of 10 short but reliable and valid tests of such variables as verbal reasoning, numerical ability, spatial visualization, and visual speed and accuracy. The occupational norms are broadly based, but not to the extent of the GATB. Crites (1984) equated the EAS to GATB, with the exception of the latter's performance measures, so that the OAP database can be used with both batteries. Thus, the EAS, supplemented as needed with performance tests such as the Purdue Pegboard (Purdue Research Foundation, 1968) and the Bennett Mechanical Comprehension Test (Bennett, 1968), gives the career specialist a viable option to the GATB. The Differential Aptitude Test for Personnel and Career Assessment (DAT for PCA; Bennett, Seashore, & Wesman, 1989) consists of eight tests that cover many of the same abilities as those reported above. The entire battery takes approximately two hours to complete, however, specific tests can be administered which makes for more efficient use of time if there is interest in just certain abilities. The DAT can also be administered with Level 2 of Career Interest Inventory (CII; The Psychological Corporation, 1991) to assess a client's vocational interest among 15 occupational groups and 20 school subjects. Using interest and aptitude measures provide data on the congruency between these two constructs. This information can assist individuals in making appropriate and realistic educational and vocational decisions.

SELF-ESTIMATES OF ABILITY AND SELF-EFFICACY

Achievement and aptitude tests are often time consuming as well as expensive. Given these limitations, self-estimates of ability are emerging as viable methods of assessing abilities in career counseling. Self-estimates of ability are an important aspect of a person's self-concept. While counselors maybe skeptical of this approach, research has supported self-estimates as an acceptable method of appraising occupationally related abilities (e.g. Mabe & West, 1982; Harrington & Schafer, 1996). Rather than objective testing, clients are asked to estimate abilities in comparison to others their age. ACT developed the Inventory of Work Relevant Abilities (IWRA; ACT, 1999) which uses the Data/Ideas –Things/ People dimensions (Prediger, 1976) that underlie the RIASEC hexagon (Holland, 1997) to assess fifteen self-estimated work abilities. Abilities that are not traditionally assessed through objective tests such as meeting people, helping others, and creativity are included in IWRA.

Although both tested and self-estimated abilities are prone to distortions as measures of "true ability," normative self-estimate scores have been found to provide acceptable hit rates in classifying people in their occupation. Self-estimates also provide additional information to tested abilities when used in combination, thus providing incremental validity in ability assessment (Prediger, 1999). Using self-estimates of ability requires that the counselor review the results with the client as they pertain to his or her experiences, grades, accomplishments, and self-concept.

Over the past 20 years measures operationalizing self-efficacy theory (Bandura, 1977, 1986, 1997) for career counseling have been developed. The Skills Confidence Inventory (SCI; Betz, Borgen, & Harmon, 1996), a sixty-item measure that is used in conjunction with the Strong Interest Inventory (SII; Harmon, Hansen, Borgen, & Hammer, 1994) provides profiles of skill confidence in the RIASEC typology. In contrast to IWRA that asks respondents to rate their abilities relative to others, the SCI asks that respondents rate their degree of confidence for tasks and activities from 1 (No Confidence at All) to 5 (Complete Confidence). Results of the SCI and the SII provide clients feedback regarding skills and interests which can be classified in terms of low, medium, and high for their respective skills and interests. For instance, low interest and low skills in Conventional occupations may rule them out for further exploration whereas high skill and interest for Enterprising occupations would be a priority for exploration. Additionally, cases where interest is high but skill is low can lead to discussion about what a client can do to augment skills in that area should they desire. In a similar fashion, the Campbell Interest and Skills Survey (CISS; Campbell, 1992) advises courses of action based upon the various interest and skill configurations such as Pursue (high interest, high skill), Develop (high interest, low skill), Explore (low interest, high skill) and Avoid (low interest, low skill) for each of it's Orientation, Basic Interest, and Occupational scales.

Vocational Interests

In the discussion that follows, the focus is on vocational interests, both expressed and inventoried, but measures of work needs and job satisfaction are also reviewed. For a comprehensive appraisal of adult career capabilities, it is often useful to assess needs that are satisfied in the work environment, as well as vocational interests.

EXPRESSED INTERESTS

For many years simply asking people questions about their interests, such as "which occupation do you intend to enter when you have completed your schooling or training?" (Crites, 1969), was considered unreliable and therefore, invalid for predicting their eventual occupation (e.g., Berdie, 1950; Darley & Hagenah, 1955; Super & Crites, 1962). Since the late 1960s, however, when Holland and Lutz (1968) compared expressed interests with Vocational Preference Inventory (VPI), regard for the predictive validity of expressed interests has increased greatly. The Holland and Lutz study indicated a much higher "hit rate" for expressed interests than the VPI against a common criterion of career choice 8 months later. With an interval of 3 years, Borgen and Seling (1978) essentially replicated this finding using the Strong Vocational Interest Blank (SVIB). And, in a review of relevant research on the comparative predictive validity of expressed and inventoried interests, Dolliver (1969, pp. 103-104) concluded:

The predictive validity of expressed interests is at least as great as the predictive validity of SVIB. In no study where direct comparison was made (Dyer, 1939; Enright & Pinneai, 1955; McArthur & Stevens, 1955) was the SVIB as accurate as the expressed interests in predicting occupation engaged in... There is no evidence to show the SVIB is superior to expressed interests.

Additionally, Apostal (1985) reported that there were few discrepancies between expressed and inventoried interests among most people. The implications of these results and conclusions certainly is that expressed interests should be elicited in any thorough appraisal of adult career capabilities and that they should be given at least as much weight as inventoried interests. The use of vocational card sorts such as the Occ-U-Sort (Jones, 1981) or the Occupational Interest Card Sort (Knowdell, 1993) provide a useful means of elucidating expressed vocational interests. There are some distinct advantages to using card sorts. For instance, card sorts provide a phenomenological perspective in assessment that permits the examination of how clients construct personal meaning of their interests. Also, card sorts can be useful in avoiding certain pitfalls such as inattention to cultural identity issues and the potential for sex bias (Hartung, 1999).

INVENTORIED INTERESTS

The question that immediately arises then is why administer interest inventories, given that expressed interests are more predictive? There are at least two answers to this question: First, some want to take an interest inventory to confirm (or reality test) their expressed interests. When inventoried and expressed interests are the same, their combined predictive efficiency is considerably greater than that of either separately. Indeed, the predictive validity of using both expressed and inventoried interests can be as high as 60 to 70 percent (Barlting & Hood, 1981; Borgen & Seling, 1978). However, when they differ, expressed interests are, of course, the better predictor in most cases (Borgen & Seling, 1978). Second, about 20 to 25 percent of adults in the career decision-making process have no expressed interests. For these individuals, interest inventories serve the very worthwhile purpose of stimulating them to explore areas of interest similarity.

At the professional, semi-professional, and managerial/white collar occupational levels, the most widely used instrument is the Strong Interest Inventory (SII; Harmon et al., 1994), but the Kuder Occupational Interest Survey (KOIS; Kuder & Zytowski, 1991) is also highly recommended. Interpretation of the SII is sometimes complicated by the percentages of Like, Indifferent, and Dislike responses, particularly if the latter is high, because the General Occupational Theme and Basic Interest Scales are scored +1 for Likes and −1 for Dislikes. A strong dislike response tendency produces, therefore, low scores on these scales, but high scores on some occupational scales such as Mathematician that are keyed to a high percentage of Dislikes (the so-called "doubting" attitude of the scientist). The SII also poses problems in the interpretation of cognate male/female scales when an individual scores higher on the opposite sex scale (Crites, 1978). The KOIS, on the other hand avoids this difficulty because of its different construction (occupation vs. occupation as compared with occupation vs. in-general groups), but it is often awkward to explain Lambda scores to clients without a lengthy discussion that interferes with the test interpretation.

At the nonprofessional occupational levels, the best available measure is the Career Assessment Inventory - Vocational Version (CAI; Johansson, 1982), which is formatted after the SII but with occupations largely within the semi-skilled range for adults desiring to enter the work force immediately following high school requiring little or no additional training. The educational ranges of occupations is extended upward in the Enhanced Version of the CAI Johansson, 1986). Some of the same problems in interpretation occur with it as with the SII, particularly if the response percentages are extreme. As Strong (1943) pointed out many years ago and Darley and Hagenah (1955) reiterated, vocational interests at these levels are largely undifferentiable. Rather, it is preference for different work environments or job conditions that is important to these individuals. Hence, it may be more important to assess work environment preferences on such dimensions as indoor-outdoor, clean-dirty, and noisy-quiet. This type of assessment may be particularly useful with adults that are unskilled and unemployed.

WORK NEEDS

The extensive and long-term research of the Work Adjustment Project at the University of Minnesota under the leadership of Dawis and Lofquist (1984) has produced several instruments to measure the variables in their "Theory of Work Adjustment." Not the least of these is the Minnesota Importance Questionnaire (MIQ; Weiss, Dawis, & Lofquist, 1975). It measures 20 needs, which are grouped into six general categories of work values: Achievement, Comfort, Status, Altruism, Safety, and Autonomy. Also listed with each need are the corresponding "Work-Related Reinforcers" that satisfy them on-the-job. The rationale for the MIQ is that individuals gain greater job satisfaction, and ultimately accrue greater tenure, if their needs are fulfilled by the appropriate occupational reinforcer pattern (ORPs). The MIQ profile indicates high and low needs that are interpreted according to these patterns. Reliability and validity data on the MIQ are limited but encouraging. The MIQ's careful development and theoretical significance certainly justify its widespread use in appraising the career capabilities of adults.

JOB SATISFACTION

Job satisfaction has been linked to employee turnover and organizational commitment (Carsten & Spector, 1987; Schlesinger & Zornitsky, 1991). Thus, examining job satisfaction with clients can be important if he or she hopes to attain tenure and success in an occupation. There are two major measures of job satisfaction: the Hoppock Job Satisfaction Blank Form 5 (JSB; Hoppock, 1935), and the Job Descriptive Index, Revised (JDI; Balzer, Kihm, Smith, Irwin, Bachiochi, Robie, Sinar, & Parra, 1997). The first of these, the JSB, provides a global assessment of job satisfaction. Based upon the individual's overall "hedonic tone" toward work (Crites, 1969). Four 7-point scale items ask workers how much they like their jobs, whether they want to change their work, and so forth. The total score is an expression of job satisfaction in relation to job dissatisfaction. In contrast the JDI uses the *summative* method to elicit satisfaction with five different facets of the work situation: 1) work on present job, 2) present pay, 3) opportunities for promotion, 4) supervision on present job, and 5) people on your present job. The assumption is that a worker can be differentially satisfied with these various components of the work environment, but provision is also made with the JDI for summing the part-scores to obtain a total job satisfaction score, which correlates highly with the JSB. The revised scale also includes the Job in General scale as a global measure of job satisfaction (Ironson, Smith, Brannick, Gibson, & Paul, 1989). Using such measures in counseling can be useful to appraise a client's satisfaction with their current position and subsequently, what can be done to increase it. Also, should a client be interested in changing occupations, these instruments can be useful in elucidating what would be important considerations in selecting a new occupation.

Personality Inventories

Unlike ability tests and vocational interest measures whose items directly sample the context of the world of work, personality inventories come from a different tradition. There is no available inventory of work personality. Rather, there are several instruments, constructed for other purposes that have been applied to the assessment of personality in the work environment. Their validity for the appraisal of the adult work personality is indirect at best. But, some of them have demonstrated usefulness for career counseling and career workshops with adults, and they are reviewed and critically evaluated here. Five personality inventories have been sufficiently researched for career purposes to include in this discussion: 1) the California Psychological Inventory, Form 434, Third Edition (CPI; Gough, 1995); 2) the Edwards Personal Preference Schedule (EPPS; Edwards, 1959); 3) the Myers Briggs Type Indicator (MBTI; Myers & Briggs, 1988); 4) the Revised NEO Personality Inventory (NEO PI-R; Costa & McCrae, 1992); and 5) the Sixteen Personality Factor Inventory, Fifth Edition (16PF; Cattell, Cattell, & Cattell, 1993).

CALIFORNIA PERSONALITY INVENTORY (CPI)

Of the personality measures available for assessing adult personality, the CPI is probably the most extensively researched. In a revision (Gough & Bradley, 1996), 28 items from Form 462 that were in conflict with fair employment practices, and the Americans with Disabilities Act were dropped. The CPI was originally standardized and validated to measure "folk concepts" of personality, such as dominance (Do) and good impression (Gi). Factor analysis indicates that these are the principal dimensions of the normal personality (Crites, Bechtoldt, Goodstein, & Heilbrun, 1961). They focus on how individuals deal with interpersonal relations, a behavioral domain that is critical to adult career adjustment. The findings of many studies (Crites, 1969; 1982) establish that more employees lose their jobs because of problems in interpersonal relations than for any other reason. In other words, coping with others on the job (superiors, subordinates, and co-workers) is more important in career success than competence for job performance, at least above a minimal level. The CPI offers an objective measurement of interpersonal areas that might directly impinge upon job adjustment. Low scores on CPI scales in both "Class I. Measures of Poise, Ascendancy, Self-Assurance, and Interpersonal Adequacy" and "Class II. Measures of Socialization, Responsibility, Intrapersonal Values, and Character" are often diagnostic of potential difficulties in human relations at the workplace. Two-scale analyses of these measures have also been related to discriminating self-descriptive adjectives, and means and standard deviations for various educational and occupational groups are given in the manual (Gough & Bradley, 1996). To augment and extend the interpretation of the CPI, the revised edition presents a conceptual schema based on factor analytically derived "Vectors."

EDWARDS PERSONAL PREFERENCE SCHEDULE (EPPS)

In contrast to the CPI, the EPPS was constructed to measure variables from an explicit personality theory – Murray's (1938) system of needs. The 15 need scales of the EPPS (e.g. autonomy, dominance, order, etc.) are not organized, however, into a readily interpretable conceptual schema. To provide such a framework, Crites (1981) arranged the needs into a circumplex that defines Horney's (1945) major orientations in interpersonal relations: (a) moving toward people, (b) moving against people, and (c) moving away from people. Used with these constructs, the EPPS gains increased diagnostic significance for identifying possible human relations' problems of adult workers. There is growing evidence, for example, that employees more frequently lose their jobs because they are nonassertive than because they are aggressive. In the circumplex (Figure 2), the EPPS Abasement and Deference scales define a self-effacing personality that may experience interpersonal problems on-the-job because of nonassertiveness and an indiscriminate tendency to move toward people. Other configurations of scores identify orientations that are likely to create different job adjustment problems. In interpreting these patterns, it is important to remember that the EPPS is ipsative, in other words, has a "forced choice" response format, and consequently only high and low scores within the individual should be reported. Normative interpretations should not be reported. For normative assessment of needs, the Personality Research Form (PRF; Jackson, 1984) should be considered. The PRF measures the same 15 needs as the EPPS along with six additional variables: Abasement, Change, Cognitive Structure, Defendence, Sentience, and Succorance.

FIGURE 2

EPPS CIRCUMPLEX FOR APPRAISAL OF WORK-RELATED
INTERPERSONAL ORIENTATIONS

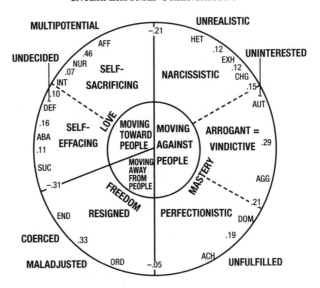

MYERS-BRIGGS TYPE INDICATOR (MBTI)

Within the last 20 years there has been an interest in the MBTI and there is accruing research on it, as well as applications in business and industry (Hirsch, 1984). The MBTI was originally designed to operationally define the major constructs in Jung's theory of personality. It yields scores on four bipolar dimensions representing these variables 1) Extraversion-Introversion; 2) Thinking-Feeling; 3) Intuition-Sensing; and 4) Judgment-Perception. From combinations of scores on these basic personality orientations, types are derived that indicate the individual's dominant modes of interacting with the world. These obviously are relevant to the work environment and suggest how an adult worker might best fit into a compatible occupational role (Hirsch, 1984). To use the MBTI for the appraisal of adult career capabilities, however, it is essential to have a thorough understanding of the Jungian concepts it measures. Making use of these concepts can be helpful in assisting the client in information gathering and decision making. For instance, preference for extraversion may indicates that a person is comfortable conducting informational interviews to gather occupational information. Conversely, a person with an introverted preference may be more at ease conducting library research for information. Results of the inventory can provide insight as to how they take in information (Sensing or Intuition) and how they prefer to make decisions (Thinking or Feeling) (McCaully & Martin, 1995). Further, preliminary research suggests that the MBTI may be useful in identifying career obstacles based upon preferences (Healy & Woodward, 1998). The Center for Applications of Psychological Type in Gainesville, Florida offers the relevant training for professionals through a variety of seminars and workshops. The center also provides information on the most and least preferred occupations by type.

THE REVISED NEO PERSONALITY INVENTORY (NEO PI –R)

In recent years there has been growing evidence to suggest that personality can be understood in terms of five fundamental dimensions (Digman, 1990): Neuroticism (e.g. anxious - calm), Extraversion (e.g. talkative - silent), Openness to Experience (e.g. curious - uncurious), Agreeableness (e.g. friendly - unfriendly), and Conscientiousness (e.g. thorough - careless). The NEO PI-R measures these five dimensions defined by 30 descriptive facets (6 per dimension) that can be used in career counseling to assist the client in making appropriate career choices (Costa, McCrae, & Kay, 1995). The NEO PI-R can be used to cross check interest inventory results. For example, it is not unusual for people who score high in Openness to Experience have a wide variety of vocational interests (Costa, McCrae, & Holland, 1984). Given that such results are endemic to high scorers on this dimension, counselors have to assist these clients in finding outlets for these interests in avocational ways as well as narrowing realistic vocational options to a manageable number. Further, information from the results may give some indication to the motivation for seeking an occupational change (Costa et al., 1995). For instance, a client scoring high in Neuroticism may generally be unhappy despite their current job, rendering an occupational change as a hopeless solution to their dissatisfaction. Accordingly, other avenues of intervention need to be pursued. Additionally, those scoring high in Neuroticism may have difficulty in coping with the demands of inherently stressful occupations such as paramedic or police officer. The Conscientiousness dimension also provides information pertinent to career decision making. High scorers in this dimension are considered to be achievement oriented and hard working (Barrick & Mount, 1991). Thus, clients may want to consider the level of their vocational aspirations and the work demands of the occupations they are considering based upon their score on this dimension.

SIXTEEN PERSONALITY FACTOR QUESTIONNAIRE, FIFTH EDITION (16PF)

The 16 PF is included here because it is widely known and has norms for occupational groups, as well as regression equations for predicting job performance criteria and other work relevant behavior. Vocationally pertinent information is available in the Personal Career Development Profile that includes: problem-solving resources, interpersonal interaction styles, coping patterns, work-setting preferences, and interest patterns using the same scheme as the CISS. Additionally, correlational data of the sixteen primary factors and the RIASEC typology (Holland, 1997) are presented in the technical manual to provide estimates for vocational interests. Additional occupational matching information can be found in Schuerger and Watterson (1998) who have compiled data from several studies to provide 16 PF profiles for 68 occupational groups. The latest version of the 16 PF has largely overcome some of the psychometric limitations of its predecessors (Conn & Rieke, 1994). Perhaps most importantly, the new edition of the 16 PF has been able to demonstrate convergent and discriminate validity with other well respected personality inventories such as the NEO PI-R, PRF, CPI, and the MBTI. Internal consistency reliability has increased substantially in the fifth edition, yet many scales are still below .80. The 16 PF makes use of five global factors that are similar to those of the NEO PI-R. These scales generally demonstrate a higher degree of temporal stability compared to the 16 primary factors.

The 16 primary factors provide information pertinent not only for a client's career decision making but also for identifying potential barriers to success and satisfaction in an occupation. Schuerger and Watterson (1998) provide an excellent summary of how the primary factors relate to vocational behavior. For instance, a person with a high score on Factor E (Dominance) indicates that job dissatisfaction is likely, particularly if the person is in a subordinate position. Considering a scale score in relation to other scales provides a more comprehensive picture of the client's personality. For example, high scores on Factor A (Warmth) can be positively related to job performance when other factors such as G (Rule Consciousness) and Q3 (Perfectionism) compensate for control over impulsiveness and factors B (Reasoning) and M (Abstractedness) indicate the person is capable of good judgement. Conversely, high scores on Factor A may indicate with out such compensatory mechanisms indicate that a person's job performance can be impaired by excessive socialization in the work place.

Conclusion

This chapter has presented a review of ability, interest, and personality appraisal instruments that may be used in the career counseling of adults. The instruments presented represent both an objective view of scientific findings and the subjective experience of the authors with the instruments. The instruments discussed are those that the authors consider the most pragmatic for career counseling practice. Readers are encouraged to continue the ongoing search for the most useful and scientifically sound tools for their professional practice.

Using assessment instruments to assist adults in making educational or vocational choices requires that the counselor know the strengths and weaknesses of assessment protocols. When selecting assessment instruments, it is important to keep in mind the relevance of the measures to the population being served. This is crucial for normed reference tests, which compare the client to the population they belong, or in some cases populations which they hope to join. Further, regardless of the type of measure used, the counselor should be familiar with the nomological network associated with scores to give an accurate and meaningful interpretation of results. In this vein, Messick (1995) points out that there are intentional and unintentional consequences of testing that can have either negative or positive effects. Inherently, all tests have limitations. Accordingly, counselors need to use the chosen measures in a manner that facilitates the attainment of client goals. Discussing results with a client provides an opportunity to corroborate or disconfirm the meaning of test scores. In the end, the goal of assessment is to help the client attain a clearer sense of their self-concept and how it can be implemented in the world-of-work.

References

American College Testing. (1999). *Career Planning Survey Technical Manual.* Iowa City, IA: Author.

Apostal, A. (1985). Expressed-inventoried interest agreement and type of Strong-Campbell Interest Inventory Scale. *Journal of Counseling Psychology, 32,* 624-336.

Balzer, W. K., Kihm, J. A., Smith, P. C., Irwin, J. L., Bachiochi, P. D., Robie, C., Sinar, E. F., & Parra, L. F. (1997). *Users' Manual for the Job Descriptive Index (JDI; 1997 Revision) and the Job In General Scales.* Bowling Green, OH: Bowling Green State University.

Bandura, A. (1977). Self-efficacy: Toward a unifying theory of behavior change. *Psychological Review, 84,* 191-215.

Bandura, A. (1986). *Social foundations of thought and action: A social cognitive view.* Englewood Cliffs, NJ: Prentice Hall.

Bandura, A. (1997). *Self-efficacy: The exercise of control.* New York: W. H. Freeman & Co. Publishers.

Barrick, M. R., & Mount, M. K. (1991). The big five personality dimensions and job performance: A meta-analysis. *Personnel Psychology, 44,* 1-26.

Bartling, H. C., & Hood, A. B. (1981). An 11-year follow up of measured interest and vocational choice. *Journal of Counseling Psychology, 28,* 27-35.

Beck, M. D. (1998). Review of the Tests of Adult Basic Education, forms 7 & 8. In J. C. Impara, & B. S. Blake (Eds.), *The thirteenth mental measurements yearbook* (pp. 1080-1083). Lincoln, NE: The University of Nebraska Lincoln.

Bennett, G. K. (1968). *Bennett Mechanical Comprehension Test.* San Antonio, TX: The Psychological Corporation.

Bennett, G. K., Seashore, H. G., & Wesman, A. G. (1989). *Differential Aptitude Tests for Personnel and Career Assessment.* San Antonio, TX: The Psychological Corporation.

Berdie, R. F. (1950). Scores on the SVIB and the Kuder Preference Record in relation to self-ratings. *Journal of Applied Psychology, 34,* 42-49.

Betz, N. E., Borgen, F. H., Harmon, L. W. (1996). *Skills Confidence Inventory.* Palo Alto, CA: Consulting Psychologists Press, Inc.

Borgen, F. H., & Seling, M. J. (1978). Expressed and inventoried interests revisited: perspicacity in the person. *Journal of Counseling Psychology,* 25, 536-543.

Campbell, D. P. (1992). *Campbell Interest and Skills Survey.* Minneapolis: NCS Assessments.

Carsten, J. M., & Spector, P. E. (1987). Unemployment, job satisfaction and employee turnover: a meta-analytic test of the Muchinsky model. *Journal of Applied Psychology,* 72, 199-212.

Cattell, R. B., Cattell, A. K., & Cattell, H. E. (1993). *Sixteen Personality factor Questionnaire, Fifth Edition.* Champaign, IL: Institute for Personality and Ability Testing, Inc.

Conn, S. R., & Rieke, M. L. (Eds.). (1994). *16 PF Fifth Edition Technical Manual.* Champaign, IL: Institute for Personality and Ability Testing, Inc.

Costa, P. T., & McCrae, R. R. (1992). *Revised NEO Personality Inventory.* Odessa, FL: Psychological Assessment Resources, Inc.

Costa, P. T., McCrae, R. R., & Holland, J. L. (1984). Personality and vocational interests in an adult sample. *Journal of Applied Psychology,* 39, 390-400.

Costa, P. T., McCrae, R. R., & Kay, G. G. (1995). Persons, places, and personality: Career assessment using the Revised NEO Personality Inventory. *Journal of Career Assessment,* 3, 123-139.

Crites, J. O. (1969). *Vocational psychology.* New York: McGraw-Hill.

Crites, J. O. (1978). *Theory and research handbook for the Career Maturity Inventory,* (2nd ed.). Monterey, CA: CTB McGraw-Hill.

Crites, J. O. (1981). *Career counseling: Models, methods, and materials.* New York: McGraw-Hill.

Crites, J. O. (1982). Testing for career adjustment and development. *Training and Development Journal,* 36, 20-24.

Crites, J. O. (1984). Instruments for assessing career development. In N. C. Gysbers and Associates, *Designing careers* (pp. 248-274). San Francisco: Jossey-Bass.

Crites, J. O., Bechtoldt, H. P., Goodstein, L. D., & Heilbrun, A. B., Jr. (1961). A factor analysis of the California Psychological Inventory. *Journal of Applied Psychology,* 45, 408-414.

CTB/McGraw-Hill. (1996). *Tests of Adult Basic Education, forms 7 & 8.* Monterey, CA: Author.

CTB/McGraw-Hill. (1996). *Tests of Adult Basic Education, Work Related Foundation Skills.* Monterey, CA: Author.

CTB/McGraw-Hill. (1996). *Tests of Adult Basic Education, Work Related Problem Solving.* Monterey, CA: Author.

Darley, J. G., & Hagenah, T. (1955). *Vocational interest measurement.* Minneapolis: University of Minnesota Press.

Dawis, R. V., & Lofquist, L. H. (1984). *A psychological theory of work adjustment.* Minneapolis: University of Minnesota Press.

Digman, J. M. (1990). Personality structure: Emergence of the five-factor model. *Annual Review of Psychology,* 41, 417-440.

Dolliver, R. H. (1969). Strong Vocational Interest Blank versus expressed vocational interests: A review. *Psychological Bulletin,* 72, 95-107.

Droege, R. C., & Padgett, A. (1979). Development of an interest-oriented occupational classification system. *Vocational Guidance Quarterly,* 27, 302-310.

Dyer, D. T. (1939). The relation between vocational interests of men in college and their subsequent histories for ten years. *Journal of Applied Psychology,* 23, 280-288.

Edwards, A. L. (1959). *Edwards Personal Preference Record.* San Antonio, TX: The Psychological Corporation.

Enright, J. B., & Pinneau, S. R. (1955). Predictive value of subjective choice of occupation and the Strong Vocational Interest Blank over fifteen years. *American Psychologist,* 10, 424-425.

Gottfredson, G. D., & Holland, J. L. (1996). *Dictionary of Holland occupational codes.* Odessa, FL: Psychological Assessment Resources, Inc.

Gough, H. G. (1995). *California Psychological Inventory,* Form 434 (3rd ed.). Palo Alto, CA: Consulting Psychologists Press, Inc.

Gough, H. G., & Bradley, P. M. (1996). *CPI manual* (3rd ed.). Palo Alto, CA: Consulting Psychologists Press, Inc.

Grimsley, G., Ruch, F. L., Warren, N. D., & Ford, J. S. (1980). *Employee Aptitude Survey.* Glendale, CA: Psychological Services, Inc.

Gysbers, N. C., & Associates. (1984). *Designing careers.* San Francisco: Jossey-Bass.

Harmon, L. W., Hansen, J. C., Borgen, F. H., & Hammer, A. L. (1994). *Strong Interest Inventory.* Palo Alto, CA: Consulting Psychologists Press, Inc.

Harrington, T. F., & Schafer, W. D. (1996). A comparison of self-reported abilities and occupational ability patterns across occupations. *Measurement and Evaluation in Counseling and Development,* 28, 180-190.

Hartung, P. J. (1999). Interest assessment using card sorts. In M. L. Savickas & A. R. Spokane (Eds.), *Vocational interests: Their meaning measurement, and counseling use* (pp. 235-252). Palo Alto, CA: Davies-Black.

Healy, C. C., & Woodward, G. A. (1998). The Myers-Briggs Type Indicator and career obstacles. *Measurement and Evaluation in Counseling and Development,* 31, 74-85.

Hirsch, S. (1984). *MBTI training guide.* Palo Alto, CA: Consulting Psychologists Press.

Holland, J. L. (1997). *Making vocational choices: A theory of vocational personalities and work environment.* Odessa, FL: Psychological Assessment Resources, Inc.

Holland, J. L., & Lutz, S. W. (1968). The predictive value of a student's choice of vocation. *Personnel and Guidance Journal,* 46, 428-436.

Hoppock, R. (1935). *Job satisfaction.* New York: Harper & Row.

Horney, K. (1945). *Our inner conflicts.* New York: Norton.

Hunter, J. E. (1983). *Overview of validity generalization for the U.S. employment service.* Washington, DC: Division of Counseling and Test Development, Employment and Training Administration, U.S. Department of Labor.

Impara, J. C., & Plake, B. S. (Eds.). (1998). *The thirteenth mental measurements yearbook.* Lincoln, NE: The University of Nebraska Press.

Ironson, G. H., Smith, P. C., Brannick, M. T., Gibson, W. M., & Paul, K. B. (1989). Construction of a job in general scale: A comparison of global, composite and specific measures. *Journal of Applied Psychology,* 74, 1-8.

Jackson, D. N. (1984). *Personality Research Form manual* (3rd ed.). Port Huron, MI: Research Psychologists Press.

Johansson, C. B. (1982). *Career Assessment Inventory – Vocational Version.* Minneapolis: NCS Assessments.

Johansson, C. B. (1986). *Career Assessment Inventory – Enhanced Version.* Minneapolis: NCS Assessments.

Jones, L. K. (1981). *Occ-U-Sort professional manual.* Monterey, CA: Publisher Test Service of CTB/McGraw-Hill.

Karlsen, B., & Gardner, E. F. (1986). *Adult Basic Learning Examination* (2nd ed.). San Antonio, TX: The Psychological Corporation.

Kaufman, A. S., & Kaufman, N. L. (1990). *Kaufman Brief Intelligence Test.* Circle Pines, MN: American Guidance Service, Inc.

Kellog, C. E., & Morton, N. W. (1999). *Beta III.* San Antonio, TX: The Psychological Corporation.

Knowdell, R. L. (1993). *Manual for Occupational Interests Card Sort Kit.* San Jose, CA: Career Research and Testing.

Kuder, F., & Zytowski, D.G. (1991). *Kuder Occupational Interest Survey Form DD general manual.* Adel, IA: National Career Assessment Associates.

Lindemann, J. E., & Matarazzo, J. D. (1990). Assessment of adult intelligence. In G. Goldstein & M. Hersen (Eds.), *Handbook of psychological assessment* (2nd ed., pp. 79-101). Elmsford, NY: Pergamon.

Lubinski, D. (2000). Scientific and social significance of assessing individual differences: Sinking shafts at a few critical points. *Annual Review of Psychology,* 51, 405-444.

Mabe, P. A., III, & West, S. G. (1982). Validity of self-evaluation of ability: A review and meta-analysis. *Journal of Applied Psychology,* 67, 280-296.

Maddox, T. (1997). *Tests: A comprehensive reference for assessments in psychology, education, and business* (4th ed.). Austin, TX: Pro-Ed.

Matarazzo, J. D. (1972). *Wechsler's measurement and appraisal of adult intelligence* (5th ed.). Baltimore: Williams & Wilkins.

McArthur, C., & Stevens, L. B. (1955). The validation of expressed interests as compared to inventoried interests: A fourteen-year-follow-up. *Journal of Applied Psychology,* 39, 184-189.

McCaully, M. H., & Martin, C. R. (1995). Career assessment and the Myers Briggs Type Indicator. *Journal of Career Assessment,* 3, 219-239.

Messick, S. (1995). Validity of psychological assessment: Validation of inferences from persons' responses as scientific inquiry into score meaning. *American Psychologist,* 50, 741-749.

Murray, H. A. (1938). *Exploration in personality.* New York: Oxford University Press.

Myers, I. B., & Briggs, K. C. (1988). *Myers–Briggs Type Indicator.* Palo Alto, CA: consulting Psychologists Press, Inc.

Osterlind, S. J. (1994). Tests of adult basic education. In J. T. Kapes, M. M. Mastie, & E. A. Whitfield (Eds.), *A counselor's guide to career assessment instruments* (3rd ed., pp. 111-114). Alexandria, VA: National Career Development Association.

Prediger, D. J. (1976). A world-of-work map for career exploration. *Vocational Guidance Quarterly,* 29, 293-306.

Prediger, D. J. (1999). Integrating interests and abilities for career exploration: General considerations. In M. L. Savickas & A. R. Spokane (Eds.), *Vocational interests: Their meaning measurement, and counseling use* (pp. 295-325). Palo Alto, CA: Davies-Black.

Purdue Research Foundation. (1968). *Purdue Pegboard.* Minneapolis: NCS Assessments.

Roe, A. (1956). *Psychology of occupations.* New York: Wiley.

Savickas, M. L. (1992). New directions in career assessment. In D. H. Montross, & C. J. Skinkman (Eds.), *Career development: Theory and practice* (pp. 336-355). Springfield, IL: Charles C. Thomas.

Savickas, M. L. (2000). Assessing career decision making. In E. Watkins, & V. Campbell (Eds.), *Testing and assessment in counseling practice* (2nd ed., pp. 429-477). Hillsdale, NJ: Erlbaum.

Schelsinger, L. A., & Zornitsky, J. (1991). Job satisfaction, service capability and customer satisfaction: an examination of linkages and management implications. *Human Resource Planning,* 14, 141-150.

Schuerger, J. M., & Watterson, D. G. (1998). *Occupational interpretation of the 16 personality factor questionnaire.* Cleveland, OH: Authors.

Strong, E. K., Jr. (1943). *Vocational interests of men and women.* Palo Alto, CA: Stanford University Press.

Super, D. E., & Crites, J. O. (1962) *Appraising vocational fitness* (rev. ed.). New York: Harper & Row.

Super, D. E., Thompson, A. S., & Lindeman, R. H. (1988). *The Adult Career Concerns Inventory.* Palo Alto, CA: Consulting Psychologists Press.

Sweetland, R. C., & Keyser, D. J. (1983). *Tests.* Kansas City, MO: Test Corporation of America.

The Psychological Corporation. (1991). *Counselor's manual for the interpretation of the Career Interest Inventory.* San Antonio, TX: Author.

Thompson, A. S., Lindeman, R. H., Super, D. E., Jordaan, J. P., & Myers, R. A. (1981). *Career Development Inventory: Vol. 1. User's manual.* Palo Alto, CA: Consulting Psychologists Press.

Thompson, A. S., Lindeman, R. H., Super, D. E., Jordaan, J. P., & Myers, R. A. (1982). *Career Development Inventory, supplement to user's manual.* Palo Alto, CA: Consulting Psychologists Press.

United States Employment Services. (1982). *USES General Aptitude Test Battery.* Salt Lake City, UT: Western Assessment Research and Development Center.

Ward, A. W. (1995). Review of the Wide Range Achievement Test 3. In J. J. Kramer, & L. L. Murphy (Eds.), *The twelfth mental measurements yearbook* (pp. 1110-1111). Lincoln, NE: The University of Nebraska Lincoln.

Wechsler, D. (1997). *Wechsler Adult Intelligence Scale – Third Edition.* San Antonio, TX: The Psychological Corporation.

Weiss, D. J., Dawis, R. V., & Lofquist, L. H. (1975). *Minnesota Importance Questionnaire.* Minneapolis: Vocational Psychology Research.

Wesman, A. G. (1965). *Wesman Personnel Classification Test.* San Antonio, TX: The Psychological Corporation.

Wilkinson, G. S. (1993). *Wide Range Achievement Test 3.* San Antonio, TX: The Psychological Corporation.

Wonderlic, E. F. (1989). *Wonderlic Personnel Test.* Northfield, IL: E. F. Wonderlic & Associates.

CHAPTER 8
An Active Engagement Counseling Approach

Norman E. Amundson
University of British Columbia

In recent years I have made a concerted effort to stand back and look at the career counseling process through fresh eyes. In following this process I have come to some new understandings with respect to client problems and the way in which clients and counselors relate to one another. I have used the term "active engagement" to capture some elements of this new perspective. Within this article I will be summarizing some of the essential elements of an active engagement approach to career counseling.

A starting point is the definition of what exactly is a career counseling problem. The distinctions between career and personal problems are much fuzzier than many counselors would like to admit. While it may be convenient at times to divide the world into career and personal problems, reality is much more complex. The person dealing with anger management issues or depression usually has to cope with certain occupational realities. Similarly, clients choosing between various career options do so within a social context (parents, spouses, friends). Problem exploration also often flows through different phases. hat starts out as a personal issue may shift into career concerns and vice versa. This integration of personal and career counseling has begun to be recognized by career theorists such as Herr (1993, 1997).

I think it is also important to recognize the broader social and economic context in which career counseling is imbedded. We are living and working in a time of rapid change in every aspect of life. Our client base is shifting and becoming more culturally diverse. The problems that clients are facing not only seem to integrate both personal and career issues, they also seem to be more challenging. In the face of this cultural diversity and problem complexity there is a need for new, more innovative approaches.

Many clients come to counseling with what I would term a "crisis of imagination." They come to counseling because they are 'stuck.' Despite their best efforts they cannot see new possibilities. In coming to counseling they are seeking help in finding their way through the quagmire that stands in front of them. Within this context, counselors reach out to offer assistance and to help their clients find a new vision. In many respects counselors are "reframing agents," persons who listen to how clients are describing (framing) their problems and then use their own creativity and imagination to help clients imagine a new reality (reframing). This process, of course, involves not only creativity and imagination on the part of the counselor but also a rekindling of the client's creative spirit.

The infusion of creativity and imagination requires innovation both within the counseling relationship and within the basic organizational structures (conventions) that serve to define the counseling process. There are many aspects of counseling that have been handed down over the years without any critical review. For example, many organizations still do not recognize that counseling begins the moment a client makes contact with the organization. Counseling is not something that can be isolated into a small room for a prescribed period of time. Efforts to make clients feel welcome and important (that they matter - Schlossberg, Lynch & Chickering, 1989) play a critical role in setting the stage for counseling success. Also, many organizations continue to follow an organizational pattern that reflects a "factory" model of production. Counseling sessions are organized for set periods of time and follow a weekly schedule. These patterns may fit for some people, but there are many people (also cultural groups) that do not readily fit within this framework. Another example cuts to the very heart of the client - counselor dialogue. As clients and counselors come together there is often the assumption that all that is needed is a couple of chairs. Counseling is viewed as a primarily verbal activity with little allowance for visual processes (flip charts) or physical activity (extra chairs or space for clients to walk their problems). It is important to set the stage for creativity and innovation by rethinking many of the counseling conventions that have come to be accepted as standard practice. This does not mean change just for the sake of changing, it does mean playing a more active role in setting the context for counseling.

Building on this foundation I would like to now turn to various phases of counseling and examine how "active engagement" principles can be applied throughout the counseling process. These phases begin with problem definition, move to problem resolution and end with problem closing tasks. It should be understood in presenting these phases that the counseling process is very dynamic and never follows a neatly defined linear process.

Defining the Problem

Many clients come to counseling ready to tell their problems and get to the "business" of seeking solutions. I have found it helpful to begin by asking clients to hold the problems for a moment and to start by simply telling me something about themselves. In this initial segment (usually about 5 or 10 minutes) I listen closely for information that might fit at some later date as well as for points where there might be some "common ground." This strategy serves two functions, first it tells clients that my interest is personal as well as professional and thus helps to build rapport; second, it often provides useful information for later in the counseling process. The importance of taking time to build this initial connection with the client is critical. Research on the effectiveness of counseling has illustrated that the strength of the counseling relationship is the primary factor in the change process (Hackney & Cormier, 1996).

There are, of course, times when this initial counseling relationship is difficult to form, particularly when the client is mandated to come for counseling (Amundson & Borgen, in press). In this situation it is critical to encourage dialogue and to listen to feelings and concerns in an open and non-judgmental fashion. It is also important to openly discuss roles and responsibilities within this structure. Success in forming a relationship is never guaranteed, but in many situations, clients appreciate being heard and having the opportunity to have an honest and open relationship with a counselor.

Non-mandated clients also appreciate the opportunity to openly discuss their expectations regarding the counselling process. For all clients the nature of the client-counselor relationship needs to be negotiated and clarified.(Vahamottonen, 1998). Many clients ascribe certain "magical" powers to counselors (i.e. belief in the power of tests) and assume that in a very short period of time advice can be dispensed and problems solved. In order to help clients appreciate the complexity of the counseling process I have found it helpful to introduce the following centric wheel as a way to frame the counseling process.

FIGURE 1
THE CENTRIC CAREER PLANNING MODEL

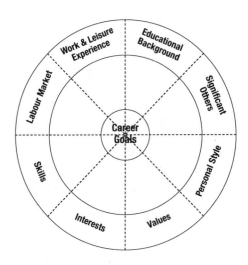

I explain to clients that before I can advance an opinion with respect to career direction I need to have background information in all eight segments of the wheel. In framing the process in this way clients learn that a wide range of information needs to be generated before proceeding with career decision making.

Other aspects of the negotiation process include a discussion about the confidentiality of information, some focus on the usual length and number of counselling sessions, and the effort that needs to be expended in and between (homework) counseling sessions. Building on this dialogue, clients and counselors work toward setting realistic and mutually determined counseling goals. Walter and Peller (1992) provide the following guidance with respect to the development of appropriate goals:

1. Use positive language.
2. Describe goals with action verbs.
3. Focus on the immediate situation.
4. Be specific and work out the details.
5. Emphasize goals that are within the control of the client.
6. Use ordinary language when stating goals.

These goals, of course, are always open for re-negotiation at any stage in the counseling process.

With a solid foundation in place (negotiated roles and goals) the counseling process shifts towards a fuller examination of the clients story. It is important at this juncture to recognize that the visit to a counselor is only one step in a process. There are many other events that need to be understood. As a starting point it is important to clarify the "triggers" that set everything in motion. These triggers can be either external or internal. Examples of external triggers include job loss, promotions, graduation, change in marital status, and so on. Internal triggers refer to events such as turning a certain age (30, 40, 50, 65) or not reaching some of the goals that were set earlier (Schlossberg & Robinson, 1996). Exploring triggers requires a systematic questioning and listening process whereby the counselor probes for thoughts, feelings and actions during the initial review of events. Some typical questions during this phase include:

a) *First Impressions:* When did you first hear about ... or When did you first realize you needed to make a change? How were you feeling at the time?
b) *Transition:* What happened between the time you first heard (thought) about it and it became a reality? What were you thinking and feeling?
c) *Significant Others:* What were the reactions (actions, thoughts, feelings) of others to what was happening?

Following this examination of triggers, there is a shift to the way in which the problem has been "framed" and some of the actions that were taken. Some of the questions that fit within this phase include:

a) *Framing:* How have you made sense of what has happened to you? What are some of the thoughts and feelings you have had about your situation?
a) *Actions:* How have you dealt with your situation? What specifically have you done?
a) *Significant Others:* How has what you are going through affected others? How have others supported you (or not) during this time period?

In exploring the action steps it is important to hear the disappointments, to remind clients of their successes, and to help clients identify what they have learned through the experience. A focus here needs to be on self-directed behavior. One of the most obvious steps (often overlooked) is the fact that they have taken the step of coming to counseling.

In listening to the story as it unfolds it is important to be listening at many different levels. At the most basic level there is simply the sequence of events that led to the problem. In addition there are the ways that the client has tried to make sense of what is happening, and the accompanying feelings. One aspect of listening that is often overlooked is the metaphoric imagery that clients are use to describe their problems. Metaphors are the ways in which we understand and experience events in terms of their connection to other events. For example, we might talk about frustration using metaphors like running into a brick wall, being caught between a rock and a hard place, running fast but getting nowhere, and so on. Metaphors are important because of their visual qualities. Images capture large amounts of information and by changing images we often can make important gains in terms of new ways of understanding (reframing) and of solving problems. The following quotation by Combs and Freedman (1990) describes the close connection between metaphors and flexibility and creativity:

> "Any single metaphor is a particular version of a particular part of the world. When people have only one metaphor for a situation, their creativity is limited. The more metaphors they have to choose from for a given situation, the more choice and flexibility they have in how to handle it. Finding multiple metaphors expands the realm of creativity." (p.32)

Within this phase counselors are merely identifying metaphors and trying to develop visual images of the problem. In the next phase working with these images can become a powerful tool for intervention.

Resolving the Problem

In some instances counselors find themselves stuck in the first counseling phase. They listen to the story, elaborate the many complexities of the problem but have no idea how to proceed from this point. Clients come to counselors to explain their problems, but the bottom line is that they are also looking for some type of resolution. At the very least counselors need to develop the skills to help clients assess their problems from different perspectives. Helping people to change the way in which they think about themselves and the problems they are facing is at the core of the counseling process.

For some counselors the problem is not the lack of a solution but rather the fact that they move too quickly to an action plan. In most instances, the counselor primarily constructs this action plan with minimal input from the client. While this has some efficiency attached to it, usually there is a breakdown because the client has little ownership of the plan that has been developed. Under these circumstances there is a need to slow the process down and spend more time in the resolving phase.

There are many different ways to proceed with this second phase. Certainly the issue of assessment is of central importance. People need to understand their abilities, interests, values and personality. They need to appreciate how family and friends influence the decisions that are made. They also need to have some understanding of the external reality. How do educational training and the labor market function; what are the local, national and global trends? Many of these factors are outlined in the "wheel" that was described earlier (Figure 1).

STRUCTURED ASSESSMENT

There are innumerable methods of facilitating the assessment process. Some are relatively straightforward and simply involve directing people to the right information i.e. through the internet, through self -help books such as Career Pathways (Amundson & Poehnell, 1996), and in some instances, through psychoeducational instruction. Other methods utilize a certain degree of structure in guiding the exploration process. An example being the questioning strategies suggested in narrative and brief/solution- focused counseling (deShazer, 1985; O'Hanlon & Weiner-Davis, 1989; White & Epston, 1990; and Friedman, 1993). The focus of solution-focused questioning is to identify personal strengths, emphasize positive changes, and suggest possible solutions. Listed below are five examples of different questioning strategies:

1. Description of between session changes - The counselor makes the assumption that positive changes are happening between sessions and asks questions to elaborate these events.

2. Coping strategies in other situations - The counselor asks questions to help clients realize that they have successfully solved problems in other situations. Many of the strategies that have worked for clients previously can be applied to their current problems.

3. Exception Finding questions - Many clients describe their situations in an overly negative fashion. There are often instances where "cracks of sunlight" shine through and the counselor helps clients to consider these more positive instances.

4. Scaling questions - Clients may have difficulties in appreciating that problem solving is often like a journey. They need to have a way of measuring where they are now, what would constitute progress and what would be a step backwards. The counselor can use questioning with scaling metaphors to help clients better formulate the change process.

5. The miracle question - Most of us usually approach problems in a linear fashion, starting with the problem and looking ahead to the solution. What would happen if the process was reversed? With this intervention the counselor helps clients to start with the solution (not worrying about how they get there - a miracle) and look backwards to the problem and the steps that would need to be taken to move forward. With this particular questioning strategy I have found it helpful to have clients actually "walk the problem." Sometimes we try to do too much at a conceptual level. By having clients actually walk around the room they have the opportunity to develop insights at many different levels.

Another structured questioning strategy is to follow what has been described as the pattern identification exercise (Amundson, 1995). The assumption here is that we need to do in-depth exploration to identify some of the key patterns which drive behavior. The counselor helps direct the process in conducting this exploration, but clients are given every opportunity to do their own analysis and application. Any number of experiences can be explored, but the most common approach is to start with personal interests. The steps of inquiry are as follows:

1. Ask the client to think about a particular activity; this activity can come from a number of different domains. Once the activity has been defined, ask the person to think about a specific time when it was very enjoyable and a time when it was less so.

2. Have the client describe in detail the positive and negative experiences. Some questions can be asked at this point to facilitate a full description of events. Ask about the people involved, feelings, thoughts, challenges, successes and motivations. What are the particular dynamics that differentiate the positive and negative dynamics? Depending on the situation, it may be helpful to extend the questioning to some of the contextual issues. Ask about how their interest developed over time and what they project for the future. As the story is told it is helpful for the counselor to write down what is being said, either on a flip chart or a large piece of paper clearly visible to the client. This information will serve as the foundation for the analysis; and, thus it is important to get down on paper everything that is said. (Generally, I am not in favor of taking notes during a

session, and it can be helpful to discuss this beforehand if it might be an issue.) Whatever is being written down should be in clear view for the client as well as the counselor.

3. After a full discussion, have the client consider what types of patterns are suggested by the information that has been generated. Give the client every opportunity to make connections and provide ongoing support and encouragement. Ask how each specific piece of information reflects something about the client, i.e. goals, values, aptitudes, personal style, interests . During this period, the counselor can provide some input. The statements made by the counselor should be tentative and be positively linked with client comments. While this can be an excellent opportunity for reframing, it is important not to lose sight of the contributions made by the client.

4. Following the identification of themes, the counselor moves to application issues. As above, the client speaks first and then the counselor follows with some comments. The issue here is how personal information relates to career choice and action planning (Amundson, 1998, 101-102).

The strength of the Pattern Identification Exercise lies in the fact that clients are actively engaged in the process of self discovery. They are not only pulling out important information but also are learning a structured self-exploration process. One limitation of this approach is the reliance on description and analysis by clients. he cognitive abilities of the client and counselor can have some influence on effectiveness of the method.

There are many more structured methods of assessment that could be discussed, some examples being task analysis, achievement profiling, identifying career anchors (values), card sorts, early recollections, and so on. Additional information on these methods is included in *Active Engagement: Enhancing the Career Counselling Process* (Amundson, 1998). What stands out about all of these methods is a structured sequence of activities that serve as a catalyst for career assessment and exploration.

DYNAMIC ASSESSMENT

There are also other methods of assessment which are more dynamic and do not have the same degree of structure. One method that was introduced earlier is the use of metaphors to help clients better understand their personal situation. Metaphors capture a great deal of information and as such, are excellent vehicles for both understanding and reframing client problems. Suppose for example, that a client is frustrated by their lack of progress in finding employment. Expressions of frustration can take many forms. Metaphorically speaking the client may describe their situation as "beating their head against a wall." It can be helpful to take this metaphor and sketch the figure on a flip chart or other piece of paper. With the client, there is then a further exploration of what it means to be beating one's head against the wall. Words such as the following may come to mind: futility, pain, isolation, confusion, and despair. Focusing on the figure, the counselor and client can then look at different ways to change the situation. Perhaps it would be helpful to simply step back from the wall and get a better perspective. Maybe it would help to have a hammer or ladder to handle the situation. Perhaps another person would be helpful to give a boost or provide a different perspective. At the most basic level, maybe there is a need for a helmet to cushion the blows to the head. These different perspectives contain within them ideas for action planning. By stepping back the client takes some time to re-assess the situation. The ladder and hammer may represent the need for new tools. Support from another person may be the realization that they are trying to do too much on their own. The helmet may be the need for an immediate change in the situation. By considering these various options (images) the client may develop a new appreciation of their situation and develop some new ideas about what needs to be done.

A key principle in working at this dynamic level is to help clients gain a better understanding of their internal world through the process of "externalization." In the above example the counselor focuses on a particular metaphor and then makes it more concrete (external) by giving it some shape through a rough sketch. The focus shifts from the internal world of the client to an external figure that can be discussed and adjusted more readily. When the client re-integrates the new figure there may be greater self understanding and the development of a new action plan.

Externalization can happen at many different levels. Sometimes it involves simply putting down on paper some of the ideas that have been swirling within the internal world. Brainstorming/mind mapping are good examples of how ideas can be generated and connected to develop new perspectives. With brainstorming the idea is simply to get ideas down on paper without evaluating them. In mind mapping there is an attempt to go beyond the words and start to draw connections. I have used mind mapping as a way to summarize the major ideas that have been discussed. By placing all of the ideas on a flip there is the opportunity to create a visual map of what has been discussed. There may also be an opportunity to develop some new connections between the ideas.

As clients confront different problems they often find themselves torn (split) between different options. On the one hand they may want to take certain actions, but something is holding them back. These moments of indecision can be frustrating and consume large amounts of time and energy. Both sides of the question can be played (another metaphor) back and forth in their mind. Working with this impasse can take many different forms. Sometimes it is sufficient to simply talk through the various issues. At a visual level it may help to draw out both sides of the question using figures on a flip chart. Working at a physical level, the counselor may decide to use a procedure of dramatic re-enactment using chairs to represent the different parts of the self (Greenberg, Rice and Elliott, 1993). With this process clients are encouraged to "act out" and give "voice" to the various positions. Of course, it is not just about having each side of an issue be clearly heard, it is also about the dialogue that needs to occur between the different positions. The counselor plays a pivotal role in facilitating the discussion that needs to occur. As a starting point the different positions need to be named. Suppose, for example, that a client was trying to decide whether to move to a new geographic area and look for work or stay where they are. The names of the chairs might be "Moving On" and "Staying Put." When sitting in one of the chairs the client should elaborate on the position (feelings as well as thoughts) and direct comments to the other chair - not to the counselor. To assist with this process the counselor can move beside the client when they are speaking and encourage the client to face the other chair and explain what they are thinking and feeling. The counselor needs to direct the discussion by moving the client from chair to chair. The dialogue that often occurs tends to follow a certain pattern. Greenberg et al. (1993) have described this pattern as follows:

1. *Predialogue Stage:* A collaborative discussion with the client about how the two-chair activity is going to proceed with some explanation of the roles that will be assumed.

2. *Opposition Stage:* The two positions often begin with different levels of power. As the discussion proceeds there is a tendency for one chair to dominate the other. Feelings as well as ideas need to be expressed at this point.

3. *Contact Stage:* The counselor helps the client become aware of the various self-criticisms and injunctions (words such as "should," "must," and "have to"). Each of the sides becomes more aware of one another.

4. *Integration Stage:* There often is a "softening" of each position and a greater acceptance of one another.

5. *Postdialogue Stage:* Creating perspective and better understanding of the situation. Helping clients reflect upon the experience.

In using a stage model approach to understand the process it is important to recognize that these are just general guidelines. The actual process is much more dynamic and depends on a combination of counselor skill and intuition i.e. when to move people from one chair to the other, what supplementary questions to ask.

The two-chair technique can be modified in many different ways depending on the particular demands of the situation. On occasion I have introduced a third chair, a mediator chair, to assist in the integration process. There also may be more than one position that needs to be expressed. Perhaps there are three or four different positions that need to be articulated. Different chairs can be used to reflect the different positions, or if this is not possible, use different crayons (placed in the hand of the client) can be used to symbolize the various stances. Whatever method is used, the basic point is to have clients assume different positions, formalize the dialogue between these positions, and facilitate greater insight and integration.

The counseling methods that have been highlighted thus far reflect the importance of externalization in working with client problems. Another related concept is that of "projection," the process of putting something of ourselves into all of our interactions. In whatever we do we respond in a unique fashion that reflects our personal perspectives. Even the simplest task contains some elements of projection. For example, when we pick up a menu in a restaurant we do so in a unique fashion that reflects our interests, background and personality. Some people start from the back of the menu, others from the front. For some people price is a determining factor, for others it is a desire to try something different. These idiosyncrasies are indicative of the process of projection.

Many dynamic self-assessment activities encourage projection by involving clients in ambiguous activities where there are no clear right or wrong answers. These activities can include certain games, photography, writing tasks (journals and poetry), story telling, drawing, and so on. As an illustration of how drawings might be used as a counseling tool consider some of the following options:

a) Using a blank sheet of paper, make a drawing of your present environment. Include in this diagram both the people and places that are important to you. (Modify by having the person look ahead to life in two to five years time).

b) Draw a picture of yourself doing something together with others (Make this drawing more specific by referring to family members or other significant others, also you may want to focus on the work place or on involvement in leisure activities).

c) Draw a life-line that illustrates your experiences (ups and downs) over a period of time (like a stock index). Describe the situations that account for the low and the high points in your drawing.

When introducing drawing tasks it is important to emphasize the voluntary nature of the activity. For some people, there are many negative associations with drawing and if this is the case other activities may be more appropriate. Usually drawings are a stimulus to story telling. After clients have completed a drawing it is important to discuss what the drawing means to them, what they felt like when doing the drawing, and maybe how the drawing might change shape in different situations. There are many elements to consider when examining a drawing. These include factors such as the size of the figures, the proximity of the figures, figures that might have been omitted, and the use of certain colors and shading. Interpreting drawings is a complex process and must be imbedded within a client-counselor collaborative relationship.

Understanding and working with projection and externalization within counseling requires both skill and creativity. While there are some general guidelines, much of the actual process is "crafted" to fit each situation. The image of "careercraft" as a metaphor for career counseling practice has been elaborated more recently by Poehnell and Amundson (in press). This image captures the elements of skill and creativity but also adds the notion of function and practicality. There certainly appears to be some strong similarities between the professional craftsperson and the actively engaged counselor.

Consider the following quotation by Else Regensteiner (1970) in *The Art of Weaving:*

"Weaving has many faces: it is a medium for working directly with fundamental materials to create joyful mixtures of textures and colors, to feel the accomplishment of mastering the tools and learning the steps, and to explore the discipline of fine craftsmanship. It is an art, an expression of our time that can have the brilliance of a painting, the dimension of sculpture, the shape of invention, and the form of imagination. It is functional, intimately related to us through our daily use of fabrics...it is as individual as its creator will make it. It is a tool for the educator and a technique for the therapist; it is romantic and sober, ancient and contemporary. As with all crafts, fundamentals and theory must be learned before the full range of creative possibilities can be embraced. But invention can start together with learning, and technical perfection does not have to be dull" (p. 9).

Many counselors do not choose to embrace the more dynamic assessment methods because they feel overwhelmed by the skill and creativity that is involved. The encouragement from Regensteiner is that becoming a craftsperson requires some basic fundamentals, but it is a journey and considerably exciting that the possibility can be generated through the learning process – the same applies in counseling. While the task may initially appear daunting, the rewards are considerable and once counselors have opened themselves up to more dynamic assessment methods the rewards are considerable.

CONNECTING TO THE LABOR MARKET

For many clients one of the main challenges is to understand and connect with the current labor market. Times have changed and labor market turbulence is an ongoing reality. Reid (1996) the CEO of the Angus Reid polling group states that "the basic rules and patterns that made our lives predictable, that imposed a sense of order and continuity, no longer seem to apply" (p. 14). Clients and counselors need to come to terms with this new economic reality. Herr (1997) suggests the need for a new occupational identity, one that includes life-long learning; defining oneself through skills and achievements rather than job titles (a portfolio worker); being open to part-time, contract and entrepreneurial opportunities; learning how to market oneself in a competitive marketplace; thinking globally; and above all being flexible.

Perhaps the starting point to understanding the labor market is to recognize that there are many different labor markets. Firstly, there is what might be described as a personal labor market. We all have opportunities that are connected to the people we know. There is no question that "knowing the right people" can make a big difference with respect to gathering information and to finding appropriate job opportunities. A starting point for many clients is to recognize the contacts that are already in place.

Of course, for many people their interests extend beyond their current group of contacts and the challenge is to expand personal connections through information networking. Most people who are working are pleased to give short interviews (about 20 minutes) describing their field of work and their particular occupational role. These interviews focus on how the person obtained their position (education, work experiences, etc.), what their duties are in the job, how the job has changed over time, what their likes and dislikes are, and what the prospects are for the future. As a concluding question, it is often helpful to inquire about whom else they would recommend for an interview. Information interviewing gives people the opportunity to enhance their occupational understanding and to expand their personal labor market.

Gathering and interpreting labor market information can be accomplished in many different ways. In addition to personal contacts there is a wealth of information in libraries, community centers, educational counseling centers, employment centers, and on the internet. These resources can help stimulate ideas about occupational options. Often one of the biggest challenges is to break outside a rather limited occupational framework. Most people when thinking of occupations think of standard jobs such as nurse, doctor, lawyer, plumber, carpenter, and so on. Moving beyond these job titles requires some exposure to new information. In some instances it is also important to broaden the image of looking for work to include making work or entrepreneurial activity. There are many situations where work is not to be "found" using the traditional methods. Encouraging and supporting entrepreneurial actions allows for greater degrees of freedom.

Interpreting labor market trends is also a skill that is well worth learning. Many clients focus only on the current opportunities and trends. While this certainly is helpful, in many cases they would be well advised to use a longer-term perspective. Positioning oneself for emerging opportunities often can lead to more satisfying results. Certainly this is the case when considering some types of educational training.

Making Decisions

The career counseling process is filled with opportunities for decision making by clients and counselors. Rather than being a specific point in time, it is often useful to look at decision making as part of a journey. There are certainly times when significant changes in direction are made, but these moments usually come as part of an ongoing process. Often clients want to limit in some ways the decision-making processes that are open to them. They want to make the "big decision" that will set a pathway for their entire life. Often all that needs to be decided is a first step; other decisions will follow, as more information becomes known. Addressing this need for pre-mature closure becomes part of the counseling process.

The way in which decisions are made has received considerable attention in recent years. Traditionally decision making has been viewed as a rational cognitive activity where clients assess the relative merits of various options. This can involve a simple list of advantages or disadvantages or it can be more complex and involve the construction of a decision making grid (Amundson & Poehenell, 1996). At the other end of the spectrum there is the intuitive approach to decision making. The dichotomy between cognitive and intuitive decision making has been challenged in recent years. H.B. Gelatt (1989, 1991) makes that point that what we need now is a more balanced approach, something that he calls "positive uncertainty." We need to use a logical process for making decisions but also maintain a certain degree of wariness and uncertainty about the decisions that are being made. This paradoxical approach relies on "both / and" rather than "either / or" thinking. The four paradoxical principles that define positive uncertainty follow:

1. Be focused and flexible about what you want
   - Know what you want but don't be sure
   - Treat goals as hypotheses
   - Balance achieving goals with discovering them
2. Be aware and wary about what you know
   - Recognize that knowledge is power and ignorance is bliss
   - Treat memory as an enemy
   - Balance using information with imagination
3. Be objective and optimistic about what you believe
   - Notice that reality is in the eye of the beholder
   - Treat beliefs as prophesy
   - Balance reality testing with wishful thinking
4. Be practical and magical about what you do
   - Learn to plan and plan to learn
   - Treat intuition as real
   - Balance responding to change with causing change (Gelatt, 1991, p. 12)

The principles of positive uncertainty have a close relationship to many of the foundational concepts of active engagement.

New Learning

There are times in the career counseling process when there is a specific need for additional learning. Clients may need to learn, as part of the job search process, how to contact employers and create a good impression in interviews. This new learning requires behavioral rehearsal training where the counselor assumes the role of "coach." In this role the counselor helps to define achievable goals and breaks down complex tasks into manageable units for learning. Encouragement and constructive feedback are provided throughout the process.

Westwood (1994) has developed a behavioral rehearsal sequence that can be applied in a number of different domains:

1. *Assess:* determine what needs to be learned
2. *Explain:* use specific examples to describe what needs to be learned.
3. *Preliminary Modeling:* demonstrate through role playing.
4. *Comment & Question:* discuss and clarify what has been observed.
5. *Initial Practice:* client's role play what they have observed.
6. *Feedback & Encouragement:* focus on the positive achievement. (Repeat as Necessary)
7. *Goal Setting & Contracting:* encourage clients to practice their skill(s) in actual situations. Allow time for additional practice as necessary.
8. *Follow-Up:* check on progress and provide additional encouragement and practice.

This comprehensive rehearsal strategy is designed to provide ample opportunity for instruction, demonstration, practice, encouragement and correction.

Using visualization to have clients imagine themselves successfully completing tasks can enrich behavioral rehearsal training. Audio/video recording and playback can also facilitate the learning process. As with the other problem resolving approaches, there are many strategies that can used as part of the process.

Closing the Problem

Most counselors operate within a limited time frame and there will come a point where there is **mutual** agreement, with respect, to ending the counseling process. The expectation here is that some gains have been made toward resolving the problem. There may be a need for further counseling at some later date, but for now enough has been accomplished to warrant closure of the counseling relationship.

The starting point for this closure phase is a summary of what has been learned during the counseling period. This learning starts with the client's perspective and then moves to what the counselor has observed. In making these observations I have found it helpful to document certain "moments of movement." These moments are indicators of a change in perspective (reframing). Listed below are some illustrative comments from clients:

"That really has got me thinking. I never looked at it that way before."

"I used to feel really down when people wouldn't take my resume. Now when I get turned down, I try to learn from it and develop new ways to make my presentation."

These special moments of movement are indicators of how change has developed.

In addition to the moments of movement this is also an opportunity for a counselor to use strength challenge to identify some of the changes that have been noted. Strength challenge is a communication skill that is based on the notion of challenging clients with observed strengths. Often clients "sell themselves short" and need to be reminded (with specific behavioral observations) of the strengths that they do possess.

Depending on the issues involved and the strength of the counseling relationship there also may be a need for acknowledgment of feelings of loss and uncertainty. A positive counseling relationship often provides some much needed support and encouragement. Under these conditions it is not surprising that some strong feelings may emerge. In dealing with these feelings it is important to have acknowledgement without dependency.

Action planning is a very significant part of the closing process. Clients need to consolidate their learning and focus their attention on concrete and attainable goals. Walter and Peller (1992) offer the following suggestions with respect to framing goals so that there is a higher likelihood of success:

1. Be positive when stating goals. Emphasize what will be accomplished through the action plan.
2. Use action words (e.g. verbs ending with "ing": researching, writing, calling) to describe intentions.
3. Focus on the present. What is going to happen after the client leaves the counseling session?
4. Be specific and think through all the details.
5. Pay particular attention to those areas that are within the client's personal control.
6. Use examples and metaphors that are within the client's experience and understanding.

In applying these suggestions it is important to keep in mind that clients need to play an integral part in the development of the action plan, otherwise there is no commitment. Also, in the development of a plan there may be a need to consider back-up options. Given the high levels of uncertainty there is a need to prepare for potential obstacles.

As a final concluding note in the counseling process there are times when some form of "ceremony" is needed to bring about proper closure. This ceremony can be as simple as the formal signing (and witnessing) of a written action plan. Again, depending on the nature of the relationship, there may be times when some food is shared to acknowledge the closure of the counseling relationship.

Case Illustration

As a brief illustration of how the Active Engagement model can be applied in career counseling consider the following case study:

BACKGROUND

Sandy is a Croatian refugee. She is 26 years old and has been in the country for 6 months. She was studying to be a doctor and was in the middle of her program when the war broke out. She fled to Romania and was living in a refugee camp prior to coming to North America.

Sandy's mother died of cancer when she was young. Her father was killed in the war. She has one younger brother who she would like to bring to North America. Her brother is currently living with an uncle.

In terms of academic studies, Sandy has always done very well. She is interested in alternative medicine and hopes that she can find something in this field. She is torn between her educational ambitions (she would like to start a training program in the fall) and her self-imposed obligations to her brother (to get a job and become a sponsor).

Sandy is trying very hard to learn English. As an expression of this desire, she found an English speaking person to room with. She connects with the Croatian community in the city but takes every opportunity to speak English. She is currently enrolled in an English course at the community college.

COUNSELING APPROACH

In the preliminary discussion with Sandy it became clear that she was very motivated to move forward with her career plans. I was responsive to this high energy but also took time at the beginning to get some of the details of her personal story. This story telling focused on her past experiences in Croatia, her present life circumstances (practical realities), as well as her hopes for the future. The focus here was very much on Sandy as a person, not just another client coming through the door. Much of the background information was generated during this first session.

At a practical level one of the issues was the length of sessions. Sandy had to come a long way by bus and it seemed worthwhile to explore the viability of longer counseling sessions. With this in mind, she was booked for a "double" appointment for the second session.

Sandy seemed very interested in the career wheel and as part of her initial homework assignment she finished most of the Career Pathways workbook (most clients would do one or two exercises, she completed the whole book!). While the information generated was important, I was most struck by her incredibly high level of motivation. During the first part of the second session we explored the information that she had generated. The values underlying her career choice was one of the more interesting pieces of information that came out of this exploration. Her mother's death was a very significant event in her life and she felt completely helpless. Medical procedures were less than ideal and there also was little consideration of alternative medical approaches. Her desire for a medical career was formulated at this early age.

During this second session we also started to focus more specifically on the push and pull of her concerns for her brother and her career ambitions. Several different activities were used to further this exploration process. Perhaps the most prominent activity was the two-chair technique. One of the chairs represented further education and the second one represented getting a job and helping her brother. The activity seemed "a bit strange" to her at the beginning, but she soon became very engaged in the dialogue process. While there was not a full integration at the end, it helped to clarify the two sides. There was the recognition that it would be possible to start with a shorter educational program and then look for work.

At the end of the second session we came back to the "wheel" and her need for more information about the labor market and educational possibilities. As homework she set off to explore various options and to also have her own educational qualifications assessed by a local university. For the next session we decided that only one time slot (50 minutes) would be necessary.

In coming to the third session Sandy was coping with some mixed emotions. She had explored some alternate medical programs and found that the cost was just too high. On a more positive note, she had found that the local university would give her two years credit for her prior medical studies in Croatia. The discussion in this third session focused on the options at the local university. One of the programs that looked interesting was a Nutrition program. It was a four-year program and if she could get credit for the first two years she would only have two years remaining. The program also seemed to fit within the alternate medicine option. Finding out more about the Nutrition program became the next priority. Enquiry phone calls were made and Sandy arranged an appointment for herself with one of the faculty members.

The fourth and final counseling session focused on the information Sandy had obtained from her meeting with the faculty member. She was very encouraged by what she had learned. The costs of the program could be covered through a student loan. The content of the program looked very interesting and fit with the interests and skills that were expressed as part of the wheel. She also was pleased that she could complete her Bachelor's degree with only two more years of study. She could then find work and begin the process of sponsoring her brother. She also had long term plans for a Masters degree. To help with short and long-term planning process I used the Miracle Question and had her "walk the problem." This visualization activity seemed to provide a concrete structure for action planning.

This last session was certainly filled with high energy, but there were also some apprehensions. She was primarily worried about her ability to handle the English language. Using a strength challenge approach I focused on what she had accomplished thus far and how these strengths would serve her further as she pursued her academic plans. This summary served as the conclusion for the session and seemed to buoy her spirits. The door was left open for further counseling sessions if there was a need.

Conclusion

The active engagement approach that is being presented here is based on a number of key principles. First, there is the recognition of the overlap between personal and career issues. There also is a focus on imagination, creativity and flexibility. This creativity is evident in both the counselor and the client and helps to define some elements of the counseling process. Lastly, the engagement of clients and counselors is designed to be active with an emphasis on full involvement through various counseling activities.

The counseling process as described here passes through the phases of problem defining, problem resolving, and problem closing. These phases represent a general progression but often do not follow a linear path. People move back and forth between the phases and counselors need to respond accordingly.

Developing the skills and attitudes for the active engagement approach requires both personal and professional development. Counselor education and development must go hand in hand with new counseling methods. The choice towards imagination, creativity, and flexibility is an exciting one but also requires its own methods, discipline, and courage. Considerable attention needs to be focused on developing a learning climate that supports reflection, exploration, and creativity. Safety, trust and risk taking are essential training conditions for this approach. There are also many different training methods that can be employed. Metaphoric case conceptualization is a good illustration of how case material can be represented and discussed using the collaborative construction of metaphors (Amundson, 1988).

References

Amundson, N. E. (1988). The use of metaphor and drawings in case conceptualization. *Journal of Counseling and Development,* 66, 391-393.

Amundson, N. E. (1995). Pattern identification exercise. *ERIC Digest, EDD-CG-95-69,* Greensboro, NC: ERIC/CASS.

Amundson, N. E. (1998). *Active engagement: Enhancing the career counselling process.* Richmond, B.C.: Ergon Communications.

Amundson, N. E., & Borgen, W. A. (in press). Mandated clients in career or employment counseling. *Journal of Employment Counseling.*

Amundson, N. E., & Poehnell, G. (1996) *Career pathways* (2nd ed.). Richmond, BC: Ergon Communications.

Combs, G., & Freedman, J. (1990). *Symbol, story & ceremony.* New York: Norton.

deShazer, S. (1985). *Keys to solution in brief therapy.* New York: Norton.

Friedman, S. (1993). *The new language of change.* New York: The Guilford Press.

Gelatt, H. B. (1989). Positive uncertainty: A new decision-making framework for counseling. *Journal of Counseling Psychology,* 33, 252-256.

Gelatt, H. B. (1991). *Creative decision making.* Los Altos, CA: Crisp Publications.

Greenberg, L. S., Rice, L. N., & Elliott, R. (1993). *Facilitating emotional change: The moment by moment process.* New York: Guilford.

Hackney, H. L., & Cormier, L. S. (1996). *The professional counselor: A process guide to helping* (3rd ed.). Boston: Allyn and Bacon.

Herr, E. L. (1993). Contexts and influences on the need for personal flexibility for the 21st century (part 1). *Canadian Journal of Counselling,* 27, 148-164.

Herr, E. L. (1997). Perspectives on career guidance and counseling in the 21st century. *Educational and Vocational Guidance Bulletin,* 60, 1-15.

O'Hanlon, W. H., & Weiner-Davis, M. (1989). *In search of solutions: A new direction in psychotherapy.* New York: Norton.

Poehnell, G., & Amundson, N. E. (in press). Careercraft: Engaging with, energizing and empowering career creativity. In M. Peiper, M. Arthur, R. Goffee, & N. Anand (Eds.), *Career creativity: Explorations in the re-making of work.* London: Oxford Press.

Regensteiner, E. (1970). *The Art of Weaving.* New York: Van Nostrand Reinhold.

Reid, A. (1996). Shakedown: *How the new economy is changing our lives.* Toronto: Doubleday.

Schlossberg, N. K., & Robinson, S. P. (1996). *Going to plan B.* New York: Simon & Schuster.

Schlossberg, N. K., Lynch, A. Q., & Chickering, A. W. (1989). *Improving higher education environments for adults.* San Francisco: Jossey-Bass.

Vahamottonen, T. (1998). *Reframing career counselling in terms of counsellor-client negotiations. Doctoral dissertation,* University of Joensuu, Finland.

Walter, J. L., & Peller, J. E. (1992). *Becoming solution-focused in brief therapy.* New York.

Westwood, M. J. (1994). *Developing skills for social-cultural competencies. Unpublished manuscript.* UBC, Vancouver.

White, M., & Epston, D. (1990). *Narrative means to therapeutic ends.* New York: Norton.

CHAPTER 9
Career Planning and Technology in the 21st Century

JoAnn Harris-Bowlsbey
Loyola College in Maryland

In the previous edition of this book this chapter discussed assumptions related to career development, a model for career planning, and the role of two different kinds of computer-assisted career planning systems in assisting individuals with career choice and planning. Expecting that a simple update would suffice in preparation for this second edition, the author read the chapter. To her surprise there had been such tremendous change in career development theory, career development assumptions, and the role of technology in the years between the first and second editions that she concluded that it was necessary to discard the previous chapter and rewrite it entirely. Thus the chapter will first deal with changes in career development theory and assumptions about career development and then discuss the role of technology in supporting this development for adults.

Career Development Theory

The earlier version of this chapter highlighted the career choice theory of John L. Holland and the career development theory of Donald E. Super. Holland's (1997) theory can be briefly described in four statements:

1. Individuals can be described as a combination of six personality types.
2. Environments can be described as a combination of the same six personality types.
3. Individuals seek environments that are compatible with their personality types.
4. To the extent that individuals are able to make this match, we may predict satisfaction in work.

This time- and research-tested theory is representative of trait-and-factor theory, first proposed by Parsons (1909), that has had very great impact on career counseling since its genesis. This approach is still very useful for assisting an individual to identify vocational options at a specific point in time; but by reviewing the career theory of the late 20th century, it is clear that career development and choice in the 21st century is considerably more than matching the characteristics of people and environments.

Super's early theory (1957) proposed that career development occurs in defined, sequential life stages, each characterized by common and necessary developmental tasks. Super proposed that performing developmental tasks appropriately and on schedule was the formula for acquiring vocational maturity. The self-concept was proposed as the catalyst and driving force of career development.

Each in its own way, the theoretical positions of Lent and colleagues (Lent,

Brown, & Hackett, 1996), Brown (1995), and Sampson and colleagues (Peterson, Sampson, & Reardon, 1991) emphasize the intention and motivation of the individual in making career choices. Lent et al. (1996) stress the role of cognitive factors in career choice and development, emphasizing self-efficacy beliefs, outcome expectations, and personal goals.

Brown (1995) proposes that values are the driving force in career choice and development and that making choices that coincide with values is essential to satisfaction. Peterson et al. (1991), in their cognitive information processing approach, also stress the role of cognitive factors in career choice. Their first three levels of cognition include the trait-and-factor components (self-knowledge, career information, and decision making); but they add a fourth level that includes self-talk, self-awareness, and the monitoring and control of cognitions.

Each of these theories places far more emphasis on the individual as the designer of his or her own career than does Holland's theory, and in so doing, moves career choice and development beyond the recognition of the influences of heredity and environment, capturing its essence in a three-letter code, and identifying matching environments. Similarly, each of these theories ignores the sequential time dimension of career development and places other constructs (self-efficacy, values, information processing, and intentionality) more central to career choice and development than self-concept. Thus these theories propose that there are additional important factors in career choice and development in the 21st century besides interests, abilities, developmental tasks, and self-concept.

Other theorists of the late 20th century—specifically, Savickas (2000) and Hansen (1997)—propose that matters related to meaning, wholeness, family, and making contributions to the global society affect career choice and planning. Savickas underscores the importance of assisting a client to identify life themes, values, and unfinished business as a way to make career choices that have meaning as individuals seek to live out themes and complete unfinished business through work. This view gives work a deeply spiritual meaning.

Hansen proposes six critical themes that should guide career choice and planning in the 21st century. These themes include finding work that needs to be done for the global good, creating career options that take family needs into consideration, weaving our lives into a meaningful whole, and exploring spirituality and life purpose. This approach is far different from the more self-centered view of assessing yourself and then making choices designed to provide the greatest personal satisfaction.

The earlier version of this chapter described a systematic process for making career choices, assuming that a left-brain, logical approach is likely to provide the best outcomes and that alternatives can be identified, enlightened by information, and selected with a high degree of certainty. At least three theorists of the late 20th century—Miller-Tiedeman (1999), Krumboltz, Mitchell, and Levin (1999), and Gelatt (1995) – are emphasizing the impossibility of planning ahead, of following step-by-step logical models, and of being able to identify the "best" alternative. Rather, they are speaking of following one's intuition, going with life's flow, devoting energy to constant exploration, and developing skills to make quick transitions. All of these positions, so briefly described, indicate that career choices and development in the 21st century are complex, ever changing, and driven by a multitude of forces, both internal and external.

These theoretical positions would lead us to make a series of assumptions about the career development of adults in the 21st century that are quite different from those of the second half of the 20th century. Some of those assumptions are as follows:

- No one rubric for guiding career choice will suffice for all. Individuals will be driven in their choices by interests, skills or abilities, values, a search for life meaning, a desire to do work that society badly needs, a desire to merge personal needs with those of family, self-concept, and a variety of other internal and external forces. Internal forces will be coordinated by the self-concept and guided by values.

- A planful decision-making process, learned and applied, will not be sufficient to assist individuals with career choices and development. Change and information will be so plentiful and pervasive that individuals will often focus on near-term transition survival rather than long-term planning.

- Given that the social contract between employers and employees has been broken, individuals and organizations will pursue their own best interests. For that reason, individuals will assume more personal responsibility for career choices and planning than ever before, and organizations will continue to deal with getting their work done in the way they assume to be more cost-efficient—including part-time work, outsourced work, and use of contingent workers.

- Individuals will make many more career changes during a lifetime than they did in the 20th century. For that reason possessing a set of transferable work skills and a model for coping with transitions may be a very important skill combination. Learning will be lifelong since work skills will need to be continually updated.

- The common definition of career as a sequence of work positions in a person's life will be replaced by a definition that stresses the expression of self through several different life roles that encompass all of life, taking into account the needs of family and society.

Just as career development theory and assumptions have changed in the last 10 years, so have the capabilities and medium of technology. The use of technology to assist individuals with career planning had its genesis in the late sixties. At that time several early developers (Super, 1970) crafted the first use of the computer to assist with career planning, occasioned by the invention of the cathode ray tube. This invention moved the computer age from batch processing—running decks of cards through a mainframe computer to execute a program—to interactive computing. Once interactive computing was possible, developers could script possible dialogues between students or clients and computer scripts and databases. This capability made possible the development of two kinds of computer-assisted career planning systems—those called *career planning systems* and those called *career information systems*. The former attempted to operationalize the developer's theory of career planning.

"Super developed a system called The Education and Career Exploration System (ECES), designed to assist students to develop a more realistic self-concept through assessment and a view of the world of work through provision of occupational descriptions, enhanced by microfiche files that included pictures of work tasks." The Information System for Vocational Decisions (ISVD), developed by Tiedeman and colleagues at Harvard, sought to teach students the Tiedeman-O'Hara (1963) decision-making paradigm, expecting that once they had internalized it, they would be able to make decisions without its prosthetic support. The System for Interactive Guidance Information (SIGI) operationalized Katz' (1966) classical model for decision making, based on the selection and prioritization of values and fixing of probabilities related to success in completing the education needed to enter occupations, identified by those values. Harris (1970) implemented Roe's (1956) classification system for occupations, assisting students to identify groups of occupations for exploration based on interest inventory scores and educational aspirations. These early systems had several things in common:

1. Each stored a personal record for each user so that the system could monitor a person's progress through the career planning process.

2. Each proposed, either explicitly or implicitly, a specific process for making career decisions.

3. Each used the results of assessment to link a user to occupational options.

Two of these systems were precursors of later systems: 1) SIGI Plus and 2) DISCOVER – which continue to be prominent in schools, colleges, and many other settings today.

In the 1970s, due to the birth of the National Occupational Information Coordinating Committee, *career information systems* were developed. These systems, customized for each state that implemented them, focused on the provision of high-quality career information. They were comprised of search strategies through databases of occupations, schools, financial aids, and military programs. Unlike the career planning systems, they did not store a user record, teach a decision-making strategy, nor use the results of assessment to identify occupational options. From the early seventies until 1999, there was a steady growth of customized versions of commercial career information systems in the states. During that same period there was a progressive move to add features to the career information systems with the result that by the decade of the 90's, there were fewer differences between the two types of systems.

The advent of common access to the Internet in the early 90's changed the scene dramatically related to technology and career planning. Several of the computer-based career information systems moved from delivery by means of stand alone and networked computers to delivery via the Internet. Websites devoted to some aspect of career information or planning began to proliferate at an astounding rate and with a wide range of quality. Counselors began to embrace the new technology, learning about existing websites and how to develop their own. Professional associations – including the National Career Development Association, the National Board for Certified Counselors, and the American Counseling Association – wrote guidelines for use of this medium for service delivery. The invention of the digital camera and access to faster modems and wider-band phone lines made cybercounseling – the provision of face-to-face counseling via the Internet – possible and cost-feasible. The development of websites that facilitate the translation of printed text from one language to many others made international communication possible.

Implications for the 21st Century

One implication of the changes in theory and assumptions is that, more than ever before in our history, adults will need assistance in career development. This is true because of the increased number of jobs they will hold in their lifetime (Rifkin, 1995). This increase is occurring because of the demise of the social contract, the continuation of the trend for computers to perform functions that reduce the number of humans needed, the behavior of organizations as they seek to find the most cost-feasible operation, and the decision making of individuals as they exert greater personal control over their career planning. Besides these trends, the lifespan will continue to lengthen, and many older persons will elect to continue to work, though perhaps in different occupations from those they pursued at an earlier age. These trends will also create a continuing need for education and training for adults as they find it necessary both to keep present skills updated and to learn new ones.

How and where will adults have access to career counseling and information in the 21st century? Some will seek face-to-face assistance from certified career counselors in private practice or in community agencies. Many will not have the money or time to take this route. The Internet will play an increasingly important role as a service provide in three distinct ways – administering assessment, providing information on a variety of topics related to career planning, serving as a conduit for interactive cybercounseling, and providing a forum for group communication. Let us examine these four roles.

The Internet as administrator of assessment inventories is currently a reality; and little by little, additional formal and informal, free and for-fee sites are becoming available. These sites offer inventories of interests; ability, values, and personality traits with complete self-help score reports. In some cases, the site also provides textual or video-based information about the occupations suggested by these instruments.

The results of these inventories or tests may be sent directly to the user (in the case of Level A instruments); to a professional counselor who will intervene in the interpretation (for Level B instruments); or to a college staff member, employer, or accrediting body in the case of assessment related to academic advising, job or school entry, or personnel selection.

Characteristics of assessment sites currently include the following:

- An increasing number of well-known, valid, and reliable instruments are being placed on the Internet on a for-fee basis.

- An increasing number of unknown and potentially invalid and unreliable instruments are being placed on the Internet without fee.

- The price of instruments of known quality varies widely – from $4.95 per administration to $25.00.

- The score report is saved on the website for a period of time so that those who took the instrument can review the results or retake the instrument.

- Unless scores have been sent to a certified counselor for interpretation to a client, there is likely to be no advance preparation for taking the instrument nor follow-through after receipt of a score report.

The Internet as information-provider requires the provision of high quality and timely information on many topics, including occupational descriptions, descriptions of educational opportunities, job-seeking instruction, and databases of jobs. The early history of websites has already created a stereotype that this information will be updated often; accessed quickly; available to all from home, work, or the community library; and free of charge.

The characteristics of the multitude of sites currently available to provide career information include the following:

- Some, such as sites developed by the Employment and Training Administration of the federal Department of Labor and state career information delivery systems, are of very high quality and feature complete occupational descriptions, labor market information, and job openings.

- There are sites that provide a search of college databases, provide detailed information about schools identified, offer online college applications, and link the user directly to the home page of the schools.

- Sites are beginning to include short videos in order to enliven the occupational and school databases.

- The Department of Defense offers the *Military Guide* online, which provides complete information about military occupations and their civilian equivalents.

- The United States Department of Education provides extensive information about federal sources of financial aid and offers the family financial aid application online.

- The *Dictionary of Occupational Titles* has been replaced by the online *O*Net,* which describes 1122 occupational groups and offers a search for occupations by skills and other characteristics. An electronic version of the *Occupational Outlook Handbook* is available online.

- The databases provided on these sites have a wide range of quality, and there is no professional review of their quality at this time.

- They are disjointed; that is, each presents information about some part of the career choice or planning process, but there is no integration of these disparate pieces.

- They are free of charge.

The third major application of the Internet for provision of career assistance to adults is using the Internet as a medium of communication with a career counselor or a career coach. Such assistance may be at a range of levels. At the lower end of that range, a counselor may answer questions or refer clients to sources of information as a result of asynchronous e-mail, that is, through e-mail exchange when clients and counselors are not at the computer at the same time. An intermediate level of assistance might be provided by synchronous e-mail; that is, the client and the counselor are at their respective computers at the same time, allowing a real-time dialogue to occur.

The advent of an inexpensive digital camera, complementary software, and wider-band phone line connections has made a third level of service, called *cybercounseling,* possible. In this mode the client and the counselor are at their respective machines at the same time. Assuming appropriate hardware and software, they can have an interview in which they see and hear each other in real time. This capability, at the time of this writing, is in its infancy, but is projected to expand greatly as technical capability improves, ethical guidelines are in place, and counselors have been trained to work with clients in this mode.

A fourth promising use of the Internet to support career development is to foster communication via-e-mail. Such communication, for example, might occur between individual clients and alumni of schools they are considering, between clients and possible employers, or between members of a support group.

Given the increased need for adults to receive career assistance or counseling and the rapid advance of technology to support its provision on the Internet, it seems very likely that this method of service provision will increase and mature in the early 21st century. This trend offers tremendous potential for increased cost-feasible service to adults. Service provision in this mode has two distinct advantages:

1. Service will be available to adults 24 hours per day and seven days per week wherever they have access to the Internet.

2. Counseling service can be combined with other functions – such as communication with others or use of assigned websites – within the same medium. Disadvantages of service delivery in this mode include a) loss of direct face-to-face contact, and b) need to know referral sources in many different geographical locations for those who are not profiting from this approach.

Another trend of the early 21st century is the development of cohesive, integrated websites to support career planning which could be called *virtual career centers.* A virtual career center is a website that supports career planning and integrates a variety of kinds of functions on one site, some developed by that site and some joined to it by a linkage. For example, such a site might include a linkage to several different assessment websites (for measurement of interests, skills, and work values, for example). Once a combination of results from these instruments identifies possible occupations, their titles may be linked to definitive sources of occupational information on the Internet. A third category of content on the virtual career center might be information about many kinds of training and linkage to existing database searches to identify these. A fourth category could be instruction on job-seeking skills. A fifth could provide linkage to one or more major sites that feature searches for job openings. A sixth capability might be locally developed information about majors and programs of study. A seventh capability might link users directly to the websites of major employers. An eighth capability might be linkage to instruction on a wide variety of topics, while a ninth might be to talk with a counselor, for a fee, about the meaning of all of this information. An integrated website could address the full range of information needed by its clientele, including individual counseling.

Predicted Impact

It seems certain that the use of the Internet with adults for the purpose of career planning and development will continue to rise, especially in conjunction with cybercounseling. This will have the effect of serving many more adults than the profession currently is serving and of serving them at times and in places that are convenient. This trend will become even more pronounced when a larger percentage of the population has access to the Internet from home.

The use of the Internet to provide instruction, counseling, information, and e-networking will stimulate research in areas such as identifying the characteristics of both counselors and clients that will profit from service best in this mode and how to screen and support those who participate in it.

Summary

The last decade of the 20th century was rich in developments that affect the field of career counseling significantly. These developments included the statement of new theories about career development and choice, significant changes in the workplace, and the advent of the Internet as a viable means of communication between clients and counselors. The first two categories of development mandate change in the assumptions that underlie career planning. This chapter has summarized these developments and assumptions and has described four different uses of the Internet to support the career planning of adults in the 21st century.

References

Brown, D. (1995). A values-based model for facilitating career transitions. *The Career Development Quarterly, 44,* 4-11.

Gelatt, H. B. (1995). Chaos and compassion. *Counseling and Values, 39,* (pp. 109-116).

Hansen, L. S. (1997). *Integrative life planning: Critical tasks for career development and changing life patterns.* San Francisco, CA: Jossey-Bass.

Harris, J. (1970). The computerization of vocational information. In D.E. Super (Ed.), *Computer-assisted counseling* (pp. 46-59). New York: Teachers College Press.

Holland, J. L. (1997). *Making vocational choices: A theory of vocational personalities and work environments* (3rd ed.). Lutz, FL: Psychological Assessment Resources.

Katz, M. (1966). A model of guidance for career decision making. *Vocational Guidance Quarterly, 15,* (pp. 2-10).

Krumboltz, J. D., Mitchell, K. E., & Levin, A. S. (1999). *Planned happenstance: Capitalizing on the unpredictable.* Paper presented at the 8th annual NCDA conference, Portland, OR.

Lent, R. W., Brown, S. D., & Hackett, G. (1996). *Career development from a cognitive perspective.* In D. Brown, L. Brooks, & Assoc. (Eds.), Career choice and development (3rd ed., pp. 373-416). San Francisco, CA:Jossey-Bass.

Miller-Tiedeman, A. (1999). *Learning, practicing, and living the new careering.* Philadelphia: Taylor & Francis.

Parsons, F. (1909). *Choosing a vocation.* Boston: Houghton-Mifflin.

Peterson, G. W., Sampson, J. P, Jr., & Reardon, R. C. (1991). *Career development and services: A cognitive approach.* Pacific Grove, CA: Brooks/Cole.

Rifkin, J. (1995). *The end of work.* New York: Putnam Publishing.

Roe, A. (1956). *The psychology of occupations.* New York: Wiley.

Savickas, M. L. (2000). *Career choice as biographical bricolage.* Paper presented at the 9th annual NCDA conference, Pittsburgh, PA.

Super, D. E. (1957). *The psychology of careers.* New York: Harper & Row.

Super, D. E. (Ed.). (1970). *Computer-assisted counseling.* New York: Teachers College Press.

Tiedeman, D. V., & O'Hara, R. P. (1963). *Career development: Choice and adjustment.* Princeton, NJ: College Entrance Examination Board.

SECTION IV:

DIVERSE POPULATIONS

CHAPTER 10
Feminism and Women's Career Development: An Ecological Perspective

Ellen P. Cook
University of Cincinnati

Mary J. Heppner
University of Missouri

Karen M. O'Brien
University of Maryland

Research on women's career development has mushroomed during the past decade, illustrating the diversity of women's career paths and the factors influencing them (Betz, 1994). Unfortunately, the French aphorism that "the more things change, the more they remain the same" describes well the status of women's careers today, despite the heady promises of the civil rights and feminist movements of recent years. Although women have entered the paid labor force in increasing numbers and have succeeded in careers virtually unimagined a generation ago, the overall pattern of gender and race discrimination remains similar (Betz, 1994; Fitzgerald, Fassinger, & Betz, 1995). By and large, women are concentrated in relatively few, poorly paid occupations, and remain largely responsible for home and family (Betz, 1994). Moreover, women continue to encounter roadblocks to their career advancement because of gender and race discrimination (Cook, Heppner, & O'Brien, in press). Numerous excellent reviews of women's career development over the past decade depict the nature and the consequences of the processes facilitating and impeding women's career development (e.g., Bingham & Ward, 1994; Fassinger & O'Brien, 2000; Fitzgerald et al., 1995; Gysbers, Heppner, & Johnston, 1998; Phillips & Imhoff, 1997).

Any framework for analyzing women's careers must accommodate a complex pattern of similarities and differences across and within diverse groups of women. For nearly three decades, feminist perspectives in psychology have provided a language and philosophy for counseling that recognize the complexity of women's lives and view a woman as a product of, but not solely determined by her environment (Betz & Fitzgerald, 1987). In this chapter, we will briefly describe core elements of feminist analysis, as a preamble to discussing a model of career development that attempts to represent the complexity of the person/context interaction shaping the career patterns of women of color and White women. We are indebted to earlier feminist analyses of career development, and will not attempt to duplicate their contributions to the field. For example, Brooks and Forrest (1994) provide a cogent feminist critique of research on women's career development and mental health practice, and Fitzgerald and Weitzman (1992) comprehensively review the literature on structural and normative constraints on women's career development. This chapter will build upon the work of many feminist scholars to propose a general framework for conceptualizing women's career development based on feminist analysis and ecological theory, to provide examples from recent career development literature illustrating this model, and to discuss implications for career counseling practice.

Feminist Analysis and Counseling

Feminist analyses of career development and vocational behavior have laid the foundation for much of the structural rethinking around gender that has occurred in the field over the last four decades (Brown & Brooks, 1991; Espín, 1994; Fitzgerald & Weitzman, 1992). Feminist critiques of dominant theories, the research process, and career counseling practice have broadened the field from a narrow focus on the individual, and most often the individual middle class, white, heterosexual male, to a much broader and more inclusive focus.

At the core of feminist philosophy is the belief in the autonomy and independence of every woman and in the right to live unhampered by artificially determined sex appropriate roles. As such feminism is "both an ideology and a movement for social political change based on a critical analysis of male privilege and women's subordination" (Offen, 1988, p. 151). Thus, the feminist movement seeks to end women's subordination to men and the myriad ways that subordination has been institutionalized and practiced. As such, feminism is a direct challenge to male authority and to hierarchical systems with which it is supported.

Out of this feminist analysis of the social and political structures came a need for a new type of therapy for women; one that did not replicate the hierarchical, patriarchal, woman blaming, focus of the dominant society. The principal tenets of this feminist theory were: a) the personal is political; b) the counseling relationship should be non-hierarchical; and c) women's problems must be placed within a larger sociopolitical environment. This listing was adapted from numerous sources (e.g., Brooks & Forrest, 1994).

THE PERSONAL IS POLITICAL

At the core of feminist analysis is the belief that individual behavior is best understood within the sociopolitical environment in which it occurs. Thus, a woman's individual career concerns are conceptualized as part of a larger context, one that includes sexist ideologies, oppressive institutions and culturally determined gender conditioning. Thus, changes in the lives of girls and women require changes in the larger environment. Within counseling, the client differentiates her individual responsibility from external sociocultural conditions that keep women from moving out of low status, low paying positions (e.g., sex stratification in the workplace, bias in hiring practices and glass ceilings). Counselors are encouraged to examine their biases, work for personal change, and advocate for societal change.

THE NON-HIERARCHICAL NATURE OF THE COUNSELING RELATIONSHIP

In a feminist approach, collaboration rather than hierarchy form the basis for the relationship between counselor and client. In the feminist approach, both client and counselor are given "equal worth." Equal worth does not mean equal competence as career counselors have levels of training and expertise that far exceed their clients and are needed for effective counseling. Rather, the inherent worth of all women and the self awareness that each woman brings to the counseling process is acknowledged in feminist therapy (Brooks & Forrest, 1994). This egalitarian approach requires the counselor to be vigilant of any behaviors that promote passivity and dependence on the part of the client and to monitor the establishment of unnecessary hierarchies in the relationship. The focus is on women's empowerment, and on assisting female clients to use inner resources to heal and grow in healthy ways. The therapeutic relationship is demystified and professional diagnosis and jargon are eliminated. In career counseling, assessments are viewed as tools of discovery rather than prescriptive measures and the client is actively involved in the interpretation process.

THE PLACEMENT OF WOMEN'S ISSUES WITHIN A LARGER SOCIOPOLITICAL CONTEXT

Perhaps the greatest contribution of feminist analysis was moving the source of all problems from the individual to the larger sociopolitical context. At the core of feminist counseling is the recognition of the ways in which a sexist society has both shaped and limited women's opportunities. Women's problems are now conceptualized as adaptive responses to an oppressive society rather than viewed as pathological. Thus, together, the career counselor and client examine the ways in which the culture has circumscribed her dreams and limited the view of her place in the world.

As we begin a new century, these tenets advanced by feminist researchers and clinicians have become embedded in the way in which effective career counseling is practiced (Brown & Brooks, 1991). However, the work of feminist scholars is not yet complete as feminism has largely spoken to the needs of white middle class, educated, women. More work is needed to explicate the experiences of women of color and of poor or working class women. As Espín (1994) argued, "Regrettably, there is much that could be said about the insensitivity, racism, and classism of feminists in psychology (e.g., Brown, 1990; Espín & Gawelek, 1992) and in the Women's Movement in general (e.g., Anzaldúa, 1990; hooks, 1984)" (p. 265). Espín goes on to say that the "near sightedness of white feminists as to the possibilities of the movement and the far-reaching consequences of its ideas is being much to blame for the narrowness of some definitions of feminism and for the movement's goals being perceived as limited and exclusionary." (Espín, p. 265).

From the early years of the feminist movement, women of color challenged the nature of a movement that asked them to sacrifice the needs of their community to support the often racist and elitist demands of a white women's movement (Taylor, 1998). While white women were perceived as seeking equality with white men, many women of color felt torn between fighting for their rights as women and identifying with the struggles of their race in a racially oppressive society. At times, the concerns of the feminist movement seemed irrelevant to the struggles that they and their male counterparts were facing. But as numerous writers argued (Anzaldúa, 1990; Espín, 1994, hooks, 1984), "White middle class women do not 'own' feminism, nor is it irrelevant to the experiences of women of color. Rather, the oppression of women of color in a white-dominated society takes on specific characteristics related to both race and gender" (Espín, 1994, p. 265).

Indeed, feminist therapy has been recognized for its positive effect on many women of color (Espín, 1994; Comas-Diaz, 1987). The emphasis on empowerment, the external environment rather than internal psychopathology, and the prominence placed on social change are all seen as positive contributions of feminist theory to the overall mental health of women of color (Comas-Diaz, 1987). But as Espín (1994) argued:

> It is rather ironic that a theory that evolved from the awareness that sociocultural factors are essential determinates in the psychology of women has been so slow to extend its own insights to sociocultural factors other than gender, thus excluding the experiences of the vast majority of women who are not white and in the process excluding the impact of sociocultural factors other than gender (e.g., race, class, ethnicity) on the lives of all women including white women (Espín & Gawelek, 1992; Spelman, 1988) (Espín, p. 274).

Thus, although feminist analysis holds promise for improving career counseling for women of color, it is also critical to expand the analysis from being gender based to incorporating the intertwined nature of race and class to better understand the career development needs of all women. A critical next step is articulating the nature of career counseling today to build the foundation for developing a theoretical framework to understand the contributions of race, gender and class in the career development of women.

The Nature of Career Counseling Practice Today

The occupational structure in the United States clearly illustrates the power of race and gender to shape life patterns. The myth of freedom of choice for all maintains that occupational success is contingent primarily on individual initiative, however, many women of color and white women continue to experience discrimination and are overrepresented in low-paying, low status occupations. The diversity of career patterns among women as a group also makes it clear that some women are undeterred – or untouched – by the gender or racial discrimination that impedes others' access to advancement. One challenge facing career development professionals is to propose a complex model of vocational development that articulates the myriad factors influencing the career paths of diverse groups of women. Cook et al. (in press) began their articulation of their ecological model of women's career development by first identifying the assumptions embodied by current career counseling practices (assumptions that often do not reflect the life realities of many women of color and white women). These assumptions were stated as follows:

> Work plays a central and pivotal role in people's lives. Individuals are responsible for making independent decisions that actualize their career potential. Knowledge about individual traits and preferences is the most important factor in optimal career decision-making. Career counseling also typically refers to counseling for work roles with little exploration of other life roles commonly assumed by adults (e.g., family, community). These rational job decisions initiate or maintain an orderly, linear progression of career development in terms of continuous, increasingly skilled and rewarding

involvement over time. Finally, career counseling perpetuates the optimistic belief that any individual, if she or he works hard enough, will be able to realize her or his occupational dreams.

Cook et al. (in press) argued that although this view of career development is consistent with the American ideal of self-sufficiency and freedom, this view may not convey the general life priorities and specific role commitments of many women of color and White women. For example, many women and people of color may define the central meaning of life as resting within a relational or collective, rather than an individualistic perspective (Helms & Cook, 1999). Many women, particularly low-income women, must make career decisions in light of also fulfilling primary responsibility for maintaining home and family. Because of culturally based world views or the exigencies of balancing multiple role responsibilities, many women may also be unable to plot an orderly, rational career trajectory as commonly recommended by career planning experts. Finally, the pervasive racial and gender discrimination still present in the labor market (Reskin & Padavic, 1999) results in social, institutional, psychological, political, and economic barriers that selectively limits the career development of women of color and White women.

Given these barriers to career development, current theories must extend beyond the examination of the individual to recognize contribution of both individual and environmental influences to career behavior (Spokane, 1994). More recently, increased attention has focused on the role of context in career development across time (e.g., Vondracek, Lerner, & Schulenberg, 1986). However, popular models have not explicitly considered the importance of race and gender in shaping career patterns, influences that a feminist perspective would place at center stage. To build on current knowledge about the career development process, models focusing on race/gender must accommodate both unique individual and shared group experiences, and dynamics varying in complexity from moment-to-moment experiencing to sociocultural influences on the national level. Thus, we propose an ecological model to stimulate new understanding about the complexities of women of color's and white women's career development.

Our intention is not to build a comprehensive theory about contextual processes within career development but to integrate feminist analysis and contextual literature from counseling and related disciplines. The constructs and processes described in this ecological model may prove helpful in understanding the contextual forces influencing the career development of women of color and white women.

The Ecological Model of Career Development

There is no single ecological theory in psychology. Ecological psychology can be thought of as either a family of models linked by a common understanding of person – environment interactions, or as a unique metatheoretical model encompassing diverse approaches to theory and research under a common rubric of shared principles. Ecological principles have been most widely accepted by human service professionals who consider environmental interventions to be crucial helping tools, for example, community psychology (e.g., Trickett, 1996), social work (e.g., Chung & Pardeck, 1997), school psychology (e.g., Schensul, 1998), and student development professionals (e.g., Delworth & Piel, 1978). Perhaps because career counseling has maintained a focus on individual change via personal or group interventions, the applicability of ecological principles has seemed less clear (for a notable exception, see Conyne, 1985). An ecological perspective offers career counselors a way to conceptualize individual or group behavior on multiple levels simultaneously. Diversity becomes the principal phenomenon to explain, rather than an exception to presumably universal rules.

OVERVIEW OF ECOLOGICAL PSYCHOLOGY

The essence of ecological psychology was neatly summarized in Kurt Lewin's (1936) famous dictum that behavior is a function of persons interacting in their environment: $B = f(PxE)$. In ecological perspectives, human behavior is seen as resulting from the ongoing, dynamic interaction between a person and the environment as multiply constituted. Behavior is considered an "act-in-context" (Landrine, 1995, p. 5) in that the context is an essential determinant of the nature, naming, and meaningfulness of individual behavior. Behavior is also multiply determined, a representation of the complex interaction among myriad factors comprising an individual's life at any given time.

In the most influential ecological model, Bronfenbrenner (1977) identified subsystems influencing behavior as nested within one another, with the microsystem (interpersonal interactions within a given environment) at the center and the macrosystem, the ideological components of a given society, as encompassing other subsystems. The individual was conceptualized primarily as a component of a subsystem. This interactional perspective is useful in reminding career counselors how all humans exist within interlocking relationships to the world around them, although implications for career counseling with individuals using such a structural perspective may be challenging to formulate. Bronfenbrenner's recent 1995 revision, the bioecological paradigm, places much more emphasis on the individual as an active agent within a reciprocal interaction process, influencing her environment as well as being acted upon in a complex set of environmental processes. Bronfenbrenner's new emphasis on the individual is consistent with Conyne's (1985) positioning of the person at the heart of the dynamic ecological interaction among subsystems.

Individuals influence, and are influenced by, their environments through their thinking processes. Constructivists (e.g., Sexton & Griffin, 1997) argued that individuals create their lives in part by how they construe what happens to them. The same environmental determinant may be perceived as facilitating, discouraging, neutral, or powerful but personally irrelevant by different individuals, or may not be perceived at all despite its impact on the individual. Herr (1999) is clear about the impact of the environment on perceptions of oneself and one's possibilities:

> Individual behavior within and across societies is a continuous response to transactions within the social context that motivate persons in positive and in negative ways, that allow them to create new meanings and reconstruct old meanings, that affirm them or demean them, that mentor or confuse them, that encourage them to be purposeful, productive, and future oriented, or that create conditions that limit their vision and aspirations to surviving physically and mentally each day or to living within very restrictive boundariesdefined by gender, class, or other attributes (p. 2).

Collin and Young (1992) described meaning as "at the heart of career" (p. 12), the interpretive process by which individuals connect with other individuals and with their society and culture in general. This is true for many, but not all people in our society and part of career counselors' jobs is to create opportunities for people to find meaning in their work. In certain work settings or demographic groups, people may develop some general consensus about shared events, but individuals' personal life goals, prior experiences, and unique interpretations maintain meaning making as a uniquely individual process (Wicker & August, 2000). Individual behaviors may reflect meaning making at multiple levels of abstraction, ranging from construals of specific events to life stories reflected in patterns of choices over time (e.g., Savickas, 1997).

In the ecological model of career development, although individual, microsystem, macrosystem, and meaning making variables are separated for discussion, they are not so distinct in reality. Career behavior does not occur within a vacuum, but rather emerges from a lifelong dynamic interaction between the person and her or his environment. The essential interactional nature of the ecological model of career development can be summarized as follows (Cook et al., in press):

- Career behavior can be thought of as determined by the interrelations between subsystems in a larger ecosystem (Bronfenbrenner, 1977).

- Interrelationships occur simultaneously on multiple levels, so that a focus on any one level of interaction is by definition a limited picture of the dynamics shaping career behavior at any one time.

- The ecological model of career development recognizes that by their very nature, humans live interactionally in a social environment.

- Every person has both a biological sex and a race. These factors decisively shape an individual's career throughout life, as he or she encounters opportunities or roadblocks because of biological sex or race.

- Although individuals of the same biological sex or race may encounter similar circumstances because of their demographics, each career path is unique because of individual circumstances, and the unique interactions of their subsystems.

- Clients bring their ecosystems into counseling primarily through conveying how they understand and react to it, for example, in how they perceive opportunities (or not), in how they compare themselves positively or negatively to desired models, conceive of the future as rosy, or a dead end, internalize others stereotypes as personally salient or dismiss them as irrelevant.

- Even when individuals are alone, their career behaviors are strongly influenced by the action of others, whether directly (e.g., racial or gender based customs delimiting their career behavior) or internally (e.g., the nature of their career self concepts shaped through previous interactions with others).

- Individuals also shape the environment around them in complex ways (e.g., overtly rewarding or punishing the career behaviors of others).

For example, the nature of relationships with others decisively shapes self-definition (Blustein, 1994; Jordan, Kaplan, Miller, Stiver, & Surrey, 1991). Personal interactions are invariably determined by other features of the environment (Bersheid, 1999) and by characteristics of the individual herself. Finally, meaning making is a cognitive process influenced by individual and environmental variables.

INDIVIDUAL VARIABLES WITHIN THE ECOLOGICAL MODEL

Individual variables including career interests, values, abilities, and occupational self-concepts (Super, Savickas, & Super, 1996) are important determinants of career behavior. These individual characteristics can be described without explicit reference to other people (e.g., interest inventories); may have some genetic determinants; and once formed tend to be relatively stable over time. However, these characteristics should be viewed as potentially changeable products of dynamic interactions between a woman and her environment over her lifetime. Individual characteristics recently determined to influence a woman's career development include ability, agentic characteristics and gender role attitudes (O'Brien & Fassinger, 1993; O'Brien, Friedman, Tipton, & Linn, 2000). In fact, researchers have shown that traditional gender role attitudes may limit women's educational and vocational aspirations (Fassinger, 1990; Murrell, Frieze, & Frost, 1991). Moreover, the ability to select a career that seems to match one's ability was correlated with confidence in choosing a career (or career decision-making self efficacy) (O'Brien, 1996).

Research within the past decade has illuminated the power of self-efficacy beliefs in women's career development (Betz & Hackett, 1983; Hackett & Betz, 1981). According to theory (Bandura, 1986), once formed, self-efficacy beliefs may exert a powerful influence on the type of careers a woman chooses to enter, her confidence in her abilities to find and succeed in a career, and the manner in which she deals with obstacles and barriers encountered on her career path. Some self-efficacy beliefs are idiosyncratic consequences of a woman's unique life history, for example, a woman may believe she cannot cook because of a disastrous attempt at entertaining. Other self-efficacy beliefs are commonly shared by women because of societal views about gender-linked skills and appropriate career pursuits, for example, women's enduring perceptions that they are not able in mathematics.

Race and gender identity development may shape what a woman at a particular stage sees as a personally satisfying and rewarding career for herself (Robinson & Howard-Hamilton, 2000). Similar to women of color, lesbian women may struggle to reconcile multiple identities (gender and sexual orientation), internalized homophobia, and race or ethnic group identity as well (e.g., Hispanic bisexual woman). These issues may influence vocational development which may be hindered by time spent integrating one's sexual orientation into one's identity, perhaps due to internalized homophobia or concerns about how their lesbian identity will affect personal and professional relationships with others (Fassinger, 1995, 1996).

A woman's sexual orientation may also influence what careers she considers as compatible with her lifestyle (Fassinger, 1996). For example, many heterosexual women limit their career paths by selecting careers that underutilize their abilities to ensure that they will be able to manage their careers and assume primary responsibility for caring for children and the home (Betz, 1994; O'Brien et al., 2000). Sexual orientation becomes a critical variable in the career development of many lesbian and bisexual women as they frequently face discrimination at multiple levels (Fassinger, 1996). At the individual level, many lesbians may self-select out of lucrative careers (e.g., pediatrician) due to realistic fears of homophobia, which can result in lesbian women selecting low-prestige, low-paying, traditional jobs for women that often do not utilize their ability or education (Morgan & Brown, 1991). Realistic fears about being discriminated against because of a lesbian or bisexual orientation may determine not only a woman's choice of occupation, but also the location of her work, the specific job setting, and the degree of openness with coworkers about many aspects of her life. Moreover, lesbian women may need to negotiate the coming out process at the same time that they are making vocational decisions, which adds an additional stressor to the already complex process of women's career development.

Another important individual factor influencing women's career development is the centrality of relationships with others to their self-perceptions and life decisions. This factor has been discussed as a relational orientation common among women (e.g., Jordan et al., 1991) and a collectivistic orientation common among people of color (Helms & Cook, 1999). Research confirms that many women rank family and connections with others as highly salient to their career decisions (O'Brien et al., 2000; Richie, Fassinger, Linn, Johnson, Prosser, & Robinson, 1997). Whether because of personal preference or necessity, women across races and ethnicities bear major responsibility for caring for home, children, and other significant relationships, and often weigh heavily what they perceive as their family's needs in their personal career plans (Betz, 1994; Cook, 1993; Shelton, 1999; Wentling, 1998). In fact, recent research suggested that women at a very young age may decide not to pursue lucrative and prestigious occupations to allow for the possibility in future relationships of assuming major responsibility for raising children and caring for the home (O'Brien et al., 2000).

Career literature within the past decade has begun to document the benefits as well as the stresses that multiple role commitments provide women (Phillips & Imhoff, 1997). Contradictory findings characterize the literature regarding the role of managing multiple roles in women's career development (Dukstein & O'Brien, 1995; Lefcourt & Harmon, 1993; Orput, 1998; Quimby & O'Brien, 2000). Several studies have noted that confidence in one's ability to manage multiple roles has an impact on women's career development, whereas other studies have failed to document a relation. More research is clearly needed. One promising concept to explore is multiple role realism (Weitzman, 1994), which may be related to personal agency (McCracken & Weitzman, 1997). This area of research may enhance understanding about how women's individual perceptions of their ability to manage multiple roles can affect decisions regarding their career paths.

MICROSYSTEM INFLUENCES WITHIN THE ECOLOGICAL MODEL

Individuals or groups with whom an individual woman interacts directly through her diverse life roles (microsystem) dramatically influence how she views herself and her career possibilities. During childhood and adolescence the expectations and support of parents and teachers shape a young woman's aspirations, confidence, and willingness to take risks (Acker & Oakley, 1993; Betz, 1994; O'Brien et al., 2000). These influences do not need to be explicit; subtle gender stereotyping within classrooms (Sadker & Sadker, 1994) or the failure to provide proactive support (rather than the presence of deliberate discouragement) (American Association of University Women, 1992; Betz, 1989) may be sufficient to dampen young women's career development. Young women are also sensitive to peer and media influences on their career influences, either changing or keeping secret those interests that might appear deviant to others.

Conversely, other individuals can facilitate young women's career development. Attachment to mother appears to be a decisive factor in young women's career development (O'Brien et al., 2000). A mother's high aspirations for her daughter can be particularly instrumental for women of color (Reid, Haritos, Kelly, & Holland, 1995; Turner, 1997). Mentors can be an invaluable source of skill development, knowledge about the career and particular work setting, and access to networks and career opportunities. It is unfortunate that finding mentors and complexities of mentoring relationships with men can be difficult for women, particularly women of color (Hansman, 1998).

During adulthood, women of color and white women regularly encounter others' expectations about their career orientation solely on the basis of their race or biological sex. Such uniformity myths effectively ignore the individuality of the woman worker, and maintain a subtle pattern of discrimination present in everyday interactions. For example, a woman may be considered more adept at handling personnel disputes than more technical tasks because of stereotypes about women's relationship orientation. Other women may not be offered career-building opportunities because bosses assume that they are not interested in working evenings or in travel because of family commitments.

On the other hand, as noted earlier, the nature and demands of her personal role commitments can decisively influence a woman's career decision making (Betz, 1994). Researchers have begun to investigate the contribution that a realistic view of the challenges inherent in managing multiple roles plays in women's career decision-making (Weitzman, 1994).

Finally, sexual harassment is a ubiquitous and pernicious influence on women's career development (Fitzgerald, 1993). Sexual harassment originates in beliefs about appropriate male-female relations and is often condoned or overlooked by organizations in which it occurs. Although sexual harassment occurs through interpersonal relationships on the job or in school (microsystem), it represents a manipulation of gender-based power common through organizations within society at large (macrosystem). Women of color may be particularly susceptible to harassment because of racial stereotypes and perceptions about their vulnerability (Paludi, DeFour, Roberts, Tedesco, Brathwaite, & Marino, 1995). Sexual harassment has traumatic consequences for its targets, including psychological distress, physical symptoms, impaired work performance, and restricted educational and career opportunities (Culbertson, Rosenfeld, Booth-Kewley, & Magnusson, 1992; Fitzgerald, 1993; Gutek & Koss, 1993; Koss, 1990).

MACROSYSTEM INFLUENCES WITHIN THE ECOLOGICAL MODEL

The career development of all individuals also occurs within a specific sociocultural context: the values, customs, norms, and preferred life paths implicitly conveying to a woman what are appropriate or inappropriate career options based on her particular cultural or gendered context. The larger culture operating as a macrosystem effectively institutionalizes forms of race/gender discrimination as prototypes of desirable behavior. In Elder's (1995) words, the life course is "worked out by the individual within a social system of institutional pathways" (p. 107). Some patterns embodied within the macrosystem are common across societies and over time, for example, that women bear primary responsibility for care of home and family. Others can be specific to a particular world view (e.g., the Western ideal of personal fulfillment through individual, goal-directed efforts), or to an ethnic group or economic class (Helms & Cook, 1999). Macrosystem values are commonly internalized by an individual, for example, as perceptions about gender or race-appropriate career choices (cf. Gottfredson, 1996). Such values also influence how a woman's relationships with family, peers, friends, and coworkers can support or thwart her career development over time, ranging from subtle messages about women's appropriate roles, to the explicit offering or withholding of emotional support and material resources crucial to her career success.

Macrosystem ideologies about race and gender are learned by individuals and codified into organizational practices and structures. Individuals internalize attitudes about race and gender appropriate occupations in early childhood (Gettys & Cann, 1981; Yager & Yager, 1985). Once perceptions about race and gender appropriate occupations become circumscribed, they are difficult to modify (Gottfredson, 1996). In adulthood macrosystem ideologies about race and gender support continued discrimination in hiring (Betz & Fitzgerald, 1987), and salaries (Eccles, 1987). Wood (1994) concluded that hostile environments devaluing women still exist, informal networks continue to exclude people of color and white women, and mentoring of women of color and white women is still rare.

It is important to recognize that macrosystem influences can change over time, leading to differences in values orientations across generations or even decades of a woman's life. Elder (1995) noted the importance of studying both "variations in place" as well as "variations in historical time" (p. 107) to understand how the impact of historical changes can vary by community, geographic region, or society. Although women entering the labor force today are still likely to encounter discrimination because of their race or gender, the range of opportunities open to them is likely to appear different from those confronting women during each of the recent decades because of the Civil Rights and feminist movements, and fluctuations in the state of the economy.

MEANING MAKING PROCESSES AND CAREER DEVELOPMENT

The nature of an individual woman's meaning making within her life is an important source of the variability of career patterns across women. In its broadest sense, meaning making can refer to any cognitions pertaining to a woman's experience, for example, commitment to a low-paying job to provide for her family, self-efficacy beliefs developed from specific life events or occupational stereotypes learned from media or one's peers. Individual women perceive their environments in ways that are unique to them: comparing themselves favorably or unfavorably to others; conceiving the future as predetermined or filled with unforeseen possibilities; internalizing others' stereotypes for women or their racial group as self-descriptive or irrelevant. An individual woman is also likely to respond uniquely to macrosystem changes depending on how they influence her daily life contingencies and future possibilities. For example, the increasing reliance on computer technology in the workplace is perceived quite differently by a woman who sees her computer skills as a way to surmount racial discrimination in her company; one who perceives computer technology as more difficult for women than for men to master; or one who recognizes an opportunity to do professional work from a home office.

Individuals do more than simply think about what happens to them; they try to make sense of life events. Constructivists note that individuals effectively construct their realities via their interpretations of life events. People plan future behaviors in light of their meaning making (Young & Vaslach, 1996). In career counseling, individuals tell stories conveying their understanding of themselves and their possibilities within the world of work. How women understand such concepts as self, work, female, and culture influences how they connect themselves to the world around them, and the range of choices available to them (Law, 1992). Individuals may also enact certain enduring life themes through their career patterns over time through diverse expressions that may either enhance or stifle their development as a whole (Savickas, 1997).

How a woman constructs an integrated mental map of herself as an individual on the basis of her unique life experiences deserves more attention in career counseling (Faltermeier, 1992; Grimstad, 1992). Statham (1992) reminded researchers that what constitutes a meaningful career from a woman worker's perspective may appear surprising to an outsider. Awareness of the process of meaning making can both affirm a woman's choices and open the door to actualizing possibilities not generally considered (Law, 1992). Savickas (1997) and Gysbers et al. (1998) provide examples of how career counselors can encourage exploration of meaning making in career counseling.

Implications for Career Counseling

To be practical for career counselors, the ecological model must meet two challenges: helping counselors to determine interventions appropriate for particular clients, and defining an appropriate scope for professional practice.

DETERMINING COUNSELING INTERVENTIONS

In ecological career counseling, career counselors recognize that the client's behavior is influenced by a host of factors inherent within her ecosystem. In particular, a woman's career development is strongly influenced from birth by ongoing interactions with significant others within her immediate environment (microsystem); broader sociocultural dynamics related to the intersection of her biological sex and race or ethnicity (macrosystem); and how she understands who she is and what happens to her within her ecosystem (meaning-making). Developmental pathways may differ remarkably for individuals in different contexts (Belsky, 1995). Although in Bronfenbrenner's (1995) words, a person is "an active agent in, and on, its own environment" (p. 634), every individual is also influenced by factors outside of her choosing and perhaps awareness.

The fact that every significant behavior is multiply determined offers both challenges and resources for the career counselor. A target behavior can be changed in numerous ways, both directly and indirectly. The nature of the client's target problem helps to determine appropriate interventions, which always occur within the context of the client's ecosystem. Changes occurring within a circumscribed area of a career client's life are likely to have reverberating consequences within the ecosystem in areas not particularly targeted by the intervention. For example, self-exploration during career counseling may alter central self-perceptions (e.g., "I am more interested in creative things than I thought"), expand the range of activities, in which a client engages, and stimulate meaningful new relationships. Certain choices may have far-reaching effects on a person's later development in unforeseen ways, for example, the impact of early education on personality characteristics as assessed years later (Kohn, 1995).

In ecological career counseling, a career counselor must determine how to best use the client's personal and environmental resources within the parameters of the counseling relationship to enhance a client's career development over time. The counselor serves as an advocate and "ecosystem liaison," working as a partner with the client to stimulate more successful and satisfying interactions within the world of work. In effect, through establishing a counseling relationship, the counselor and client become a microsystem, with functions and skills determined by the counselor – client role interaction. Both the counselor and client negotiate what can be done within the confines of their relationship to enhance other client – environment interactions.

Career change, whether in the form of a new choice or an adjustment within an existing job, requires mobilization and enhancement of the client's personal resources (e.g., decision-making skills) and environmentally based resources, particularly supportive relationships with others (see Moen & Erickson, 1995, for a relevant discussion of personal resilience). In ecological career counseling, the counselor typically helps the client gain skills or knowledge needed to cope more successfully, or to reshape cognitive processes influencing the nature of the client's interactions within the environment. The counselor must help the client determine what resources are needed and how to use or obtain them.

An ecological perspective reminds the career counselor to consider the possibility of changes on a number of different levels. For example, a woman might need to learn job search skills, or to identify unique abilities and values she has developed through hobbies or volunteer activities. Other clients may benefit from role playing exercises preparing them to confront peers or family members about career plans likely to arouse opposition. A woman may also need to confront gender or racial stereotypes limiting the range of possibilities she sees as appropriate for herself, or self-limiting conclusions about her mathematics abilities because of negative early educational experiences. A bicultural client may explore conflicting images of working women implicit in her family of origin and American culture.

These person-focused interventions are consistent with a broader feminist goal of personal empowerment. The intention is to stimulate a certain type of career planning process rather than a particular type of choice per se. A woman may decide to make career development the top priority in her life, or may choose a career compatible with prioritizing other values or commitments. The career counselor's challenge is to ensure that she considers the full range of factors influencing her life, and that she is better equipped to face the challenges ahead of her in an environment that places obstacles in her way because of her sex or her race. The literature now contains some excellent sources of techniques for exploring microsystem, macrosystem, and meaning making with a client, in addition to more familiar strategies for career self-exploration (e.g., Bingham & Ward, 1996; Brown & Brooks, 1991; Helms & Cook, 1999; Gysbers et al., 1998; Subich, 1996).

DEFINING THE SCOPE OF CAREER COUNSELING PRACTICE

In ecological career counseling, a counselor may also consider how to make the environment more helpful and affirming to an individual. The most common way this occurs in career counseling is when a client decides to seek another job, to optimize the match between job requirements and her personal qualities, for example, or to leave a workplace that discriminates against individuals of her gender or race. Career counselors may also consider promoting changes in the environment itself to remediate or prevent certain career related problems (Fassinger & O'Brien, 2000). School career guidance programs designed to promote sex equity may be focused on the students' career plans, but may also train school personnel about how to create more equitable classrooms (e.g., Sadker & Sadker, 1994). Human resource development experts within organizations can provide opportunities for informal learning and support, mentoring, re-education of management about diversity issues, and training programs (McDonald & Hite, 1998).

In an ecological approach to counseling, then, an individual client's self-knowledge and decision-making capacities remains an important, but not an exclusive target of change. Diverse settings and functions can potentially constitute career counseling practice. Conyne (1985) utilized Morrill, Oetting, and Hurst's (1974) counseling cube to illustrate the range of targets, methods, and purposes of ecological counseling. Career counselors could conceivably use direct (e.g., group counseling) or indirect (e.g., consultation) methods with the person, environment, or both as targets of either remedial, developmental, or preventive focused interventions. Such interventions may render some distinctions between career and noncareer counseling meaningless. For example, the best way to enhance a woman's career development may be to use couples or family counseling to explore restrictive role allocations influencing communications in general, and most specifically about who cares for the children and who does the housework.

Environmentally targeted interventions provide an affirmative response to feminists' call for social action. It is not enough to change persons to cope more effectively with environments that oppress them; we are also enjoined to correct social injustices using our professional expertise. Moen (1995) pointed out how ecological psychology "stands at the nexus of basic science and social policy... (ecologists) are concerned with questions of "how" precisely because of the possibilities for interventions that the answers suggest" (p. 4). The ecological counseling perspective provides a language for conceptualizing such social changes and translating our good intentions into counseling interventions. These interventions may coax us out of our comfort zones within schools or agency offices to become change advocates. For example, women today still struggle to reconcile their traditional responsibilities for childcare with demands of the paid labor force. Some economically privileged women may benefit from career counseling exploring the conflicting, absolutistic standards of work in a competitive marketplace versus idealistic prototypes of fulltime motherhood as vocation. Women living in poverty typically have little choice: they must work outside of the home for their family's survival, and affordable, quality day care is scarce to nonexistent. In some cases, career counselors might be able to empower them to design ingenious solutions to their daycare dilemmas, for example, developing daycare collaboratives within their religious organizations or neighborhoods.

The ultimate – and best – solutions may rest instead in changing the environmental conditions trapping women in no-win situations because of their multiple commitments. Organizations should view balancing work and family as a human issue rather than a woman's issue, and consider the possible benefits to the workplace of adopting family friendly practices (Wentling, 1998). Counselors might consult with businesses on developing more family-supportive benefits, for example, or work on legislation mandating affordable daycare for everyone. Changing the workplace ultimately requires changing broader societal attitudes about the intersection of family and work (Wentling, 1998).

Career counselors have long understood that intrapsychic processes account for only a portion of a client's career development. The purest individual intentions must be negotiated within the contexts of an imperfect world. Career counseling interventions have always had an impact beyond the individual making the decision, if only through the financial support provided to dependents or by the addition of a new individual to a particular working environment. An ecological perspective invites counselors to ponder how professional skills might be used to change the environment in which a client lives and works in more intentional ways.

References

Acker, S., & Oatley, K. (1993). Gender issues in education for science and technology: Current situation and prospects for change. *Canada Journal of Education, 18,* 255-272.

American Association of University Women. (1992). *How schools shortchange girls.* AAUW Educational Foundation.

Anzaldúa, G. (Ed.). (1990). *Making face, making soul – Haciendo caras: Creative and critical perspectives by feminists of color.* San Francisco: Aunt Lute Foundation.

Bandura, A. (1986). *Social foundations of thought and action: A social cognitive theory.* Englewood Cliffs, NJ: Prentice Hall.

Belsky, J. (1995). Expanding the ecology of human development: An evolutionary perspective. In P. Moen, G. H. Elder, Jr., & K. Luscher (Eds.), *Examining lives in context: Perspectives on the ecology of human development* (pp. 545-561). Washington, DC: American Psychological Association.

Berscheid, E. (1999). The greening of relationship science. *American Psychologist, 54,* 260-266.

Betz, N. E. (1989). Implications of the null environment hypothesis for women's career development and for counseling psychology. *The Counseling Psychologist, 17,* 136-144.

Betz, N. E. (1994). Basic issues and concepts in career counseling for women. In W. B. Walsh & S. H. Osipow (Eds.), *Career counseling for women* (pp.1-42). Hillsdale, NJ: Erlbaum.

Betz, N. E., & Hackett, G. (1983). The relationship of career-related self-efficacy expectations to perceived career options in college women and men. *Journal of Counseling Psychology, 28,* 399-410.

Betz, N. E., & Fitzgerald, L. F. (1987). *The career psychology of women.* Orlando, FL: Academic Press.

Bingham, R. P., & Ward, C. M. (1994). Career counseling with ethnic minority women. In W. B. Walsh & S. H. Osipow (Eds.), *Career counseling for women* (pp.165-195). Hillsdale, NJ: Erlbaum.

Bingham, R. P., & Ward, C. M. (1996). Practical applications of career counseling with ethnic minority women. In M. L. Savickas & W. B. Walsh (Eds.), *Handbook of career counseling theory and practice* (pp. 291-313). Palo Alto, CA: Davies-Black.

Blustein, D. L. (1994). "Who am I?" The question of self and identity in career development. In M. L. Savickas & R. W. Lent (Eds.), *Convergence in career development theories: Implications for science and practice* (pp. 139-154). Palo Alto, CA: CPP Books.

Bronfenbrenner, U. (1977). Toward an experimental ecology of human development. *American Psychologist, 32*(7), 513-531.

Bronfenbrenner, U. (1995). Developmental ecology through space and time: A future perspective. In P. Moen, G. H. Elder, Jr., & K. Luscher (Eds.), *Examining lives in context: Perspectives on the ecology of human development* (pp. 619-647). Washington, DC: American Psychological Association.

Brooks, L., & Forrest, L. (1994). Feminism and career counseling. In W. B. Walsh & S. H. Osipow (Eds.), *Career counseling for women* (pp. 87-134). Hillsdale, NJ: Erlbaum.

Brown, D., & Brooks, L. (1991). *Career counseling techniques.* Boston: Allyn & Bacon.

Brown, L. S. (1990). The meaning of a multicultural perspective for theory building in feminist therapy. In L. S. Brown & M. P. Root (Eds.), *Diversity and complexity in feminist therapy* (pp. 1-21). New York: Harrington Park Press.

Conyne, R. (1985). The counseling ecologist: Helping people and environments. *Counseling and Human Development, 18*(2), 1-12.

Chung, W. S., & Pardeck, J. T. (1997). Treating powerless minorities through an ecosystem approach. *Adolescence, 32*, 625-634.

Collins, A., & Young, R. A. (1992). Constructing career through narrative and context: An interpretive perspective. In R. A. Young & A. Collins (Eds.), *Interpreting career: Hermeneutical studies of lives in context* (pp. 1-13). Westport, CN: Praeger.

Comas-Díaz, L. (1987). Feminist therapy with Hispanic/Latina women: Myth or reality? *Women and Therapy, 6*(4), 39-61.

Cook, E. P. (1993). The gendered context of life: Implications for women's and men's career-life plans. *The Career Development Quarterly, 41*, 227-237.

Cook, E. P., Heppner, M. J., & O'Brien, K. M. (in press). Career development of women of color and white women: Assumptions, conceptualizations, and interventions from an ecological perspective. *Journal of Multicultural Counseling and Development.*

Culbertson, A. L., Rosenfeld, P., Booth-Kewley, S., & Magnusson, P. (1992). *Assessment of sexual harassment in the Navy: Results of the 1989 Navy-wide survey. TR-92-11.* San Diego, CA: Naval Personnel Research and Development Center.

Delworth, U., & Piel, E. (1978). Students and their institutions: An interactive perspective. In C. A. Parker (Ed.), *Encouraging development in college students* (pp. 235-249). Minneapolis: University of Minnesota Press.

Dukstein, R. D., & O-Brien, K. M. (1994). *The contribution of multiple role self-efficacy and gender role attitudes to women's career development.* Unpublished manuscript.

Eccles, J. (1987). Gender roles and women's achievement-related decisions. *Psychology of Women Quarterly,* 11, 135-172

Elder, G. H., Jr. (1995). The life course paradigm: Social change and individual development. In P. Moen, G. H. Elder, Jr., & K. Luscher (Eds.), *Examining lives in context: Perspectives on the ecology of human development* (pp. 101-140). Washington, DC: American Psychological Association.

Espín, O. M. (1994). Feminist approaches. In L. Comas-Díaz and B. Greene (Eds.), *Women of color: Integrating ethnic and gender identities in psychotherapy* (pp. 265-318). New York: Guilford Press.

Espín, O. M., & Gawelek, M. A. (1992). Women's diversity: Ethnicity, race, class and gender in theories of feminist psychology. In M. Ballou & L. S. Brown (Eds.), *Personality and psychopathology: Feminist reappraisals* (pp. 88-107). New York: Guilford Press.

Faltermeier, T. (1992). Developmental processes of young women in a caring profession: A qualitative life event study. In R. A. Young & A. Collins (Eds.), *Interpreting career: Hermeneutical studies of lives in context* (pp. 48-61). Westport, CN: Praeger.

Fassinger, R. E. (1990). Causal models of career choice in two samples of college women. *Journal of Vocational Behavior,* 36, 225-248.

Fassinger, R. E. (1995). From invisibility to integration: Lesbian identity in the workplace. *The Career Development Quarterly,* 44, 148-167.

Fassinger, R. E. (1996). Notes from the margins: Integrating lesbian experience into the vocational psychology of women. *Journal of Vocational Behavior,* 48, 160-175.

Fassinger, R. E., & O'Brien, K. M. (2000). Career counseling with college women: A scientist – practitioner – advocate model of intervention. In D. A. Luzzo (Ed.), *Career counseling of college students: An empirical guide to strategies that work* (pp. 253-265). Washington, DC: American Psychological Association.

Fitzgerald, L. F. (1993). *The last great open secret: Sexual harassment of women in the workplace and academia.* Washington, DC: Federation of Behavioral, Psychological and Cognitive Science.

Fitzgerald, L. F., Fassinger, R. E., & Betz, N. E. (1995). Theoretical advances in the study of women's career development. In W. B. Walsh & S. H. Osipow (Eds.), *Handbook of vocational psychology.*

Fitzgerald, L. F., & Weitzman, L. M. (1992). Women's career development: Theory and practice from a feminist perspective. In H. D. Lea, L. B. Leibowitz (Eds.), *Adult career development: Concepts, issues and practices* (pp. 125-160). Alexandria, VA: National Career Development Association.

Gettys, L. D., & Cann, A. (1981). Children's perceptions of occupational sex stereotypes. *Sex Roles,* 7, 301-308.

Gottfredson, L. S. (1996). Gottfredson's theory of circumscription and compromise. In D. Brown, L. Brooks & Associates, *Career choice and development* (3rd ed., pp. 179-232). San Francisco: Jossey-Bass.

Greene, B. A. (1986). When the therapist is white and the patient is Black: Considerations for psychotherapy in the feminist heterosexual and lesbian communities. In D. Howard (Ed.), *The dynamics of feminist therapy* (pp. 41-65). New York: Harrington Park Press.

Greene, B. (1994). Lesbian women of color: Triple jeopardy. In L. Comas-Díaz and B. Greene (Eds.), *Women of color: Integrating ethnic and gender identities in psychotherapy* (pp. 389-427). New York: Guilford Press.

Grimstad, J. A. (1992). Advancing an ecological perspective of vocational development: The construction of work. In R. A. Young & A. Collins (Eds.), *Interpreting career: Hermeneutical studies of lives in context* (pp. 79-97). Westport, CN: Praeger.

Gutek, B., & Koss, M. P. (1993). Changed women and changed organizations: consequences of and coping with sexual harassment. *Journal of Vocational Behavior, 42*, 28-48.

Gysbers, N. C., Heppner, M. J., & Johnston, J. A. (1998). *Career counseling: Process, issues, and techniques.* Boston: Allyn & Bacon.

Hackett, G., & Betz, N. E. (1981). A self-efficacy approach to the career development of women. *Journal of Vocational Behavior, 18*, 326-339.

Hansman, C. A. (1998). Mentoring and women's career development. In L. L. Bierma (Vol. Ed.). *New directions for adult and continuing education. Women's career development across the lifespan: Insights and strategies for women, organizations, and adult educators, 80*, 63-72. San Francisco: Jossey-Bass.

Helms, J. E., & Cook, D. A. (1999). *Using race and culture in counseling and psychotherapy.* Boston: Allyn & Bacon.

Herr, E. (1999). *Counseling in a dynamic society: contexts and practices for the 21st century* (2nd ed.). Alexandria, VA: American Counseling Association.

Hooks, B. (1984). *Feminist theory: From margin to center.* Boston: South End Press.

Jordan, J., Kaplan, A., Miller, J. B., Stiver, I., & Surrey, J. (1991). *Women's growth in connection: Writings from the Stone Center.* New York: Guilford.

Kohn, M. L. (1995). Social structure and personality through time and space. In P. Moen, G. H. Elder, Jr., & K. Luscher (Eds.), *Examining lives in context: Perspectives on the ecology of human development* (pp. 141-168). Washington, DC: American Psychological Association.

Koss, M. P. (1990). Changed lives: The psychological impact of sexual harassment. In M. Paludi (Ed.), *Ivory power: Sex and gender harassment in the academy.* New York: SUNY.

Landrine, H. (1995). Introduction: Cultural diversity, contextualism, and feminist psychology. In H. Landrine (Ed.), *Bringing cultural diversity to feminist psychology: theory, research, and practice* (pp. 1- 20). Washington, DC: American Psychological Association.

Law, B. (1992). Autonomy and learning about work. In R. A. Young & A. Collins (Eds.), *Interpreting career: Hermeneutical studies of lives in context* (pp. 151-167). Westport, CN: Praeger.

Lefcourt, L. A., & Harmon, L. W. (1993, August). *Self-efficacy expectations for role management measure (SEERM): Measure development.* Paper presented at the 101st Annual Convention of the American Psychological Association, Toronto, Canada.

Lewin, K. (1936). *Principles of topological psychology.* New York: McGraw-Hill.

McCracken, R. S., & Weitzman, L. M. (1997). Relationship of personal agency, problem-solving appraisal, and traditionality of career choice to women's attitudes toward multiple role planning. *Journal of Counseling Psychology, 44*, 1149-159.

McDonald, K. S., & Hite, L. M. (1998). Human resource development's role in women's career progress. In L. L. Bierma (Vol. Ed.). *New directions for adult and continuing education. Women's career development across the lifespan: Insights and strategies for women, organizations, and adult educators, 80,* 53-62. San Francisco: Jossey-Bass.

Moen, P. (1995). Introduction. In P. Moen, G. H. Elder, Jr., & K. Luscher (Eds.), *Examining lives in context: Perspectives on the ecology of human development* (pp. 1-11). Washington, DC: American Psychological Association.

Moen, P., & Erickson, M. A. (1995). Linked lives: A transgenerational approach to resilience. In P. Moen, G. H. Elder, Jr., & K. Luscher (Eds.), *Examining lives in context: Perspectives on the ecology of human development* (pp. 169-210). Washington, DC: American Psychological Association.

Morgan, K. S., & Brown, L. S. (1991). Lesbian career development, work behavior, and vocational counseling. *The Counseling Psychologist, 19,* 273-291.

Morrill, W. H., Oetting, E. R., & Hurst, J. C. (1974). Dimensions of counselor functioning. *Personnel and Guidance Journal, 52,* 354-359.

Murrell, A. J., Frieze, I. H., & Frost, J. L. (1991). Aspiring to careers in male- and female-dominated professions: A study of Black and White college women. *Psychology of Women Quarterly, 15,* 103-126.

O'Brien, K. M. (1996). The influence of psychological separation and parental attachment on the career development of adolescent women. *Journal of Vocational Behavior, 48,* 257-274.

O'Brien, K. M., & Fassinger, R. E. (1993). A causal model of the career orientation and career choice of adolescent women. *Journal of Counseling Psychology, 40,* 456-469.

O'Brien, K. M., Friedman, S. M., Tipton, L. C., & Linn, S. G. (2000). Attachment, separation, and women's vocational development: A longitudinal analysis. *Journal of Counseling Psychology, 47,* 301-315.

Offen, K. (1988). Defining feminism: A comparative historical approach. *Signs: Journal of Women in Culture & Society, 14,* 119-157.

Orput, D. (1998). *Women at work: Multiple roles and development.* Unpublished doctoral dissertation.

Paludi, M. A., DeFour, D. C., Roberts, R., Tedesco, A. M., Brathwaite, J., & Marino, A. (1995). Academic sexual harassment: From theory and research to program implementation. In H. Landrine (Ed.), *Bringing cultural diversity to feminist psychology: theory, research, and practice* (pp. 177-192). Washington, DC: American Psychological Association.

Phillips, S. D., & Imhoff, A. R. (1997). Women and career development: A decade of research. *Annual Review of Psychology, 48,* 31-59.

Quimby, J. L., & O'Brien, K. M. (2000). *A structural model of the psychological health of reentry women balancing multiple roles.* Manuscript in preparation.

Reid, P. T., Haritos, C., Kelly, E., & Holland, N. E. (1995). Socialization of girls: Issues of ethnicity in gender development. In H. Landrine (Ed.), *Bringing cultural diversity to feminist psychology: theory, research, and practice* (pp. 93-112). Washington, DC: American Psychological Association.

Reskin, B. F., & Padavic, I. (1999). Sex, race, and ethnic inequality in the United States workplace. In J. S. Chafetz (Ed.), *Handbook of the sociology of gender* (pp. 343-374). New York: Kluwer/Plenum.

Richie, B. S., Fassinger, R. E., Linn, S. G., Johnson, J., Prosser, J., & Robinson, S. (1997). Persistence, connection, and passion: A qualitative study of the career development of highly achieving African American-Black and White Women. *Journal of Counseling Psychology, 44,* 133-148.

Robinson, T. L., & Howard-Hamilton, M. F. (2000). *The convergence of race, identity, and gender: Multiple identities in counseling.* Columbus, OH: Merrill.

Sadker, M., & Sadker, D. (1994). *Failing at fairness: How American schools cheat girls.* New York: Charles Scribner's Sons.

Savickas, M. L. (1997). The spirit in career counseling: Fostering self-completion through work. In D. P. Bloch & L. Richmond (Eds.), *Connections between spirit and work in career development* (pp. 3-25). Palo Alto, CA: Davies-Black.

Schensul, J. J. (1998). Community-based risk prevention with urban youth. *School Psychology Review, 27,* 233-245.

Sexton, T. L., & Griffin, B. L. (Eds.). (1997). *Constructivist thinking in counseling practice, research, and training.* New York: Teachers College Press.

Shelton, B. A. (1999). Gender and unpaid work. In J. S. Chafetz (Ed.), *Handbook of the sociology of gender* (pp. 375-390). New York: Kluwer/Plenum.

Spelman, E. V. (1988). *The inessential woman: Problems of exclusion in feminist thought.* Boston: Beacon Press.

Spokane, A. R. (1994). The resolution of incongruence and the dynamics of person-environment fit. In M. L. Savickas & R. W. Lent (Eds.), *Convergence in career development theories* (pp. 119-137). Palo Alto, CA: CPP Books.

Statham, A. (1992). The notion of managerial and clerical careers as they emerge from descriptions of self and coworkers. In L. L. Bierma (Vol. Ed.). *New directions for adult and continuing education. Women's career development across the lifespan: Insights and strategies for women, organizations, and adult educators, 80,* 63-78. San Francisco: Jossey-Bass.

Subich, L. M. (1996). Addressing diversity in the process of career development. In M. L. Savickas & W. B. Walsh (Eds.), *Handbook of career counseling theory and practice* (pp. 277-289). Palo Alto, CA: Davies-Black.

Super, D. E., Savickas, M. L., & Super, C. M. (1996). The life-span, life-space approach to careers. In D. Brown, L. Brooks & Associates, *Career choice and development* (3rd ed., pp. 121-178). San Francisco: Jossey-Bass.

Taylor, U. (1998). The historical evolution of Black feminist theory and praxis. *Journal of Black Studies, 29,* 234-253.

Trickett, E. J. (1996). A future for community psychology: The contexts of diversity and the diversity of contexts. *American Journal of Community Psychology, 24,* 209-218.

Turner, C. W (1997). Psychosocial barriers to Black women's career development. In J. V. Jordan (Ed.), *Women's growth in diversity: More writings from the Stone Center* (pp. 162-175). New York: Guilford.

Vondracek, F. W., Lerner, R. M., & Schulenberg, J. E. (1986). *Career development: A life span developmental approach.* Hillsdale, NJ: Erlbaum.

Weitzman, L. M. (1994). Multiple role realism: A theoretical framework for the process of planning to combine career and family roles. *Applied and Preventive Psychology, 3,* 15-25.

Wentling, R. M. (1998). Work and family issues: Their impact on women's career development. In L. L. Bierma (Vol. Ed.). *New directions for adult and continuing education. Women's career development across the lifespan: Insights and strategies for women, organizations, and adult educators, 80,* 15-24. San Francisco: Jossey-Bass.

Wicker, A. W., & August, R. A. (2000). Working lives in context: Engaging the views of participants and analysts. In W. B. Walsh, K. H. Craik, & R. H. Price (Eds.), *Person-environment psychology: New directions and perspectives* (2nd ed., pp. 197-232). Mahwah, NJ: Erlbaum.

Wood, J. T. (1994). *Gendered lives: Communication, gender, and culture.* Belmont, CA: Wadsworth.

Yager, R.E., & Yager, S. O. (1985). Changes in perceptions of science for third, seventh, and eleventh grade students. *Journal of Research in Science Teaching, 22(4),* 347-358.

Young, R. A., & Vaslach, L. (1996). Interpretation and action in career counseling. In M. L. Savickas & W. B. Walsh (Eds.), *Handbook of career counseling theory and practice* (pp. 361-375). Palo Alto, CA: Davies-Black.

CHAPTER 11
Counseling for Career Development With Persons of Color

Jerry Trusty
Pennsylvania State University

Throughout the history of the United States, persons of color have been viewed and treated by mainstream society in varying ways, with the variability of these views depending heavily on the economic and political needs of the time (see Axelson, 1999; Ramirez, 1991). As cultural entities, counseling and psychology have also taken variable views on persons of color; and through history, these views to a large extent reflect the concurrent economic, social, and political perspectives of mainstream American society (see Ivey, 1995; Jackson, 1995; Ramirez, 1991, 1999; Sue & Sue, 1999).

Jackson (1995) asserted that until the latter decades of the twentieth century, the perspective of counseling was **monolithic.** That is, counseling was based on a single view of the world, the Anglo-European view. Ivey (1995) termed this the **naïve Eurocentric approach;** and Sue and Sue (1999) referred to this phenomenon as **ethnocentric monoculturalism.** Counseling, according to Jackson (1995) and Ivey (1995), is now shifting to a pluralistic or multicultural perspective, a perspective that is more flexible in addressing the needs of persons of color. This multicultural perspective involves focusing on the commonalities as well as differences across cultures and groups, and within cultures and groups. This perspective involves seeing our clients and ourselves as cultural beings (Ivey, Ivey, & Simek-Morgan, 1993; Ramirez, 1991, 1999).

This chapter covers research, theory, and practical considerations in working with persons of color. It begins with common experiences of persons of color, followed by presentation and discussion of conceptual frameworks. The chapter concludes with material on researching the career development of persons of color. For the purposes of this chapter, a broad and longitudinal-developmental view on working with adult persons of color is taken. Rather than presenting thorough and detailed information on one or a few models, I present an overview of several models and their applicability for working with various groups. Material for this chapter was drawn from literature in several areas, including multicultural counseling, career development counseling and vocational psychology, developmental psychology, social psychology, sociology, and education. Frequently, readers are referred to resources for expanding their knowledge and understanding of perspectives, models, frameworks, and approaches used in counseling persons of color.

In this chapter, the designations that I use for the four major U.S. racial-ethnic groups of color are African Americans, Hispanics, Asian Americans, and Native American Indians. It is desired that readers recognize that the four designations used for groups are (a) not necessarily the designations preferred by all people who are commonly or "officially" included in those groups, and (b) not necessarily reflections of the cultural, racial, and ethnic heritages of persons commonly or "officially" included in those groups.

Experiences of Persons of Color

The career-related perceptions and the vocational behavior of adult persons of color are inextricably tied to their previous experiences. For example, Arbona (1996) pointed out that career counseling—including theory, research, and practice—has little to offer for many, if not most, persons of color. The cycle of persistent poverty and low educational attainment experienced by many persons of color often precludes the opportunity to make an educational or vocational choice. Only those young people who have exceptional talent, resilience, and bravery will escape the cycle. And by becoming socially mobile, persons of color face discrimination from mainstream society and possibly from within their own group (see Arbona, 1995; Cohn, 1997; Davis, 2000; Fordham & Ogbu, 1986).

DISCRIMINATION

Racism is the basis for discrimination; and racism results from an ideological, biological conceptualization of race (Atkinson, Morten, & Sue, 1993). Authors (Atkinson et al., 1993; Cameron & Wycoff, 1998; Dobbins & Skillings, 1991; Helms, 1997; Johnson, 1990) agree that a purely biological definition of race is not useful in counseling, nor is it scientifically valid. Dobbins and Skillings and Helms define race as a social construct based on biological characteristics. Authors (e.g., Atkinson et al., 1993; Johnson, 1990) have presented a logical rationale for using terms and conceptualizations other than race (e.g., ethnicity, culture) for designating and understanding groups of people. However, many persons of color choose to define themselves based on their race (Atkinson et al., 1993); and in U.S. society, the effects of "race" are much greater than the effects of ethnicity and culture (Helms, 1997). Several authors (e.g., Arbona, 1995; Brown, 1995; Helms & Piper, 1994; Leung, 1995; Oakes, 1990) agree that in contemporary U.S. society, visible physical characteristics are used to make social distinctions, and these judgments are often the basis for discrimination and blocked opportunity. Although many White Americans express lower levels of overt racism than in years past, racism and discrimination continue, but in a new, more indirect and complex form (Dovidio & Gaertner, 1991). White Americans now are likely to deny the existence of prejudice against persons of color in today's social structure, and likely to deny their own prejudices (Ponterotto & Pedersen, 1993).

Brown (1995) discussed discrimination against African Americans based on colorism (skin tone) and other physical characteristics. Discrimination on these bases is also evident within some African American groups (Brown, 1995; Davis, 2000). Similarly, Arbona (1995) noted that Hispanic Americans with lighter skin tone experience less discrimination than do Hispanic Americans with darker skin. In addition, Hispanic Americans with Native American Indian ancestry and features may be treated differently than Hispanics with Spanish ancestry and features.

Leong and Serafica (1995) noted that Asian Americans have often been labeled as a "model minority." Although this may seem an enviable label, it has two subtle negative consequences. First, it tends to conceal the fact that there is much variability in levels of educational and economic success between and within Asian American groups. Second, this label creates the illusion that there is no discrimination against Asian Americans. Leong and Serafica provided evidence that a high level of income inequity exists for Asian Americans. That is, educational attainment bears fewer economic rewards for Asian Americans than for European Americans.

The U.S. has a long history of discrimination against Native Americans Indians; and although societal attitudes toward Native Americans may have improved somewhat in recent years, more change is needed (Watts, 1993). To demonstrate, Markstrom-Adams (1990) examined attitudes toward Native American Indians reflected in novels published in the 1970s and 1980s. A less stereotypical and more culturally sensitive attitude was reflected in these novels as compared to earlier works. However, a study by Haertel, Douthitt, Haertel, and Douthitt (1999) demonstrates the subtle nature of contemporary gender-racial discrimination. They found that research participants rated a Native American Indian woman job candidate lower than a White man, although the two candidates had identical vitae and audiotapes.

Discrimination experienced early in the lives of persons of color can have pervasive and lasting effects on their career development. Cohn (1997), through a qualitative study of young adults, observed that participants who experienced discrimination early in their lives came to expect discrimination later. Participants felt powerless to stop it. Discrimination undermined participants' goal-setting processes. When students were in high school, they had no future focus; all they wanted was to get out of school. Similarly, discrimination experienced in college and later in work undermined career interests, vocational self-concepts, and identity. Authors (Chung, Baskin, & Case, 1999; Cohn, 1997; Bowman, 1995; Brown, 1995; Leung, 1995) contend that persons of color tend to avoid occupational or educational environments that they experience and perceive as discriminatory.

Given these wide-reaching and enduring effects of discrimination, it is paramount that counselors—in order to understand and help their clients—devote attention to the perceptions, emotions, and behavior associated with discrimination experiences. Many of our traditional assessments and counseling methods lead us to ignore discrimination. In fact, multicultural counseling authors and leaders have been criticized (e.g., Weinrach & Thomas, 1998) for being overly focused on racism and discrimination. If discrimination experiences are ignored, we likely become instruments of discrimination and oppression.

Racism, prejudice, and discrimination are difficult to address; and they are even more difficult to change. Vontress, in the foreward to Ponterotto's and Pedersen's (1993) work on prejudice prevention, noted that racism, prejudice, and discrimination are part of our American heritage and our human heritage. Therefore, this humanly damaging phenomenon is not only subtle but also ubiquitous. We counselors will need to consistently focus attention on:

    a) our own prejudices and discriminatory practices,
    b) intentional and unintentional prejudice and discrimination,
    c) the collective prejudices of the world,
    d) discrimination from individuals and from institutions, and

e) how our clients experience, perceive, and respond to all types of racism, prejudice, and discrimination.

Counselors' roles in addressing discrimination should be broad, and should include individual counseling, group counseling, consultation, training, and individual and social advocacy (Ponterotto, 1991).

EDUCATIONAL ATTAINMENT

One manifestation of discrimination and inequity is lower educational attainment. Educational aspirations, expectations, choices, and attainment are salient to the career development of most people. If educational development is viewed in a broad sense, and not necessarily as formal education, it is salient for the career development of all people. Educational choices and attainment are primal in the hierarchy inherent in the occupational choice process. For example, Johnson, Swartz, and Martin (1995) described education as the "gatekeeper" for Native American Indians. Educational choices and attainment serve to set parameters for—or define the range of—subsequent occupational choices.

For a large percentage of persons of color in this country, these parameters are extremely narrow. For example, the U.S. Census Bureau (2000) reported that for White American adults ages 25 to 29, approximately 34 percent hold at least a bachelor's degree. In this same age range, approximately 18 percent of African Americans and 10 percent of Hispanic Americans hold a bachelor's or higher degree. When these percentages are compared to corresponding percentages for prior years, Whites and African Americans show some improvement, however, Hispanic Americans do not.

The negative economic consequences of low educational attainment have been increasing. Snyder and Shafer (1996) presented data showing that in the U.S., the earnings of those who have attained postsecondary degrees have remained relatively steady (in constant U.S. dollars) across the last three decades, while earnings of those without degrees have declined substantially.

The educational aspirations, expectations, and attainment of young people in the U.S. have been studied extensively, and some researchers have focused upon persons of color. Earlier research (e.g., Hafner, Ingels, Sneider, & Stevenson, 1990; Mickelson, 1990) led to the conclusion that students from some non-White groups were likely to be unrealistic in their educational expectations and aspirations. However, recent research with national samples (Hanson, 1994; Trusty, 2000; Trusty & Harris, 1999) has not supported this conclusion. These researchers studied expectations for postsecondary educational attainment across time. They found that Whites were more likely than non-Whites to lower their expectations. Also, Hanson found that non-Whites were more likely than Whites to actually attain postsecondary education at their level of expectation. It is important to recognize that these researchers studied only young people who, early on, had high expectations for postsecondary attainment. Also, at the high-school level and beyond, individuals become more realistic in their expectations and aspirations (Hanson, 1994; Trusty, 2000).

Socioeconomic status (SES) is the variable with a strong and pervasive influence on educational and career development, noting that many persons of color in the

U.S. are of lower SES. Researchers using national samples (Hanson, 1994; Trusty & Harris, 1999) reported that of several variables included in models, SES had strongest effects on lowered educational expectations and unrealized expectations. Other research (e.g., Adelman, 1999; Kao & Tienda, 1998; Trusty, 1999, 2000; Wong, 1990) supports the powerful influences of SES on postsecondary educational expectations and attainment.

Understanding the strong influences of SES is salient to helping many persons of color in their career development. Most obviously, lower SES means fewer economic and social resources for postsecondary education. Over the last three decades, adults (parents, school counselors, teachers) have been increasingly advising students toward more postsecondary education (Rasinski, Ingels, Rock, Pollack, & Wu, 1993). Young people of lower SES probably understand the logic behind this advice. However, for them, postsecondary education may seem like "pie-in-the-sky" because they have not experienced the rewards that postsecondary education brings. Additionally, their information resources and learning experiences are likely limited.

Young people of lower SES lack modeling influences from parents and others (see Smith, 1991; Wilson & Wilson, 1992). It is likely that the educational attainment of young people is influenced by parents' levels of educational attainment, as well as by parents' goals for their children. It seems that parents would have more difficulty transmitting high goals to their children if those goals extend beyond parents' levels of educational attainment. Researchers (e.g., Smith, 1991; Trusty, 1999; Trusty & Pirtle, 1998) have reported that parents' influences were weaker at lower levels of SES. Although lower SES tends to dampen the ability of parents to transmit high educational goals to their children, parents' influences on their children's educational development are particularly strong (positively or negatively) for some persons of color (e.g., Mexican Americans; see McWhirter, Hackett, & Bandalos, 1998; Trusty, Plata, & Salazar, in press). And parents, through support of their children's education and through communication with their children, serve to protect them from the negative educational consequences associated with lower SES (Trusty, 1998).

There also may be cultural reasons for the lower educational attainment of people who are of lower SES. If they pursue educational attainment beyond the norm for their culture, they may risk alienating themselves from their culture (Arbona, 1995; Fordham & Ogbu, 1986; Trusty, 1996). Additional cultural pressure against achievement comes from our society at large. Through our schools and other means, our society socializes academic inferiority into our lower SES students (Brantlinger, 1990). That is, through social messages, lower SES students come to believe that they are inferior, and that attainment is not for them. Therefore, cultural pressures both from within and outside people's cultures may negatively influence their educational attainment.

SES also influences educational choices in a dynamic way. Using a national sample, Trusty, Ng, and Plata (2000) found a three-way interaction among SES, gender, and race-ethnicity in predicting choice of college major. SES had a stronger effect on men's choices than on women's choices. At higher levels of SES, racial-ethnic differences in choices became much smaller. For example, in the career literature, it is commonly accepted that African Americans tend to choose social-type majors and occupations such as teaching and social service (e.g., see Brown, 1995;

Thomas, 1985). Trusty et al. found that this was true only at the lowest level of SES. At middle and high SES, African Americans differed little from other racial-ethnic groups in frequency of choice of social majors. In this example and others, increases in SES led to homogeneity across racial-ethnic groups in choices of majors. Likewise, SES contributed to within-group heterogeneity in choices.

Although the focus here is on the earlier educational experiences of persons of color, SES and other family influences extend well into adulthood. The traditional, Euro-American view of human development prizes psychological separation and independence from parents in early adulthood; whereas the contemporary view is more consistent with a multicultural perspective. The contemporary view prizes healthy dependencies among parents and their children (see Baumrind, 1991; Trusty & Lampe, 1997 for a comparison of the two theoretical perspectives). Counseling approaches that focus upon family, SES, gender, culture, and other relational influences (e.g., Arbona, 1995; Blustein, 1997; Brown, 1995; Hartung et al., 1998; Ivey, 2000; Leong & Serafica, 1995; Ramirez, 1999; Vondracek & Fouad, 1994) are potentially more efficacious than individual-focused approaches when working with persons of color. Also, this is likely for many White persons. All career theories recognize that environment and experiences play a role in career decisions and career development, but all theories do not focus upon or characterize these influences.

To summarize, lack of educational attainment can and does subvert the career development process. Counselors should explore the early educational experiences, behavior, perceptions, and goals of persons of color; and they should seek to understand how circumstances may have constricted development. Attention should be devoted to availability of a broad range of potential resources, including personal, family, social, educational, and economic resources. Counselors should explore the influences of clients' cultures and the dominant culture on clients' educational development. Clients should be viewed from a theoretical context that focuses upon the interplay among personal, familial, cultural, and environmental variables.

Conceptual Frameworks

There are numerous conceptual frameworks, theories, strategies, and approaches for working with persons of color. Some frameworks come from multicultural counseling; Some are career-development frameworks that have particular applicability to working with persons of color; Still others are general approaches and strategies that have applicability to career development contexts. I first present and discuss conceptual approaches that, by design, are effective for working with persons of color. I then discuss traditional career approaches and how they are applied when working with the groups addressed.

READILY APPLICABLE FRAMEWORKS

Opportunity, familiarity, and values. One very basic and simple framework comes from research on occupational interests and choices (Day & Rounds, 1998); and it readily applies to career counseling with persons of color. Differences in interests, preferences, and choices among racial-ethnic or cultural groups arise from three major socially-driven variables: (a) differences in the real and perceived social and economic opportunity structure, sometimes referred to in the literature as barriers (e.g., Arbona, 1990; Luzzo, 1993); (b) familiarity or unfamiliarity with educational and occupational options, and (c) differences in the value placed upon various options.

The first of these, opportunity, is closely related to experiences and perceptions of discrimination. It also extends into other areas that may or may not stem from discrimination. For example, Suzuki (1994) pointed out that many Asian Americans face verbal-linguistic barriers in social-service occupations, and therefore tend to choose occupations of a more quantitative nature; Martin (1991) noted that the geographic restrictions of Native American Indians living on reservations narrow their real and perceived range of occupational options.

The second category in this model, familiarity, is commonly found in the literature on career development of persons of color. For example, Arbona (1990) showed evidence that limited life experiences and lack of role models impede the career development of some, especially poorer, Hispanic Americans; Bowman (1995) and McCollum (1998) expressed concerns regarding the accessibility of career information and role models for African Americans; Johnson et al. (1995) cited similar concerns for Native American Indians. The reader should note that the two categories, opportunity and familiarity, are closely related. That is, barriers to opportunity not only restrict options, they limit knowledge regarding options.

The third category is values; and again, there is considerable literature that supports the salient role of culturally-related values in the career development of persons of color. For example, strong family values in Hispanic American cultures are reflected in strong influences of parents on their children's postsecondary education (e.g., Arellano & Padilla, 1996; Fisher & Padmawidjaja, 1999: Trusty et al., in press); Quantitative fields offer occupational security and extrinsic rewards which are, in general, valued by Asian Americans (Leong, 1991); Native American Indian's beliefs may take precedence over career attainment (Johnson et al., 1995).

These three variables—opportunities, familiarity, values—therefore offer a useful basic focal point for career counseling with persons of color. It is likely that exploration of these three will reveal clients' discrimination experiences and perceptions, and it may reveal information regarding clients' racial or ethnic identity development. However, this may not happen with all clients. Counselors should keep in mind that gender and SES are related to the three variables. In applying this framework, counselors should not assume that persons of color have had limited opportunities or have low familiarity with particular occupations, and not assume that clients' values are consistent with those of their identified group or groups.

Krumboltz' Social Learning Theory of Career Decision Making (SLTCDM). Krumboltz' (1979) SLTCDM is a model that has particular applicability for working with persons of color. In this approach, environmental influences receive close attention. Learning experiences, interpreted broadly, drive the career development process. Learning experiences lead to self-perceptions, preferences and interests, and values—all of which are termed *self-observation generalizations*. These, along with skills developed from learning experiences, lead to career-related actions. Recent research supports the predictive power of self-observation generalizations for career-related choices (e.g., Trusty & Ng, 2000; Trusty, in press-b). In fact, self-observation generalizations are often a stronger predictor of career choices than measured abilities (Prediger, 1999); and counselors can easily and inexpensively assess clients' self-estimates of their abilities and other self-observation generalizations.

Based on his decision-making theory, Krumboltz (1996) provided a theory of career counseling. These two theories—or this approach—seem particularly efficacious for working with persons of color whose learning experiences have been constrained. For example, if the counselor finds that barriers to opportunity and low familiarity with the range of educational or occupational choices have limited the client's career development, then the counselor facilitates clients in broadening their learning experiences and perceptions. From Krumboltz' (1996) perspective, interests and preferences are not outcomes. They are a starting point for structuring new learning experiences. For persons of color—particularly if they are of lower SES—interests and preferences are likely symptoms of environmental constraints. If we treat scores on an interest inventory as an outcome or summative evaluation, then we may stifle growth.

Also, Krumboltz (1996) posited that people tend to have inaccurate and misleading beliefs about themselves and their educational and career development. For persons of color, debilitating beliefs may be a product of discrimination experiences. Whereas it is important for counselors to validate clients' discrimination experiences and perceptions, the counselor's role is to help clients challenge debilitating beliefs and encourage facilitative beliefs.

Multicultural Counseling and Therapy (MCT). Sue, Ivey, and Pedersen (1996) presented MCT theory as a framework, or metatheory, for using various theories, techniques, and strategies in counseling. MCT recognizes that existing theories represent worldviews, and that counselors and clients are cultural beings. Person-environment dynamics are a particular focus for this framework, and racial-ethnic identity development is incorporated. Similar to models developed by Ivey (Ivey, 1987, 2000; Ivey et al., 1993), counseling is seen as a coconstruction of counselor and client; and counselors are flexible regarding clients' worldviews, identities, and needs; and counselors are therefore flexible in their own roles. For example, a counselor may engage in community advocacy and may use helping models that are consistent with the culture and experiences of the client.

Although MCT is not specific to counseling for career development, it is certainly applicable. For example, Blustein and Noumair (1996), in a review of self and identity constructs in career development, noted a shift in perspective on how these are viewed. Whereas self and identity are important constructs in well-established career theories, this new perspective takes a stronger focus on how multiple contexts (e.g., family, culture, gender, SES) actually influence self and identity. This perspective is more relativistic than individualistic; and because it is more relativistic, it is a more pragmatic way of conceptualizing career development in a rapidly changing social and economic environment (see Blustein, 1997). It seems logical that in different cultures, self and identity would be defined in different ways, based on the values and worldviews held in those cultures. All people in all cultures do not perceive themselves and work the way self and work are perceived in Western culture—with many or most of our theories being a manifestation of that Western perception (see Cohn, 1997). Therefore, counselors should be flexible in how they define self and identity in career development; and consistent with MCT, they should let definitions emanate from the counselor-client coconstruction.

Racial and ethnic identity development. Racial and ethnic identity development theories are promising frameworks for understanding the career development of persons of color (Osipow & Littlejohn, 1995). In any general discussion of racial and ethnic identity development, it is important to recognize that there are similarities and differences among various models. Some models were designed as generic models, for example, the Minority Identity Development (MID) model of Atkinson et al. (1993), and the Phinney (1990, 1993) model of ethnic identity development. Several models have been developed for specific groups, for example, Cross's Nigrescence theory for African Americans (Cross, 1995; Vandiver, Fhagen-Smith, Cokley, Cross, & Worrell, 2001), Helms's models of Black and White racial identity (Helms, 1995; Helms & Cook, 1999); models of Biracial identity (Henriksen, 2001; Kerwin & Ponterotto, 1995; Root, 1990, 1996), multidimensional models of Asian American identity (Sodowsky, Kwan, & Pannu, 1995), models applied to Hispanic American groups (Casas & Pytluk, 1995; Ruiz, 1990), and identity and acculturation models for Native American Indians (Choney, Berryhill-Paapke, & Robbins, 1995). These resources offer more explicit description of the models than is provided in this chapter.

Most theories of racial-ethnic identity development were influenced by the early Nigrescence models of Cross (1971) and Thomas (1971). Although any brief description could not articulate the complex and dynamic interactional nature of actual racial identity development, I provide a brief and general summary of Nigrescence models to serve as an example. Nigrescence models begin with people placing little importance on race or on being Black—a rejection of self, or at least having an identity centered on some other focal point to the exclusion of racial-being consciousness. After some salient event (discrimination experience), or encounter, there is an awakening to racial being, and people discover that they have denied themselves. This stage is fraught with conflict and confusion between the old and the new self. When the new identity is internalized, some degree of comfort is realized. This new identity is embedded in the Black group. If the person gains a high level of security and integration in the new identity, the person may evolve to a multicultural identity, an identity characterized by felt connections to all humans and increased perceptiveness of qualities of all people and interactions among people. This identity may evolve further, through a dialectical process that crosses the life-span (Cross, 1994; Parham & Austin, 1994).

Racial-ethnic identity development is a relatively new and evolving area of study and application, and many of the constructs arising from theoretical formulations have proven difficult to quantify (e.g., encounter attitudes, see Fischer, Tokar, & Serna, 1998). Much more research is needed. However, there is sound logical basis for the utility of racial-ethnic identity development theory in counseling in general and in counseling for career development in particular. The Nigrescence model, as well as other models, acknowledge that racism and discrimination mediate movement through identity processes (Helms & Piper, 1994; Leong & Chou, 1994). Also, positive experiences of people within their own group and with other groups mediate movement (Parham & Austin, 1994). One quality of racial-ethnic identity development models that renders them useful in career development counseling is that they address experience, cognition, affect, and overt behavior in terms of people's selves, their own and other racial-ethnic group cultures, and the mainstream or dominant culture. The world of work exists mainly, but not exclusively, in and for mainstream culture. As Helms and Piper noted, it is necessary for most persons of color in the U.S. to function in a work environment over which they have little control. According to Helms and Piper, racial identity ego-statuses should influence how people experience and perceive discrimination; and these perceptions, in turn, influence career-related variables such as perceived opportunity, choices, and job satisfaction.

Bicultural models. Bicultural models are similar in several aspects to identity development models and acculturation models. Phinney (1990) described two basic, common models of acculturation. The first is a bipolar model, in which acculturation is conceptualized on a linear continuum, with a strong allegiance to the heritage culture on one end, and a strong embracing of mainstream culture on the other end. In this model, the person forsakes the heritage culture as the person becomes acculturated into mainstream culture. The two cultures, therefore, are mutually exclusive of one another, and identifying with one culture is dependent on not identifying with the other. LaFromboise, Coleman, and Gerton (1993) refered to this model as the *acculturation model*. The second model described by Phinney is the two-dimensional model (see Berry, Trimble, & Almedo, 1986). In this model, the two cultures are not mutually exclusive of one another, and identifying with one culture is independent of identifying with the other. A person may embrace both cultures strongly, embrace one culture or the other, or embrace neither culture. LaFromboise et al. (1993) termed this model the *alternation model,* or bicultural model. LaFromboise et al. examined several theoretical models of second-culture acquisition, and determined that the alternation model had the greatest potential for helping clients. This bicultural model encourages clients to choose their degree of involvement in each culture, and it tends to enhance feelings of belonging and cultural groundedness.

This bicultural model is similar to Ramirez' (1991, 1999) cognitive and cultural theory of personality. As in the alternation model of LaFromboise et al. (1993), people do not forsake one culture for the other. Ramirez' model focuses on the cognitive and cultural flexibility that persons of color need to effectively adapt to and function in a bicultural world. As people gain flexibility, they develop multicultural coping skills and a multicultural identity.

These models termed bicultural models readily apply to the career development contexts of persons of color. Work environments and educational environments reflect a particular culture or cultures, and most reflect mainstream culture to a great extent. Operating from a bicultural model, counselors would first ensure that clients have a positive identity in their heritage culture. Counselors would then facilitate clients in choosing their desired levels of involvement in both cultures. These desired levels would be mediated by work requirements, responsibilities, and interactions with others. Next counselors would help clients in developing cognitive and cultural flexibility for functioning in the two cultural environments. The Ramirez model includes a component in which clients and counselors become agents of change in response to insensitive and restricting environments (see Arbona, 1995; Johnson et al., 1995; LaFromboise et al., 1993; Leong & Gim-Chung, 1995; Martin, 1995; Ramirez, 1991, 1999; Trusty, 1996 for more detailed application of bicultural and acculturation models).

There are similarities and differences between the bicultural models and racial-ethnic identity models. Regarding similarities, if individuals have developed

identity and coping skills in both cultures, the individual is bicultural, a concept which is consistent with the advanced stages of the racial and ethnic identity development models. For example, the MID model of Atkinson et al. (1993) ends with the *synergistic stage*. In this stage, individuals take a broad view on society and cultures, incorporate positive elements from both cultures, gain more cultural flexibility, and are committed to pluralism. Other models (e.g., Cross, 1995; Helms, 1995; Phinney, 1990) have a similar final stage, status, or goal.

Regarding differences, bicultural models do not have fixed stages, and identity development is not conceptualized as a sequential phenomenon, as in some identity models. However, some identity development theorists have moved away from linear sequences of stages (e.g., see Helms, 1995). In the bicultural models, no dominant culture is assumed, in contrast to identity development models (see LaFromboise et al., 1993; Ramirez, 1991). Admittedly, assuming that there is no dominant culture in this country is erroneous. However, there are advantages in operating from this assumption. This assumption implies no hierarchy between cultures. It places no judgments upon either culture. Thus, clients are freer to take on new perspectives on themselves and the cultures. Because consistencies and inconsistencies between the cultures are defined by clients and not by the models, clients naturally feel more empowered to choose their levels of involvement in the cultures; and they feel more empowered to develop coping skills, make decisions, and become change agents. It is important to note that bicultural models are more appropriate after clients have recognized and negotiated their discrimination experiences—an area more readily addressed through racial and ethnic identity development models.

Bicultural models and racial-ethnic identity development models may not apply for some persons of color (Phinney, 1989; Ying & Lee, 1999). For example, some persons may interact little with people and institutions outside their own culture. Therefore, they may have little need for flexibility; and their identity may be tied closely to their heritage culture. In applying bicultural and identity development models, counselors should be aware that contexts such as gender and SES affect processes (Phinney, 1990; Jackson & Neville, 1998).

The status attainment model. Leung (1995), in his work on multicultural career development, extolled the usefulness of sociological models for understanding the career development of persons of color. In particular, the Status Attainment Model (Portes & Wilson, 1976; Sewell, Haller, & Portes, 1969; Sewell & Shah, 1968) is useful because it takes a broad and longitudinal perspective on the educational and occupational attainment process. The status attainment model is a well-established model supported by extensive research across several decades (Hotchkiss & Borow, 1996). In this model, SES and early academic performance are exogenous variables. These affect parents' expectations for their children. Parents, through their expectations for their children and through involvement in their children's education, influence their children's educational and occupational aspirations and expectations; and significant others, such as teachers and peers, influence aspirations and expectations. SES and early academic performance also affect students' expectations directly (Sewell & Shah, 1968). Educational expectations and attainment lead to occupational attainment. Over the years, variables have been added to the status attainment model, including personal resources (psychological) variables, and behavioral and attitudinal variables such as educational involvement (Hanson, 1994; Trusty, in press-a; Wong, 1990). Other models (e.g., social-cognitive models, Bandura, Barbaranelli, Caprara, & Pastorelli, 1996; Super's, 1990 model) have commonality with the status attainment model.

One observation by earlier researchers is that the status attainment model does not seem to fit as well for women and persons of color as it does for White men (e.g., Portes & Wilson, 1976). Recent research using national samples (Trusty, in press-a; Trusty et al., in press), however, reveals a relatively close fit of the model for particular groups. Trusty found that the model fits well for African American men and not quite as well for African American women. Trusty also found a stronger relationship between African Americans' achievement and educational expectations than found by Portes and Wilson, using a national sample from the 1960s. This result is encouraging, and may reflect some erosion of barriers to educational attainment for some African Americans. Results of McWhirter et al. (1998) and Trusty et al. (in press) show that the status attainment model fits reasonably well for Mexican Americans.

Leung (1995) noted that the status attainment model is not deterministic, and he suggested three points of intervention based on the model. First, exploration of clients' aspirations and expectations could lead clients toward generating realistic long-term and short-terms goals and plans. Processing discrepancies between aspirations (the ideal) and expectations (the realistic) should enhance clients' self-awareness and counselors' understanding. Second, enlisting the help of significant others (parents, teachers, peers, adult educators, mentors, etc.) could empower individuals in implementing plans and reaching goals. Third, a focus on educational attainment is crucial. Educational attainment is often the only means of social mobility for persons of color (Crowley & Shapiro, 1982). In addition, variables added to the model (e.g., self-perceptions, attributions, educational attitudes and behavior) are also points of intervention.

TRADITIONAL, ESTABLISHED APPROACHES

Much has been written and reported on the applicability and non-applicability of traditional career development models to persons of color (e.g., Brown, 1995; Arbona, 1995; Cohn, 1997; Day & Rounds, 1998; Day, Rounds, & Swaney, K., 1998; Leong & Chou, 1994; Luzzo, 1992; Tinsley, 1994). The preceding sections of this chapter have illuminated the limits of traditional approaches. If the preceding material is used as a lens for viewing the career development of persons of color, then traditional approaches become more applicable. I choose to hold a positive and pragmatic view of established theories, and thus I now focus on their applicability. Readers should access Leong (1995) for a more thorough coverage of the applicability of traditional career development theories to African Americans, Hispanic Americans, Asian Americans, and Native American Indians. In the multicultural counseling and career development literature, the traditional theories most often addressed regarding applicability to persons of color are Holland's theory and Super's approach.

HOLLAND'S THEORY

Holland (1966, 1997) classified occupations and postsecondary education majors into six types, realistic (R), investigative (I), artistic (A), social (S), enterprising (E), and conventional (C). There are six corresponding personality types of occupation-education seekers. These types form Holland's hexagonal model. Holland (1997) recognized the importance of gender, SES, and racial-ethnic contexts in personality development, career choice, and career development. Some of Gottfredson's (e.g., Gottfredson, 1981) work on SES and occupational prestige is incorporated into the model. Holland recognized the stifling nature of racism and discrimination, and he suggested that there is a dynamic interplay among these and other variables, resulting in personalities, interests, and choices.

One salient question surrounding Holland's (1997) theory is whether the hexagonal model is applicable to various racial-ethnic and gender groups. There is support for the validity of Holland's R-I-A-S-E-C, hexagonal model across U.S. racial-ethnic/gender groups. Day and Rounds (1998) and Day et al. (1998) did large-scale quantitative studies of interest inventory scores from males and females in the five major racial-ethnic groups in the U.S. Their results provided strong support for the universality of Holland's (1966, 1997) structural model. Although U.S. racial-ethnic/gender groups differ in their interests associated with Holland types of occupations, their interests reflect a common cognitive organization. In addition, Arbona (1990), in reviewing research literature on the career development of Hispanic Americans, noted that Holland's hexagonal model seems valid for Hispanic Americans.

Brown (1995) observed that research has supported the applicability of Holland's (1997) concept of congruence for African Americans. More research on congruence is needed for other racial-ethnic groups; and for all racial-ethnic groups, more study is needed on the concepts of consistency and differentiation. Leong and Serafica (1995) noted that whereas Holland's theory does account for the effects of culture on the personality development of individuals, it does not account for the direct effects of culture on work environments.

Overall, however, it appears that Holland's (1966, 1997) model does have applicability for persons of color. His adjustments and refined delineations of the theory have produced a theory more sensitive to environmental influences and varying world-views. Although some of the constructs in Holland's theory have not been adequately studied in particular groups, the basic structural components of the theory appear valid for many persons of color.

SUPER'S APPROACH

Super's approach (Super, 1990; Super, Savickas, & Super, 1996) is very comprehensive in that it acknowledges the influences of many variables across the life-span. One quality that enhances the applicability of Super's approach is that it is a segmented approach; and therefore it is flexible. Counselors can readily adjust, expand, or otherwise mold the approach to fit particular clients, groups, or perspectives. For example, Blustein (1997) used Super's model as a guide to develop a contextual, relativistic framework for career exploration; and authors (Arbona, 1995; Foaud & Arbona, 1994) have suggested that racial-ethnic identity development be viewed as a developmental task within Super's approach. It seems that the developmental, person-environment dynamics perspectives of Super make for theoretical compatibility with MCT and bicultural and acculturation models.

Much of the research on Super's model has centered around key constructs such as occupational self-concept, career maturity, and adult career concerns. However, little of this research has been done with racially and ethnically diverse or lower

SES populations. Career maturity, for example, seems to be mediated by racial-ethnic identity development (Arbona, 1995; Brown, 1995). Additionally, across cultures, differing value placed on social roles influence various developmental tasks (Leong & Serafica, 1995). The self-concept is a key construct in Super's approach, and it is not clear how lower SES and discrimination affect occupational self-concepts (Brown, 1995). For the self-concept construct to be more viable in working with persons of color, it seems that a more relativistic (as opposed to than individualistic) perspective is needed (see Blustein & Noumair, 1996; Brown, 1995; Cohn, 1997; Foaud & Arbona, 1994).

Leong and Serafica (1995) asserted that Super's (1990) maxicycle concept has potential applicability for Asian Americans who were raised in the U.S.; however, Asian Americans may move through the stages of the maxicycle at a slower rate than Whites. Leong and Serafica noted that the minicycle concept seems applicable for all Asian Americans. The minicycle may be a particularly useful structural sequence for working with Asians, and perhaps others, who are new to the U.S. Super's approach and its accompanying theoretical formulations seem most applicable to middle and upper SES persons of color, to individuals for which educational and occupational attainment are highly valued, and to individuals who have higher levels of acculturation or biculturalism (Brown, 1995; Arbona, 1990; 1995; Leong & Serafica, 1995). Although many research questions remain unanswered, and some constructs in their present form may be inadequate, several theoretical formulations from Super's approach hold promise for guiding the work of counselors in helping persons of color in their career development (Arbona, 1995; Blustein, 1997; Bowman, 1995; Leong & Serafica, 1995).

Perspectives on Research

As mentioned and implied at several points earlier in this chapter, there is dire need for research in many areas relating to the career development of persons of color. In many of these areas, studies have been done only on Whites and African Americans. In taking a critical, global view on existing research, several problems and needs emerge:

1. Comparison studies have limited usefulness. The majority of studies in the literature that address career variables for persons of color are comparison studies. These studies tell us that one group scores higher or lower than some other group on some variable. These studies generally give counselors little information on how career development processes operate, and they provide few implications for helping persons of color. Often, these studies may only add to general stereotypes because they rarely account for contexts such as SES or gender; and studies that compare persons of color to whites may perpetuate the idea of the "white standard."

   If a study is comparing the fit of a theoretical model for one group to the model fit for another group, then this type of comparison is very useful because it speaks to processes and applicability of theory to groups. For example, it is more useful to know what variables influence the postsecondary educational attainment of African American men and African American women than it is to know how African American men and women differ in their attainment.

2. <u>Many studies are piecemeal.</u> Often, studies include only a few variables. Authors in multicultural counseling argue for context. However, many studies do not include the variables that supply the context. Our theories specify the variables that influence career outcomes. If all specified variables are not included, then the research suffers from specification error. Specification error is a particularly insidious problem when unspecified, unmeasured variables influence an observed relationship or difference; and the reported relationship or difference is erroneously attributed to some specified, measured variable, when the actual relationship should be attributed to a variable or variables that the researcher did not include. The most frequently cited case in the multicultural career literature is the exclusion of SES (e.g., see Brown, 1995; Leung, 1995). Several studies also ignore gender (Trusty, Robinson, Plata, & Ng, 2000). The solution to this problem is to build models that are firmly grounded in theory, and test these models and theories as a whole. Generally, studies of this type include many variables; and analysis procedures are relatively complex, leading to longer manuscripts. Therefore, journal editors, editorial boards, and other decision-makers should not force authors into a piecemeal publication mode.

3. <u>Researchers often ignore the possibility of interactions or other curvilinear relationships.</u> Interactions, or conditional relationships, are important in counseling for career development. Statistical interactions reveal context. For example, it would be informative to know if the effect of acculturation on satisfaction was conditional on country of birth for Asians who have come to the U.S. This is a time in which linear structural equation models are popular. This type of analysis is very useful for building models and testing theories. However, the assumption of linear structural models is that there are no curvilinear relationships, including interactions. Therefore, researchers should carefully examine data, especially if the theory or earlier research specifies an interaction or other curvilinear relationship.

4. <u>Too little attention is paid to external validity-transferability of findings.</u> In the past, when psychological studies were mostly studies of psychological variables, external validity (generalizability) of studies was less a concern than internal validity. However, authors and researchers are now realizing the importance of environmental and other contextual variables in psychological processes. Multicultural counseling has been one discipline that has taken the lead in this area. Naturally, environmental variables depend on particular environments; whereas some psychological variables may be universal (although universality is increasingly rare). Findings regarding psychological variables may generalize somewhat from students in an introductory psychology course in a large Midwestern university; but findings regarding environmental variables are very unlikely to generalize. This is probably one major reason for the inconsistency of findings across studies. If journals published only studies with random, representative samples, journals would be much smaller. The solution lies between these two extremes. Researchers should work to have their samples as representative as possible, and they should qualify the external validity of their findings. It seems that many researchers have forgotten that most all statistical analyses are for simple random samples, and that representativeness is required for generalization.

Qualitative research paradigms have philosophical consistency with multicultural counseling, and several are promising for building theory and addressing complex questions in the career development of persons of color. In qualitative studies, transferability is the concern. Qualitative researchers should be careful to support the validity of their findings and qualify the transferability of their results. When quantitative and qualitative research support one another, our knowledge base benefits.

5. Research and theory from areas other than multicultural and career counseling are often ignored. Phinney (1990) illuminated this problem regarding ethnic identity development. There is a rich knowledge base in social psychology and sociology that is pertinent to multicultural counseling and career development, and it is underutilized. Sometimes, applicable theory and research from developmental psychology, education, and other fields are not used. Also, researchers and theorists sometimes build models and theories and fail to credit others where credit is due.

6. There is a double standard regarding cause in correlational studies. Some stick to the old axioms that "correlation does not mean causation" and "only experimental studies can show cause." Pedhazur (1982), Asher (1983), and Arbukle and Wothke (1999), among others, have discussed qualifiers for these axioms. Cause is a controversial subject in quantitative research. All theories, however, delineate cause. They describe causal sequence and causal direction. If researchers are forced to "stick their heads in sand" and ignore theory and cause, then the likelihood that they can make any meaningful contribution is near zero. A more realistic scenario would be that researchers build models based on theories, and test the causal linkages specified by those theories. If a theorist can theorize—hopefully based on some data—that one set of variables causes some other variable, then a researcher should surely be able to do research seeking to support or disconfirm that theory. As implied earlier, research testing the adequacy of theories for persons of color are sorely needed (see Leong & Serafica, 1995).

7. We need more studies that focus on the effectiveness of interventions. Most of these studies would be experimental or quasi-experimental studies. This statement of need has become a mantra when suggestions for research are included in works. However, it is an important statement to make. Internally valid experimental studies do speak to cause, and they often provide information on what interventions work best. This information is salient for career-development counseling with persons of color.

8. More research is needed on developmental processes. Foaud and Arbona (1994) pointed out this need. Most of these studies would either be quantitative-longitudinal or qualitative. With regard to quantitative research, too many of our models are tested with cross-sectional samples, and temporal sequence is inferred from the theory or model being tested. Method variance problems arise in these studies when all variables are measured simultaneously, and the requirement of temporal asymmetry (see Asher, 1983) is violated. Retrospective studies may also be useful, and they are usually less time-consuming than longitudinal studies. With regard to qualitative research, retrospective studies are also useful in describing developmental processes, and this type of qualitative study is fairly common (participants' recollections of career-related influences

and experiences). However, actually following participants through processes longitudinally should produce richer data. As stated earlier, if quantitative and qualitative research can work together toward common goals, we will all benefit. Whereas much of the quantitative-qualitative philosophical controversy has been intellectually stimulating; it can also be inhibiting; and the product is that knowledge suffers.

It is encouraging that research on specific racial, ethnic, and cultural groups is growing. With the recent explosion in available quantitative analysis procedures and qualitative methodologies, it is hoped that our knowledge base can grow at a similar exponential rate. As the diversity of the U.S. population increases, the need for knowledge on the career development of persons of color increases likewise.

References

Adelman, C. (1999). *Answers in the tool box: Academic intensity, attendance patterns, and bachelor's degree attainment.* U.S. Department of Education, Office of Educational Research and Improvement. Retrieved December 18, 1999, from http://www.ed.gov/ pubs/Toolbox/Title.html.

Arbona, C. (1990). Career counseling research and Hispanics: A review of the literature. *The Counseling Psychologist, 18,* 300-323.

Arbona, C. (1995). Theory and research on racial and ethnic minorities: Hispanic Americans. In F. T. L. Leong (Ed.), *Career development and vocational behavior of racial and ethnic minorities* (pp. 37-66). Mahwah, NJ: Erlbaum.

Arbona, C. (1996). Career theory and practice in a multicultural context. In M. L. Savickas, & W. B. Walsh (Eds.), *Handbook of career counseling theory and practice* (pp. 45-54). Palo Alto, CA: Davies-Black.

Arbuckle, J. L., & Wothke, W. (1999). *Amos 4.0 user's guide.* Chicago: SPSS.

Arellano, A. R., & Padilla, A. M. (1996). Academic invulnerability among a select group of Latino university students. *Hispanic Journal of Behavioral Sciences, 18,* 485-507.

Asher, H. B. (1983). *Causal modeling* (2nd ed.). Newbury Park, CA: Sage.

Atkinson, D. R., Morten, G., & Sue, D. W. (1993). *Counseling American minorities: A cross-cultural perspective* (4th ed.). Madison, WI: Brown & Benchmark.

Axelson, J. A. (1999). *Counseling and development in a multicultural society* (3rd ed.). Pacific Grove, CA: Brooks/Cole.

Bandura, A., Barbaranelli, C., Caprara, G. V., & Pastorelli, C. (1996). Multifaceted impact of self-efficacy beliefs on academic functioning. *Child Development, 67,* 1206-1222.

Baumrind, D. (1991). The influence of parenting style on adolescent competence and substance use. *Journal of Early Adolescence, 11,* 56-95.

Berry, J. W., Trimble, J. E., & Olmedo, E. L. (1986). Assessment of acculturation. In W. L. Lonner & J. W. Berry (Eds.), *Field methods in cross-cultural research* (pp. 291-324). Beverly Hills, CA: Sage.

Blustein, D. L. (1997). A context-rich perspective of career exploration across the life-roles. *Career Development Quarterly, 45,* 260-274.

Blustein, D. L., & Noumair, D. A. (1996). Self and identity in career development: Implications for theory and practice. *Journal of Counseling and Development, 74,* 433-441.

Bowman, S. L. (1995). Career intervention strategies and assessment issues for African Americans. In F. T. L. Leong (Ed.), *Career development and vocational behavior of racial and ethnic minorities,* (pp. 137-164). Mahwah, NJ: Erlbaum.

Brantlinger, E. (1990). Low-income adolescents' perceptions of school, intelligence, and themselves as students. *Curriculum Inquiry, 20,* 305-324.

Brown, M. T. (1995). The career development of African Americans: Theoretical and empirical issues. In F. T. L. Leong (Ed.), *Career development and vocational behavior of racial and ethnic minorities,* (pp. 7-36). Mahwah, NJ: Erlbaum.

Cameron, S. C., & Wycoff, S. M. (1998). The destructive nature of the term race: Growing beyond a false paradigm. *Journal of Counseling & Development, 76,* 277-285.

Casas, J. M., & Pytluk, S. D. (1995). Hispanic identity development: Implications for research and practice. In J. G. Ponterotto, J. M. Casas, L. A. Suzuki, & C. M. Alexander (Eds.), *Handbook of multicultural counseling* (pp. 155-180). Thousand Oaks, CA: Sage.

Choney, S. K., Berryhill-Paapke, E., & Robbins, R. R. (1995). The acculturation of American Indians. In J. G. Ponterotto, J. M. Casas, L. A. Suzuki, & C. M. Alexander (Eds.), *Handbook of multicultural counseling* (pp. 73-92). Thousand Oaks, CA: Sage.

Chung, Y. B., Baskin, M. L., & Case, A. B. (1999). Career development of Black males: Case studies. *Journal of Career Development, 25,* 161-171.

Cohn, J. (1997). The effects of racial and ethnic discrimination on the career development of minority persons. In H. S. Farmer (Ed.), *Diversity & women's career development* (pp. 161-171). Thousand Oaks, CA: Sage.

Cross, W. E. (1971). The Negro to Black conversion experience. *Black World, 20(9),* 13-27.

Cross, W. E., Jr. (1994). Nigrescence theory: Historical and explanatory notes. *Journal of Vocational Behavior, 44,* 119-123.

Cross, W. E., Jr. (1995). The psychology of Nigrescence: Revising the Cross model. In J.G. Ponterotto, J.M. Casas, L.A. Suzuki, & C.M. Alexander (Eds.), *Handbook of multicultural counseling* (pp. 93-122). Thousand Oaks, CA: Sage.

Crowley, J. E., & Shapiro, D. (1982). Aspirations and expectations of youth in the United States. *Youth & Society, 13,* 391-422.

Davis, P. E. (2000). *The impact of cultural forces on the academic performance of African Americans in higher education.* Unpublished doctoral dissertation, Texas A&M University-Commerce, TX.

Day, S. X., & Rounds, J. (1998). Universality of vocational interest structure among racial and ethnic minorities. *American Psychologist, 53,* 728-736.

Day, S. X., Rounds, J., & Swaney, K. (1998). The structure of vocational interests for diverse racial-ethnic groups. *Psychological Science: a Journal of the American Psychological Society, 9,* 40-44.

Dobbins, J. E., & Skillings, J. H. (1991). The utility of race labeling in understanding cultural identity: A conceptual tool for the social science practitioner. *Journal of Counseling & Development, 70,* 37-44.

Dovidido, J. F., & Gaertner, S. L. (1991). Changes in the expression and assessment of racial prejudice. In H. J. Knopke, R. J. Norrell, & R. W. Rogers (Eds.), *Opening doors: Perspectives on race relations in contemporary America* (pp. 119-148). Tuscaloosa, AL: University of Alabama Press.

Fischer, A. R., Tokar, D. M., & Serna, G. S. (1998). Validity and construct contamination of the Racial Identity Attitude Scale—Long Form. *Journal of Counseling Psychology, 45,* 212-224.

Fisher, T. A., & Padmawidjaja, I. (1999). Parental influences on career development perceived by African American and Mexican American college students. *Journal of Multicultural Counseling and Development, 27,* 136-152.

Foaud, N. A., & Arbona, C. (1994). Careers in a cultural context. *The Career Development Quarterly, 43,* 98-112.

Fordham, S., & Ogbu, J. U. (1986). Black students' school success: Coping with the "burden of 'acting White.'" *The Urban Review, 18,* 178-206.

Gottfredson, L. S. (1981). Circumscription and compromise: A developmental theory of occupational aspirations. *Journal of Counseling Psychology, 28,* 545-579.

Haertel, C. E. J., Douthitt, S. S., Haertel, G., & Douthitt, S. Y. (1999). Equally qualified but unequally perceived: Openness to perceived dissimilarity as a predictor of race and sex discrimination in performance judgments. *Human Resource Development Quarterly, 10,* 79-89.

Hafner, A., Ingels, S., Schneider, B., & Stevenson, D. (1990). A profile of the American eighth grader: NELS:88 student descriptive summary. (NCES Publication No. 90-458). Washington, DC: U.S. Government Printing Office.

Hanson, S. L. (1994). Lost talent: Unrealized educational aspirations and expectations among U.S. youths. *Sociology of Education, 67,* 159-183.

Hartung, P. J., Vandiver, B. J., Leong, F. T. L., Pope, M., Niles, S. G., & Farrow, B. (1998). Appraising cultural identity in career-development assessment and counseling. *The Career Development Quarterly, 46,* 276-293.

Helms, J. E. (1995). An update of Helms's White and people of color racial identity models. In J. G. Ponterotto, J. M. Casas, L. A. Suzuki, & C. M. Alexander (Eds.), *Handbook of multicultural counseling* (pp. 181-198). Thousand Oaks, CA: Sage.

Helms, J. E. (1997). Race is not ethnicity. *American Psychologist, 52,* 1246-1247.

Helms, J. E., & Cook, D. A. (1999). *Using race and culture in counseling and psychotherapy: Theory and process.* Boston: Allyn & Bacon.

Helms, J. E., & Piper, R. E. (1994). Implications of racial identity theory for vocational psychology. *Journal of Vocational Behavior, 44,* 124-138.

Henriksen, R. C., Jr. (2001). Black/white biracial identity development: A grounded theory study. *Dissertation Abstracts International, 67,* 2605.

Holland, J. L. (1966). A psychological classification scheme for vocations and major fields. *Journal of Counseling Psychology, 13,* 278-288.

Holland, J. L. (1997). *Making vocational choices* (3rd ed.). Odessa, FL: Psychological Assessment Resources.

Hotchkiss, L., & Borow, H. (1996). Sociological perspective on work and career development. In D. Brown, L. Brooks, & Associates (Eds.), *Career choice and development* (3rd ed., pp. 281-334). San Francisco: Jossey-Bass.

Ivey, A. E. (1987). The multicultural practice of therapy: Ethics, empathy, and dialectics. *Journal of Social and Clinical Psychology, 5,* 195-204.

Ivey, A. E. (1995). Psychotherapy as liberation. In J. G. Ponterotto, J. M. Casas, L. A. Suzuki, & C. M. Alexander (Eds.), *Handbook of multicultural counseling* (pp. 53-72). Thousand Oaks, CA: Sage.

Ivey, A. E. (2000). *Developmental therapy: Theory into practice.* North Amherst, MA: Microtraining Associates.

Ivey, A. E., Ivey, M. B., & Simek-Morgan, L. (1993). *Counseling and psychotherapy: A multicultural perspective* (3rd ed.). Boston: Allyn & Bacon.

Jackson, C. C., & Neville, H. A. (1998). Influence of racial identity attitudes on African American college students' vocational identity and hope. *Journal of Vocational Behavior, 53,* 97-113.

Jackson, M. L. (1995). Multicultural counseling: Historical perspectives. In J. G. Ponterotto, J. M. Casas, L. A. Suzuki, & C. M. Alexander (Eds.), *Handbook of multicultural counseling* (pp. 3-16). Thousand Oaks, CA: Sage.

Johnson, M. J., Swartz, J. L., & Martin, W. E., Jr. (1995). Applications of psychological theories for career development with Native Americans. In F. T. L. Leong (Ed.), *Career development and vocational behavior of racial and ethnic minorities,* (pp. 103-133). Mahwah, NJ: Erlbaum.

Johnson, S. D. (1990). Toward clarifying culture, race, and ethnicity in the context of multicultural counseling. *Journal of Multicultural Counseling and Development, 18,* 41-50.

Kao, G., & Tienda, M. (1998). Educational aspirations of minority youth. *American Journal of Education, 106,* 349-384.

Kerwin, C., & Ponterotto, J. G. (1995). Biracial identity development: Theory and research. In J. G. Ponterotto, J. M. Casas, L. A. Suzuki, & C. M. Alexander (Eds.), *Handbook of multicultural counseling* (pp. 199-217). Thousand Oaks, CA: Sage.

Krumboltz, J. D. (1979). A social learning theory of career decision making. In A. M. Mitchell, G. B. Jones, & J. D. Krumboltz (Eds.), *Social learning and career decision making* (pp. 19-49). Cranston, RI: Carroll Press.

Krumboltz, J. D. (1996). A learning theory of career counseling. In M. L. Savickas & W. B. Walsh (Eds.), *Handbook of career counseling theory and practice* (pp. 55-80). Palo Alto, CA: Davies-Black.

LaFromboise, T., Coleman, H. L. K., & Gerton, J. (1993). Psychological impact of biculturalism: Evidence and theory. *Psychological Bulletin, 144,* 395-412.

Leong, F. T. L. (1991). Career development attributes and occupational values of Asian American and White American college students. *The Career Development Quarterly, 39,* 221-230.

Leong, F. T. L. (Ed.). (1995). *Career development and vocational behavior of racial and ethnic minorities.* Mahwah, NJ: Erlbaum.

Leong, F. T. L., & Gim-Chung, R. H. (1995). Career assessment and intervention with Asian Americans. In F. T. L. Leong (Ed.), *Career development and vocational behavior of racial and ethnic minorities,* (pp. 193-226). Mahwah, NJ: Erlbaum.

Leong, F. T. L., & Serafica, F. C. (1995). Career development of Asian Americans: A research area in need of a good theory. In F. T. L. Leong (Ed.), *Career development and vocational behavior of racial and ethnic minorities,* (pp. 67-102). Mahwah, NJ: Erlbaum.

Leong, F. T. L., & Chou, E. L. (1994). The role of ethnic identity and acculturation in the vocational behavior of Asian Americans: An integrative review. *Journal of Vocational Behavior, 44,* 155-172.

Leung, S. A. (1995). Career development and counseling: A multicultural perspective. In J. G. Ponterotto, J. M. Casas, L. A. Suzuki, & C. M. Alexander (Eds.), *Handbook of multicultural counseling* (pp. 549-566). Thousand Oaks, CA: Sage.

Luzzo, D. A. (1992). Ethnic group and social class differences in college students' career development. *The Career Development Quarterly, 41,* 161-173.

Luzzo, D. A. (1993). Ethnic differences in college students' perceptions of barriers to career development. *Journal of Multicultural Counseling and Development, 21,* 227-236.

Markstrom-Adams, C. (1990). Coming-of-age among contemporary American Indians as portrayed in adolescent fiction. *Adolescence, 25,* 225-237.

Martin, W. E., Jr. (1991). Career development and American Indians living on reservations: Cross-cultural factors to consider. *The Career Development Quarterly, 39,* 273-283.

Martin, W. E., Jr. (1995). Career development assessment and intervention strategies with American Indians. In F. T. L. Leong (Ed.), *Career development and vocational behavior of racial and ethnic minorities,* (pp. 227-248). Mahwah, NJ: Erlbaum.

McCollum,V. J. C. (1998). Career development issues and strategies for counseling African Americans. *Journal of Career Development, 25,* 41-52.

McWhirter, E. H., Hackett, G., & Bandalos, D. L. (1998). A causal model of the educational plans and career expectations of Mexican American high school girls. *Journal of Counseling Psychology, 45,* 166-181.

Mickelson, R. A. (1990). The attitude-achievement paradox among black adolescents. *Sociology of Education, 63,* 44-61.

Oakes, J. (1990). Opportunities, achievement, and choices: Women and minority students in science and mathematics. In C. B. Cazden (Ed.), *Review of Research in Education,* (Vol 16, pp. 153-222). Itasca, IL: F. E. Peacock Publishers.

Osipow, S. H., & Littlejohn, E. M. (1995). Toward a multicultural theory of career development: Prospects and dilemmas. In F. T. L. Leong (Ed.), *Career development and vocational behavior of racial and ethnic minorities,* (pp. 251-261). Mahwah, NJ: Erlbaum.

Parham, T. A., & Austin, N. L. (1994). Career development and African Americans: A contextual reappraisal using the Nigrescence construct. *Journal of Vocational Behavior, 44,* 139-154.

Pedhazur, E. J. (1982). *Multiple regression in behavioral research.* Fort Worth: Holt, Rinehart & Winston.

Phinney, J. S. (1989). Stages of ethnic identity development in minority group adolescents. *Journal of Early Adolescence, 9,* 34-39.

Phinney, J. S. (1990). Ethnic identity in adolescents and adults: Review of research. *Psychological Bulletin, 108,* 499-514.

Phinney, J. S. (1993). A three-stage model of ethnic identity development in adolescence. In M. Bernal & G. Knight (Eds.), *Ethnic identity: Formation and transmission among Hispanics and other minorities* (pp. 61-79). Albany, NY: State University of New York Press.

Ponterotto, J.G. (1991). The nature of prejudice revisited: Implications for counseling intervention. *Journal of Counseling and Development, 70,* 216-224.

Ponterotto, J. G., & Pedersen, P. B. (1993). *Preventing prejudice: A guide for counselors and educators.* Newbury Park, CA: Sage.

Portes, A., & Wilson, K. L. (1976). Black-White differences in educational attainment. *American Sociological Review, 41,* 414-431.

Prediger, D. J. (1999). Basic structure of work-relevant abilities. *Journal of Counseling Psychology, 46,* 173-184.

Ramirez, M., III. (1991). *Psychotherapy and counseling with minorities: A cognitive approach to individual and cultural differences.* New York: Pergamon Press.

Ramirez, M., III. (1999). *Multicultural psychotherapy: An approach to individual and cultural differences* (2nd ed.). Boston: Allyn & Bacon.

Rasinski, K. A., Ingels, S. J., Rock, D. A., Pollack, J. M., & Wu, S. (1993). *America's high school sophomores: A ten year comparison* (NCES Publication No. 93-087). Washington, DC: U.S. Government Printing Office.

Root, M. P. P. (1990). Resolving "other" status: Identity development of biracial individuals. In L. Brown, & M. P. P. Root (Eds.), *Diversity and complexity in feminist therapy*. New York: Harrington Park Press.

Root, M. P. P. (1996). *The multiracial experience*. Thousand Oaks, CA: Sage.

Ruiz, A. S. (1990). Ethnic identity: Crisis and resolution. *Journal of Multicultural Counseling and Development, 18,* 29-40.

Sewell, W. H., Haller, A. O., & Portes, A. (1969). The educational and early occupational attainment process. *American Sociological Review, 34,* 82-92.

Sewell, W. H., & Shah, V. P. (1968). Social class, parental encouragement, and educational aspirations. *American Journal of Sociology, 73,* 559-572.

Smith, T. E. (1991). Agreement of adolescent educational expectations with perceived maternal and paternal educational goals. *Youth & Society, 23,* 155-174.

Snyder, T., & Shafer, L. (1996). *Youth indicators 1996: Trends in the well-being of American youth* (NCES Publication No. 96-027). Washington, DC: U.S. Government Printing Office.

Sodowsky, G. R., Kwan, K. K., & Pannu, R. (1995). Ethnic identity of Asians in the United States. In J. G. Ponterotto, J. M. Casas, L. A. Suzuki, & C. M. Alexander (Eds.), *Handbook of multicultural counseling* (pp. 123-154). Thousand Oaks, CA: Sage.

Sue, D. W., Ivey, A. E., & Pedersen, P. B. (Eds.). (1996). *A theory of multicultural counseling and therapy*. Pacific Grove, CA: Brooks/Cole.

Sue, D. W., & Sue, D. (1999). *Counseling the culturally different: Theory and Practice* (3rd ed.). New York: Wiley.

Super, D. E. (1990). A life-span, life-space approach to career development. In D. Brown, L. Brooks, & Associates (Eds.), *Career choice and development* (pp. 197-261). San Francisco: Jossey-Bass.

Super, D. E., Savickas, M. L., & Super, C. M. (1996). The life-span, life-space approach to careers. In D. Brown, L. Brooks, & Associates (Eds.), *Career choice and development* (3rd ed., pp. 121-178). San Francisco: Jossey-Bass.

Suzuki, B. H. (1994). Higher education issues in the Asian American community. In M. .J. Justiz, R. Wilson, & L. G. Bjork (Eds.), *Minorities in higher education* (pp. 258-285). Phoenix, AZ: Oryx Press.

Thomas, C. W. (1971). *Boys no more*. Beverly Hills, CA: Glencoe Press.

Thomas, G. E. (1985). College major and career inequality: Implications for Black students. *Journal of Negro Education, 54,* 537-547.

Tinsley, H. E. A. (1994). Racial identity and vocational behavior. *Journal of Vocational Behavior, 44,* 115-117.

Trusty, J. (1996). Counseling for dropout prevention: Applications from multicultural counseling. *Journal of Multicultural Counseling and Development, 24,* 105-117.

Trusty, J. (1998). Family influences on educational expectations of late adolescents. *Journal of Educational Research 91,* 260-270.

Trusty, J. (1999). Effects of eighth-grade parental involvement on late adolescents' educational expectations. *Journal of Research and Development in Education, 32,* 224-233.

Trusty, J. (2000). High educational expectations and low achievement: Stability of educational goals across adolescence. *Journal of Educational Research, 93,* 356-365.

Trusty, J. (in press-a). African Americans' educational expectations: Longitudinal causal models for women and men. *Journal of Counseling & Development*.

Trusty, J. (in press-b). Effects of high-school course-taking and other variables on choice of science and mathematics college majors. *Journal of Counseling & Development.*

Trusty, J., & Harris, M. B. C. (1999). Lost talent: Predictors of the stability of educational expectations across adolescence. *Journal of Adolescent Research, 14,* 359-382.

Trusty, J., & Lampe, R. E. (1997). Relationship of adolescents' perceptions of parental involvement and control to adolescents' locus of control. *Journal of Counseling & Development, 75,* 375-384.

Trusty, J., & Ng, K. (2000). Longitudinal effects of achievement perceptions on choice of postsecondary major. *Journal of Vocational Behavior, 57,* 123-135.

Trusty, J., Ng, K., & Plata, M. (2000). Interaction effects of gender, SES, and race-ethnicity on post-secondary educational choices of U.S. students. *The Career Development Quarterly, 49,* 45-59.

Trusty, J., & Pirtle, T. (1998). Parents' transmission of educational goals to their adolescent children. *Journal of Research and Development in Education, 32,* 53-65.

Trusty, J., Plata, M., & Salazar, C. (in press). Modeling Mexican Americans' Educational Expectations: Longitudinal effects across adolescence. *Journal of Adolescent Research.*

Trusty, J., Robinson, C., Plata, M., & Ng, K. (2000). Effects of gender, SES, and early academic performance on post-secondary educational choice. *Journal of Counseling & Development, 76,* 463-472.

U.S. Census Bureau. (2000). Educational attainment in the United States (update). U.S. Census Bureau, Educational Attainment. Retrieved July 6, 2001, from http://www.census.gov/population/www/socdemo/educ-attn.html.

Vandiver, B. J., Fhagen-Smith, K. O., Cross, W. E., Jr., & Worrell, F. C. (2001). Cross's Nigrescence model: From theory to scale to theory. *Journal of Multicultural Counseling and Development, 29,* 174-213.

Vondracek, R. W., & Fouad, N. A. (1994). Developmental contextualism: An integrative framework for theory and practice. In M. L. Savickas, & R. W. Lent (Eds.), *Convergence in career development theories: Implications for science and practice* (pp. 207-214). Palo Alto, CA: Consulting Psychologists Press.

Watts, T. D. (1993). Native Americans today: An outer view. *Journal of Alcohol & Drug Education, 38,*125-130.

Weinrach, S. G., & Thomas, K. R. (1998). Diversity-sensitive counseling today: A postmodern clash of values. *Journal of Counseling & Development, 76,* 115-122.

Wilson, P. M., & Wilson, J. R. (1992). Environmental influences on adolescent educational aspirations. *Youth & Society, 24,* 52-70.

Wong, M. G. (1990). The education of White, Chinese, Filipino, and Japanese students: A look at High School and Beyond. *Sociological Perspectives, 33,* 355-374.

Ying, Y., & Lee, P. A. (1999). The development of ethnic identity in Asian American Adolescents: Status and outcome. *American Journal of Orthopsychiatry, 69,* 194-208.

CHAPTER 12
Providing Career Counseling Services to Gay and Lesbian Clients

Mark Pope
University of Missouri-St. Louis
Bob Barret
University of North Carolina-Charlotte

At first glance, providing career counseling to gay and lesbian clients may appear to be largely the same as helping non-gay clients identify and pursue their career goals. In the past several years the emergence of an identifiable gay and lesbian community in most medium to large size metropolitan areas in the U.S. has dispelled the long-held negative stereotype of gay men as effeminate and lesbians as overly masculine (Barret & Logan, 2001). In other than large cities such as New York, San Francisco, and Boston, gay men and lesbians generally kept their sexual orientation a closely guarded secret on the job. Many of them fabricated social lives that included dates with persons of the opposite sex and rarely would share their vacation photographs with their co-workers. If there were a social event with co-workers, many would bring opposite sex "dates" that had been secured to help "cover" their secret. Some even chose careers on the basis of its "safety" in the event they did decide to come out. For example, it was not unusual to hear young gay men or lesbians speak of avoiding careers that involved working with children or commenting on "conservative" corporations that would not deal with their sexual orientation easily. Others carefully guarded their sexual orientation for fear that the promotions would be denied them if they were more out. Fortunately today, for many lesbian and gay clients, much of this is changing, as it is not unusual to hear casual conversations about the social and relationship aspects of gay and lesbian co-workers in the workplace. That too, however, would suggest that the special career needs of gay men and lesbians are rapidly changing.

In spite of this increased visibility and acceptance, gay men and lesbians continue to experience difficulty in the workplace. The failure to pass laws such as the Employment Non-discrimination Act by the U.S. Congress attests to the lack of acceptance of the needs of gay men and lesbians in the workplace. On the other side many national corporations are including sexual orientation in their non-discrimination personnel policies and many are providing domestic partner benefits. It would appear that gay and lesbian professionals have entered a new rather

Correspondence regarding this article should be addressed to Mark Pope, Ed.D., Associate Professor, Division of Counseling & Family Therapy, College of Education, University of Missouri - St. Louis, 8001 Natural Bridge Road, St. Louis, Missouri 63121-4499, USA, pope@umsl.edu.

contradictory era where their sexual orientation may or may not be an issue in the workplace (Diamant, 1993; Lee & Brown, 1993; Schneider, 1987). It just depends.

Unfortunately, discrimination continues to exist. Nationally there are only 90 state and local governments that provide domestic partner benefits to their gay and lesbian employees. In spite of the fact that professional athletes like Martina Navratilova and Greg Louganis have come out, most other gay and lesbian sports figures, like most stage and screen actors, keep their sexual orientation a closely guarded secret. Going to work for a religious organization or even some government agencies would pose risks for gay and lesbian clients. Given the negative notion of the so-called gay and lesbian "lifestyle" promoted by more conservative political and religious organizations, being "out" in that workplace would result in significant stress. Dual career gay and lesbian couples face particular challenges when one partner is offered a promotion that demands a move to another city. Formerly married gay men and lesbians who have children may also experience difficulty when faced with a job choice that involves moving. And the kinds of tension that results when one partner is more out than the other can quickly make the workplace more complicated (Croteau & Thiel, 1993; Milburn, 1993; Pope, 1996). For example, when Jim is invited to the company party and his "partner," Dave, is also explicitly invited. Jim who is really "out" wants to bring his partner, Dave, who is very closeted, to show how proud he is of Dave, to acknowledge that they are a couple, to acknowledge that they should not be treated any differently than the male/female couples, to acknowledge that the company has made strides in using nondiscriminatory language, but all Dave can think about is someone seeing him at Jim's office who knows Dave from his work where he is not out. This is a common dilemma.

Less than ten years ago there was little research addressing career counseling with lesbian and gay clients (Chojnacki & Gelberg, 1994; Croteau & Thiel, 1993; Etringer, Hillerbrand, & Hetherington, 1990; Lonborg & Phillips, 1996; Pope 1995a). This lack of professional information paralleled the general lack of published research about all sexual minorities (Bowman, 1993; Phillips, Strohner, Berthaume, & O'Leary, 1983; Pope, 1995c). As attention to the unique needs of gay and lesbian persons has expanded, a similar trend can be identified within the career development field. The movement towards change began when Pope (1995a, b) organized a unique event in the history of career counseling. A panel of career development researchers who would review the extant knowledge on lesbian and gay career counseling was selected to present their findings at the 1994 annual conference of the National Career Development Association meeting in Albuquerque, New Mexico (Chung, 1995; Fassinger, 1995; Pope, 1995a, b; Prince, 1995). The findings of that panel were later published as a special section of The *Career Development Quarterly* (Pope, 1995b).

Pope (1995b) discussed the extant literature on providing career counseling interventions with gay and lesbian clients. Prince (1995) discussed the developmental issues associated with gay men, especially identity and career development. Fassinger (1995) looked at lesbian identity development issues as it has been described in the career development literature. Chung (1995) reported on the literature available on the career decision making of lesbians and gay men. In each of these four presentations, the panel members reviewed what had already been done in their area and made concrete recommendations for what research remained to be done. These four presentations laid the groundwork for future researchers and established that there were the beginnings of a coherent group of literature in lesbian and gay career development.

That historic panel presentation led to a boom in research on this important topic. For example, Croteau and Bieschke (1996) developed a special issue of the *Journal of Vocational Behavior* that followed the Pope panel and quoted extensively from those findings. The American Counseling Association published a "how-to" book on career counseling with gay and lesbian clients (Gelberg & Chojnacki, 1996). A second panel which included Mark Pope, Michael Mobley, Hillary Williams Ford, Sue Morrow, and Brian Campbell was selected for presentation at NCDA's 1995 San Francisco conference (Ford, 1996; Mobley & Slaney, 1996; Morrow, Gore, & Campbell, 1996). This second panel reported on research in progress as a result of the first panel's presentations. Chernin, Holden, and Chandler (1997) authored the lead article in a special section on assessment with lesbians and gays in the Association for Assessment in Counseling's journal, *Measurement and Evaluation in Counseling and Development*. A gay male case study was included as part of a multicultural presentation at the American Counseling Association's annual convention on applying Donald Super's Career Development and Counseling model (C-DAC) (Hartung, Vandiver, Leong, Pope, Niles, & Farrow, 1998). In Ron Sanlo's book (1998) on working with lesbian and gay college students, two chapters were included to address the career development issues of gay, lesbian, bisexual, and transgender students (Taylor, Borland, & Vaughters, 1998; Worthington, McCrary, & Howard, 1998). Luzzo (2000) included a chapter on providing career counseling to gay and lesbian college students in his book on career counseling for college students published by the American Psychological Association. Dissertations were beginning to address this topic (Adams, 1997; Button, 1996; Ford, 1996; Ormerod, 1996; Shallenberger, 1998; Terndrup, 1998; Thiel, 1995). These publications and conference proceedings provide evidence that the topic of gay and lesbian career development had now become part of the mainstream in career counseling. For the career counselor or vocational psychologist who is seeking practical advise on how to provide such career counseling services, there is now a large and growing body of literature to plumb for knowledge of how to intervene appropriately in the lives of our lesbian and gay clients.

This chapter details the current collected knowledge that is available regarding the provision of career services to gay and lesbian clients. This chapter is divided into four parts: counselor preparation for working with gay and lesbian clients, individual counseling interventions useful for counseling with gay and lesbian clients, workplace programs useful to address the special issues which this group presents, and appropriate advocacy or social action interventions.

Counselor Self-Preparation

The first step for counselors who want to work with gay and lesbian clients is to take a personal inventory of the ways often subtle or unconscious biases may influence the counseling process (Bieschke & Matthews, 1996; Buhrke & Douce, 1991; Gelberg & Chojnacki, 1995; Prince, 1997a). Previous research studies have documented the mental health profession's poor treatment of all sexual minorities (Barret & Logan, 2001). Bias towards this oppressed minority will impact interventions which the individual career counselor chooses to use (Belz, 1993;

Brown, 1975; Chung & Harmon, 1994; Hetherington, Hillerbrand, & Etringer, 1989; Hetherington & Orzek, 1989; Morgan & Brown, 1991; Pope, 1992). For example, Pope (1992) used the example of how heterosexually-oriented counselors may have the idea that if they can help a young man become more masculine in his behaviors, he can change his sexual orientation and will not have to deal with all of the problems that being gay brings for him. They are just trying to help in their own heavy-handed, heterosexist way, but they are letting their own prejudices get in the way of making decisions about what is best for their young client.

Living in communities that routinely discriminate against gay men and lesbians it is virtually impossible to avoid internalizing negative stereotypes or attitudes. Misinformation or misunderstanding will quickly be evident to sexual minority clients and may cause them to seek help elsewhere or not to get help at all.

Counselors must be familiar with gay and lesbian culture so they are credible and congruent in their attitudes (Pope, 1992). Attending a workshop, reading the literature, and participating in lesbian/gay culture are effective ways to acquire knowledge about gay men and lesbians. Former clients and friends who are gay or lesbian will be an invaluable source of information. In particular, career counselors who work with gays and lesbians must understand the process of developing a gay/lesbian cultural identity (Cass, 1979; Driscoll, Kelley, & Fassinger, 1996; Dunkle, 1996; Fassinger, 1991; Fassinger, 1996; Pope, 1996).

Morgan and Brown (1991) reanalyzed data from two previously gathered, large lesbian samples and concluded that the lesbian career development process seemed both similar to and different from previously published minority group models of career development. These authors identified the process of identity development as critical in the lives of lesbian women. Because age cannot be a predictor of gay identity development, career counselors need to be aware of their clients' stage of gay/lesbian identity development to provide effective career counseling. Counselors who cannot be gay/lesbian affirmative in their attitudes are ethically required to refer the client to a career counselor who has experience with sexual minorities (Pope, 1995a).

Interventions

CLIENT-FOCUSED INTERVENTIONS

From the earliest (Brown, 1975) to the most recent articles in this domain (Pope, Prince, & Mitchell, 2000), the issue of "coming out" has been central for gays and lesbians who are seeking career counseling. Even if unstated, it is important for the counselor to recommend this topic for discussion as part of the career counseling process.

Issues to address in this discussion include "how to" (Croteau & Hedstrom, 1993; Pope & Schecter, 1992) and the "why's" associated with deciding to come out (Brown, 1975; Hetherington et al., 1989; Pope, 1995b). Counselor can help their clients consider the advantages and disadvantages of "coming out" in the workplace (Belz, 1993; Brown, 1975; Croteau & Hedstrom, 1993; Elliott, 1993; Hetherington et al.; Morgan & Brown, 1991; Pope, 1992; Pope, Rodriguez, & Chang, 1992; Pope & Schecter, 1992; Savin-Williams, 1993). Counselors can provide clients with opportunities for behavioral rehearsals directed toward developing and training strategies for informing others.

Further, it is important for counselors to recognize that there are two different types of "coming out" (Pope, 1995a). On the one hand, "coming out" has been discussed as a developmental task for gay and lesbian individuals to successfully complete. This "coming out" involves a self-acceptance of the individual's own sexual orientation and might be better termed "coming out to self." On the other hand, "coming out" has also been discussed as disclosing to others. Such disclosure might be accomplished by verbal or written, private or public statements to other individuals. By this action, individuals inform other persons of their sexual orientation. This might be better termed "coming out to others". For many, the final step in this process is coming out in the workplace.

Pope (1995a) and Gonsiorek (1993) identified some inherent problems in delayed mastery of the developmental task of accepting one's sexual orientation ("coming out to self") along with the concomitant development of appropriate dating and relationship strategies with same sex partners. This may cause a "developmental domino effect" whereby the inadequate completion of a particular task, causes the next important developmental task to be delayed, missed, or inadequately completed. These delayed or skipped developmental tasks may have long term and pervasive effects for individuals who come out in their 30s, 40s, 50s, or even later. For example, Elizabeth came out when she was 45. She had never been married to a man. She had never had sex with another human being. On her first date with a woman, she was unsure of who paid for what and who was supposed to lead when they danced as well as utterly petrified when her female date walked her to the door of her apartment, because she did not know what to do.

Other career counseling recommendations include having the career counselor:

1. give information on how to go about "coming out" (Croteau & Hedstrom, 1993; Elliott, 1993; Pope & Schecter, 1992);

2. train clients in asking and responding to informational interview and job interview questions like "are you married?" and "how many children do you have?" (Hetherington & Orzek, 1989); and

3. offer special programming to meet the career development needs of lesbians and gays (D'Augelli, 1993; Evans & D'Augelli, 1996) including special programming on: (a) resume writing addressing issues of how far out to be on the resume, or how many times to mention the word "gay" in one page (research on gay issues, teaching gay topics) (Elliott, 1993; Hetherington et al., 1989; Pope et al., 1992), and (b) interviewing (Hetherington et al.; Pope et al., 1992).

What about the client who has not completed the coming out tasks and keeps his or her sexual orientation private? There is no guaranteed way career counselors can elicit this information. There are, however, specifics that will help create a supportive atmosphere. Having gay and lesbian books which address career development on the bookshelf, along with other professional literature, will help some clients realize that you are prepared to work with sexual minorities. (See Appendix A.) Placing gay and lesbian literature in the office waiting room will send a very overt signal that the counselor is gay-affirmative. (See Appendix B.) Popular magazines such as *Advocate* and *Genre* send obvious signals to all clients and may help non-gay clients gain more information about gay and lesbian co-workers.

Discrimination against individuals on the basis of their race, ethnic origin, gender, handicapping condition, religion, political affiliation, or sexual orientation is a fact of life in U.S. society. Career counselors who fail to recognize this and do not assist their clients in coping with this reality do a disservice to their clients. As simple as it may seem, talking openly with gay or lesbian clients about issues of employment discrimination is very important. Even if clients do not bring it up, the issues ought to be discussed so that the client is aware of the career counselor's sensitivity and knowledge in this area (Brown, 1975; Croteau & Hedstrom, 1993; Elliott, 1993; Hetherington et al., 1989; Pope, 1991; Pope et al., 1992).

Providing couples counseling with dual career couples or discordant couples (one person is "out", the other is "closeted") is an important intervention. It is important to work with both individuals in a relationship on dual career couple issues (Belz, 1993; Eldridge, 1987; Elliott, 1993; Hetherington et al., 1989; Morgan & Brown, 1991; Orzek, 1992). The issues are important ones for the male couple or female couple with no experience and only few "out" dual career couple role models. Two other special issues identified involved differences in socio-economic status between the partners and spouse relocation. Cheryl has just been offered a position as a faculty member in counseling at a major university. Her partner, Melissa, is currently a physician with her own private practice of 15 years. Melissa is willing to move with Cheryl, but will require spouse relocation counseling to assist with finding a placement. Cheryl's new department does not know that she is a lesbian.

Hetherington et al. (1989) highlighted the issues facing men in male dual-career couples — how to present the relationship, how to introduce one's partner, whether to openly acknowledge the lover relationship, and how to deal with social events. Belz (1993) discussed male dual career couple issues as well, including geographic location, lifestyle that he would want to maintain while employed, problems that his job may cause for a partner who may not want to be as open about this orientation, when to tell people at work, and how to handle situations which may arise at work for which he has to involve his partner.

For example, Roger had a wonderful job as a graphic design artist working for Disney waiting for him in Los Angeles, but Patrick was an attorney with an established practice in Columbus, Ohio. They currently live in Ohio. For Roger, this was the job of which he had dreamed all of his life, but Patrick had been the primary breadwinner during the entire 11 years of the relationship. Roger had "come out" during the interview and was ecstatic when they offered him the job because he felt that it was on his own terms and he did not have to hide his sexual orientation. Patrick was not out in his attorney's practice and had pictures of his college women friends out on his desk in his office while Roger's picture was never in the office. Now, they must decide what to do about Roger's job offer in Los Angeles. These are common issues that dual career gay males couples must face.

Another aspect of providing career counseling to gay men are the special procedures have been recommended for using psychological tests with gays and lesbians (Belz, 1993; Chung & Harmon, 1994; Pope, 1992; Pope & Jelly, 1991; Pope et al., 1992; Pope, 1993; Prince, 1997a; Prince, 1997b). Counselors need to know what special procedures are required in order to get accurate results or to make accurate interpretations. Because the use of career interest inventories, other personality tests, and card sorts are all important interventions in the arsenal of career counselors, how these items are used with lesbian women and gay men is becoming an important issue. Pope (1992) identified and analyzed the use and misuse of specific subscales on five major psychological inventories used in career counseling and personnel selection (Strong Interest Inventory, Myers-Briggs Type Indicator, Edwards Personal Preference Schedule, California Psychological Inventory, and Minnesota Multiphasic Personality Inventory). Using a case study methodology, Pope wove into the cases technical and psychometric data to illustrate how psychological tests have been misused with gay and lesbian clients. He identified the following issues: fear of identification/exposure of sexual orientation especially in the highly sensitive personnel selection area, bias and prejudice (heterosexism) of the counselor, appropriate interpretation based on identification of client response set, issues of sex-role and "sexual orientation" stereotyping (male feeling types and females thinking types), and generally the appropriate interpretation of psychological tests with a gay male or lesbian client.

Other research on the use of psychological assessment with gay men have included Pope and Jelly's (1991) discussion of the use of the Myers-Briggs Type Indicator (MBTI) with gay and lesbian clients. These authors reported preliminary data suggesting that not "coming out" for a gay man or lesbian woman may mask a true understanding of self and, therefore, be a source of distortions on self-report inventories like the MBTI. This may be lead to changes in self-report inventories after the developmental task of "coming out to self" is accomplished. Belz (1993) also identified special assessment procedures to be used with gay and lesbian clients such as making new cards in a values card sort, for example, "being out on the job."

Chung and Harmon (1994) used the Self-Directed Search (SDS; Holland, 1995) and compared gay and heterosexual men of equivalent age, socioeconomic background, ethnicity, student status, and education and reported that gay men scored higher on Artistic and Social scales of the SDS and lower on the Realistic and Investigative scales. They concluded that gay men's aspirations were less traditional for men, yet their aspirations were not lower in status than those of the heterosexual men.

Other special counseling interventions such as bibliotherapy (Belz, 1993; Brown, 1975; Croteau & Hedstrom, 1993) and cross-cultural counseling for gay men of color (Pope et al., 1992) have also been identified in the literature. These recommended special counseling interventions included bibliotherapy, in which gay/lesbian clients read biographies and autobiographies of lesbians or gays who did not conceal their sexual orientation from others and society (Belz, 1993; Croteau & Hedstrom, 1993), and distribution of a bibliography containing factual references on gay/lesbian issues such as the references on the etiology of sexual orientation (Brown, 1975). Belz (1993) and Croteau and Hedstrom (1993) suggested that role models of an integrated and open sexual orientation for gays and lesbians were useful to clients in enhancing their options and educating them about living a positive, mentally healthy, and well integrated life. Other counseling interventions included recommendations that gay men of color have special issues such as multiple identities and special oppression (Pope et al., 1992).

Helping clients overcome internalized negative stereotypes is another task of the career counselor (Chung & Harmon, 1994; Hetherington & Orzek, 1989; Morgan & Brown, 1991; Pope et al., 1992). Pope (1995a) reported that it is important for the career counselor to understand the concept of internalized homophobia for gay and lesbian clients as this may affect the client's life and occupational choices.

Oppression oppresses even the mentally healthy and well-adjusted people in cultural minorities. Societal messages repeated over and over again about "evil, sick, and sinful" people may be believed and accepted at some conscious or unconscious level and these messages permeate the U.S. dominant culture. Internalized homophobia, when it occurs, cannot be overcome easily. It is important that career counselors understand and appreciate the effect that these messages can and do have on their gay and lesbian clients as well as all cultural minorities in the U.S. (Pope, 1995a). Any type of self-esteem intervention (e.g. positive self-talk; reframing; forgivenesses) can be used here to overcome these internalized negative stereotypes.

PROGRAM-FOCUSED INTERVENTIONS

Program-focused interventions include interventions that are programmatic in scope and can be implemented in an agency or institution. All of the recommended interventions in this area have one commonality: each tries to create more options for the gay man or lesbian woman making a career decision. Even with gay male clients who need more focus in their decision making, the procedures identified here are important ones to precede the decision making stage of career counseling as they may suggest options which the client may not have explored. The interventions recommended here for the career counseling include: support and encourage gay/lesbian professionals as role models for students (Chung & Harmon, 1994; Elliott, 1993; Hetherington et al., 1989; Morgan & Brown, 1991); provide information on national lesbian/gay networks of professionals and community people such as the Association for Gay, Lesbian, Bisexual Issues in Counseling (gay/lesbian/bisexual counselors in the American Counseling Association) and the Golden Gate Business Association (gay/lesbian Chamber of Commerce in San Francisco) (Belz, 1993; Elliott, 1993; Hetherington & Orzek, 1989); share information on existing local gay/lesbian community resources (Elliott, 1993; Hetherington et al.; Morgan & Brown, 1991); offer special programming such as talks by lesbian/gay professionals (Hetherington et al.); arrange career shadowing opportunities with other gay/lesbian professionals (Belz, 1993); facilitate externships or cooperative education placements in gay/lesbian owned or operated businesses (Hetherington et al.); and establish mentoring programs (Elliott, 1993).

Other recommendations include having the career counselor: publish a list of "out" gay/lesbian individuals who would be available for informational interviews with clients (Belz, 1993; Croteau & Hedstrom, 1993; Hetherington et al., 1989) and offer special programming to meet the career development needs of lesbians and gays including special programming on: (a) job fairs (Elliott, 1993; Hetherington et al.), and (b) support groups (Croteau & Hedstrom, 1993; Hetherington et al.).

Occupational role model and networking interventions are very important for special populations that have historically been limited in their occupational choices by some type of societal stereotyping (Brown, 1975; Hetherington & Orzek, 1989). Gay men have been stereotyped as hairdressers, florists, dancers, actors, secretaries, nurses, and other occupations traditionally held by females. Lesbian women have been stereotyped as truck drivers, athletes, mechanics, and other occupations traditionally held by males. These very narrow stereotypes serve as "safe" occupations, in which lesbian/gay people may feel more accepted, more able to truly be themselves; however, these occupations can also limit the occupational choices of gay/lesbian individuals who are "coming out to self" and beginning to make choices based on a changing identity. For some individuals, however, they are seen as the only possible choices.

ADVOCACY OR SOCIAL ACTION INTERVENTIONS

Advocacy or social action interventions include interventions which are focused on the external, social environment of the client (Herr & Niles, 1998; Pope, 1995a). Positive social advocacy for our gay and lesbian clients could include lobbying for the inclusion of sexual orientation in the nondiscrimination policies of local employers or picketing a speech made by an ex-gay who claims to have become a happy, fully-functioning heterosexual. Some gay male clients will need basic information on the gay and lesbian community as well as the facts on sexual orientation discrimination.

Such interventions could include counselors knowing and providing client information on the geographic location and the size of the gay and lesbian communities in their area (Belz, 1993; Elliott, 1993; Hetherington et al., 1989), information on the employment policies and EEO statements of local businesses (Elliott, 1993), information on local and federal anti-discrimination laws (Morgan & Brown, 1991), assistance on clients' avoiding arrest (Brown, 1975), and assistance to clients about constructing affirming work environments (Croteau & Hedstrom, 1993).

Career counselors working with this special population must be gay/lesbian affirmative going beyond the "do no harm" admonition to encompass a positive advocacy for gay and lesbian clients and their rights (Belz, 1993; Brown, 1975; Croteau & Hedstrom, 1993; Hetherington et al., 1989, Hetherington & Orzek, 1989). Examples of such a positive advocacy include working toward changing the laws which criminalize certain sexual acts between two consenting adults as well as working to stop police entrapment (Brown, 1975; Pope & Schecter, 1992). These laws are often used to deny gay men and lesbian women employment as teachers, counselors, police officers, and other professionals. Even if these laws are rescinded, gay men and lesbian women who have had these laws used against them are subject to continued problems because violations may remain on computerized police records for years. A gay or lesbian professional who faces a background investigation as a routine part of employment may freeze due to fear that previous entrapment will lead to renewed public humiliation.

For example, a gay male client who worked in the finance industry had been arrested 15 years before when he was kissing his boyfriend goodnight after a date. Charged with public indecency this client felt trapped in his current position and accepting a job from a bank in another community seemed impossible. This client was referred to a gay-affirming attorney who ultimately had the client's record expunged. Other clients may decide to take the risk that previous histories may not be discovered. Whatever the course of action selected, the career counselor can expect to experience significant anxiety and anger that this injustice may continue to limit the client. While not routine, situations like this may lead some clients to choose to remain in unsatisfying or limited careers. Counselors have an opportunity to lobby law enforcement officials to stop entrapments and the unequal enforcement of laws.

Summary

In this chapter we have recommended specific interventions directed at counselors themselves, at individual counseling activities, at career counseling programs within institutions, and at advocacy or social/community action. Those interventions aimed at counselors themselves or the type of activities employed with gay and lesbian career counseling clients must either be learned during graduate school education or through continuing professional development at conferences or workshops. Interventions directed at institutions or programs and at social/community action have implications for school-based career education programs, career planning texts used in colleges and universities, and for occupational information.

Providing effective career counseling services for our lesbian and gay clients is not an easy task. It is fraught with personal and social issues including internalized homophobia and employment discrimination and much more. The career counselor who directly addresses these issues will find the path smoother and rewards greater for their clients who are seeking help with their career decisions.

References

Adams, K. V. (1997). The impact of work on gay male identity among male flight attendants (Doctoral dissertation, Loyola University of Chicago, 1997). *Dissertation Abstracts International, 57-12,* 7754.

Barret, B., & Logan, C. (2001). *Counseling gay men and lesbians: A practice primer.* Belmont CA: Brooks/Cole.

Belz, J. R. (1993). Sexual orientation as a factor in career development. *The Career Development Quarterly, 41,* 197-200.

Bieschke, K. J., & Matthews, C. (1996). Career counselor attitudes and behaviors toward gay, lesbian, and bisexual clients. *Journal of Vocational Behavior, 48,* 243-255.

Boatwright, K. J., Gilbert, M. S., Forrest, L., & Ketzenberger, K. (1996). Impact of identity development upon career trajectory: Listening to the voices of lesbian women. *Journal of Vocational Behavior, 48,* 210-228.

Bowman, S. L. (1993). Career intervention strategies for ethnic minorities. *The Career Development Quarterly, 42,* 14-25.

Brown, D. A. (1975). Career counseling for the homosexual. In R. D. Burack & R. C. Reardon (Eds.), *Facilitating career development,* (pp. 234-247). Springfield, IL: Charles C. Thomas.

Buhrke, R. A., & Douce, L. A. (1991). Training issues for counseling psychologists in working with lesbians and gay men. *The Counseling Psychologist, 19,* 216-234.

Button, S. B. (1996). Organizational efforts to affirm sexual diversity: A multi-level examination (Doctoral dissertation, The Pennsylvania State University, 1996). *Dissertation Abstracts International, 57-08,* 5373.

Cass, V. (1979). Homosexual identity formation: A theoretical model. *Journal of Homosexuality, 4,* 219-235.

Chernin, J., Holden, J. M., & Chandler, C. (1997). Bias in psychological assessment: Heterosexism. *Measurement and Evaluation in Counseling and Development, 30,* 68-76.

Chojnacki, J. T., & Gelberg, S. (1994). Toward a conceptualization of career counseling with gay/lesbian/bisexual persons. *Journal of Career Development, 21,* 3-10.

Croteau, J. M. (1996). Research on the work experiences of lesbian, gay, and bisexual people: An integrative review of methodology and findings. *Journal of Vocational Behavior, 48,* 195-209.

Croteau, J. M., & Thiel, M. J. (1993). Integrating sexual orientation in career counseling: Acting to end a form of the personal-career dichotomy. *Career Development Quarterly, 42,* 174-179.

Chung, Y. B. (1995). Career decision making of lesbian, gay, and bisexual individuals. *The Career Development Quarterly, 44,* 178-190.

Chung, Y. B., & Harmon, L. W. (1994). The career interests and aspirations of gay men: How sex-role orientation is related. *Journal of Vocational Behavior, 45,* 223-239.

Croteau, J. M., & Bieschke, K. J. (Eds.). (1996). Beyond pioneering: An introduction to the special issue on the vocational issues of lesbian women and gay men. *Journal of Vocational Behavior, 48,* 119-124.

Croteau, J. M., & Hedstrom, S. M. (1993). Integrating commonality and difference: The key to career counseling with lesbian women and gay men. *The Career Development Quarterly, 41,* 201-209.

D'Augelli, A. R. (1993). Preventing mental health problems among lesbian and gay college students. *Journal of Primary Prevention, 13,* 245-261.

Diamant, L. (Ed.). (1993). *Homosexual issues in the workplace.* Washington, DC: Taylor & Francis.

Driscoll, J. M., Kelley, F. A., & Fassinger, R. E. (1996). Lesbian identity and disclosure in the workplace: Relation to occupational stress and satisfaction. *Journal of Vocational Behavior, 48,* 229-242.

Dunkle, J. H. (1996). Toward an integration of gay and lesbian identity development and Super's life-span approach. *Journal of Vocational Behavior, 48,* 1149-159.

Eldridge, N. S. (1987). *Correlates of relation satisfaction and role conflict in dual-career lesbian couples.* Unpublished doctoral dissertation, University of Texas, Austin.

Elliott, J. E. (1993). Career development with lesbian and gay clients. *The Career Development Quarterly, 41,* 210-226.

Etringer, B. D., Hillerbrand, E., & Hetherington, C. (1990). The influence of sexual orientation on career decision-making: A research note. *Journal of Homosexuality, 19,* 103-111.

Evans, N. J., & D'Augelli, A. R. (1996). Lesbians, gay men, and bisexual people in college. In R. C. Savin-Williams & K. M. Cohen (Eds.), *The lives of lesbians, gays, and bisexuals: Children to adults* (pp. 201-226). Fort Worth, TX: Harcourt Brace College Publishers.

Fassinger, R. E. (1991). The hidden minority: Issues and challenges in working with lesbian women and gay men. *The Counseling Psychologist, 19,* 157-176.

Fassinger, R. E. (1995). From invisibility to integration: Lesbian identity in the workplace. *The Career Development Quarterly, 44,* 148-167.

Fassinger, R. E. (1996). Notes from the margins: Integrating lesbian experience into the vocational psychology of women. *Journal of Vocational Behavior, 48,* 160-175.

Ford, H. W. (1996). The influence of sexual orientation on the early occupational choices of young lesbians using Astin's model of career choice and work behavior

(Doctoral dissertation, University of San Francisco, 1996). *Dissertation Abstracts International, 57-12,* 5061.

Gelberg, S., & Chojnacki, J. T. (1995). Developmental transitions of gay/ lesbian/bisexual-affirmative, heterosexual career counselors. *Career Development Quarterly, 43,* 267-273.

Gelberg, S., & Chojnacki, J. T. (1996). *Career and life planning with gay, lesbian, and bisexual persons.* Alexandria, VA: American Counseling Association.

Gonsiorek, J. C. (1993). Threat, stress, and adjustment: Mental health and the workplace for gay and lesbian individuals. In L. Diamant (Ed.), *Homosexual issues in the workplace,* (pp. 243-264). Washington, DC: Taylor & Francis.

Hartung, P. J., Vandiver, B. J., Leong, F. T. L., Pope, M., Niles, S. G., & Farrow, B. (1998). Appraising cultural identity in Career-Development Assessment and Counseling. *The Career Development Quarterly, 46,* 276-293.

Herr, E., & Niles, S. (1998). Career: A source of hope and empowerment in a time of despair. In C. Lee & G. Walz (Eds.), *Social action: A mandate for counselors* (pp. 117-136). Greensboro, NC: ERIC/CASS.

Hunt, M. (1987). *Gay: What teenagers should know about homosexuality and AIDS.* (2nd ed.). New York: Farrar, Straus, & Giroux.

Hetherington, C., Hillerbrand, E., & Etringer, B. (1989). Career counseling with gay men: Issues and recommendations for research. *Journal of Counseling & Development, 67,* 452-454.

Hetherington, D., & Orzek, A. M. (1989). Career counseling and life planning with lesbian women. *Journal of Counseling & Development, 68,* 52-57.

Holland, J. L. (1995). *Self-directed search.* Lutz, FL: Psychological Assessment Resources.

Lee, J. A., & Brown, R. G. (1993). Hiring, firing, and promoting. In L. Diamant (Ed.), *Homosexual issues in the workplace,* (pp. 45-64). Washington, DC: Taylor & Francis.

Lonborg, S. D., & Phillips, J. M. (1996). Investigating the career development of gay, lesbian, and bisexual people: Methodological considerations and recommendations. *Journal of Vocational Behavior, 48,* 176-194.

Luzzo, D. A. (Ed.). (2000). *Career counseling of college students: An empirical guide to strategies that work.* Washington, DC: American Psychological Association.

Milburn, L. (1993). Career issues of a gay man: Case of Allan. *Career Development Quarterly, 41,* 195-196.

Mobley, M., & Slaney, R. B. (1996). Holland's theory: Its relevance for lesbian women and gay men. *Journal of Vocational Behavior, 48,* 125-135.

Morgan, K. S., & Brown, L. S. (1991). Lesbian career development, work behavior, and vocational counseling. *The Counseling Psychologist, 19,* 273-291.

Morrow, S. L., Gore, P. A., & Campbell, B. W. (1996). The application of a sociocognitive framework to the career development of lesbian women and gay men. *Journal of Vocational Behavior, 48,* 136-148.

Ormerod, A. J. (1996). The role of sexual orientation in women's career choice: A covariance structure analysis (Doctoral dissertation, University of Illinois at Urbana-Champaign). *Dissertation Abstracts International, 57-08,* 3405.

Orzek, A. M. (1992). Career counseling for the gay and lesbian community. In S. Dworkin & F. Gutierrez (Eds.), *Counseling gay men & lesbians: Journey to the end of the rainbow,* (pp. 23-34). Alexandria, VA: American Counseling Association.

Phillips, S. D., Strohner, D. C., Berthaume, B. L. J., & O'Leary, J. (1983). Career development of special populations: A framework for research. *Journal of Vocational Behavior, 22,* 12-27.

Pope, M. (1991, December). *Issues in career development for gay males and lesbians.* Paper presented at the Multicultural Counseling Conference, San Jose State University, Gilroy, CA.

Pope, M. (1992). Bias in the interpretation of psychological tests. In S. Dworkin & F. Gutierrez (Eds.), *Counseling gay men & lesbians: Journey to the end of the rainbow,* (pp. 277-292). Alexandria, VA: American Counseling Association.

Pope, M. (1993, June). *Testing and assessment issues of gays and lesbians.* Paper presented at the CSUN Career Conference '93, California State University, Northridge, CA.

Pope, M. (1995a). Career interventions for gay and lesbian clients: A synopsis of practice knowledge and research needs. *The Career Development Quarterly, 44,* 191-203.

Pope, M. (1995b). Gay and lesbian career development: Introduction to the special section. *The Career Development Quarterly, 44,* 146-147.

Pope, M. (1995c). The "salad bowl" is big enough for us all: An argument for the inclusion of lesbians and gays in any definition of multiculturalism. *Journal of Counseling & Development, 73,* 301-304.

Pope, M. (1996). Gay and lesbian career counseling: Special career counseling issues. *Journal of Gay and Lesbian Social Services, 4,* 91-105.

Pope, M., & Jelly, J. (1991). *MBTI, sexual orientation, and career development* [Summary]. Proceedings of the 9th International Biennial Conference of the Association for Psychological Type, 9, 231-238.

Pope, M., Prince, J. P., & Mitchell, K. (2000). *Responsible career counseling with lesbian and gay students.* In D. A. Luzzo (Ed.), Career counseling of college students: An empirical guide to strategies that work (pp. 267-284). Washington, DC: American Psychological Association.

Pope, M., Rodriguez, S., & Chang, A. P. C. (1992, September). *Special issues in career development and planning for gay men.* Presented at the meeting of International Pacific Friends Societies, International Friendship Weekend 1992, San Francisco, CA.

Pope, M., & Schecter, E. (1992, October). *Career strategies: Career suicide or career success.* Paper presented at the 2nd Annual Lesbian and Gay Workplace Issues Conference, Stanford, CA.

Prince, J. P. (1995). Influences on the career development of gay men. *The Career Development Quarterly, 44,* 168-177.

Prince, J. P. (1997a). Assessment bias affecting lesbian , gay male and bisexual individuals. *Measurement and Evaluation in Counseling and Development, 30,* 82-87.

Prince, J. P. (1997b). Career assessment with lesbian, gay and bisexual individuals. *Journal of Career Assessment, 5,* 225-238.

Savin-Williams, R. C. (1993). Personal reflections on coming out, prejudice, and homophobia in the academic workplace. In L. Diamant (Ed.), *Homosexual issues in the workplace,* (pp. 225-242). Washington, DC: Taylor & Francis.

Schneider, B. E. (1987). Coming out at work: Bridging the private/public gap. *Work and Occupations, 13,* 463-487.

Shallenberger, K. L. (1998). Career development of lesbians: Is there a relationship between lesbian identity development and the career development process?

(Doctoral dissertation, State University of New York at Buffalo, 1998). *Dissertation Abstracts International, 59-05,* 1475.

Taylor, S. H., Borland, K. M., & Vaughters, S. D. (1998). Addressing the career needs of lesbian, gay, bisexual, and transgender college students. In R. Sanlo (Ed.), *Working with lesbian, gay, bisexual, and transgender college students: A handbook for faculty and administrators* (pp. 123-133). Westport, CT: Greenwood Press.

Terndrup, A. I. (1998). Factors that influence career choice and development for gay male school teachers: A qualitative investigation (Doctoral dissertation, Oregon State University, 1998). *Dissertation Abstracts International, 59-12,* 4371.

Thiel, M. J. (1995). Lesbian identity development and career experiences (Doctoral dissertation, Western Michigan University, 1995). *Dissertation Abstracts International, 56-12,* 4665.

Worthington, R. L., McCrary, S. I., & Howard, K. A. (1998). Becoming an LGBT affirmative career adviser: Guidelines for faculty, staff, and administrators. In R. Sanlo (Ed.), *Working with lesbian, gay, bisexual, and transgender college students: A handbook for faculty and administrators* (pp. 135-143). Westport, CT: Greenwood Press.

Appendix A

POPULAR CAREER BOOKS FOR GAYS AND LESBIANS

Besner, H. F., & Spungin, C. I. (1995). Gay & lesbian students: *Understanding their needs.* Washington, DC: Taylor & Francis.

Coville, B. (Ed.). (1995). *Am I blue? Coming out from the silence.* New York: Harper Collins.

DeCrescenzo, T. (Ed.) (1994). *Helping gay and lesbian youth: New policies, new programs, new practices.* New York: Harrington.

Diamant, L. (Ed.). (1993). *Homosexual issues in the workplace.* Washington, DC: Taylor & Francis.

Ellis, A. L., & Riggle, E. D. (Eds.). (1996). *Sexual identity on the job: Issues and services.* New York: Haworth.

Harbeck, K. M. (Ed.). (1992). *Coming out of the classroom closet: Gay and lesbian students, teachers and curricula.* New York: Harrington.

Harris, M. B. (Ed.). (1997). *School experiences of gay and lesbian youth: The invisible minority.* New York: Harrington.

Herdt, G., & Boxer, A. (1996). *Children of horizons: How gay and lesbian teens are leading a new way out of the closet* (2nd ed.). New York: Beacon Press.

Heron, A. (Ed.). (1983). *One teenager in 10: Testimony of gay and lesbian youth.* New York: Warner Books.

Heron, A. (Ed.). (1994). *Two teenagers in 20: Writings by gay and lesbian youth.* Boston: Alyson.

Gelberg, S., & Chojnacki, J. T. (1996). *Career and life planning with gay, lesbian, and bisexual persons.* Alexandria, VA: American Counseling Association.

Jennings, K. (1994). *Becoming visible: A reader in gay and lesbian history for high school and college students.* Boston: Alyson.

Jennings, K. (1994). *One teacher in ten.* Boston: Alyson.

Katz, J. (1976). *Gay American history.* New York: Crowell.

McNaught, B. (1993). *Gay issues in the workplace.* New York: St. Martins.

Rasi, R. A., & Rodriguez-Nogues, L. (1995). *Out in the workplace: The pleasures and perils of coming out on the job.* Los Angeles: Alyson.

Appendix B

POPULAR BOOKS AND ARTICLES FOR GAYS AND LESBIANS

Aarons, L. (1995). *Prayers for Bobby: A mother's coming to terms with the suicide of her gay son.* San Francisco: Harper.

Abelowe, H., Barale, M. A., & Halperin, D. M. (1993). *The lesbian and gay studies reader.* New York: Routledge.

Alyson, S. (Ed.). (1985). *Young, gay and proud!* Boston: Alyson.

Bailey, N. J., & Phariss, T. (1996, January). *Breaking through the wall of silence: Gay, lesbian, and bisexual Issues for middle level educators.* Middle School Journal, (pp. 38-46). Washington, DC: National Middle School Association.

Bass, E., & Kaufman, K. (1996). *Free your mind: The book for gay, lesbian, and bisexual youth — and their allies.* New York: HarperPerennial.

Bernstein, R. (1995). *Straight parents/gay children: Keeping families together.* Emeryville, CA: Thunder's Mouth Press.

Besner, H. F., & Spungin, C. I. (1995). *Gay & lesbian students: Understanding their needs.* Washington, DC: Taylor & Francis.

Coville, B. (Ed.). (1995). *Am I blue? Coming out from the silence.* New York: Harper Collins.

DeCrescenzo, T. (Ed.). (1994). *Helping gay and lesbian youth: New policies, new programs, new practices.* New York: Harrington.

Dew, R. F. (1995). *The family heart: A memoir of when our son came out.* New York: Ballantine.

Due, L. (1995). *Joining the tribe: Growing up gay & lesbian in the '90s.* New York: Anchor.

Elliott, L., & Brantley, C. (1997). *Sex on campus: The naked truth about the real sex lives of college students.* New York: Random House.

Fricke, A. (1992). *Sudden strangers: The story of a gay son and his father.* New York: St. Martin's Press.

Fricke, A. (1981). *Reflections of a rock lobster: A story about growing up gay.* Boston: Alyson.

Garber, L. (1994). *Tilting the tower: Lesbians teaching queer subjects.* New York: Routledge.

Gibson, P. (1989). Gay male and lesbian youth suicide. In M. R. Feinleib (Ed.), *Report of the Secretary's task force on youth suicide. Volume 3: Preventions and interventions in youth suicide* (pp. 110-142). (U. S. Department of Health and Human Services Pub. No. ADM 89-1623). Washington, DC: U. S. Government Printing Office.

Gray, M. L. (Ed.). (1999). *In your face: Stories from the lives of queer youth.* New York: Harrington.

Griffin, C. W., Wirth, M. J., & Wirth, A. G. (1986). *Beyond acceptance: Parents of lesbians and gays talk about their experiences.* Englewood Cliffs, NJ: Prentice-Hall.

Grima, T. (Ed.). (1994). *Not the only one: Lesbian and gay fiction for teens.* Boston: Alyson.

Harbeck, K. M. (Ed.). (1992). *Coming out of the classroom closet: Gay and lesbian students, teachers and curricula.* New York: Harrington.

Harris, M. B. (Ed.). (1997). *School experiences of gay and lesbian youth: The invisible minority.* New York: Harrington.

Herdt, G., & Boxer, A. (1996). *Children of horizons: How gay and lesbian teens are leading a new way out of the closet* (2nd ed.). New York: Beacon Press.

Heron, A. (Ed.). (1983). *One teenager in 10: Testimony of gay and lesbian youth.* New York: Warner Books.

Heron, A. (Ed.). (1994). *Two teenagers in 20: Writings by gay and lesbian youth.* Boston: Alyson.

Heron, A., & Maran, M. (1991). *How would you feel if your dad was gay?* Boston: Alyson.

Herr, E., & Niles, S. (1998). Career: A source of hope and empowerment in a time of despair. In C. Lee & G. Walz (Eds.), *Social action: A mandate for counselors* (pp. 117-136). Greensboro, NC: ERIC/CASS.

Hunt, M. (1987). *Gay: What teenagers should know about homosexuality and AIDS.* (2nd ed.). New York: Farrar, Straus, & Giroux.

Jennings, K. (1994). *Becoming visible: A reader in gay and lesbian history for high school and college students.* Boston: Alyson.

Jennings, K. (1994). *One teacher in ten.* Boston: Alyson.

Katz, J. (1976). *Gay American history.* New York: Crowell.

Lorde, A. (1984). *Sister outsider.* Freedom, CA: The Crossing Press.

Marcus, E. (1993). *Is it a choice? Answers to 300 of the most frequently asked questions about gays and lesbians.* San Francisco: Harper.

Marsiglio, W. (1993). Attitudes toward homosexual activity and gays as friends: A national survey of heterosexual 15- to 19-year-old males. *Journal of Sex Research, 30*(1), p. 12.

Martin, A. D. (1982). Learning to hide: The socialization of the gay adolescent. In S. C. Feinstein, J. G. Looney, A. Z. Schwartenberg, & A. D. Sorosky (Eds.), *Adolescent psychiatry: Development and clinical studies* (pp. 52-65). Chicago: University of Chicago Press.

Mondimore, F. M. (1996). *A natural history of homosexuality.* Baltimore: Johns Hopkins University Press.

Muller, A. (1987). *Parents matters: Parents relationships with lesbian daughters and gay sons.* Tallahassee, FL: Naiad.

Munchmore, W., & Hanson, W. (1982). *Coming out right: A handbook for the gay male.* Boston: Alyson.

Newman, B. S., & Muzzonigro, P. G. (1993). The effects of traditional family values on the coming out process of gay male adolescents. *Adolescence, 28,* 213-226.

O'Conor, A. (1994). Who gets called queer in school? Lesbian, gay and bisexual teenagers, homophobia, and high school. *The High School Journal, 77,* 7-12.

Owens, R. E. (1998). *Queer kids: The challenges and promise for lesbian, gay, and bisexual youth.* New York: Harrington.

Pollack, W. (1998). *Real boys: Rescuing our sons from the myths of boyhood.* New York: Random House.

Pope, M. (1995). The "salad bowl" is big enough for us all: An argument for the inclusion of lesbians and gays in any definition of multiculturalism. *Journal of Counseling & Development, 73*(3), 301-304.

Savin-Williams, R. C. (1990). *Gay and lesbian youth: Expressions of identity.* Washington, DC: Hemisphere.

Sherman, P., & Bernstein, S. (Eds.). (1994). *Uncommon heroes: A celebration of heroes and role models for gay and lesbian Americans.* New York: Fletcher.

Sherrill, J. (1994). *The gay, lesbian, and bisexual students' guide to colleges, universities, and graduate schools.* New York: New York University Press.

SIECUS. (1995). (Sexuality Information and Education Council of the United States.) *Facts about sexual health for America's adolescents*, p. 12. New York: SIECUS.

Silverstein, C. (1977). *A family matter: A parents guide to homosexuality.* New York: McGraw-Hill.

Slater, E. (1958). Sibs and children of homosexuals. In D. R. Smith (Ed.), *Symposium on Nuclear Sex,* pp. 79-83. New York: Interscience Publishers.

Sloan, L. M., & Gustavsson, N. S. (Eds.). (1998). *Violence and social injustice against lesbian, gay and bisexual people.* New York: Harrington.

Tsang, D. (Ed.). (1981). *The age taboo: Gay male sexuality, power and consent.* Boston: Alyson.

Unks, G. (Ed.). (1995). *The gay teen: Educational practice and theory for lesbian, gay, and bisexual adolescents.* New York: Routledge.

Walling, D. R. (Ed.). (1996). *Open lives, safe schools.* Bloomington, IN: Phi Delta Kappa Educational Foundation.

Woog, D. (1995). *School's out: The impact of gay and lesbian issues on America's schools.* Boston: Alyson.

CHAPTER 13
Career Development Interventions For Young Adults With Disabilities

Edward M. Levinson
Indiana University of Pennsylvania

Unfortunately, many young adults leave school unprepared for a career. The United States General Accounting Office (1993) reported that one third of young workers ages 16 to 24 do not have the skills they need to perform entry-level, semiskilled jobs. A series of nationwide studies commissioned by the National Career Development Association and carried out by the Gallup Organization (Brown & Minor, 1989; Hoyt & Lester, 1995) revealed that only one-third of adults are in their current jobs as a result of conscious planning. The remaining two thirds entered their jobs because of chance factors, the influence of others, or because they took the only job available. Only about half of these workers reported that they were satisfied with their jobs.

Adults with disabilities are at even greater risk for experiencing career difficulties. Though the career development of individuals with disabilities has been given "scant attention" in the literature (Patton & McMahon, 1999, p. 157), studies have consistently demonstrated that compared to their non-disabled peers, individuals with mild disabilities experience a higher rate of unemployment and underemployment, lower pay, more dissatisfaction with employment (Collet-Kingenberg, 1998; Dunn, 1996) and are viewed by their employers less positively than other workers (Minskoff, 1994). A recent survey by Louis Harris and Associates indicated that two thirds of Americans with disabilities between the ages of 16 and 64 were not working (Taylor, 1994), though 79 percent indicated that they wanted to work.

One factor that has historically contributed to the lack of career preparedness among adults with disabilities is the elevated school drop out rate that characterizes this population. Studies that have compared school drop out rates of individuals with disabilities with control group drop out rates or normative data have consistently demonstrated that those with disabilities leave school more often than individuals without disabilities (Ysseldyke, Algozzine, & Thurlow, 1992). Individuals with learning disabilities and emotional disabilities appear to be at particularly high risk for dropping out of school. Drop out rates for individuals with these disabilities have been reported to exceed 40 percent and 50 percent respectively (Gajar, Goodman, & McAfee, 1993). As Szymanski, Ryan, Merz, Trevino, and Johnson-Rodriquez (1996) clearly note, educational limitations inhibit employment options for adults with disabilities, and negatively affect their income and overall quality of life. In contrast to 37 percent of adults without disabilities, 59 percent of adults with disabilities lived in households earning less than $25,000 per year (Taylor, 1994). In contrast, only 37 percent of employed adults with disabilities lived in such households.

But why do individuals with disabilities drop out of school? One reason is that for the majority of students who do NOT plan to go on to college, schools are particularly ineffective in addressing their educational and career needs. A 1993 Gallup Poll (Hoyt & Lester, 1995) indicated that 60 percent of American adults said high schools devote enough attention to preparing students for college, but NOT enough attention to helping non-college bound students get jobs. Schools direct most of their resources toward preparing students for college. Yet only about 15 percent of incoming ninth graders go on to graduate from high school and then obtain a 4-year college degree within 6 years of their high school graduation (Morra, 1993). Hence, schools focus their curriculum more on the educational needs of the college-bound minority than on the educational needs of the work-bound majority This is particularly problematic for young adults with disabilities, the vast majority of whom do not go on to college.

Among young adults with disabilities, the need to address career and vocational skills rather than the academic skills necessary for entrance into college is essential. The 21st Annual Report to Congress on the Implementation of the IDEA (U.S. Department of Education, 1999) reported that only 24.5 percent of students with disabilities ages 17 years and older graduated from high school with a diploma (a prerequisite for college entrance). This report also indicated that individuals with disabilities were less likely to drop out of school and more likely to be competitively employed after high school if they received adequate vocational and career education in high school. The report concluded that at the systems level, major changes are needed in schools, adult service agencies and in the community if the vocational and career needs of individuals with disabilities are to be met.

As such, this chapter will take a proactive and preventative perspective rather than a reactive and remedial perspective in addressing career development interventions for adults. It will emphasize actions that can be taken with YOUNG adults with disabilities, actions that are designed to facilitate career development and reduce the risk of vocational and career problems later in life. Also, there will be no attempt to discuss interventions specific to a disability type. The number of disability types and the heterogeneous nature of each disability clearly precludes such an approach in a chapter such as this. As Conyers, Koch, and Szymanski (1998) note, people with disabilities are a heterogeneous population; therefore disability itself does not determine career development. Rather, disability should be viewed as a risk factor, which may or may not influence an individual's career development (Conyers, Koch, & Szymanski, 1998). "The heterogeneity of people with disabilities...means that there can be no simple application of any [career] theory...Theories do, however, suggest lines of inquiry for clinical practice" (Szymanski, Hershenson, Enright & Ettinger, 1996, pp.104-105).

This chapter will begin by briefly addressing issues associated with career development and interventions among adults with disabilities, and the more significant pieces of legislation designed to assist in efforts to address the career development needs of this population. This will be followed by a discussion of a transdisciplinary career planning model. This model consists of the following phases: assessment, planning, intervention, and follow-up. Each of these phases will be briefly described, and issues associated with implementation of each phase with young adults with disabilities will be discussed.

Issues Associated with Career Development and Interventions Among Young Adults with Disabilities

Comparatively little research has been conducted on the career development processes which characterize individuals with disabilities. As Szymanski, Hershenson, Enright and Ettinger (1996) explain, research on the career development of individuals with disabilities presents some unique methodological problems. As a consequence, much of the research that has been conducted has been plagued by poor research design, conceptual ambiguities, and methodological weaknesses. Many of the career development theories that guide the interventions we use with clients were meant to be applied to the general population, and as such, may have only partial application to individuals with disabilities. Over twenty-five years ago, Osipow (1976) suggested, for example, that the career development process among individuals with disabilities was less likely to be systematic, and more likely to be stressful than was the career development process of individuals without disabilities. He also suggested that the career options of individuals with disabilities were more likely to be limited than were those for individuals without disabilities, and were likely to be overly influenced by the individual's disability.

Since most career development theories are an attempt to explain factors that influence the career development of the general population, application of each of them in full to individuals with disabilities would clearly be inappropriate. The career development process among individuals with disabilities may not be nearly as orderly and as systematic as is suggested by developmental theory, for example. Many individuals with disabilities have been restricted in their career exploration and limited in terms of their range of experiences. As a consequence, these individuals may progress through the developmental stages cited by Super and others at a slowed rate, or not at all. Whereas the developmental tasks cited in each of these stages MIGHT be equally applicable to individuals with disabilities, the ages at which these developmental tasks are confronted may deviate significantly from what is true for those without disabilities.

Holland's (1985) theory, as do most trait-factor approaches, emphasizes testing, the provision of occupational information, and a process of "matching" the individual to a particular job. This perspective's emphasis on testing, and on a self-directed approach to exploration and intervention renders it inappropriate for many individuals with disabilities. The utility of a test-match-place orientation to the career assessment and intervention of individuals with severe disabilities has especially been questioned. Likewise, the self-directedness inherent in decision-making theory limits it's usefulness with many individuals with disabilities, especially those who lack the cognitive and intellectual capabilities required for independent use of occupational information.

Although inappropriate when applied in full, many of the popular career development theories offer a perspective which can be modified and adapted for use with individuals with disabilities. Age ranges aside, developmental theory would seem to suggest that increasing self and occupational awareness, facilitating occupational exploration, implementing an occupational choice, and facilitating adjustment within that occupation would be sequentially appropriate developmental tasks for all individuals regardless of disability. The ages at which these tasks may be appropriate for a given individual may deviate significantly from what is the norm, however, and may be influenced by type and severity of disability, and range of occupational and life experience. Decision-making theory may be most appropriately applied within this developmental framework at logical decision points, such as the time at which decisions need to be made about which occupational areas a particular individual should explore, which of these are realistic options, and which of these options should be pursued. Although some individuals with disabilities may not be able to independently apply such a decision making approach, those assisting young adults with disabilities can utilize decision-making theory as a guide to making such decisions, and can involve the young adult in the process to the maximum extent possible. Trait factor approaches seem to have their greatest utility within this decision-making framework, specifically in terms of identifying realistic options for individuals. Testing and other forms of assessment can be utilized to identify the specific traits possessed by the individual, and how these traits compare to the traits required for successful adjustment to various occupations and jobs. From such an assessment, realistic options can be identified. The social learning/learning theory perspective would seem to have its greatest utility in training young adults with disabilities to function within a previously identified and appropriate occupational training program or job and to assist them in making a successful transition to life in the community. The behavioral and learning principles, which form the foundation of social learning/learning theory, can be utilized to facilitate acquisition of the skills necessary to complete the vocationally appropriate developmental tasks specified in developmental theory.

Legislation Pertinent to Career Development and Interventions With Young Adults With Disabilities

Considerable legislation has been passed in the last ten to fifteen years designed to improve the vocational and career assistance provided to individuals with disabilities. The Vocational Rehabilitation Act, the Education of the Handicapped Act, the Vocational Education Amendments Act, and the Career Education Incentive Act have combined to provide federal funding assistance to assist individuals with disabilities to prepare for work.

More recently, the Carl D. Perkins Vocational Education Act, and the Individuals with Disabilities Education Act have contributed to the development of school-based career services. The Perkins Act requires that information about vocational and career education opportunities be provided to parents and students no later than the beginning of the ninth grade or at least one year before the student enters the grade in which vocational education is offered. The Act also requires that information about eligibility requirements for enrolling in vocational education programs be provided to parents and students, and that once enrolled in vocational education, students receive an assessment of interests, abilities, and special needs and other special services designed to facilitate transition from school to post-school employment or training.

The Individuals with Disabilities Education Act (IDEA) was originally passed in 1990, and amendments to it were passed in 1997. IDEA incorporates requirements for the establishment of services designed to assist students in making a successful transition from school to work and community living. Under this law, plans for a student's transition from school to work and community living must be initiated by age 14. Under this law, young adults with disabilities are eligible for services through age 21.

Career Interventions for Adults with Disabilities: A Transdisciplinary Career Planning Model

Given the complexity, diversity, and heterogeneous nature of disabilities in general, a career development professional cannot hope to be familiar with all of the career-related issues that any one disability type is likely to present. Hence, when working with adults with disabilities, it is important that the career development professional be familiar with other professionals with whom they can consult and actively involve them when planning and implementing career interventions with this population.

As such, I advocate a Transdisciplinary Career Planning Model (TCPM) when working with young adults with disabilities. This model allows the career development professional to work as part of a team of professionals, and to draw upon the expertise of other team members who may be more familiar with some of the issues which may impact the career development of an individual with a specific type of disability. The term "transdisciplinary" is used instead of "multidisciplinary" in order depict the need to involve professionals "across disciplines" in the career planning and intervention process. Traditionally, the term "multidisciplinary" has been used in education to depict the need to involve educators from different fields *within* education in a particular process. For example, "multidisciplinary teams" responsible for identifying individuals with disabilities are often comprised of school psychologists, teachers, counselors, nurses, and administrators, all of whom are educational personnel based in schools. These multidisciplinary teams do not typically include professionals from outside of the schools. Instead, the TCPM model encompasses services from a variety of community agencies in addition to the schools, and consists of the following phases: Assessment, Planning, Intervention, and Follow-up. The reader should note that these phases are not conceptualized as separate processes that occur at only one distinct point in time. Rather they are considered to be ongoing interacting processes that effect each other and may occur repeatedly over the course of an individual's career. As such, the model is consistent with the life to death perspective inherent in most theories of career development. This entire process (assessment, planning, intervention, and follow-up) may be repeated at different points during one's life and for different aspects of career development. For example, it may occur when a young adult with disabilities is considering entry into college, an initial job placement, a job change, relocation, or retirement.

The remainder of this chapter will be organized around each of the TCPM phases. Each phase will be discussed, and issues associated with implementing each phase with young adults with disabilities will be highlighted.

ASSESSMENT

Given the heterogeneous nature of disabilities, a necessary first step in identifying the career interventions necessary for a particular individual is assessment (Levinson, 1998). Given that all career intervention planning should be based upon some assessment, a thorough and valid assessment of needs is a necessary prerequisite and important first step in the planning of career interventions with young adults with disabilities. In that assessment data often facilitate career exploration and increase an individuals self awareness and overall level of career maturity, assessment can in and of itself be conceptualized as one type of career intervention. However, assessment is more problematic with individuals with disabilities than it is with the non-disabled population. Hence, this section will begin with an overview of some of these problems. This will be followed by a discussion of assessment practices that have been recommended in the literature for young adults with disabilities. Included in this section will be a brief discussion of the following: community-referenced (environmental) assessment, functional assessment, and multitrait, multimethod, multifactored assessment. This section will conclude with an overview of the domains and traits that may be targeted for assessment when working with young adults with disabilities.

PROBLEMS ASSOCIATED WITH THE CAREER ASSESSMENT OF INDIVIDUALS WITH DISABILITIES

Career assessment with young adults with disabilities is more difficult and problematic than it is with the non-disabled population. Many of the assessment instruments and techniques that are appropriately used with most non-disabled clients are inappropriate for use with individuals with disabilities. In particular, the use of traditional paper-pencil, norm referenced assessment procedures with many individuals with disabilities, especially those with more severe disabilities, is especially problematic (Parker, Szymanski. & Hanley-Maxwell, 1989; Power, 2000; Rogan & Hagner, 1990). Many assessment instruments and techniques have not been validated for use with this population (and hence, have unknown psychometric properties when used with disabled clients), have been standardized and normed on samples that have excluded those with disabilities (rendering the norms and scores derived from them invalid for this population), are based upon theories of career development which may or may not be applicable to individuals with disabilities, and require tasks (like reading, writing, etc.) which may exceed the individual's capabilities.

Moreover, the standardized method for administering traditional assessment instruments often penalizes clients because of their disability. Clients with physical disabilities, for example, are often penalized on timed tasks for slow responses. In such cases, test scores reflect the physical disability rather than the trait purported to be measured by the test. Hence, the score becomes an invalid measure of the trait assessed by the test.

For this reason, test administration procedures often need to be modified and adapted when certain tests are used with clients with disabilities. For example, time limits may need to be relaxed or eliminated, instructions may need to be simplified and or repeated, items may need to be read and responses recorded for clients, etc. Often, pre-trials need to be employed to "teach" the client about the nature of the task and how to respond to test items. However, use of such modifications may invalidate the norms associated with many tests because these tests were not standardized using such adapted testing procedures. Hence, the use of such norms following the implementation of such adapted testing procedures is often inappropriate.

Additionally, many career assessment instruments make assumptions about individuals taking the test that are not true for individuals with disabilities. For example, many interest inventories assume that individuals taking the test have had a certain set of life experiences that have exposed them to a range of careers. Unfortunately, many young adults with disabilities have had a restricted range of life experiences and are more limited in their knowledge of careers than are their non-disabled peers. As a consequence, one typically finds a pattern of uniformly low interest scores across interest areas when using interest inventories with many young adults with disabilities. Such a pattern of scores usually reflects a lack of knowledge and exposure to occupations rather than lack of interest in those occupations.

Because of the problems just discussed, both a functional assessment approach and a community-referenced assessment model have been advocated in lieu of a traditional career assessment model for clients with some disabilities, especially those with severe disabilities (Rudrud, Ziarnik, Bernstein, & Ferrara, 1984). As Rogan and Hagner (1990) state "the most fair, reliable, and useful way to evaluate an individual with severe disabilities is within the actual work setting using materials that are naturally present" (p. 64). Though several different terms, such as "assessment with an environmental focus" (Power, 2000), "on-site assessment" (Power, 2000), and "ecological assessment" (Parker, Szymanski, & Hanley-Maxwell, 1989; Menchetti & Uduari-Solner, 1990) have all been used to describe assessment within the natural work or community setting, the community-referenced approach will be briefly described here. This will be followed by a brief discussion of functional assessment.

COMMUNITY-REFERENCED ASSESSMENT

According to Rudrud et al (1984), a community-referenced assessment system provides a proactive alternative to traditional career assessment (which relies heavily on standardized norm-referenced procedures), and is designed to answer the following key questions:

1. What local job opportunities/residential placement options exist into which clients with severe disabilities can be successfully placed, following appropriate training?
2. Which of the available jobs/residential placement options does the client prefer?
3. Which tasks associated with both job and residential living can the client competently perform and, conversely, which of these tasks will the client need to be trained to perform?
4. How well is the client progressing toward acquiring the skills needed to competently perform all necessary tasks?

There are several steps involved in implementing a community-referenced assessment. These include:

1. surveying the community to identify local job opportunities and residential placement options;
2. screening all identified jobs/residential placement options;
3. identifying the skills needed to perform each task associated with the job or residential placement option;
4. identifying which job/residential placement option the individual prefers;
5. assessing the individual's ability to perform the job/tasks associated with living in the preferred residential placement option, and
6. training the individual to perform all necessary tasks.

FUNCTIONAL ASSESSMENT

Functional assessment may be defined as the analysis and measurement of specific behaviors that occur in real environments and are relevant to life or career goals (Halpern & Fuhrer, 1984). Put simply, functional assessment is designed to identify what individuals can and cannot do in particular situations, under certain conditions and in light of unique demands. As defined by Gaylord-Ross and Browder (1991), functional assessment has the following main characteristics:

1. It focuses on practical, independent living skills that enable the person to survive and succeed in the real world.
2. It has an ecological emphasis that looks at the individual's functioning in his or her surrounding environment.
3. It examines the process of learning.
4. It suggests intervention techniques that may be successful.
5. It specifies ongoing monitoring procedures that can evaluate treatment progress.

In particular, this form of assessment is one that focuses on skills that allow an individual to "function" successfully in a variety of settings necessary for independent, self-sufficient functioning. As such, it focuses on only the academic, social and career-related skills that are necessary for day-to-day functioning at school, at home, in the community, and on the job. Skills which have little relationship to successful functioning in these settings would not be targeted for assessment or training. Additionally, a functional approach to assessment will often assess the individual in the environment in which the individual will be required to perform the skill, and will utilize the materials the individual will use when performing the skill in the real world. For example, housekeeping skills will often be assessed and taught in the group or residential home in which an individual is likely to be placed following the completion of school, rather than in a classroom or office setting. Measurement skills will often be assessed and taught within the context of a job-training program or on the job itself, using the same equipment the individual will be required to use once placed on the job. Clearly, one drawback of such an approach is the logistics associated with arranging and implementing a functional community-based assessment. As an alternative, Wissick, Gardner, and Langone (1999) have suggested the use of video-based multimedia simulations. Such simulations can be used to augment assessment and training that might take place in community settings.

MULTITRAIT, MULTIMETHOD, MULTIFACTORED ASSESSMENT

When gathering assessment data for intervention planning, a multitrait, multimethod, multifactored (MTMM) approach to the career assessment of young adults with disabilities is advocated (Levinson 1998; 1993). Such an approach assesses a variety of traits (to be discussed next), using multiple assessment methods (observations, interviews, rating scales, etc.), and employs a team of professionals. This approach encourages overlap among the traits assessed by different professionals so that the consistency of the information across assessors and assessment techniques can be evaluated. Such an approach allows professionals to determine the extent to which assessment results may have been affected by assessor or instrumentation variables and increases the overall reliability and validity of the assessment process.

In particular, the MTMM approach can sometimes be used to overcome the problem of technically inadequate tests. For example, assume an interest inventory which possesses unknown or less than desirable psychometric properties for a client with disabilities is used in an assessment, and that the results indicate high interest in art. While it would be inadvisable to place much confidence in the interest inventory results alone, assume that the client had also indicated high interest in art in an interview with the counselor, and had been observed painting, drawing and sketching by parents. These multiple methods of assessing interests (test, interviews, and observations) all yielded similar results and suggest that the interest inventory results, in this instance, may be reliable and valid. Had there not been agreement among the results of these different assessment techniques, the validity of the assessment would be in question, and considerably less confidence could be placed in any interventions that were based on the results. Moreover, that results are consistent across assessors suggests that the results are not a function of the individual gathering the data.

AREAS/TRAITS TO BE ASSESSED

A variety of domains need to be assessed when considering what career interventions might be appropriate for a young adult with disabilities. More generally, these include the following: intellectual/cognitive, educational/academic, social/interpersonal, occupational/vocational, independent living, and physical/sensory (Levinson, 1993; 1998). Different assessment approaches and techniques can be utilized to gather information about an individual, different domains may be targeted for assessment at different points in the client's career, and the purposes of assessment may vary from one assessment to another. As an example of the domains that might be specifically targeted as part of a functional assessment for an individual with severe disabilities, the following describes the Iowa Department of Education's ten critical areas of need which should be the focus of any functional assessment designed to assist in developing interventions for this population.

DEFINITIONS

Following are the ten critical areas and their definitions.

Self Determination. Competencies needed to understand one's abilities, needs, and rights; to speak for one's self; and to act as one's own advocate. Competencies needed for problem solving and decision making.

Mobility. Academic and functional competencies to interact and travel within and outside the community.

Daily Living. Academic and functional competencies needed to live as independently as possible and desired.

Health and Physical Care. Academic and functional competencies needed to maintain the full range of physical, emotional, and mental well being of an individual, such as selecting health care professionals, determining whom to contact in the case of an emergency, obtaining assistive devices, and using personal hygiene skills.

Money Management. Academic and functional competencies such as budgeting, balancing a checkbook, and doing insurance planning.

Social Interaction. Competencies needed to participate and interact in a variety of settings in society.

Workplace Readiness. Academic and functional competencies and basic work behaviors, such as staying on task as expected, responding appropriately to instructions, and working under pressure. Knowledge of occupational alternatives and self awareness of needs, preferences, and abilities related to occupational alternatives.

Occupationally Specific Skills. Academic and functional competencies required in specific occupations or clusters of occupations.

Academic and Lifelong Learning. Academic and functional competencies needed to pursue and benefit from future educational and learning opportunities.

Leisure. Academic and functional competencies, interests, and self expression of the individual that can lead to enjoyable and constructive use of leisure time.

Planning

As stated earlier, career development professionals are unlikely to have all of the knowledge and skills necessary to adequately assist in career planning for young adults with disabilities. Hence, best practice dictates that career development professionals work as a member of a transdisciplinary career planning team when working with young adults with disabilities. Both school and community agency personnel are also likely to participate on these teams. Appropriate educational personnel include instructors, (regular, special education, and vocational education), counselors, psychologists, and administrators. Representatives from community agencies such as Mental Health/Mental Retardation, Vocational Rehabilitation, and Social Services are also likely to participate on these teams. Parents should also be active participants in planning meetings since research has indicated that family involvement is critical (Morningstar, Turnbull, & Turnbull, 1996) and parental participation increases the effectiveness of service delivery (Burkhead & Wilson, 1995; Hasazi, Gordon, & Roe, 1985; Schalock & Lilley, 1986). Lastly, the client should also be encouraged to be an active team participant.

As Levinson, Peterson, and Elston (1994) have suggested, the extent to which assessment data are successfully used to plan for a young adult's transition from school to work and community living, and for any subsequent career interventions, may depend upon the attitudes and values possessed by the professionals involved in the planning. Professionals must believe that, with proper training and support services, all individuals with disabilities can be fully employed and can be active and contributing members of the community. Professionals should be familiar with best practices in providing vocational training and support services, preferably have direct experience with individuals with disabilities who have been successfully employed, and understand the increasing range of jobs in which these individuals have been successfully placed. Professionals working with individuals with disabilities should also have a commitment to the community integration of these individuals. This includes a belief that individuals with disabilities, both mildly and severely disabled, should have opportunities for interactions with nondisabled persons in integrated settings.

Professionals should encourage individuals with disabilities to be involved in the career planning process to the maximum extent possible. This means that individuals with disabilities should be invited to all planning meetings, should be fully informed of assessment results, and should be actively involved in establishing career goals. Too often, individuals with disabilities are considered incapable of making their own career decisions. As a result, professionals and family members have assumed this decision-making role for them. Certainly, many individuals with disabilities may have difficulty processing the information needed when making decisions and may need assistance from others in simplifying and clarifying decisions and options. Two very real dangers exist in this process. On the one hand, parents and professionals sometimes encourage an individual with disabilities to accept options in which they are not interested. On the other hand, without assistance, individuals with disabilities may flounder and select options that are clearly unrealistic in light of local resources and opportunities. Professionals must walk a tightrope between these two extremes when involving individuals with disabilities in career planning.

Though young adults with disabilities are sometimes involved in career planning meetings, they are seldom active participants. Given the lack of emphasis on career development and career education in the schools, particularly for individuals with disabilities, this should not be surprising. It is unrealistic to expect individuals with disabilities, who have not been afforded career development activities, to have the knowledge and skills necessary to be active participants in the career planning process. If we want to prepare young adults with disabilities to assist in their own planning, we need to afford them experiences that will increase their level of career maturity. In short, this entails increasing their self-awareness, occupational awareness, and decision-making skills. If young adults with disabilities are taught how to make decisions, are provided with activities that allow them to become aware of their interests, skills, values, and personality characteristics, and are allowed to explore the various occupational and job training opportunities available to them, they are armed with knowledge that will allow them to assist in making the kinds of decisions that career planning entails. Without such experiences, however, young adults with disabilities are unlikely to develop the requisite skills necessary for active participation in the career planning process (Levinson & Brandt, 1997; Szymanski, 1994).

As stated earlier, P.L. 101-476, the Individuals with Disabilities Education Act (IDEA; passed in October, 1990), requires that a disabled student's Individual

Education Plan (IEP) address the issue of transition from school to work and community living by age 14, and that continued planning and service delivery be offered to young adults through age 21. Plans must include a statement of services the student needs to make a successful transition from school to work and community living. Plans developed for a client are required to list outcomes as long term goals and for each long term goal need to cite sequential actions which will be taken to accomplish these goals. Timelines associated with implementation of each service are to be included in these plans, as are the specific agencies and professionals responsible for intervention implementation. Plans must be reviewed, revised, and updated annually. Rehabilitation personnel for clients with disabilities often write individualized Written Rehabilitation Plans, which are similar to the Individual Education Plans written by school personnel.

Intervention

As suggested earlier, the extent to which a disability influences an individual's career development will depend on several factors. In some instances, a disability has little effect on an individual's career development. In such instances, many of the career interventions discussed in other chapters of this book are applicable to young adults with disabilities. Even in cases where one's disability does affect career development, many of the interventions discussed in other chapters of this book are still applicable. These interventions will not be reiterated here. Instead, this section will first address general principles and considerations when intervening with young adults with disabilities. This will be followed by a discussion of both systemic and individual interventions that are pertinent to clients with disabilities.

GENERAL PRINCIPLES AND CONSIDERATIONS WHEN IMPLEMENTING CAREER INTERVENTIONS FOR YOUNG ADULTS WITH DISABILITIES

As Mastie (1994) reminds us, unless we plan to work with an ever increasingly dependent client over and over again across the decades, our professional responsibility is to assure that each person learns the career planning process. For many young adults with disabilities, for whom dependence on the system is increasingly likely, this is a particularly important consideration. As suggested earlier, individuals with disabilities should be involved, to the maximum extent possible, in the planning and implementation of interventions. Interventions should have the goal of providing the client with the knowledge and skills they need to make career decisions in an increasingly independent manner. Interventions which rely too heavily on implementation by professionals and which do not teach clients the skills needed to manage their own career development may provide short-term assistance, but are not beneficial in the long run (Szymanski, Hershenson, Enright, & Ettinger, 1996). As such, Szymanski & Parker (1989) have suggested that interventions for young adults with disabilities should be maximally under control of the client, least intrusive, and most natural for the setting. Though interventions that require the active participation of a counselor or job coach may be beneficial at times for some clients, we must remember that such interventions may also call negative attention to the client, especially when they appear unnatural or overly obtrusive in the work environment.

Spekman, Goldberg, and Herman (1992) found that young adults with disabilities tended to deny the challenges associated with their disability and did not seem to recognize that they could alter their current situations and solve their own problems. These young adults had neither the knowledge necessary to act upon career goals nor the knowledge of how to develop or use their support systems. Based upon Spekman et al.'s and other's research, Morningstar (1997) identified the following factors associated with successful career adjustment for some adults with disabilities:

a) self awareness,
b) creative adaptation and reframing of one's disability,
c) persistence and perseverance,
d) a proactive and systematic approach to goal attainment,
e) a desire to succeed,
f) a goodness of fit between abilities and career choice, and
g) the presence and use of support systems.

As such, Blustein (1992) has formulated the following general recommendations for those professionals formulating interventions for persons with disabilities, many of which will be discussed in more detail in the next section:

1. Enhance client sense of control – in addition to increasing motivation and empowering the client, it encourages independence in future decision making.
2. Enhance client competence in self exploration – disability conditions change and competence in self exploration/self awareness can increase the client's ability to make ongoing disability-related decisions.
3. Enhance client competence in environmental exploration – many individuals with disabilities have a restricted range of experiences; moreover, many environments present limitations and barriers for individuals with disabilities that are best evaluated by the individual themselves.
4. Help clients avoid premature closure – many individuals with disabilities inappropriately rule out occupations or quickly settle on one because of their disability.

SYSTEMIC INTERVENTIONS

I have already discussed the importance of working within the context of a transdisciplinary team when planning and implementing interventions for young adults with disabilities. Perhaps the most important intervention when working with this population is the establishment of such a team, and with it, the establishment of interagency agreements. Family involvement on the team is essential, and family support must be encouraged. It is also important to establish a longitudinal service delivery system that is available to provide services to young adults with disabilities throughout the life-span, and is designed to create (not just identify) career options. Lastly, attempts must be made to reduce the disincentive to work that many young adults with disabilities experience.

ESTABLISH A TEAM AND INTERAGENCY AGREEMENTS

In order to provide for the career development needs of young adults with disabilities, a variety of professionals and agencies need to be involved.

Professionals from the fields of education (regular education, special education, and vocational education), vocational rehabilitation, social services, mental health/mental retardation all have expertise and offer services that can assist in furthering the career development of young adults with disabilities. However, lack of coordination between these professionals and agencies has traditionally hampered career planning efforts with this population. Hence, it is important that the role of each of these professional/agencies be clearly delineated and agreed to in writing, and that a process for joint planning be established.

ENCOURAGE FAMILY SUPPORT AND INVOLVEMENT

Research results indicate that family involvement is a critical factor influencing the success of career interventions for young adults with disabilities (Burkhead & Wilson, 1995; Hasazi et al., 1985; Schalock & Lilley, 1986). Family members must be encouraged to be active team members in planning and implementing interventions. Family members can be encouraged to act as role models for their children, and can be taught how to encourage career development by assisting their children in self and occupational exploration and by encouraging and supporting early work experiences (Morningstar, 1997). Teams should also assist families in establishing appropriate and realistic expectations for their children.

ENCOURAGE LONGITUDINAL AND LIFE-SPAN SERVICE DELIVERY

Because many young adults with disabilities will need ongoing services, a system must be in place where the client can seek services throughout adulthood. One agency should serve as the primary contact for the client and act as a liaison to other agencies that provide services.

REDUCE DISINCENTIVES TO WORK

Many of the federal and state services that young adults with disabilities take advantage of provide a financial disincentive to work. Though such services will often provide young adults with opportunities for job training, they will often place a limit on how much money they can earn before services are discontinued. From a financial perspective, young adults with disabilities are often no better working than not working. Professionals must advocate for the removal of financial disincentives to career advancement in disability policy if significant strides are to be made in the career development of young adults with disabilities (Conyers, Koch, & Szymanski, 1998).

INDIVIDUAL INTERVENTIONS

As stated previously, many of the career interventions used with the general population are often equally applicable for individuals with disabilities. Interventions designed to increase career maturity by providing opportunities for clients to improve self awareness, occupational awareness and decision making skills may be even more important for young adults with disabilities than they are for other clients. However, young adults with disabilities also need to be taught to advocate for themselves and to recognize the accommodations they need in order to successfully function in work and community life. Efforts also must be made to improve self-efficacy among individuals with disabilities. Lastly, young adults with disabilities need to be knowledgeable about the service delivery system with which they must interact.

INCREASE CAREER MATURITY

Because they often have a more limited range of life experiences than do many individuals without disabilities, interventions with young adults with disabilities need to focus on improving self and occupational awareness and decision making skills. Self and occupational awareness can be facilitated via assessment, individual career counseling, the use of career planning systems, career planning books/exercises, career classes or workshops, and via use of computer-assisted career information systems (like SIGI-PLUS and DISCOVER) (Szymanski, Hershenson, Enright, & Ettinger, 1996). For many individuals with disabilities, particularly those with cognitive disabilities, experiential interventions may be preferable to verbal interventions (Szymanski et al, 1996) especially when attempting to facilitate self and occupational awareness. Integrated work experiences, job tryouts, and on-the-job training have long been considered to be critical indicators of successful post-school employment outcomes (Morningstar, 1997). Job tryouts can be developed in such a way so as to allow clients to test out assumptions they have made about their interests, values, and skills (Hagner & Salomone, 1989). Work experiences can be structured so as to allow clients to express interests and preferences and to assess their satisfaction and success with the work (Hagner & Salomone, 1989). Additionally, work experiences can be structured so that they provide knowledge that is broader than just the job itself, offer opportunities to assess and acquire socialization skills (critical to the placement success for many individuals with disabilities), offer exposure to positive adult role models and mentors and individuals without disabilities, and offer the client feedback on their performance (Morningstar, 1997). When structuring work experiences for young adults with disabilities, one should emphasize the importance of advanced planning and problem solving in the workplace, encourage motivation through providing ample opportunities for success, teach goal setting and action planning, develop skills for positive reframing of one's challenges and difficulties, and support persistence and perseverance (Reiff, Gerber, & Ginsberg, 1996). On-the-job training and work experiences also offer the opportunity to teach decision-making skills and afford young adults with disabilities an opportunity to learn the meaning and value of work. It also provides them with an opportunity to experience the satisfaction that can be gained from work.

PROVIDE ACCOMMODATIONS NEEDED FOR SUCCESS

Career development professionals must identify and make arrangements to provide the accommodations young adults with disabilities need in order to be successful in work and community settings. Obviously, the accommodations needed will vary depending upon the nature and type of disability possessed. Accommodations may range from a notetaker and books on tape for a young adult college student with a learning disability to a communication system for an individual with cerebral palsy. The specific accommodations needed by an individual should be a major goal of assessment. Career development professionals must insure that young adults with disabilities are aware of their rights to reasonable accommodations under the law, are knowledgeable about the specific accommodations they need to be successful, are capable of using these accommodations independently to the maximum extent possible, and can clearly articulate and advocate their need for these accommodations. Clients should also be encouraged to develop and experiment with new ways to ameliorate the limitations of their disability. Professionals must also continually assess client's skills at identifying, requesting and implementing accommodations in various contexts (Conyers, Koch, & Szymanski, 1998). They should also assist clients in accommodations planning by staying informed of resources, validating the benefits of needed accommodations, modeling effective communication strategies when advocating for accommodations, and engaging clients in role-playing activities to help them develop effective communication strategies (Conyers, Koch, & Szymanski, 1998).

TEACH ADVOCACY SKILLS

Unfortunately, many young adults with disabilities develop a sense of dependency on the agencies that service them and over rely on professionals to advocate for their needs. As a result, it is important for professionals to assist clients in developing a sense of self-determination and to develop a strong sense of self-advocacy. Self advocacy has been described as "the ability of an individual to effectively communicate, convey, negotiate, or assert one's own interests, desires, needs, and rights. The term assumes the ability to make informed decisions. It also means taking responsibility for those decisions" (Van Reusen, Bos, Schumaker, & Deshler, 1995, p. 6). Wilson (1994) described successful self advocates as individuals who understand their personal strengths, weaknesses, and coping strategies, and who are actively involved in goal setting and planning. Self advocates have been described as taking responsibility for oneself, separating from parental control and values, separating from control of the school system and other agencies, and developing an internal locus of control (Michaels, 1997).

Though it may take some young adults with disabilities years to become successful self advocates, this process can be facilitated by involving clients in all planning to the maximum extent possible. Insuring that clients have adequate opportunities to increase self awareness, are well aware of their functional limitations, and are knowledgeable about accommodations that are effective for them, can also assist. As suggested earlier, role-playing can be an effective technique for modeling and having client's practice effective communication strategies they can use to advocate for themselves.

IMPROVE SELF EFFICACY

Many individuals with disabilities have diminished self-efficacy beliefs which become detrimental to career development (Hershenson & Szymanski, 1992). Though individual counseling can be used to remedy this, experiential interventions are likely to also prove effective. By providing clients with a) a variety of experiences, b) developing opportunities for them to be successful in a vast array of situations, and c) exposing them to a wide variety of options previously unconsidered, self-efficacy can be improved (Szymanski, Hershenson, Enright, & Ettinger, 1996). Additionally, professionals can improve client self efficacy by conveying belief in the client's ability to succeed and including others on the transdisciplinary team who share this view; teaching clients to view their functional limitations as challenges that they are able to successfully overcome rather than as barriers that hold them back; setting realistic expectations that increase the likelihood of success; and by providing adequate support, assistance, and accommodations (Conyers, Koch, & Szymanski, 1998).

TEACH THE SYSTEM

In order to be successful advocates, clients must first understand the services various agencies provide, and understand their rights to these services under the law. Researchers have found that the degree of skill one has in accessing and using disability services is a major influence on career development and occupational self-efficacy (Conyers, Koch, & Szymanski, 1998). Given the interaction of financial issues, health-related concerns, employment training, and education, the disability system is complex, highly politicized, and difficult to understand and negotiate. The workings of this system are usually communicated to clients in a haphazard, poorly organized manner, and most frequently by "word of mouth" (Conyers, Koch, & Szymanski, 1998).

Young adults with disabilities need to be taught "the system" in a systematic and direct manner. This can be facilitated by having clients participate in all team meetings in which service delivery is to be discussed and planned. All team members and service providers should clearly communicate a) the services they offer, b) eligibility requirements for these services, c) application procedures, d) and any other assistance the agency provides in accessing its services. One member of the team should act as the liaison to all agencies, and should involve the client in all contacts. The liaison should use these contacts as an opportunity to teach the client about the disability service delivery system and give the client an opportunity to practice accessing services on their own (under supervision). As the client becomes more knowledgeable and skilled in working within the system, the liaison should gradually reduce their involvement.

FOLLOW-UP

Follow-up is the final component of the TCPM and is often the most neglected by professionals. Historically, interventions have often been implemented with young adults with disabilities without any follow-up. Once interventions have been implemented, it is essential that professionals assess the effectiveness of the interventions and identify any modifications that need to be made in order to increase their effectiveness. Additionally, follow-up allows professionals to address and react to ongoing concerns and needs, and to increase, add, or revise interventions as appropriate (Levinson, 1998).

Summary

The career development of individuals with disabilities is not well understood and has been given scant attention in the literature. Efforts to address the career development needs of this population have been largely unsuccessful. Though there are many reasons for this, one reason is that service delivery has been hampered by a lack of coordination among the various professionals that work with this population. As such, a transdisciplinary career planning model has been advocated in this chapter. Prior to planning interventions, a thorough assessment should be conducted by the transdisciplinary team. This assessment should be the basis for intervention planning and should be functional, incorporate an environmental focus, and assess multiple traits using multiple assessment methods. To the maximum extent possible, clients should be actively involved in their own career planning. When appropriate, family members should also be involved. Service delivery plans should identify which agency and professional is responsible for each intervention to be implemented, and plans should be reviewed and revised annually. Interventions should be designed to:

a) increase career maturity and teach the knowledge and skills clients need to make career decisions independently,
b) enhance client control,
c) provide accommodations needed for success in work and community settings,
d) teach clients self advocacy skills,
e) improve client self efficacy, and
f) teach clients how to negotiate the system.

References

Blustein, D. L. (1992). Applying current theory and research in career exploration to practice. *The Career Development Quarterly, 41,* 174-185.

Brown, D., & Minor, C.W. (Eds.). (1989). *Working in America: A status report.* Alexandria, VA: National Career Development Association.

Burkhead, E., & Wilson, L. (1995). The family as a developmental system: Impact on the career development of individuals with disabilities. *Journal of Career Development, 21,* 187-199.

Collet-Klingenberg, L. L. (1998). The reality of best practices in transition: A case study. *Exceptional Children, 65,* 67-79.

Conyers, L., Koch, L, & Szymanski, E. M. (1998). Life-span perspectives on disability and work: A qualitative study. *Rehabilitation Counseling Bulletin, 42,* 51-75.

Dunn, C. (1996). A status report on transition planning for individuals with learning disabilities. *Journal of Learning Disabilities, 29,* 17-30.

Gajar, A., Goodman, L., & McAfee, J. (1993). *Secondary schools and beyond: Transition of individuals with mild disabilities.* New York: Macmillan.

Gaylord-Ross, R., & Browder, D. (1991). Functional assessment: Dynamic and domain Properties. In L. H. Meyer, C. A. Peck, and L. Brown (Eds.), *Critical issues in the lives of people with severe disabilities.* Baltimore: P. H. Brookes.

General Accounting Office. (1993). *Vocational rehabilitation: Evidence for Federal program's effectiveness is mixed* (GAO/PEMD-93-19). Washington DC: Author.

Hagner, D., & Salomone, P. (1989). Issues in career decision making for workers with developmental disabilities. *The Career Development Quarterly, 38,* 148-159.

Halpern, A., & Fuhrqer, M. J. (1984). *Functional assessment in rehabilitation.* Baltimore: Brookes.

Hasazi, S. B., Gordon, L. R., & Roe, C. A. (1985). Factors associated with the employment status of handicapped youth exiting high school from 1979 to 1983. *Exceptional Children, 51,* 455-469.

Hershenson, D. B., & Szymanski, E. M. (1992). Career development of people with disabilities. In R. M. Parker & E. M. Szymanski (Eds.), *Rehabilitation counseling: Basics and beyond* (2nd ed., pp. 273-303). Austin, TX: PRO-ED.

Holland, J. L. (1985). *Making vocational choices: A theory of vocational personalities and work environments* (2nd ed.). Englewood Cliffs, NJ: Prentice-Hall.

Hoyt, K., & Lester, J. (1995). Learning to work: The NCDA Gallup Survey. Alexandria, VA: National Career Development Association.

Individuals with Disabilities Education Act of 1990. 20 U.S.C. 1400 *et seq.*

Levinson, E. M. (1993). *Transdisciplinary vocational assessment: Issues in school-base programs.* Brandon, VT: Clinical Psychology Publishing.

Levinson, E. M. (1998). *Transition: Facilitating the postschool adjustment of students with disabilities.* Boulder, CO: Westview Press.

Levinson, E. M., & Brandt, J. (1997). Career development. In G. Bear, K. Menke, and A. Thomas (Eds.), *Children's needs: Psychological perspectives II.* Washington, DC: National Association of School Psychologists.

Levinson, E. M., Peterson, M., & Elston, R. (1994). Vocational counseling with the mentally retarded. In D.C. Strohmer and H. T. Prout (Eds.), *Counseling and psychotherapy with mentally retarded persons.* Clinical Psychology Publishing.

Mastie, M. M. (1994). Using assessment instruments in career counseling: Career assessment as compass, credential, process and empowerment. In J. T. Kapes, M. M. Mastie, & E. A. Whitfield (Eds.), *A counselor's guide to career assessment instruments* (3rd ed., pp. 31-40). Alexandria, VA: The National Career Development Association.

Menchetti, B., & Uduari-Solner. (1990). Supported employment: New challenges for vocational evaluation. *Rehabilitation Education, 4,* 301-317.

Michaels, C. A. (1997). Preparation for employment: Counseling practices for promoting personal competency. In P. J. Gerber, & D. S. Brown (Eds.), *Learning disabilities and employment* (pp. 187-212). Austin, TX: PRO-ED.

Minskoff, E. H. (1994). Postsecondary education and vocational training: Keys to success for adults with learning disabilities. In P. J. Gerber, & H. B. Reiff (Eds.), *Learning disabilities in adulthood: Persisting problems and evolving issues* (pp. 111-120). Boston: Andover Medical Publishers.

Morningstar, M. (1997). Critical issues in career development and employment preparation for adolescents with disabilities. *Remedial and Special Education, 18,* 307-320.

Morningstar, M., Turnbull, A., & Turnbull, H. (1996). What do students with disabilities tell us about the importance of family involvement in the transition from school to adult life? *Exceptional Children, 62,* 249-260.

Morra, L. G. (1993). *Transition from school to work.* General Accounting Office, Washington, DC: Human Resources Division.

Osipow, S. H. (1976). Vocational development problems of the handicapped. In H. Rusalem & D. Malikin (Eds.), *Contemporary vocational rehabilitation* (pp. 51-60). New York: New York University Press.

Parker, R. M., Szymanski, E. M., & Hanley-Maxwell, C. (1989). Ecological assessment in supported employment. *Journal of Applied Rehabilitation Counseling, 20,* 26-33.

Patton, W., & McMahon, M. (1999). *Career development and systems theory: A new relationship.* Pacific Grove, CA: Brooks/Cole.

Power, P. (2000). *A guide to vocational assessment.* Austin, TX: PRO-ED.

Reiff, H. B., Gerber, P. J., & Ginsburg, R. (1996). What successful adults with learning disabilities can tell us about teaching children. *Teaching Exceptional Children, 29,* 10-17.

Rogan, P., & Hagner, D. (1990). Vocational evaluation in supported employment. *Journal of Rehabilitation, 56,* 45-51.

Rudrud, E., Ziarnik, J., Bernstein, G., & Ferrara, J. (1984). *Proactive vocational habilitation.* Baltimore, MD: Paul H. Brookes.

Schalock, R. L., & Lilley, M. A. (1986). Placement from community-based mental retardation programs: How well do clients do after 8 to 10 years? *American Journal of Mental Deficiency, 90,* 669-676.

Spekman, N., Goldberg, R., & Herman, K. (1992). Learning disabled children grow up: A search for factors related to success in the young adult years. *Learning Disabilities Research and Practice, 7,* 161-170.

Szymanski, E. M. (1994). Transition: Life-span and life-space considerations for empowerment. *Exceptional Children, 60*(5), 402-410.

Szymanski, E., Hershenson, D., Enright, M., Ettinger, J. (1996). Career development theories, constructs, and research: Implications for people with disabilities. In E. M. Szymanski, & Parker, R. (Eds.), *Work and disabilities: Issues and strategies in career development and job placement* (pp. 9-38). Texas: PRO-ED.

Szymanski, E., & Parker, R. M. (1989). Rehabilitation counseling in supported employment. *Journal of Applied Rehabilitation Counseling, 20,* 65-72.

Szymanski, E., Ryan, C., Merz, M., Trevino, B., & Johnston-Rodriguez, S. (1996). Psychosocial and economic aspects of work: Implications for people with disabilities. In E. M. Szymanski & R. Parker (Eds.), *Work and disabilities: Issues and strategies in career development and job placement* (pp. 9-38). Texas: PRO-ED.

Taylor, H. (1994). N.O.D. Survey of Americans with disabilities: Employment related highlights. [special advertising section]. *Business Week.*

Van Reusen, A., Bos, C., Schumaker, J., & Deshler, D. (1995). *The self-advocacy strategy.* Lawrence, KS: Excell Enterprises.

Wilson, G. L. (1994). Self-advocacy skills. In C. A. Michaels (Ed.), *Transition strategies for persons with learning disabilities* (pp. 153-184). San Diego, CA: Singular.

Wissick, C., Gardner, J., Langone, J. (1999). Video-based simulations: Considerations for teaching students with development disabilities. *Career Development for Exceptional Individuals, 22*(2), 233-249.

Ysseldyke, J., Algozzine, B., & Thurlow, M. (1992). *Critical issues in special education* (2nd ed.). Princeton, NJ: Houghton Mifflin.

CHAPTER 14
Career Counseling with Military Personnel and Their Dependents

Dennis W. Engels
Henry L. Harris
University of North Texas

This chapter describes the vast population of military personnel and their dependents and discusses aspects of their many and diverse need for career counseling and related services. This description is followed with a series of questions and discussions related to issues and concerns confronting military personnel and their dependents, all of who are in the unending process of career planning and resolving career and other life issues. Contemporary mainstream economic, technical and related contextual workplace concerns are discussed with an eye to their relationship to and commonality with the military workplace. Common career and related counseling principles and practices that are appropriate for counseling with the military are also discussed, with concluding remarks focused on general and specific implications for providing personal and career counseling services for military personnel and their dependents. Attention is focused on general and specific needs and services for military personnel and their dependents. This chapter closes with implications for counseling practice, research and public policy.

THE NUMBERS

More than 1.3 million dedicated men and women serve on active duty in the U.S. military (Military Family Resource Center, 2000). The Army, the largest branch of the military, comprises 34.5 percent of active duty members, followed, respectively, by the Navy, with 26.9 percent, Air Force, with 26 percent, and the Marine Corps, with 12.6 percent (Military Family Resource Center, 2000; U.S. Department of Labor, 2000). Military personnel are classified in two major categories, enlisted and officers, with approximately 85 percent of Armed Forces personnel in enlisted ranks and the remaining 15 percent serving as officers. More than 50 percent of the enlisted personnel are considered junior enlisted, falling in low-end pay grades E-1 through E-4. From the educational perspective, 91.5 percent of enlisted members are high school graduates, 3 percent hold a Baccalaureate Degree, and a small percentage .3 percent, have an advanced degree. The majority of officers (approximately 90 percent) hold either a Baccalaureate or an advanced degree.

Approximately 80 percent of active duty military service members range in age from 18 to 35 (Military Family Resource Center, 2000). Women comprise slightly over 14 percent of the military population. Racial and ethnic demographics of the Armed Forces indicate 66 percent of active duty members are Caucasian, and 34 percent are minorities (Military Family Resource Center, 2000). Over 30 percent of current military personnel are located in Virginia, North Carolina, Texas, and California. Approximately 258,000 military personnel were stationed outside the

U.S. in 1998, with over 116,000 in Europe, mainly in Germany, and another 96,000 assigned predominantly in Japan and the Republic of Korea (Military Family Resource Center, 2000). Suffice it to say the Defense Department is the U.S.' largest public sector employer, and the U.S. has a substantial active duty military force.

RELEVANCE FOR ALL COUNSELORS

In this chapter, two counselor educators who are veteran military officers, one of whom is a retired reserve colonel, whose son is a reserve captain on active duty as a dentist, look at a topic that may seem very narrow on the surface. In actuality, career counseling with military personnel and their dependents has many dimensions and venues.

Because this chapter emphasizes career counseling for the military, many readers may conclude that it is only of interest to counselors employed by the Department of Defense (DOD) to serve the counseling needs of active duty military personnel; but a broad range of counselors have opportunities to provide counseling and related services for military personnel and their dependents. As is commonly reported in contemporary media, today's military depends increasingly on a combination of active and reserve component forces, with dedicated and regular combined active-reserve component integration, to a point where many active duty military personnel are reservists on extended active duty tours. When one adds members of the reserve components, the civilian "citizen soldiers" of the Army, Air Force, Navy and Marines, to the force structure, the numbers increase dramatically. If one expands beyond the traditional sense of 1.3 million active duty personnel to this fuller range of active and inactive guard and reserve and other sectors of the military, possible needs for career counseling and related services expand rapidly and extensively (Yip, 2001a).

Counseling military personnel and their dependents takes on added poignancy and viability in the face of the fall, 2000, American Counseling Association and American Mental Health Counseling Association public policy breakthrough on the TRICARE DOD health care program as defined in Public Law 106-398 of the laws of 2000. This law requires that the DOD conduct a demonstration project on independent reimbursement of Licensed Professional Counselors. Provisions of this law direct the Secretary of Defense to conduct this demonstration project in one TRICARE region over a two year period to determine effects of increasing access to licensed professional counselors by removing the requirement for physician referral prior to engaging a counselor under the TRICARE program. This demonstration project has great potential for including licensed professional counselors as approved TRICARE providers. Although the TRICARE DOD mental health care program is a small element of the massive TRICARE system, providing military and other DOD employees the right to choose licensed counseling providers constitutes a landmark event in the history of the counseling profession and enhances the likelihood that a growing number of counselors will provide professional services to military personnel and their dependents.

International headlines, such as, "Three U.S. teens on trial in Germany: Soldiers' sons charged with murder of 2 motorists killed by stones," (Associated Press and *Dallas Morning News,* 2000, December 2, p. 29), bespeak a crucial need for counseling military dependents. Obviously, school children that are military dependents require the services of school counselors, and other dependents may need a variety of counseling services. School counselors and other counselors commonly work with prospective members of the military, as well, during their formative years. Hence, it would behoove all counselors working with young adults to be familiar with aspects of potential career opportunities and resources available to prospective and actual members of the military. The senior author's son, for example, obtained a U.S. Air Force scholarship that fully funded two of his four years of very expensive dental study in exchange for three years of service as a captain in the USAF, the first year of which is advanced training at a highly specialized USAF health services facility. For many, military educational benefits can provide basic and advanced education not otherwise available. Seen in light of the massive size of the U.S. current and prospective military force structure and all the immediate and extended families of military personnel, this chapter has relevance for many counselors and other mental health professionals. With this contextual background in mind, the narrative now turns to general mainstream economic and other market factors impacting career development for military personnel.

Economic and Related Factors

Hansen et al. (2001), Engels and Harris (1999), and Feller and Walz (1997) noted how current robust, yet turbulent, economic, labor, and related circumstances such as the "temping" or contracting of the work force and labor market projections (Bridges, 1994; Ettinger, 1996; Rifkin, 1995) suggest major, unprecedented changes in employee expectations and entitlements in an era of dwindling employee loyalty to employers and an erosion of traditional employee safety nets and other benefits commensurate with long term continuous employment. Two major dimensions of this unprecedented change lie in fundamental aspects of work, itself, and in how people might earn a living. Technological advances contributing to and stimulating continuous increases of new knowledge, the global economy, changing traditional rules and removal of many conventional boundaries for exchange of goods and services, all these factors influence military and other public and private sector employment. Significant recruiting and retention pressures in the military relate to the general U.S. economy and employment levels and suggest that the military is in no way immune from civilian sector social, economic and labor factors. Hence, military counselors and all who work with the military need to know about these changes and forces for change. Along with these complex change factors comes the need for U.S. policy makers and all citizens to consider how best to attain high skills needed for a high-wage economy (Commission on Skills of the American Workforce, 1990).

America's Choice: High Skills or Low Wages!, a major influential work by the Commission on Skills of the American Workforce (1990), says that the U.S. needs workers with high-level skills and knowledge to compete in global, high wage, markets, where new technologies, emerging communications and other factors radically change the means and strategies for work. As noted in this 1990 report's title, America's choice is profound, fundamental and universal because almost everyone in the military and civilian sectors needs high skills. Persons with high skills have high marketability, and many skills attained in the military make military personnel very attractive prospective employees for private sector employers.

REDEFINING CAREER

In view of unprecedented changes and instability in the nature and performance of work today (Feller & Walz, 1997), the general public may be ready for a longstanding concept of career counselors who note that each person has one career that is life-long (Engels, 1994, Hansen 1997), manifest in a variety of work and related tasks, settings and roles throughout one's life. If each person has one career that is life-long, counselors may need to help military personnel see the importance of and commit to taking personal responsibility for individual career ownership and stewardship.

Although this book's emphasis on adult career development might lead to reader inference of working only with adults, emphases in current professional literature on integrating work roles and responsibilities with other life roles and responsibilities (Hansen, 1997, Hansen et al., 2001, Super & Sverko, 1995), and application of systems theory suggest that counselors need to focus attention on family members and other dependents in addressing the life/career needs of their military clients. Hence, in this chapter, we consider the encompassing context of military life and military career fields on both the immediate and the overall life-career development of military personnel and their dependents.

In addition to contextual considerations, the concept of a single, life-long, career has many implications for all counselors. Helping military personnel see their military service as one part of their overall, continuous, life-long career could afford increased stimulation and incentives for personal life-career ownership and personal life-career responsibility. Helping military personnel see simultaneous connections with all prior, current and future career and life-role development could afford a sense of stability, a sense of wholeness and continuity, in an otherwise highly mobile, transitory and relatively brief military tenure. Helping military personnel acknowledge responsibility, plan and care for their careers in this manner might readily enhance an individual's investment in all facets of military life, including a smooth transition from the military at some point. Helping military clients focus on balancing and even integrating family and other life roles could stimulate and accentuate both near term and long term life-career planning. With this sense of multiple life roles and responsibilities and individual career ownership and stewardship as a definitional nuance and a guide, it seems appropriate to move toward some specific life-career counseling strategies for military personnel and their dependents.

PRACTICAL QUESTIONS AND ISSUES

Having looked at who the military are and appreciating their multiple life-roles and their one-owner, life-long, career development context, the following focus questions might be useful in organizing this chapter for practitioners, scholars and researchers:

1. What are some key issues and strategies and resources for life-career planning and development in the military today?
2. How do military counselors and other counselors working with military personnel and their dependents promote and provide effective life-career planning and development services?

3. What role might counselors play in helping policy makers and military leaders and personnel create and implement life-career visions, goals and plans, address current life-career trends and implement career development programs that are both nationally sensitive and locally appropriate in scope, focus and thrust?

In view of the major human, economic, technological and other changes cited above, the military might need to consider new ways of promoting individual career ownership and stewardship.

MULTI-FACETED PHENOMENON

In many domestic and overseas circumstances and situations, career counseling with active duty military personnel may require working with service members as though they are developing two or more career paths simultaneously. Among the many factors prompting this dual or multiple career path focus are: the fixed temporal nature of active military service; relatively brief enlistment-reenlistment periods for many, relatively frequent assignment or duty station changes; retirement options available as early as 18 years of service, occasional buy-outs and other reductions in force; incremental scarcity of openings at higher ranks; installation closings, available modified military career path alternatives via reserve service, and rich career opportunities in non-military sectors of the U.S.

Of course, the constant possibility of mobilization, of movement to and engagement in conflicts and combat, is the one aspect of military and military reserve life that seems most unique, sobering and dramatic in terms of overall human impact. While many occupations include health hazards and physical safety hazards, and while all workplaces today guard against increasing instances of human violence, only front line local, state, and federal police and other public safety and protection occupations and career fields seem to approach the violence and combat potential of military career fields. Military personnel are always "on call" and need to be ready for high-risk activities in actual conflict and in preparation for conflict. Freedom, indeed, is not free, and this potential for risk sets military duties in a special category for military personnel and all that serve military personnel. In light of this partial list of variables in military career fields and job status dimensions, one can see the wide array of permutations and combinations in military career paths, and one can infer a wide array of possibilities and needs for various counseling services and approaches related to many of these aspects of active duty, as well as extensions of and transitions to or from active duty.

RESOURCES

Staffing, preparing, maintaining and improving military force requirements, competence and readiness for mobilization are of paramount importance to the DOD and the U.S. This system affords a wide array of career opportunities for a wide array of U.S. citizens. Active duty and, to some extent, reserve personnel, their dependents and their counselors must be concerned with current and long term military career progression, assignments, education and training requirements and related military occupational specialty and promotion opportunities. All military branches spend tremendous sums of money for basic and specialized education programs and resources, and members of the military can have access to abundant educational and training opportunities.

Specific military resources are well documented within the military and in numerous world-wide-web sites for DOD and each respective service branch, as well. DOD and other government sponsored information resources abound, including general and specific Internet websites, such as, *www.todaysmilitary.com/jobs, www.hrsc.osd.mil/empinfo.htm,* or the DOD Voluntary Education site, *www.voled.doded.mil* and *www.gibillexpress.com.* These and other electronic, print and non-print resources, such as those listed in the appendix of this book, are vital for military personnel and all counselors who work with military personnel and their dependents. Many of these DOD and private and public sector resources are noted in a number of sources, including books, such as, *The Military Advantage: Your Path to an Education and a Great Civilian Career,* (Vincent, 2001), *The Military Family: A Practice Guide for Human Service Providers,* (Martin, Rosen & Sparacino, 2000), *Out of Uniform* (Drier, 1995), as well as officer and non-commissioned officer guides, soldier's handbooks, similar documents, numerous DOD videos and popular press articles (Yip, 2001a&b). These and other information and self help resources afford counselors and military personnel and dependents valuable, current and accurate information, often from an "insider's" point of view. Suffice it to say, good, current, accurate life-career development resources are abundant and, in many cases, military personnel and their dependents can use a self-service, self-help, approach to these resources. Counselors who are familiar with such resources can help members of the military and dependents find and use resources, combinations of resources and unique aspects of resources and programs that afford a win-win outcome for military personnel, their dependents and the U.S. In turn, after personnel use these resources, counselors can help military personnel with planning and decision making.

ADVOCACY

While resource awareness, access and proper exploitation are crucial in any counseling situation, the bureaucratic nature of all governmental entities, including the military, mandate that all counselors working with military personnel be advocates for those they serve. As any veteran can testify, bureaucracy abounds within the military, and many resources remain merely potential sources for those unable to navigate the bureaucracy. Counselors who learn appropriate means to identify, access and exploit resources for military personnel can be invaluable to those personnel. Counselors who learn key phrases and other strategies for sidestepping the bureaucracy in articulating and documenting military client needs and entitlements can serve an invaluable role in helping clients and in helping clients help themselves. Additionally, some military clients, especially the least educated and those with the lowest ranks or greatest needs for resources, may need considerable help articulating their needs and accessing and exploiting resources. For these and other most vulnerable military clients and dependents, it is imperative that counselors serve as advocates in the fullest sense, lest their clients' needs and potentials be squandered in opportunities not recognized, possibilities not explored and horizons not expanded. Due to the bureaucratic nature of the military system, advocacy for individuals seems mandatory, especially for the least able and the neediest military personnel and dependents. In brief, empathy, warmth, and genuineness and other counseling characteristics and skills are as important in counseling with the military as with civilians. Motivation and inspiration are also highly important.

INSPIRATION

While career counseling, resource brokering, and related activities might become routine, counselors of military clients need to maintain respect for the motivation and dedication inherent in service to country. Counselors who need motivation and inspiration to advocate for clients might do well to mark the words and work of Henry Scheible, Denton County, Texas, Veterans' Service Officer. Scheible says he always keeps in mind that people who serve in the military keep the U.S. free, face unique risks and noble obligations unlike any risks in the civilian sector, and frequently distinguish themselves with their sense of duty, honor, country and personal acts of sacrifice, bravery and heroics (Henry Scheible, personal communication, July 18, 2001).

POST-MILITARY SERVICE OPPORTUNITIES AND TRANSITIONS

In view of the considerable post-military and post-military-retirement life expectancy and general economic necessity for gainful employment to supplement military retirement income (Yip, 2001b), active component officer and enlisted personnel may need help seeing connections between military and civilian sector skills, knowledge, experience, opportunities and overall lifestyle, as well as advance preparations and planning for their post military career development and career paths. Career planning is a core element of career counseling, and counselors working with military personnel, before, during and following military service, need to help those they counsel with career planning. High school counselors can find ways to help students anticipate pros and cons of military career fields. Veterans' Counselors and county veterans' service officers can help military veterans and their dependents with continued planning and resource identification and exploitation. Some state laws, such as the laws of Texas, require county veterans' service officers, and have a veteran's commission with access to numerous information and other resources. Counselors working with prospective, active, and veteran members of the military would do well to become familiar with these and related resources and resource persons to help broker career, educational and other developmental resources and the overall military system prior to, during and following active military service.

Approximately 88 percent of all military jobs have equivalent matches in the civilian world (Occupational Outlook Handbook 2000). In many cases, there may be considerable overlap between military occupational specialty knowledge and skills and civilian occupational requirements, (e.g. a military pilot's work may have considerable similarity with piloting in the civilian sector, a military officer may have many of the very same or highly similar responsibilities as a person in management, a cook or food service worker may have competencies identical to a variety of food handling and preparation occupations), and all these skills and this knowledge overlap may relate readily to current and future paths within and outside the military.

In other cases, military and civilian sector occupational skills and knowledge may have few similarities or be very different, almost to a point of seeming mutual exclusivity, (e.g. selected combat infantry, artillery, bombardier or assault combat competencies). In these latter cases, military personnel may need considerable help from career counselors to see knowledge, skill, and application overlaps and bridges among and between military and civilian sector career fields (e.g., munitions and demolition experts, armored soldiers assigned to gunnery duties on a tank, naval or Air Force gunners, combat infantry soldiers). Additionally, active duty personnel may have plans for post-military civilian work that are very different from their military work, and they may need counselors to assist them in identifying career options, building and implementing career plans and making decisions. Post-military service can be post-enlistment, post-obligation, post-disability, post-retirement or some other status, with some commitment similarities to contemporary civilian sector trends toward an increasingly large contract or temporary workforce. Education and training might be direct means to help military personnel prepare for civilian career fields (e.g. an infantry soldier who aspires to high level technology related work following military service). As noted earlier, a number of publications and other resources can help military personnel and their counselors attend to maximizing development before, during and following the active service commitment, with attention to many useful transition resources, as well (Drier, 1995, Martin, Rosen and Sparacino, 2000, Vincent, 2001).

KNOWLEDGE AND SKILLS FOR THE FUTURE

Military basic training, entry level skill and education programs, occupational specialties, command and general staff and other highly refined educational preparatory and continuing education programs provide general, specific and highly specialized knowledge and skills, and counselors may need to help military personnel see direct and subtle connections between military and civilian competencies. If one were looking for a single base for comparison of military competencies with skills and knowledge that will be needed in the future, one very useful resource could be the extensive Department of Labor Secretary's Commission on Achieving Necessary Skills, (SCANS) reports (SCANS, 1991, 1992a, 1992b). In the SCANS, reports, spokespersons for major corporate and other private and some public sector entities identified general and specific competencies in the form of skills, knowledge and characteristics which will be necessary for workplace success in the near and distant future. These reports make it clear that all workers in all elements of the private and public sectors, including the military, will need high skills to earn and command high wages. Civilian and military personnel will also need to depend increasingly on themselves and their personal capabilities, resources and assets for career ownership, stewardship, planning and stability.

SCANS competencies greatly expand educational "basics" into a three-part necessary skill foundation, which includes:

1. the "3 Rs" plus speaking and listening,
2. thinking skills, such as reasoning, decision making, problem solving and learning to learn, and
3. personal qualities, such as integrity, respect for self and others and honesty.

Continuous advances in the human knowledge base point out the vital importance of learning how to learn so that one can continue to learn throughout one's lifespan. At the most basic level, counselors and others working with the military need to promote and provide teaching and practice with fundamental study skills, such as, efficient and effective reading and note taking. At the highest level, thinking skills relate to philosophical inquiry and love for the pursuit of truth. Suffice it to say, thinking and learning skills are fundamental, especially as specific knowledge and information become increasingly perishable and at risk of obsolescence in this rapidly changing world. Basic skills and personal characteristics, too, may require considerable attention in helping some members of the military enhance their career development.

Beyond this three-part foundation, of 1) the revised basics, 2) thinking-learning skills and 3) personal characteristics, SCANS leaders identified five areas of additional competencies required for successful participation in a smart or high-skills workforce: Resources, Interpersonal, Information, Systems, and Technology competencies. These general competencies encompass the following:

RESOURCES: identifying, organizing, planning and allocating time, money, material and human resources;

INTERPERSONAL: working with others as, a team member, a teacher, a service provider, a leader and a negotiator who works well with men and women from diverse backgrounds;

INFORMATION: using computers and other means for acquiring, evaluating, maintaining, interpreting, communicating and using information;

SYSTEMS: understanding, monitoring, correcting, designing and improving social, organizational, technological and other complex interrelationships; and

TECHNOLOGY: selecting, applying, and maintaining technological tools and equipment (SCANS, 1991).

While some educators and counselors have been familiar with many of these necessary knowledge and skill components for a long time (Foster, 1979; Hartz, 1978a, 1978b, NOICC, 1989, 1997; Texas Advisory Council 1975, 1985), these SCANS competencies seem increasingly important to career development in preparing our military and in helping our military personnel and dependents transition back into civilian sector employment. Current deficits and voids in the education of far too many (Isaacson & Brown, 1997; Hoyt & Lester, 1995, National Alliance of Business, 1990) highlight major aspects of the challenge of empowering Americans with high skills and knowledge. To help military personnel meet, acquire, refine and maintain these competencies and capacities, counselors will need to consider new paradigms, such as, a one-owner, life-long career for each person. New paradigms and approaches can help counselors develop, foster, promote and deliver individual and group career development services and programs for all military personnel.

IMPLEMENTATION STRATEGIES

Career counselors working with the military will likely see the need for continuing to provide traditional employability, career and personal development services while expanding to a more holistic emphasis promoting balanced and integrated one-owner life-career development. Among its reorganized priorities, this holistic approach requires greater attention to helping military personnel and their dependents:

1. See themselves as individual owners and stewards of their own lives and careers;
2. Identify, understand and assess personal characteristics, competencies, interests, and values;

3. Plan their short term and long term career development;
4. Balance and integrate work roles and responsibilities with other life roles and responsibilities;
5. Take responsibility for developing career plans and decisions, technical, graduate/professional school plans, employment plans, and job search competencies;
6. See connections among and between military experiences and other public and private sector opportunities;
7. Acquire skills for accessing educational and occupational information to aid career and educational planning and to develop an understanding of the world of work;
8. Select personally suitable military and civilian academic programs and experiential training opportunities, such as, entry/progression in an appropriate educational, graduate, or professional program designed to optimize a soldier, sailor, airman or marine's human capacity as well as future educational and employment options;
9. Prepare for finding suitable employment by developing job-search skills, effective candidate presentations skills, and an understanding of the fit among and between personal attributes and competencies and occupational and job requirements;
10. Manage their careers during and following military service; link with veterans, employers, professional organizations, and others who will provide opportunities to develop professional interests and competencies, integrate academic learning with work, and explore future career possibilities (Engels, Kern, & Jacobs, 2000).

As noted earlier, many traditional career counseling resources complement DOD and other military specific counseling and career resources. Many of these conventional resources, such as, assessment tools, interactive guidance information software programs and employability skills materials lend themselves to use with military personnel. Contemporary career counseling resources, such as career development and career counseling theories and techniques also lend themselves to use with military personnel. Military clients might readily benefit from such standard points of focus in adult career counseling, as, self knowledge, information skills, employability skills, decision making and planning skills and other facets of the SCANS competencies. Additional points of focus might encompass: relative satisfaction, challenge and sense of future development seen in current, past and future work; attention to life-career balance and life role integration; processes for improving one's perspective and performance of current work; elaboration of a personal life-career vision and goals; stated ownership and commitment to personal responsibility in career planning; and near term and far term prospects and plans for continued career development and appropriate career transitions. Such career focused approaches and directions seem to have obvious value for career counselors in all settings and with almost all client bases, including military personnel and their dependents.

SUMMARY, CONCLUSIONS, AND IMPLICATIONS

Whereas, *America's Choice: High Skills or Low Wages!* (Commission on Skills of the American Workforce, 1990) addresses general public and private policy issues, little of the attention in and to this highly pivotal strategic U.S. economic document attends directly to individuals. Moreover, the general, macro-economic focus of this document and labor market economics, in general, seems to miss a vital implication for individuals, including military personnel. Today, even individuals in relatively constricted environments such as the military, need to depend less on external or standing policies, dictates and conventions, and more on internal, personal resources. As the workplace moves increasingly toward shrinking job duration, increasing job shifts and changes, contract labor of skilled workers, and related paradigm shifts in creation and distribution of goods, services, and wealth, global markets and numerous other factors noted in the references cited above, one new paradigm seems at hand. In the face of such systemic changes, one major imperative centers on an increasing need for personal, individual, career ownership and stewardship. The National Career Development Association's concept of each person having one career that is life-long (Engels, 1994) takes on dramatic proportion in terms of individual self-governance, as do constructivist perspectives in contemporary career development literature (Savickas & Walsh, 1996, Hansen et al., 2001). Fortunately, good counseling resources are readily available, and some longstanding career development concepts and goals afford contemporary direction for counseling practitioners, researchers and educators.

Seen in light of the many sweeping changes noted throughout this chapter and book, counselors serving career planning and development needs of the military in the 21st Century may be facing some of the most critical factors ever. Contemporary workforce challenges in all facets of work and work settings, including the military, require new perspectives and some paradigm shifts in moving past traditional approaches. Military personnel who miss early and focused attention to the SCANS competencies and other basic and specialized knowledge and skills may be at risk of limited and sporadic unemployment and/or time in dead end jobs at poverty level and lower incomes with limited or no benefits (Hoyt & Lester, 1995; Rifkin, 1995), to say nothing of the quality of life issues attendant to low income, especially for high school and college dropouts. Marshaling resources and identifying and creating opportunities to meet challenges, problems and barriers is a perennial top priority for counselors in many settings.

From a programmatic standpoint, the National Occupational Information Coordinating Committee's (NOICC, 1989, 1997) National Career Development Guidelines (NCDG) constitute one blueprint for facilitating acquisition and mastery of the SCANS competencies across the entire lifespan and might be highly adaptable to military programs and settings. Acknowledging that no one size fits all, the NCDG are designed for state and local adaptation to accommodate, accentuate and tailor the guidelines to local needs and circumstances, and many state career development guidelines reflect the efficacy of adapting the NCDG.

Those who counsel with the military need to help people with future career planning and balancing and integrating life-work roles and responsibilities with other life roles and responsibilities, e.g. family membership, parenting and citizenship (Hansen 1997). While some career counselors have been attuned to this message, military counselors may have to shift from traditional linear and compartmentalized paradigms to fully embrace and model these concepts. Counselors in the civilian sector, too, need to attend to possible responsibilities and opportunities in working with military personnel, including reservists, and their dependents. Career development literature provides increasing recognition of inseparable linkages and overlaps between career and personal counseling

(Isaacson & Brown, 1997; Subich, 1993). Career development is not merely about current jobs and present time, it is very much about a core area of life that dramatically impacts other areas of life now and in the future. Additionally, career development is so vital, so fundamental, that military counselors need to consider how best to help the entire military community embrace life-career counseling for its pivotal importance for both individual and force well being and development. Again, counselors working with military personnel may find good reason to consider the National Career Development Association's view that each person has only one life-long career (Engels, 1994).

Because of their educational backgrounds and their familiarity with the resources mentioned here, and in view of their dedication to promoting the worth, dignity, uniqueness and potential of human beings (American Counseling Association, 1997), counselors are well prepared and may be well positioned to serve as major catalysts in helping to build and implement comprehensive developmental life-career programs, with a healthy dedication to the individual career development of today's and tomorrow's military and their dependents. In many respects, counselors need to afford clients in all settings, including the military, a contextual perspective that encompasses the rapid human and economic changes cited earlier. Attention to the whole person, to a one-owner, life-long career consciously integrating military work roles and responsibilities with current, past and future life roles, can afford new horizons for military personnel, their dependents, their counselors and their leaders. Similarly, and no less important, is the obligation of counselors working with the military to develop and maintain an understanding of the culture of the military environment. This understanding can help counselors better comprehend life-career concerns of military personnel and their dependents. As opportunities increase for more counselor involvement with military personnel and their dependents, the counseling community needs to consider partnering with this major human segment of U.S. society.

References

American Counseling Association. (1997). *Ethical standards.* Alexandria, VA

Bridges, W. (1994). *Job shift.* New York: Addison-Wesley.

Commission on Skills of the American Workforce. (1990). *America's choice: High skills or low wages!* Rochester, NY: National Center on Education and the Economy.

Drier, H. (1995). *Out of uniform.* Lincolnwood, IL: VGM Career Horizons.

Engels, D. W. (1994). *The Professional practice of career counseling and consultation: A Resource document.* Alexandria, VA: National Career Development Association.

Engels, D. W., & Harris, H. L. (1999). Career Development: A Vital Part of Contemporary Education. *National Association of Secondary School Principal Bulletin, 83,* 70-77.

Engels, D. W., Kern, C. W., & Jacobs, B. C. (2000). *Life-career development counseling.* Alexandria, VA: American Counseling Association.

Ettinger, J. M. (1996). *Improved career decision making in a changing world* (2nd ed.) Garrett Park, MD: Garrett Park Press.

Feller, R., & Walz, G. R. (Eds). (1997). *Career transitions in turbulent times.* Greensboro: University of North Carolina Educational Resource Information Clearinghouse.

Foster, D. E. (1979). *Assessment of knowledge acquired in employability skills training program.* Unpublished dissertation, University of North Texas, Denton.

Hansen, L. S. (1997). *Integrative life planning: Critical tasks for career development and changing life patterns.* San Francisco: Jossey-Bass.

Hansen, L. S. et al. (2001). *ACES/NCDA Commission on Preparing Counselors for Career Development in the New Millennium.* Unpublished position paper. Alexandria, VA: Association for Counselor Education and Supervision.

Hartz, J. D. (1978a). *Instructor's guide to employability skills.* Madison: University of Wisconsin Vocational Studies Center.

Hartz, J. D. (1978b). *Employability inventory: Findings and analysis.* Madison: University of Wisconsin Vocational Studies Center.

Hoyt, K. B., & Lester, J. L. (1995). *Learning to work: The NCDA Gallup survey.* Alexandria, VA: National Career Development Association.

Isaacson, L. E., & Brown, D. (1997). *Career information, career counseling, and career development.* (6th ed.). Boston: Allyn and Bacon.

Martin, J. A., Rosen, L. N., & Sparacino, L. R. (Des). (2000). *The Military family: A Practice guide for human service providers.* Westport, CT: Praeger.

Military Family Resource Center. (2000). *Profile of the military community: 1999 Demographics.* Arlington, VA: Author.

National Alliance of Business. (1990). *Employment policies: Looking to the year 2000.* Washington, DC: Author.

National Occupational Information Coordinating Committee. (1989). *National Career Development Guidelines.* Washington, DC: Author.

National Occupational Information Coordinating Committee. (1997). *National Career Development Guidelines* (2nd ed.). Washington, DC: Author.

Rifkin, J. (1995). *End of work: Decline of the global labor force and the dawn of the post-market era.* New York: G. P. Putnam Sons.

Savickas, M., & Walsh, W. B. (Eds.). (1996). *Handbook of career counseling theory and practice.* Palo Alto, CA: Consulting Psychologists.

Secretary's Commission on Achieving Necessary Skills. (1991). *What work requires of schools.* Washington, DC: U.S. Department of Labor.

Secretary's Commission on Achieving Necessary Skills. (1992a). *Learning a living.* Washington, DC: U.S. Department of Labor.

Secretary's Commission on Achieving Necessary Skills. (1992b). *Skills and tasks for jobs: A SCANS report for America 2000.* Washington, DC: U.S. Department of Labor.

Subich, L. M. (1993). How personal is career counseling? *The Career Development Quarterly, 42,* 129-131.

Super, D. E., & Sverko, B. (Eds.). (1995). *Life roles, values and careers.* San Francisco: Jossey Bass.

Texas Advisory Council for Technical-Vocational Education. (1975). *Qualities employers like and dislike in job applicants: Final report of a statewide employer survey.* Austin: Texas Board of Education.

Texas Advisory Council for Technical-Vocational Education. (1985). *Qualities employers like and dislike in job applicants: Final report of a statewide employer survey.* Austin: Texas Board of Education.

Three U.S. teens on trial in Germany: Soldiers' sons charged with murder of 2 motorists killed by stones. (2000, December 2). *Dallas Morning News,* p. 29.

U.S. Department of Labor. (2000). *Occupational outlook handbook.* Washington, DC: Author.

Vincent, L. (2001). *The Military advantage: Your path to an education and a great civilian career.* New York: Learning Express.

Yip, P. (2001, January 15). Guard deployment taught family to plan. *Dallas Morning News,* pp. D1&2.

Yip, P. (2001, January 15). Personal finance: Active duty: Military families must take extra steps when planning financial futures. *Dallas Morning News,* pp. D1&2.

CHAPTER 15
Career Counseling For Mature Workers

Juliet V. Miller
Worthington, OH

The practice of career counseling with clients in the mature years (over age 50) is being influenced by several trends including the increasing number of mature workers as the baby boom ages, changing attitudes toward and understanding of aging, current revisions of adult and career development theory, rapid changes in the world of work, and fluctuating retirement benefits. While much of what we currently know is applicable to counseling the mature workers, counselors are being called upon to review new information and to revise goals and strategies for assisting mature adults with life career planning and transitions. The purpose of this chapter is to help counselors update their knowledge and skills for helping mature workers by providing information on the:

1) Current social context for career counseling,
2) Adult career development theories,
3) Career counseling approaches with mature adults, and
4) Career counseling goals with mature adults.

Current Social Context for Career Counseling with Mature Adults

The baby boom is now maturing, thus creating a much larger number of mature adults who are grappling with a variety of life decisions. Moen (1998) indicates that the values and characteristics of this age cohort are reinventing the nature of various adult life transitions. In addition to these changing values, the social context in which these changes occur is reshaping the nature of work, family, careers and retirement. Collard (1996) suggests that information technology, globalization, and workplace reengineering are reshaping the concept of jobs, organizations and even careers. Bridges (1991) introduces the concept of "dejobbing" of America, and questions the continuing existence of stable, long-terms jobs as we have known them in the past.

The American Association of Retired Persons (AARP) Public Policy Institute publishes many reports that describe the employment and retirement trends among mature adults. In one of these reports, Rix (1999) summarizes the data on the employment of older adults. Employment opportunities have been increasing recently which has helped to reverse a negative trend in the employment of members between the ages of 55 to 64. The unemployment rates for this age group dropped to 2.7 percent compared with 4.3 percent five years earlier. Fewer older Americans who are not working indicate that they wish that they were.

Older workers who become unemployed spend a longer time in finding a new job than younger workers. While jobs have been more plentiful, the average length of unemployment for older job seekers fell from about 22 weeks in 1997 to 21.8 weeks in 1998 (Rix, 1999). The length of job tenure has shown a steady decline over time. This decline is challenging older notions of job stability. According to the U.S. Bureau of Labor Statistics (reported in Rix 1999), in 1983 the median job tenure for mature adult men was 15.3 years compared to 11.2 years in 1998. Older workers are more likely to be in nontraditional work arrangements, such as contract work, which offer fewer benefits and less job stability. Eleven percent of workers over age 55 are in these arrangements, compared to 6 percent of workers under 55.

For several years there has been a trend toward earlier retirement, but many experts agree that this trend has slowed or possibly reversed. The early retirement trends are attributed to such factors as long-term increase in Americans' wealth, expansion of Social Security and employer-sponsored pensions, and recent early retirement and layoff plans. A major driver in the slowing of the early retirement rates is the age-dependency ratio (the ratio of Americans older than 64 compared to Americans aged 20 to 64) that will increase to almost 70 percent between 2000 and 2030. This burden, a smaller number of employed supporting a larger number of retired, will be relieved if more older workers can be persuaded to delay their retirements and continue contributing to the health and pension systems.

Uccello and Mix (1998) investigated the impact of higher normal retirement ages on workers. Their data indicate that individuals who are in poorer health and in physically demanding jobs are apt to retire early without adequate financial support. Unmarried women and nonwhites are also vulnerable to lack of retirement benefits. The good news is that the trend toward a lower percentage of physically demanding jobs will increase the ability of workers to expand their working lives by holding jobs that require a lower level of physical capability.

The definition of retirement is also changing. Increasingly, retirement is seen as a flexible process rather than a single event. Stein (2000) suggests a model that sees older workers as remaining in, retiring from, or returning to the workplace. Weckerle and Schultz (1999) use the term, bridge employment, to reflect partial retirement in which an older worker alternates periods of engagement and disengagement in the workplace. They found that, among workers over age 60, more than 50 percent retire from a career job but only one in nine actually disengage from all work activity. Older workers who chose not to retire cite reasons such as not planning wisely for retirement, need to contribute, appreciation from others, and the desire to create something. In an AARP (2000) study, eight in ten baby boomers say they plan to work at least part-time during their retirement years. Curnow and Fox (1994) refer to the importance of planning for the "Third Age," a period beyond career job and parenting that can last for up to 30 years.

The latest trends indicate that there will be several pressures to keep older adults in the labor force for longer periods of time. Is the work place recognizing and responding to this trend? Stein (2000) feels that organizations need to rethink the need to provide opportunities to older workers as well as changing the attitudes and expectations of managers and younger employees toward older workers. Flexible schedules, job sharing, reduced loads, and seasonal employment may be options that older workers will demand.

The AARP (2000) completed a study of "American Business and Older Employees." Phone interviews were conducted with human resource managers in 400 U.S. organizations. Respondents indicated that older employees possess all but one of the top seven general qualities that companies see as being most desirable in any employee. They rated older employees positively on commitment to doing quality work, get along with coworkers, solid performance record, basic skills, someone you can count on in a crisis, and loyalty to the company. Older employees were rated low only on willingness to be flexible about doing different tasks. However, older employees were also rated lower on skill-related qualities such as trying new approaches, learning new technologies, and having up-to-date job skills.

Although the workforce is aging and there will be a smaller pool of younger workers, HR staff do not yet perceive this as a problem. Few companies have specific programs to support fuller use of older workers. The survey (AARP, 2000) indicated that about 50 percent of HR staff recognized the value of strategies for more fully utilizing older employees, but a much lower percentage has implemented approaches such as special benefits packages, part-time arrangements, educating mangers about older employees, and skill training for older workers.

IMPLICATIONS OF THE CURRENT SOCIAL CONTEXT FOR ADULT CAREER COUNSELING

The following trends need to be considered by counselors when working with the mature adult population:

- The population of mature adults is increasing rapidly as the baby boom ages.

- Although it is possible to make some generalizations about the mature adult group, there are great differences within groups including work values, health conditions, financial resources, and educational and skill levels.

- Mature workers are living in a context of very rapid changes in the nature of work including a blurring of the definitions of job, increased technological demands, need for continuous learning, and changes in the basic contract between employer and employee. Adults are struggling to understand these trends and to track them over time in a meaningful way.

- Because of these changes, many mature workers have experienced involuntary job loss and change while others are redefining their career goals and directions to respond proactively to these changes.

- There has been a trend toward earlier retirement, but this has slowed and is expected to reverse as the balance between over 50 and under 50 workers changes. This demographic trend makes it increasingly important to retain mature workers in the labor force.

- There is an important population of adults whose employment is not protected by adequate retirement benefits. This includes mature adults who have health problems and are working in physically demanding jobs. Unmarried women and nonwhites are also vulnerable to inadequate pensions and health care.

- Retirement is being viewed as a process rather than a single event. Most baby boomers intend to continue some type of employment after leaving their "career job." Adults cite not only financial considerations but also needs such as personal meaning, meaningful human contact, and service to others as reasons for continuing employment.

- Social security and pension programs are adopting policies to increase the age of retirement.

- Employers perceive mature adults as having important general work skills and attitudes but are uncertain about the adequacy of their job specific skills.

- Although employers are experiencing a serious shortage of available workers, few have implemented benefit plans and flexible work arrangements that support the employment of older workers.

Adult Development Theories

Career counseling has been based primarily on psychological perspectives of human development with recognition of the effects of biological and social factors. This section discusses adult development theories including: 1) sequential theories, 2) life events and transition theories, 3) relational theories, and 4) emerging theories.

SEQUENTIAL THEORIES

Erick Erikson's (1959) developmental framework included descriptions of stages and associated tasks. Each of his eight stages is identified by a pair of opposite outcomes, one positive or healthy and the other negative or less desirable. The last two stages relate directly to mature adults. The second stage of adulthood at midlife is generativity versus stagnation. In this stage, the individual is involved in finding ways to support the next generation by shifting the focus from self to others. Failure to achieve generativity results in stagnation or being stuck in issues of personal success or failure. The final stage, old age, is described as integrity versus despair. Integrity arises from the capacity to look back over one's life with satisfaction. Failure to achieve integrity results despair over what might have been. Erikson's view is that, if all life stages have been addressed positively, the mature adult nearing the end of life will accept himself or herself as he or she is.

Levinson (1986) describes the concept of life structure, the underlying pattern or design of a person's life at a given time. He describes development as including periods of relative stability (structure building) and transition (structure changing). The life structure includes the individual's relations with others including persons and groups, institutions, and cultures. Periods in the life structure are described in terms of developmental tasks. Periods end when a task loses its importance and other tasks emerge.

Levinson describes four eras of alternating periods of stability and transition. Two of these eras describe the mature adult. Middle adulthood lasts from ages 40 to 65. The biological capacities of adults diminish during this period but are still sufficient to have an energetic and satisfying life. At this time, most adults become senior members of their group. In addition to responsibility for their own work, they tend to be involved in the development of young adults. Late adulthood begins at approximately age 60. The goal during this time is to confront self and make peace with the world. Most of Levinson's research was conducted with men.

Super (1990) applied the notions of life stages and life space to adult career development. He described the major career development stages as birth, growth, exploration, establishment, maintenance, decline and death. Super acknowledged that the timing of these stages varies according to the individual and that, with the changing nature of the labor market resulting in more rapid and frequent career change, individuals might cycle through these stages several times. Super also described the developmental tasks associated with each stage. He further defined the concept of career adaptability as the extent to which one is ready to cope with these tasks is an indication of career maturity. In addressing life space, Super (1990) conceptualized the Life-Career Rainbow. In the Life-Career Rainbow he described the interaction and predominance at various life stages of various life roles including child, student, leisurite, citizen, worker, and homemaker. His "Segmental Model of Career Development" (Super, 1990) combines personality (self) and social policy (social factors). Osborne (1996) summarizes the comprehensive contributions of Super as including: "1) trying to understand the many determinants of career development, 2) tying all of these together in a "segmental theory," and 3) devising a career counseling approach that addresses these determinants." (p. 71)

TRANSITION THEORIES

Another group of adult development theorists has focused on life events and transitions. Life events create the motivation for change and transition. Schlossberg (1996) states, "thinking about adult career development as a transition process of moving in, through and out of the workforce helps explain what is a highly fluid process" (p.94). Individuals have both strengths and weaknesses that affect the transition process. Schlossberg (1984) provides a framework for organizing these around four S's including situation, self, support and strategies. Reviewing strengths and weaknesses using these categories can help highlight areas of needed support and areas of strength that can support the transition process.

Bridges (1991) also sees transitions as the motivation for adult development. He views transition as a process including an ending, a neutral zone, and a new beginning. It is important to acknowledge that the first stage of a transition is letting go of something. Next, the neutral zone is a period where old patterns that no longer work are released and new patterns are developed. The final phase, the new beginning, emerges only after the individual has let go of the old and spent some time in the neutral zone.

Hudson (1991) views adult development as a cyclical process. He states that this includes five major characteristics:

1. life is a complex, pluralistic, flow,
2. life proceeds through cycles of change and continuity rather than in a straight line,
3. both life's ups and downs should be honored,
4. it views humans as flexible and resilient permitting continuous adaptations, and
5. continuous learning is essential to adult development.

Hudson describes a cycle of change with ten personal skills. He suggests the notion of mini changes (within an existing life structure) verses major life transitions (that call for the development of new life structures). The ten skills are organized into four phases:

Phase 1 – Alignment, includes beginning, launching, and plateauing.

Phase 2 – Out of synch, includes managing the doldrums, sorting things out, ending, and restructuring.

Phase 3 – Disengagement, includes cocooning and self renewal.

Phase 4 – Reintegration, includes self-renewal and experimenting, networking and creativity leading to a new beginning.

RELATIONAL THEORIES

Most adult development research has been conducted using male populations. For example, Reeves (1999) observes that, "the desired outcomes in many development theories (for example, autonomy, independence and separateness) typify the male experience and, but the course of female development, with its emphasis on relationships, empathy, interdependence, and attachment, is rarely equated with healthy adulthood" (p. 24). In response to this concern, several theories based on women's development have emerged that include both separation and connection as the developmental goals. For instance, Peck (1986) discusses women's need for attachment without loss of self. Peck suggests that, although a woman's identity as expanding as she grows, it is influenced by family and cultural influences. A flexible sphere of influence supports healthy development. The most important developmental goal is to maintain attachment while achieving separation or individuation.

Jordan, Kaplan, Miller, Stiver, and Surrey (1991) suggest replacing traditional definitions of self with the idea of relational self. Empathy is the key to developing and maintaining the relationship. Some people experience empathic failure by being so open to other people that they lose their own sense of self. The goal is to have both ego flexibility (allowing connection with others) and ego strength (ability to maintain self).

EMERGING THEORIES

Kegan (1982) describes a cognitive-developmental theory that focuses on the way that the self constructs meaning across cognitive, affective, and moral domains. Development is seen as the evolution of meaning making. He describes five orders or stages of consciousness which achieve increasingly more expansive, open and inclusive understandings of self and the world. The last three orders relate directly to adult development.

Persons who make meaning from a third order operates from a dependent stance. They tend to make decisions tied to the perspective of various reference groups such as parents, peers, bosses, and other social groups. At some point, usually in a transition such as attending college or job change, persons meet with several conflicting group standards and are forced to look within for answers within. This leads to the fourth order, referred to as the self-authoring order, when individuals can more clearly define their own purpose. This is period of increased personal independence. However, this leads to living a fixed role or persona. As Marshall (1997) states, during this time people develop greater independence but may become rather rigidly identified with specific role such as a career role. This inhibits their ability to fully see all aspects of themselves and alternate live possibilities. At midlife individuals begin to wonder if there is more to life than they are currently experiencing in their fixed roles. This marks the transition to the fifth order that is characterized great personal flexibility and interdependence with others. At this stage, the self does not have a particular form, but is "like figure upon a ground, a moving ground more committed to culturing a process than preserving a product" (p. 204). During the fifth order, openness to contradiction and flexible movement are evident.

Marshall (1997) suggests that Kegan's theory is important to adult career transitions. Counselors need not only to consider the client and his or her context but also to understand, "what people are experiencing in the way that they themselves understand it. This means having some idea of how they structure meaning in their lives" (p. 112). Transitions may become opportunities for growth, for transforming the meaning-making structure that the client is using, and for moving toward flexible knowledge structures.

Kegan (1994) contends that the current social and career context requires at least fourth order or self-authoring level cognitive functioning. He indicates that only one-half to two-thirds of adults are operating at the fourth order of consciousness. He also that only a small percentage of adults reach fifth order functioning, and that this never occurs before age 40. Therefore, a large number of adults are dealing with complex career challenges without the level of cognitive skills needed

Another emerging perspective on development is the narrative orientation. This approach reverses the orientation used to understand development from an external, observational approach to an internal, meaning-making approach. Rossiter (1999) suggests:

> The process of human meaning-making takes a narrative form and people understand the changes over the course of their own lives narratively... Developmental change is experienced through a constructed personal narrative that is revised and enlarged over time to accommodate new insights, unanticipated events, and transformed perspectives. (p. 78)

Rossiter (1999) summarizes several important implications of the narrative perspective for working with adults. First, she indicates that adults are the experts on their own development. Counselors need to honor the therapeutic benefits for clients of telling their own life story. Secondly, narratives mediate change. Transitions, whether anticipated or unanticipated, stimulate the story-telling function. It is through these personal stories that adults broaden and revise their meaning systems. Thirdly, telling one's life narrative leads to development. "The act of telling one's story externalizes it so that one becomes more aware of the themes and topics that dominate one's life" (p.83).

IMPLICATIONS OF ADULT CAREER DEVELOPMENT THEORIES

The following summarizes the major conclusions found in adult career development theories.

- Development is a lifelong process.
- It is more accurate to view development as cyclical rather than linear with cycles repeating as new choices arise and with the timing of various stages depending on individual and social factors.

- Many developmental theories recognize that growth and change arise both from changes within the self (including psychological, cognitive, social, and biological changes) and within the social context.

- As the self develops, life structures and cognitive processes change. This affects the individual's perspective and life goals. Several theorists agree that in the later stages of adult development, the individual becomes more complex, open, flexible and process oriented.

- Some theorists have focused on transitions, both expected and unexpected, and suggest that these transitions drive the development process.

- Transitions have stages and characteristics. Some transitions have little effect on the life structure of the individual while other transitions have a major impact. It is important to note that the transition process requires time. Transitions start with a letting-go process, followed by a "neutral zone" or "cocooning stage." It is possible to move forward into the new situation only after these stages have been completed.

- Recent theorists have re-examined the goals of development. The concept of the relational self reflects the importance of both being connected with others while maintaining a strong sense of self.

- Modern social and workplace changes are challenging the cognitive developmental capacity of mature adults. Many adults may not be at a cognitive-developmental stage required to deal with change. Providing experiences and framing counseling goals to encourage development shifts become important.

- Most writing and research on development has been from an external, observational perspective. However, individuals use personal story as a way to look at changes and life structures. Counselors need to honor this perspective and use counseling approaches to help clients clarify and author their own stories.

Career Counseling Approaches with Mature Adults

DEFINITIONS OF CAREER COUNSELING

Cochran (1994) suggests that adult career counseling needs to focus on the both the immediate career problem and the broader the viewpoint of the total life course. This dual counseling focus can result in a more meaningful, productive, and fulfilling life direction that informs both current and future career directions. He further suggests that an important outcome of career counseling is, "to encourage the position of the agent of one's own career course" (p. 209).

Savickas (1991) also expresses the notion that career counseling results in a kind of double vision. The process focuses on more immediate actions that have career meaning, as well as on plots that are concerned with the total view of life. This can result in an integration of past, present, and future life events and directions.

Several writers stress the importance of considering both the cognitive and emotional aspects in career counseling. Spokane (1991) suggests that the stages of the career counseling process parallel the stages of the psychotherapy process. During the beginning stage, the first goal is to establish a therapeutic context and an environment of trust. The second goal in this stage is to encourage clients to recognize the discrepancies between their current situations and stated aspirations. During this beginning stage, effective counseling techniques include showing empathy, reflecting feelings, and helping clients process emotions. During the second (or activation) phase, the goal of career counseling is focused on generating, testing, and sharing hypotheses and encouraging action. The counselor becomes more cognitively challenging during this phase.

Loman (1993) thinks that the emotional component of career counseling is now becoming more important than in the past. He suggests that working functionally will be increasingly difficult in this period of rapid social change and redefinition of workplace. Career counselors need to be skilled in diagnosing effects of workplace stresses such as depression, anxiety, and other work-related mental disorders. He provides a framework that is very useful in identifying and addressing specific work dysfunctions.

CAREER COUNSELING GOALS FOR MATURE ADULTS

It is important to set career counseling goals for mature adults that are based upon trends in demographics of the older population, public and employment policies that affect mature adults, and workforce participation of older adults as well as the most current adult development theories. The following list suggests a set of understandings, attitudes and behaviors that reflect positive later-life career development. As a result of career counseling, the mature adults will:

1. Embrace career goals that support the next generation and development of the young as well as personal achievement.
2. Look back at their life with satisfaction.
3. Appreciate and accept the cyclical nature of development, honor both the ups and downs of development, and experience comfort in both periods of change and of continuity.
4. Show flexibility and willingness to expand and redefine their life structures as either personal and/or contextual changes prove their current life structures inadequate for new developmental tasks and life situations.
5. Accept and adapt to physical and cognitive life changes associated with the aging process with realism and hope.
6. Demonstrate the ability to manage and coordinate various life roles over time, and demonstrate the flexibility needed to change and modify life roles throughout the life span.
7. Appreciate that some changes are mini-changes that do not include change in life structure, while others are major and do require time for major life structure change.
8. Understand the nature of the transition process including the need for letting-go, or ending the old and taking time in a neutral zone before a new beginning can emerge.
9. View transitions as a process rather than an event, and develop a plan for using both internal (self) and external (other) resources to support the process.
10. Develop an understanding of the importance of both attachment and separation in self-development. Show both ego flexibility (allowing connection with others) and ego strength (allowing return to self).

11. Progress developmentally from other-directed (I am what others expect me to be) to self-directed (I am what I do) to a self-in-process (what I do is only part of who I am).

12. Engage in telling their life story with others, thus expanding their perspective and understanding of their lives.

CAREER PROBLEMS AND MATURE ADULTS

Krumboltz (1993) outlines several categories of career problems that clients may bring to counseling. These include locus of control, career direction, career obstacles, job search knowledge, job search motivation, job relationships, job burnout, occupational advancement, and retirement planning. He stresses the importance of recognizing that there is an emotional and informational component to each career problem. Krumboltz's categories can provide a useful structure for understanding the types of career problems confronted by mature adults.

During the early phases of the career counseling process, it is helpful to encourage clients to talk about any aspect of their career that they feel is most important for them at this time. In addition, they can explore the major career needs that they anticipate arising in the future. As counselors listen to clients' career stories, they note specific career problem areas that seem to be the most important for each client. Counselors can use Krumboltz's career problem areas as a framework for exploring specific career problem areas. For example, counselors can explore locus of control concerns by asking clients the following questions:

1. Do you feel that you are able to influence your career in a positive direction?
2. Are you able to cooperatively plan various life roles with other key people in your life such as your spouse or partner?
3. Do you value yourself for reasons other than career achievements?
4. Do you feel that you can direct your career in the changing workplace?

To explore concerns related to career direction or advancement counselors can ask clients the following questions:

1. How important is career to you at this point in your life?
2. Are you aware of various types of career redirection including moving up, downshifting, moving sideways, or enriching the status quo? (Hudson, 1996)
3. What is the effect of the new workplace on your vision of career advancement?
4. What unrealized dreams do you still want to fulfill?
5. What future legacy do you want to leave to new generations?

Questions that counselors can ask about career obstacles include:

1. How is the changing workplace affecting your levels of and stress and emotional stability?
2. What personal changes are you experiencing at this point in your life (physical, cognitive, or emotional), and what do they mean for your career goals?
3. How do you feel about aging, and what are you self messages about the aging process?
4. How do you see others in the workplace responding to you as a mature worker?

5. Which factors seem to support your career direction and which seem to inhibit it?

Inquiries addressing job search knowledge and motivation might include:

1. What recent experiences have you had that make it difficult for you to want to conduct a job search?
2. Do you need to find a way to translate your current skills into new job or occupational goals?
3. Do you see career change as positive or negative?
4. What do you think the current attitude of employers is about career change?
5. Are you comfortable with using new Internet technology in your job search?
6. Are you comfortable with the idea of requesting specific work conditions during the job interview?

To address job relationships counselors can ask their clients questions such as:

1. How is your relationship with others at work influencing your career satisfaction?
2. Are there specific work-related relationships that are difficult for you?
3. Are these problem related to differences between you as a mature worker and other-aged people in your workplace?
4. Do you think that your current age is negatively influencing your opportunities for job advancement or enrichment?
5. Does your employer have specific age-discrimination policies in place?

Questions pertaining to job burnout can include:

1. How do you feel about your job at this point in time?
2. What is most stressful for you?
3. What is most motivating for you?
4. What is your image of an ideal job for yourself at this point in your life?
5. How can other life roles provide the meaning for you that may be missing in your job?
6. What immediate actions can you take to provide support for yourself?
7. How can you move closer to the your current ideal career goal?

To help clients explore issues related to retirement planning, counselors can ask questions such as:

1. When you think about retiring, how do you feel?
2. What does retirement mean to you?
3. Are you aware that many people are looking at retirement in new ways (as a process rather than an event)?
4. Are you experiencing physical health or working conditions that make it hard for you to continue in your current job?
5. Have you discussed possible work adaptations with your employer?
6. Have you reviewed your retirement benefits and return-to-work policies?
7. Have you received other benefits for which you are eligible?
8. Why would it be important or not important for you to engage in some paid work in the future?
9. When you review your career plan at this point in your life, what goals do you have?
10. How can you fulfill these in other than paid work situations?

The Case of Kate: A Maturing Adult

INTRODUCTION TO KATE

Kate called the office of my counseling practice to schedule an appointment to begin career counseling. On the phone, she said that she was in the middle of a very important life transition. She had resigned from the career position at a university research center and wanted to work on better aligning her career, that had become very dominant in her life, and other aspects of her life.

During the initial interview, I learned the following about Kate. She is 55 years old, has sustained a successful career for over 30 years, has been married to the same person for 30 years and has one child, a son, who is currently away at college.

Kate is from a family that valued education very highly. Both of her parents were college graduates and it was assumed that she would be too. Her mother had an active career as a teacher before marrying in her late 30's and having two children, an older brother Kevin, and Kate. Her mother did not work after she was married but held many volunteer leadership positions in the community. Her father was very intellectual but also had emotional problems and experienced very limited career success.

Kate went to the same state university that all of her family attended having no choice in this decision. She initially started to major in medical technology because her mother thought that it was a good career field for a woman. She hated the coursework and made her own decision in her junior year to major in English. After graduating, she taught for one year and returned to work on a master's degree in special education. She loved the work and the university atmosphere. She had a professor who was an important mentor. Through his encouragement, she completed a Ph.D.

During the next 25 years, she was successful in establishing herself in interesting work positions. She conducted research, directed several projects, and held increasingly demanding administrative and leadership positions. She did find it somewhat difficult to stay in a position for more 5-10 years but the job changes always resulted in better positions. In retrospect she recognized a pattern of getting a job, setting very demanding goals for herself, getting recognition from others, and then feeling exhausted and burdened by the job. Rather than being able to negotiate her expectations of herself and talk to others about the need to modify the workload, she tended to leave the position with hopes that the next time it would be different.

During her late 40's Kate started to experience some depression and sought therapy. Through therapy she realized a need to find more balance in her life. Specifically, she wanted to spend more time with her child who has then in high schools and her husband, to cultivate non-work friends, and to begin to explore some of her interests such as art that she had not had time to cultivate. By the time she came to career counseling, she had started to work on these new goals and was developing a greater commitment to them than to her previous career achievement goals. Although her health is good, she had recently gained some unwanted weight. As she said, "I just can't keep being the whiz kid any longer. In fact, I'm not a kid any more."

Kate was able to state some clear themes that she wanted to address with in counseling. First, she shared a dream she had where she realized that she had been living in a duplex but lived only on one side. She wanted to explore the other side of the duplex. She suspected that the unlived half was her creative side. She also mentioned that she was becoming interested in mentoring others and having a more direct helping role with growth. Kate mentioned with pleasure that a young professional had recently said that she was her professional grandmother because she had mentored the young students doctoral advisor.

As the initial interview ended, Kate asked, " Can you help me plan were I go from here with my life? I quit a stressful job to make time to balance my life, to explore the unused parts of myself, and to develop new life goals. I really want to be faithful to these goals. It just won't work to repeat the old patterns."

STRATEGIES FOR HELPING KATE BASED ON MATURE ADULT DEVELOPMENT

Developmental Theory suggests that in the later stages of life individuals become more pen, flexible and process-oriented. At these stages healthy individuals show an increased interest in supporting next generation (rather to focus primarily on personal achievement) and in developing a capacity to look back at life with satisfaction. This is a time when some physical diminishment is experienced and processed. People tend to reassess their involvement in various life roles and to reallocate time to various roles according to their emerging need to more toward wholeness.

Kate is on-track with this developmental picture. I note that she has expressed an interest in balancing her life, is finding satisfaction through giving to the next generation, and in committing to the process of making a successful transition toward more balance among life roles. I do note the dysfunctional work pattern of getting a job, setting very demanding goals for herself, getting recognition, feeling overwhelmed, and leaving.

Developmental career counseling approaches would include having Kate review life roles and set new goals in for activities and use of time within life roles. I would focus with Kate on her good feeling about being an effective mentor to others and help her to set new career goals for supporting the needs of the next generation. It would be helpful to Kate to complete a thorough review as her career history for the purposes of consolidating and accepting personal achievements to date. In a counseling session, we would review the history and talk about how this is time to accept both personal achievements as well and disappointments so that she can look back on her life with satisfaction. I would spend some time with Kate looking at her dysfunction career pattern of getting a job, setting very demanding goals for herself, getting recognition, feeling overwhelmed, and then withdrawing. I would check in with her early in each counseling session for evidence of whether the old pattern is emerging to sabotage her positive developmental course.

Transition Theory suggests that it is important to help clients understand that a transition is a process including an ending, a neutral zone, and a beginning. Some transitions are larger than others and encompass major shifts in life structures. A specific approach to helping clients with transition is the Schlossberg (1984) 4S approach of looking at the situation, self, support and strategies. Kate has just resigned from a job. This is a major transition because she is not only ending a job but try to establish and move of forward on new life goals. I would help support her in the "neutral zone" which is stressful and takes time. Keeping a daily journal or noting dreams, and discussing themes in counseling sessions would be a good way of listening to her inner urging about new directions. I would also encourage her to develop a specific transition plan including self-care strategies and use of friend and family support networks.

Relational Theories stress the need to honor both relational and separation goals. The goal is to learn to connect with others while maintaining strong sense of self. This is an important concept for Kate at this stage of life. She has a history of forgetting about her own personal needs and getting lost in work. In counseling we will check during each session in to see how Kate is doing on maintaining separation while connecting with others.

Cognitive-Developmental Theory views development as evolution of meaning making. Early in Kate's career her decisions were strongly tied to family. During her middle career years, she became increasingly self-directed. The current time, she has become somewhat rigidly tied to her career role but her recent resignation is an attempt to more toward a more open and flexible view of self that is not so rigidly ties to roles. In counseling, small experiments in taking small activities that take Kate outside of her comfort zone will be helpful. She might take some art classes to explore the creative part of herself that has not been developed. It will be very important to process her feelings during these experiments. For example, she may not like the feeling of being a novice but we can discuss that idea that being a learner and being in process has benefits that more rigid roles and self-definitions do not such as greater flexibility, more fun and increased creativity.

Narrative Orientation proposes that change occurs through telling your own story. Kate is at a point in life where reviewing her story to date will be important to helping her move toward the healthy future that she envisions. Counseling approaches discussed earlier including the review of career achievements, exploring dysfunctional work patterns, and setting more balanced life goals draw on the narrative approach. The narrative approach will require not only written life/career review but adequate time for Kate to "tell her story" during the counseling process.

Summary

This chapter has described the current social context in which mature adults will make career decisions, reviewed adult career development theories, proposed a set of career counseling goals for mature adults, and discussed career counseling approaches with mature adults.

Counselors who work with mature adults need to understand the changing context for work as well as the developmental changes that mature adults experience. The goal of career counseling is to assist with current career concerns in the context of life career development. It is important that career counseling help clients resolve current career concerns and also move toward more mature and flexible life structures. Career counseling can help clients understand the development process, including its cyclical nature, and view current concerns from an increased appreciation of the nature of growth and change. A major challenge at this point in history is for career counseling to help clients revise their assumptions about work in light of the changing workplace and changing attitudes toward aging.

Mature adults are being doubly challenged at this time to define and enact their own careers in the context of a rapidly changing workplace. One scenario is that adults will be unable to meet these challenges and will experience increasing levels of dysfunction and despair. A more positive scenario is that mature adults, with assistance from counselors and new workplace policies and structures, will develop the following characteristics that are the hallmarks of the mature adults who can respond proactively in the rapidly changing workplace (Miller, 1996). First, it is important to develop resilience — the capacity to adapt to a changing situation while maintaining and nurturing one's core self. Next, clients need to develop a balanced perspective that allows them to hold opposites with comfort. Since change has become a way of life, clients need to appreciate the cyclical nature of change and to understand that they will experience many change cycles throughout the life span. This includes a capacity to observe where they are in the cycle and honor current needs during each stage of transition. Finally, our clients need to develop a healthy sense of community that enables them to maintain closeness to others while also maintaining a strong sense of self.

References

American Association of Retired Persons. (2000). *American business and older employees: A summary of findings.* Washington, DC: AARP.

Bridges, W. (1991). *Managing transitions: Making the most of change.* Reading, MA: Addison-Wesley.

Cochran, L. (1994). What is a career problem? *The Career Development Quarterly, 42,* 204-215.

Collard, B. (1996). *Forces driving change in the workplace.* Columbus, OH: ERIC Clearinghouse on Adult, Career and Vocational Education, Ohio State University.

Curnow, B., & Fox, J. M. (1994). *Third age careers.* Brookfield, VT: Gower.

Erikson, E. (1959). *Identity and the life cycle.* New York: Norton.

Hudson, F. M. (1991). *The adult years: Mastering the art of self-renewal.* San Francisco: Jossey-Bass.

Hudson, F. M. (1996). Career plateau transitions in midlife, and how to manage them. In R. Feller & G. R. Walz (Eds.), *Career Transitions in Turbulent Times.* (pp. 257-266). Greensboro, NC: ERIC Counseling and Student Services Clearinghouse, University of North Carolina.

Jordan, J. S., Kaplan, A. G., Miller, J. B., Stiver, I. P, & Surrey, J. L. (1991). *Women's growth in connection.* New York: Guilford Press.

Kegan, R. (1982). *The evolving self: Problem and process in human development.* Cambridge: Harvard University Press.

Kegan, R. (1994). *In over our heads. The mental demands of modern life.* Cambridge, MA: Harvard University Press.

Krumboltz, J. D. (1993). Integrating career and personal counseling. *The Career Development Quarterly, 42,* 143-153.

Levinson, D. J. (1986). A conception of adult development. *American Psychologist. 41* (1), 3-13.

Loman, R. L. (1993). *Counseling and psychotherapy of work dysfunctions.* Washington, DC: American Psychological Association.

Marshall, A. (1997). Kegan's constructive developmental framework for adult career transitions. Paper presented at the NATCON conference, Ottawa, Canada. Available in full text through the International Career Development Library Website at www.icdl.uncg.edu.

Miller, J. V. (1996). A career counseling collage for the next century: Professional issues shaping career development. In R. Feller & G. R. Walz (Eds.), *Career Transitions in Turbulent Times*. (pp. 395-404). Greensboro, NC: ERIC Counseling and Student Services Clearinghouse, University of North Carolina.

Moen, P. (1998). Work in progress: The changing nature of work. *Issue Brief, 1*(1), 1-4. Cornell Employment and Family Careers Institute.

Osborne, L. (1996). Donald. E. Super: Yesterday and tomorrow. In R. Feller & G. R. Walz (Eds.), *Career Transitions in Turbulent Times*. (pp. 67-76). Greensboro, NC: ERIC Counseling and Student Services Clearinghouse, University of North Carolina.

Peck, T. A. (1986). Women's self-definition: From a different model? *Psychology of Women Quarterly, 10,* 274-284.

Reeves, P. M. (1999). Psychological development: Becoming a person. In M. C. Clark & R. S. Caffarella (Eds.), *An update on adult development theory: New ways of thinking about life course. New Directions for Adult and Continuing Education,* (Winter) *84,* 19-27. San Francisco: Jossey-Bass.

Rix, S. E. (1999). *Update on the older worker: 1998 – employment gains continue.* Washington, DC: American Association of Retired Persons.

Rossiter, M. (1999). Understanding adult development as narrative. In M. C. Clark & R. S. Caffarella, *An update on adult development theory: New ways of thinking about life course. New Directions for Adult and Continuing Education,* (Winter) *84,* 77-87. San Francisco: Jossey-Bass.

Savickas, M. (1991). Improving career time perspective. In D. Brown & L. Brooks (Eds.), *Career Counseling Techniques* (pp. 236-249). Needham Heights, MA: Allyn & Bacon.

Schlossberg, N. K. (1984). *Counseling adults in transition.* New York: Springer.

Schlossberg, N. K. (1996). A model of worklife transitions. In R. Feller & G. R. Walz (Eds.), *Career Transitions in Turbulent Times*. Greensboro, NC: ERIC Counseling and Student Services Clearinghouse, University of North Carolina.

Spokane, A. R. (1991). *Career interventions.* Englewood Cliffs, NY: Prentice-Hall.

Stein, D. (2000). *The new meaning of retirement.* ERIC Digest 217. Columbus, OH: ERIC Clearinghouse on Adult, Career and Vocational Education, Ohio State University.

Super, D. E. (1990). A life-span, life-space approach to career development. In D. Brown & Brooks, L. (Eds.), *Career Choice and Development.* (2nd ed., pp. 197-261). San Francisco, CA: Jossey-Bass.

Uccello, C. E., & Mix, S. E. (1998). Washington, D.C. American Association of Retired Persons.

Weckerle, K. A., & Shultz, S. (1999). Influences on bridge employment decisions among older USA workers. *Journal of Occupational Psychology, 72,* 317-329.

SECTION V:
DIVERSE SETTINGS

CHAPTER 16
Career Development: Extending The "Organizational Careers" Framework

Kerr Inkson
Massey University
New Zealand

Michael B. Arthur
Suffolk University

Business school researchers and management practitioners such as human resource managers have always taken a rather different view of careers from that taken by educational psychologists and career counselors. This is largely a matter of starting point. The classic psychological theories, whether developmental (e.g. Super, 1957; Levinson et al., 1978) or trait (e.g. Holland, 1973), take as their starting-point the *individual career actor,* and as their criteria of success the adjustment and satisfaction of that person as he or she moves through the career. In this view, career development is largely the responsibility of the individual, assisted perhaps by skilled guidance practitioners. Management researchers and practitioners, in contrast, see the welfare and performance of employing organizations as a key issue. In the managerial view, career planning and development involves two protagonists, the individual and the organization.

This does not mean there is no convergence between the two views. In both views the two protagonists may work in harmony, to mutual benefit. Psychological theorists and practitioners can see that a well-disposed organization, with good career development processes, can contribute enormously to satisfying and effective careers for individuals. Management advocates recognize that individuals who go about their careers in an orderly way and make good decisions have much to offer. Both groups tend to believe that people are more likely to experience ongoing career satisfaction when the organizations in which they work are performing well, and that effective career adjustment tends to lead to such performance. The difference is one of emphasis.

However, careers no longer have, if they ever did have, the degree of stability and predictability once associated with them. The employment environment is transformed ever more quickly, through globalization, restructuring, outsourcing, downsizing, technological advance, contingency employment and feminization of the workforce. The implicitly lifelong "vocations" around which Crites (1969) and Holland (1973) developed their theories are transformed and destabilized, and the predictable "seasons" into which Levinson et al. (1978) and others divided careers are disrupted by constant imperatives to career actors to re-invent themselves. Organizations appear ephemeral, and the relatively recently envisioned "organizational society" (Presthus, 1978) appears to be in retreat. These changes present challenges for both traditionally based and organizationally based views of career development (Sullivan, 1999).

In this chapter we trace the evolution and subsequent revision of organizational career thinking. We will then propose what we see as a more constructive alternative concerned with *inter*-organizational careers. We close by suggesting some new possibilities for career development relevant to both traditional and organizational thinkers.

Traditional "Organizational Career" Thinking

In the emergence of "organizational career" thinking since around the middle of the nineteenth century, four phases can be identified. An initial phase was the establishment of what may be called an "organizational imperative" concerning the dominance and influence of large private and public organizations in economic life. A second phase involved the subsequent articulation of theory on "organizational careers." The next phase saw the absorption of organizational thinking into mainstream ideas about human resource management. A final phase involved the subsequent decline of organizational career thinking and its underlying assumptions.

THE ORGANIZATIONAL IMPERATIVE

Historically, companies have rarely undertaken to sponsor career development out of a beneficent desire to assist their staff to have more satisfying working lives. They have done so in order to build more strongly committed workforces better able to meet the company's needs. They have recognized that money spent on the training and development of the workforce could be regarded as an investment, and sought to ensure their return on investment through the retention of the personnel involved. In the interests of company performance, they have sought to influence, or even control, the career decision-making of individuals. And they have offered rewards, such as employment security, social programs, promotion prospects, a sense of identity, and the kind of benefits which encouraged long-term, even lifetime, loyalty.

The traditional career arrangements are epitomized by the fabled 'salarymen' of large post-war Japanese manufacturing companies (Ouchi, 1981). These workers typically committed themselves to lifetime employment with one company, accepted implicit guarantees of security, waited patiently to be advanced by seniority-based promotion, made loyalty to the collective the primary principle of their careers, and effectively ceded control of those careers to the superior logic of the company's managers. In America and Europe, most large corporations of the post-1945 era adopted more meritocratic but basically similar philosophies and practices, particularly in relation to their white-collar workers. The success of such companies depended on strong socialization practices to engender loyalty, and central systems for the support and development of staff in a close relationship with company planning.

The loyalty-oriented companies were described, and implicitly criticized, in popular ethnographic works of the fifties and sixties, particularly Whyte's *The Organization Man* (1956) and Packard's *The Pyramid Climbers* (1964). Such books described a developing world of corporate careers characterized by a strong ethos of hierarchical control, individual conformity to organizational norms, and career development through status acquisition. These works preceded Galbraith's *The New Industrial State* (1971) which claimed that the large corporation held a distinct economic advantage over its smaller counterparts in its capacity for planning, and, implicitly at least, for the planning of its members' careers.

THE "ORGANIZATIONAL CAREERS" PERSPECTIVE

It was not until the middle 1970s that the term "career" began to figure substantially in the research or the curriculum of the business schools. However, the groundwork had been laid by the expansionist post-1945 environment, as well as by the incorporation of models of employee motivation asserting that "challenge," "achievement," or "recognition" (Herzberg, Mausner, & Snyderman, 1959) or more broadly "esteem" and "self-actualization" (Maslow, 197064) were central to effective employment practice. The new interest in careers was aided by the emergence of "organization development", ambiguously labeled to suggest that the development of the capabilities of both people and their employer organizations could be mutually beneficial (French & Bell, 1973). Almost all of this thinking presumed that the relationship between the employee and the organization was permanent.

However, the root models of employee motivation and organizational development left issues about work and time unresolved. What could be done if a succession of jobs up an organizational hierarchy did not connect with an employee's vision of his or her own future growth? How could people experience the benefits of variety in a single setting?

The business schools' interest was to explore these questions from both sides of the employment contract. The interest became manifest in the late 1970s in the publication of three related books: Hall's *Careers in Organizations* (1976); Van Maanen's *Organizational Careers: Some New Perspectives* (1977); and Schein's *Career Dynamics: Matching Individual and Organizational Needs* (1978). The emphasis on "organization," in contrast to other academics' emphasis on "vocation," signaled the business schools' interest in promoting individual careers as a means of advancing organizational as well as individual ends.

Much of the excitement of the emerging organizational career thinking stemmed from the hope its proponents held to extend traditional "vocational" career theory. The vision was that understanding careers – in particular, understanding how complex patterns of human decision making and development around the person's core identity intersect with the day-to-day experience of company life – provided new and exciting perspectives on the workings of organizations. With this new understanding, organizations could be managed better, to the mutual benefit of their owners, their managers, and their employees. Schein (1978, pp. 6-12), for example, urged managers to take a "career development perspective," because it would enable them to "manage the whole person," to "integrate the contributions of diverse and specialized resources.... (by) understanding that people... differ because of their career history." He further argued that managers "enlarge the concept of organizational development," an "facilitate the analysis and understanding of organization climate or culture."

Thus, managers could utilize truths derived from conventional psychological career theory, and could use organizational resources and know-how to develop applications designed to put the individual's career, rather than merely his or her momentary energies, into the service of the company. Furthermore, just as Hughes (1937) and others from the Chicago School of Sociology had seen the potential to treat careers as fundamental building-blocks of societal phenomena (Barley, 1989), so did Schein and others see career processes as being central to the understanding of wider organizational phenomena. This provided a potential key to effective managerial action, on systemic as well as individual issues.

Accordingly, theories of vocational fit developed to help employees find satisfying careers have their counterparts in company career systems. A first step is the selection of the new recruit according to the company's criteria. Thereafter, note is taken of concepts of career and life 'stages' as companies plan the continuing development, assignment, and promotion of their staff or try to enable employees to continue to be productive through any career 'plateau'. The observation that people whose careers are deemed 'successful' often have important older mentors at an early stage in their career (Kram, 1985) pushes companies to encourage internal mentoring. "Dual career ladders" (Dalton & Thompson, 1986) and even "jungle gyms" with a whole variety of ladders, not all vertical (Gunz, 1989) are seen as making creative use of the organizational hierarchy while accommodating a range of employee preferences.

ABSORPTION INTO HUMAN RESOURCE MANAGEMENT

Schein (1978, p. 191) provided an early model of a "human resource planning and development system" which is still cited in contemporary texts (Greenhaus et al., 2000, p. 403). Schein's model intertwines organizational activities such as human resource planning and workforce assessment, with individual activities such as self-assessment and personal career planning. Through a series of "matching processes" – performance appraisal, talent identification, jointly negotiated development programs etc. – an appropriate symbiosis may be arrived at in which both individual and organizational needs are accommodated to mutual benefit.

Mainstream human resource management absorbed Schein's perspective. This acknowledges the individual's own interests in career self-management, at the same time as the descriptor "human resources" identifies the sponsoring company as a co-participant in, and a beneficiary of, the management involved. Heneman et al.'s (1989) view is representative of this kind of approach:

> The duration and pattern of individuals' organizational careers are shaped by organizations' internal staffing decisions which determine the nature of the career opportunities that are (or are not) offered. But, of course, individuals have much to say about their own careers, partly through the action they take to develop or create career opportunities for movement and advancement and partly through their responses to the various opportunities that materialize (p. 403).

Heneman et al. (1989) elaborate that from a typical human resource management perspective, "the moment an individual accepts a job" with an employer "his or her organizational career begins." They see real advantages to the company of "a comprehensive effort (at) being systematic ... in planning employees' careers (and) facilitating career moves and adjustment." These advantages are the easier ⚡ attraction of good employees, reduced undesirable turnover, higher performance through better job matching, and better outcomes for minorities. Although career planning may be viewed as an individual responsibility, "there is much that organizations can do to help."

Heneman et al. (1989) provide a visual 'organization chart' example of employees in an insurance company progressing through various clerical jobs to the position of "assistant administrative supervisor". It appears from this description that the potential usefulness of career planning is confined to stable organizations, most likely with long hierarchies, where there are job descriptions within which employees are encouraged to stay, and where historical patterns of career progression will continue to be valid. Writing with the benefit of some twelve years hindsight, it is easy for us to question how long the kind of positions and hierarchies described in the above example might prevail.

Succession planning of the above type, and formal programs governing such human resource management activities as training and development, performance evaluation, and advancement, provide a basis for managers to exercise considerable influence on employees' careers. The philosophy involved is reflected in the transition in terminology from "people" to "employees" to "personnel" to "human resources." However, the term "human resource" depersonalizes. "Resource" means "a stock or supply that can be drawn on" *(Concise Oxford Dictionary)*. Its use in the context of organizational management suggests that the person is part of the company's stock, which can be drawn on, but also developed, for organizational ends. In such a context, career development appears to be the long-term development (or sometimes non-development, if that is in the company's interests) of employees for the primary purpose of achieving the company's objectives. Schein's ideal of "managing the whole person" seems endangered.

THE APPARENT DEMISE OF ORGANIZATIONAL CAREERS

Since the middle 1980s, this relatively comfortable view of careers unfolding within a single and largely benevolent corporate setting has been jolted. In many countries, the business landscape has been changed by downsizing (reducing staff numbers), delayering (reducing the number of hierarchical levels), outsourcing (putting out to competitive contract work which was previously done by company employees), and contingency employment (through temporary help agencies). At the same time, globalization has altered international patterns of employment, information technology has displaced traditional skills and required new ones, new emphases on 'multi-skilling' and teamwork have abolished traditional demarcations around jobs, occupations, and professions, and the feminization of the workforce has introduced employees who needed new, more flexible patterns of work.

The effect of organizational restructuring has been to increase involuntary turnover and inter-company movements, to de-stabilize workforces, and to seriously threaten the continuing existence of the organizational career (Hall, 1996). In addition, the bonds of loyalty which many employees had felt towards their employers had in many cases been severed, and the new generation of employment relationships are characterized by psychological contracts which are "transactional" rather than "relational" (Rousseau, 1995).

Some of these forces were may be seen as temporary, as contributions to company "re-engineering" (Hammer & Champy, 1993) which, once achieved, could perhaps allow a company to settle once more into a more stable configuration. However other forces were may be seen as enduring, as contributions to the "flexible specialization" considered necessary for organizational health, and to the emergence of adaptive inter-company networks to challenge the presumed power and industry leadership of large corporations.

The new challenge to organizational career thinking was epitomized by the development in the 1980s of Silicon Valley (e.g. Rogers & Larsen, 1984, Delbecq & Weiss, 1988). To some observers, this burgeoning high-technology region around San Jose and Stanford University was more than a region hosting successful corporations such as Hewlett-Packard. It was seen in addition as a successful alternative model of industrial organizing, in which for its participant firms and workers the host industry region, or cluster, is pre-eminent. Silicon Valley employees, typically highly-qualified experts in aspects of the semiconductor industry, showed new patterns of high mobility between employers and projects in careers based on constant new learning (Saxenian, 1996). Faced with such rapid turnover, Silicon Valley employers needed news ways to understand not just their employees' careers, but their whole "human resource" situation. We will return to this example later.

The 1980s were turbulent years for organizational career theory. They began with an endorsement from the hugely influential *In Search of Excellence* (Peters & Waterman, 1982, p. 77) that the person's "need to control one's destiny" obliged the organization to provide employment security. However, no sooner had the world heard the message than the first author of the "excellence" tract reversed himself, citing "an enormous error" in his celebration of large manufacturing firms over smaller, more adaptive alternatives (Peters, 1987). In another remarkable switch, strategic management guru Michael Porter turned from thinking about the "competitive advantage" of the single firm (Porter, 1985) to the "competitive advantage of nations" (Porter, 1990) and of industry regions of interdependent companies. A further reversal came from long-standing management guru Peter Drucker. In his classic 1954 work "The Practice of Management" Drucker had insisted that it was necessary for companies to take responsibility for their employees' welfare. Forty years on, Drucker (1994) volunteered that he now considered taking such responsibility impractical, and claiming to do so immoral. These represented major challenges to the traditional management focus on "the organization," and consequently to the primacy of organizational careers.

The Revision of Organizational Career Thinking

What can be done with traditional organizational career thinking, and its associated human resource systems, to adapt or supplement them to fit the new situation? Recent management literature suggests four overlapping responses, concerned with affirming the organization's "core competencies," broadening interventions to effect managerial influence through organizational career development programs, developing new models of career, and meeting the obligation to provide employees with new learning.

AFFIRMING "CORE COMPETENCIES"

A first response has been to attempt to shore up the company-centric ground which Michael Porter vacated at the end of the 1980s. In particular, Hamel and Prahalad (1989, p. 66) lamented that in the "Silicon Valley" approach to innovation "the only role for top managers (was) to retrofit their corporate strategy to the entrepreneurial successes that emerged from below." In contrast, these authors saw a role for top managers in shaping the "strategic intent" of their companies and nurturing the "core competencies" through which that intent could be pursued Hamel & Prahalad, 1994). Such initiatives led to a growing emphasis on the skills and knowledge of key staff, whereby the ability to acquire, develop and deploy appropriate people was seen as a major source of competitive advantage. In contrast to earlier approaches which stressed business strategy in terms of the company's responses to external business conditions, such as market opportunities and competition, the new approach took a "resource-based view of the firm" (Wright, McMahan, & McWilliams, 1994), and identified the workforce as key.

In the long-term, these competencies could be shaped and increased by means of the development which employees underwent on their company's behalf. The focus was on competencies which were "firm-specific, embedded in a firm's history and culture, and (generating) ... organizational knowledge" (Lado & Wilson, 1994, p. 599). As far as careers were concerned, there were clear advantages for organizations in fostering the organizational careers of loyal company employees in whom the desired competencies could be deliberately inculcated, and which could be altered as the company's needs changed. In this scenario the career is again cast as a consequence of *organizational* goals, even though those goals are seen as more dynamic than before. Recent claims to foster "the individualized organization" Bartlett & Ghoshal, 1999) remain concerned with the collective success of supposedly individualized agendas.

BROADENING CAREER DEVELOPMENT INTERVENTIONS

A second response to the new situation has been to broaden the basis of company interventions in individual career development. The upheaval of recent years has moved discussion of career management in organizations toward a smorgasbord rather than a set menu, embodying traditional "organizational career" thinking as far as possible, but modifying it to reflect the experience of employment turbulence. Contemporary approaches suggest a range of organizational "interventions" which the company can provide as either optional or required components of its human resource management, often as free or subsidized opportunities. Arnold (1997) provides a list of the most popular items on the organizational career development table (Table 1).

These interventions consist largely of:

(a) information about the organization and possible career opportunities within it;

(b) voluntary programs for participants to apply structured ways of thinking to their careers;

(c) access to persons skilled at facilitating career development;

(d) on-the-job and off-the-job development opportunities.

TABLE 1
CAREER MANAGEMENT INTERVENTIONS
IN ORGANIZATIONS

Internal vacancy notification. Information about jobs available in the organization, normally in advance of any external advertising, and with some details of preferred experience, qualifications, and a job description.

Career paths. Information about the sequences of jobs that a person can do, or competencies he or she can acquire, in the organization. This should include details of how high in the organization any path goes, the kinds of inter-department transfers that are possible, and perhaps the skills/experience required to follow various paths.

Career workbooks. These consist of questions and exercises designed to guide individuals in determining their strengths and weaknesses, identifying job and career opportunities, and identifying necessary steps for reaching their goals.

Career planning workshops. Cover some of the same ground as workbooks, but offer more chance for discussion, feedback from others, information about organization-specific opportunities and policies. May include psychometric testing.

Computer-assisted career management. Various packages exist for helping employees to assess their skills, interests and values, and translate these into job options. Sometimes these options are customized to a particular organization. A few packages designed for personnel or manpower planning also include some career-relevant facilities.

Individual counseling. Can be done by specialists from inside or outside the organization, or by line managers who have received training. May include psychometric testing.

Training and educational opportunities. Information and financial support about, and possibly delivery of, courses in the organization or outside it. These can enable employees to update, retrain or deepen their knowledge in particular fields. In keeping with the notion of careers involving sequences, training in this context is not solely to improve the performance in a person's present job.

Personal development plans (PDPs). These often arise from the appraisal process and other sources such as development centers. PDPs are statements of how a person's skills and knowledge might appropriately develop, and how this development could occur, in a given timescale.

Career action centers. Resources such as literature, videos, and CD ROMS and perhaps more personal inputs such as counseling available to employees on a drop-in basis.

Development centers. Like assessment centers in that participants are assessed on the basis of their performance in a number of exercises and tests. However, development centers focus more on identifying a person's strengths, weaknesses and styles for the purpose of development, not selection.

Mentoring programs. Attaching employees to more senior ones who act as advisers, and perhaps also as advocates, protectors and counselors.

Succession planning. The identification of individuals who are expected to occupy key posts in the future, and who are used to experiences which prepare them appropriately.

Job assignment/rotation. Careful use of work tasks to help a person stay employable for the future, and an organization to benefit from the adaptability of staff.

Outplacement. This may involve several interventions listed above. Its purpose is to support people who are leaving the organization to clarify and implement plans for their future.

It lies beyond the scope of this paper to comment in detail on the incidence and efficacy of such techniques. However, the central challenge for any organizational career initiative seems clear. It is to build internal practices that effectively interface with the outside pace of economic and technological change.

The same challenge applies at the level of the individual. At this level, contemporary business school perspectives still suggest a conventional wisdom that there is a "desired career goal" (Greenhaus, Callanan, & Godschalk, 2000, p. 25) and that individual career management involves a "problem-solving, decision-making process." However, factors such as new educational opportunities, new technologies, new industries, and the disappearance of geographical and distance barriers to information create new and shifting challenges for many of today's workers. These challenges make career problems harder to define, decisions more complex, and fixed goals almost impossible to delineate. Perhaps, even at the individual level, more flexible conceptualizations of career management are necessary.

DEVELOPING NEW MODELS

The third response from the business schools was the development of new models of career that challenged the conventional wisdom. For example, Kanter (1989) predicted the potentially terminal decline of the "bureaucratic" career model based on status acquisition within organizations and the corresponding growth of an "entrepreneurial" model based on "adding value" either within or between organizations. Another response – led, coincidentally, by the second author of *In Search of Excellence* – was the encouragement of organizations to promote "career resilience" in employees and to recognize the legitimacy of their often inter-organizational career aspirations (Waterman, Waterman, & Collard, 1994).

A further response was the conceptualization of "boundaryless careers" (Arthur & Rousseau, 1996) offering an alternative career theory that seeks to take account of the new economic environment, particularly the loss of loyalty to employing companies (Altman & Post, 1996), the growth of career mobility between organizations (Nicholson & West, 1988), the more flexible career behavior of the new generation of 'knowledge' workers (Lee & Maurer, 1997), and a growing recognition of the importance of wide networks as a means of career development (Burt, 1997). Boundaryless careers are both an outcome and a cause of the increasing dissolution and permeability of external and internal organizational boundaries. Boundaryless careers are made possible by the willingness of people to cross boundaries – between jobs, between occupations, between organizations, and between industries. They are in contrast to the organizational career emphases on hierarchical movement and the acquisition of company-relevant competencies, and to the occupational career emphasis on continuing specialization within narrow professional or trade competencies. The boundaryless career actor seeks career development informed by a much wider range of opportunities.

The influential organization theorist Karl Weick (1996) extended the argument further by applying the principle of "enactment" to career development. In traditional organization theory, organizations are considered to be continually constrained by larger forces in their economic environments. Enactment theory holds that the organization enacts itself, and in so doing enacts the environment of which it is part. Applying the same principle to the individual, Weick's thinking moves us from considering the individual career as a predestined outcome of wider organizational forces, to understanding that individuals, in their career behavior, enact the organizations in which they work. An organization can thus be considered as the enacted product of a complex system of interacting careers – a nice reversal of conventional business thinking.

THE LEARNING OBLIGATION

The fourth response to the new situation has been for companies to recognize that they have a social responsibility to provide employees with the opportunities to learn broadly, and beyond conventional organizational curricula. A major problem posed by organizational career thinking for career actors is the contrast between organizationally-imposed limitations on new learning and skill acquisition, and the wider learning requirements of the new economic environment. In this environment, success rather than advancement becomes the criterion on which a career is judged (Zabusky & Barley, 1996), and employability rather than employment is crucial (Kanter, 1989). Those who can best preserve their employability are those who have a broad range of learning, those whose learning is portable between settings, and those who have the flexibility to learn quickly in any new setting. Any single organization has natural restrictions in the number and range of settings it can provide, and this puts all organizations at a disadvantage in trying to retain the loyalty of the 'savvy' employee.

Waterman, Waterman, and Collard (1994), Parker and Inkson (1999), and others argue that in order to cater for the new types of learning-oriented employees, organizations must increasingly see themselves as hosting learning rather than hosting employment. Traditional practices include restricting discussion of individual career progression to intra-company moves, encouraging specialization, and supporting only staff development which can be shown to be directly related to the needs of the organization. These may be counter-productive because they give employees the message that the company is not interested in their careers. To engender a new sort of loyalty, the organization must accept that, in the long-term, most employees will go elsewhere. In the short- and medium-term, however, they may be encouraged to stay with an organization that in matters such as new project opportunities, formal support for development, and career discussion and mentoring, shows real concern for their real career needs. Paradoxically, the open support and acknowledgement of the individual's potential mobility may be the first step in strengthening his or her loyalty to the organization.

However, the loyalty of individuals is changing. Increasingly they see their loyalty as being to themselves and their own development and performance; to specific projects, particularly those with good learning opportunities; to the changing teams which undertake them; and to host industries in which they can gather expertise across a wider range of settings. Imaginative organizations can find ways of responding to capitalize on these new loyalties: valuing individuals for the excellence of their short-term contribution rather than for the continuation of their employment; encouraging project organization; ensuring that excellent but mobile individuals are encouraged to pass on and institutionalize their learning before they leave; and being positive non-defensive contributors in industry labor markets.

To return to the example of Silicon Valley, it seems that companies in the region gained a developing competitive advantage over those from Boston's more conservative Route 128, where companies such as DEC continued to attempt to operate a traditional organizationally-based human resource and career management system (Saxenian, 1996). The entrepreneurial companies of Silicon Valley, in contrast, understood that their competitive advantage did not lie only in their current labor resource, but in the resource of the industry region as a whole, and the norms of career mobility and inter-organizational learning on which they could capitalize. Organizational learning in rapid-turnover situations is essential, but organizational learning may in the end be less important than *regional* learning or (semi-conductor) *industry* learning. Porter's (1990) inquiries into national competitive advantage offered widespread evidence of Silicon Valley look-alikes - regional clusters of firms – and region-specific rather than company-specific skill sets, and therefore careers.

Working with Inter-Organizational Careers

Organizations may still want to invest in people's careers, and people may still want to invest in organizations' success, but neither party can sensibly assume that the employment relationship will last forever. How, then, can we work with the employment relationship as a temporary one, which nevertheless brings long-term advantages to both parties? Can career development by organizations, for organizational purposes, benefit individuals who have *inter*-organizational careers? Can those benefits in turn benefit employing organizations, even when people persistently move to new employment?

In the last section of this chapter, we will describe our own recent engagement with these questions. What follows has an autobiographical flavor and may seem partisan, reflecting as it does our own struggles to make sense of the new career arrangements. Our purpose is to share our enthusiasm that more liberating and viable models of individual-organization engagement are coming into view. Individuals and organizations still need each other, but the way they need each other brings about new possibilities.

THREE "WAYS OF KNOWING"

By the early 1990s not only were public perceptions about career mobility changing (Arthur, 1994), but it was evident that such mobility had been a feature of organizational careers for some time: only the extent had changed (Nicholson & West, 1988; Inkson, 1995). Moreover, substantial proportions of employment changes were undertaken voluntarily. Some organizations saw benefits in recruiting people who brought career experience from outside, and some people saw benefits in taking their career experience to a new organization. These observations appeared to challenge the cozy assumptions of organizational career theory, and to invite a new approach.

One point of departure is the emerging work on "core competencies," already cited. However, instead of asking what is particular to any one organization, we can ask what is *generalizable* among organizations. Core competencies can be categorized in three overlapping arenas. These are:

- a company's *culture* – its mission, values, beliefs, and strategic purpose;
- a company's *know-how* – its accumulated skills, expertise, and areas of special competence; and
- a company's *networks* – its relationships with suppliers, customers, other companies and others (Hall, 1992).

The career actor has the opportunity to align his or her career investments with the organization's competencies, but to emphasize transferable rather than company-specific investments. This thinking provides a framework that seems helpful to understand career dynamics beyond rather than within single organizational settings.

Corresponding to the organization's competencies, DeFillippi and Arthur (1996) conceptualize three types of individual competency:

- *Knowing-why* (corresponding to company culture): the ever-changing energies, values, interests, motivations and personal circumstances and goals which an individual brings to work;
- *Knowing-how* (corresponding to company know-how): the individual abilities, qualifications, skills, and expertise, accumulated as a result of career and life experience;
- *Knowing-whom* (corresponding to company networks): the reputation and networks that an individual develops within and beyond the employing company.

In our original conception we called these ways of knowing "career competencies" to relate them to the matching framework of company competencies. However, our emphasis on transferable skills made our conception distinct from other views that used similar language, views concerned with "job competencies" or "managerial competencies." Those views not only tend to focus on firm-specific competencies, but also to emphasize "knowing-how" over "knowing-why" and "knowing-whom." In our more recent work (Arthur, Inkson, & Pringle, 1999; Inkson & Arthur, in press) we describe the three ways of knowing as repositories for the accumulation and investment of *career capital* on which we elaborate below. We further emphasize not only the importance of all three ways of knowing, but also the way that they may interact with, and stimulate, each other as the career progresses (see Figure 1).

EXAMPLE: GAINING "OVERSEAS EXPERIENCE"

As an illustration of the above framework, we offer a recent study of the contrast between company-sponsored "expatriate assignments" and the personal pursuit of "overseas experience." In a 1997 paper we noted that the phenomenon of working abroad, much studied in business research, was invariably conceived as "expatriate assignment" – the organizational practice of assigning corporate employees to temporary overseas postings and projects (Inkson, Arthur, Pringle, & Barry, 1997). However, an alternative conception – familiar among Australians and New Zealanders - is to see such work as "overseas experience," – a term for people traveling on their own volition to live in other countries.

In the study and practice of expatriate assignment, the career is considered an organizational career, the property of the company, and an aspect of its human resource management. Yet our data suggested that the constrained posting of an individual to a predetermined overseas position with a clear company job description (an organizational career move) was less common and arguably less beneficial than the spontaneous habit of young people worldwide in going overseas to see the world and gathering new career experiences along the way (a boundaryless career move).

The working conditions of broadly directed, improvisational, 'do-it-yourself' travel make it a fine analogue for the ambiguous, complex working world of the twenty-first century. Although the young may view travel as a form of personal and cultural stimulation and enrichment, it may inadvertently also provide an important career development activity. "Knowing-why" – the urge to travel, to cross boundaries – inevitably facilitates the development of "knowing-how" skills in the new cross-cultural career experiences the traveler engages in, and new "knowing-whom" networks of overseas contacts and fellow travelers. Thus, self-determined travel adds to the stock of knowing-why, knowing-how and knowing-whom with which the travelers return, and which they invest anew in the companies, industries, and society in which they now work.

The example of overseas travel demonstrates how the traditional organizational perspective limits the perception of careers as potential contributors to individual, industry, and societal welfare. We believe this perspective also handicaps the organization. In the case of organizational approaches to overseas travel, for example, attention is directed to controlling human initiative (typically via "strategic human resource management") rather than to capitalizing on the self-initiated career-relevant learning which most travelers engage in spontaneously. In contrast, some firms do identify with Weick's enactment perspective, and appreciate the contributions that could stem from the career experience people might bring. For example, a prominent New Zealand law firm tells exceptional but travel-hungry job applicants "You have a job, now come back in ten years time and tell us what you will make if it."

FIGURE 1
THREE WAYS OF KNOWING AND THE
ACCUMULATION OF CAREER CAPITAL

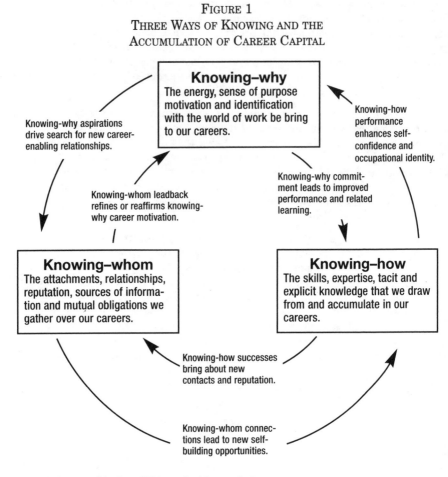

Source: Inkson and Arthur, 2001, used with permission.

INVESTING "CAREER CAPITAL"

Self-directed overseas travel was but one example of career practices that may be suitable for the new Millennium. In these practices, described in more detail in our book *The New Careers* (Arthur, Inkson, & Pringle, 1999), idiosyncrasy is valued above convention, discontinuity above continuity, and improvisation above planning. Many career actors design their own apprenticeships rather than following the dictates of organizational, academic, or professional curricula. They offer their services for low pay in situations where they believe the learning will exceed the cost. They volunteer for 'crisis' projects where the work is hard but the accumulation of career experience great. They choose their own mentors from a range of settings rather than accepting assigned mentors from organizational settings. They recycle the 'exploration' phase of the career so that it does not cease at age 30 as older theories suggest, but continues to inform their career choices throughout their lives. When their learning is stifled by circumstance, they rattle the bars in appeal for new learning opportunities, or they leave the company in search of better.

Career experiences potentially provide new career capital (Inkson & Arthur, in press). At any given time, career investors may choose from different investment opportunities – educational programs, jobs, companies, occupations, industries, personal interests, even family activities – to add to their career capital. The career theory and counselling of the past have encouraged individuals to make substantial investments in the 'secure" institutions of occupation, profession, or company. Those who make good choices and monitor their learning acquisitions are often still able to grow their investments in these conventional ways.

But others may choose not to invest all available resources in a single company in a specialized industry (or a narrow or obsolescent occupation) whose returns are in currencies not easily tradeable elsewhere. They may feel that to cultivate an organizational career is to overexpose oneself in a small market sector. A career that is mobile between different companies, industries, or types of work may seem a better spread of risk, as well as a means whereby asset gains can be more quickly made.

One caveat which must be entered to the "career capitalism" scenario is that like all market models it is subject to cyclic peaks and troughs. At times of industry boom, career capital may inflate in perceived value, encouraging mobility either within or outside the company as investors seek an even better return on their resources of scarce knowledge. At times of recession, force of circumstance may drive them to more conservative behavior, and they may feel content to hold their position with a current employer; or they may be displaced, and may struggle to find suitable opportunities in which to place their depleted capital.

The world of boundaryless careers and career capital investment opportunities does not bring positive results for all. Among those who may have difficulty in adjusting to the new arrangements are those who have already made substantial investments in traditional careers (Hirsch & Shanley, 1996), older workers seeking stability rather than turbulence in their careers (Carson & Carson, 1997), and low-skill workers hitherto protected to some extent by traditional arrangements. As far as gender is concerned, the jury is still out, but there are suggestions that womens' more flexible career expectations may enable them to work more effectively in the newer organizational forms (Fletcher, 1996).

The notion of the mobile individual investing in the company rather than the company investing in the immobile individual changes the psychology of the situation. It reflects and accentuates the shift of responsibility for career development from the company-investor in employees to the employee-investor in companies. The individual will appraise the career development opportunities afforded by the company from a viewpoint that may be very different from the company's careful plan. A range of career self-development strategies may result that are quite different from the political organizational-climbing recommended by traditional organizational career protagonists (Inkson, 2000).

PROJECT-BASED LEARNING

The imagery of firms waiting for people to join up and bring their career capital with them asks new questions of organizational managers. What is their role in the new order? As indicated earlier, in a world of temporary rather than permanent jobs, an important answer may be to offer good projects and use those projects well.

Evidence from the independent film-making industry, Silicon Valley and elsewhere is that in some industries, possibly an increasing number, projects may be more important than permanent firms. For example it is only a modest exaggeration to suggest that independent film-making provides for a healthy industry without the existence of any permanent firms. Films get made one project at a time, and upon completion the projects and their film-making firms are disbanded. The workers – enriched by their experience and sustained by industry rather than company networks – move on to new challenges (Jones, 1996; DeFillippi & Arthur, 1998). The same may be argued for Silicon Valley projects.

The ideal-typical Silicon Valley worker is one who completes his or her project duties and moves on, cross-fertilizing new projects and the industry region with the learning gained from previous projects. Moreover, this kind of behavior is not seen as disloyal. Rather, loyalty is vested in the project, and industry networks can be very harsh on people who get a reputation for moving on before their work is done (Saxenian, 1996). Arguably, world-wide moves to more flexible and temporary company and project structures, collaborative industry regions, and outsourcing to small niche ventures and contract employees, will make the film industry and Silicon Valley scenarios more and more common.

Projects have traditionally been viewed as challenges in efficiency - to finish the project on time, under budget, and with the anticipated product or service outcomes. However, in a knowledge society projects may be as important for their learning potential, for both individuals and organizations. For the individual, projects provide a distinctive opportunity for the investment and upgrading of career capital, where the project and fellow project participants provide a rich source for further knowing-why, knowing-how and knowing-whom career capital accumulations. In the ideal case, the project team becomes a temporary "community of practice" (ref.Arthur, DeFillippi, & Lindsay, 2001) where members invest in one-another's learning as the project unfolds, and where communal attachments often endure for long after the project is finished. Thus, individually-driven, project-based careers seem a straightforward extension of the "career capital" argument.

Projects also represent potential episodes for rapid organizational learning. Consider for example the growing ranks of mobile project professionals. As organizational 'cores' of long-term loyalists decline, and 'peripheries' of short-term consultants, contractors, and contingent workers grow, more and more individuals must construct their careers not on a 'job-to-job' basis but on a 'project-to-project' or 'opportunity-to-opportunity' basis. Inkson et al. (2000) show that the careers of such workers – at least where they are skilled professionals - are typically informed by an explicit philosophy of personal learning. In this respect, independent project contractors may well be "prototypes of the 21st century worker" (Inkson et al., 2001, p. 259). For the organization, the apparent costs as these workers take away the stock of learning they have acquired in the organization are offset by the benefits of the varied learning and flexibility which they bring with them, and the incorporation of their new knowing-why, knowing-how, and knowing-whom in the developing process of organizational learning. However, there is a danger, if such an approach is taken too far, of allowing flexibility to be valued at the expense of performance (Tsui et al., 1997). To gain the full benefit of the new situation, organizations need to conceptualize themselves in new ways – not as controllers of skilled resources, but as progenitors of open-ended collaborative behavior (Miles & Snow, 1996).

Summary

At the outset of the early work on organizational careers, Hall (1976) had this to say to the individual career actor:

If you don't care where you go, the organization you work for will be only too happy to determine your moves for you. Having personal plans and goals is one important way to reduce the control of the organization over the management of your life (Hall, 1976, pp. 179-180).

A quarter-century later we would concur, but would add that in the new environment, having firm "plans and goals" may be too difficult, or even inappropriate, in the contemporary era. The emphasis needs to be not on plans but on proactive individual behavior. The key may be to stay adaptive, and to control one's own destiny through persistent, self-directed learning. In a world of increasingly mobile careers, organizational career mechanisms are better looked at not as "one-stop-career-shops" offering secure pathways and progressions within a secure corporate framework, but as means for individual career actors to acquire self-selected career development benefits.

It may be inevitable for organizations to attempt to secure competitive advantage and future staffing by expropriating all or part of an individual's career. However, this can have potentially negative outcomes for all parties. Individuals may develop too narrow a career focus or become over-dependent. Meanwhile organizations, the professions, industry, or society as a whole may miss out on the increased learning that comes from cross-fertilization across boundaries. Moreover, we are beginning to see how organizations can benefit from this cross-fertilization through their sponsorship of learning activities, including the sponsorship of project-based learning that is also good for the host industry and the project participants' careers.

In the new environment, organizations need the autonomous enterprise of mobile individuals, the experience and skill they have gained in their multiple work encounters, and the networks and links that they bring with them. Individuals need the sense of larger purpose, the opportunities for practice, innovation, and self-development, and the new contacts that organizations can bring. Both companies and people need projects to serve as learning episodes. While the opportunities for companies to control members' careers may never have been less, the opportunities for company-to-person career collaboration may never have been greater.

References

Altman, B. W., & Post, J. E. (1996). Beyond the social contract: an analysis of the executive view at twenty-five larger organizations. In D. T. Hall (Ed.) *The Career is Dead: Long Live the Career.* San Francisco: Jossey-Bass.

Arnold, J. M. (1997). *Managing Careers into the Twenty-First Century.* London: Paul Chapman.

Arthur, M. B. (1994). The boundaryless career: A new perspective for organizational inquiry. *Journal of Organizational Behavior, 15,* 295-306.

Arthur, M. B., DeFillippi, R. J., & Lindsay, V. (2001). Careers, communities and industry evolution: Links to complexity theory. *International Journal of Innovation Management, 5*(2), 239-255.

Arthur, M. B., Inkson, K., & Pringle, J. K. (1999). *The New Careers: Individual Action and Economic Change*. London: Sage.

Arthur, M. B., & Rousseau, D. M. (Eds.). (1996). *The Boundaryless Career: A New Employment Principle for a New Organizational Era*. New York: Oxford.

Barley, S. R. (1989). Careers, identities, and institutions: the legacy of the Chicago School of Sociology. In M. B. Arthur, D. T. Hall, & B. S. Lawrence (Eds.), *Handbook of Career Theory* (pp. 41-65). Cambridge: Cambridge University Press.

Bartlett, C. A., & Ghoshal, S. (1999). *The Individualized Corporation*. New York: HarperBusiness.

Burt, R. S. (1997). The contingency value of social capital. *Administrative Science Quarterly, 42*, 339-365.

Carson, K. D., & Carson, P. P. (1997). Career entrenchment: a quiet march toward occupational death? *Academy of Management Executive, 11*, 62-75.

Crites, J. O. (1969). *Vocational Psychology*. New York: McGraw-Hill.

Dalton, G., & Thompson, P. (1986). *Novations: Strategies for Career Development*. Glenview, IL: Scott Foresman.

DeFillippi, R. J., & Arthur, M. B. (1996). The boundaryless career: a competency-based perspective. In M. B. Arthur & D. M. Rousseau (Eds.), *The Boundaryless Career: A New Employment Principle for a New Organizational Era* (pp. 116-131). New York: Oxford.

DeFillippi, R. J., & Arthur, M. B. (1998). Paradox in project-based enterprise: The case of film-making. *California Management Review, 40*(2), 125-139.

Delbecq, A., & Weiss, J. (1988). The business culture of Silicon Valley: Is it a model for the future. In J. Weiss (Ed.), *Regional Cultures, Managerial Behavior and Entrepreneurship*. New York: Quorum.

Drucker, P. F. (1954). *The Practice of Management*. New York: Harper & Row.

Drucker, P. F. (1994, November). The age of social transformation. *The Atlantic Monthly*, 53-80.

Fletcher, J. K. (1996). A relational approach to the protean worker. In D. T. Hall & Associates (Eds.), *The Career is Dead: Long Live the Career* (pp. 105-131). San Francisco: Jossey-Bass.

French, W. L., & Bell, C. H. (1973). *Organizational Development*. Englewood Cliffs, NJ: Prentice-Hall.

Galbraith, J. K. (1971). *The New Industrial State* (2nd ed.). Boston: Houghton Mifflin.

Greenhaus, J. H., Callanan, G. A., & Godschalk, V. M. (2000). *Career Management* (3rd ed.). Fort Worth: Dryden Press.

Gunz, H. P. (1989). *Careers and Corporate Cultures: Managerial Mobility in Large Corporations*. Oxford: Basil Blackwell.

Hall, D. T. (1976). *Careers in Organizations*. Pacific Pallisades, CA: Goodyear.

Hall, D. T. (1996). *The Career is Dead: Long Live the Career*. San Francisco: Jossey-Bass.

Hall, R. (1992). The strategic analysis of intangible resources. *Strategic Management Journal, 13*, 135-44.

Hamel, G., & Prahalad, C. K. (1989). Strategic intent. *Harvard Business Review, 67*(3), 63-76.

Hamel, G., & Prahalad, C. K. (1994) *Competing for the Future*. Boston, MA: Harvard.

Hammer, M., & Champy, J. (1993). *Re-engineering the Corporation: A Manifesto for Business Revolution*. New York: Harper Business.

Heneman, H. G., Schwab, D. P., Fossum, J. A., & Dyer, L. D. (1989). *Personnel/Human Resource Management* (4th ed.). Homewood, IL: Irwin.

Herzberg, F., Mausner, B., & Snyderman, B. (1959). *The Motivation to Work.* New York: Wiley.

Hirsch, P. M., & Shanley, M. (1996). The rhetoric of boundarylessness – or how the newly empowered managerial class bought into its own marginalization. In M. B. Arthur & D. M. Rousseau (Eds.), *The Boundaryless Career: A New Employment Principle for a New Organizational Era* (pp. 218-233). New York: Oxford.

Holland, J. L. (1973). *Making Vocational Choices.* Englewood Cliffs, NJ: Prentice-Hall.

Hughes, E. C. (1937). Institutional office and the person. *American Journal of Sociology, 43,* 404-43.

Inkson, K. (1995). The effects of economic recession on managerial job change and careers. *British Journal of Management, 6,* 183-194.

Inkson, K. (2000). Rewriting career development principles for the new Millennium. In R. Weisner & B. Millett (Eds.), *Contemporary Challenges and Future Directions in Management and Organizational Behaviour* (pp. 11-22). Sydney: Wiley.

Inkson, K., & Arthur, M. B. (2001). How to be a successful career capitalist. *Organizational Dynamics, 30*(1), 48-61.

Inkson, K., Arthur, M. B., Pringle, J. K., & Barry, S. (1997). Expatriate assignment versus overseas experience: Contrasting models of human resource development. *Journal of World Business, 14*(4), 151-68.

Inkson, K., Heising, A., & Rousseau, D. M. (2001). The interim manager: prototype of the twenty-first century worker? *Human Relations, 54*(3), 259-285.

Jones, C. (1996). Careers in project networks: The case of the film industry. In M. B. Arthur & D. M. Rousseau (Eds.), *The Boundaryless Career: A New Employment Principle for a New Organizational Era* (pp. 23-39). New York: Oxford.

Kanter, R. M. (1989). Careers and the wealth of nations: a macro-perspective on the structure and implications of career forms. In M. B. Arthur, D. T. Hall, and B. S. Lawrence (Eds.), *Handbook of Career Theory* (pp. 506-521). Cambridge: Cambridge University Press.

Kram, K. E. (1985) *Mentoring at Work. Developmental Relationships in Organizational Life.* Glenview, IL: Scott Foresman.

Lado, A., & Wilson, M. (1994). Human resource systems and sustained competitive advantage: A competency-based perspective. *Academy of Management Review, 19*(4), 699-727.

Lee, T. W., & Maurer, S. D. (1997). The retention of knowledge workers with the unfolding model of voluntary turnover. *Human Resource Management Review, 7,* 247-275.

Levinson, D. J., Darrow, C. N., Klein, E. B., Levinson, M. H., & McKee, B. (1978). *The Seasons of a Man's Life.* New York: Knopf.

Maslow, A. H. (1970). *Motivation and Personality* (2nd ed.). New York: Harper & Row.

Miles, R. E., & Snow, C. C. (1996). Twenty-first century careers. In M. B. Arthur & D. M. Rousseau (Eds.), *The Boundaryless Career: A New Employment Principle for a New Organizational Era* (pp. 97-115). New York: Oxford.

Nicholson, N., & West, M. (1988). *Managerial Job Change: Men and Women in Transition.* Cambridge: Cambridge University Press.

Ouchi, W. (1981). *Theory Z: How American Business can meet the Japanese Challenge.* Reading, MA: Addison Wesley.

Packard, V. (1964). *The Pyramid Climbers.* London: Pelican.

Parker, P., & Inkson, K. (1999). New forms of career: the challenge to Human Resource Management. *Asia-Pacific Journal of Human Resources, 37*(1), 76-85.

Peters, T. (1987). *Thriving on Chaos.* New York: Knopf.

Peters, T., & Waterman, R. H. (1982). *In Search of Excellence: Lessons form America's Best-Run Companies.* New York: Harper & Row.

Porter, M. E. (1985). *Competitive Advantage: Creating and Sustaining Superior Performance.* New York: Free Press.

Porter, M. E. (1990). *The Competitive Advantage of Nations.* New York: Free Press.

Presthus, R. (1978). *The Organizational Society.* (Revised Edition.) New York: St. Martins.

Rogers, E., & Larsen, J. (1984) *Silicon Valley Fever: Growth of High Technology Culture.* New York: Basic Books.

Rousseau, D. M. (1995). *Psychological Contracts in Organizations.* Thousand Oaks, CA: Sage.

Saxenian, A. L. (1996). Beyond boundaries: open labor markets and learning is Silicon Valley. In M. B. Arthur & D. M. Rousseau (Eds.), *The Boundaryless Career: A New Employment Principle for a New Organizational Era* (pp. 23-39). New York: Oxford.

Schein, E. H. (1978). *Career Dynamics: Matching Individual and Organizational Needs.* Reading, MA: Addison Wesley.

Sullivan, S. E. (1999). The changing nature of careers: a review and a research agenda. *Journal of Management, 25*(3), 457-484.

Super, D. E. (1957). *The Psychology of Careers.* New York: Harper & Row.

Tsui, A. S., Pearce, J. L, Porter, L. W., & Tripoli, A. M. (1997). Alternative approaches to the employee-organization relationship: Does investment in employees pay off? *Academy of Management Journal, 40,* 1089-1121.

Van Maanen, J. (Ed.). (1977). *Organizational Careers: Some New Perspectives.* New York: Wiley.

Waterman, R. H., Waterman, J. S., & Collard, B. A. (1994). Toward a career-resilient workforce. *Harvard Business Review, 72*(4), 87-95.

Weick, K. E. (1996). Enactment and the boundaryless career: organizing as we work. In M. B. Arthur & D. M. Rousseau (Eds.), *The Boundaryless Career: A New Employment Principle for a New Organizational Era* (pp. 40-57). New York: Oxford.

Whyte, W. H. (1956). *The Organization Man.* New York: Simon & Schuster.

Wright, P., McMahan, G., & McWilliams, A. (1994). Human resource management and sustained competitive advantage. *International Journal of Human Resource Management, 5*(2), 301-326.

Zabusky, S. E., & Barley, S. R. (1996). Redefining success: Ethnographic observations on the careers of technicians. In P. Osterman (Ed.), *Broken Ladders* (pp. 185-214). New York: Oxford.

CHAPTER 17
Community-Based Adult Career Counseling

Jane Goodman
Sandra McClurg
Oakland University

The focus of this chapter is on organizations that provide career development services to adults who may not be affiliated with the sponsoring organization. The key is open access. Many organizations that employ adults, and many educational institutions that teach adults, have career development programs. However, most do not. In addition, adults who are self-employed, unemployed, or work for no monetary compensation as homemakers or volunteers have no institutional affiliation. A school district, college or university may have an adult career development program, but it would be considered community-based only it if were open to non-students.

In the chapter we identify some parameters that program planners need to consider in developing their community-based approaches. We look at the needs of adults related to entering and leaving the work force. We present four case studies of programs in Michigan to provide a picture of several different approaches to community based programs.

Needs of Adults

Over the years the concept of what constitutes career development for adults has changed and expanded. Many of these changes have come in response to an increasingly rapidly changing society where "future shock" is indeed a present reality. Although as we write this chapter we are in a time of little unemployment, many are employed at poverty level wages and all face a changing definition of job security. These changing notions of the meaning of work and expectations of the work environment have been amply discussed in the media and in top selling works such as Rifkin's *The End of Work* (1995) and Bridges, *JobShift* (1994). Some experts say that adults will experience as many as seven major career shifts during a work life (Bureau of Labor Statistics, 1998; Peterson, 1995).

According to Richard Bolles, *What Color is Your Parachute,* (2000) about 10 percent of U.S. workers change careers yearly. Of these, 5.3 million changed voluntarily, 1.3 million changed involuntarily, and 3.4 million changed careers for a "mixture" of voluntary or involuntary reasons. These changes mean that "career development services are now concerned to help individuals not to *choose* careers but to *construct* them" (Watts, 2000, p. 13).

While not the focus of this chapter, it is important to keep in mind both family and cultural influences on career development. Evans and Rotter (2000) identify areas to consider when working with families from a variety of cultures socioeconomic status, language barriers, generational conflicts, and discrimination (pp. 68-69). Clearly, all of these have an influence on career decision making. They conclude, "Choosing a job is but the end result of a dynamic process of self-awareness, exploration, planning, and decision making. This process can only be effective when cultural, ethnic, and familial themes are addressed" (p. 70).

Furthermore, it is in the best interest of a global society that career development services are available to adults. Watts (2000) argued that career development services should meet the needs of both individuals and the wider society, that is "that they represent a public good as well as a private good" (p. 11). He stated that these benefits can be organized into two categories – economic efficiency and social equity. It is arguable that the *economic efficiency* of a society can be improved if its citizens make better career decisions. There will be less waste in education and training programs if they are well chosen; individuals are more likely to complete the programs successfully if there is a good match with their skill and interest level. Furthermore, good occupational information can assist individuals in choosing work where they are more likely to find employment, again increasing the efficiency of the "system."

Social equity is advanced when individuals make occupational decisions based on job availability, training availability, and their own personal attributes, rather than on social class, differing abilities or other potentially disadvantaging characteristics. Lack of access to good information has been endemic in several societal substrata; lack of assistance in decision making has also pervaded the lives of many people. Having effective and available career assistance could mitigate both of these circumstances.

Globalization is affecting not only the ways organizations conduct business, but also the need for individuals to have access to career information to help meet their needs. Reardon, Lenz, Sampson and Peterson (2000) believe that the ever-increasing number of multi-national companies will greatly affect work activity and production around the world. For example, companies, work and production will move effortlessly across international borders. The concept of a strictly "American company or product" will be non-existent. Career information and knowledge about growth in both occupations and industries will be necessary for individual career planning for future employment.

Organizations are becoming increasingly concerned about employees having access to career development services. According to Gilley and Eggland, (1997) many performance problems on the job are career related. They state that employees often feel trapped, stagnated or overlooked in their present jobs or occupations. Many people feel little pleasure in their work, and they concur that this contributes to increased stress and lowered output. They conclude that many people do not work to their full potential and often fail to meet organizational expectations.

It would be helpful if organizations were able to provide career services on site, but most do not. It then becomes the responsibility of the individual to find career services in the community. Acquisition of career information not only helps individuals to further their careers, but also meets the needs of the organization. Gilley and Eggland (1997) emphasize this by stating that it is "the employee" who is responsible for his or her career planning.

A National Public Radio report (August 23, 2000) stated that only 1/3 of workers in California work at typical nine to five jobs, salaried by the organization for whom they work. The rest are free lance, portfolio, temporary, leased, on-call, interim, or contract workers. According to an Upjohn Institute Study, flexible staffing arrangements were widely used (78 percent) in all kinds of organizations. Forty-six percent of companies used workers from temp agencies and 44 percent used independent contractors (Reardon, Lenz, Sampson, & Peterson, 2000).

These new work modalities meet the needs of many workers for autonomy and flexibility, and they clearly meet the needs of employers for a flexible, just in time, work force. Such new work structures, with their lack of a predictable income, benefits, or a retirement plan, create insecurity and distress for many workers. While higher paid workers may be able to weather this situation and purchase their own benefits, lower paid workers often live in hopes of staying healthy and without provision for retirement. A Bureau of Labor Statistics study reported in the Monthly Labor Review, that more than 60 percent of contingent workers preferred to have permanent jobs (Reardon, Lenz, Sampson, Peterson, 2000).

Clearly, the need for career assistance is there. What is being done to address that need? Arbeiter, Aslanian, Schmerbeck, and Brickell (1978) found that the primary service requested by adults to be lists of available jobs. A National Career Development Association (NCDA) commissioned Gallup Poll (Miller, 2000) found that one tenth of Americans stated that they needed assistance with career planning in the past year. Furthermore, 69 percent say that if they were starting over, they "would try to get more information about the job and career options open to them than they got the first time..." Additionally, "These data point to an unevenness of exposure to career information" (Herr, 2000) with minorities and youth receiving substantially less help than the population in general (p. 6).

Typically adult clients, particularly those adults whose career change is not voluntary, want help in finding a job. Adult career counselors, on the other hand, usually believe in teaching the career development process and want their clients to invest themselves in discovering their interests, values, skills, temperaments, and the like. They want clients to make *good* decisions, not only *expedient* ones. They see the need for adults to learn decision-making and job seeking processes to be a result of this more fluid workforce. At the same time, adult career counselors must understand the sense of urgency many adults experience when they seek help with their careers. In many cases this sense of urgency stems from real survival needs, as laid off and displaced workers experience long term unemployment and exhausted benefits. Ironically in a time of full employment, those workers are often overlooked. The plethora of help wanted signs persuades many policy makers and citizens that assistance is not longer necessary. Most of these jobs are, however, at minimum or close to minimum wage – not one that allows the worker to rise above the poverty level.

Both the immediate needs of the clients and their longer-range interests can be served, however. The traditional adage, "Give me a fish and I'll eat for today; teach me to fish and I'll eat for the rest of my life" needs to be amended. If you feed people while you are teaching them, they are better apt to learn. Thus, finding clients immediate work may become a priority, at the same time the counselor encourages them to continue the career exploration process so they may make good long term decisions about training and work.

Career counselors also may need to become advocates for their clients. They need to know about survival resources (i.e., where to get food clothing and shelter) as well as occupational and educational resources. Even when poverty and unemployment are not a reality, adults anticipating or experiencing change may feel a sense of panic. This could be related to a sudden perception of running out of time to make and implement career decisions. To meet both these short term and long term needs, it is important that career counselors have an overview of the whole career development process. Such an overview is provided by the guidelines described below.

Adult Career Development Competencies

The National Occupational Information Coordinating Committee (NOICC) developed a series of career development competencies (1992). The 12 competencies for the adult level are:

Self Knowledge:
Skills to maintain a positive self-concept.
Skills to maintain effective behaviors.
Understanding developmental changes and transitions.

Educational and Occupational Exploration:
Skills to enter and participate in education and training
Skills to participate in work and life-long learning.
Skills to locate, evaluate, and interpret career information.
Skills to prepare to seek, obtain, maintain, and change jobs.
Understanding how the needs and functions of society influence the nature and structure of work.

Career Planning:
Skills to make decisions.
Understanding the impact of work on individual and family life.
Understanding the continuing changes in male/female roles.
Skills to make career transitions.

Each of these competencies implies a number of activities and counseling interventions. For example, the last mentioned, "skills to make career transitions," includes some intangible emotional components. Transitions often engender a grieving process that arouses such emotions as denial, anger, panic, and acceptance. A model for assisting people to cope with transitions was developed and described by Schlossberg (1984) and Schlossberg, Waters, and Goodman (1995). This model identifies a number of attributes of the situation, the person, and his or her support system that both predict and can be used to enhance the successful navigation of a particular transition. In developing programs, adult career counselors should consider how each of the NOICC competencies will be achieved, and develop an action strategy based on that analysis.

What's Out There?

By its very nature, community-based adult career counseling is delivered in many ways to a wide variety of clients. In this section, a schematic way of looking at an array of services will be presented, along with several illustrations of how components of this array can be put together.

In Table 1, programmatic components are listed, using four basic parameters of program planning: organizational sponsor, clientele, services provided, and method of delivery. Program planners may view this table as a "menu" – choose at least one appetizer, main course, dessert, and beverage. The lists in each category are not exhaustive, but we hope they are comprehensive enough to be useful for program planning. Used with the NOICC guidelines, they can help service providers plan a comprehensive program rather than simply offer an array of services.

Program planners usually do not have a choice as to their organizational sponsor, because this is usually where they begin. Funding may come from a university or community college; funding may come from a state or federal agency. Private philanthropies, e.g., Jewish Vocational Service described later, also can be a program sponsor. In most cases planners also have little choice regarding clientele. That is often fixed by the funding sources or by the basic mission of their organization. Choices are more likely to exist with regard to services provided and method of delivery. Program planners who wish to include one of more vocational guidance instruments among their services may find the Kapes, Mastie, and Whitfield (1994) *Counselors Guide to Career Assessment Instruments* to be a useful resource.

To illustrate the way in which the "menu" approach to planning works, four "meals" are described in the following cases studies.

Different Approaces to Program Planning

The following case studies represent different decisions made by program planners with respect to the components listed in Table 1. Although all of the programs operate in southeastern Michigan, they differ markedly in terms of sponsorship, clientele, services and methods of delivery.

TABLE 1
PROGRAMMATIC COMPONENTS

Organizational Sponsor	Clientele	Services Provided	Methods of Delivery
Private agencies	All Adults	Formal assessment	Individual
Business and Industry Unions	Women Minorities	Emotional support Self-assessment	Group Face-to-face
"Y"s	Older people	Decision-making skills	Telephone
Public agencies e.g., vocational rehabilitation	Displaced Workers	Job seeking information	Television
Schools	Physically or emotionally disabled	Job retention techniques	Professional/ Paraprofessional
College and Universities	Prisoners and ex-offenders	Retirement planning	

OAKLAND UNIVERSITY'S ADULT CAREER COUNSELING CENTER

The Adult Career Counseling Center (ACCC) was founded in 1982 as a community service of Oakland University, to "Provide career exploration and planning opportunities to community adults at no cost" (Berg, Cunningham, & Frick, 1998-99, p.4). Four students in the master's level counseling program are employed for two years as graduate assistant advisors to implement the program. They are supervised by a faculty member in the Counseling Department, but take full responsibility for the day to day operations of the Center. Over 12,000 clients have used the services of the ACCC since its inception. The Center is supported by Oakland University funds, with the Counseling Department contributing the services of the faculty supervisor through released time from teaching.

Originally planned as a computer dependent service, with only minimal assistance available from Center staff, the Center has evolved into a true career counseling center, with the typical client coming for three to five sessions and taking advantage of a variety of services. These include 1) talking with the advisor, 2) using computer assisted and Internet-based career guidance programs, 3) taking paper and pencil inventories, 4) conducting traditional and Internet-based job search activities, and 5) using role rehearsal and videotape to practice job interviews. All sessions are provided individually and face to face. Although job placement is not provided, clients often seek help in resume preparation and in learning to use the Internet to identify openings. Referrals are also made to One Stop Centers, like the Troy Career Center, described in this chapter, as well as to Oakland University's Counseling Practicum Center for those who need more extensive personal help.

The Center is marketed through traditional means, such as press releases to radio and television, especially cable television, as well as through an annual open house, held during National Career Development Month. The majority of clients, however, hear about the Center's services through "word-of-mouth," usually from past clients who were pleased with the service they received. The Center is open 60 hours per week, including four evenings and Saturday. These extended hours provide access to working adults, as well as to those who need to wait for a spouse to return from work to take care of young children.

Additionally, the Center is expected to provide training to Counseling Practicum students and part time faculty in the use of computer and Internet assisted career guidance programs, as well as to conduct research that supports the Center's mission of providing career guidance assistance to adults. The Center's annual report is available through the ERIC system (Berg et al, 1998-99) and has been described, more fully in Goodman and Savage (1999).

OPERATION ABLE: AN OLDER WORKER PROGRAM

While the definition of when a person qualifies as an older worker varies from one government program to another, it seems clear that older adults have some special problems in identifying new career arenas and/or seeking new jobs. The mission of Operation ABLE, designed to assist workers over 40, is, "To provide market responsive programs to meet the employment needs of mature individuals along their career paths, to promote lifelong learning among individuals, businesses and government and to assist the employer community in developing a competent workforce" (1999, unpaginated).

ABLE provides classroom based training and self paced instruction in a variety of computer applications, such as Introduction to Windows, Microsoft Word, Excel, PowerPoint, Access, and Outlook. Classes are also offered in basic skills such as reading, math, and grammar. They also house a "Career Resilience Center" for older workers who need assistance with employment and career decisions, resume development, interview preparation and coaching, and job search assistance (Operation ABLE, 2000, p. 13). The Resilience Center offers skills and aptitude testing and professional career counseling, provided by Licensed Professional Counselors. Members of the Career Resilience Center pay a fee, and have access to networking meetings, phones, Internet, and FAX, and receive a discount on ABLE's training programs.

ABLE staff believes that the reason that they are successful is that they understand the needs of adult learners, using a self-paced approach in an adult learning environment. "Classes are small, to allow for significant one-on-one instruction and to provide a non-threatening and supportive environment" (Operation ABLE, 2000, p. 8). They also place a great emphasis on working with the employer community, guided by a Board of Directors that includes a broad array of business and industry representatives. This enables them to offer training that meets the needs of employers, and provides their clients with greater employability (Freedman, personal communication).

In 1999 ABLE helped more than 500 people, the majority under 60 years of age. To quote from their annual report, "Their needs were as varied as their backgrounds. While some enrolled in a single computer class to learn a new software program, others signed up for membership in the Career Resilience Center for help with their resumes, interviewing techniques and online job searches. Most of our customers were looking for employment and participated in all of Operation ABLE's services: counseling and assessment, computer classes and job search assistance"(1999, unpaginated). ABLE is funded through a combination of contracts, grants and individual and corporate donations.

TROY CAREER CENTER

The Troy Career Center is a grant funded career center based in Troy, Michigan. The center was established in 1976 as a community resource to help job seekers achieve their career goals. In 1976, there were five staff members serving about 500 clients a year. In 2000, there were eighteen full time staff members serving more than 2000 clients yearly. All of the staff are career management specialists and possess a master's degree in counseling, career development facilitation certification or are licensed professional counselors.

Many different grants have funded the Troy Career Center. Workforce Investment Act (WIA), North American Free Trade Act/Trade Act Assistance (NAFTA/TAA), Work First, Welfare to Work, Veteran's Employment Services are examples of funding sources in addition to many state and federal programs. The grants are administered by Troy Public Schools, Office of Continuing Education, but the center is self-supporting and self-sustaining. As a result of the relationship with the school system, cooperative programs are available for clients in the areas of childcare, English as Second Language (ESL), and high school certification and alternative education.

Any U.S. resident is eligible to receive the free services from the career center and they offer a "seamless system" of support to clients regardless of their career development needs. This means that all support services for clients are integrated in the one career center. This enables the individual to get any help they might need, such as information about additional training, college courses, or other services, by going to only one place. The services are specialized, yet multi-faceted, enabling the center to meet a variety of workforce developmental needs. Services include career counseling and management, a statewide talent bank and resource center, workshops and outplacement services, job bulletins and postings, university job bulletins and newspaper classifieds.

The center also provides job clubs for clients with opportunities for networking and presentation of job search skill information, career search programs such as the Michigan Occupational Information System (MOIS), System of Interactive Guidance and Information (SIGI), DISCOVER and an extensive collection of library references and resource materials. Access is available to training services which include academic or occupational training, financial aid information, and veteran's services. Tuition assistance is available for a variety of colleges, universities and vocational schools to enable clients to gain new skills, upgrade current skills and enhance marketability.

The Troy Career Center is a "Michigan Works! One-stop program." "Michigan Works!" is a state initiated and supported program that enables career centers to refer clients to many community/support programs such as transportation, medical services, housing, child or dependent care, work attire or tools and other community service organizations.

Workshops are available which include Internet Job Search. The Internet training helps clients with ways to use the Internet for writing resumes and cover letters, obtain job leads, etc. There are also tutorial workshops that introduce clients to the Internet, Windows and Microsoft Office. Regularly held job fairs for job seekers and employers are organized to match clients with job opportunities.

The Troy Career Center is open daily from 8:00-5:00 with evening hours on certain nights and other hours available by appointment. The career management services are individualized to help clients determine their career direction. Resources are introduced to enable achievement of career goals. Full office services are available which includes telephones, fax machines, copiers and computer workstations.

Clients are seen as often as needed by a member of the career center staff to support career needs. There are three categories of services that are available on an ongoing daily basis. These services are as follows:

1 *Core Services:* Self-serve resources, computers, library, job leads, and compiled resources.
2. *Career Management and Development:* Career counseling and skill assessment, career planning and exploration, follow-up and case management.
3. *Training:* Support and tuition assistance for any education or training needed to obtain new skills or upgrade existing ones. This training can range from a specific skill such as computer training to a bachelor or master's degree.

Clients are free to use all of the services of the Troy Career Center independently or with the help of staff, who are available at all times. There is no fee for any of the basic services.

JEWISH VOCATIONAL SERVICE

Jewish Vocational Service (JVS) is an $18 million, non-profit organization that has been providing vocational services in the metropolitan Detroit area for 59 years. During 1999-2000, JVS served more than 20,800 people from Macomb, Oakland and Wayne counties at six JVS centers (Jewish Vocational Services, 2000 Annual Report). JVS receives funding from Jewish Federation of Metropolitan Detroit, The Jewish Fund, United Way Community Services and many other community partners, local businesses, health and community service organizations, foundations and government departments and agencies.

The mission of JVS is to "help people meet life challenges affecting their self-sufficiency through counseling, training and support services" and the belief that "the best way to help people is to make it possible for them to help themselves" (JVS 2000 Annual Report). Examples of clients served were people looking for better jobs, unemployed workers, employers with job vacancies, at-risk teenagers from the former Soviet Union, women out of the workforce and high school students with severe disabilities and special needs.

The career services offered by JVS include complete employment services such as electronic job bank, career and educational counseling, occupational resource library centers, career fairs, and skill development for conducting job searches. In addition to individual and group career counseling, JVS operates a number of programs targeted to a particular clientele. The following are examples.

Job Link targets food stamp recipients who do not have dependents. The program provides job skills training and placement services to help find job placements for the clients. Employment Link works with homeless individuals referred by Med-Link and provides job skills training and placement services to help find job placements.

Work Connect helps hard-to-place individuals with histories of incarceration, substance abuse and other obstacles to find jobs. Skills remediation and employment services help them successfully enter the job market.

JVS is committed to equipping youth for the workforce. To accomplish this goal, several partnerships have been formed with schools and community organizations. A few examples follow.

- Partnering with Oakland Technical Center, JVS helps upper class high school students with diverse learning styles make a smooth transition from school to employment.

- A community training project with several local schools provides at-risk high school students and those with learning disabilities with on-the-job experience at an automotive center and local hospital.

- Oakland County high school students with severe autism are provided job training and placement with area businesses to determine their vocational skills and strengths.

- Young immigrants from the former Soviet Union find jobs and learn about the US job market and receive career guidance and counseling to help develop future educational and employment goals.

Each client at JVS is offered a variety of programs ranging from basic skills remediation to advanced technology training. Customized services such as testing and assessment, job readiness seminars, computer labs, interview and resume writing and job placement are offered both individually and in small group workshops. All services are available on a sliding scale, based on the individual's ability to pay.

Implications for Program Planners

Program planners have a challenge! They are often asked to develop the best programs for the least money in the shortest time for the most people. How can the necessary decisions and compromises be made to ensure good programs, at an affordable cost, in a reasonable time, for a sufficient number of people? Some of the decisions to be made are discussed in the following sections.

Individual versus group counseling. Working with individuals provides the most flexibility of programming. Each individual's personal requirements are addressed. For some people, the confidentiality of individual sessions is crucial. Furthermore, participants can progress at their own pace. Groups, however, provide an opportunity for support and caring confrontation that is difficult to match in an individual session. For many people who learn more by listening than by talking, the advantage of groups is obvious. In addition, the group can provide a richness of resources, ideas, contacts, and connections that no individual helper could master. A further consideration is the efficiency of service. Groups use less staff time. As Jacobs, Masson, and Harvill (1998) stated in regard to group versus individual counseling, "Sometimes one or the other is best, and sometimes the combination of group and individual counseling produces the most benefit" (p. 20).

Face to face versus technological intermediary. Direct personal contact with clients is certainly the mode with which most of us are comfortable. The advantages are: 1) familiarity for both counselor and client, 2) the ability to use nonverbal communication and to give feedback on nonverbal behavior, for example, in rehearsing an interview, 3) the ability to change and modify a program based on changing client needs and, most intangible but perhaps most important, 4) the personal support conveyed by a counselor. Some of the pros and cons – or blessings or banes as she put it – of cybercounseling were summarized by Harris-Bowlsbey (1999).

The advantages of a technological approach are also many. Sampson, Kolodinsky, and Greeno (1997) discussed the future trends in career counseling in relation to computer use, the information highway and career practice. They suggested that this technology will open up possibilities for marketing, service delivery, self-help resources, supervision, and case conferencing and research. They suggest, for example, that it will no longer be necessary for the counselor to be in the same room as a client; a supervisor could be located on the other side of the world; and clients could access career information without ever seeing a career professional. An advantage of this approach is that individuals in remote areas can now have access to a career counseling service previously unavailable to them.

Television is another method for delivering career services. It is anonymously accessible to most clients without travel and, like the Internet, fits the needs of a growing number of people. This at-home access may be particularly useful for the disabled, homemakers with young children, people in rural areas, and others for whom personal access to career services is a problem. Another advantage of television is that it can provide information efficiently to large numbers of people. This information can be delivered by skillful presenters in a format to which the American public has become accustomed.

Using the Internet, especially the World Wide Web, can be a useful method of searching for a job. Most of the websites offer a variety of services such as general information about finding a job, locating resources and information about specific positions, finding networking companies and contacts, and providing information and feedback about resumes and cover letters. Dolan and Schumacher (1994) queried people on several Internet listservs about finding jobs and found that 20 percent had a found a job on the Internet. Respondents indicated that it was a good resource because some positions are only listed on the Net and that ads on the Net usually come out in advance of print copy.

The computer, with its interactive properties, offers other advantages. It can store large amounts of information and retrieve it on demand. Through its branched design capabilities, it can allow a client to determine the direction of exploration or information. It can provide on command a written record of all transactions. Also, it never gets tired, bored, or takes a vacation! Kennedy and Morrow (1994) summarized that technology, while promising many positive developments for the modern job seeker, is not enough. They stressed the importance of coupling technology with traditional methods of job hunting and recruiting.

Cybercounseling, as is becoming called, is a growing part of the delivery system for career counseling, as well as for those with other intra- or inter-personal issues. The provision of counseling over the Internet, certainly fits within the purview of this chapter on community based career development for adults. But exactly what it is and how effective it is, is still quite controversial. In summarizing a long book on the topic, Walz (Bloom & Walz, 2000) stated, "Cybercounseling is an idea whose time has come, but we as counselors are not yet ready to say with conviction what it really is or how it should be employed" (p. 406).

In response to the increasing availability of the Internet to adults, many individuals are offering services via that medium. Indeed the Readers Digest, (October 2000) reprinted an article from Fast Company on using the Internet to "Keep your career clicking" (p. 82). It suggested that individuals use the Internet to: identify your passion; tap insiders; determine your value; and gain an edge (pp. 84-86). It further suggested finding a cyber counselor, identified as a member of the International Coach Foundation. This identification demonstrates one of the difficulties of this medium. In most states the title and the practice of counseling are only permitted to be used by Licensed Professional Counselors, a credential not required by the International Coach Foundation. On line assessments are suggested and web addresses given. Although we are skeptical about the ability of the general public to interpret assessment instruments appropriately and effectively, this type of web information is certain to increase. In response to such proliferation of use, the National Career Development Association has developed Guidelines for the Use of the Internet for the Provision of Career Information and Planning Services (www.ncda.org), and The American Counseling Association has developed Ethical Guidelines for Internet On-Line Counseling (www.counseling.org).

Professional versus paraprofessional counselors. Ideally, professional counselors have expertise in counseling and group work, along with the ability to make presentations and give feedback. They also have a storehouse of career development information and knowledge of how to access the rest. They have the capability to administer and interpret tests. For all of these reasons they are often the "method of choice."

Paraprofessional counselors can be an important asset, however, to the professional counselor and the client in many ways. Assistance with research and Web-based searches, help with resume and cover letter information and editing and securing information about companies and employment information are a few of the ways that the "team approach" enhances the career process.

A new type of service provider has emerged in recent years, that is Career Development Facilitator (CDF), a non professional occupation developed under contract with the National Occupational Coordinating Committee (Hoppin and Splete, 1996) and credentialed by the Center for Credentialing and Education (CCE). CDFs work under the supervision of a licensed or certified masters level counselor and provide a variety of services to clients. These may include conducting intake interviews; helping the client to identify interests, skills, barriers, and resources; helping clients with job search activities including researching the job market, writing resumes, and preparing for interviews; and helping clients find and keep jobs. CDFs work in a variety of settings, some like the ones profiled here, such as one-stop centers, career resource centers, government agencies, and community colleges.

The CDF training is extensive and intensive. It consists of 120 clock hours and addresses the following competency areas: helping skills, diverse populations, ethical and legal issues, consultation, career development models, assessment, labor market information and resources, technology, employability skills, training clients and peers, program management and implementation, and promotion and public relations (Harris-Bowlsbey, Suddarth, & Reile, 2000, pp. 4-6).

Summary

In all of the foregoing we have only touched on the plethora of different programs that can exist for adults in the community at large. This variety is exciting, yet it also contributes to confusion as to what is best in setting up new programs or evaluating existing programs. It has been our aim to provide some dimensions to use in decision making and some examples of the range of possible alternatives. The examples cited will, we hope, provide practitioners with some new ideas or possible resources.

References

Arbeiter, S., Aslanian, C.C., Schmerbeck, F. A., & Brickell, H. M. (1978). *Forty million Americans in career transition: The need for information.* New York: College Examination Board.

Berg, F., Cunningham, M. & Frick, B. (1998-99). *Adult Career Counseling Center: Sixteenth Annual Report.* Rochester, MI: Oakland University.

Bloom, J. W., & Walz, G. R. (Eds.). (2000). *Cybercounseling and cyberlearning.* Alexandria, VA: American Counseling Association.

Bolles, R. (2000). *What color is your parachute?* Berkeley, CA: Ten Speed Press

Bridges, W. (1994). *JobShift.* Reading, MA: Addison-Wesley.

Bureau of Labor Statistics. (1998). News: *United States Department of Labor.* USDL Publication No. 98-253. Washington, D.C.: U.S. Government Printing Office.

Dolan, D.R., & Schumacher, J. E. (1994, October-November). *Top U.S. sources for an online job search 17*(5), pp. 34-38, 40-43.

Gilley, J., & Eggland, S. (1997). *Principles of human resource development.* Reading, MA: Addison-Wesley.

Goodman, J., & Savage, N. (1999). Responding to a community need: Oakland University's adult career counseling center. *The Career Development Quarterly, 48*(1), 19-30.

Harris-Bowlsbey, J. (1999). *The Internet: A tool for career planning.* Columbus, OH: National Career Development Association.

Harris-Bowlsbey, J., Reile, D. M., & Suddarth, B. H. (2000). *Facilitating Career Development.* Columbus, OH: National Career Development Association.

Herr, E. (2000, Summer). The Career Practitioner. *Career Developments.* In J. Miller Career trends: The fourth NCDA/Gallup national survey of working America.

Hoppin, J., & Splete, H. (Eds). (1996). *Curriculum for career development facilitators.* Washington, D.C.: National Occupational Information Coordinating Committee.

Imperto, G. (2000, October.) Get your career clicking. *Readers Digest.*

Jacobs, E. E., Masson, R. L., & Harvill, R. L. (1998). *Group counseling: Strategies and skills.* Pacific Grove, CA: Brooks/Cole.

Jewish Vocational Service. (2000). *Annual Report.* Rose and Sidney Diem Building, 29699 Southfield Road, Southfield, Michigan 48076.

Kapes, J. L., Mastie, M. M., & Whitfield, E. A. (1994). *A counselors guide to career assessment instruments* (3rd ed.). Alexandria, VA: National Career Development Association.

Kennedy, J. L., & Morrow, T. J. (1994). *Electronic job search revolution.* New York: Wiley.

Miller, J. V. (2000). Career trends: The fourth NCDA/Gallup national survey of working America. *Career Developments* (Summer).

National Occupational Information Coordinating Committee (NOICC), United States Department of Labor. (1992). *National Career Development Guidelines.* Washington, DC: U.S. Department of Labor.

Operation ABLE Annual Report. (1999). Operation ABLE of Michigan, 17117 West Nine Mile Road, Suite 200 Southfield, MI.

Operation ABLE Annual Report. (2000). Operation ABLE of Michigan, 17117 West Nine Mile Road, Suite 200 Southfield, MI.

Peterson, L. (1995) *Starting out, starting over.* Palo Alto, CA: Davies-Black.

Reardon, R., Lenz. J., Sampson, J., & Peterson, G. (2000). *Career development and planning: A comprehensive approach.* Brooks/Cole, Thompson Learning.

Rifkin, J. (1995). *The End of Work.* New York: Putnam.

Sampson, J. P., Kolodinsky, R. W., & Greeno, B. P. (1997). Counseling on the information highway: Future possibilities and potential problems. *Journal of Counseling and Development, 75*, 203-212.

Schlossberg, N. K. (1984). *Counseling adults in transition: Linking practice with theory.* New York: Springer.

Schlossberg, N. K., Waters, E. B., & Goodman J. (1995). *Counseling adults in transition: Linking practice with theory* (2nd ed.). New York: Springer.

Watts, A.G. (2000). Career development and public policy. *Educational and vocational guidance bulletin,* 64, 9-21.

CHAPTER 18
Addressing the Career Development Needs of Adult Students in Research University Settings

Deborah J. Marron
Jack R. Rayman
The Pennsylvania State University

During the past two decades, global economic forces, technological advances, fluctuations in population, and changes in occupational characteristics have significantly impacted the enrollment patterns at institutions of higher education throughout the U.S. Enrollment in four-year institutions swelled from 7.7 million in 1985 to nearly 9 million in 1998 and is expected to increase to nearly 11 million by 2010 (U.S. Department of Education, 2000). As predicted, adult learners (students age 25 and older) now comprise more than 42 percent of the student population in higher education (U.S. department of Education 2000; U.S. Department of Education, 1989). Aslanian (2001) reports that from 1970 to 2000, the enrollment of adult students increased 170 percent. Moreover, the growth was both at the undergraduate and graduate levels. In 1998, the non-traditional age undergraduate student population at four-year institutions comprised 15 percent of full-time students and 65 percent of part-time students. At the graduate level, however, adult learner enrollments accounted for 62 percent of full-time students and 92 percent of part-time graduate students (The Chronicle of Higher Education, 2000).

Researchers have generally defined the nontraditional student as an undergraduate student who is at least 25 years of age (Hughes, 1983; Krager, Wrenn, & Hirt, 1990). In view of the fact that adult learners constitute the majority of graduate students, administrators of four-year institutions have a mandate to include the needs of graduate students when considering and addressing the career development needs of adult learners. Adult learners at the graduate level represent a significant force on university campuses, particularly at major research universities. This chapter focuses on the career development needs of adult learners at major research universities. Recommendations are suggested for improving career services that are targeted to both the undergraduate and graduate level students with an emphasis on the graduate student population. This cohort, including international graduate students, comprises an important element of this discussion.

Defining Major Research Universities

The Carnegie Classification of Higher Education (Carnegie Foundation for the Advancement of Teaching, 1994) is a system for categorizing American colleges and universities that are accredited, degree-granting institutions. According to this classification system, major research universities are defined as those that "offer a full range of baccalaureate degree programs, are committed to graduate education through the doctorate, and give high priority to research" (p. xix). These research-intensive institutions award 50 or more doctoral degrees each year and receive a minimum of $15.5 million to a maximum of $40 million in federal support each year. The 125 institutions that fall within these categories of Research I and Research II universities enroll more than 500,000 graduate students, grant 79 percent of all doctoral degrees and 83 percent of doctoral degrees in science and engineering. The list of member universities includes University of California at Los Angeles; University of Maryland, College Park; Temple University; the University of Massachusetts at Amherst; and the eleven "Big 10" universities (e.g. University of Iowa, University of Michigan, Purdue University, etc.).

Learning More About Adult Learners

Gaff and Gaff (1981) identified characteristics that differentiate older students from traditional age students. They postulate that many adult learners have extensive life experience, derived from work, family responsibilities, or personal crises. Adult learners may also have developed a broader range of interests, concerns, and values as a result of their life experiences. They may experience competing demands from obligations outside of school, such as dependent family members, employment, or both. They also tend to be involved in community or cultural activities. In her study of 1500 adult learners, Aslanian (2001), discovered that adult learners are typically prompted to return to school by some triggering event in their lives. Approximately 85 percent indicated that they sought additional education in response to career transitions. They tend to have a higher degree of career orientation and have returned to school to advance their careers or in response to the need to combat obsolescence (Aslanian, 2001). Aslanian and Brickell (1980), concluded that adults return to formal education for several reasons: to use the knowledge they acquire; to cope with changes in their lives such as illness or relocation; to accomplish transitions that may accompany that change such as job loss or divorce; and the most commonly cited purpose for adult learning pertains to careers. In short, adult learners seek to acquire career related skills; they view education as the means to enable them to move from one status or stage in life to another.

Aslanian's (2001) study identified an interesting profile of the adult learner as more often white, female, balancing multiple roles including parent and volunteer, possessing a higher than average income level and high levels of education. They seek degrees and additional credentials in order to advance their careers. They seek accelerated course programs and are willing to engage in distance instruction, though only twenty percent do so at this time.

Career Development Issues of Adult Undergraduate Students

The National Center for Educational Statistics (NCES) reported that the enrollment of undergraduate college students 25 years of age and over increased five percent from 5.8 million in 1990 to 6.1 million in 1998, and this trend is predicted to increase through the year 2010 to 6.8 million (Gerald & Hussar, 2000). In response to this trend, several publications over the past 20 years have addressed the career needs of adult learners with chapters focusing on the unique population of adult learners in university settings (Nowack & Shriberg, 1981; Keierleber & Sundal-Hansen, 1986; Keierleber & Hansen, 1992). Aslanian (2001) developed a profile of the undergraduate student as having multiple roles, with most of their focus on career and family, although many are active in community activities as well.

Aslanian and Brickell (1988) identified specific needs of undergraduate adult students. As a result of their multiple roles, these students experience tremendous demands on their time and require services that directly address their individual concerns. The students in their study expressed the desire for assistance in managing their time, focusing on career issues, and balancing multiple demands.

In the two previous editions of this publication, for example, Keierleber and Sundal-Hansen (1986) and Keierleber and Hansen (1992) provided a comprehensive discussion of the issues faced by the nontraditional student population and identified trends and recommendations for the future that specifically addressed the unique needs of the growing number of adult undergraduate students in university settings. Their recommendations included improving the information and assessment tools available for adult learners to learn more about themselves, the world of work, and the career choice implementation process. They suggested that career services providers incorporate knowledge and processes within the framework of adult development and adult learning theory and that these services reflect the growing knowledge of gender differences in learning styles, self exploration, and career decision making. Also proposed to career professionals was adopting a more holistic approach for providing comprehensive services to include advocacy, outreach on behalf of the students, and referral to other services and programs internal and external to the university. Aslanian (2001) would add that career services and programs should be designed to be convenient and accessible. An example of that type of program would be a drop-in, career counseling service.

The recommendations for addressing the career development needs of adult learners have been broad ranging and innovative but there are signs that there has been little follow through on the part of career professionals. A survey by Seifried and Rayman (1998) of career services professionals at 35 universities reveals a dearth of specialized services and programs for this cohort. Only ten of the institutions surveyed had specified the "official" age to identify a student as an adult learner. In most cases, the staff estimates of the adult populations at their institution were grossly miscalculated. For example, at one major research university, the number of nontraditional students was reported to be "miniscule" when in reality, adult learners comprised 27 percent of their 35,000 student population. Seifried and Rayman (1998), concluded that the scope of career services offered for adult learners should differ from those offered to traditional age students.

In addition, they recommend that the service delivery used in working with adult learners should reflect the learning style of the adult student and that the methods employed to inform adult students of available services should utilize good marketing strategies that are targeted to that market. Aslanian (2001) reports that only 20 percent of the 1500 adult learners surveyed reported utilizing career services and the least-used services reported included job placement, child care, family programs or events, and recreational facilities. More than 65 percent reported no involvement in campus activities or events even though they may have been aware of them. This would also suggest implications for programming of career related events for career services providers.

Career development professionals must be cognizant of these characteristics and needs as well as the underlying developmental stages and tasks that are associated with these life stages, in order to adequately address the unique set of experiences and issues that adult students present. Discussions of adult career development theory and issues related to particular target populations are discussed at length in other chapters in this book and are, therefore, beyond the scope of this discussion. However, another critically important population that presents a special set of needs and challenges for career services professionals is that of graduate students, including international students. The following section focuses on that population.

Career Development Issues of Adult Graduate Students

When considering the adult student makeup of major research universities, it is important to include students who are pursuing careers in academia or who are responding to external or internal forces by enrolling in graduate and first-professional programs. According to a survey of graduate and professional programs by Peterson (1998), the majority of nontraditional students are students enrolled in graduate and professional programs. Baird (1993) reported that approximately twenty five percent of college graduates continue on to graduate or first-professional programs. According to a report by the U.S. Department of Education (2000), in 1998, 2.1 million students were enrolled in first-professional and graduate degree programs with fifty six percent of those enrolled in master's degree programs. More than twelve percent were enrolled in doctoral programs and another twelve percent pursued first-professional degree programs. More than 50 percent of the students in both the master's and doctoral programs were enrolled on a part-time basis; depending upon the academic program and degree, the adult students categorized themselves as either student or employee. The projections for both graduate and first-professional programs are expected to increase by more than 10 percent during the period from 1998 to 2010.

Seifried and Rayman (1998) conducted a survey of career services professionals at 35 universities, including many of those aforementioned institutions. Their research revealed that the majority of career professionals underestimated the number of adult students at their institution and that the graduate population is generally overlooked. It would appear that research universities are continuing to target career assistance only to their traditional age undergraduate population. Given that graduate students comprise a "silent majority" of nontraditional students, it appears that the specific needs of the graduate student population must be identified to increase awareness and to develop remediation strategies. This chapter, therefore, expands the definition of nontraditional students to include masters, doctoral, and post-doctoral students. The demographics of the graduate student population have evolved beyond the white, traditional age, male student to include women, members of underrepresented groups, and non-native born students Fischer & Zigmond, 1998).

ISSUES FACING GRADUATE STUDENTS

Adjusting to graduate school. Aslanian and Brickell (1980) identified three factors that may compel adults to return to school:

1. Career changes or implementations,
2. Transitions in their family lives, or
3. Transitions in their leisure patterns.

Adult learners often have not anticipated the need to redirect their career or make a voluntary career change and return to school (Nowak & Shriberg, 1981). There may be dissonance between the adult learner's self-concept and career identity and uniformed expectations about life's career stages and their concomitant tasks. They must reconcile their earlier career expectations with the crystallization of their own career identity and the realities of the job market. When graduate education is determined to be the necessary next step in responding to those factors identified by Aslanian and Brickell (1980), adult learners are faced with the prospect of learning a new set of adaptive skills to ensure success.

Fischer and Zigmond, (1998) grouped these "survival skills" into four categories. They identified a set of basic skills for success that include the need to develop a new style of learning as they transition from "consumers" of knowledge to "creators" of knowledge. Their typical patterns that developed as undergraduate students may need to be revised to address their greater responsibilities and increased level of professionalism. As graduate students move into the role of researchers, they must also learn to communicate at a more advanced, professional level through classroom and oral presentations as well as in proposals and publications. Other than the required course in speech communications, undergraduate students may not have had experiences that enabled them to acquire skills in developing and delivering presentations on course content or research findings. Many graduate students who assume teaching assistantships must also develop skills in teaching, personnel management, and grant writing. As undergraduates, students rarely have the opportunity to learn and develop such skill sets. The fourth category that Fischer and Zigmond (1998) identified focuses on the need to develop job related skills to secure and maintain employment. These "job getting and keeping" skills include such activities as composing a resume or curriculum vitae and interviewing for positions. Numerous variables impact the prospects of employment inside or outside of the academy after graduate school. This issue is discussed in more detail in the following section.

As reported by Boyle and Boice (1998), collegiality with fellow students has been linked to academic achievement and career development. In addition to the emotional and social support provided by peers, fellow students can assist newer students in learning and understanding the departmental culture and negotiating the bureaucratic process of academic paperwork. Social interaction with fellow students can foster new students' integration into the culture of the academic department and facilitate understanding of specific research and learning opportunities.

For students from other countries, the challenges of adapting to life in graduate school at major research universities are compounded by a wide variety of factors. International students are faced with the additional, not inconsequential, burden of adapting not only to the American culture, but to the American educational system as well. Although individual differences among foreign students determine the nature and severity of the barriers they encounter, the challenges typically involve their level of proficiency in English and knowledge of American customs, their academic discipline and level of study, their cultural and religious perspectives, and their maturity and ability to operate autonomously (Althen, 1995). Lack of proficiency in speaking English may make it difficult to establish collegial relationships that have the potential to delay or prevent international students' assimilation into the culture of the academic department.

Foreign students may require time to adjust to the nuances of the American educational system, in which policies and procedures, research methods, and accepted practices for building relationships within the academic department may be very different than the systems they know. They may also experience difficulties in establishing friendships with native students or other foreign students because of prejudice or political events occurring in their home countries (Althen, 1995).

Although all graduate students may face reduced financial resources when returning to school, international students may encounter financial difficulties due to unexpected expenses for food or housing and few resources may be available to them in their native country. Regardless of nationality, many graduate students at major research universities may also be faced with balancing the additional roles of spouse and/or parent. Relocation to attend school may have resulted in the loss of a support network for childcare and, perhaps, loss of income on the part of a trailing spouse. All of these factors can compound the stress of transitioning to a new environment and culture.

Employment. Schuster (1997) suggests that various factors exist that will significantly impact the employment opportunities for graduate degree holders in the academy. He notes that two strong demographic forces, replacement-driven demand and enrollment-driven demand, will converge to create a volatile employment market. In addition, he has identified eight other factors that either dampen or enhance the demand for more faculty:

1. Economic and political conditions
2. Early retirement
3. End of mandatory retirement
4. Immigration and naturalization issues
5. Needs for flexibility in staffing
6. Reemphasis on teaching
7. Quality, and "the competition" (with the private sector for qualified candidates)
8. Technology

Anderson and Swazey (1998) found that of the 2000 graduate students in major research universities that they surveyed, 78 percent indicated they attended graduate school to gain knowledge in the field and that 40 percent indicated the desire to teach in higher education. However, recent trends reported by Nerad, June, and Miller (1997) indicated that the demand for Ph.D.s in university settings is slowing. Concurrently, enhanced relationships between the U.S. and other countries have resulted in an unprecedented number of international students receiving masters and doctoral level degrees from American universities. Approximately 54 percent of international doctoral students plan to remain in the U.S. after graduation (Young, 1997). These factors seem to indicate that for those who intend to pursue a career in academia, competition for jobs may be stiff.

Nerad, June, and Miller (1997) suggest that universities have operated too long on the premise that their primary role is to prepare the next generation of academic researchers for careers in academia. In doing so, major research universities have produced graduates, particularly at the doctoral level, whose research and academic training is too narrowly defined for the range of tasks that they will encounter in a nonacademic setting. In addition, they have difficulty adjusting to jobs that are not research-based or that require applied research and development skills rather than pure research skills. LaPidus (1995) concluded that graduate students who are enrolled in major research institutions tend to focus on coursework and research projects and devote little attention to their own career planning and employment issues. As a result, they have not developed work-related skills and are not prepared to make the transition from academia to the workplace upon graduation.

In their review of employment trends of graduate students, Fischer and Zigmond (1998) found that a majority of students who received their doctoral degrees in science and engineering in the mid 1980's are not working outside of academia. Similarly, Nerad, June, and Miller (1997) found that the majority of new Ph.D. graduates (more than 50 percent) are finding employment outside of the academy. Clearly, a significant number have made the transition to the world outside of academia. However, many graduate students are developing knowledge and skill sets in preparation for academic careers that may not materialize for them. The traditional model of graduate education with its focus on "learning more and more about less and less" may not meet the changing demands of American industrial and commercial life, particularly for engineers and scientists at the doctoral level. Because graduate education is vital to the economic, cultural, technological, and educational goals of the nation, preparation for employment both outside of and inside academia for graduate students is imperative (Nerad, June, & Miller, 1997). Thus, because of the need to pursue "non-traditional" careers outside of academia, graduate students today face very different career challenges than those of previous generations.

Major research institutions are experiencing an increase in the percentage of international graduate students. Enrollments of foreign graduate students in science and engineering programs increased more rapidly than the comparable numbers of U.S. citizens from 1982 to 1992 and that trend continues (Nerad, June, & Miller, 1997). For non-U.S. citizens, the employment preparation process is more complex and more difficult. International students face the additional challenges of navigating the complex maze of immigration laws in order to secure the appropriate visa that will enable them to work legally while they are in the U.S.

Graduate Student Work Load. "Graduate students are often the most overworked people on a university campus...This is particularly true if they have teaching assistantships" (Barnes, 1991, p. 159). The teaching assistantship responsibilities add the dimension of at least six hours of teaching per week (Barnes). However, the need for preparation and follow-up increases the teaching-related time to close to 40 hours per week. This workload is typically in addition to carrying a full course load. Consequently, graduate students often lack time to enjoy personal relationships and intimacy with others and may have limited opportunities to meet others outside of a core of fellow students with whom they attend classes or share offices (Barnes).

It is no surprise then, that there is a strong unionization movement by teaching assistants across the country that is engaging university administrators in reviewing and revising policies to address these issues of heavy work load, little socialization time, and other related issues such as health care benefit packages and wages (Leatherman, 2000).

Role Reversal and Conflict. Professionals who have returned to graduate school after several years in the workforce may encounter difficulties in adjusting to the new role of student. Graduate students have reported the experience of "divestiture" (Anderson & Swazey, 1998). Divestiture involves revising previous self-concepts and taking on new views of self that reflects new roles and membership in the graduate student group. Those who have achieved a moderate to high level of responsibility and status in their organization must adapt to a new role in which they are learners. In the academic culture, faculty are often awarded high status level and associated power. Professionals who relinquish their own high status position to return to school full time or, even those who retain their position and attend graduate school on a part-time basis, must "play by another set of rules" where they have little power and no longer enjoy high status; rather they are the protégées.

International students may share the experience of divestiture if they have worked in their field for several years and have achieved an advanced professional level as well as the accompanying level of respect or if they have attended schools at which graduate students are awarded a relatively high status. This experience may create a role conflict for some graduate students as they may experience feelings of reduced status and less control over their lives than when they were employed full time (Althen, 1995). Both groups may be disillusioned to learn that the status of graduate students in American research universities is typically low (Althen).

The difficulties associated with this change in role from professional to student may be compounded by the need to relearn the student skills that they adopted as undergraduates, but within the culture of graduate school. Postgraduate education brings with it a certain level of expectations on the part of faculty who can have a powerful impact on the degree of success or failure a graduate student may experience. New graduate students must learn how to develop and maintain relationships with faculty whose support can lead directly to employment in or out of academia. Students may feel a sense of concern about their ability to meet the expectations of faculty in order to garner their support. They must also learn the process of choosing an advisor, developing a plan-of-study, selecting a dissertation topic, taking the comprehensive exams and completing the doctoral dissertation (Fischer & Zigmond, 1998).

Redirection from Academic Career Paths. As adults advance through their careers, their needs and goals change as a result of external factors, internal factors, or a combination of the two. Gaff and Gaff (1981) suggest that adult students are often more goal-oriented than traditional age students due to the possession of a greater degree of pragmatism about jobs and careers. They typically return to school to gain skills necessary to advance in their careers. Often they seek to combat obsolescence in response to changes in the work place. Such external factors as economic fluctuations, organizational restructuring, emerging technologies, or the globalization of the marketplace often impact the career path of adult workers forcing an unplanned change. Other workers determine that their current position or even their occupation is not congruent with personal qualities or interests, thereby preventing them from attaining professional goals while satisfying personal values such as leisure or family (Goodman & Savage, 1999). These employees may voluntarily redirect their career path in order to find a better "fit" in the job market.

These variables have contributed to a transitory trend among workers whose goals "have often become more focused on the transferability and portability of their skills from business to business, industry to industry, and country to country" (Goodman & Savage, 1999, p. 20).

For many graduate students, a career in a tenure stream faculty position represents the implementation of self-concept and the realization of career goals. In view of the data on employment trends in academia, less than one half (40 percent), of graduate students will work in an academic setting. Graduate students who have worked hard to pursue careers in academia and must redirect their career path due to the realities of the academic job market, may experience reduced self esteem and a sense of failure.

Graduate Students as Temporary Workers. In an overview of the education of graduate scientists and engineers, reported by Nerad, June, and Miller (1997), it was noted that the average time to complete a doctoral degree has increased for graduate students in all science and engineering fields. One reason for the increase in registered time to degree (RTTD) is that more Ph.D.s in many fields enter into postdoctoral study, work in temporary research positions, and take temporary, usually one-year, faculty positions while seeking tenure-track opportunities. The evidence suggests that the increase in postdoctoral study is due to difficulties in securing appropriate employment after graduation.

This section identified several issues that graduate students may encounter as they enter and negotiate the new learning environment. They must adjust to new identities of student, learner, teacher, researcher, and new group member, in addition to roles that they may already be operating in such as spouse, professional, and parent. Depending upon their reasons for returning to school, graduate students may need to work through issues of changing self-concepts, role reversals, reduced status level, and adapting to new cultures and traditions. Some may be facing involuntary career transitions due to increasing technology and globalization, reduced financial resources, career redirections; still others may be working through the stages of grief related to job loss or unrealized career ambitions. Graduate students who planned to pursue an academic career may realize little potential job market for their discipline either internal or external to academia. They must often learn how to be students again while perhaps working as teaching assistants and learning to be teachers and researchers. In addition, they must negotiate the processes and procedures to attain the masters or doctoral degree and must establish relationships with peers and faculty to advance their academic goals. Because of their unique standing in the academic setting, their associated responsibilities and tasks, and their individual motivators and ambitions, graduate students face many challenges and, in turn, present unique challenges to the career development professionals who work with them. The following section details some specific programs and services that address the special needs of graduate students in major research universities and presents some recommendations for other initiatives.

Recommendations for Career Services Practitioners in University Settings

In October 1999, the American Association of University Professors drafted a supplemental statement to the Joint Statement on Rights and Freedoms of Students (Anonymous, 2000). The recommended standards comprising the statement address many of the issues discussed previously relative to academic freedom, employment, degree requirement clarification, advising, intellectual property, training, collective bargaining rights, compensation, and benefits. The association recommends that universities with graduate programs should adopt these standards to foster sound academic policies. While it remains to be seen what progress will be made in ensuring the implementation of policies and procedures consistent with these standards, other programs and services that support the career development needs of graduate students in major research universities have been initiated. Although at times more specifically designed to address graduate student issues, these interventions are most often appropriate for adult learners at the undergraduate level as well.

In her synthesis of career development theories, Minor (1992) identified many common elements that when merged into one model may assist counselors in developing interventions for adults. Several concepts that emerged include the influence that external factors such as economic and social conditions have on an individual's career decisions; the expectations that the adult has about the work environment and the degree of congruence with what actually exists; and that the adult's professional career is intertwined with one's personal career. "The interactions of occupational and family life cycles, life style, leisure, and other issues cannot be separated. They must be considered together in career planning" (p. 38).

This approach suggests that counselors at major research universities must consider the issues that graduate students, including international students, may be encountering in all facets of their lives to assist them most effectively. Counselors can assist their graduate student clients in career decision making and planning by working with them to identify and comprehend their own characteristics, the characteristics of their work environment, and other external forces impacting their career planning. Counselors also need to educate graduate students regarding the availability of occupational and employment information as well as resources for training. Perhaps most importantly, counselors must ensure that graduate level clients have a clear understanding of the implications and consequences that occupational choice may have on other aspects of their lives.

MODEL PROGRAMS

Several schools have identified the need to provide services specifically designed for graduate students. Some of the most notable programs include the University of Chicago and the University of Pennsylvania that have large graduate student populations.

The University of Chicago has developed a career development program for graduate students that many major research institutions may wish to emulate. Graduate and professional students comprise two thirds of the University's total enrollments. Approximately one third of all students are graduate students in Arts and Sciences; one third are professional students in Medicine, Law, and Business Administration; and one third of all students are undergraduates. The University's Career and Placement Services (CAPS) has dedicated four full-time counselors to provide individual career counseling assistance, workshops and programs, reference file services, and publications and internet resources geared to the job market in and outside of academia. Workshops focus on two areas:

1. The Academic Job Search Process, and
2. Exploring Options Outside of Academia

Specific topics include:

1. Preparing for the Academic Job Search
2. The Campus Visit
3. Negotiating and Offer
4. Getting Published: An Insider's Guide
5. Within and Beyond the Ivory Tower

In addition, CAPS recently launched an annual Science Career Forum that brought together Ph.D. candidates and post-doctoral fellows in the physical and biological sciences with executives and scientists in research and technology. CAPS also sponsors a Business Management Seminar with includes five two-hour seminars that are led by faculty, Ph.D. alumni, and former graduate students.

The University of Pennsylvania offers services to its masters and doctoral students through a centralized career services center. Counselors who serve specific schools within the university such as Medicine, Business, Fine Arts, Education, Arts and Sciences, Engineering and Applied Science, and Communication conduct individual career counseling sessions. Services and programs include career information, postings of summer and permanent jobs as well as job search related workshops, publications, and internet resources. In addition, the staff of the Career Planning and Placement Service at the University of Pennsylvania has published "The Academic Job Search Handbook" which was first published in 1992 (Heiberger & Vick, 1996). This publication leads the graduate job seeker through the entire process of planning for and implementing the job search targeted to academia. Indeed, there is an emerging awakening among major research universities to the fact that adult graduate students have career development needs that in may ways are more complex and challenging than those faced by undergraduates.

The University of Chicago and the University of Pennsylvania developed these programs in direct response to the needs of graduate students including international graduate students. The following are additional recommendations for other types of programs and services to support and assist all adult learners with a special focus on graduate student populations:

1. *Establish an Adult Learner Center that serves as an entry point for traditional adult students and serves as a referral agency for them.* The Pennsylvania State University provides support to undergraduate and graduate students through the Center for Adult Learner Services. Sixteen percent of undergraduates and eighty-eight percent of graduate students at Penn State are adult learners. The center assists students in the preparation for entry into the university, supports students in transitioning into their new roles and environment, and advises students regarding educational and career choices while referring them to other appropriate university services. They also advocate for adult learners on issues involving university policies and practices. Staff provides information on financial aid, admission policies and procedures, community resources, housing, and childcare. The center facilitates collegiality by enabling students to connect with other adult learners in the lounge, study area with computer access, and through shared use of kitchen facilities.

2. *Provide specialized staff at the career center that caters to the unique needs of adult students, especially graduate and international students.* Counselors should be experienced in providing individual career counseling to adult populations. When working with adult students, it is incumbent upon career counseling practitioners to explore and consider the unique set of circumstances that form the client's career perspectives. In his summary of career services imperatives for the 1990's, Rayman (1993) recommends that career services professionals educate clients about the life-long process of career development and design programs and services that support clients in every developmental stage. Hansen (1997) emphasizes the need to use an integrative approach when working with clients as they plan their careers so that they consider the various facets and span of their lives. Kerka (1995) posits that counselors must be familiar with adult development and adult learning theories as a way of mining the older students' life experiences as a source of career information. Traditional counseling had a focus on the individual's interest, skills, and values; adult career counseling must take into account the link between work and family life for both men and women. In addition, Schlossberg (1984) advises that counselors who work with adults in career transition should be cognizant of the issue of age as it relates to career decision making and to employment.

3. *Create or purchase publications that are targeted specifically to adult learners and to graduate student populations.* Depending upon the demographics of a specific university, those populations may be very similar so that marketing strategies targeted for one group may also address the other. An example of a publication for international students is published by Drexel University entitled "The International Student's Guide to the American University" (Barnes, 1991). Another book entitled *A Ph.D. is Not Enough! A Guide to Survival in Science* (Feibelman, 1993), provides advice for pursuing careers is science within academia as well as in the private and public sectors. Major research universities that enroll large numbers of graduate students may look to spend limited funding for career literature and job related resources in proportion to the student population and target some resources to support the career development needs of their graduate students.

4. *Establish credential services to support graduate and professional school applications and job applications within higher education.* Placement offices across the country have been providing credential services for undergraduate and graduate students for years. Many adult students who are new to the university may not be aware that such services exist. The application process for employment within academia is not an intuitive process and most graduate students are unfamiliar with the steps involved such as preparing a curriculum vita and interviewing. To augment the credentials services, career services professionals may wish to offer workshops and seminars targeted to careers in academia for graduate students.

5. *Develop and deliver a series of relevant workshops and seminars for the adult learner using an androgogical framework on such topics as: employment trends, job search strategies, identifying alternative career plans.* The Pennsylvania State University has developed a Job Search Strategies workshop specifically designed for international students. Workshop content includes two sections relative to potential barriers: (a) Acknowledge the Obstacles of citizenship requirements, cultural differences, and language barriers, and (b) Overcome the Obstacles by developing an understanding of how the U.S. job search process works and how international students can take advantage of that process. The third component of the workshop includes a comprehensive discussion of services and resources available to assist the students in implementing a job search plan.

6. *Provide assistance to graduate students in securing post-doctoral opportunities and employment in business, industry, and government.* Many graduate students who are pursuing careers in academia may encounter a tight job market or may determine that their career goals should be revised to better reflect personal interests and abilities. Those who have pursued an academia career to the exclusion of other alternatives may have no frame of reference or requisite knowledge with which to crystallize new career goals and develop a plan to realize those goals. Graduate students must be educated about the career development process that includes self exploration as well as exploration of career pathways that are alternatives to careers in academia. Career counselors would serve graduate students well by working with them to develop career development plans and by supporting graduate students in the implementation of those plans.

7. *Develop programs and services that are targeted to underrepresented adult undergraduate and graduate populations.* The impact of the increasing number of women, people of color, and international adults in higher education and in the workforce creates challenges and opportunities for these graduate students. Issues of potential obstacles, such as glass ceiling or racial segregation along disciplinary lines in the academic labor market, as well as in private industry, and the strategies to manage careers around those obstacles must be taught to adult students who may have little prior knowledge of the issues. Career planning professionals should identify benchmark programs such as those at the University of Chicago and the University of Pennsylvania to stimulate programs appropriate for their own student populations.

8. *Implement experiential education and practical training programs for American and international graduate students.* Experiential education programs include Cooperative Education and Internships and can be developed across all disciplines within the university. These programs give graduate students the opportunity to see first hand the practical applications of theory, deepen their understanding of the discipline, and inform them of career opportunities in the private or government sectors. The experience may also provide the opportunity for designing research that can be incorporated into the curriculum or form the basis of masters or doctoral theses. The visa status of international students allows for time in the U.S. to work in a position related to the course of study. Practical training is an integral part of the curriculum for international students yet they often experience difficulty in securing this training. Career services professionals play an important role in connecting graduate students to these career development opportunities.

9. *Coordinate mentoring and networking programs that provide opportunities for graduate students to connect with advanced level graduate students within the same college or discipline or that enable graduates to connect with professionals who have been working in the field for several years.* The Pennsylvania State University sponsors a mentoring program for first year undergraduate students of color to assist them in adjusting to the university environment. This may serve as a model for similar programs that target first year graduate students and connect them with faculty mentors and alumni mentors in their same field. This type of program may be especially helpful to address the unique needs of part-time graduate students whose connections to their academic departments may not be as strong due to lack of time on campus to develop collegial relationships.

10. *Aggressively market programs and services to adult undergraduate and graduate students.* Graduate students are not accustomed to receiving services that are targeted to their special needs so they may not seek them out. Career development professionals need to think creatively about how to reach their desired market. Engaging in market research to identify the specific demographic profiles of the adult learner population would enable career professionals to then target their marketing efforts to that population. Rayman (1993) suggests forging cooperative relationships with faculty, administrators, and other university representatives to take advantage of the "multiplier effect" that will further the goal of enhanced student career development. By managing relationships with centers of influence throughout the university system, career counselors may nurture advocates to promote career services by various channels. The key is to identify and develop innovative means of informing graduate students about programs and seminars that are targeted specifically to them.

According to Seifried and Rayman (1998), a survey of 35 major research institutions revealed that there is a dearth of programs that comprehensively address the unique career development requirements of graduate students. It is clear that the presence of adult learners at many research universities will continue to increase, it is incumbent upon career development professionals at major research universities to address the unique career development needs of their adult students at the undergraduate and graduate levels.

In identifying career services imperatives for the next millennium, Rayman (1999) suggested that career services professionals acknowledge the life-long nature of career development and initiate programs that engage students at any age and encourage them to take responsibility for their own destiny. He also suggests that counselors continue their own professional development to prepare themselves to address the changing career needs of an increasingly diverse population of students at all levels of learning at any stage of the lifespan.

References

Althen, G. (1995). *The handbook of foreign student advising* (Rev. ed.). Maine: Intercultural Press, Inc.

Anderson, M. S., & Swazey, J. P. (1998). Reflections on the graduate student experience: An overview. In M. S. Anderson (Ed.), *The experience of being in graduate school: An exploration* (pp. 3-13). San Francisco: Jossey-Bass.

Anonymous. (2000). Statement on graduate students. *Academe, 86*, 64-65.

Aslanian, C. B. (2001). *Adult students today.* New York: The College Board.

Aslanian, C. B., & Brickell, H. M. (1980). *Americans in transition: Life changes and reasons for adult learning.* New York: The College Board.

Aslanian, C. B., & Brickell, H. M. (1988). *How Americans in transition study for college credit.* New York: The College Board.

Baird, L. L. (1993). Using research and theoretical models of graduate student progress. In L. L. Baird (Ed.), *Increasing graduate student retention and degree attainment* (pp. 3-12). San Francisco: Jossey-Bass.

Barnes, G. A. (1991). *The international student's guide to the American university.* Lincolnwood, IL: National Textbook Company.

Boyle, P., & Boice, B. (1998). Best practices for enculturation: collegiality, mentoring, and structure. In M. S. Anderson (Ed.), *The experience of being in graduate school: An exploration* (pp. 87-94). San Francisco: Jossey-Bass.

Carnegie Foundation for the Advancement of Teaching. (1994). *A classification of institutions of higher education.* Princeton, NJ: Author.

College Enrollment by Age of Students. (1998, Fall). *The Chronicle of Higher Education Almanac* (2000).

Feibelman, P. J. (1993). *A Ph.D. is Not Enough! A Guide to Survival in Science.* Reading, MA: Perseus Books.

Fischer, B. A., & Zigmond, M. J. (1998). Survival skills for graduate school and beyond. In M. S. Anderson (Ed.), *The experience of being in graduate school: An exploration.* San Francisco: Jossey-Bass.

Gaff, J. G., & Gaff, S. S. (1981). Student-faculty relationships. In Arthur W. Chickering & Associates, *The Modern American College.* San Francisco: Jossey-Bass.

Gerald, D. E., & Hussar, W. J. (2000). *Projections of Education Statistics to 2001* (NCES No. 2000-071). Washington, DC: National Center for Education Statistics.

Goodman, J., & Savage, N. (1999). Responding to a Community Need: Oakland University's Adult Career Counseling Center. *The Career Development Quarterly, 48,* 19-29.

Hansen, L. S. (1997). *Integrative Life Planning.* San Francisco: Jossey-Bass.

Heiberger, M., & Vick, J. (1996). *The academic job search handbook* (2nd ed.). Philadelphia: University of Pennsylvania Press.

Hughes, R. (1983). The nontraditional student in higher education: A synthesis of the literature. *NASPA Journal, 20,* 51-64.

Keierleber, D. L., & Hansen, L. S. (1992). A coming of age: Addressing the needs of the adult learner in university settings. In H. D. Lea & Z. B. Leibowitz, (Eds.), *Adult Career Development: Concepts, Issues, and Practices* (2nd ed., pp. 312-339). Alexandria, VA: National Career Development Association.

Keierleber, D. L., & Sundal-Hansen, L. S. (1986). Adult career development in university settings: practical perspectives. In Z. B. Leibowitz & H. D. Lea, (Eds.), *Adult Career Development: Concepts, Issues, and Practices* (pp. 249-271). Alexandria, VA: National Career Development Association.

Kerka, S. (1995). *Adult Career Counseling in a New Age.* ERIC Digest No. 167. (ERIC Document Reproduction Service No. ED 389 881).

Krager, L., Wrenn, R., & Hirt, J. (1990). Perspectives on Age Differences. *New Directions for Student Services, 51,* 37-47.

LaPidus, J. B. (1995). Doctoral education and student career needs. *New Directions for Student Services, 72,* 33-41.

Leatherman, C. (2000, March 31). For T. A.'s winning the right to unionize is only half the battle. *The Chronicle of Higher Education, 46,* A16-A17.

Minor, C. W. (1992). Career development theories and models. In h. D. Lea & Z. B. Leibowitz, (Eds.), *Adult Career Development* (2nd ed., pp. 17-41). Alexandria, VA: National Career Development Association.

Nerad, M., June, R., & Miller, D. S. (1997). Volume Introduction. In M. Nerad, R. June, & D. S. Miller (Eds.), *Graduate Education in the United States* (pp. vii-xiv). New York: Garland.

Nowack, J., & Shriberg, A. (1981). Providing services for the adult learner in the university. In F. R. DiSilvestro (Ed.), *Advising and Counseling Adult Learners* (pp. 43-50). San Francisco: Jossey-Bass.

Peterson's Guide to Four-Year Colleges. (1998). (28th ed.). Princeton, NJ: Peterson's.

Rayman, J. R. (1993). Concluding remarks and career services imperatives for the 1990's. In J. R. Rayman (Ed.), *The Changing Role of Career Services* (pp. 101-108). San Francisco: Jossey-Bass.

Rayman, J. R. (1999). Career services imperatives for the next millennium. *The Career Development Quarterly, 48,* 175-184.

Schlossberg, N. K. (1994). *Counseling Adults in Transition: Linking Practice With Theory.* New York: Springer.

Schuster, J. H. (1997). Speculating about the labor market for academic humanists: Once more unto the breach. In M. Nerad, R. June, & D. S. Miller (Eds.), *Graduate Education in the United States* (pp. 92-97). New York: Garland.

Seifried, T. J., & Rayman, J. R. (1998). *Career Services for Adult Learners: A Survey of 35 Colleges and Universities.* The Pennsylvania State University, University Park: Student Affairs.

U.S. Department of Education, National Center for Education Statistics. (1989). *Digest of Educational Statistics* (25th ed.) (NCES Publication No. 89-642). Washington, D.C.: U.S. Government Printing Office.

U.S. Department of Education, National Center for Education Statistics. (2000). *The Condition of Education 2000.* (NCES Publication No. 2000-602). Washington, D.C.: U.S. Government Printing Office.

Young, B. A. (1997). *Degrees Earned by Foreign Graduate Students: Fields of Study and Plans After Graduation* (NCES Publication No. 98-042). Washington, D.C.: U.S. Government Printing Office.

CHAPTER 19
Facilitating the Career Development Of Adults Attending Two-Year Colleges

Darrell Anthony Luzzo
Junior Achievement, Inc.

Across all levels of higher education, the number of adults over the age of 25 has steadily climbed in recent years to record levels (Luzzo, 1999; Rathus & Fichner-Rathus, 1997). The majority of adults returning to the educational arena, often referred to in the literature as *non-traditional students,* tend to select two-year (i.e., community or technical) colleges as their educational environment of choice as they work to identify and pursue their career goals.

Researchers and college student affairs professionals have long recognized many personal and psychological characteristics that differentiate college students of traditional age (i.e., those under the age of 25) and adult students (Ashar & Skenes, 1993; Chartrand, 1992; Chickering & Havighurst, 1981; Miller & Winston, 1990). Among these characteristics is the consistently cited (and fairly intuitive) observation that adult students often have work, family, and community responsibilities outside of the college environment. Accompanying these responsibilities is much less of a concern among adult students in the areas of establishing an identity or engaging in college-sponsored social activities—two of the hallmarks of younger, more traditional aged students. Instead, adult students in two-year college settings are likely to be much more concerned with managing the stress associated with competing work, family, and community responsibilities.

These types of differences led Chartrand (1992) to argue that traditional models of student development (e.g., Pascarella, 1980; Tinto, 1975) may focus too exclusively on developmental factors associated with late adolescence and, as such, may ignore many of the issues that are salient in the lives of most adult college students. Miller and Winston (1990) expressed this same concern:

> This older adult group...reflects a population that is experiencing considerably different developmental needs and tasks than those of students of traditional college age. Because these nontraditional students are at different developmental levels, it is important that psychosocial assessment strategies and instrumentation be geared to the special characteristics and life patterns of these different age cohorts (p. 109).

Darrell Anthony Luzzo, Ph.D., NCC, is the Senior Vice President of Education for Junior Achievement Inc., and editor of *Career Counseling of College Students: An Empirical Guide to Strategies That Work* (published by APA Books). Correspondence regarding this chapter should be sent to Darrell Anthony Luzzo, One Education Way, Colorado Springs, CO 80906; E-mail: dluzzo@ja.org.

As with other specifically identified populations, adults attending two-year colleges exhibit a variety of characteristics that counselors need to consider when developing and providing career services. The purpose of this chapter is to discuss several of these defining characteristics and to present specific strategies for addressing the career decision-making needs of adults attending two year/community colleges.

Factors Associated with the Career Development of Adults Attending Two-Year Colleges

For many adult students attending two-year colleges, the decision to pursue additional educational training is often motivated by economic needs and/or concerns (Ashar & Skenes, 1993). Adults re-entering college after several years away from education may view their enrollment in college courses or programs of study as a means for enhancing their job security by updating their skills in a particular area or completing a degree that was initially sought several years prior. For many other adult students, the loss of a job may be accompanied by a severance package that includes fees for education or other training. Still others may return to college for the primary purpose of lifelong learning or the pursuit of a leisure or hobby. Because of the flexible scheduling of courses and the relatively low cost of enrolling at two-year colleges, many adults consider such a setting as an ideal environment for achieving their goals.

As research conducted over the past 15 years has revealed, the majority of adult students attending college are not necessarily any more advanced in their career exploration and planning than their younger counterparts (Ashar & Skenes, 1993; Brock & Davis, 1987; Healy & Reilly, 1989; Luzzo, 2000; Mounty, 1991). Still, there are several distinct factors that differentiate the career development of adult students attending two-year colleges and the career development of younger students. Because the majority of two-year college career counseling programs have traditionally focused on the needs of traditional aged students (defined in the literature as students under the age of 25), it is imperative that career counselors develop career development programs and interventions geared specifically to the expanding population of adult college students (Ginter & Brown, 1996; Luzzo, 2000; Mounty, 1991).

Evidence exists to support the notion that traditional and non-traditional college students, many of whom attend two-year colleges, exhibit at least some similarities in their career exploration and planning needs. Results of empirical studies have generally revealed the absence of a relationship between the age of college students and their knowledge of career decision-making principles (Healy, Mitchell, & Mourton, 1987; Luzzo, 1993a), knowledge of their preferred occupation (Greenhaus, Hawkins, & Brenner, 1983), and career decidedness (Slaney, 1986; Zagora & Cramer, 1994). In other words, younger, more traditionally aged college students—as well as adults attending college—exhibit nearly equal levels of knowledge of career decision-making principles, knowledge of the career they are most likely to pursue, and indecision regarding their career goals.

On the other hand, researchers have uncovered several career decision-making factors that differentiate adult students attending two-year colleges and younger, more traditionally aged students. Gaining an enhanced understanding of these differences can be especially useful in developing appropriate career counseling interventions for adult students in two-year college settings.

One of the basic tenets of the late Donald Super's (1984) theory of career development is that as one matures over time (i.e., as one grows older), she or he benefits from earlier career-related experiences in a manner that allows that individual to build upon previously learned principles of career exploration and planning. A student entering a community college directly upon graduation for high school is likely to have considerably fewer on-the-job experiences (as well as general life experiences) than an adult in her or his late 20s or early 30s who is returning to school after several years away from education. Not only are older adult students more likely to be in the establishment or maintenance stage of career development, but they are also likely to exhibit more appropriate attitudes toward career decision making, a concept Super initially referred to as *career maturity* and later referred to as *career adaptability*.

Super (1984) also believed that adult students are more likely than younger students to be engaged in *recycling,* the process of re-experiencing earlier stages of career development. Because returning adult students are hypothesized to use their accumulated knowledge from previous career decision-making experiences, it is often assumed (albeit incorrectly at times) that they are considerably more effective and perhaps even more efficient in repeating earlier stages of career development, such as the process of exploring career options, becoming established within a chosen career, or experiencing a career transition (Healy & Reilly, 1989). On the other hand, one might argue that recycling is even *more* challenging than initially experiencing the early stages career development, primarily because of the additional responsibilities associated with multiple life roles.

John Crites, a student of Super's who later went on to achieve notoriety in the field of career development in his own right, further developed the concept of career maturity. According to Crites (1971), an individual's attitudes and emotional reactions toward making career decisions comprise one of the two primary domains of career maturity (with the other domain being the cognitive or decision-making domain). Crites, like Super, argued that as persons mature over time (i.e., grow older), their work-related and general life experiences help them to develop more appropriate attitudes toward career decision-making.

Numerous research investigations—several of which have analyzed data gathered from community college students—have revealed a positive relationship between college students' ages and their attitudes toward career decision making attitudes (Blustein, 1988; Guthrie & Herman, 1982; Healy, O'Shea, & Crook, 1985; Luzzo, 1993b), thereby lending support to the arguments forwarded by Super and Crites—at least as far as the affective domain (i.e., attitudes, feelings) of career maturity is concerned. Adult students generally exhibit attitudes toward the career exploration and planning process that demonstrate a general sense of security and comfort with career decision making, whereas younger students are more likely to exhibit attitudes indicative of insecurity and anxiety associated with making career decisions.

Another student of Donald Super's, Charles Healy, and several of Healy's colleagues (Healy, 1991; Healy, Mitchell, & Mourton, 1987; Healy & Mourton, 1987;

Healy et al., 1985; Healy & Reilly, 1989) conducted a series of investigations in the mid 1980s and early 1990s that provided career counselors with a much clearer understanding of the role that age plays in the career development of two-year college students. In a study published in 1985, Healy et al. asked participants to complete the Attitude Scale of the *Career Maturity Inventory* (CMI; Crites, 1978) and a demographic form that asked for information regarding age, grade point average (GPA), and occupational status. Results revealed a positive correlation between age and career decision-making attitudes ($\underline{r}$ = .48, $\underline{p}$ < .01). A path analysis also showed a direct link between age and occupational level as well as linkages between age, career attitudes, and GPA. The two major findings associated with this investigation revealed that: (a) the affective component of career maturity is, in fact, associated with the age of two-year college students (with adults exhibiting more mature attitudes toward career decision-making than younger students), and (b) more mature attitudes toward the career decision-making process enhance employability and facilitate academic achievement.

In a non-community college student sample, Blustein (1988) asked university students to complete measures of career indecision, career commitment, and career maturity. Consistent with the findings reported by Healy et al. (1985) in their two-year college sample, findings revealed a significant, positive relationship between age and career maturity, with age accounting for nearly five percent of the variance in career maturity scores. Finally, in a more recent study, Luzzo (1993b) provided additional evidence that age may be an influential factor in determining college students' attitudes toward career decision making. Students completed several measures of career development as well as a demographic questionnaire. Results revealed that the age of participants was positively correlated with attitudes toward career decision-making ($\underline{r}$ = .31, $\underline{p}$ < .001), with age accounting for over nine percent of the variance in students' career decision-making attitudes. Once again, older students in the study were more likely than their younger, traditional classmates to exhibit mature attitudes toward career decision-making tasks.

Traditional and nontraditional students attending college also appear to differ in other aspects of career development, including career commitment, vocational identity, career decision-making self-efficacy, and perceived career counseling needs (Colarelli & Bishop, 1990; Greenhaus, Hawkins, & Brenner, 1983; Haviland & Mahaffy, 1985; Luzzo, 1993a; Peterson, 1993). In a study of 341 students working towards their Master's of Business Administration (MBA) degree, Colarelli and Bishop (1990) asked participants to complete two measures of career commitment as well as psychological measures of locus of control, role conflict, and role ambiguity. Results indicated that adult students were more committed than traditional students to their identified career choice. Results also suggested the importance of considering important personal (e.g., gender, ethnicity) and psychological characteristics (e.g., locus of control, multiple role conflict) when providing career counseling services to adults students in community (and other) college settings.

Haviland and Mahaffy (1985) had participants in their study—all of whom were adult college students—complete the *My Vocational Situation* (MVS) Inventory (Holland, Daiger, & Power, 1980). Completion of the MVS allowed the researchers to evaluate participants' vocational identity, knowledge of occupational information, and perceived barriers to occupational goals. Participants' scores were contrasted with the scores of traditional college students represented in the MVS norming group (as reported in the MVS manual). Results revealed several findings important to consider when designing career interventions for adult students attending two-year colleges. When contrasted with younger students in the norming sample, participants in Haviland and Mahaffy's investigation reported the perception of more barriers to reaching their chosen occupational goal and a greater need for occupational information. Haviland and Mahaffy concluded that adult students would probably benefit from discussing perceived barriers in career counseling contexts and from receiving an abundance of occupational information associated with the careers they are considering.

Two studies published in 1993 (Luzzo, 1993a; Peterson, 1993) evaluated the relationship between college students' ages and their *career decision-making self-efficacy*. Career decision-making self-efficacy, a term first coined by Taylor and Betz (1983), is based on Bandura's (1977) self-efficacy theory. It refers to an individual's confidence in her or his ability to engage in career decision-making tasks. College students' level of career decision-making self-efficacy is moderately associated with several other indices of career development and maturity, including career exploration behavior (Blustein, 1989), career decidedness (Taylor & Betz, 1983), and career locus of control (Luzzo, 1995). Results of both the Luzzo (1993a) and Peterson (1993) studies revealed a significant relationship between age and career decision-making self-efficacy among college students, indicating that adult students are more likely than traditional students to possess confidence in their ability to engage in the career decision-making process. The one limitation associated with both of these studies, however, is that the samples consisted of non-traditional and traditional students attending four-year colleges and universities, thereby limiting the generalizability of the findings to students in the two-year college setting.

In several recent studies specifically designed to increase our understanding of the career development of two-year college students, researchers have identified additional personal and psychological factors that warrant the attention of career counselors. Ryan, Solberg, and Brown (1996), for example, examined the relationship between family dysfunction, parental attachment, and career search self-efficacy among a sample of 220 community college students. Results of the investigation revealed that attachment to parents and degree of family dysfunction significantly predicted participants' level of career search self-efficacy. Results of Ryan et al.'s (1996) study emphasize the importance of incorporating mental health and relationship issues into the context of career counseling.

More recently, Newman and Lucero-Miller (1999) evaluated the relationship between several career variables, as well as family cohesion and acculturation level, among Mexican American community college students. The results of their study indicated the importance of considering sociocultural variables (e.g., family cohesion, ethnic identity, acculturation) when providing career services to adults in two-year college settings.

Over a decade ago, Healy and Reilly (1989) conducted what was then—and continues to be—the most comprehensive analysis of the career decision-making needs of students enrolled at two-year colleges. Over 2,900 students attending 10 different community colleges in California responded to several questions about career counseling needs and services. Participants rated their needs (as a *major* need, a *minor* need, or *no need at all*) in seven career areas: knowing more about interests and abilities, understanding how to decide on career goals, becoming more certain of career plans, exploring careers related to interests and abilities, selecting courses relevant to career goals, developing job finding skills, and obtaining a job.

Findings of Healy and Reilly's (1989) investigation—although published several years ago—provide career counselors with useful information about the career development of adult students attending two-year colleges and suggest a number of strategies that might be employed to more effectively meet adult students' career decision-making needs. As hypothesized, results generally supported the notion that the career needs of two-year college students decrease in magnitude with age. For the most part, younger students are more likely than adult students in the two-year college setting to cite major needs in the career areas of (a) knowing more about interests and abilities, (b) understanding how to decide on a career goal, and (c) developing job finding skills. However, the results of Healy and Reilly's study also revealed that the *majority* of participants in *each* of the age groups (17-19, 20-23, 24-29, 30-40, 41-50) reported at least minor needs in *all seven* of the career areas!

> Tasks thought to pose minimal concern if repeated during the adult years are instead reported as major needs by 25 to 35 percent of the adults over 30 years of age in the sample. More striking, the need to explore jobs related to interests and abilities looms important for nearly 40 percent of the 40 to 50 year olds. Apparently, many of these adult students are adopting an exploratory posture toward our changing opportunity structure, seeking and anticipating work experiences through which they can develop and discover new potentials in themselves (Healy & Reilly, 1989, p. 544).

Healy and Reilly (1989) also observed several noteworthy differences in the career exploration and planning needs of women and men. Specifically, the women in the study reported less certainty about career plans than the men reported. Healy and Reilly interpreted this finding in the context of career self-efficacy, noting the following: "Less certainty among women about career plans may stem from [women's] ... apprehensions about advancing in a work system that retains many biases against women, or difficulty integrating career, marriage, and children" (p. 544).

The other observed difference in Healy and Reilly's (1989) investigation regarding women's and men's expressed career needs was in the area of obtaining a job. Men in the 24-29 and 41-50 age groups were considerably more likely than women in these same age groups to cite "obtaining a job" as a *major* career need. In the 30-40 age group, on the other hand, women were more likely than men to cite "obtaining a job" as a *major need*. This particular set of findings emphasizes the need to consider multiple factors (e.g., age, gender, etc.) when providing career counseling services to adult students in two-year college settings. Assuming that one type of career intervention or career counseling strategy is appropriate for all students—even for all *adult* students—would be a mistake.

PRACTICAL CAREER COUNSELING IMPLICATIONS OF PREVIOUS RESEARCH

Unfortunately, the majority of existing two- and four-year college career development programs and career counseling interventions tend to focus on the career decision-making needs of traditionally aged (i.e., younger) students (Luzzo

2000). As such, there is a growing need to respond to the expanding population of returning adult students in two-year college settings by developing more age-appropriate career development programs for them (Ginter & Brown, 1996; Griff, 1987; Mounty, 1991).

On the basis of the research summarized in this chapter, it seems likely that developing career counseling interventions designed to address issues specifically relevant to adult student populations is warranted (Mounty, 1991). Adult students are more likely to consider career services relevant and useful for their academic and vocational development if available interventions and services are specifically geared to their needs. The more resources that career counselors in two-year college settings devote to understanding adult students' needs, the more likely such counselors will be to develop effective career interventions that adult students will access. Fortunately, career counselors and vocational psychologists have suggested a variety of resourceful and creative career intervention strategies to consider when working with adult students in two-year colleges. In this section of the chapter, several such ideas are discussed.

First and foremost, it is important to acknowledge that adult students represent diverse backgrounds and motivations for attending college (Luzzo, 2000). An adult student attending a two-year college may be a downsized factory worker who needs to obtain a certificate in a particular field to qualify for advanced positions in her or his field or to enter a new field altogether with more promising occupational opportunities. An adult student attending a community college may be a successful, long-term employee in a well-established corporation who is merely unable to receive a promotion without first completing an associate's degree. An adult student may be someone who graduated from high school, worked for several years in or out of the home, and recently decided to return to school to pursue a professional degree, possibly selecting a two-year college as a starting point. With the apparent diversity of persons referred to as "adult students," it seems critical that we increase our ability to provide high quality career counseling services to this growing population.

Because of the many unique characteristics exhibited by individual adult students in two-year college settings, initial assessment of career related needs and concerns is critical. Rather than assuming each adult student who accesses career services would benefit from completing an interest inventory, discussing past employment experiences, or accessing labor market information, career counselors should determine the particular needs presented by each and every client and develop an intervention strategy accordingly.

Despite some of the significant differences in career development that exist between younger students attending two-year colleges and their older adult counterparts, it is clear that adult students are not so advanced in their career development that they need *substantially* less guidance in career planning and decision making (Healy et al., 1987; Healy & Reilly, 1989; Luzzo, 1993a). Furthermore, based on the research reviewed in this chapter, it would be *inappropriate* to assume that adult students in two-year college settings possess *completely different* career decision-making needs than their younger classmates. In other words, considering the age of a student alone may be insufficient for designing appropriate career interventions. There isn't any reason, for example, to assume that only adult students are concerned with economic factors associated with career decisions. "All students, both from traditional and nontraditional perspectives, expect that college will enhance their career plans and goals in today's competitive marketplace" (Mounty, 1991, p. 43). In essence, career counselors working in two-year college environments need to recognize the widespread need for career exploration and academic assistance (e.g., course selection) among college students of all ages.

The results of Healy and Reilly's (1989) investigation suggest that many adult students who are attending two-year colleges are contemplating career changes and, as such, may need guidance into learning and employment opportunities just as traditional students often require. By coordinating services with other campus agencies, counselors can help establish a network of resources that can be used by students of all ages for obtaining valuable experiences in career exploration and planning. For example, by establishing ongoing liaison relationships with vocational and academic departments at the two-year college, career counselors can ensure an awareness of the content of such courses and can help ensure that accurate and useful information is available to students.

Davies and Feller (1999), fearing that many two-year colleges offer fragmented services that may marginalize non-traditional students, strongly suggested this type of collaboration and coordination of services across multiple student service departments within the two-year college setting. They specifically argued for the creation of comprehensive career assistance centers in two-year colleges that provide integrated academic, career, and personal services. Davies and Feller's model recognizes the importance of considering a wide range of educational and psychosocial factors when providing career counseling services to adults in two-year college settings.

Another strategy for increasing adult students' access to career development programs and activities is to expand career placement and counseling service hours to include evenings and weekends. By doing so, career counselors at two-year colleges can help ensure that working adult students are able to access career counseling services at times that may be considerably more convenient than traditional 9:00-5:00 operating hours. Similarly, offering evening and weekend orientation sessions to returning adult students will provide them with the opportunity to become better acquainted with the many adjustments and life changes that often take place when reentering school.

Counseling workshops, seminars, and courses designed for adult students attending two-year colleges should include well-established methods for addressing some of the specific career-related concerns identified by adults in previously published research studies (Haviland & Mahaffy, 1985; Healy & Reilly, 1989; Luzzo, 1993a). The results of Healy and Reilly's investigation of community college students can be especially useful in this regard. For example, although adult students at two-year colleges tend to view selecting a career goal, becoming certain of those plans, and searching for jobs as *less important* activities than traditional students view them, adult students do place a strong emphasis on the need to explore jobs related to their interests and skills. Older two-year college students also perceive a significant need to learn about the process of selecting appropriate courses to prepare for specific careers. Such topics should be the focus of workshops and seminars specifically targeted to meet the needs of adults in two-year college settings.

Results of Haviland and Mahaffy's (1985) research suggest that one of the most influential factors in adult college students' career development is the perception of career-related barriers. As such, counselors should consider integrating a discussion of perceived barriers into the career counseling process and should assist older adult clients in developing strategies for addressing and overcoming career-related barriers. Albert and Luzzo (1999) recently proposed several strategies that might be used for this purpose, such as encouraging clients to keep a journal of barriers they have encountered in the past. The journal might include a personal explanation regarding how these barriers were confronted and handled. Counselors might then encourage their clients to list additional ways in which specific barriers could have been managed or prevented.

Counselors also can help bolster adult college students' confidence in their ability to successfully encounter career-related barriers by discussing barrier perceptions from an attributional perspective, helping clients evaluate the degree to which they have control over the career decision-making process (Albert & Luzzo, 1999). Such strategies might help adult students begin to gain an increased sense of control over and responsibility for those barriers for which they might actually be able to overcome with increased effort or training.

Career counselors also need to remember that a host of other psychological characteristics can have a meaningful influence on the career development of adults attending two-year colleges. As discussed earlier in the chapter, many career counselors and vocational psychologists are beginning to recognize the importance of integrating psychosocial, academic, and vocational issues into career interventions (Davies & Feller, 1999; Newman & Lucero-Miller, 1999; Ryan et al., 1996). When working with adult college students, counselors need to consider the role that psychological factors such as multiple role conflict, ethnic identity, family cohesion, and acculturation play in students' career decision making. Integrating a discussion of these types of psychological characteristics into the career counseling process can serve a valuable purpose by helping older students consider the interaction between personal and career-related issues in their lives.

Counseling workshops and seminars for adult students in two-year colleges also should include well-planned strategies for addressing the *specific* career-related concerns identified by the students themselves. Career counselors can rely on previous research that has identified such concerns (e.g., Haviland & Mahaffy, 1985; Healy & Reilly, 1989). Or, better yet, counselors can conduct on-site investigations at their own campus to ensure that students' needs are met through program offerings. This strategy can be especially important when providing career development services to special sub-populations that exist within the broader context of the adult two-year college student population. In recent years, reports published in professional journals have included references to the development of specific programs designed to address the career decision-making needs of identified groups such as the "working poor" (Johnson, 2000) or students with disabilities (Norton & Field, 1998; Trach & Harney, 1998). By providing career services specifically designed for particular populations, career counselors can help ensure that the most effective career interventions are available for as many members of the student body as possible.

Finally, it would be particularly useful for two-year college career centers to recruit and hire counselors who have expertise in working with the unique problems and concerns of adult students. Two-year college counselors who are keenly aware of the career-related issues that are common to older student populations will be respected and appreciated by the adult clients who seek their services. Counseling training programs, which are exclusively offered at four-year institutions, may need to increase their coverage of non-traditional student populations and two-year college counseling services in theory and practice courses. Practicum and internship opportunities at two-year colleges provide an optimal training ground for graduate students who possess a particular interest in working in such settings. Peer mentoring is another strategy that might be considered for assisting college counselors to learn more about adult students' needs and develop effective career intervention strategies.

NEED FOR CONTINUED RESEARCH AND EVALUATION OF CAREER INTERVENTIONS FOR ADULT STUDENTS

With the ever-increasing number of adult students attending colleges and universities of all types—most notably two-year colleges—it is important that career counselors determine whether traditional career counseling interventions (e.g., small group interpretation of assessments, one-on-one counseling) are appropriate strategies for older student populations. Experimental research conducted by career counseling practitioners is especially warranted in this regard.

Two-year college career counselors are particularly encouraged to design and implement research studies at their home institutions. Counselors might want to consider partnering with faculty members at the college as well as with professors at the local university who are knowledgeable about research methodology. Such collaborations can prove particularly useful as career counselors engage in the initial stages of a research project. Results of research conducted by career counselors will help to determine whether traditional interventions are as effective for adult students as they are for the younger students for whom they were originally conceived.

Furthermore, counselors working in two-year college settings are urged to present the results of their research at relevant professional conferences (e.g., the annual conferences of the American Association for Community Colleges, American College Personnel Association, National Career Development Association, National Association of Student Personnel Administrators, American Counseling Association) and publish the results of their research in professional journals (e.g., the *Journal of College Student Development, Journal of Career Development, The Career Development Quarterly*). By so doing, two-year college career counselors can contribute to the knowledge base and help their colleagues to provide effective career counseling services to all students

Future research efforts should specifically target many of the unanswered questions regarding the ways in which younger and older adult students attending two-year colleges engage in the career decision-making process (Healy & Reilly, 1989). Do younger and older students explore careers through the same or different means? Do they ask the same or different questions about possible careers and courses that will assist them in preparing for careers? Are traditional and nontraditional students equally concerned about economic issues? Do they exhibit a comparable degree of understanding the world of work and current employment trends? In what ways does racial/ethnic diversity affect the career development needs of adult students? Answers to these and other important questions will help counselors working in two-year college settings to develop and implement the most effective career counseling interventions that they possibly can.

Career counselors and vocational psychologists have argued for many years that the influence of contextual factors in career exploration and planning has been traditionally ignored in career development research and practice (Blustein & Phillips, 1988; Morrow, Gore, & Campbell, 1996; Parham & Austin, 1994). It will become increasingly important to integrate such variables into future investigations. For example, we still know relatively little about the role that family members play in the career development of adult students. Similarly, only a few studies have examined the ways in which an individual's sense of personal agency towards career decision making, role ambiguity, sexual orientation, cultural identity, and socioeconomic status influence the career decisions of adult students (Blustein, 1988; Colarelli & Bishop, 1990; Healy & Reilly, 1989).

Similarly, career counselors would most certainly benefit from an examination of variables that have emerged in the student development literature as especially relevant to adult populations (Ashar & Skenes, 1993; Chartrand, 1992; Miller & Winston, 1990). The stress associated with competing work, family, and community responsibilities and the lack of social integration to college and university life need to be evaluated in the context of adult students' career development.

There is no question that the number of adult students attending college—particularly two-year colleges—will continue to increase in the years ahead (Ashar & Skenes, 1993; Luzzo, 2000). Along with this expanding population of adult students comes the challenge of building on existing two-year college programs and counseling services to more effectively address adults' career decision-making needs (Griff, 1987). Research focusing on the career development of adult students attending two-year colleges will play an important role in meeting that challenge and will serve as a critical factor in the development of effective career counseling services for college students of all ages.

References

Albert, K. A., & Luzzo, D. A. (1999). The role of perceived barriers in career development: A social-cognitive perspective. *Journal of Counseling and Development, 77,* 431-436.

Ashar, H., & Skenes, R. (1993). Can Tinto's student departure model be applied to nontraditional students? *Adult Education Quarterly, 43,* 90-100.

Bandura, A. (1977). Self-efficacy: Toward a unifying theory of behavioral change. *Psychological Review, 84,* 191-215.

Blustein, D. L. (1988). A canonical analysis of career choice crystallization and vocational maturity. *Journal of Counseling Psychology, 35,* 294-297.

Blustein, D. L. (1989). The role of goal instability and career self-efficacy in the career exploration process. *Journal of Vocational Behavior, 35,* 194-203.

Blustein, D. L., & Phillips, S. D. (1988). Individual and contextual factors in career exploration. *Journal of Vocational Behavior, 33,* 203-216.

Brock, S. B., & Davis, E. M. (1987). Adapting career services for the adult student. *Journal of College Student Personnel, 28,* 87-89.

Chartrand, J. M. (1992). An empirical test of a model of nontraditional student adjustment. *Journal of Counseling Psychology, 39,* 193-202.

Chickering, A. W., & Havighurst, R. J. (1981). The life cycle. In A. W. Chickering & Associates (Eds.), *The modern American college.* (pp. 16-50). San Francisco: Jossey-Bass.

Colarelli, S. M., & Bishop, R. C. (1990). Functions, correlates, and management. *Group and Organizational Studies, 15,* 158-176.

Crites, J. O. (1971). *The maturity of vocational attitudes in adolescence.* Washington, DC: American Personnel and Guidance Association.

Crites, J. O. (1978). *The Career Maturity Inventory.* Monterey, CA: CTB/McGraw Hill.

Davies, T. G., & Feller, R. (1999). Community colleges need comprehensive career assistance centers. *Career Planning and Adult Development Journal, 15*(2), 87-97.

Ginter, E. J., & Brown, S. (1996, August). *Lifestyle assessment and planning utilizing Super's C-DAC model and a life-skills model.* Presentation made at the 3rd International Congress on Integrative and Eclectic Psychotherapy, Huatulco, Mexico.

Greenhaus, J. H., Hawkins, B. L., & Brenner, O. C. (1983). The impact of career exploration on the career decision-making process. *Journal of College Student Personnel, 24,* 494-502.

Griff, N. (1987). Meeting the career development needs of returning students. *Journal of College Student Personnel, 28,* 469-470.

Guthrie, W. R., & Herman, A. (1982). Vocational maturity and its relationship to vocational choice. *Journal of Vocational Behavior, 21,* 196-205.

Haviland, M. G., & Mahaffy, J. E. (1985). The use of My Vocational Situation with nontraditional college students. *Journal of College Student Personnel, 26,* 169-170.

Healy, C. C. (1991). Exploring a path linking anxiety, career maturity, grade point average, and life satisfaction in a community college population. *Journal of College Student Development, 32,* 207-211.

Healy, C. C., Mitchell, J. M., & Mourton, D. L. (1987). Age and grade differences in career development among community college students. *Review of Higher Education, 10,* 247-258.

Healy, C. C., & Mourton, D. L. (1987). The relationship of career exploration, college jobs, and grade point average. *Journal of College Student Personnel, 28,* 28-34.

Healy, C. C., O'Shea, D., & Crook, R. H. (1985). Relation of career attitudes to age and career progress during college. *Journal of Counseling Psychology, 32,* 239-244.

Healy, C. C., & Reilly, K. C. (1989). Career needs of community college students: Implications for services and theory. *Journal of College Student Development, 30,* 541-545.

Holland, J., Daiger, D., & Power, P. (1980). *My Vocational Situation.* Palo Alto, CA: Consulting Psychologists Press.

Johnson, R. H. (2000). CareersNOW! *Community College Journal, 70*(6), 32-36.

Luzzo, D. A. (1993a). Career decision-making differences between traditional and nontraditional college students. *Journal of Career Development, 20,* 113-120.

Luzzo, D. A. (1993b). Value of career decision-making self-efficacy in predicting career decision-making attitudes and skills. *Journal of Counseling Psychology, 40,* 194-199.

Luzzo, D. A. (1995). The relative contributions of self-efficacy and locus of control to the prediction of career maturity. *Journal of College Student Development, 36,* 61-66.

Luzzo, D. A. (1999). Identifying the career decision-making needs of nontraditional college students. *Journal of Counseling and Development, 77,* 135-140.

Luzzo, D. A. (2000). Career development of returning adult and graduate students. In D. A. Luzzo (Ed.), *Career counseling of college students: An empirical guide to strategies that work* (pp. 191-200). Washington, DC: American Psychological Association.

Miller, T. K., & Winston, R. B., Jr. (1990). Assessing development from a psychosocial perspective. In D. G. Creamer (Ed.), *College student development: Theory and practice for the 1990s* (pp. 89-126). Washington, DC: American College Personnel Association.

Morrow, S. L., Gore, P. A., & Campbell, B. W. (1996). The application of a sociocognitive framework to the career development of lesbian women and gay men. *Journal of Vocational Behavior, 48,* 136-148.

Mounty, L. H. (1991). Involving nontraditional commuting students in the career planning process at an urban institution. *Journal of Higher Education Management, 6,* 43-48.

Newman, J. L., & Lucero-Miller, D. (1999). Predicting acculturation using career, family, and demographic variables in a sample of Mexican American students. *Journal of Multicultural Counseling and Development, 27,* 75-92.

Norton, S. C., & Field, K. F. (1998). Career placement project: A career readiness program for community college students with disabilities. *Journal of Employment Counseling, 35,* 40-44.

Parham, T. A., & Austin, N. L. (1994). Career development and African Americans: A contextual reappraisal using the nigrescence construct. *Journal of Vocational Behavior, 44,* 139-154.

Pascarella, E. T. (1980). Student-faculty informal contact and college outcomes. *Review of Educational Research, 50,* 545-595.

Peterson, S. L. (1993). Career decision-making self-efficacy and institutional integration of underprepared college students. *Research in Higher Education, 34,* 659-685.

Rathus, S. A., & Fichner-Rathus, L. (1997). *The right start.* New York: Addison Wesley Longman.

Ryan, N. E., Solberg, V. S., & Brown, S. D. (1996). Family dysfunction, parental attachment, and career search self-efficacy among community college students. *Journal of Counseling Psychology, 43,* 84-89.

Slaney, F. M. (1986). Career indecision in reentry and undergraduate women. *Journal of College Student Personnel, 27,* 114-119.

Super, D. E. (1984). Career and life development. In D. Brown, L. Brooks, & Associates (Eds.), *Career choice and development* (pp. 192-234). San Francisco: Jossey-Bass.

Taylor, K. M., & Betz, N. E. (1983). Applications of self-efficacy theory to the understanding and treatment of career indecision. *Journal of Vocational Behavior, 22,* 63-81.

Tinto, V. (1975). Dropout from higher education: A theoretical synthesis of recent research. *Review of Educational Research, 45,* 89-125.

Trach, J. S., & Harney, J. Y. (1998). Impact of cooperative education on career development for community college students with and without disabilities. *Journal of Vocational Education Research, 23,* 147-158.

Zagora, M. Z., & Cramer, S. H. (1994). The effects of vocational identity status on outcomes of a career decision-making intervention for community college students. *Journal of College Student Development, 35,* 239-247.

SECTION VI:

TRAINING COUNSELORS, EVALUATING PROGRAMS, AND FUTURE SCENARIOS

CHAPTER 20
Training Career Counselors: Meeting the Challenges of Clients in the 21st Century

Jane L. Swanson
Southern Illinois University at Carbondale

Karen M. O'Brien
University of Maryland

Individuals in the 21st century face many changes in how careers are structured over the lifespan, including fundamental shifts in the way that work itself is conceptualized. These changes have important implications for career professionals, as we need to pay attention to the increasingly diverse needs that clients bring to career counseling.

In this chapter, we address issues in training career counselors to work with a diverse range of adult clients. We begin the chapter with a discussion of the activity of career counseling itself, including a brief historical perspective, a variety of current conceptualizations, and our views about the complexity of career counseling. This discussion sets the context for the subsequent section, in which we focus specifically on the training of career counselors, including [what] presenting a model of career counseling training, discussing the changes that are needed in faculty attitudes, coursework, supervision, and research, and describing several exemplary programs. Finally, we offer suggestions for developing a model training program for career counselors.

The Past, Present, and Future of Career Counseling

Career counseling as a professional activity is typically traced back to Frank Parsons's pioneering work as a social reformer in Boston in the early 1900s (Brewer, 1942; Dawis, 2000). Parsons (1909), recently outed as a gay man, laid the groundwork for the way in which career counseling was conceptualized and practiced in the remainder of the 20th century. His tripartite model – understanding of oneself, knowledge of the world of work, and the "true reasoning" necessary to connect the two domains – permeated the establishment of career counseling and vocational guidance, and signs of his continued influence are is evident today in theories of person-environment fit (Dawis, 2000; Swanson, 1996). For many years, the trait-factor approach was the sole method of career counseling; however, other approaches have supplemented – some would say supplanted – trait-factor/person-environment fit career counseling. In particular, developmental, social learning, and social cognitive theories have strongly influenced the way in which career development is conceptualized and career counseling is practiced.

It is important to distinguish between theories of career *development* and theories of career *counseling*. Theories of career development were devised to explain vocational behavior, such as initial career choice, work adjustment, or lifespan career progress. These theories are well articulated and have received a considerable amount of attention from researchers (Swanson & Gore, 2000). The goal of theories of career counseling, on the other hand, is to provide counselors with direction for how to work with clients. These theories are less well developed, leading at least one author to conclude that there *is* no existing theory of career counseling (Osipow, 1996).

Several recently developed models, however, appear to truly be theories of career counseling, rather than theories of career development, because their purpose is to outline how counseling might proceed (Gysbersg, Heppner, & Johnston, 1998; Krumboltz, 1996; Spokane, 1991). In general, career counseling models are structured around a phase of introduction and relationship-building, a phase devoted to exploration of the client's work-related problem, and a phase devoted to helping the client move toward resolution of the problem.

These career counseling models provide useful paradigms to help counselors work with clients who have career concerns. The models They contain an implicit acknowledgement that there is a continuum of career-related issues that individuals bring to counseling.(Perhaps clarify previous sentence – I am not completely sure I know what you are intending to say.) Often, Clients clients seek help assistance for career-related problems that are intricately intertwined with their personal lives. Gysbers et al. (1998) noted that to work effectively with clients, counselors need to combine skills in career counseling with skills in personal-emotional emotional-social counseling. (I really think we should NOT use "personal" to describe noncareer counseling. I'm not sure that emotional-social works, but using personal seems to go against a lot of what we are trying to communicate and change.) They echo Blustein and Spengler's (1995) call for domain-sensitive counseling, which "refers to a way of intervening with clients such that the full array of human experiences is encompassed" (p. 316). In other words, effective career counselors take the client's concerns as the beginning point of therapy, and develop interventions in to address both career and noncareer domains as is appropriate for depending on the needs of the client (Swanson & Fouad, 1999).

However, because career counseling and personal-emotional emotional-social counseling developed from different historical traditions and within different professional specialties, they often are viewed as independent activities. A long-standing debate exists regarding whether career counseling and personal counseling are identical, subsets of one another, or distinct activities (Brown & Krane, 2000; Swanson, 1995). Haverkamp and Moore (1993) discussed the perceptual dichotomy existing in the profession in which career counseling and personal emotional-social counseling appear to function as distinct cognitive schemas. They argued that the implicit definition of personal emotional-social counseling is too broad, consisting of anything not directly related to career, whereas the implicit definition of career counseling is too narrow, consisting primarily of initial career choices of young adults and neglecting adult work adjustment or the intersection of work and nonwork.

Relatedly, consensus has not been reached regarding the amount of overlap between career counseling and personal emotional-social counseling (Hackett, 1993;

Subich, 1993; Super, 1993; Swanson, 1995). One view is that career counseling and personal emotional-social counseling are, if not identical, then quite similar. Rounds and Tinsley (1984) argued that career intervention is a "form of *psychotherapy* and should be viewed as a method of behavior change and tied to psychotherapy theory" (p. 138). Empirical comparisons of cases of career counseling and personal emotional-social counseling provide support for the similarity between these two domains (Anderson & Niles, 1995; Kirschner, Hoffman, & Hill, 1994; Nagel, Hoffman, & Hill, 1995).

A recent trend in the literature is to encourage the integration of personal issues into career counseling (Imbimbo, 1994; Krumboltz, 1993). Betz and Corning (1993) used the variables of gender and race to illustrate the need for a holistic approach to the inseparability of career and personal emotional-social issues in counseling. Several studies suggest that it is counselors would be unwise to view clients with career issues as fundamentally different from those with personal emotional-social issues (Gold & Scanlon; Lucas, 1992), and clients may be less satisfied with career counseling when evident salient personal emotional-social issues are not addressed in counseling (Phillips, Friedlander, Kost, Specterman, & Robbins, 1988).

A related area of literature highlights the connections between career counseling and mental health outcomes. There is increasing recognition that work and mental health are interwoven and that adult vocational needs are complex (Davidson & Gilbert, 1993; Flamer, 1986; Hackett, 1993; Haverkamp & Moore, 1993; Herr, 1989). Brown and Brooks (1985) argued that career counseling with adults may be a viable alternative to stress management and even to personal emotional-social counseling. Furthermore, they argued that mental health professionals have overlooked the potential value of career counseling.

A different perspective (Crites, 1981; Hackett, 1993; Spokane, 1989, 1991) advocates for a clear distinction between career and personal emotional-social counseling. These authors proposed that career counseling is more difficult than personal emotional-social counseling because it requires expertise in a broader range of domains (Crites, 1981; Hackett, 1993). Similarly, Crites (1981) asserted that career counseling often embraces, but goes beyond, personal emotional-social counseling to explore the client's role in the world of work.

Brown and Krane (2000) also argued recently for a separation of career and personal emotional-social counseling. They concluded that the "effort to equate career counseling and psychotherapy may be premature and tends to focus more on the needs of our field than on the needs of our clients" (p. 740). They argued that proponents of blurring the distinction between career and personal-emotional emotional-social counseling are doing so simply to make career counseling a more attractive activity for counseling professionals. Although counseling psychologists have been concerned about enhancing interest and efficacy in career counseling among trainees (Heppner, O'Brien, Hinkelman & Flores, 1996; O'Brien, Heppner, Flores, & Bikos, 1997), we believe that the needs of clients, rather than the needs of counseling professionals, drive the movement to provide a more integrated approach to career counseling (Blustein, 1987; Blustein & Spengler, 1995; Dorn, 1992; Lucas, 1993). Interestingly, Brown and Krane They define the important goals of career counseling as "helping people make goal-congruent work or career choices that will allow them to experience work, career, and life satisfaction in a changing society" (p. 740). Although they caution against viewing career and personal-emotional

emotional-social counseling as identical activities, they do acknowledged that there are a number of questions that merit further attention, including when and whether to focus on noncareer issues and the types of personal emotional-social issues that are important within the context of career counseling.

Brown and Krane (2000) also described meta-analytic evidence, aggregated across many independent studies, that supporteds the effectiveness of career counseling (Ryan, 1999). Moreover, they concluded that five treatment components were crucial in determining effective outcomes:

1. written exercises,
2. individualized inventory interpretation and feedback,
3. information about the world of world,
4. modeling, and
5. building support within the context of clients' lives.

Based on these results, counselors can be assured that the activity of career counseling generally have positive effects on clients, particularly when the aforementioned features are included. Unfortunately, however, two crucial factors were missing from Ryan's (1999) analyses, primarily because of inadequate attention by researchers. First, the review did not examine any factors related to counseling process or to the counselor-client relationship, key therapeutic ingredients not yet fully studied in career counseling (Heppner & Hendricks, 1995; Hill & Corbett, 1993; Meara & Patton, 1994). Second, little information was available about client (and counselor) characteristics that relate to differential outcomes. Calls for research focused on attribute-by-treatment interactions (Fretz, 1981) have apparently gone unheeded, with a few notable exceptions (e.g., Heppner & Hendricks, 1995).

THE COMPLEXITY OF CAREER COUNSELING

Our perspective of career counseling acknowledges the existence of important connections between "career counseling" and "personal emotional-social counseling," or between "career issues" and "personal emotional-social issues." Clients enter career counseling with a number of presenting issues, some of which clearly fit a narrowly drawn definition of career counseling and others which require a broader view because they are intricately intertwined with clients' personal lives. Counselors need to be aware of how career and personal emotional-social factors are connected in their clients' lives, and to clearly address the spectrum of issues that clients are experiencing.

Thus, we define career counseling can be defined as an ongoing, face-to-face interaction between counselor and client, with career- or work-related issues as the primary (but not necessarily the sole) focus (Swanson, 1995) during which counselors address issues and concerns that interfere with clients' ability to maximize their potential in work and in love. Career counseling is thus a subset of career interventions; the definition excludes other interventions such as computer-based guidance systems, didactic experiences such as ongoing courses or single-session workshops, and self-guided career instruments. Another definition, offered by the National Career Development Association (1997), highlighted the importance of placing career issues within the broader context of individuals' lives: "career counseling is defined as the process of assisting individuals in the development of a ife-career with focus on the definition of the worker role and how that role interacts with other life roles" (p. 1). Imbimbo (1994) suggested framing career counseling as an "eclectic counseling intervention in which the counselor is free to draw from a wide variety of theories and techniques" (p. 51).

A central assumption of these definitions relates to the interaction between counselor and client. In other words, although career counseling may include activities such as information giving and computer-based exploration, it is not limited to these activities. More importantly, these activities take place within the context of a relationship or working alliance between counselor and client. Furthermore, career counseling may encompass a wide range of client issues, counselor techniques, and contextual factors.

Many authors have discussed the importance of recognizing the complexity of career counseling, discussing a wide variety of dimensions along which clients – and therefore the process and outcome of career counseling – vary. Race/ethnicity, sex, age, sexual orientation all define the type of past and future opportunities open to individuals, and are crucial to address in career counseling. The overlap of one's working life with other roles and functions creates conflict and tension that can be resolved in counseling. It is precisely because of these factors that we believe career counseling is rarely a straightforward task that can be accomplished in a formulaic manner or in a few sessions.

Those who argue against incorporating personal concerns into career counseling may be concerned about diluting the effectiveness of career counseling interventions, as suggested by evidence regarding the overshadowing of vocational issues by personal emotional-social issues (Spengler, Blustein, & Strohmer, 1990; Spengler, 2000). However, there is an equally important concern involved in ignoring the interconnectedness between career and personal issues in individuals' lives, that occurs when counselors do not recognize the complexity of individuals' lives and do not attempt to integrate career and personal emotional-social issues in counseling. As Hackett (1993) noted, "we are undoubtedly doing our clients a disservice by any attempt to neatly compartmentalize their lives" (p. 110). This is particularly evident when considering the lives of adults who seek career counseling services. It is difficult to imagine how career counseling could be effective without direct and explicit attention to what else is occurring in clients' lives.

FUTURE TRENDS AND ISSUES IN CAREER COUNSELING

Use of the Internet and other information-rich technologies will change how clients gather occupational information and how career counselors work with their clients (Gore & Leuwerke, 2000). For example, the forthcoming O*NET will put an enormous amount of occupational information directly into the hands of counselors and clients. Virtual reality technology has been applied to assist clients in exploring potential work activities and environments (Krumboltz, 1997). Such unprecedented access to information about the world of work will not, however, obviate the need for counselors; in fact, clients will be more in have a greater need for an avenue to evaluate and act on the information that they have received. Although the explosion of Internet-based information makes information more readily available to a greater number of people, the accuracy and useful of such information has yet to be addressed (Robinson, Meyer, Prince, McLean, & Low, 2000).

We are confronted by new challenges at the beginning of the 21st century that will shape the future of career counseling. The very nature of the workforce is changing — increasing diversity in terms of race/ethnicity, sex, and age, temporary vs. permanent workers, and part-time vs. full-time workers. Workers' skills become obsolete as they are outpaced by rapid technological changes. Global economic factors influence the nature of job markets at home. All of these factors influence the practice of career counseling, both in the types of clients who will seek counseling as well as the issues they will address.

An additional challenge will result from the changing nature of the employment contract and of the meaning of "career" (Arthur & Rousseau, 1996; Hall, 1996 Rifkin, 1995). Changes also are likely to occur in the nature of work itself, including an increase in contingent workforce, new challenges in managing other workers (telecommuting, job sharing), salience and balance of work vs. other life roles, and the meaning of "career" to marginalized groups (Swanson & Gore, 2000).

Training Career Counselors

Given the multitude of challenges facing diverse groups of adult career clients today, the ways in which we train career counselors must be evaluated and changed Historically, career counselors were trained in the trait factor model of career development (Gerstein, 1992). Although this model works extremely well for many career clients, there appear to be a number of clients adults seeking vocational services who may need more than a person-environment fit approach to career counseling. Specifically, these clients adults may present with chronic indecision emotional difficulties, low self-esteem, and/or academic and family problems (Zamostny, O'Brien, & Tomlinson, 2000). Although providing interest and skill inventories and educating these clients about the world of work may be useful, their difficulties in selecting and succeeding in a career require a more comprehensive approach to career counseling.

In addition, for many years, models of career development and vocational interventions were developed and implemented with European-American men (Cook, Heppner, & O'Brien, 2000). Given the many demographic changes in the United States, increasing numbers of people of color and White women need assistance from career counselors (Gysbers et al., , Heppner, & Johnston, 1998). The vocational development of these diverse clients seems to diverge from the more linear model often used to describe the vocational paths of European-American men Moreover, due to the many changes in the workplace and in society, individualized career interventions in school settings no longer meet the needs of many career clients career clients (construed broadly to include individuals, groups, and organizations). Vocational interventions now occur in employment settings, welfare offices, battered women's shelters, and countless other nontraditional settings Given that a large number of vocational help-seekers are representative of diverse populations and that the needs of help-seekers adults in general may be more comprehensive than a need for information about self and the world of work, the method in which career counselors are trained must change to address the complex needs of diverse populations of career clients in a variety of settings.

A MODEL OF CAREER COUNSELING TRAINING

As Chiappone (1992) aptly noted, career counselors now need skills that were not necessary in the past as vocational professionals today must help clients deal with change and view career development as a lifelong process. Ideally, career counselors would be educated in a comprehensive manner that would include training in career development and organizational theory, basic and advanced helping skills (perhaps using the Hill and O'Brien (1999) model), assessment, multicultural counseling, evaluation and research. Moreover, students would learn about group interventions, program development, ethical behavior, information and resources related to the world of work, technology, consultation and supervision (National Career Development Association Professional Standards Committee, 1992, 1997). Most importantly, students would be taught to base their conceptualization of clients and interventions with clients in theory and previous research findings.

When beginning work with clients (again, clients should be construed broadly as an individual, group, or organization), career counselors would spend several sessions engaged in a comprehensive assessment of each client's history, personality, psychological/organizational health, ability, skills, interests, goals, and values. Moreover, a thorough assessment of the contextual forces that have operated on clients would be conducted (Cook et al., 2000). During the assessment, career counselors would attend to the development of a working alliance with their clients (the importance of which is supported by the work of Bikos, O'Brien, & Heppner, 1997; Heppner & Hendricks, 1995; Meara & Patton, 1994). Only after this comprehensive assessment (which we argue would be helpful for any adult client) is completed would the counselor develop a specialized intervention strategy for each client. Those clients who simply needed information about themselves and the world of work would be provided with this information in an interactive and creative manner. The vast majority of adult clients, however, consistent with much of the recent thinking in career counseling, would receive an integrative approach to career counseling (Anderson & Niles, 1995; Betz & Corning, 1993; Blustein, 1987; Dorn, 1992; Krumboltz, 1993). Career counselors would be encouraged and trained to address the multitude of career issues raised by the client without having to refer them to a "real" counselor for additional, disconnected sessions. In the work of these career counselors, creativity would be encouraged (Heppner, O'Brien, Hinkelman, & Humphrey, 1994) and a more holistic approach to counseling in which the intangibles of the client's life were understood would be employed (Wrenn, 1988). In addition, career counselors would use their research skills to think scientifically about their interventions and to evaluate the effectiveness of their work. Perhaps most radically, career counselors would be encouraged to intervene on a broader societal level by becoming advocates for career clients and working to change laws and societal expectations that hinder opportunities for all clients adults (Fassinger & O'Brien, 2000).

In reality, few programs offer the kind of training that is needed to enable counselors to provide a comprehensive, holistic, and ecological approach to career counseling. To do so would require changes in faculty attitudes, program curricula, supervision and research. Unfortunately, universities and faculty are often very slow to adapt curricular change (Goodyear et al., 2000). Nevertheless, in the following sections, we propose a number of changes that would enhance the ability of career counselors to attend to the changing demographics and needs of individuals adults with vocational concerns.

Changes in Faculty Attitudes

The training that career counselors receive in graduate programs will most certainly influences their ability to provide quality interventions to diverse groups of adult career clients. In a recent study of counseling psychologist psychology graduate students, Heppner and her colleagues (1996) noted that harmful influences on attitudes toward career counseling in graduate training included negative attitudes from professors or mentors about career counseling and poorly taught, uninteresting career counseling courses. One of the first (and perhaps least expensive) changes in training career counselors would be increasing the interest and excitement of professors in career counseling. Ideally, only professors who demonstrated a passion for career counseling would teach these courses. Alternatively, exceptional professors who teach career counseling could share innovative ideas that might enhance enthusiasm for the content area. Career counseling courses are taught at the University of Maryland by professors who are experts in this field. These professors use a didactic-practicum training model where in which students learn about theories and research related to vocational psychology while working with clients who present with career concerns. Similarly Swanson and Fouad (1999) advocated for integrating theory and clinical work when teaching career counseling, through the use of case studies to highlight the application of vocational theories. In addition, a series of casebooks that integrate multiculturalism and feminism into the practice of career counseling are being published for use in training (e.g., Cook et al., 2000).

Faculty might also consider using advances in technology when training career counselors. For example, Larrabee and Blanton (1999) proposed a method for enhancing the training of career counselors through use of a CD-ROM that includes 10 modules related to facilitating career development (e.g., career development theory, individual and group counseling skills, consultation and supervision, and multicultural career counseling).

In addition to altering faculty attitudes and behaviors, Heppner et al. (1996) noted that changes are needed in students' perceptions perceived that they were less skilled in performing career counseling than emotional-social counseling. Thus faculty could attend to students' levels of self-efficacy regarding career counseling as efficacy may very well influence their interest, persistence, performance, aand participation in career counseling. Faculty could consider administering the Career Counseling Self-Efficacy Scale (O'Brien , Heppner, Flores & Bikoset al., 1997) to assess confidence in basic counseling skills, vocational assessment and interpretation skills, multicultural competency skills, and knowledge about the world of work, ethics and career research. The usefulness of this scale was recently demonstrated with a large sample of predominantly masters'- level career counselors in a midwestern state was recently demonstrated (Perrone, Perrone Chan, & Thomas, 2000).

Changes in Coursework

Beyond changes in faculty and graduate student attitudes, alterations in coursework could provide career counselors with skills needed to address the myriad problems of adult career clients. In the Heppner et al. (1996) study, students rated practicing as a career counselor as the most positive experience affecting attitudes toward career counseling. To enhance interest and skill in career counseling students should have the opportunity to work with clients who differ in ethnicity gendersex, and sexual orientation, and whose levels of problems range from need for information to struggles with larger emotional (e.g., depression, chronic indecision and contextual factors (e.g., exposure to racism or sexual harassment on the job, negotiating dual career and parenting issues). Additionally, students might be educated about Savickas' (1991) proposition that a primary function of career counselors is to help adult clients examine their beliefs about and succeed in both work and love.

Also, a practicum experience in the workplace could assist enable students in understanding to understand the diverse needs of adult clients. Graduate students might assist career counselors in developing programs for employees who have lost their jobs, facilitating adjustment to retirement seminars, identifying quality day child care options for employees, and researching the impact of managing multiple roles on the productivity of management staff.

An additional consideration for training programs is the scheduling of the career counseling practica experiences. Many programs schedule the career practicum before the emotional-social practicum thus implying that career counseling is more basic, less challenging and easier than emotional-social counseling. In reality, career counseling, if done well and in a comprehensive manner, can be as (if not more) challenging for graduate students and seasoned professionals (Anderson, 1998; Crites, 1981). Anderson (1998) aptly noted the surprise of the students when they discovered the relative difficulty of the career counseling practicum when compared to other experiences with clients who were not having career concerns. Interestingly, Phillips and her colleagues (1988) suggested that career counseling be provided only by more experienced counselors as their research found that client satisfaction with career counseling was related to level of experience of the counselor.

Most importantly, changes would be needed in countless universities across the country where career and emotional social counseling are separated and provided in isolation from one another. We believe that separating counseling services contributes to an artificial and perhaps harmful dichotomization that fails to reflect the needs of (and perhaps the most effective treatment of) help-seekers. We advocate an integrated approach to providing counseling performed by counselors trained in the aforementioned model of to address the complexities of career counseling when adult clients need more than a trait-factor approach.

Training in multicultural issues is of critical importance to career counselors. Swanson (1993) provided guidelines for incorporating multicultural training throughout the curricula for career counselors. Specifically, she suggested that training programs make a programmatic commitment to multicultural training that would involve increasing the diversity of students and faculty, integrating multicultural issues in the curriculum and also providing individual courses, practica and internship experiences that address multicultural issues. Moreover, Swanson called for routine evaluations of multicultural sensitivity and competence among students.

Supervision of Career Counselors

Very little attention has focused on the supervision of career counselors and even less attention has examined methods for training students to supervise career counselors. In a thoughtful assessment of the supervision of career counselors, Bronson (2000) provided suggestions for how supervision of career counselors can be improved. Consistent with our model of training career counselingcounselors,

Bronson proposed that supervision of career counseling must take into account the complexity of the career counseling intervention. She identified ten components of effective career counseling supervision (i.e., "the supervisory relationship, counseling skills, case conceptualization, assessment skills, resources and information, the interconnection between personal and career issues, promoting supervised interest in career counseling, addressing career issues in age-appropriate ways, multicultural issues, and ethics", p. 224-225).

Attention to the training of supervisors of career counseling is necessary if students are to develop the comprehensive skills needed to perform this necessary and valuable service. Osborne and Usher (1994) described a model where advanced doctoral students were provided with experience in supervising the career counseling of masters' level trainees. Specifically, they reported on the implementation of a three academic course sequence that enhanced the career development process for undergraduates, provided masters students with experience in facilitating career development, and trained doctoral students in the supervision of career counseling.

Research Suggestions for the Evaluation of Training Programs

Clearly, the proposed model of career counseling is more comprehensive and integrative than previously employed by most training programs. Research is needed to evaluate this method of training and the interventions that stem from this comprehensive approach. When pursuing these studies, researchers should attend to the issues and problems related to research in career counseling described by Osipow (1982). In addition to learning how to conduct research, students should be educated about how to use research when planning interventions for adult career clients. For example, students might consider incorporating the factors that Ryan (1999) found to be effective predictors of helpful group interventions for clients with career choice concerns (e.g., writing exercises, interpreting tests, enhancing support networks, modeling and providing information about the world of work).

Example Programs. Although no graduate program exists that implements our proposed model of training career counselors, Anderson (1998) describes a training program at the University of Missouri-Columbia that attends carefully to the development of career counselors. Throughout graduate training, students in counseling psychology are exposed to research related to career counseling and their work is based on a foundation of theory and relevant research. The practicum in the career center is labeled a "counseling psychology practicum" and is based on a holistic counseling agency and holistic model center approach that focuses on the integration of vocational and mental health concerns. The counseling psychology practicum is offered every semester during which students attend classes (to discuss cases and learn about theory, interventions and professional development), receive supervision, and spend the majority of their time preparing for and working with clients. The professors emphasize the importance of counseling skills (e.g., the development of the relationship between client and counselor) and they attend to the contextual influences on the client's life. Students are exposed to a diverse group of adult clients with a wide range of problems. Also, graduate students are trained to use assessment tools in an interactive and creative manner and they receive supervision from faculty and advanced students who believe in the importance and value of career counseling.

In addition, students-in-training are exposed to a state-of-the-art career center that subscribes to the criteria outlined by Heppner and Johnston (1994) for career centers on college campuses. In particular, Heppner and Johnston argued that college career centers should be developed based on solid research and solid philosophical and psychological bases as well as the developmental needs of the clients. They advocated for the importance of advanced diagnostic systems, ongoing staff training, attention to multicultural issues and diversity of clientele, and perhaps most importantly, clinical practice that is informed by research. Finally, they proposed that research should be conducted in all career centers.

Chiappone (1992) also outlined a model of for training master's level career counselors that was implemented with master's level students at John F. Kennedy University. She described the program as focusing on career development while incorporating many positive components of a counseling graduate program. A comprehensive range of coursework is offered (e.g., basic listening and counseling skills, assessment, world of work information, job search strategies, consultation, management, evaluation, and multicultural issues). Students also complete a supervised internship and external fieldwork, as well as a career development project. A summer institute is held annually and often attended by career professionals from across the country. Students who complete this program can receive a master's degree and a post-master's certificate in career development.

The example programs highlighted in this section have made a concerted effort to enhance the training of career counselors. Following is a list of recommendations that may be used to assist graduate schools in developing a model training program for career counselors.

Summary of Recommendations for a Model Training Program for Career Counselors

1. Similar to one approach to multicultural counseling training (Abreu, Gim Chung, & Atkinson, 2000), graduate programs should adopt an integrative approach to training career counselors ing in which career-related issues are incorporated throughout the program wherever possible and appropriate (e.g., in all practica courses, in research courses). In addition, a multicultural, contextual, holistic and ecological approach to career counseling should be taught and students should have experience working with diverse adult clients with differing needs and problems.

2. Career counselors should be trained in basic and advanced helping skills so they will be competent in addressing vocational and mental health concerns (Niles & Pate, 1989). The false dichotomy of career versus emotional-social counseling should be eliminated and career and non-career counseling services should be provided at the same site by the same counselors.

3. Courses focused on career counseling should emulate a didactic-practicum model in which students learn about theory and research while serving as career counselors and/or working on related case studies. Only professors who feel passionate about career counseling should teach these courses.

4. Career counselors should be educated to complete a thorough assessment of the adult client prior to the development and implementation of a vocational

intervention. All interventions should be based in theory and research and should acknowledge the contextual forces influencing the client.

5. Students should receive training in the supervision of career counselors. Supervision practica should be offered at internship sites to provide interested students with experience in supervising beginning and advanced career counselors.

6. Career counselors should be trained to integrate research findings into their work. In addition, research should investigate the effectiveness of our proposed approach tocareer counseling and the training of career counselors. Researchers should also study training programs that graduate talented scholars and clinicians in vocational psychology to assess the factors that contributed to the success of these programs.

7. Finally, career counselors should be encouraged to advocate for social changes to enhance opportunities for all adult clients to access quality education and find meaningful work.

Conclusion

Recently, career counselors have begun to acknowledge the complexity of forces that affect adult clients' access to opportunities, decision-making abilities, and pursuit of paths that lead to the actualization of potential in both work and in love. To do this complex and important work, training programs must be reevaluated and restructured to enable career counselors to provide comprehensive services to diverse clients in need of a wide range of vocational interventions.

References

Abreu, J. M., Gim Chung, R. H., & Atkinson, D. R. (2000). Multicultural counseling training: Past, present, and future directions. *The Counseling Psychologist, 28,* 641-656.

Anderson, D. C. (1998). A focus on career: Graduate training in counseling psychology. *Journal of Career Development, 25,* 101-110.

Anderson, W. P., & Niles, S. G. (1995). Career and personal concerns expressed by career counseling clients. *The Career Development Quarterly, 43,* 240-245.

Arthur, M. B., & Rousseau, D. M. (1996). *The boundaryless career: A new employment principle for a new organizational era.* New York: Oxford University Press.

Betz, N. E., & Corning, A. F. (1993). The inseparability of "career" and "personal" counseling. *The Career Development Quarterly, 42,* 137-142.

Bikos, L. H., O'Brien, K. M., & Heppner, M. J. (1997, January). *Evaluating process and outcome variables in counseling for career development.* Paper presented at the annual meeting of the National Career Development Association, Daytona, FL.

Blustein, D. L. (1987). Integrating career counseling and psychotherapy: A comprehensive treatment strategy. *Psychotherapy, 24,* 794-799.

Blustein, D. L., & Spengler, P. M. (1995). Personal adjustment: Career counseling and psychotherapy. In W. B. Walsh & S. H. Osipow (Eds.), *Handbook of vocational psychology* (2nd ed., pp. 295-329). Mahweh, NJ: Erlbaum.

Brewer, J. M. (1942). *History of vocational guidance.* New York: Harper & Row.

Bronson, M. K. (2000). Supervision of career counseling. In L. J. Bradley & N. Ladany (Eds.), *Counselor supervision: Principles, process and practice* (pp. 222-244). Philadelphia: Accelerated Development.

Brown, D., & Brooks, L. (1985). Career counseling as a mental health intervention. *Professional Psychology: Research and Practice, 16,* 860-867.

Brown, S. D., & Krane, N. E. R. (2000). Four (or five) sessions and a cloud of dust: Old assumptions and new observations about career counseling. In S. D. Brown & R. W. Lent (Eds.), *Handbook of counseling psychology* (3rd ed., pp. 740-766). New York: Wiley.

Chiappone, J. M. (1992). The career development professional of the 1990s: A training model. In H. D. Lea & Z. B. Leibowitz (Eds.), *Adult career development: Concepts, issues, and practices* (pp. 364-379). Alexandria, VA: The National Career Development Association.

Cook, E. P., Heppner, M. J., & O'Brien, K. M. (2000). *Understanding diversity within women's career development: An ecological perspective.* Unpublished manuscript.

Crites, J. O. (1981). *Career counseling: Models, methods, and materials.* New York: McGraw-Hill.

Davidson, S. L., & Gilbert, L. A. (1993). Career counseling is a personal matter. *The Career Development Quarterly, 42,* 149-155.

Dawis, R. V. (2000). The person-environment tradition in counseling psychology. In W. E. Martin, Jr. & J. L. Swartz-Kulstad (Eds.), *Person-environment psychology and mental health: Assessment and intervention* (pp. 91-111). Mahweh, NJ: Erlbaum.

Dorn, F. J. (1992). Occupational wellness: The integration of career identity and personal identity. *Journal of Counseling and Development, 71,* 176-178.

Fassinger, R. E., & O'Brien, K. M. (2000). Career counseling with college women: A scientist-practitioner-advocate model of intervention. In D. A. Luzzo (Ed.), *Career development of college students: Translating theory and research into practice* (pp. 253-265). Washington, DC: American Psychological Association.

Flamer, S. (1986). Clinical-career intervention with adults: Low visibility, high need? *Journal of Community Psychology, 14,* 224-227.

Fretz, B. R. (1981). Evaluating the effectiveness of career interventions. *Journal of Counseling Psychology, 28,* 77-90.

Gerstein, M. (1992). Training professionals for career development responsibilities in business and industry: An update. In H. D. Lea & Z. B. Leibowitz (Eds.), *Adult career development: Concepts, issues, and practices* (pp. 364-379). Alexandria, VA: The National Career Development Association.

Gold, J. M., & Scanlon, C. R. (1993). Psychological distress and counseling duration of career and noncareer clients. *The Career Development Quarterly, 42,* 186-191.

Goodyear, R. K., Cortese, J. R., Guzzardo, C. R., Allison, R. D., Claiborn, C. D., & Packard, T. (2000). Factors, trends, and topics in the evolution of counseling psychology training. *The Counseling Psychologist, 28,* 603-621.

Gore, P. A., Jr., & Leuwerke, W. C. (2000). Information technology for career assessment on the Internet. *Journal of Career Assessment, 8,* 3-19.

Gysbers, N. C., Heppner, M. J., & Johnston, J. A. (1998). *Career counseling: Process, issues, and techniques.* Boston: Allyn & Bacon.

Hackett, G. (1993). Career counseling and psychotherapy: False dichotomies and recommended remedies. *Journal of Career Assessment, 1,* 105-117.

Hall, D. T. (1996). *The career is dead. Long live the career.* San Francisco: Jossey-Bass.

Haverkamp, B. E., & Moore, D. (1993). The career-personal dichotomy: Perceptual reality, practical illusion, and workplace integration. *The Career Development Quarterly, 42,* 154-160.

Heppner, M. J., & Hendricks, F. (1995). A process and outcome study examining career indecision and indecisiveness. *Journal of Counseling and Development, 73,* 426-437.

Heppner, M. J., & Johnston, J. A. (1994). Evaluating elements of career planning centers: Eight critical issues. *Journal of Career Development, 21,* 175-183.

Heppner, M. J., O'Brien, K. M., Hinkelman, J. M., & Flores, L. Y. (1996). Training counseling psychologists in career development: Are we our own worst enemies? *The Counseling Psychologist, 24,* 105-125.

Heppner, M. J., O'Brien, K. M., Hinkelman, J. M., & Humphrey, C. F. (1994). Shifting the paradigm: The use of creativity in career counseling. *Journal of Career Development, 21,* 77-86.

Herr, E. L. (1989). Career development and mental health. *Journal of Career Development, 16,* 5-18.

Hill, C. E., & Corbett, M. M. (1993). A perspective of the history of process and outcome research in counseling psychology. *Journal of Counseling Psychology, 40,* 3-24.

Hill, C. E., & O'Brien, K. M. (1999). *Helping skills: Facilitating exploration, insight, and action.* Washington, DC: American Psychological Association.

Imbimbo, P. V. (1994). Integrating personal and career counseling: A challenge for counselors. *Journal of Employment Counseling, 31,* 50-59.

Kirschner, T., Hoffman, M. A., & Hill, C. E. (1994). Case study of the process and outcome of career counseling. *Journal of Counseling Psychology, 41,* 216-226.

Krumboltz, J. D. (1993). Integrating career and personal counseling. *The Career Development Quarterly, 42,* 143-148.

Krumboltz, J. D. (1996). A learning theory of career counseling. In M. L. Savickas & W. B. Walsh (Eds.), *Handbook of career counseling theory and practice* (pp. 55-80). Palo Alto, CA: Davies-Black.

Krumboltz, J. D. (1997, August). Virtual job experience. In G. Hackett (Chair), *Information Highways, Byways, and Cul de Sacs in Counseling Psychology.* Symposium presented at the annual meeting of the American Psychological Association, Chicago, IL.

Larrabee, M. J., & Blanton, B. L. (1999). Innovations for enhancing education of career counselors using technology. *Journal of Employment Counseling, 36,* 13-23.

Lucas, M. S. (1992). Problems expressed by career and non-career help seekers: A comparison. *Journal of Counseling and Development, 70,* 417-420.

Lucas, M. S. (1993). Personal aspects of career counseling: Three examples. *The Career Development Quarterly, 42,* 161-166.

Meara, N. M., & Patton, M. J. (1994). Contributions of the working alliance in the practice of career counseling. *The Career Development Quarterly, 43,* 161-177.

Nagel, D. P., Hoffman, M. A., & Hill, C. E. (1995). A comparison of verbal response modes used by mater's-level career counselors and other helpers. *Journal of Counseling and Development, 74,* 101-104.

National Career Development Association. (1992). Career counseling competencies. *The Career Development Quarterly, 40,* 378-386.

National Career Development Association. (1997). *Career counseling competencies.* Columbus, OH: Author.

Niles, S. G., & Pate, R. H. (1989). Competency and training issues related to the integration of career counseling and mental health counseling. *Journal of Career Development, 16,* 63-71.

O'Brien, K. M., Heppner, M. J., Flores, L. Y., & Bikos, L. H. (1997). The Career Counseling Self-Efficacy Scale: Instrument development and training applications. *Journal of Counseling Psychology, 44,* 20-31.

Osborne, W. L., & Usher, C. H. (1994). A Super approach: Training career educators, career counselors and researchers. *Journal of Career Development, 20,* 219-225.

Osipow, S. H. (1982). Research in career counseling: An analysis of issues and problems. *The Counseling Psychologist, 10,* 27-34.

Osipow, S. H. (1996). Does career theory guide practice or does career practice guide theory? In M. L. Savickas & W. B. Walsh (Eds.), *Handbook of career counseling theory and practice* (pp. 403-409). Palo Alto, CA: Davies-Black.

Parsons, F. (1909). *Choosing a vocation.* Boston: Houghton Mifflin.

Perrone, K. M., Perrone, P. A., Chan. F., & Thomas, K. R. (2000). Assessing efficacy and importance of career counseling competencies. *The Career Development Quarterly, 48,* 212-225.

Phillips, S. D., Friedlander, M. L., Kost, P. P., Specterman, R. V., & Robbins, E. S. (1988). Personal versus vocational focus in career counseling: A retrospective outcome study. *Journal of Counseling and Development, 67,* 169-173.

Rifkin, J. (1995). *The End of Work.* New York: Putnam.

Robinson, N. K., Meyer, D., Prince, J. P., McLean, C., & Low, R. (2000). Mining the Internet for career information: A model approach for college students. *Journal of Career Assessment, 8,* 37-54.

Rounds, J. B., Jr., & Tinsley, H. E. A. (1984). Diagnosis and treatment of vocational problems. In S. D. Brown & R. W. Lent (Eds.), *Handbook of counseling psychology* (pp. 137-177). New York: Wiley.

Ryan, N. E. (1999). *Career counseling and career choice goal attainment: A meta-analytically derived model for career counseling practice.* Unpublished doctoral dissertation, Loyola University, Chicago.

Savickas, M. L. (1991). The meaning of work and love: Career issues and interventions. *The Career Development Quarterly, 39,* 315-324.

Spengler, P. M. (2000). Does vocational overshadowing even exist? A test of the robustness of the vocational overshadowing bias. *Journal of Counseling Psychology, 47,* 342-351.

Spengler, P. M., Blustein, D. L., & Strohmer, D. C. (1990). Diagnostic and treatment overshadowing of vocational problems by personal problems. *Journal of Counseling Psychology, 37,* 372-381.

Spokane, A. R. (1989). Are there psychological and mental health consequences of difficult career decisions? *Journal of Career Development, 16*(1), 19-23.

Spokane, A. R. (1991). *Career intervention.* Englewood Cliffs, NJ: Allyn & Bacon.

Subich, L. M. (1993). How personal is career counseling? *The Career Development Quarterly, 42,* 129-131.

Super, D. E. (1993). The two faces of counseling: Or is it three? *The Career Development Quarterly, 42,* 132-136.

Swanson, J. L. (1993). Integrating a multicultural perspective into training for career counseling: Programmatic and individual interventions. *The Career Development Quarterly, 42,* 41-49.

Swanson, J. L. (1995). The process and outcome of career counseling. In W. B. Walsh & S. H. Osipow (Eds.), *Handbook of vocational psychology* (2nd ed., pp. 217-259). Mahweh, NJ: Erlbaum.

Swanson, J. L. (1996). The theory is the practice: Trait-and-factor/Person-environment fit counseling. In M. L. Savickas & W. B. Walsh (Eds.), *Handbook of career counseling theory and practice* (pp. 93-108). Palo Alto, CA: Davies-Black.

Swanson, J. L., & Fouad, N. A. (1999). *Career theory and practice: Learning through case studies.* Thousand Oaks, CA: Sage.

Swanson, J. L., & Gore, P. (2000). Advances in career development theory and research. In S. D. Brown and R. W. Lent (Eds), *Handbook of counseling psychology* (3rd ed., pp. 233-269). New York: Wiley.

Wrenn, C. G. (1988). The person in career counseling. *The Career Development Quarterly, 36,* 337-342.

Zamostny, K. P., O'Brien, K. M., & Tomlinson, M. J. (2000, August). *Career problems among help-seekers: An integrative approach.* Paper presented at the annual convention of the American Psychological Association, Washington, DC.

CHAPTER 21
Evaluating the Effectiveness of Adult Career Development Programs

Susan C. Whiston
Briana K. Brecheisen
Indiana University

In many settings that assist adults in their career development, practitioners not only need to provide career counseling but they must also document that the services they provide are effective. The previous chapters of this book have addressed numerous methods for assisting adults in their career development, but these chapters have yet to address the important topic of how to evaluate career development programs for adults. In almost all settings in which adults receive career assistance, there are requirements related to evaluating programs and providing accountability information. Furthermore, in many career development settings, there are insufficient funds to hire professional evaluators and thus clinicians must perform these activities. This chapter is designed to assist career development practitioners in evaluating adult career development programs.

Program evaluation may be viewed as a laborious task designed only for supplying administrators, funding agencies, or administrative boards with trivial information. Evaluation studies, however, can also provide information that can be used to increase practitioners' effectiveness and enhance career services provided to clients. Sometimes practitioners may procrastinate in conducting evaluations of career programs because they feel less confident in this area as compared to other counseling related activities. Previously, Whiston (1996) proposed that there were many similarities between the process of counseling and the research process. We propose that this same similarity applies to the process of career counseling and program evaluation (see Table 1). In career counseling, a counselor begins by identifying pertinent career issues; whereas in program evaluation, the practitioner identifies the focus of the evaluation. In career counseling, the counselor then begins to formulate counseling goals, which is analogous to the program evaluation step of formulating the evaluation design. In formulating the evaluation design, the evaluator must also choose evaluation instruments or outcome measures, which is similar to identifying methods for gauging the progress of the counseling. In both career counseling and program evaluation, the next step involves gathering information. As a part of career counseling, the clinician often gathers data relating to clients (e.g., interests, values); whereas in program evaluation, the evaluator gathers information or data about a program rather than about clients. These same similarities continue into the next stage, where the analysis and interpretation of the information gathered either involves client information or program information. The parallel process continues through the final stage. In career counseling, the final stage concerns clients using the information gained in counseling in making career/lifestyle decisions and implementing career goals; whereas in evaluation, the final stage concerns using the information gained through the evaluation process to enhance the program and achieve programmatic goals.

TABLE 1
SIMILARITIES BETWEEN CAREER COUNSELING
AND PROGRAM EVALUATION

Career Counseling	Program Evaluation
Step 1: Identify pertinent career issues	Step 1: Identify focus of evaluation
Step 2: Formulate counseling goals	Step 2: Formulate the evaluation design and procedures
Step 3: Determine ways of gauging counseling progress toward goals	Step 3: Determine evaluation or outcome measures
Step 4: Gather client information	Step 4: Gather program information
Step 5: Analyze and interpret the information	Step 5: Analyze and interpret the program information
Step 6: Use the information gained in counseling to make career/lifestyle decisions	Step 6: Use information gained from program evaluation to make decisions

Steps in Evaluating Career Development Programs

The general steps in conducting an evaluation of a career development program included in Table 1 can be adapted and modified to meet the unique needs of a variety of programs and services provided to adults. It is important, however, to proceed through the steps sequentially because the steps are designed in a developmental progression. In progressing through this framework, there should be an understanding that some phases may already exist within an organization and can quickly be accomplished, while other steps may be more time consuming. Quality program evaluation often does involve a commitment of time and resources, but that does not necessarily mean that all quality evaluations are expensive (Joint Committee on Standards for Educational Evaluation, 1994). With sufficient planning and creative resource allocations, program evaluations can be conducted that provide useful, and often financially beneficial, information.

IDENTIFY THE FOCUS OF THE EVALUATION

The initial step in evaluating any career development program is determining what needs to be evaluated and what specific information is needed. This fundamental step is sometimes omitted because individuals launch into an evaluation in order to meet a deadline or to respond to some external pressure (e.g., annual evaluations or reports to funding organizations). The purpose of evaluation is to gather information and it is important to consider what information is needed and why. Rossi and Freeman (1982) contended that there is no universal template for conducting an evaluation study; rather the focus of every evaluation needs to be tailored to the program being evaluated. In most evaluations, there needs to be a direct connection between the program goals and/or objectives and the evaluation. In this era of accountability, those involved in a career development program should ensure that the objectives of the program are measurable. In career development programs, developing program objectives simply means stating programmatic goals in quantifiable terms, such as determining the number of clients the program anticipates serving, identifying indicators that the program provides quality services, and specifying the expected outcomes of those career services. The reviewing of program goals and objectives can often assist in identifying the focus or central purpose of the evaluation. Furthermore, analyzing program goals and objectives can often facilitate program enhancement by simply requiring individuals to reflect on processes and procedures of their program.

In clarifying the focus of the evaluation, one of the initial factors an evaluator needs to consider is whether the evaluation needs to be *formative* or *summative*. According to the Joint Committee on Standards for Educational Evaluation (1994), formative evaluation or feedback concerns the improvement of an ongoing program, whereas, summative evaluation pertains to drawing conclusions about the overall worth or merit of a program. In formative evaluation, the goal is to evaluate an ongoing program and provide recommendations for improvement. The term summative evaluation is used when the intent is to evaluate the merits of the program, which is often accompanied by decisions to retain, alter, or eliminate the program.

Benkofski and Heppner (1999) suggested soliciting input from stakeholders concerning both the focus of the evaluation and the methods for collecting and analyzing data. In evaluating adult career development programs, it is often helpful to get information from those providing the direct services (e.g., counselors), clerical staff that assists in program delivery, and a sampling of clients who have been the recipients of the services. Although Benkofski and Heppner (1999) contended that evaluators should gain information from stakeholders, they also suggested that evaluators set boundaries before progressing into design and methodologies issues. It is difficult to conceptualize an effective evaluation design if there is a lack of clarity related to the focus of the evaluation study. Furthermore, evaluation studies can quickly become overly complex and unwieldy if parameters are not set.

In human service programs, Yates (1996) argued that in these days of accountability and fiscal responsibility, managers and practitioners need to gather information on effectiveness, benefits, cost-effectiveness, and cost-benefits. Some stakeholders (e.g., administrators, advisory boards, funding agents) are more interested in the cost effectiveness or cost benefits of a career development program, as compared to information on the intrinsic merits or general effectiveness of the program. Thus, in many situations the focus of the evaluation will be determining whether the benefits of the career development program outweigh the cost of the program. Yates contended that in order to determine effectiveness, benefits, cost-effectiveness and cost-benefits, one must first determine the costs of the program, understand the procedures or program provided to the clients, identify the processes that result in client change, and measure the outcomes or effects of the program.

FORMULATE THE EVALUATION DESIGN AND PROCEDURES

The selection of the evaluation design and methodologies is guided by the focus of the evaluation, the setting, and the availability of evaluation resources. Designing an evaluation of a career development program is more complex than simply selecting one outcome or criterion measure that indicates whether the program was successful. One of the areas to consider in designing an evaluation study is the type of information desired. This decision making process can be initiated by determining if descriptive information is sufficient or if comparison data are needed. In certain situations, it will suffice to describe the program and summarize the outcome or evaluative information. Providing descriptive information about clients after they have completed the program can often provide useful information, but it is difficult to attribute positive results directly to the career development program. For sake of illustration, let us assume a program designed to assist clients with interviewing skills finds through an outcome assessment that 25 out of 30 participants are employed one month after completing the program. Without comparison data it is impossible to confirm that the positive outcome of being employed is a result of the career development program. Comparison data that contrasts participants' employment status before the program or compares their employment status to others who have not completed the program will provide more compelling findings. If an evaluator determines that comparison data would be desirable, then he or she needs to consider whether an *intersubject* (variations across subjects that usually take the form of some group comparison) or *intrasubject* (variation within subjects that usually focuses on the temporal unfolding of variables within individual subjects) design is preferable.

In *intersubject* designs, there needs to be a comparison group in which the evaluator will determine if those receiving the career interventions have better outcomes than the comparison group. Some evaluators may avoid intersubject designs because of the difficulties associated with gathering data from an appropriate comparison group. In outcome research, researchers often use a wait-list control group in order to address both ethical concerns and group equivalency issues. Some evaluators may avoid intersubject or group comparison designs because of ethical or practical issues related to having a control group that does not receive the career program. In a wait-list control group design, participants are randomly assigned to either the treatment or wait-list control group and after the treatment phase and the posttests are administered, the treatment is made available to the wait-list control group (Heppner, Kivlighan, & Wampold, 1999). The use of random assignment to either the treatment or the wait-list control group addresses group equivalency concerns. Furthermore, members of the wait-list control group do receive services, thus diminishing the difficulties associated with not providing services to individuals in need of those services.

In some settings, however, a wait-list control group may not be a viable alternative. Another option in using intersubject designs involves varying treatments so that knowledge can be gained concerning the effects of various career interventions. For example, a community college may want to investigate whether the use of a computerized career guidance program is worth the financial investment. In this case, they might compare the outcomes of students who were required to use a computerized career guidance program in a career exploration course as compared to students who were not required in their courses to use the system. Another example of an intersubject design would be to compare those who received a more traditional approach to job search training to the outcomes of those who participated in a more comprehensive and intensive program.

Examining group differences is not the only evaluation design available. Evaluators can also use *intrasubject* research designs, which concern variations within each subject or participant. A common approach in intrasubject designs is to pretest individuals before they participate in the program and then posttest them at the conclusion of the career development program. The problem with a pretest-posttest design is that without a control group, it is impossible to rule out the possibility that client changes are due to other factors. Another approach to intrasubject designs concerns time-series approaches, where information on individuals is collected over a period of time to see if change occurs as a result of the program. An example of a time-series approach would be to monitor adults' job search behaviors over a number of months and see if the number of applications increased after participation in a career development program.

An additional approach to intrasubject designs is to use a single-subject or single-case design. In counseling research, there has been increasing interest in using single-subject designs (Heppner et al., 1999). Although single-subject designs are not commonly used in evaluation studies, there are circumstances where gathering in-depth information on one individual can be useful. Single case designs may seem less foreign to a clinician than other research designs since historically this method has been the basic model for teaching, learning, and supervision (Jones, 1993). Single-case studies can be either quantitative, qualitative, or a combination, and those who are interested are directed to Hillard (1993) and Galassi and Gersh (1993).

Another factor to consider in the design of an evaluation study is whether cost-effectiveness or cost-benefit information is needed. Specific information needs to be gathered if the evaluation study is going to include analyses of the relationship between the cost of the career development program and the effectiveness of the services and/or benefits to a specific organization (e.g., agency or educational institution) or to society (e.g., reduction in state and federal spending). Specifically, the evaluator will need to gather information on the cost of the career development program, which Yates (1996) found should include costs of personnel, facilities and utilities, equipment, and supplies. Moreover, the design of the evaluation also will need to include methods for gathering outcome information that can be transformed into tangible benefits and monetary units.

A final factor to consider in designing an evaluation study concerns how information is going to be gathered about the program and the services clients receive. Results of an evaluation study are meaningless if there is not a clear description of what services clients actually received and some documentation that they indeed received those services. Rossi and Freeman (1982) indicated that one of the reasons programs fail is the treatment is unstandardized, uncontrolled, or varies across target populations. Sometimes evaluation results can reflect difficulties within a system where clients are receiving quite different services or, in some cases, less than optimal services. Yates (1996) suggested that very specific information about program procedures must be gathered in cost-benefit analyses in order to examine the relationship between the cost of the procedures and the benefits of the program. Examining the implementation of a program is similar to ensuring treatment integrity in counseling research. In counseling research, treatment manuals or supervision and training of those delivering the counseling services are some of the more common methods for ensuring that the counseling treatment is provided consistently and appropriately (Lambert & Hill, 1994).

DETERMINING EVALUATION OR OUTCOME MEASURES

The legitimate effect of a career development program cannot be determined without sound evaluative measures or procedures. The selection of appropriate measures is not an easy task and sometimes individuals will avoid evaluation of career programs because they are unfamiliar with appropriate instruments or measures. Outcome research conducted over the last 50 years on the effectiveness of career interventions can assist evaluators in selecting reliable and valid measures. In terms of measuring outcome, the trend is to use more than one outcome measure and to gather information from more than source (Lambert & Hill, 1994; Oliver, 1979).

Whiston (in press) designed an organization scheme to assist evaluators in selecting multiple career outcome assessments. Table 2 contains an overview of the organizational scheme, which includes the four domains of content, source, focus, and time-orientation. Within each of the four domains are categories for the evaluator to consider in selecting outcome measures. In using this scheme, an individual would consider each of the four domains and would attempt to select outcome measures that measure different categories within that domain. In an ideal world, career practitioners would select instruments so that all of the categories in each of the domains were addressed in measuring outcome. This goal is fairly unrealistic, as practical limitations (e.g., time, expenses, and lack of sound instruments) will influence instrument selection. The organizational scheme, however, can be used to systematically select diverse outcome measures that address different facets of the career process and to avoid needless duplication of certain outcome categories. Although common practice is to use more than one outcome measure, this organizational scheme also can be used in situations where only one outcome assessment is being selected in order to select the instrument that is the most comprehensive measure.

It is often helpful in evaluating career development programs to gather information from different perspectives. In Whiston's organizational scheme, the first domain to consider is the **Content Domain,** which includes the categories of *career knowledge and skills,* career behaviors, sentiments, and effective role functioning. These categories are drawn from Fretz's (1981) classic monograph. The first category, career knowledge and skills, concerns a frequent goal of career counseling, which is to increase clients' knowledge of self and the world of work. The intent of this organizational system is to assist practitioners in selecting multiple outcome measures that assess pertinent, yet, different aspects of client change. Hence in the Content Domain, when an evaluator has selected one outcome assessment that measures career knowledge and skills (e.g., knowledge of the job search process), he or she would want to select a second measure that would assess either career behaviors, sentiments, or effective role functioning.

The second category within the Content Domain is *career behaviors.* Here the focus is not on acquisition of knowledge or skills but on the career behaviors exhibited by clients. Examples of outcomes included in this area are: performance in a training program, career information behaviors, performance in a mock interview, seeking initial/new job, job ratings, or occupational promotion. The third category within the Content Domain is *sentiments and beliefs* and involves attitudes, beliefs, perceptions, and other affective responses. Included in this category are attitudes toward certainty, commitment, and career salience and measures such as the *Career Decision Scale* (Osipow, 1987) or the Vocational Identity Scale from *My Vocational Situation* (Holland, Daiger, & Power, 1980). This category also includes beliefs, so measures of self-efficacy, such as the *Career Decision Making Self-Efficacy Scale*

(Taylor & Betz, 1983) could be selected to measure whether the career program being evaluated influenced clients' beliefs. The last category in the Content Domain is *effective role functioning.* This category concerns whether career program produces changes in clients' abilities to function, with the understanding that effective role functioning will vary depending on the client's age and developmental level. Career maturity measures are often used as outcome measures in career counseling research and would be considered indicators of effective role functioning. Other measures of effective role functioning are self-concept, locus of control, and measures of adjustment.

In counseling and psychotherapy outcome research, the trend is to measure change from multiple perspectives (Lambert & Hill, 1994). One of the major reasons for this practice is studies have found that the effects of the interventions vary depending on who is evaluating the counseling. As Table 2 reflects, the categories in the **Source Domain** are client, counselor, trained observer, relevant other, and institutional/archival information. Most instruments used in the career area involve client self-report, while very few instruments have been designed for others to complete (Oliver, 1979). In evaluating adult career programs, instructors, employers, peers, and family members can often provide unique perspectives on the effects of the career counseling. Furthermore, institutional or archival information (e.g., employment records, salary, time spent unemployed) may also be available and contribute to the overall evaluation of the career program.

In selecting career outcome measures, Oliver (1978, 1979) suggested that individuals use both global and specific measures. The third dimension of the model is the **Focus Domain,** which encourages evaluators to consider both global and specific evaluative measures. Typically, global measures have included numerous behaviors, whereas specific measures incorporate only a few (Gelso, 1979). An example of a global measure is the *Multidimensional Career Behavior Scales* (Spokane, 1990), which assesses various factors related to career choice. Concerning program specific goals, an evaluator may want to consider adapting an approach commonly used in psychotherapy research called Goal Attainment Scaling (Kiresuk & Sherman, 1968). Goal Attainment Scaling requires the formulation of specific goals with the grading of a scale on likely outcomes. The goals are then prioritized with higher priority goals receiving more weight in the evaluation of outcome. There are a few examples of goal attainment scales in career research, such as the Self-Directed Vocational Goal Attainment Scale (Hoffman, Magoon, & Spokane, 1981). Although goal attainment scaling is difficult to implement, it has the advantage of measuring the unique goals of a specific career development program.

The last domain in the classification model is **Time Orientation,** which emphasizes the importance of both short-term and long-term program goals. Kidd and Killeen (1992) argued that not all criterion measures are equal and that more efforts should be devoted to using meaningful measures. Often in career development programs for adults, practitioners assist clients in developing skills (e.g., resume writing), but the long-term goals are related to gaining employment or career satisfaction. Whiston (in press) labeled the categories in this domain macro-outcomes and micro-outcomes to distinguish between more significant and less consequential measures. Micro-outcome measures are less significant than macro-outcome assessments and reflect short-term changes that hopefully contribute to those more consequential effects. Examples of micro-outcomes would be decreasing career indecision, increasing networking skills, and increasing career decision-making self-efficacy; whereas, macro-outcomes would measure more long-term or ultimate criteria, such as gaining employment.

TABLE 2

CAREER OUTCOME MEASURES SCHEME

Content	Source	Focus	Time Orientation
Career Knowledge & Skills	Client	General	Macro-outcome
Career Behaviors	Counselor	Specific	Micro-outcome
Sentiments & Beliefs	Trained Observer		
Effective Role Functioning	Relevant Other		
	Institutional/ Archival		

This classification scheme is designed to assist evaluators in considering using multiple measures from multiple perspectives. It does, however, assume that all of the evaluative measures are psychometrically sound and pertinent to the program being evaluated. It is particularly important that evaluators select evaluative measures that are appropriate for adults in their specific career program. Whiston, Sexton, and Lasoff (1998) found evidence of researchers using outcome measures that were not developmentally appropriate for the participants in the study.

GATHERING INFORMATION

According to Benkofske and Heppner (1999), data collection can be rather straightforward with proper planning and preparation. As the previous steps emphasized, it is important to determine what information is needed and the most appropriate methods for gathering that information *before* any data is collected. The actual gathering of information or data can be an arduous and challenging task. Problematic situations that arise during the collection of data can undermine the entire evaluative process, which, in turn, may result in negative consequences for the career development program (e.g., insufficient data to support ongoing funding). Numerous pitfalls can be avoided by ensuring that those individuals who are collecting the data are thoroughly trained and prepared to deal with potential problems. Benkofske and Heppner (1999) suggested piloting the data collection process in order to identify problems when there still is sufficient time to adjust the process. Piloting the data collection process will also identify problems, such as participants not understanding the instructions or survey questions; observation techniques that are too cumbersome; or difficulties in retrieving institutional data (e.g., graduation rate, employment record).

DATA ANALYSES AND INTERPRETATION

After the data is collected, the next step is to analyze the data and interpret the results. Some practitioners may shy away from conducting an evaluation study because of their uneasiness with statistics and data analysis. In some circumstances, evaluators can rely on descriptive statistics (e.g., mean, standard deviation) or qualitative data analyses procedures that do not involve inferential statistics. New statistical packages for the computer, however, make data analysis more simple and user friendly. Individuals with limited training in using statistics may want to consult with an experienced researcher since statistical decisions are complex and involve issues related to statistical power, such as (a) the particular statistical test used; (b) the alpha level; (c) the directionality of the statistical test (d) the size of the effect; and (e) the number of participants (Heppner et al., 1999). Practitioners may also want to consider following the suggestions of some researchers (e.g., Thompson & Snyder, 1998) and calculate effect sizes. The *Publication Manual of the American Psychological Association* (American Psychological Association, 1994) encourages the reporting of effect sizes, which also have the advantage of being relatively easy to compute. Effect sizes are typically calculated by subtracting the mean of the control group from the mean of the experimental group and dividing that by either the pooled standard deviation of the two groups or by the standard deviation of the control group. Effect sizes, hence, provide an indication of the magnitude of difference between program participants and nonparticipants on the outcome measures used.

For evaluators with more statistical sophistication, correlational and regression analyses can often provide important data, particularly related to the relationships between the cost and benefits of a program. It is also imperative in the field of career counseling for there to be efforts devoted to demonstrating the monetary benefits of individuals making effective career choices. Researchers should be encouraged to further explore the financial benefits of career counseling (e.g., reducing absenteeism, medical expenses related to job stress, cost of replacing employees) and share these calculations and linear models with practitioners. Additional findings that indicate that career development programs produce both personal and financial benefits could assist individuals in justifying their current programs and assist those who are arguing for expanding career development services for adults.

Once the data are analyzed, the crucial task of fully interpreting the results should begin. In the early stages of interpreting the results, it is also important to consider a context for explaining the results to pertinent stakeholders. Benkofski and Heppner (1999) suggested that all evaluation reports should: (a) describe the program, (b) summarize the evaluation process, (c) discuss the data collection procedures, and (d) provide the results and findings of the evaluation. They also suggested that reports contain an executive summary and a list of recommendations that include the positive aspects of the program as well as the areas that may need improvement. Any report, however, needs to be geared to the potential audience(s) with an understanding of the "lens" the readers will use in reading the report. Gearing the report toward an audience does not mean that results are distorted or findings misrepresented, for accurate representation of the findings of an evaluation study is consistent with ethical standards in the profession.

USING THE INFORMATION

An evaluation should not stop after the final draft of the report has been written because the purpose of an evaluation study is to use the information generated in the evaluation. Once the data have been analyzed and interpreted, career development personnel need to consider disseminating information to shareholders and other appropriate individuals. Sometimes evaluation studies that indicate programs are providing needed services to clients are not disseminated to individuals who make funding decisions. The purpose of evaluation is often not to just identify weaknesses but, also, to identify strengths. Sometimes those in the helping professions concentrate on providing quality services to clients and miss opportunities to promote their programs. Furthermore, evaluation studies can provide needed information that documents the need for additional resources.

Applying the Evaluation Model

The following section contains an illustrative model to aid in the effective evaluation of adult career development programs. As mentioned earlier, there are six steps in program evaluation:

1. Identifying the focus of the evaluation.
2. Formulating the evaluation design and procedures.
3. Determining the evaluation or outcome measures.
4. Gathering program information.
5. Analyzing and interpreting the program information.
6. Using the information gained from program evaluation to make decisions.

An example of evaluating a welfare-to-work program was chosen to illustrate the proposed steps in evaluation. The evaluation of individual welfare-to-work sites has become increasingly important over the past two decades because the results of such research provides policy makers with answers to basic questions regarding the effectiveness and efficiency of the welfare-to-work system (Riccio & Orenstein, 1996). Furthermore, many of the issues pertinent to evaluating welfare-to-work programs and sites are germane to other career development programs serving adults.

STEP 1: IDENTIFYING THE FOCUS OF THE EVALUATION.

In beginning to evaluate a welfare-to-work program, an evaluator must decide on the focus of the evaluation. One of the first considerations is whether the evaluation needs to be summative or formative. If the goal of the evaluation is to determine the effectiveness of the welfare-to-work program with the intent of seeking continued funding, then the evaluation would be summative. If, on the other hand, the evaluation is going to be conducted to finds ways of improving the program, the evaluation would be formative. Depending on the focus of the evaluation, it is not uncommon for evaluators to incorporate both summative and formative aspects in the evaluation process.

Sometimes evaluators may have a vague sense of what they believe the focus of evaluation study should be, but may have difficulty precisely articulating that focus. For these individuals, examining previous research on welfare-to-work programs may assist them in clarifying the evaluation needs of their own welfare-to-work program. In reviewing the research in this area, there appears to be four major categories of welfare-to-work evaluation studies. The first category involves evaluating overall program effectiveness. For those interested in overall program evaluation, helpful information may be retrieved by a recent study initiated by the U.S. Department of Health and Human Services to evaluate the overall effectiveness of welfare-to-work initiatives (http://wtw.doleta.gov/wtweval/evalsum.htm). This study involves examining all welfare-to-work grantees, an in-depth analysis of creative programs, and an evaluation of the impact of welfare-to-work programs and the cost effectiveness of these programs. Evaluation studies of this nature often aim to determine whether the benefits of the program outweigh the costs. The second category, illustrated by Hollister, Kemper, and Woodridge (1979), involves using case studies to measure the association between level and duration of participation in the program and various program outcomes such as employment and earnings. The third category of evaluation research in this area entails comparing individual welfare-to-work sites to one another. For example, Mead (1983) examined the association between individual site characteristics and outcome measures such as the proportion of participants placed in jobs. The final category of research involves comparing services and interventions within a welfare-to-work site. Riccio and Orenstein (1996) suggested that this type of research is powerful because it results in unbiased estimates of the effects of various treatment strategies, and critical because identifying what works is necessary to the development of stronger welfare-to-work programs. For the purpose of illustrating the steps in evaluating an adult career development program, the following sections will discuss an example of research within this last welfare-to-work evaluation category. Specifically, the focus of this pseudo evaluation study will involve comparing the effects of counseling related services, such as case management, support groups, substance abuse treatment, and workplace mediation, to the effects of non-counseling related services, such as basic skills training, transportation assistance, and childcare assistance.

STEP 2: FORMULATING THE EVALUATION DESIGN AND PROCEDURES.

After the focus of the evaluation study has been specified, the evaluation design and methodologies can be selected. The first factor to consider when designing an evaluation study is the type of information needed. In comparing the effects of counseling related welfare-to-work services to the effects of non-counseling related services, descriptive information would most likely not be sufficient. Rather, comparison data on two or more groups would probably be needed and, hence, an intersubject design would need to be employed. More specifically, outcome data would need to be collected on participants involved in counseling related services and on those involved in non-counseling related services. This would enable researchers to compare the two groups with the goal of determining the differential outcomes of the two categories of services. However, while an intersubject design would be the most appropriate when evaluating various welfare-to-work services, researchers interested in measuring change promoted by counseling and non-counseling related interventions could also consider an intrasubject design. This would involve pre and post-testing participants who received various interventions with the goal of measuring individual change, rather than comparing those involved in counseling related interventions to those involved in non-counseling related interventions.

The second factor to consider in designing an evaluation study is whether cost-effectiveness or cost-benefit information is needed. In comparing counseling related services to non-counseling related services within the welfare-to-work program, cost-benefit information would likely be of interest. Therefore, evaluators first need to gather information on the cost of offering various counseling and non-counseling related services. This would include the cost of personnel, facilities, and supplies necessary to provide each service. Second, evaluators need to formulate methods by which to translate outcome information into monetary units. In other words, they need to quantify the benefits of the program services. In welfare-to-work programs, many recipients would no longer need services such as Aid to Family with Dependent Children (AFDC), Temporary Assistance to Needy Families (TANF), and Food Stamps and those economic savings can be calculated. Benefits to individuals, such as income and duration of employment, can also be calculated. These types of variables lend themselves to statistical analyses and interpretation. If evaluators, however, are also interested in intangible outcomes such as job satisfaction and congruence, as Edwards, Rachal, and Dixon (1999) say they should be, this task can be complex. These variables would need to be coded and assigned numerical figures in rank order so that they may be included in statistical analyses.

A number of additional factors should also be considered when designing an evaluation study: confidentiality, treatment integrity, and generalizability. First, evaluators should assure welfare-to-work participants that the information they provide during the study will not be provided to their case manager and will not be used against them. Second, individuals should design studies with attention to treatment integrity and methods for ensuring that the interventions are implemented in the manner intended. For instance, if a program administrator wishes to determine the impact of support groups on job satisfaction, he/she must ensure that the support groups are conducted in a systematic, standard fashion and that the welfare recipients actually attend the group meetings. The evaluation process needs to include detailed descriptions of the services provided so that other welfare-to-work offices have procedures to follow in implementing the services that are found to be effective.

STEP 3: DETERMINING THE EVALUATION OR OUTCOME MEASURES

The effectiveness of any welfare-to-work program cannot be determined without sound evaluation measures. Edwards, Rachal, and Dixon (1999) argued that welfare-to-work programs should not be judged successful merely because they lead to a job with a "good" salary. They further argued that welfare-to-work programs should be assessed based on the programs' ability to address both personal and workplace issues of welfare recipients. This section will suggest possible outcome measures that could be used in the example of comparing the outcomes of those who received counseling in a welfare-to-work program to those who did not receive counseling services. Many states already have a mandated state reporting requirement and none of these suggestions are designed to lessen the importance of those outcome measures.

In using the outcome scheme suggested by Whiston (in press), an individual would first consider the Content Domain (see Table 2) and the categories of career knowledge and skills, career behaviors, sentiments and beliefs, and effective role functions. Typical evaluation information gathered in welfare-to-work programs are how many recipients find jobs, job wages, number of average hours worked per week, and length of employment (Ganzglass, Golonka, Tweedie, & Falk, 1998). All of these outcomes would be classified as career behaviors and, thus, welfare-to-work personnel might consider the other categories within the Content Domain. There are a number of instruments that can be used to see if participants' sentiments and beliefs change as a result of the welfare-to work program. Examples of instruments in the category of sentiments and beliefs are the *Career Transition Inventory* (Heppner, 1998), *Barriers to Employment Success* (Liptak, 1996), or the *Career Aptitude Scale* (Bonett & Stickel, 1992). Whiston also suggested that outcome measures should consider measures of effective role functioning. Outcome measures in this area could include overall measures of functioning such as the *Brief Symptoms Inventory 18* (Derogatis, 1999) or the *Quality of Life Inventory* (Frisch, 1994). In comparing the outcomes of counseling versus non-counseling services, it also would be important to include measures in the category of knowledge and skills. There are numerous methods and instruments that measure knowledge and skills that participants may have developed through the training they received as a part of the welfare-to work program. For example, Hamilton et al. (1997) found that many welfare-to-work programs involve adult basic education and these services could be evaluated using measures of adult achievement, such as the *Test of Adult Basic Education* (CTB/McGraw-Hill, 1994).

In using Whiston's (in press) model to select multiple outcome measures, an individual evaluating a welfare-to-work program would consider the Source Domain second. The Source Domain encourages evaluators to gather information from different viewpoints or perspectives (e.g., client, counselor, relevant other). In the evaluation of welfare-to-work programs, it is not unusual to gather evaluative information from participants and their employers (Freedman et al., 2000). In an innovative evaluation that included a nontraditional source, Zaslow, McGroder and Moore (2000) examined the effects of three welfare-to-work programs on the development and well-being of the children of program participants. This Child Outcomes Study of the National Evaluation of Welfare-to-Work Strategies examined whether children can be affected by their mother's participation in a welfare-to-work program, which included an examination of how children are affected and the ways in which those impacts came about in children. Outcome measures included children's cognitive development, academic achievement, behavioral adjustment, emotional adjustment, and global health ratings.

The Focus Domain is the third domain in the outcome scheme proposed by Whiston (in press) and entails including both global and specific measures of outcome. A specific measure assesses more of a defined outcome that typically is related to the intervention. Examples of specific outcomes that could be used in welfare-to-work programs are participation in job search activities, GED certificate attainment, and measures of self-efficacy. Global measures are more general and some examples in welfare-to-work programs concern the number of participants who gain employment, reductions in welfare recipients, increased earnings, and number of individuals who have jobs with benefits. In evaluating a career development program, it is often useful to include both global and specific measures, particularly when there is some questions about whether specific treatments produce specific outcomes.

In using Whiston's (in press) outcome scheme, the last domain to consider is the Time Orientation Domain, which involves including both macro-outcomes and micro-outcomes. Macro-outcomes are the more consequential outcomes, and in the welfare-to-work example of comparing counseling services to non-counseling services, they might include such outcomes measures as job placement rate, wages, job satisfaction, and employment advancements. Micro-outcomes are more short-term goals and less noteworthy indicators of success. While micro-outcomes are not as significant as macro-outcomes, they can still provide needed information.

Examples of micro-outcomes in the comparison of counseling and non-counseling activities could include indicators such as level of satisfaction with services provided, commitment to job or occupational saliency, and increases in self-efficacy. In selecting outcome measures, it is important to use psychometrically sound measures that assess pertinent domains or constructs. Typically a single measure will not be sufficient for assessing the complex effects of career interventions and, thus, evaluators will need to use multiple measures from multiple perspectives.

STEP 4: GATHERING PROGRAM INFORMATION.

After determining the outcome measures, the next step in evaluating the counseling versus non-counseling components of a welfare-to-work program would be to gather the evaluative information. The key to completing a useful evaluation study is careful planning and attention to detail. In collecting evaluative data, evaluators need to ensure that the individuals actually gathering the data are adequately trained. For instance, if welfare-to-work participants will be observed on the job and their performance judged using a coding system, the observers should be trained in how to observe and code the behaviors. Second, the data gathering methods should be piloted. Referring to the preceding example, the researchers should be allowed to practice using the coding system with fake data so the coding system can be revised if necessary. Third, involving the program employees and participants early on can enhance the data gathering process. Providing all participants with the rationale and purpose of the study will most likely increase the level of effort they put forth in the study. Finally, researchers should always make sure the participants give their informed consent prior to the beginning of the evaluation study and should try to ensure their individual confidentiality. If welfare-to-work participants think program administrators will have access to the information they provide to the researchers, they may resist divulging negative information about the program for fear they will be adversely affected by the program administrators. Participants may be honest in their disclosures if evaluative information is gathered by nonwelfare-to-work personnel and the measures are completed immediately after services are rendered.

Welfare-to-work programs may have an advantage over some other career development programs in data collection opportunities, as there are materials and databases available through both the U.S. Department of Health and Human Services and the Department of Labor. Both of these federal departments have websites for Welfare-to-Work programs (i.e., http://wtw.doleta.gov/ and http://aspe.hhs.gov/hsp/hspwelfare.htm) that provide information on evaluating welfare-to-work programs (e.g., how to track employment outcomes). Furthermore, these websites include numerous examples of evaluative reports of diverse welfare-to-work programs. These sample evaluative reports can also provide information on effective methods for gathering evaluative data. Career development professionals working in settings other than welfare-to-work programs may benefit from examining these sites and exploring the policies and procedures used in evaluating welfare-to-work programs.

STEP 5: ANALYZING AND INTERPRETING THE PROGRAM INFORMATION.

Once information on the effects of counseling related services and non-counseling related services within the welfare-to-work system has been collected, the information needs to be analyzed using inferential statistics. A multivariate analysis of variance (MANOVA) would probably be the most appropriate statistical test in which to analyze the results of the example study because more than one dependent variable will likely be incorporated into the analyses. Evaluators might also consider multivariate analysis of covariance (MANCOVA), which includes the addition of a covariant. This type of statistical test can be used to control extraneous variables, such as background characteristics, thus enabling researchers to be fairly confident that the amount of variance found between the effects of program services are actually due to the program services rather than to other variables. Effect sizes could also be calculated. Effect sizes would indicate the magnitude of difference between those who participated in counseling related activities and those who participated in non-counseling related activities on a variety of outcome measures. Finally, for purposes of predicting which welfare-to-work services will lead future participants to successful outcomes, a multiple regression analyses could be conducted.

The interpretation of results can be one of the more exciting aspects of program evaluation. However, interpretations should only be made by people who fully understand the statistical results. For instance, if a welfare-to-work program administrator hires a statistician to analyze the results, he or she should also enlist the help of that statistician when interpreting the data. Several considerations need to be made when interpreting the results. First, an evaluator should gear his or her report to the audience (e.g., in-house administrators, other site administrators, governmental officials). In the welfare-to-work example, the administrator may consider extracting pertinent portions of the report and forwarding them to appropriate individuals. For example, a brief summary could be sent to local newspapers or to state legislators who serve on important legislative committees. Second, in interpreting the results of an evaluation study, individuals must be careful not to overstate or understate the impact of various services. The findings that support the effectiveness of a welfare-to-work program should not be unduly glorified, just as the results that do not support the efficacy of a welfare-to-work program should not be ignored. In addition, the results need to be interpreted within an appropriate context and should not be overgeneralized. For example, the findings of a study conducted on a rural Midwest welfare-to-work program should not be generalized to an urban California program. Finally, the interpretation of results needs to consider practical or clinical significance within a welfare-to-work program. This often means explaining the positive benefits of a welfare-to-work program so that readers of the report can understand the clients' needs and how the outcome results reflect positive changes for clients.

STEP 6: USING THE INFORMATION GAINED FROM PROGRAM EVALUATION TO MAKE DECISIONS.

An evaluation study is only useful if the results lend themselves to practical recommendations and, subsequently, those recommendations then are acted upon. Once the program information has been collected, analyzed, and interpreted, evaluators and program administrators should be willing to translate the results into action through program modifications. For instance, if the results of the example study suggest that individual career counseling is significantly related to a number of outcomes, the program administrators should consider reallocating funds so that career counseling is more of a program focus. On the other hand, if career counseling activities are less related to various outcomes than non-counseling services, then the program administrator needs to enhance the services that are shown to be most effective.

The information gained from an evaluation can be used for more than program modification and improvement. In our opinion, career development personnel need to do a better job of informing the public of the benefits of career development activities. This applies to the welfare-to-work example that has been used as an example. There are a number of evaluative studies indicating the effectiveness of welfare-to-work programs (Michalopoulos, Schwartz, & Adams-Ciardullo, 2000); yet, these findings are not commonly known. Given the current focus on empirically-supported interventions, it seems that it would be worthwhile to more effectively publicize these positive findings. In fact, all types of career development would most likely profit if researchers and practitioners increased their efforts in publicizing the positive effects of career development programs.

Conclusion

This chapter has focused on the process of evaluating a career development program for adults. The need to provide accountability information will most likely continue and those programs that do not have readily available evidence documenting the program's effectiveness are at risk. Conducting evaluations should not be viewed as an isolated activity, for it should be seen as a continual process that complements program services. This chapter suggested steps for instituting program evaluation. For career development programs currently conducting program evaluation, it may be time to revisit that process and see if the procedures can be improved and better information can be gathered. Administrators of career development programs not currently gathering evaluative information are encouraged to promptly begin the process before their programs are in jeopardy and they need evaluative information immediately.

References

American Psychological Association. (1994). *Publication Manual of the American Psychological Association.* Washington, DC: Author.

Benkofski, M., & Heppner, C. C. (1999). Program evaluation. In P. P. Heppner, D. M. Kivlighan, & B. E. Wampold (Eds.), *Research design in counseling* (pp. 488-513). Belmont, CA: Wadsworth.

Bonett, R. M., & Stickel, S. A. (1992). A psychometric analysis of the Career Aptitude Scale. *Measurement and Evaluation in Counseling and Development, 25,* 14-26.

CTB/McGraw-Hill. (1994). *Test of Adult Basic Education.* Monterey, CA: Author.

Derogatis, L. R. (1999). *Brief Symptoms Inventory 18.* Minneapolis, MN: National Computer Systems.

Edwards, S. A., Rachal, K. C., & Dixon, D. N. (1999). Counseling psychology and welfare reform: Implications and opportunities. *The Counseling Psychologist, 27*(2), 263-284.

Freedman, S., Friedlander, D., Hamilton, G., Rock J., Mitchell, M., Nudelman, J., Schweder, A., & Storto, L. (2000). *Evaluating alternative welfare-to-work approaches: Two-year impacts of eleven programs (executive summary)* [Online]. Available: http://aspe.hhs.gov/hsp/NEWWS/11-prog-es00/index.htm.

Fretz, B. R. (1981). Evaluating the effectiveness of career interventions [Monograph]. *Journal of Counseling, 28,* 77-90.

Frisch, M. B. (1994). *Quality of Life Inventory.* Minneapolis, MN: National Computer Systems.

Galassi, J. P., & Gersh, T. L. (1993). Myths, misconceptions, and missed opportunity: Single-case designs and counseling psychology. *Journal of Counseling Psychology, 40,* 525-531.

Ganzglass, E., Golonka, S., Tweedie, J., & Falk, S. (1998). Tracking welfare reform: Designing followup studies of recipients who leave welfare. Retrieved November 16, 2000 from Department of Health and Human Services, Office for the Assistant Secretary for Planning and Evaluation Web site: http://aspe.hhs.gov/hsp/isp/ ngancsl.htm.

Gelso, C. J. (1979). Research in counseling: Methodological and professional issues. *The Counseling Psychologist, 8*(3), 7-35.

Hamilton, G., Brock, T., Farrell, M., Friedlander, D., Harkneet, K., Hunter-Manns, J., Walter, J., & Weisman, J. (1997). *Evaluating two welfare-to-work program approaches: Two-year findings on the labor force attachment and human capital development programs in three sites* [On-line]. Available: http://aspa.hha.gov/hsp/ isp/2yrwtw97/exsum.htm.

Heppner, M. J. (1998). The Career Transitions Inventory: Measuring internal resources in adulthood. *Journal of Career Assessment, 6,* 135-145.

Heppner, P. P., Kivlighan, D. M., & Wampold, B. E. (1999). *Research design in counseling* (2nd ed.). Belmont, CA: Wadsworth.

Hillard, R. B. (1993). Single-case methodology in psychotherapy process and outcome research. *Journal of Consulting and Clinical Psychology, 61,* 373-380.

Hoffman, J. L., Magoon, T. M., & Spokane, A. R. (1981). Effects of feedback mode on counseling outcomes using the Strong-Campbell Interest Inventory: Does the counselor really matter? *Journal of Counseling Psychology, 28,* 119-125.

Hollister, G. R., Kemper, P., & Woodridge, J. (1979). Linking process and impact analysis: The case of supported work. In T. D. Cook & C. S. Reichardt (Eds.), *Qualitative and quantitative methods in evaluation research* (pp. 234-253). Beverly Hills, CA: Sage.

Joint Committee on Standards for Educational Evaluation. (1994). *The program evaluation* (2nd ed.). Thousand Oaks, CA: Sage.

Jones, E. E. (1993). Introduction to special section: Single-case research in psychotherapy. *Journal of Consulting and Clinical Psychology, 61,* 371-372.

Kidd, J. M., & Killeen, J. (1992). Are the effects of career guidance worth having? Changes in practice and outcomes. *Journal of Organizational Psychology, 65,* 219-234.

Kiresuk, D. J., & Sherman, R. E. (1968). Goal attainment scaling: A general method for evaluating comprehensive community mental health programs. *Community Mental Health Journal, 4,* 443-453.

Lambert, M. J., & Hill, C. E. (1994). Assessing psychotherapy outcome and process. In A. E. Bergin & S. L. Garfield (Eds.), *Handbook of psychotherapy and behavior change* (4th ed., pp. 72-113). New York: Wiley.

Liptak, J. J. (1996). *Barriers to Employment Success Inventory.* Indianapolis, IN: Jist Publishing.

Mead, L. M. (1983). Expectations and welfare work: WIN in New York City. *Policy Studies Review, 2*(4), 648-688.

Michalopoulos, C., Schwartz, C., & Adams-Ciardullo, D. (2000). *What works best for whom: Impacts of 20 welfare-to-work programs by subgroups* [On-line]. Available: http://aspe.hhs.gov/hsp/NEWWS/synthesises-00/index.htm.

Oliver, L. W. (1978). *Outcome measures for career counseling research* (Technical Paper 316). Alexandria, VA: U.S. Army Research Institute.

Oliver, L. W. (1979). Outcome measurement in career counseling research. *Journal of Counseling Psychology, 26*, 217-226.

Osipow, S. H. (1987). *Career Decision Scale Manual.* Odessa, FL: Psychological Assessment Resources.

Riccio, J. A., & Orenstein, A. (1996). Understanding the best practices for operating welfare-to-work programs. *Evaluation Review, 20*(1), 3-28.

Rossi, P. H., & Freeman, H. E. (1982). *Evaluation: A systematic approach.* Beverly Hills, CA: Sage.

Spokane, A. R. (1990). *Multidimensional Career Behavior Scales.* Unpublished scale available from author.

Taylor, K. M., & Betz, N. E. (1983). Application of self-efficacy theory to understanding and treatment of career indecision. *Journal of Vocational Behavior, 22*, 63-81.

Thompson, B., & Snyder, P. A. (1998). Statistical significance and reliability analyses in recent Journal of Counseling & Development research articles. *Journal of Counseling and Development, 76*, 436-441.

Whiston, S. C. (1996). Accountability through action research: Research methods for practitioners. *Journal of Counseling and Development, 74*, 616-623.

Whiston, S. C. (in press). Selecting career outcome assessments: An organizational scheme. *Journal of Career Assessment.*

Whiston, S. C., Sexton, T. L., & Lasoff, D. L. (1998). Career-intervention outcome: A replication and extension of Oliver and Spokane (1988). *Journal of Counseling Psychology, 45*, 150-165.

Yates, B. T. (1996). *Analyzing costs, procedures, processes, and outcomes in human services.* Thousand Oaks, CA: Sage.

Zaslow, M. J., McGroder, S. M., & Moore, K. A. (2000). *Impact on young children and their families two years after enrollment: Summary report.* [On-line]. Available: http://aspe.hhs.gov/hsp/NEWWS/child-outcomes/summary.htm#overview.

CHAPTER 22
Adult Career Development: Some Perspectives On The Future

Edwin L. Herr
The Pennsylvania State University

As a context for looking to the future of adult career development, it is useful to use the recent past as a frame of reference. In such a context, adult career development is, in relative terms, a new term and a new concept. A generation or so ago, the term "adult career development" would have been rarely used. At that time, the focus tended to be on the expectation that most individuals made their choice of an occupation and an employer in late adolescence and in their early 20s and then in adulthood they implemented the career path that followed from these earlier choices. The implicit assumption, with few exceptions, was that the importance of career exploration and choice tended to be at the front end of one's career, not distributed throughout the life span. The periods of the middle adult years and later years were described by a language that emphasized linear careers, stability (usually defined by long-term employment in one firm or workplace), a steady and predictable rise in responsibilities and income, and such perspectives were captured in words like consolidation, maintenance, plateauing, deceleration.

Further, most theoretical perspectives in the middle third of the 20th century spoke to the career development of men, typically white and relatively well educated, not to the career development of women, persons of color, or poor persons. Again, with important exceptions (Super, 1957; Krumboltz, 1979, 1994; Vondracek, Lerner, & Schulenberg, 1986), the emphasis was on individual career development, not on the interaction of individual, corporate and societal career development as interactive. In an overly caricatured sense, conceptions of adult career development were not sufficiently *contextualized*. A lack of *contextualization* of human behavior fails to fully embrace the view that neither theories nor the problems that people bring to counselors exist in a vacuum. Within such a limited perspective of the influences on individuals, career development can be seen as homogenized, similar for all people in all places, cultural factors and gender can be downplayed as major influences on career identity and the actions that ensue, the effects of the environment in which people live are benign, and change is rare, not a constant in one's life.

In contrast to such views, the theories and interventions presented in the earlier chapters of this book paint a different view of adult career development. We have learned that adulthood is dynamic: workers make choices, enter and leave different jobs and career paths, explore and reinvent themselves. Many of the jobs and the processes used at work were not known and could not be explored when the typical 50 year old worker of today was entering the workforce 30 or more years ago. But, they have had to adapt to and learn to implement organizational forms and job tools that did not exist when they were beginning to forge their careers. When they entered their careers, the contemporary pervasiveness of computer technology, telecommunications, satellites, the global economy were not yet issues. Until 1995, there was no Internet available for general application in the workplace. Jobs and workplaces were considered bound by location, geography, and political sovereignty. No longer are these things true. Indeed, the effects of advanced technology and international economic competition have changed the language of work, the organization of work, how and where work is done, and by whom.

Specific elements of the context in which adult career development is shaped and executed are wide-ranging. Examples include the accelerated change in the nature of the work available to be done; the steady decline of jobs available in certain sectors (e.g., manufacturing); the emerging skills and preparation required to work in many occupations and settings,; the shifting of selected jobs from one nation to another; the high unemployment rates in many parts of the world; the current affirmation that in a global economy the primary asset in the economic development of any nation is the literacy, numeracy, communication and computer skills of its workforce.

The technological and political factors that are rapidly changing the occupational structures of the world are also changing the types of jobs and work arrangements available to people in different nations (Rifkin, 1996). For example, Handy, a British scholar of management, (1994) has suggested a conceptualization of the workforces in most of Europe and North America as being divided into three concentric rings: the small circle in the middle is the permanent workforce needed by employers to do the critical tasks required in a particular work organization. These are the people with relatively long-term security, excellent benefits and income and with support for their learning and re-learning as the organizational work processes change. The second ring is comprised of contingent workers: essentially part-time workers whose skills are purchased for limited amounts of time (e.g., retail workers for the winter holiday season; farm workers for the summer harvesting season; workers to do specific projects of a time-limited nature). These are persons who frequently have several part-time jobs, but no long-term institutional identity; they frequently lack health and other benefits available to permanent workers and have little employment security. The third ring of workers is identified with specialty firms that do outsourcing: they take on particular functions that employers traditionally handled in-house with a permanent workforce but now find it less expensive to subcontract with another firm to handle for them (e.g., accounting, advertising, food services, marketing, security, legal services, custodial services). The persons working for outsourcing firms may also be contingent, part-time workers or they may be more permanent employees with outsourcing firms who are assigned to fulfill contracted tasks with specific firms or workplaces with which they have no long-term identity.

The outcomes of Handy's conceptualization of the occupational structure or of a particular firm have many corollary implications. One is that the traditional image of employment—long-term, full and permanent employment with one employer—is no longer a reality for most persons and it gives rise to many forms of alternate employment patterns. In a special issue of the *Monthly Labor Review* (Hipple, 2001), some of these patterns were discussed. Some 5.6 million workers, some 4.3 percent of total employment in 1999, held contingent jobs, jobs structured to be short-term r temporary, not expected to continue. As full-time unemployment rates rise, the percentage of contingent workers also rises. Many of these persons work through temporary help agencies and range in skills across occupations such as those of physicians, biological and life scientists, actors and directors, construction workers, library clerks, interviewers, general office clerks, receptionists, and typists. Contingent workers are much more likely to hold multiple jobs than non-contingent workers, be younger, earn less, have no employer-provided health insurance or pension plans, be foreign born or minority. Within the broad spectrum of contingency workers are several categories used by the U.S. government. They include independent contractors; consultants and freelance workers who are essentially self-employed; on-call workers who are called into work only when needed; temporary help agency workers who are paid by a temporary help agency; workers provided by contract firms, who may work for only one customer at the customer's work site or for several customers (DiNatale, 2001). Almost 10 percent of the workforce now has workweeks that are variable and thus unpredictable from week to week (Golden, 2001).

While there is much more that could be said about the three rings—permanent, contingent, outsource workers—suggested by Handy, it seems clear that the workers in each of these categories have in common the need to keep their skills current and focused in areas that employers, temporary help agencies, outsource firms want to purchase on a contingent or non-contingent basis. Many of these workers must be committed to continuous learning in order to possess the competencies that can be sold to employers. And, there is the added implication that increasingly each of these categories of workers is his or her own career manager. That is to say that many employers do not accept responsibility for their employees' career development; they see this as the individual employee's responsibility if they want to remain employed. In such a context, the fundamental relationship between employer and employee changes and the role of the employee in maintaining competencies that are salable and current becomes a major prerequisite to remaining employed. Some observers would argue that the employee, in addition to technical skills, must possess the personal flexibility (Herr & Cramer, 1996) by which to cope with constantly changing employment conditions and requirements.

Such perspectives have led some researchers to argue that new patterns of careers are taking place that are qualitatively different from those traditionally assumed by many adult career development theories. For example, Arnold and Jackson (1997) have argued that the changes in the way work is organized and structured have affected how notions of "new careers" need to be conceived in many nations. They state:

> The changes taking place in the structure of employment opportunities mean a widening diversity of career patterns and experiences ... more and different sorts of career transitions will be taking place. One consequence may be that in the future more men will experience the kind of fragmented careers that many women have experienced (p. 428) ... more people will be working for small and medium-sized employers, and there will be more people who are self-employed ... they highlight the need for lifelong learning and an appropriate strategy for career guidance to support people especially during career transitions ... the new career recognizes both the changed objective realities in which careers are being developed and also the universality of people's intense involvement with the subjective aspects of their careers (p. 429).

In essentially a parallel perspective, Hall and Associates (1996) discuss *Protea Careers.* They suggest that:

> People's careers increasingly will become a succession of 'ministages' (or shor cycle learning stages) of exploration-trial-mastery-exit, as they move into an out of various product areas, technologies, functions, organizations, and othe work environments (p.33) . . . this protean form of career involves horizonta growth, expanding one's range of competencies and ways of connecting to wor and other people, as opposed to the more traditional vertical growth of succes (upward mobility). In the protean form of growth, the goal is learning psychological success, and expansion of the identity. In the more traditiona form, the goal was advancement, success and esteem in the eyes of others, an power (p. 35).

It might be noted here that the use of the term "protean" by Hall and hi Associates is derived from the mythology of the Greek Sea God Proteus who wa believed to have a many-sided self and was able to transform himself into man forms as circumstances required (Lifton, 1993). Although constancy and stabilit have frequently been touted in the psychological literature as desirable traits fo individual growth and development, adult career development in the future is likel to be more ad hoc, more spontaneous, more embedded in environmental an organizational flux, unpredictability and turbulence.

An obvious point here is that persons are shaped by the environmental condition to which they are exposed and which they must learn to manage. Super (1984 addressed such a point as follows:

> Career behavior and development do not unfold separately and independentl from the world of work and the personal, social, and economic environment and sanctions within it. The relationship is reciprocal and interactive. As . result, professions need a thorough understanding of the work world so tha they are able 1) to appreciate its impact on the dynamics of career behavior an development and 2) to empower individuals with whom they work to becom competent, achieving persons by effectively managing their talents in the worl environment (Super, 1984, p. 25).

Implications for Adult Career Development Theory

Super's comments obviously have implications for theory in adult caree development just as do the comments about the Protean Self, the individual as hi or her own career manager, the changing work patterns—permanent, contingen outsource—now arising around the world, who populates what occupational strata and needs for personal flexibility.

These issues raise serious questions about the content and breadth of perspectiv of contemporary adult career development theories. In particular, do availabl theories adequately reflect the changing nature of work—as contingent, potentiall more fragmented and multi-staged; the changing relationships between worker and employers; the need for individual workers to have greater personal flexibility and be their own career manager; and the increasing need for many workers to conceptualize the work they do as not bound by geographic or time constraints, but to occur within the global environment with its attendant competitive pressures from other nations and workers for American jobs and processes?

There are also other implications for such theory that include:

1. To understand human behavior and the potential influences on career development is to understand that people live in various social, cultural, political, and economic environments. These environments exert influence or apply limits to the conceptions of work roles and work ethics, the achievement images being reinforced, the cognitive and interpersonal styles rewarded, the resources available, and the forms and comprehensiveness of information provided. The mixes of environments through which persons negotiate their identity are affected by birth order, place of birth, cultural traditions, socioeconomic status, history and many other factors. "Such environments are not static. They are constantly changing, and individuals are under constant pressure to receive, interpret, and act upon messages related to personal behavior that emanate from these environmental mixes" (Herr, 1999, p. 6).

2. The issue of how persons think about the environments they occupy is also relevant here. Do they conceptualize themselves as bound to a specific physical location, a particular town or city, that determines the skills they will need to forge and to play out their career aspirations. If so, how do they interpret their role in a world of global competitiveness, in which the products or services they help to produce are likely to be part of a complex import-export network which changes and makes more important the issues of quality standards, production costs, understanding of one's competitors and potential consumers, the economies and social systems in which these competitors and consumers function? Do these workers consider the implications for them of the globalization of the workforce and the growing cross-national mobility of workers; the growing labor surplus, frequently including highly trained and skilled workers, many of whom seek to obtain work in the United States or other developed, industrial nations; the rising importance of the knowledge worker and of literacy, numeracy, communication, and computer literacy skills as prerequisites for employability and lifelong training in many of the emerging occupations; the need for workers to have a world view that facilitates adaptation and flexibility to deal with change? Should these perspectives be understood by workers? Should they be incorporated into adult career development theory? In a world filled with economic systems and occupational structures in flux, such dynamics would appear to have increasing relevance to the future understanding of adult career development and its transactional quality.

3. Views of the transactional nature of human behavior have been undergoing change as the psychology of human behavior has been increasingly informed by the sociology of human behavior. In a narrow sense, the psychology of human behavior can be seen as primarily concerned with individual actions and their origins and effects. The sociology of human behavior is instead more concerned with the context, with the socializing factors that are related

to individual actions and that stimulate and shape or limit them (Herr 1999). In the case of adult career development, which occupations and which work behaviors are most likely to be effected by the changes in the organization of work, its processes and its role expectations? Adult career development theory needs to address such issues as: How do individuals anticipate such changes, prepare themselves to be both secure and personally flexible in the face of change, and accept change as a challenge not a threat?

4. An emerging theoretical issue is whether the construction of adult career development theory should rest primarily on psychological assumptions about the primacy of individual action or on interactional sociological anthropological, organizational, or economic perspectives. The latter serve to clarify the contextual factors that shape or restrict individual action and create barriers and obstacles that must be understood and surmounted They also reflect more directly the transactions between individual and environment that shape behavior.

   As the context, as well as individual actions, become the focus of theories of adult career development, they broaden the interventions required to recognize that individuals engage in a constant array of adaptive interchanges with the multiple environments which they occupy. These include the family, community, institutional settings, governmental agencies, workplaces, and social policy. Each of these environments is potentially a target of career interventions designed to help facilitate adult career development. The broadening of concern for interventions that address both the individuals and the contexts they occupy, raises new questions about the types of information adults need and the mode of delivery, the uses of advanced technology (e.g., computer-assisted career guidance systems, the Internet) as primary career interventions, and the differing roles of counselors with individuals, groups, and social/economic environments (e.g., workplaces, schools, agencies) that can facilitate or thwart individual career development. Such perspectives affirm the need for the construction of a comprehensive matrix of interventions that are related to specific presenting problems, client characteristics, and settings. The purpose of such a matrix is to classify in accessible ways the science associated with adult career development in order to translate theory and research, what we know and its practical relevance, into systems of practice defined by categories of problems and the location of such problems, within the individual or in the environment.

5. To be successful in creating such a matrix of presenting problems x treatments/interventions x client characteristics x settings requires additional knowledge about populations that are not well represented in existing theory or research. For example, we have relatively few examples of research addressing the adult career development of poor persons, persons with a high school education or less, immigrant and domestic populations from different cultural backgrounds, Gay, Lesbian, and transgendered populations. Research about the career behavior and the "lived experiences" of persons in these populations needs significant attention if adult career development theory is to more fully reflect the differences in barriers,

reinforcements, and other factors related to the career development of these subpopulations.

The need for increased attention to he variations in the career development of different sub-groups in the population may mean the need for more segmented theories rather than a theory or theories that are all-encompassing in their coverage. Segmented theories would focus more directly on the specific forms of obstacles, barriers, reinforcements, received messages, and other variables affecting the career behavior of women, racial and ethnic minorities, persons with disabilities, persons of alternative sexual orientations, by level of education, socioeconomic level, and other indices (Herr, 1996). The results of such studies need to be compared to constructs already validated in existing career theory and reported in syntheses of career concepts that are well established (Herr, 1997; Savickas, 1999).

There also will need to be greater theoretical attention to the elements and the processes by which personal flexibility is achieved. Will this require new adaptations of human capital theory which emphasizes the "worker as investor" (Davenport, 1999). In such a context, the worker is in control of the "human capital" he or she possesses and can apply to different work settings, problems, or expectations. Human capital in this case means one's *ability* (knowledge, skill, talent), *behavior* (how we perform in contributing to a task), *effort* (the conscious application of our mental and physical resources to accomplish particular tasks, our work ethic), *time* (how much time are we willing to invest in a particular job), and what does the worker expect as a *return on investment* (e.g., intrinsic job fulfillment, opportunity for growth, recognition for accomplishments, financial rewards)? In such a paradigm, one can draw a parallel between the worker as an investor and the worker as a career manager. In the latter case, the task is to apply the human capital in those cases where the return on investment is expected to be appropriate. To remain flexible, however, the career manager also must be constantly improving and adding to his or her supply of human capital to make it more attractive to changing employers. To the degree one can engage in lifelong learning to improve one's human capital is in essence to be personally flexible. Such a perspective can also be considered in relation to motivation or to self-efficacy theory. The concept of motivation in industrial-organizational psychology as proposed by Lawler (1973) and in self-efficacy theory as originally proposed by Bandura (1977) essentially includes the same elements. Lawler's model of motivation is characterized by the equation (E?P) (P?O). Basically, such a framework indicates that the tendency to act in a certain way depends on the expectancy that the act will be followed by a given consequence (or outcome) and on the value or attractiveness of the consequence (or outcome) to the actor. Thus, there are two expectancies involved in motivation. The first, Effort?Performance, reflects the person's estimation of the probability that he or she can accomplish the tasks required in a particular job or other situation. The essential question is: Is the human capital I have to invest going to allow me to perform adequately in this situation? This is what Bandura (1977) and others such as Betz and Hackett (1986) refer to as self-efficacy, the beliefs one has that he or she can or can not perform a given behavior. The second dimension of motivation then is captured by the notation, Performance?Outcomes. Here the emphasis is on the subjective probability one has that if a particular performance can be achieved (if one's human capital is adequate), it will lead to certain desired outcomes (one will achieve the return on investment desired). In this segment of the motivation process, the issue is one's beliefs about what outcomes are valued. In this paradigm, the career manager engaged in reinforcing his or her personal flexibility would be concerned about enlarging one's possible performance and clarifying one's values and being able to apply them to a large range of potential work performance options and settings.

Obviously, there are many other possible ways to consider the substance and processes of achieving personal flexibility. However, the individual ability to adapt to change, to be able to reinvent oneself as necessary, to be personally flexible, will be critical to conceptions of adult career development in the future. Thus, such a concept deserves significant theoretical and research attention.

Conclusion

The processes and conceptions of adult career development are likely to vary in different time periods, cross-generationally, and across nations. It is likely that in a world of economic systems and occupational structures in significant turbulence, the contexts in which career development is forged will be qualitatively different from those about which much adult career development theory has been formulated in the past. This chapter has attempted to identify some of the dynamic influences that will affect the nature and outcomes of adult career development. More specifically, this chapter has focused on areas in which theory development and research need further attention and refinement, has examined selected concepts (e.g., personal flexibility), and identified subpopulations (e.g., poor, immigrants, etc.) whose life experiences and career behavior must be more fully incorporated in adult career development theory.

References

Arnold, J., & Jackson, C. (1997). The new career: Issues and challenges. *British Journal of Guidance and Counselling, 25*(4), 427-434.

Bandura, A. (1977). Self-efficacy: Toward a unifying theory of behavioral change. *Psychological Review, 84,* 191-215.

Betz, N. E., & Hackett, G. (1986). Applications of self-efficacy theory to understanding career choice behavior. *Journal of Social and Clinical Psychology, 4,* 279-289.

Davenport, T. O. (1999). *Human capital. What it is and why people invest in it.* San Francisco: Jossey-Bass.

DiNatale, M. (2001). Alternative work arrangements. *Monthly Labor Review, 124*(3), 28-49.

Golden, L. (2001). Flexible work schedules: What are trading off to get them? *Monthly Labor Review, 124*(3), 50-67.

Hall, D. T., & Associates (Eds.). (1996). *The career is dead—long live the career. A relational approach to careers.* San Francisco: Jossey-Bass.

Handy, C. (1994). *The age of paradox.* Boston, MA: Harvard Business School Press.

Herr, E. L. (1996). Toward the convergence of career theory and practice: Mythology, issues, and possibilities. In M. Savickas & W. B. Walsh (Eds.), *Handbook of career counseling theory and practice.* Palo Alto, CA: Davies-Black.

Herr, E. L. (1997). Perspectives on career guidance and counselling in the 21st century. *Educational and Vocational Guidance, 60,* 1-15.

Herr, E. L. (1999). *Counseling in a dynamic society. Contexts and practices for the 21st century.* Alexandria, VA: American Counseling Association.

Herr, E. L., & Cramer, S. H. (1996). *Career guidance and counseling through the lifespan: Systematic approaches.* New York: Harper Collins.

Hipple, S. (2001). Contingent work. *Monthly Labor Review, 124*(3), 3-27.

Krumboltz, J. D. (1979). A social learning theory of career decision making. In A. M. Mitchell, G. G. Jame, & J. D. Krumboltz (Eds.), *Social learning and career decision making* (pp. 19-49). Cranston, RI: Carrole Press.

Krumboltz, J. D. (1994). Improving career development theory from a social learning perspective. In M. L. Savickas & R. W. Lent (Eds.), *Convergence in career development theories. Implications for science and practice* (pp. 9-31). Palo Alto, CA: CPP Books.

Lawler, E. E. (1973). *Motivation in work organizations.* Monterey, CA: Brooks/Cole.

Lifton, R. J. (1993). *The protean self: Human resilience in an age of fragmentation.* New York: Basic Books.

Rifkin, J. (1996). *The end of work. The decline of the global labor force and the dawn of the post-market era.* New York: Tarcher/Putnam.

Savickas, M. (1999). Career development and public policy: The role of values, theory and research. *Making waves: Career development and public policy. International Symposium 1999 Papers, Proceedings and Strategies.* Ottawa, Canada: Canadian Career Development Foundation.

Super, D. E. (1957). *The psychology of careers.* New York: Harper & Row.

Super, D. E. (1984). *Career and life development.* In D. Brown & L. Brooks (Eds.), Career choice and development: Applying contemporary approaches to practice. San Francisco: Jossey Bass.

Vondracek, F. W., Lerner, R. M., & Schulenberg, J. E. (1986) *Career development: A life-span developmental approach.* Hillsdale, NJ: Erlbaum.